CHINESE MUSEUMS ASSOCIATION GUIDE

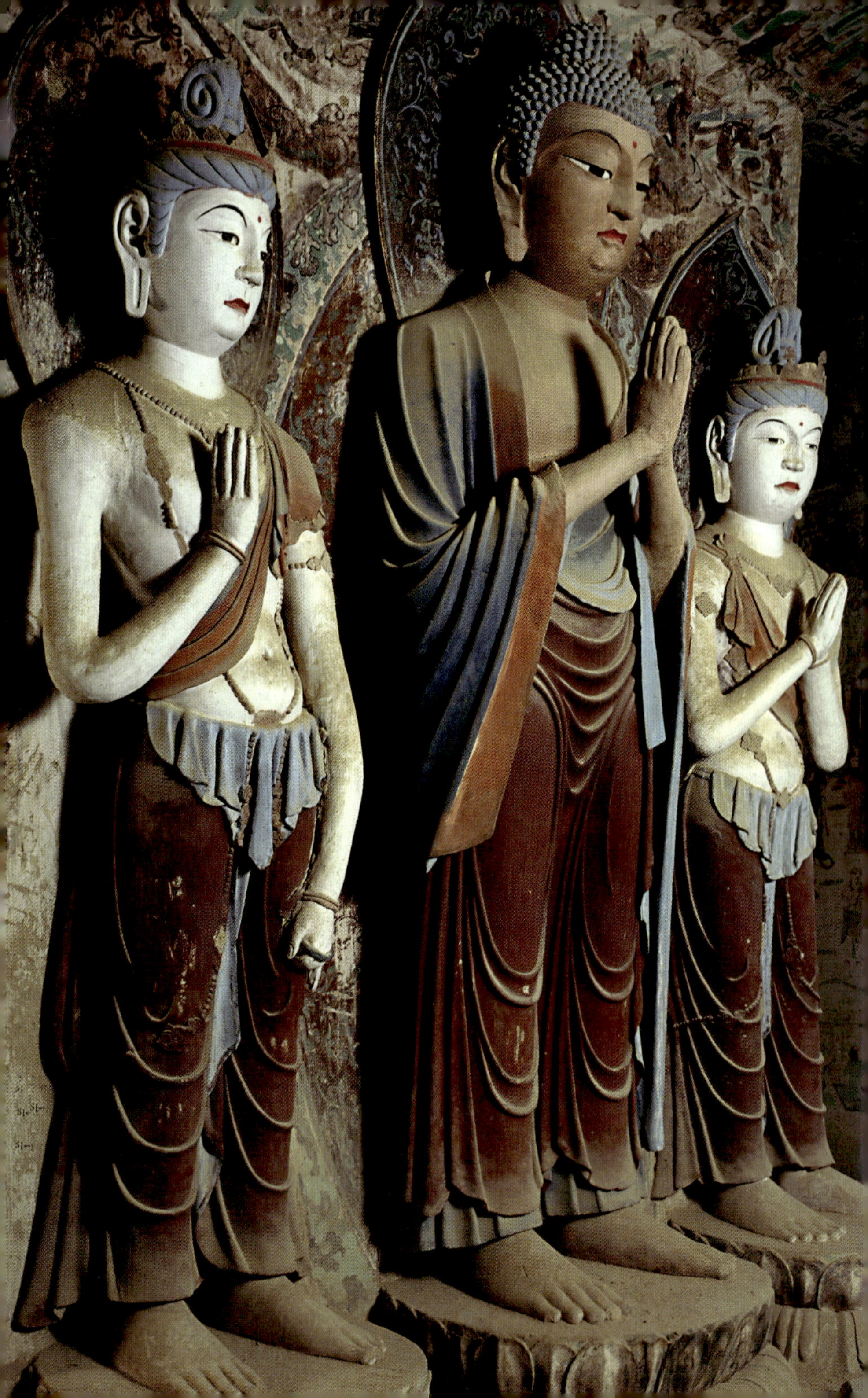

CHINESE MUSEUMS ASSOCIATION GUIDE

edited by CMA

Miriam Clifford, Cathy Giangrande, Antony White

SCALA

Yilin Press

图书在版编目（CIP）数据

中国博物馆导览 = Chinese Museums Association Guide：英文 /（美）克利福德 (Clifford,M.)，（美）詹格兰德 (Giangrande,C.)，（英）怀特 (White,A.) 著；中国博物馆协会编. — 南京：译林出版社，2013.8
ISBN 978-7-5447-4059-3

Ⅰ. ①中… Ⅱ. ①克… ②詹… ③怀… ④中… Ⅲ. ①博物馆—介绍—中国—英文 Ⅳ. ① G269.26
中国版本图书馆CIP数据核字(2013)第174518号

CHINESE MUSEUMS ASSOCIATION GUIDE
Edited by Chinese Museums Association with Bookshow Culture Ltd.
Copyright © Miriam Clifford, Cathy Giangrande and Antony White 2013
Copyright license arranged through Andrew Nurnberg Associates International Limited
English edition (in mainland China) copyright © 2013 by Yilin Press, Ltd
ALL RIGHTS RESERVED

著作权合同登记号：10-2013-165 号

书　　　名	CHINESE MUSEUMS ASSOCIATION GUIDE
作　　　者	［美国］米里亚姆·克利福德 (Miriam Clifford)
	［美国］凯西·詹格兰德 (Cathy Giangrande)
	［英国］安东尼·怀特 (Antony White)
编　　　者	中国博物馆协会
责 任 编 辑	陆晨希　费明燕
英 文 校 对	［英国］彼得·布朗 (Peter Brown)　许冬平
书 籍 设 计	邱雪峰
出 版 发 行	凤凰出版传媒股份有限公司
	译林出版社
出版社地址	南京市湖南路1 号A 楼，邮编：210009
电 子 邮 箱	yilin@yilin.com
出版社网址	http://www.yilin.com
经　　　销	凤凰出版传媒股份有限公司
印　　　刷	南京凯德印刷有限公司
开　　　本	889 毫米×1194毫米　1/32
印　　　张	12.5
版　　　次	2013 年8 月第1 版　2013 年8 月第1 次印刷
书　　　号	ISBN 978-7-5447-4059-3
定　　　价	88.00元

译林版图书若有印装错误可向出版社调换
（电话：025-83658316）

Contents

Introduction

Section 1 — Beijing and the North — 2

1. Arthur M. Sackler Museum of Art and Archaeology
2. Beijing Ancient Architecture Museum
3. Beijing Ancient Coins Museum
4. Beijing Art Museum
5. Beijing Aviation Museum
6. Beijing Museum of Natural History
7. Beijing Planetarium
8. Beijing Police Museum
9. Beijing Stone Carving Museum
10. Beijing Tap Water Museum
11. CAFA Art Museum
12. Capital Museum
13. China Agricultural Museum
14. China Aviation Museum
15. China Millennium Monument World Art Museum
16. China National Film Museum
17. China National Post and Postage Stamp Museum
18. China Printing Museum
19. China Railway Museum
20. Dabaotai Western Han Tomb Museum
21. Forbidden City and the Palace Museum
22. Geological Museum of China
23. Guanfu Museum
24. Jiaozhuanghu Underground Tunnel War Remains Museum
25. Lao She Museum
26. Lu Xun Museum Beijing

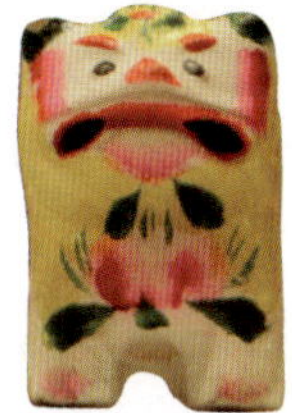

27. Mei Lanfang Memorial Museum

28. Military Museum of the Chinese People's Revolution

29. Ethnic Costumes Museum of BIFT

30. National Art Museum of China (NAMOC)

31. National Museum of China

32. National Museum of Modern Chinese Literature

33. New Culture Movement Memorial Museum

34. Poly Art Museum

35. Sino-Japanese War Memorial Museum / Marco Polo Bridge

36. Soong Ching Ling's Former Residence

37. Tank Museum

38. Xu Beihong Museum

39. Zhoukoudian Site Museum

40. Museum of Chinese Opera

41. Tianjin Academy of Fine Arts Gallery

42. Tianjin Museum

43. Tianjin Natural History Museum

44. Tianjin Science and Technology Museum

45. Hebei Provincial Museum

46. Chengde Imperial Summer Resort Museum

47. Henan Museum

48. Kaifeng Museum

49. Longmen Grottoes

50. Luoyang Museum

51. Luoyang Museum of Ancient Arts

52. Museum of Zhou Capital and Royal Six-Horse Chariot

53. Yinxu Museum

54. Linzi Funerary Horse Pit Museum of the Eastern Zhou

55. Linzi Museum of Chinese Ancient Chariots

56. Sino-Japanese War (1894-1895) Museum

57. Qi State History Museum

58. Shandong Museum

59. Qingdao Municipal Museum

60. Qingdao Naval Museum

61. Qingzhou Municipal Museum

62. Coal Museum of China

63. Pingyao Confucius Temple Museum

64. Pingyao Museum (Qingxu Temple)

65. Shanxi Museum

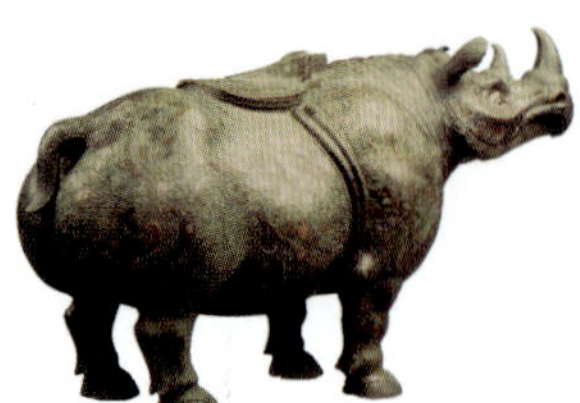

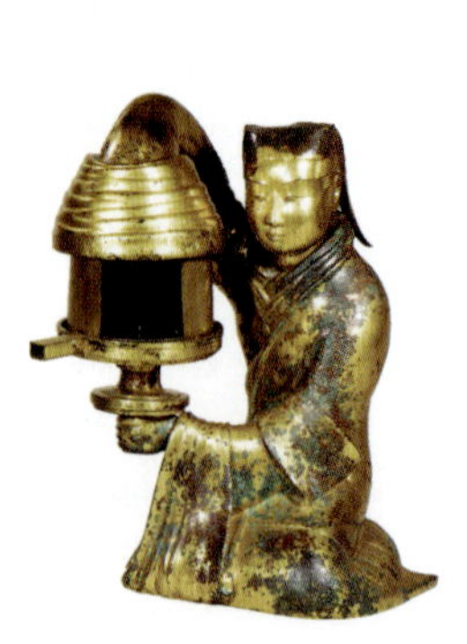

<table>
<tr><td>**Section 2**</td><td>**The Northeast**</td><td>**128**</td></tr>
</table>

66. Aihui History Museum

67. Harbin Architectural Museum

68. Heilongjiang Provincial Museum

69. Japanese Germ Warfare Museum Unit 731

70. Northeast China Revolutionary Martyrs Memorial Hall

71. American POW Memorial Museum-Mukden Prison Camp

72. Chinese Memorial Hall of the War to Resist US Aggression and Aid Korea

73. Liaoning Provincial Museum

74. Lüshun Museum

75. September 18 History Museum

76. Shenyang Imperial Palace Museum

77. Jilin Provincial Museum

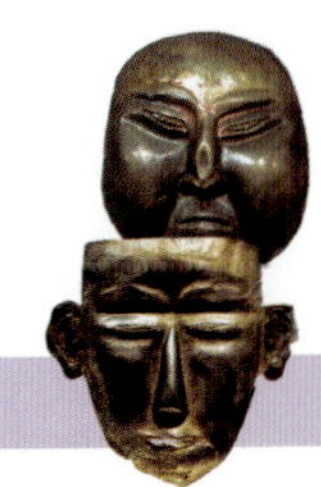

<table>
<tr><td>**Section 3**</td><td>**Shanghai and East China**</td><td>**146**</td></tr>
</table>

78. China Art Museum

79. China Tobacco Museum

80. Himalayas Art Museum

81. MoCA Shanghai

82. Memorial Hall of First National Congress of Communist Party of China

83. Museum of Oriental Musical Instruments

84. Shanghai Auto Museum

85. Shanghai Bank Museum

86. Shanghai Kids' Museum

87. Shanghai Lu Xun Memorial Hall (Final Residence/The Tomb of Lu Xun)

88. Shanghai Museum

89. Shanghai Museum of Public Security

90. Shikumen Open House Museum

91. Soong Ching Ling Memorial Residence in Shanghai /Soong Ching Ling Mausoleum

92. Sun Yat-sen's Former Residence and Museum in Shanghai

93. The Memorial Hall to the Victims in the Nanjing Massacre by Japanese Invaders

94. Nanjing Cloud Brocade Museum and Research Institute

95. Nanjing Museum

96. Taiping Heavenly Kingdom Historical Museum

97. Nantong Abacus Museum

98. Nantong Kite Museum

99. Nantong Museum

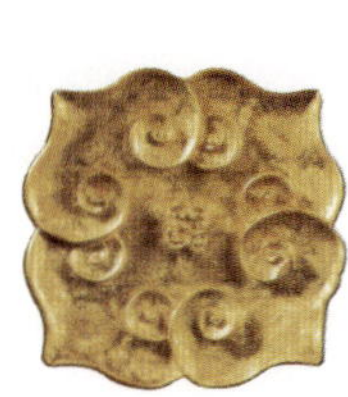

100. Nantong Textile Museum

101. Suzhou Museum

102. Suzhou Opera Museum

103. Xuzhou Museum

104. Yangzhou Museum / China Block-printing Museum

105. China Grand Canal Museum

106. China National Silk Museum

107. China National Tea Museum

108. Hu Qingyu Tang Traditional Chinese Medicine Museum

109. Pan Tianshou Memorial Hall

110. Southern Song Dynasty Guan Kiln Museum in Hangzhou

111. Zhejiang Museum of Natural History

112. Zhejiang Provincial Museum

113. Ningbo Museum

114. The Museum of Hemudu Site

115. Liangzhu Museum

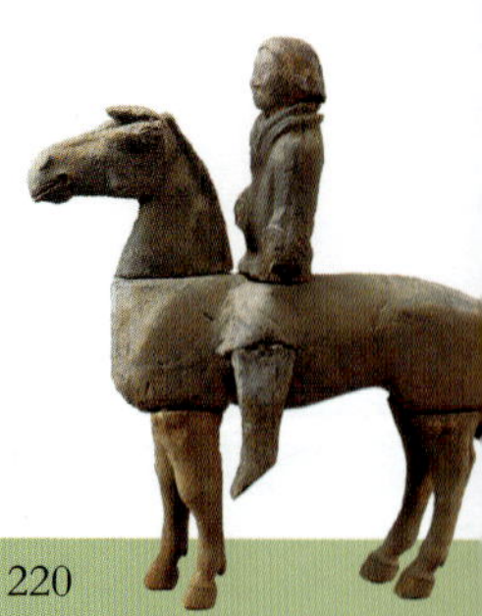

| Section 4 | The Yangtze | 220 |

116. Anhui Museum

117. Hubei Provincial Museum

118. Memorial Hall of Wuchang Uprising of 1911 Revolution

119. Tonglushan Ancient Metallurgy Museum

120. China Lantern Museum

121. Chengdu City Museum

122. Chengdu Shu Brocade and Embroidery Museum

123. Chengdu Wuhou Shrine Museum

124. Dayi Liu Family Estate Museum / Rent Collection Courtyard

125. Jianchuan Museum Cluster

126. Jinsha Archaeological Site Museum

127. Liangshan Yi Ethnic Group's Slavery Museum

128. Sanxingdui Museum

129. Sichuan Museum

130. Sichuan University Museum

131. Zigong Dinosaur Museum

132. Zigong Salt History Museum

133. Baiheliang Underwater Museum

134. Chongqing Huguang Guildhall Complex

135. Chongqing Three Gorges Museum

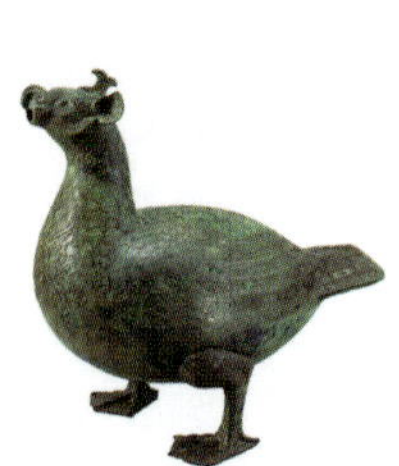

136. Overseas Chinese Museum

137. Quanzhou Maritime Museum

138. Guangdong Marine Silk Road Museum

139. Guangzhou Museum of Art

140. Guangdong Provincial Museum

141. Guangzhou City Museum

142. Guangdong Museum of Art

143. The Museum of the Mausoleum of the Nanyue King of the Western Han Dynasty

144. The Museum of Dr. Sun Yat-Sen

145. Opium War Museum

146. Shenzhen Museum

147. Hunan Provincial Museum

148. Shaoshan Mao Zedong Memorial Museum

149. Jingdezhen Folk Kiln Museum (Hutian Kiln Site)

150. Jingdezhen Imperial Porcelain Museum

151. Jingdezhen Porcelain Museum

152. Lushan Conference Site Memorial Museum

153. Lushan Museum

154. Bada Shanren Memorial Hall

155. Nanchang Bayi (August 1st) Uprising Museum

156. Jiangxi Provincial Museum

157. Kunming City Museum

158. Yunnan Nationalities Museum

159. Yunnan Provincial Museum

160. Lijiang Municipal Museum

161. Guizhou Provincial Museum

162. The Memorial of Zunyi Meeting

163. The Museum of Guangxi Zhuang Autonomous Region

164. Guangxi Museum of Natural History

165. Hainan Museum

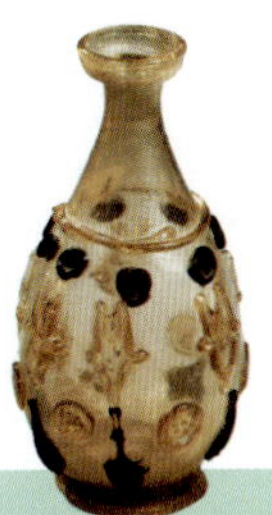

166. Baoji Bronze Museum

167. Emperor Qinshihuang's Terracotta Warriors and Horses and Mausoleum Site Museum

168. Famen Temple Museum

169. Hanyangling Museum

170. Shaanxi History Museum

171. Xi'an Banpo Museum

172. Xi'an Beilin Museum

173. Xi'an Museum

174. Yaozhou Kiln Museum

175. Inner Mongolia Museum

176. Ordos Bronze Museum

177. Guyuan Museum

178. Ningxia Hui Autonomous Region Museum

179. Dunhuang Museum

180. Mogao Grottoes/ Dunhuang Academy

181. Jiayuguan Great Wall Museum

182. Gansu Provincial Museum

183. Liuwan Painted Pottery Museum

184. Hotan Museum

185. Turpan Prefecture Museum

186. Xinjiang Ili Kazakh Autonomous Prefecture Museum

187. Xinjiang Uygur Autonomous Region Museum

Section 7   Tibet   356

188. Potala Palace
189. Tibet Museum

Section 8   Hong Kong, Macao, Taiwan   364

190. Hongkong Museum of History
191. Macao Museum
192. National Palace Museum in Taipei

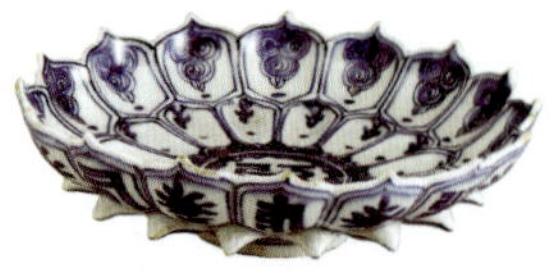

Photographic Credits   374

Glossary   378

Chronology   380

Acknowledgements   382

Index to Art Spaces, Museums and Sites   383

Introduction

This book, edited by the Chinese Museums Association (CMA), is based on *China: Museums* published in 2009. All the museums included are related to the CMA, so a number of the original entries have been deleted, while others have been added.

Since our first edition, China's museum building explosion has continued. In 2008, the official count was 2,310 and by 2012 had increased to over 3,000 with about 100 new museums being built annually. This official count excludes private museums, new art centres and vibrant districts and villages dedicated to contemporary art and culture.

Beginning in the Republican Period and accelerating after 1949, China established a system of national, provincial and city museums. New museums of world-class quality were opened, such as those in Nanjing and Shanghai.

Unlike in the West, these museums collected, almost exclusively, Chinese art and artefacts. This is still the case, in large part, but the situation is evolving, as Chinese audiences are exposed to more travelling exhibitions from the finest museums in the world and as galleries and individuals begin to collect from other cultures as well as their own.

Out-of-date exhibition practices are quickly disappearing from Chinese museums and being replaced with more modern displays which are attracting large numbers of people. Additionally, the Chinese government has made all state museums and memorials (except ancient architecture and site museums) free of charge. The number of buildings undergoing renovation and modernization, as well as the construction of compelling and innovative new structures, is staggering. Every day, new private collections and government-sponsored museums open their doors.

The key national and provincial museums, e.g. the Capital Museum in Beijing and the Shaanxi History Museum in Xi'an, present their displays historically. Every province has its own museum dedicated to the history and culture of that region. Exhibitions are didactic in nature, showing the development of Chinese history through its art, neatly compartmentalized by dynasty or material. Over time, these museums have also acquired newly excavated treasures in the wave of stunning archaeological finds after 1949. From this period as well, a fervent pride in the new state and its institutions emerged, leading to the founding of institutions such as the Military Museum in Beijing and the Naval Museum in Qingdao. Is the government's purpose to use the artefacts in these venues to highlight the creation of China as a unified centralized state, in addition to showing their aesthetic value? Foreign visitors are often left with this impression. The emphasis on viewing objects with an eye to history rather than for its own sake can be seen in the common practice among Chinese museums of exhibiting copies of originals – and not always thus marked. This can occur even in a so-called 'Treasure Room', where a copy or cast is lovingly displayed as the real thing; it is not necessarily meant as a deception, rather the object itself may be deemed too valuable to risk exposure. This situation is likely to change with the creation of more modern museums, with ever better methods of conservation and tighter security.

Archaeological sites are now some of the most exciting art destinations in China, as new museums are built *in situ* and excavation pits are opened to the public – a trend that began with the Terracotta Warriors. Although, traditionally, the best finds went to the provincial museum or to Beijing, site museums are now able to start displaying their treasures in newly built, state-of-the-art galleries located at the excavation site. Great exhibitions of Chinese art are now being shown in the West, but, if able, do see the original collections *in situ*. No travelling exhibition can give more than a vestigial understanding of the impact of the Terracotta Warriors amassed in their burial pit the size of an aircraft hangar; or of the alternating intimacy and grandeur of the Forbidden City; or of the radiant magic of the great ancient bronze collection in Shanghai.

It is intended that the selection and presentation of museums will contribute to the quality of a visit to China and to the beginning of an enhanced understanding of Chinese art, culture, society and history.

Miriam Clifford, Cathy Giangrande, Antony White

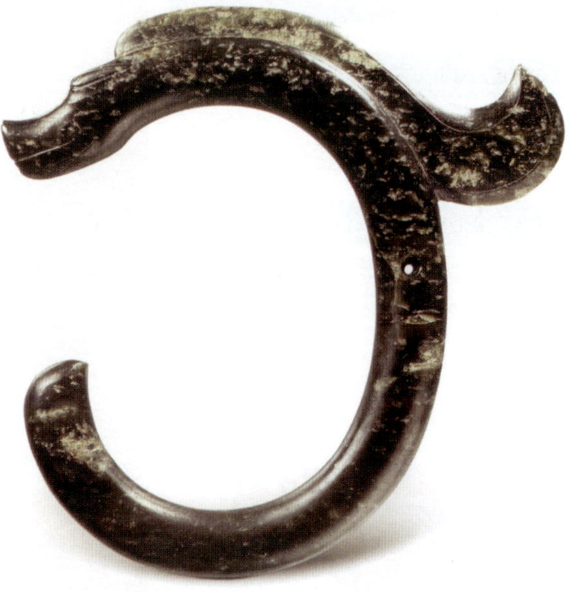

Jade dragon, Neolithic period, Hongshan Culture
National Museum of China (no. 31), Beijing

CHINESE MUSEUMS ASSOCIATION GUIDE

BEIJING AND THE NORTH

THE NORTHEAST

SHANGHAI AND EAST CHINA

THE YANGTZE

THE SOUTH

THE SILK ROAD AND THE NORTHWEST

TIBET

HONG KONG, MACAO, TAIWAN

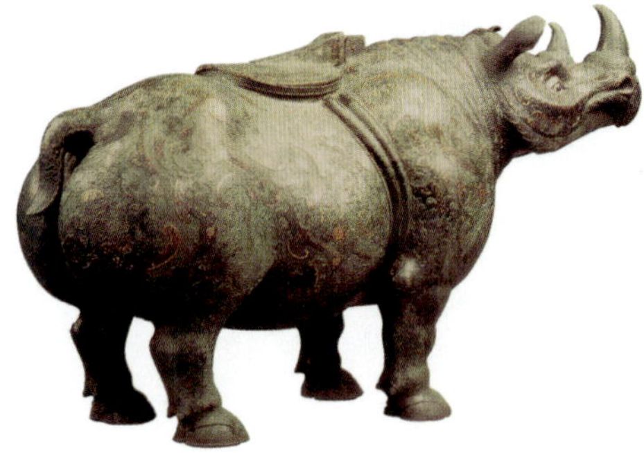

北京与北方

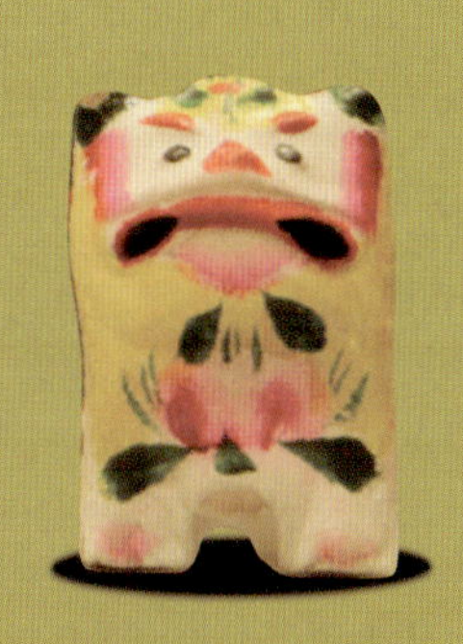
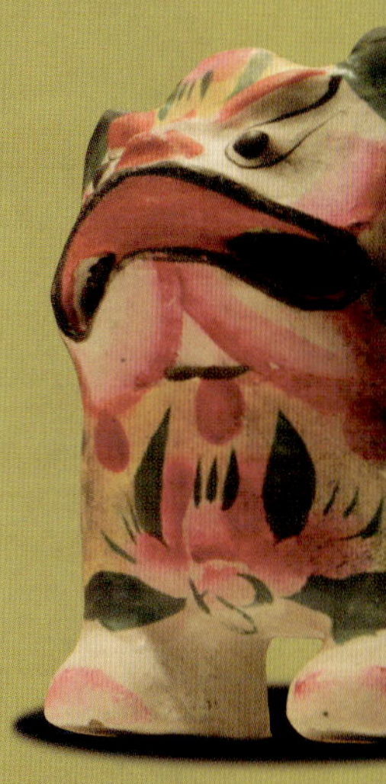

Arthur M. Sackler Museum of Art and Archaeology

北京大学赛克勒考古与艺术博物馆 *Beijing daxue Saikele kaogu yu yishu bowugua*

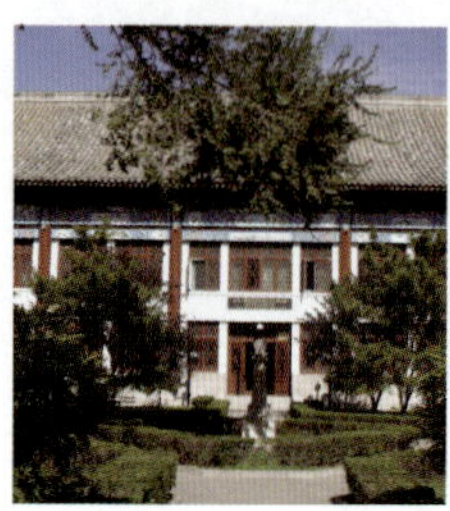

Inside the West Gate, Beijing University, Haidian District, Beijing
北京市海淀区北京大学西校门内
Tel: (010) 6275 1667
Open: 9.00–16.30 except public holidays, last entry 16.00
www.sackler.org/china/amschina.htm
Bookshop / gift shop

Arthur M. Sackler (1913–1987) was an American scientist, physician, collector, philanthropist and benefactor of the arts. Besides the numerous medical institutions he established, there are galleries and museums in New York, Princeton, Cambridge, MA, London and Washington, DC bearing his name. The idea for a *teaching* museum at Beijing University sprung from his desire to create a bond between people through art and archaeology. Completed in 1993, the museum was built by Sackler's wife, Jill, together with Beijing University after his death.

Because this museum was set up with a didactic purpose, it is the perfect place to begin one's journey through the art museums of China; a visit to the Sackler Museum offers a potted course in Chinese art history. When you have absorbed the information offered here, you are ready to tackle any of the larger, more complex museums you might visit, as well as appreciate more focused collections. This is certainly one of the 'must see' museums of Beijing due to the quality of the collection and its modern, uncomplicated and informative presentation.

The museum is set within the University grounds. Walk past the lovely Weiming Lake – The Unnamed Lake – which when frozen in winter becomes the University's skating park. It is well worth exploring the campus, which was once part of the Imperial Parklands. The American writer Edgar Snow, author of *Red Star over China* (1936) and protégé of Mao Zedong, is buried on a small hillside by the lake.

The Sackler Museum, carefully designed to be in harmony with the surrounding University buildings, is based on a courtyard plan of the Ming dynasty. The Gillian Sackler Sculpture Garden adjoining the museum lies in part of the grounds of the Yuanming Yuan, the Old Summer Palace. The collection originally contained objects from the holdings and excavations of the University but has been expanded to include artefacts from other archaeological institutes and museums. As you enter, a sign

Pottery figure, Northern Qi burial, Hebei

explains the chronological layout of the galleries, which are arranged according to the archaeological periods used when teaching: Palaeolithic; Neolithic; Xia, Shang and Zhou; The Warring States; Qin and Han; The Six Dynasties, Sui and Tang; Song, Liao, Jin, Yuan and Ming. There are also three separate exhibitions illustrating the fieldwork carried out by the University: the Early Palaeolithic site of Jinniushan Man in Liaoning; the Neolithic village of Beizhuang in Shandong; and the Bronze Age (Western Zhou) Jin State site of Tianma-Qucun in Shanxi.

The Palaeolithic galleries contain stone tools and grinding stones, and human and animal fossils from Jinniushan, while the Neolithic galleries have many fine pottery vessels from the Dawenkou, Yangshao and Longshan Cultures. Note the huge cooking vessel from Dawenkou marked with striations and a ring round the circumference, and the bold, geometric painted ceramics of the Yangshao.

In the Xia, Shang and Zhou gallery there are beautiful and characteristic examples of pottery and bronze vessels typical of the period. Notice the wonderful jumbo cooking pots, one with distinctive 'rope' decoration. Look for the red-painted ceramic vessel with tripod legs from the Lower Xiajiadian Culture.

The time-line continues with objects from the Warring States period – note the ceramic roof tiles decorated with animals and birds, and the bronze mirrors.

Many bronze objects, jewellery and horse trappings are exhibited, while the Qin and Han Gallery includes material from the burial pit of the famous Empress Dou of the Early Western Han. The faces of the ceramic figurines are serene, and their robes are expressive with their natural flowing lines.

The Six Dynasties and Sui–Tang period rooms contain wonderful examples of typical Tang ceramics: vessels, horses, camels and warriors. There is a large collection of figurines and ox-drawn carts in procession from a Northern Qi burial at Wanzhang in Hebei. Also included are some lovely celadon pieces and, notably, two formidable Tang *sancai* tomb guardians. The final gallery contains objects from the Song to the Ming dynasties. There are porcelains including Jingdezhen imperial ware and a Liao dynasty *sancai* plate.

Western Jin pottery warrior

Signage in each gallery, in both Chinese and English, offers a short explanation of the relevant period or excavation, and describes the highlights of the accompanying material culture. Lastly, there is a room for temporary exhibitions. The collection is a great pleasure to visit with its tasteful displays in well-lit cases, excellent and consistent English signage, and high-quality and well-labelled artefacts.

2

Beijing Ancient Architecture Museum

北京古代建筑博物馆 *Beijing gudai jianzhu bowuguan*

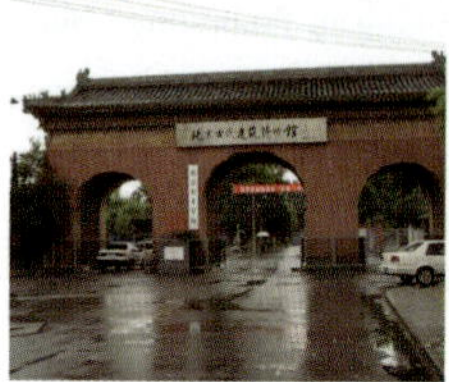

21 Dongjing Road, Xiannongtan, Xuanwu District, Beijing
北京市宣武区先农坛东经路21号
Tel: (010) 6304 5608
Open: 9.00–15.40 except Mon and Spring Festival
www.bjgjg.com
Audio guide (English, French, Japanese, Korean, German, Italian, Spanish, Arabic)

China's traditional architecture is a key component of its unique cultural make-up, from its walled towns, buildings set around courtyards and formal city layouts to the vast array of decorative elements and structural parts which meld together to produce a distinct style. As you wander round the country's temples, pavilions, hidden gardens and palaces, a better understanding of the elements of Chinese architecture will lead to a deeper comprehension of the two contrasting philosophies reflected throughout architectural settings: the Taoist belief that humanity and nature are one, and the need for order and harmony as laid down by Confucius. Insight into these schools of thought and the architectures based on them can be reached both inside the Hall of Jupiter (where this museum is located) and by exploring the surrounding complex of buildings – all that remains of the *Xiannongtan*, or Altar to Agriculture, which once occupied 3 square km. Unfortunately, signage throughout the complex is primarily in Chinese, but a good axonometric plan showing how this vast complex looked during the Qing dynasty can be seen directly ahead from the ticket booth at the entrance.

Even if you decide to skip the museum, this sister site to the Temple of Heaven, situated on the west side of the central axis leading south from the Forbidden City, is historically as significant and is certainly worth a visit. It was here that since 1420 the Emperors performed agricultural rituals and sacrifices at the vernal equinox. Clad in the yellow imperial silk robe and a blue coat, the Emperor would make his way from the Forbidden City with an escort of high officials and courtiers. Upon arrival he would proceed to the Altar to Agriculture, where he would make animal sacrifices to Xiannong, the legendary inventor of agriculture, and then perform the Tiling ritual, which consisted of ploughing furrows in the earth with the help of oxen followed by officials who would plant seeds and an old peasant who would cover them with earth. Once this was completed, the Emperor would celebrate in the Hall of Feasting. The Empress' duties involved feeding mulberry leaves to silkworms raised at the Altar of Silkworms and performing related rituals appropriate to women. Over the years, buildings were added and existing ones were renamed. During the Reign of Emperor

Qianlong, the Ming wooden viewing platform was rebuilt in stone (it can still be seen surrounded by a white marble balustrade). Here a tent would be erected with an ancestor tablet inscribed with Xiannong's name in the centre and a table bearing meat from the sacrificed animals and dishes of cereals and vegetables as offerings to the gods. The last time the altar was used was in 1906 by Emperor Guangxu.

Unfortunately, until the Hall of Jupiter was renovated in 1979, the site was subjected to all kinds of abuse. Since 1997 various donations from international charities, including the World Monuments Fund, have helped to fund the restoration of the Ju Fu Hall, the Divine Tablet Depository, the Divine Kitchen and its main gate, the Holy Granary and the Hall of Feasting, among others. A team of Chinese conservators have done their best to save as much of the original structures, paint work and mural paintings as possible. The Divine Tablet Repository and the Holy Granary are now museums, displaying objects relating to the First Agriculturalist.

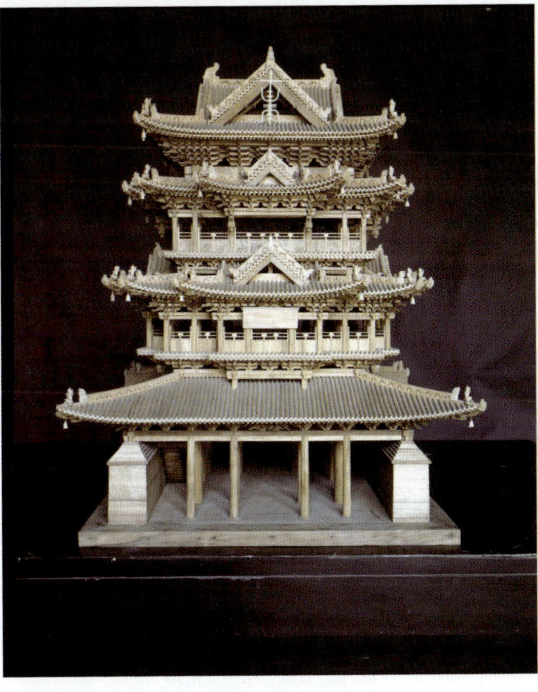

Wooden model of the Flying Cloud Tower, Wanrong County, Shanxi

The Hall of Jupiter is one of four halls enclosing a large paved courtyard, all exquisitely restored to their original kaleidoscope of colours, with tiled roofs and fabulous decorative features. The holdings include numerous beautifully executed models, images and diagrams which illustrate architectural advances as well as specific elements. Part 1 takes you swiftly through a survey of China's traditional architecture. One of the key displays here consists of wooden models illustrating the various shapes of *dougong* – a bracket used at the top of a column and composed of two elements: a rectangular block (*dou*) and a bow-shaped cross-bar (*gong*). Originating in early times, the *dougong* came into its own in the Tang dynasty, appearing more decorative and used according to sets of ratios graded to match the importance of particular buildings.

A selection of drawings and images illustrates the skills and the artistic input

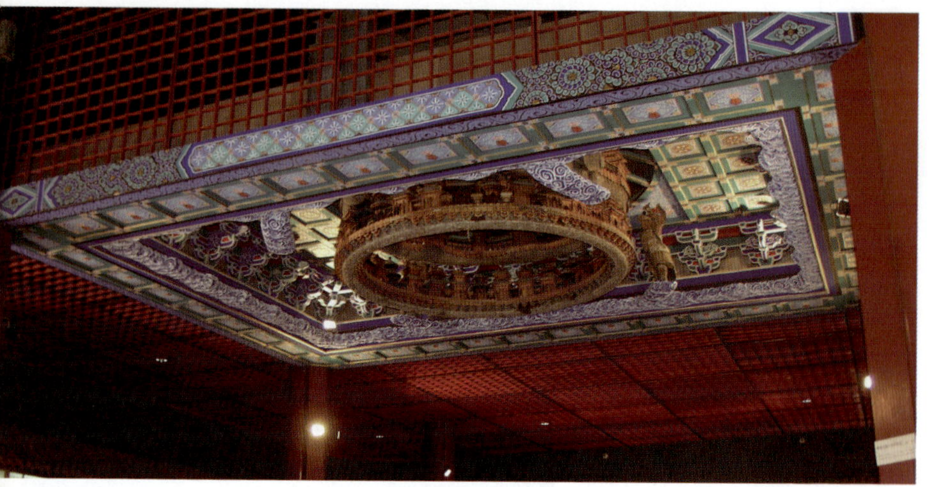

required for designing a Chinese garden. Further on is a much larger section devoted to the architectural evolution of the residence, starting with a Han dynasty funerary model of a multi-storey mansion which provides a useful glimpse of what buildings at that time looked like. The tiled roofs were supported by beams, and there were latticed windows as well as porches. Central to the elevated gallery in the exhibition hall is a 1:1000 three-dimensional map of Beijing as it looked in 1949 with its fortified wall still in place (it was removed in 1965 to build one of the outer ring roads). A stunning model of a corner watchtower of the Forbidden City built in 1368 shows its turret-style structure including its complicated triple-eave cross-ridged roof. Other models include the main hall of the Foguang Temple at Foguang Mountain near Wutai Mountain in Shanxi, one of the most important remaining wooden structures representing the apogee of Buddhist art and architecture during the Tang dynasty.

Walking back outside, you can examine several of the construction features you just saw in the gallery. These enormous wooden structures are true marvels. Take the time to notice the decorative paintings on the Hall of Jupiter: Qing-style *hexi* painting with golden dragon patterns, divided by 'W' shapes, is the highest-ranked decorative painting, representing supreme nobility. The central sections of the beams show a pair of running dragons facing each other, as well as ascending dragons (facing upwards) on a blue background (heaven) and descending dragons painted on green backgrounds (water).

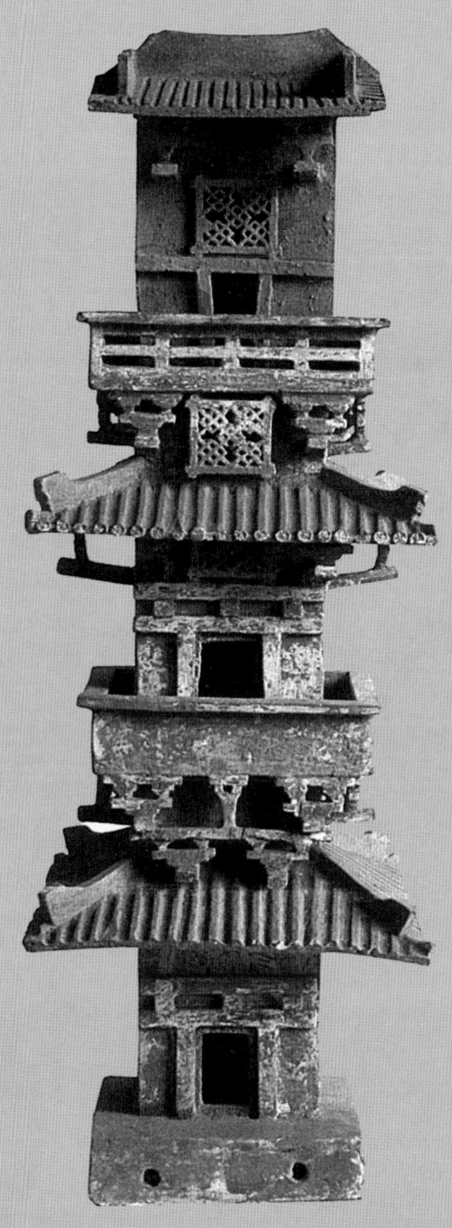

Han dynasty model of a multi-storey mansion

Beijing Ancient Coins Museum

北京古代钱币博物馆 *Beijing gudai qianbi bowuguan*

3

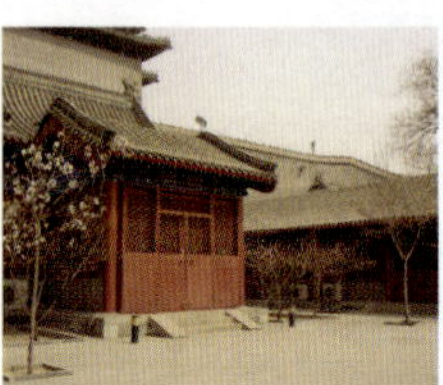

Arrow Tower, Desheng Gate, 9 Dongda Street, Xicheng District, Beijing
北京市西城区德胜门东大街9号箭楼
Tel: (010) 6201 8073
Open: 9.00–16.00 except Mon
English pamphlet available

The Beijing Ancient Coins Museum is located within the Desheng Gate, one of the two remaining arrow towers from the old Beijing inner-city wall, with eighty-two ports from which to shoot arrows. Imperial troops marched out of the city for battle through the Anding Gate and returned in victory through Desheng Gate. In 1664, when the rebel leader Li Zicheng led his army into the city to overthrow the Ming dynasty, he entered the city through this gate.

In 1993, the city government reconstructed the Zhenwu Temple and placed the Beijing Ancient Coins Museum here. On first entering the museum, there is a small pavilion consisting of a book and gift shop, which also has some introductory material displayed and a replica of a Qing dynasty bank from Pingyao, an ancient city in Shanxi, where the first banks in China were located until they were sidelined by the rise of a new up-and-coming financial centre: Shanghai. These privately owned banks, in Pingyao known as *piaohao*, date from the late Ming to early Qing period. Their existence is very important to Chinese Marxist historians, who point to them as evidence that China had developed its own brand of capitalism from feudalism. There is some English signage in this room, mainly just the titling. More detailed explanations of the displays are in Chinese only. There are also some numismatics books on sale, as well as various other small things and what the sales staff insists are genuine antique coins.

'*Shuntian*' Coin (front), Five Dynasties

'*Shuntian*' Coin (back), Five Dynasties

The galleries consist of two small halls in which more than a thousand ancient coins and paper money from the past 2,500 years are displayed. Metal coins in China date back to the Spring and Autumn period, when commerce first developed. Different types of coins were in use in different parts of

China and at different times. In the north, the design of coins was based on agricultural implements, such as the spade. These types of coins, known as *bu* coins, were common during the Zhou, Zheng, Jin and Wei. In the south, coins shaped like a knife were used.

After China was unified under the Qin dynasty, round coins with a square hole were introduced. This design was based on the Emperor Qin Shihuang's belief that the sky was round and the earth square. This model of coin, one of the most common in the museum, remained in use for some 2,000 years. The history of currency is illustrated including the earliest paper currency, which dates to the Northern Song dynasty. These first notes, distributed from Chengdu in Sichuan Province, were called *jiaozi* – a word which readers may recognize as meaning dumpling. There is a fascinating but complicated etymological connection between the paper money, the ingots of gold or silver used before the *jiaozi* as currency, and the dumpling, traditionally eaten during the Lunar New Year because its shape is reminiscent of money and prosperity.

Among the many coins exhibited are copper coins that were cast in the Republican period (1911–1949) and 'folklore' coins, first minted in the Han dynasty, which feature dragons or phoenixes.These were not used as legal tender but as precious objects to be given as gifts or collected. There is also an interesting display on the ancient technology used to cast coins, with an explanation in English.

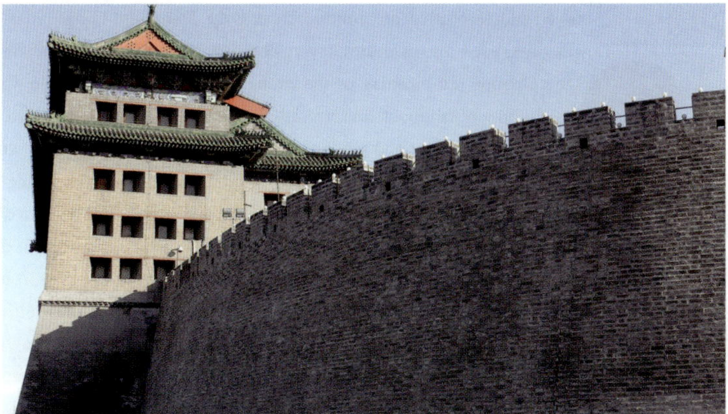

The collection is neatly displayed, but more detailed English signage would be helpful for the foreign visitor. Also within the Desheng Gate grounds, to the left of the museum entrance, is a little tourist market hawking copies of ancient coins and other knick-knacks. In 1994, the museum established the first authorized coin-transaction market here. The museum's brochure says the market offers coin aficionados an ideal place to buy and sell coins, but our advice is: Buyer beware!

If you climb the steps to the watchtower above the temple area, there is a good view of the city below. In the tower is a privately owned contemporary art gallery called Beijing East Gallery.

Beijing Art Museum

北京艺术博物馆 *Beijing yishu bowuguan*

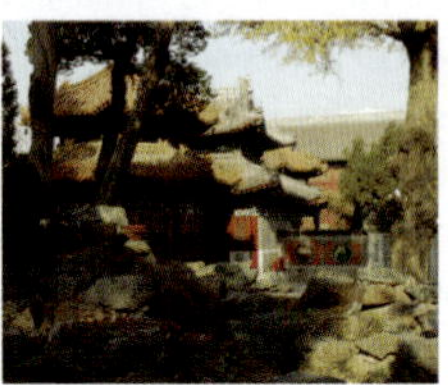

Wanshou Temple, Suzhou Street, Haidian District, Beijing
北京市海淀区苏州街万寿寺
Tel: (010) 6841 3380 / 6845 6997
Open: 9.00–16.30 except Mon, last entry 16.00
An introductory pamphlet is available but not on display

This lovely, uncrowded museum, set within a charming temple, is definitely worth the trip out to western Beijing. Sometimes called the 'mini-Forbidden City', it is built on the edge of the Changhe Canal, which connects the Summer Palace and the Forbidden City. It was once one of many temples lining the canal shore, almost all of which are now gone. The Wanshou Temple (Temple of Longevity) was built in 1577 during the Ming dynasty by Emperor Wanli for the purpose of storing Buddhist sutras and scriptures written in Chinese. During the Ming and Qing dynasties, the temple was often used for royal birthday celebrations; a thousand monks would chant sutras to celebrate the birthday of the Emperor's mother. The temple was continuously repaired and enlarged, and was used not only as a temple but also as a temporary imperial palace and garden; here the Empress Dowager Cixi would rest on her way to the Summer Palace from the Forbidden City. During the Republican period, the temple fell into disrepair, mainly owing to a fire in 1937 and the building's use by the Kuomintang army as an opium den. After 1949, it was used as a nursery school. In the 1960s and '70s, it became an army barracks. In 1979 the site was rescued when the Beijing government earmarked it as a 'key cultural heritage preservation site', and in 1987 the Beijing Art Museum was opened. Preservation and reconstruction of the buildings is still in progress.

When entering the first courtyard, visitors are directed to the Prologue Hall, where the history of the temple is explained and they can get a feel for the atmosphere of the Ming and Qing periods. There are excellent English translations and explanations of the exhibits throughout the museum.

The art is exhibited in the temple halls along the sides of the beautifully landscaped courtyards. The halls of Ming and Qing Buddhist art contain gilded bronze, stone, wood and crystal Tibetan and Han objects of worship. Some of these were not originally the property of the temple but come from the Bureau of Cultural Relics and are on permanent display here.

Glass snuff bottles

There is a Gallery of Ming and Qing Arts and Crafts displaying wooden brush pots, ivory work, bamboo, inkstands and other objects. Alongside the artefacts are explanations of the use of some of the more obscure items; for instance, there is a display of thimbles made of a variety of materials such as jade or stone that were worn by ancient warriors as protection for their right thumbs when shooting arrows and which, in later periods, became valued as ornaments. Also on display are snuff bottles, bowls and cloisonné.

The Ming and Qing Porcelain Gallery displays mostly imperial porcelain, some of which was actually used by the Empress Dowager herself. Again, the exhibit is sensitively displayed with enlightening explanations of seals and especially interesting details regarding glazes and manufacturing or historical details. In the centre of the courtyard complex sits a large Ming period Buddhist temple. As you enter, you see a seated Buddha figure atop a bronze base of a thousand Sakyamunis. This exquisite and atmospheric old hall has eighteen *Luohans* lined up on either side and three big Buddhas behind. Note the beautifully painted ceiling. Be sure to walk behind the big Buddha and see the painted wooden bodhisattva Guanyin, the goddess of mercy.

The Wanshou Temple's Bell Tower was built as part of the original Ming temple and repaired in the Qing period. Tradition has it that the famous big bell of the Emperor Yongle's Reign – the so-called 'king of bells' – was hung in this tower and was to be rung by six monks every day. However, during the Reign of Qianlong, it was decided that the temple's location was inauspicious for the ringing of the bell, so it was laid on the ground. In 1743 it was moved to the Juesheng Temple, where it can be seen today in the Ancient Bell Museum.

In the temple grounds you can sit in the rock garden surrounded by magnolia trees and breathe in the atmosphere of Ming dynasty China. The eastern and western portions of the original temple grounds have, over the years, been taken over as residences; after you have looked at the museum itself, you can wander through the surrounding *hutongs*. People are living in the old temple buildings, which are now dilapidated, and you can see the ancient peeling paint, rotting roofs and pillars of the once grand structures among the detritus of modern life. On some walls you can even see the faint remains of slogans from the Cultural Revolution.

Enamel hand-warmer, Qing dynasty

5

Beijing Aviation Museum

北京航空航天博物馆 *Beijing hangkonghangtian bowuguan*

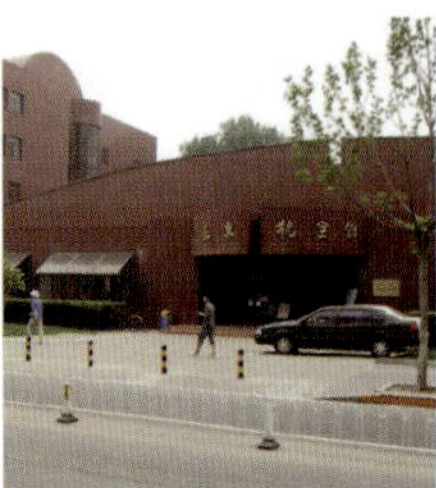

Beijing University of Aeronautics and Astronautics,
37 Xueyuan Road, Haidian District, Beijing
北京市海淀区学院路37号 北京航空航天大学
Tel: (010) 8231 7114
Open: 9.00–12.00 Tues & Sat (book on line ahead)
http://airandspacemuseum.buaa.edu.cn/ (Chinese only)
Kids

The Beijing Aviation Museum was used by Beijing University of Aeronautics and Astronautics as a showroom for teaching, practice and structural-design reference until 1986, when it was opened to the public. Unfortunately, there are no English explanations for any of the exhibitions.

The museum is divided into indoor and outdoor exhibition areas. The East Hall displays models and photos of various aircraft, as well as a model of the Chinese experimental communications satellite that was sent into orbit in 1984. In the West Hall are super-light aircraft which hang from the ceiling. The most interesting exhibits can be found in the yard to the back of the museum. On display are various aircraft from around the world and dating as far back as the 1940s. One of the most interesting is the P-61 night fighter, dubbed the 'Black Widow'. This name and a spider's web are prominently displayed on the front of this twin-prop plane, which was the first radar-equipped aircraft used by the Americans in the 1940s. Also of interest is a British Harrier jet. The P-47D fighter, aka the Thunderbolt, is easily identified by its chequered nose. Despite looking quite bulky, the P-47 was a fast aircraft and was used a good deal in Europe in World War II. The museum is also home to several MiG fighters, including the MiG-15, which saw heavy duty in the Korean War. The sole helicopter in the collection was the first such aircraft to be developed by China.

Photography is permitted.

MiG-15 fighter

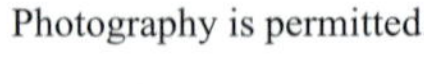

P-61 Night Fighter,
'Black Widow'

Beijing Museum of Natural History

北京自然博物馆 *Beijing ziran bowuguan*

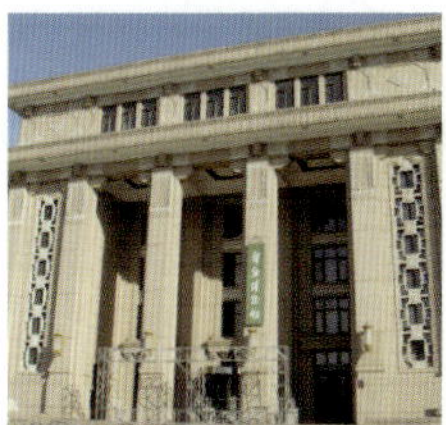

126 Tianqiao South Street, Chongwen District, Beijing
北京市崇文区天桥南大街126号
Tel: (010) 6702 4431
Open: 9.00–17.00 except Mon, last entry 16.00
www.bmnh.org.cn
Gift shop / café on second floor
Kids

Like so many museums of natural history, visiting this one is like walking into an oversized cabinet of curiosities, each exhibition hall – from the Ancient Reptiles and Invertebrates halls to Discovery World and the Aquarium – displaying the rare, the curious and the beautiful. This collection, however, unlike those founded in the great European cities, did not grow out of the wonders gathered by eighteenth-century men of science. Rather, it developed out of the National Central Museum of Natural History (founded in 1951) and consists primarily of indigenous specimens. Today, the museum boasts more than 200,000 items – a modest number compared to the many millions found in comparable natural history museums elsewhere – but its many unique specimens make it worthy of a visit.

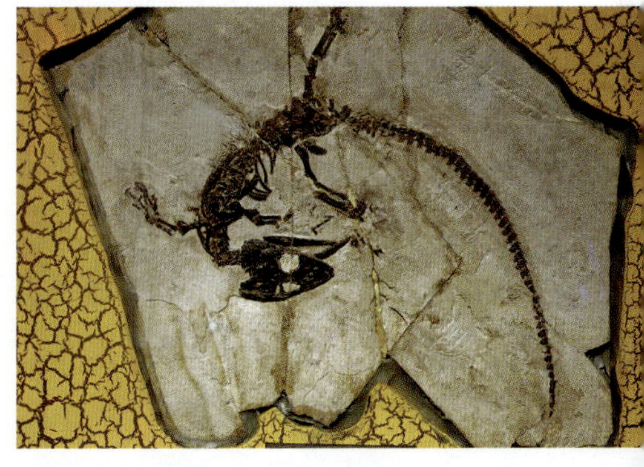

'onjurosuchus
lendens,
oto bird fossil

Displays vary in quality; many of the newer ones, like those in the Palaeontology Hall and Discovery World, make use of ultra-modern methods of introducing collections to the lay visitor and in particular to children. The vanishing Manchurian tiger is shown in its natural wilderness, while dinosaurs come to life – complete with sound effects and moving parts. Interactive displays allow school groups to learn through handling fossils and examining specimens, no doubt one of the reasons this is one of China's National Youth Science and Technology Education bases.

Overall the displays are well lit and described thoroughly in accompanying text, although only the main panels have highlights in English. Useful signage in the stairwells provides a layout of the museum indicating your current position and suggesting routes to follow, making it relatively easy to navigate the labyrinthine halls and exhibition areas.

If time is pressing, move to the large central dinosaur display entitled 'Dinosaur World' with full-size skeletons of a whole range of Chinese dinosaurs, some of which come alive as you approach, issuing sounds as they might have done in life. The long-necked *Mamenchisaurus jingyanensis* stands out. A gargantuan herbivore that lived around 150 million years ago, it had one of the longest necks of all known dinosaurs – 9 m in length – which allowed it to reach high in the trees to feed on leaves. Its 'second brain' in the hip area allowed it to control the movement of its hind legs and long, whip-shaped tail.

Another giant is the *Lufengosaurus huenei*, discovered by a Chinese dinosaur specialist and named after Lufeng, where it was found. Also plant-eating, its small, flat teeth with serrated edges enabled it to shred the plants it was able to reach while standing on its strong hind legs and using its big tail for balance. Also among the mix is the lake-dwelling *Tsintaosaurus spinorhinus*, discovered in and named after Qingdao in Shandong Province. Armed with a unicorn-like crest to which its name refers, this creature's large tail and paddle-like forelegs enabled it to swim.

Upstairs are displays of *Macroolithus* dinosaur-egg nests – the largest dinosaur eggs found in the world to date. Such nests have been found in various locations in China buried in sand or mud, sometimes as many as three deep, and date from the Late Cretaceous period.

Worth seeing are the cases crammed with beautifully displayed fossilized ammonites, sponges, shells and huge crinoids, or sea lilies. The computer-generated images of these early sea creatures are stunning. Fossils of *Archaefructus liaoningensis* – an extinct genus of herbaceous aquatic seed plant from the Yixian Formation in western Liaoning Province – date from the Jurassic and are said to be the first flowers.

Stringcephalus obesus, Chinese Devonian brachiopod

The basement aquarium is shabby but worth a visit if only to see the range of live specimens of fresh- and seawater fish; most impressive are the tropical fish. Also worth looking at, although rather dull in their formaldehyde-filled cases, are the two coelacanth specimens. A fish thought to be extinct since the time of the dinosaurs but rediscovered off the east coast of South Africa in 1938 when one was caught in a fishing net, these 'living fossils' date back 360 million years.

The Russian Tsar Peter the Great, who was renowned for his cabinet of human oddities, would have enjoyed seeing the hall entitled 'The Mystery of Humans' on the top floor. Displays of pickled body parts line cases around the walls while in the centre of the room, human cadavers with their heads hooded in black and feet covered with socks float serenely in coffin-shaped glass cases. Perhaps like Peter the curators hope these displays will inspire and above all educate; deformed fetuses and diseased organs are still used to support medical education and training.

The museum is active in scientific research across the disciplines of zoology,

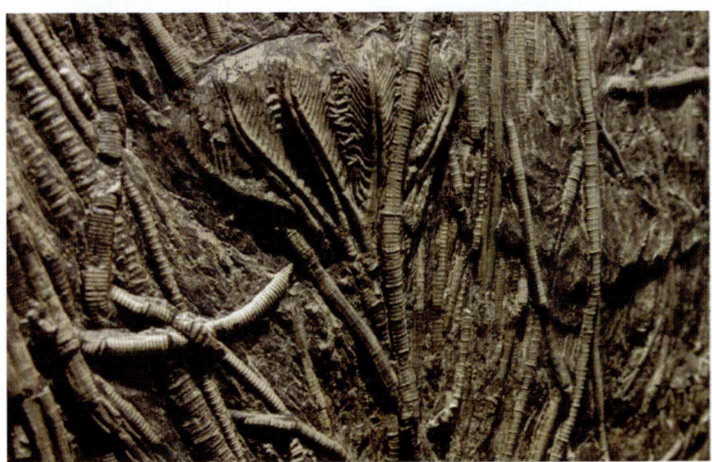

ossilized crinoids

botany, palaeontology and anthropology. Fieldwork, often together with visiting scientists from institutions abroad, is conducted across China, and provides a constant stream of new discoveries. A host of publications highlights the latest research achievements, and the museum, in collaboration with the China Association of Natural Science Museums and the China Association of Wildlife Protection, publishes the scholarly journal *Nature* alongside more popular scientific books and papers. Mounting exhibitions abroad serves to not only publicize the collections and latest research but also to play an essential role as 'cultural ambassadors', promoting international collaboration.

As you leave the museum, look at the specimens of fossilized trunks of petrified conifers, some well over a metre high, standing outside in the forecourt. These are from the Mesozoic period and were found in western Liaoning Province, one of the most abundant areas in China for fossilized wood from the Jurassic – Early Cretaceous formation.

7

Beijing Planetarium

北京天文馆 *Beijing tianwenguan*

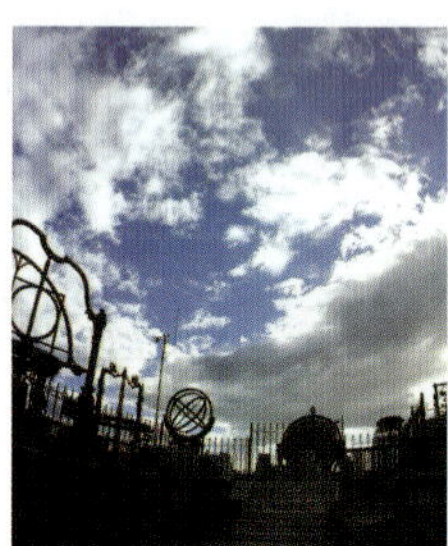

138 Xizhimenwai Street, Beijing
北京市西直门外大街138号
Tel: (010) 5158 3311
Open: 9.30–15.30 Wed–Fri, last entry 15.00; 9.30–16.30 Sat
& Sun, last entry 16.30; closed on Mon & Tues. 9.00–17.00
summer vacation; 9.30–17.00 winter vacation
www.bjp.org.cn/en
Gift shop / restaurant

A paradise for kids and young adults alike, this is a science museum with all the usual gimmicks, including interactive screens galore and state-of-the art projection. Whether you want to understand the fundamentals of the universe or learn more about the heavens and planets, this is a good place to spend a day. Much of the information is in both Chinese and English.

Built in 1957, the planetarium has since been re-fitted several times and now incorporates what the museum claims is one of the most advanced projection systems in the world. This planetary projector has 30 motors controlled by 45 computers and can project a 9,100 sun-star field made up of high-intensity white lights projected through fibre-optic cables, making a brilliant night sky. It can even recreate the twinkling of starlight and take viewers on a journey through a 3-D universe.

Move to the SGI – that is, Silicon Graphics Digital Space Theatre – where visitors

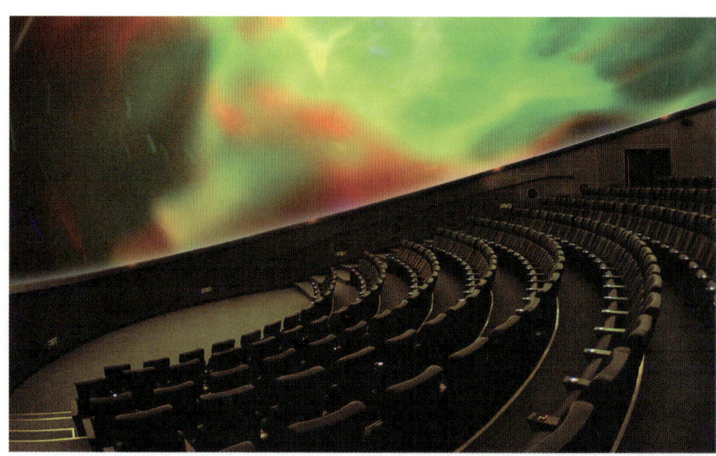

The fantastic
Silicon Graphics
Digital Space
Theatre

are treated to high-contrast colour images including tens of thousands of stars, 30,000 galaxies, nebulae, and spacecraft powered by a Zeiss All Dome Laser Image projection system. Together these technologies combine to bring the viewer into the vastness of the universe.

Not to be missed, especially by budding astronauts, is the 3-D theatre with turbo ride space ship shaped motion seats that simulate flights through space. If you fancy the experience of free-fall, swing and rotation, this is the place for you. If that is not enough, there is also a 4D theatre where added special effects including streams of air, smoke and sprays of water complete the experience.

If all this is overwhelming, you can come back to Earth and see the collection of meteorites or visit the Beijing Ancient Observatory. The observatory showcases a collection of Qing Dynasty astronomical instruments located at the top of a corner watchtower set in the ancient city wall. This was the city's first observatory and since 1949 has been run as part of the Beijing Planetarium.

Beijing Police Museum

北京警察博物馆 *Beijing jingcha bowuguan*

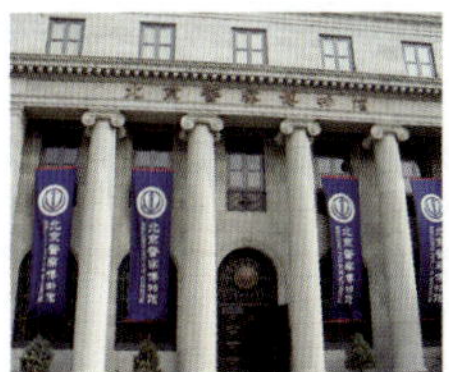

36 Dongjiaominxiang Lane, Dongcheng District, Beijing
北京市东城区东交民巷36号
Tel: (010) 8522 5001
Open: 9.00–16.00 except Mon

Situated on three floors, the Beijing Police Museum is thoroughly modern with well-lit cases, almost all with English signage. The content is thoroughly Chinese, including much political propaganda.

The ground floor shows the history of the Beijing police from its beginnings in 1947. There are many photographs as well as documents, uniforms and old guns. On the wall is a huge photo taken from Tiananmen on the occasion of the 1 October 1949 ceremony in which Mao declared the beginning of the Republic. Also displayed are cannons, uniforms and other objects used by the participants in the ceremony. In contrast there are weapons, radio equipment, signed confessions, photos, signed denials and other relics of recalcitrant Nationalist agents, spies and leaders. The usual pictures of visits to the museum by government officials and the high and mighty, including Mao Zedong and Deng Xiaoping, are also displayed on this level.

Upstairs there is a display of 'Judicial and Public Security Systems of Ancient

Chinese Society'. There are a number of ancient artefacts such as a stone tablet dating from the Eastern Han found in 'a criminal's tomb' and inscribed with an account of his misdeeds. Also noteworthy is a Jin dynasty terracotta figurine of a man in handcuffs. There are Ming dynasty suits of armour, police documents from the 1920s and 1930s, old maps of Beijing and photos of parades. Also displayed are some palace-guard uniforms and Qing dynasty police uniforms. Documents and photographs concern the travails of the police during the Cultural Revolution, when many members of the force were under attack. Even the Beijing police chief was persecuted and imprisoned. There are also some especially gory, graphic photographs depicting bombings, public uprisings, torture and murder – several of which are terribly gruesome and not suitable for children.

Photographs of and relics from particular crime investigations are displayed – such items can have a morbid fascination.

At the top of the building is an exhibition of guns used by the Public Security Bureau from the past to the present. There is also a shooting gallery in which you can try your luck shooting at bad guys on a video screen.

Beijing Concession District

This museum is housed in a former bank building in the old Legation Quarter of Beijing, an area well worth exploring as this neighbourhood is key to understanding China's domination by foreign powers. It begins on the southern edge of Tiananmen Square – called Qianmen – and is easily identified by the tower and clock of the old railway station – Qianmen Train Station – which has been recently restored.

After the First Opium War (1840–42) and the humiliating Treaty of Nanjing, the Qing government was forced, along with other degrading concessions, to allow foreigners to create a walled legation quarter in Beijing. All Chinese living in this district had to leave; no Chinese were permitted to enter without permission. Separated by walls, cannon and armed guards, the area became an international town within Beijing – outside the jurisdiction of Chinese law. There were restaurants, hotels, cafés, delicatessens, post offices and banks in addition to the offices of the occupying governments which included Britain, France, Japan, Sweden and Russia. The tremendous resentment such indignities caused came to a head during the Boxer Rebellion of 1900 when the Legation Quarter in Beijing was besieged and the German ambassador among others was killed. After months of fighting and many deaths throughout China, the rebellion was ultimately crushed by an international force which sailed into Tianjin, and then marched to Beijing to lift the siege, looting and pillaging on their way.

Although Beijing's Legation area is much smaller than that of Guangzhou and the Western-style architecture less remarkable than much of Shanghai, it still has an old world, colonial atmosphere. The streets are filled with solid old Western-style civic buildings and influences from German, British and French architecture can easily be spotted. Many of these buildings now house Chinese government offices. Some of the buildings that remain of the period include the Catholic Church of St Michael on the corner of Taijichang toutiao and Dongjiaominxiang, the buildings of the Belgian Embassy and a former French post office at 19 Dongjiao minxiang. The former Japanese Legation is on Zhengyi Lu and is now part of the Public Security Bureau. The Huafeng Hotel on Zhengyi Lu is still a hotel but was once the Grand Hotel des Wagon-Lits and was built in 1905.

Beijing Stone Carving Museum

北京石刻艺术博物馆 *Beijing shike yishu bowuguan*

9

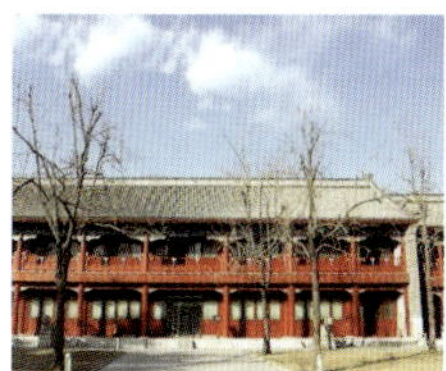

24 Wutasi Village, Baishiqiao, Haidian District, Beijing
北京市海淀区白石桥五塔寺村24号
Tel: (010) 6217 3543
Open: 9.00–16.00 except Mon
Delightful tea house

The National Library looming large on the north side of the Purple Bamboo Garden is your cue that across the street, along a rather quiet road and over the White Stone Bridge, is this museum within a temple complex. Unexpectedly peaceful and with a vegetarian restaurant attached, this delightful site is highly recommended for a brief respite.

Central to the complex is the handsome Wuta Si Temple, also known as the Five Pagoda Temple. Explore this first by going up the spiral staircase inside, as you will not only be enthralled by its carved decoration but from the top you will get a bird's eye view of the museum's mostly open-air layout. Built in the fifteenth century to house five golden Buddhas and a miniature model of the famous temple of Mahabodhi at Bodh Gaya in India (where the Buddha attained enlightenment), it was originally known as the Zhenjue Temple. The building was renovated in the Qing dynasty, when it was used as an important imperial religious venue. It was badly damaged during the Japanese War, and what remains is a pagoda

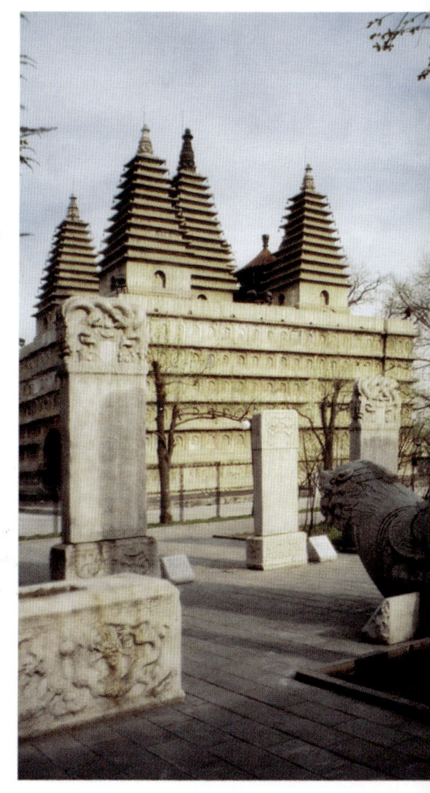

with a square base or throne and a large *shikhara* rising from four smaller ones. An enormous artwork in its own right, its surfaces are covered with the five sacred animals of Buddhism (lion, elephant, phoenix, horse, peacock), as well as the Buddha's

ve Pagoda
emple

footprints surrounded by lotus motifs, symbolizing his universal presence. Under each of the eaves are small shrines containing Buddhas.

The museum is divided into eight sections; displays range from tombstones to tools used to carve stone and fine examples of gilded stone tablets, all with very good explanations in English. A majority of the works are from the Beijing region with representative examples from various periods, many unearthed in recent years during construction work in the city. The stone tablets include one inscribed for a eunuch and others listing moral disciplines. Among the finest are twelve Ming and Qing tablets given by Emperors to their officials and generals and praising their achievements. Among the larger exhibits in the second hall is that containing more than a hundred stelae from the Tang to the Qing dynasties with inscriptions offering an encyclopaedic insight into the history, geography and politics of Beijing.

Decorative stone carvings for buildings and gardens (including arches, watchtowers, railings, balustrades and motifs such as dragons) demonstrate a diversity of styles and uses. Many of these were unearthed when demolishing the Ming wall in Beijing; particularly noteworthy are the stone lions which originally sat at the corners of foundation platforms in front of grand houses in the Yuan dynasty; the white marble decorated balustrade slabs engraved with dragons, phoenix and flowers; and the Song stone table listing acupuncture points. The third hall is devoted to the investigation and protection of carved stone objects in Beijing. In the 1950s surveys of carvings were launched in eighteen districts of the city to record, photograph and in some cases take rubbings. A map shows the distribution of these cultural relics. The survey's findings prompted the city to establish this museum in 1987.

The area entitled 'The Art of Stone Carving' includes the oldest stone carvings in Beijing – from the Eastern Han dynasty – as well as Buddha statues from the Northern Qi and Northern Wei dynasties. Further on, gilded stone tablets from eight different provinces demonstrate the intriguing differences in regional cultures. There are stelae with Buddhist and Taoist inscriptions and images of the tombstones belonging to the Jesuits once buried in a graveyard here, thus demonstrating the cultural interactions between China and Europe.

Beijing Tap Water Museum

北京自来水博物馆 *Beijing zilaishui bowuguan*

10

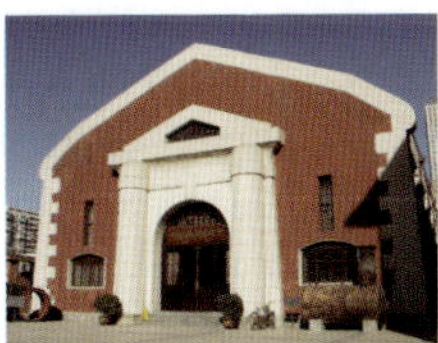

Inside the Qingshuiyuan, A6 Dongzhimen North Street, Dongcheng District, Beijing
北京市东城区东直门北大街甲6号 清水苑内
Tel: (010) 6465 0787
Open: 9.00–16.00 Wed–Sun

This is one of Beijing's newer technology-based museums. The subject may sound odd, especially given the fact that many people do not drink tap water in Beijing, but in fact the museum offers a compelling narrative of how this vital resource was and is delivered to the city's massive population.

Before there was any organized urban water infrastructure, Beijing's residents got their water from wells dug to reach underground springs. By around 1885 there were more than 1,200 such wells in the city. The water wasn't particularly satisfactory as it had a salty and bitter taste. Naturally, this would not have been suitable for the imperial family; their water was brought from a spring on Mt Yuquanshan in the west of Beijing.

How was the first public water system created? Apparently in the early twentieth century the Empress Cixi decided that a fire-protection system was needed for Beijing. For this purpose a source of water had to be available on the streets. This was achieved in 1907–08 when Yuan Shikai, the top Qing general who later became the first President of the Republic, initiated a tap-water system providing reliable, safe (as it was treated with calcium chloride) and plentiful water. The company created for this job, the Jingshi Tap Water Co. Ltd, was the country's first limited company.

The museum is housed in the original pump house of the Beijing Water Plant, making it close to a hundred years old. Built in partnership with the Germans, it is tucked inside a little courtyard – now an oasis – surrounded by high-rise apartment blocks and the Second Ring Road. Its location is evident from afar due to the tall brick steam pipe rising into the sky.

The exhibition is divided into three

Original equipment in the outside yard

sections. First is the history of tap water in Beijing. On display are photos and artefacts as well as stock certificates from the Jingshi Tap Water Co. Ltd. There is a life-size model of a Beijing street illustrating how water was dispersed early in the twentieth century; it was available from a central public tap, where a man was stationed to distribute it. Residents had to buy water tickets. If they were unable to carry the water back to their homes themselves, they employed others to carry it for them. If you were wealthy, you could have your water delivered by standing order. A blue metal sign was posted above your door (all this can be seen on the reconstructed street corner). The process of retrieving, storing, purifying and delivering the water is described and illustrated with original objects, photos and models. A model of the original 54-m-high water tower is also on exhibit.

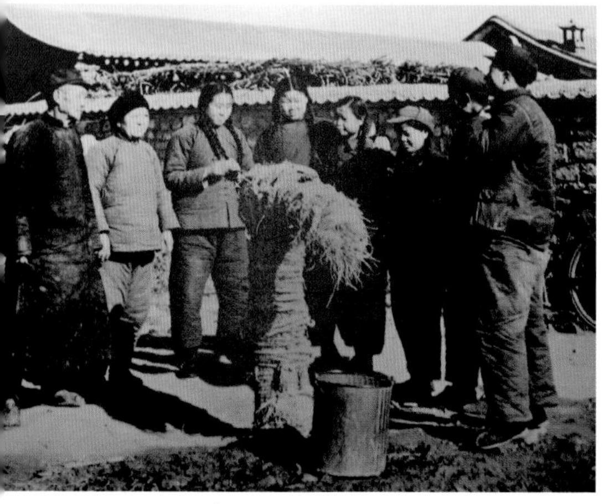

A public tap
in old Beijing

The second section of the museum deals with the period from 1949 to 1979. Following the inception of the Republic, the Capital Iron and Steel Co. was established in Beijing, and the importation of foreign equipment for the city's tap-water system was stopped. The People's Army was ordered to take over water disbursement in the capital; there is a photo of the original document dated 17 March 1949 giving this order. They had their work cut out for them as only about 30 per cent of the population had access to tap water – even at this time most people were still getting their water from wells.

The final section of the museum deals with the present and the need for water conservation. There are models of Beijing No. 8 Water Factory, which uses water from thirty-seven deep wells, and No. 9 Water Plant, which uses surface water and is one of the biggest in Asia.

There is a lovely circular pillared building at the entrance of the complex built as a shrine to Guanyin. This building stood before the pool where water was collected in the early days. The original statue within it was destroyed, but the building and charming park surrounding the pump house have been restored. Although the museum does not have much English signage, it is absolutely worth a visit, especially if you can bring a translator.

CAFA Art Museum

11

中央美术学院美术馆 *Zhongyang meishuxueyuan meishuguan*

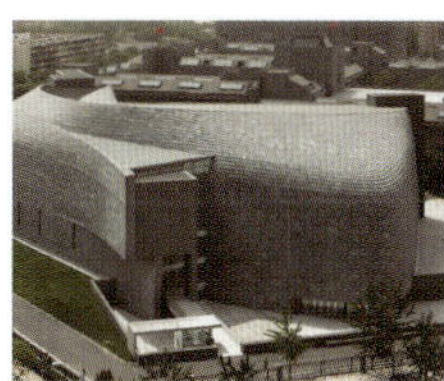

8 Huajiadi South Street, Chaoyang District, Beijing
北京市朝阳区花家地南街8号
Tel: (010) 6477 1575
Open: 9.30–17.30 except Mon, last entry 17.00
www.cafamuseum.org

This striking museum was designed by the prominent architect Arata Isozaki, whose work includes the Museum of Contemporary Art, Los Angeles. As an essential component of the Academy of Fine Arts, the museum's missions are to serve its

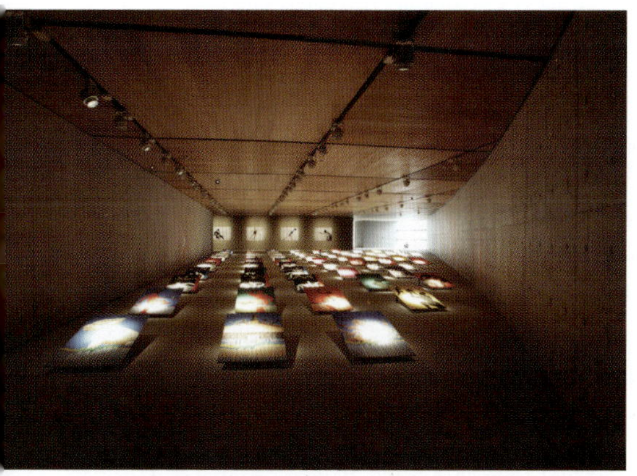

students and provide visitors with an educational experience. CAFA is the only art and design institute in the country directly under the supervision of the Ministry of Education. Its goals are to improve communication between artists and the public, and to educate the younger generation from Beijing and the provinces.

The museum has a collection of more than 13,000 pieces covering a wide variety of genres and styles from ancient to present, China to western countries, and all art fields, including representative works of maestros, contemporary artists, as well as fine art students since the foundation of the Academy. Tradition has it that graduates donate examples of their work to their alma mater, as well as a bequest after they die. As many of China's most famous artists attended the school, it has amassed a first-rate archive. The museum incorporates vast galleries with flowing lines and sharp angles – a feast for the eyes and a challenge for exhibition designers. The galleries are on four floors, with the second floor exhibiting local masters and the permanent collection. On the third and fourth floors the work of professors and teachers from CAFA is shown, as well as visiting contemporary exhibitions. Architecture, design, fashion and visual arts are all meant be represented in this venue, one of China's premier art establishments.

12

Capital Museum

首都博物馆 *Shoudu bowuguan*

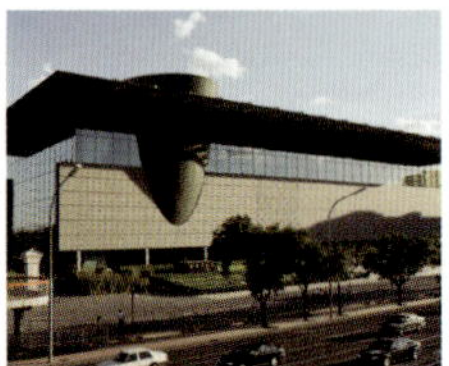

16 Fuxingmenwai Street, Xicheng District, Beijing
北京市西城区复兴门外大街16号
Tel: (010) 6339 3339
Open: 9.00–17.00 except Mon, last entry 16.00
www.capitalmuseum.org.cn

The original Capital Museum, although planned since 1953, was not opened until 1981. It was housed in the side halls of the Confucius Temple, one of the last idyllic sites of old Beijing. The original concept for the museum was twofold: to present a history of the development of the city of Beijing, its people, buildings and art; and to present a history of Chinese art, with an emphasis on artefacts collected in, or excavated in or near, the capital. The scale was small, the presentation and display unadventurous. The place was seldom crowded, and its charm was enhanced by the tranquillity of the surroundings.

From 1999 onwards both the municipal and state governments planned to move the museum to an altogether more grandiose site in Muxidi, west of Tiananmen and in the heart of modern Beijing. Construction began in December 2001. The new museum was designed by AREP together with China Architecture Design and Research. AREP, a Paris-based company specializing in transport projects, has had substantial experience in China, including work on the Xidan Bookstore a few kilometres down the road to the east on Chang'an Avenue, Beijing's central thoroughfare. The aim was to produce an intermingling of classic Chinese and modern architecture, in terms of both style and materials. Stone, bricks, timber and bronze are the major elements. The stone, from the Fangshan region, was commonly used in Beijing throughout its history. Elm, the most usual local construction material, is also used here. Decorative bronze features mirror locally unearthed Western Zhou ritual vessels. The massive overhanging roof is a modern essay on traditional low-slung Chinese roofs with eaves; the long stone curtain wall is intended to represent the ancient Chinese city wall, and a massive piece of stone carved with images such as dragons, phoenixes or clouds has been placed in the ground in front of the north gate. The basic two-part collection remains the same as at the Confucius Temple. Although the physical plant and tech services are world-class (and designed to rival China's

Jingdezhen ceramic kettle, Yuan dynasty

most modern museum to date in Shanghai), its scale (40-m high and 64,000 sq m) is deliberately in excess of the size of the collection. The museum's new building is therefore inextricably linked to its ambitious new exhibition programme.

The museum is made up of three main buildings: the Rectangular Exhibition Hall, the Oval Exhibition Hall, and the Office and Scientific Research Building. They are linked by a vast, towering reception hall and a naturally lit bamboo courtyard. The galleries devoted to the history of Beijing, housed on the second to the fifth floors of the Rectangular Hall, are the most interesting (sensitively and entertainingly arranged, they give a real picture of life in old Beijing, with a mass of architectural details, furniture, fittings, reconstructions of rooms and streets, toys, textiles, the Beijing Opera, and food and drink) and give a charming picture of the life and folk culture of the city as it was. They are not to be missed. The Beijing galleries are divided into History and Culture (second floor), Urban Construction (third floor), Chinaware and the Stage (fourth floor) and Old Stories and Folk Costumes (fifth floor). The exhibitions of fine art show highlights from the old Capital Museum on five floors of the Oval Hall and include painting, calligraphy, bronzes, jades, Buddhist art, and ancient stationery, writing materials and scholars' objects.

Gold and silver mask, Liao dynasty

Folk culture of old Beijing

The building's huge scale leaves ample accommodation for multiple temporary exhibitions, and it has got off to a cracking start with major shows from the British Museum and the National Museum of Mexico, as well as some great provincial shows. Such high-quality exhibitions from around China will be of particular interest to the overseas visitor.

China Agricultural Museum

13

中国农业博物馆 *Zhongguo nongye bowuguan*

16 East Third Ring Road, Chaoyang District, Beijing
北京市朝阳区东三环北路16号
Tel: (010) 6509 6067 / 6068
Open: 9.00–16.00 except Mon and Spring Festival
www.zgnybwg.com.cn
Gift shop

If you happened to be staying in the Chaoyang District during the summer months, you might find this museum a welcome relief from the congestion of central Beijing, as it situated in a green oasis of pine trees and cypresses offering shade and relatively fresh air. In fact, you may choose to spend longer outside than in, walking on the surrounding footpaths admiring a whole host of fruit trees, such as persimmons, apples and pears or, noticing the ornamental designs on the buildings of corn, grapes, sunflowers and fish symbolizing China's varied agricultural output.

Those not interested in natural history, be it animals or related subjects, might find this museum rather staid, but for those who wish to understand how China has fed its massive population several sections are very informative. You will, however be overwhelmed, as the main octagon shaped building connects through a series of corridors to ten additional buildings each hosting a number of halls harmoniously integrated with lake views, so it's best to choose the subjects you would like to explore most and head straight to these.

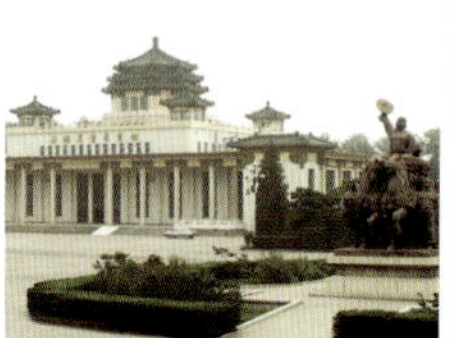

Animal-drawn seeding plough, a traditional Chinese farm tool

The museum is located in the National Agricultural Exhibition Centre, one of the 10 large public buildings constructed in Beijing in 1959 to commemorate the 10th anniversary of the People's Republic. The Centre is attached to the Ministry of Agriculture, and in addition to the museum it includes research and educational facilities where lectures, temporary displays and summer camps are held to disseminate agricultural science and foster international exchanges on agriculture. Trade exhibitions on agricultural equipment are also held on the site.

In the museum itself, for students and young people there are several halls explaining modern methods of farming which is a comprehensive course in agricultural science. There are also galleries highlighting China's marine resources and most recently, and of great interest, a section on energy and water resources. But it's not all about the present; in fact the museum prides itself on its holdings of traditional Chinese agricultural tools from all over the country. Cases are crammed with iron tools from the Liao and Jin dynasties to bronze implements, and cooking and food vessels. Halls displaying hundreds of implements are hard to take in, so it's best to concentrate on the exceptional examples. These include sacrificial relics that were buried in Shang dynasty tombs including bronze cooking and wine vessels, as well as dings from the Western Zhou. The Warring States are well represented too with bronze bells and other vessels serving as ritual food containers.

For historians of agriculture and rural life, the library holds the one of the most comprehensive collections of books on ancient agriculture in China. Here too, are New Year pictures known as nianhua. These bright and colourful prints, from ancient times to the present, are pasted on doors during the Lunar New Year to bring good luck, longevity and prosperity to the family.

The museum has also amassed an impressive collection of over 2,000 propaganda posters. These cover the initial land reform, then collectivization and the People's Communes. They depict idyllic scenes of bronzed peasants amid agricultural plenty: farm animals, ripening grain and experimental agricultural stations. But that system did not achieve the plenty the posters depict and shortages were typical. The museum has a large collection of small multi-coloured ration coupons, printed on thin paper, that were used during the period of the planned economy, for rice, wheat, pork, cooking oil, cotton cloth, even bicycles.

Foreign visitors will want to see the collection of stuffed rare animal, bird and marine specimens including the giant panda, Asian black bear, golden snub-nosed monkey, Tibetan antelope and the red-crowned crane.

The scope of the museum is enormous. The soil samples are the richest set of specimens in China – from the black soil of Northeast China, to the laterite filled soil from the South. These, along with the examples of hundreds of varieties of fruits made in wax and samples of trees, make an important collection for researchers and scientists.

Oddly for such a museum, but of great artistic significance, is the collection of ink-stones, used for grinding ink-sticks to produce ink for calligraphy and painting.

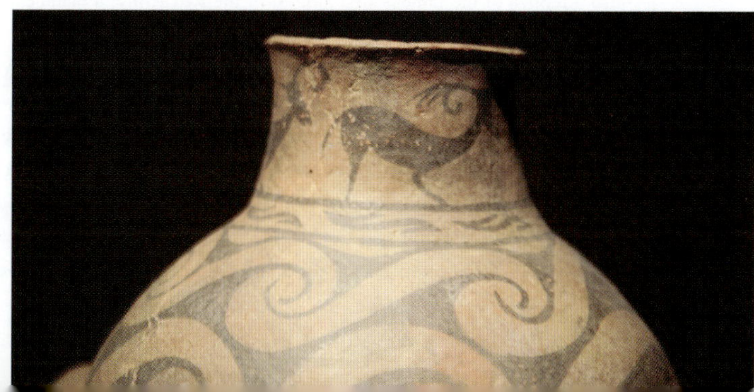
Neolithic pottery vessel with hunting and fishing pattern

China Aviation Museum

14

中国航空博物馆 *Zhongguo hangkong bowuguan*

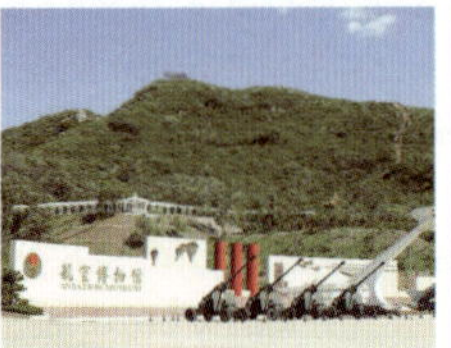

Datangshan, Xiaotangshan Town, Changping District, Beijing
北京市昌平区小汤山镇大汤山
Tel: (010) 6178 4882
Open: 8.30–17.30 except Mon
www.chn-am.com
Kids

Located about 64 km north of Beijing – approximately an hour's ride out of town – is the China Aviation Museum, among the finest aviation museums in the world. The museum displays more than 200 airplanes of a hundred different types, and provides an exciting hands-on look at the history of Chinese aviation. Opened in 1989, on the occasion of the fortieth anniversary of the Chinese air force, it is located on a former military air base at the foot of Datangshan.

The first thing you see upon arriving in the forecourt is a dramatic queue of surface-to-air missiles, anti-aircraft guns and a Chinese F-12 fighter. You then enter an enormous, dark concrete hangar hewn out of the mountain with double anti-blast doors at both ends. Here, more than fifty airplanes, parked side by side in two rows, trace the development of Chinese aviation and the indigenous aircraft-manufacturing industry. The exhibit begins with a replica of a biplane, made of bamboo by Feng Ru, China's first aircraft designer and aviator. Born in Guangzhou, Feng (1883–1912) emigrated to the US as a child. In 1907 he began to manufacture airplanes in Oakland, California with a company he named the Guangdong Air Vehicle Company. In 1911, he returned to China with two planes and began to work with the Guangdong revolutionary government. In August 1912 he was killed in a plane crash while staging a performance.

The historical time-line continues with a replica of the first plane manufactured in China, 'The Rosamonde', named for Sun Yat-sen's wife, Soong Ching Ling. There is also a replica of the famous first aircraft of the Red Army: a plane captured from the Nationalist army and renamed 'Lenin'.

Following World War II, China obtained its aircraft from the Soviet Union, but the country soon began its own production, manufacturing Russian models under license. Therefore many early Chinese-made planes are very similar to their Russian counterparts. In the hangar can be seen the Chinese versions of Soviet F-2, F-5, F-6, F-7 and F-8 fighter planes. Also on exhibit are a Russian La-11 fighter, a Tu-2 bomber and a Mi-4 helicopter. Of special interest are MiG-15 and -17 fighter planes flown by Chinese and Soviet pilots during the Korean War. Some of these have stars painted below the cockpit – known as 'MiG Kills'– indicating how many American and South Korean planes they had shot down. Signage by the planes gives the names of the pilots responsible. Also notable is an American Mustang captured from the Nationalist army in 1949 and a Japanese Tachikawa Ki-36 used by the Japanese against Chinese guerrilla fighters, as well as an Italian fighter aircraft – an F-104S – donated by the Italian air force.

Leaving the hangar, you see – parked by the side on the taxiway across from some gift shops and drink stands – a line-up of fighter planes from China and North Korea, including a rare FT-6 training plane. Finally you can wander out to the field where large aircraft of all sorts are parked. There are planes used during World War II and the early years of the People's Republic to transport senior leaders such as Mao Zedong, Zhou Enlai and Zhu De (commander-in-chief of the PLA). Here is an Li-2 used by Mao to inspect Guangzhou, Changsha, Wuhan and other areas in 1956. There is an Il-14 also used by Mao in 1957–58 which you can enter and see just as it was when Mao flew in it, his desk and bed, the carpet and upholstery all authentic and surprisingly austere. Displayed as well is the Y-5 transport, an all-purpose plane modelled on the Soviet An-2 which was used to scatter the ashes of Premier Zhou Enlai in 1976. You can even see a C-46 Transport Commando, flown over 'the Hump' by the US air force in World War II. After the Japanese took control of the Burma Road, the allies kept the Chinese Nationalists supplied by flying this treacherous route over the Himalayas. By the end of the war, more than 44,000 tons a month were being delivered, with a plane taking off every three minutes. More than 600 planes were lost.

The huge field is filled with every conceivable type of plane, both commercial and military, dating from World War II and later (helicopters, bombers and passenger planes; B-29 bombers from the 1940s, a MiG-21, a Red Flag F-20 fighter, even a water-ready flying boat). The list goes on and on. The planes have been left out in various states of decay. You can board many of them or clamber around outside, offering excellent photo opportunities and a great deal of fun. English labelling accompanies many displays.

For those with an interest in planes and aviation history, this experience is not to be missed.

15

China Millennium Monument World Art Museum

中华世纪坛世界艺术馆 *Zhonghua shijitan shijie yishuguan*

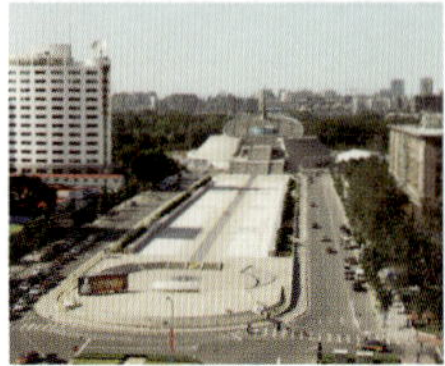

A9 Fuxing Road, Haidian District, Beijing
北京市海淀区复兴路甲9号
Tel: (010) 5980 2222
Open: 9.00–17.00 except Mon, last entry 16.10
www.worldartmuseum.cn
Gift shop / bookshop

Built to celebrate the millennium this venue often hosts world-class national and international travelling art exhibitions. In 2001 it was the venue for the inaugural Beijing Biennale and has, over the years, hosted many high-calibre shows featuring contemporary, modern, classical and archaeological art both from China and abroad.

Check local listings to see what is on during your stay in Beijing.

Statues of
well-known
Chinese artists
in the gallery

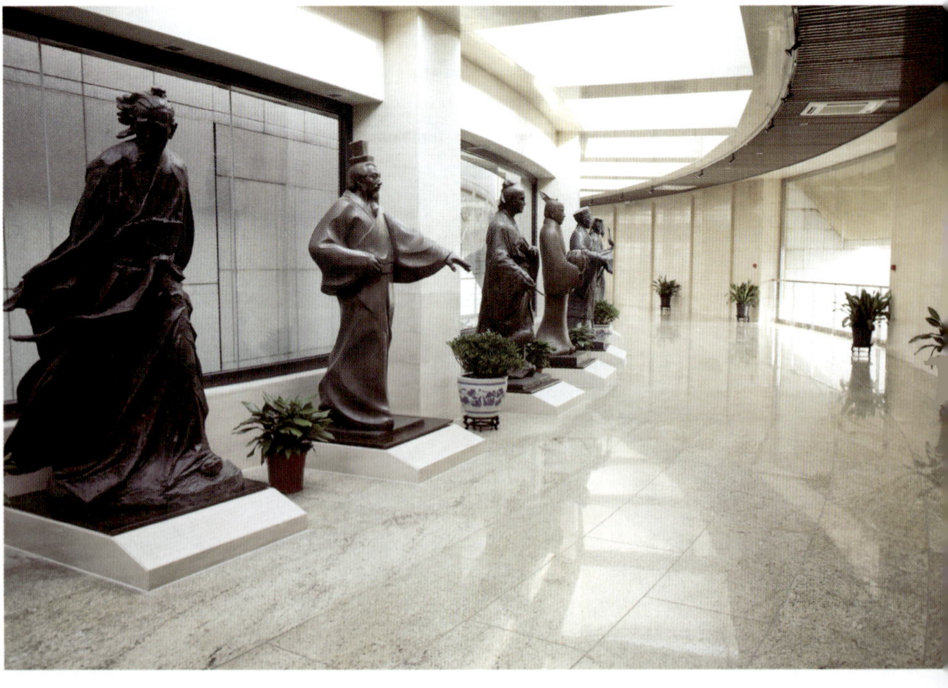

China National Film Museum

中国电影博物馆 *Zhongguo dianying bowuguan*

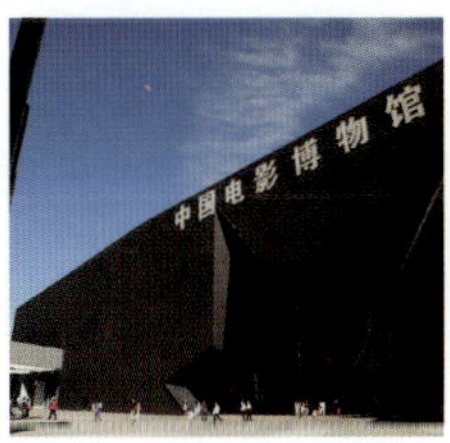

9 Nanying Road, Chaoyang District, Beijing
北京市朝阳区南影路9号
Tel: (010) 8435 5959
Open: 9.00–16.30 except Mon
www.cnfm.org.cn
Gift shop with legitimate DVDs / cafeteria / snack shops (including popcorn for movie viewing)   Kids

Since the release of *Ding Jun Shan*, China's first feature film, in 1905, China has had a thriving and innovative cinema industry. The film museum and cinema complex celebrates this past and present through exhibits and screenings. Unfortunately, there is little in English, but you can learn a lot walking through the museum's twenty exhibition halls with a Chinese friend. Content includes the history of Chinese cinema from its inception, animated and documentary films, the Hong Kong and Macao film industry and so on. Biographical information on stars and directors is displayed, as well as exhibits on special effects, sets and costumes, animation and the science of film photography. Hands-on interactive exhibits, which the kids might enjoy, allow you to try out camera and film technologies while making your own film. Shooting, editing, music, special effects and developing are covered. (Some of these exhibits are not always available during the week and when available may involve waiting in a long queue.) A variety of movies are also available for viewing. The museum has three 35-mm projection theatres, a digital-projection theatre screening panorama-format films with surround sound, and an IMAX theatre.

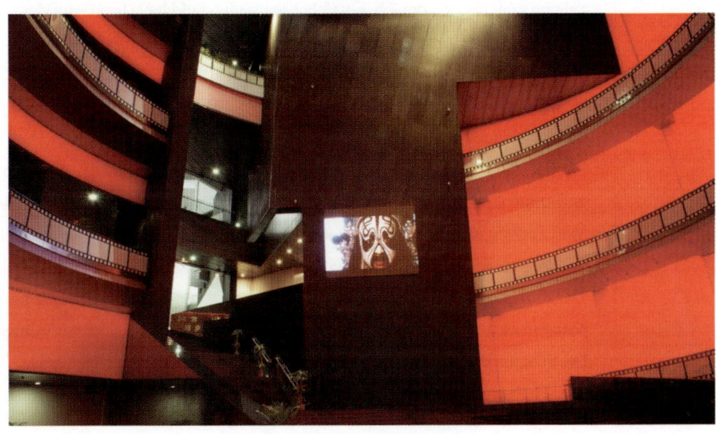

China National Post and Postage Stamp Museum

中国邮政邮票博物馆 *Zhongguo youzheng youpiao bowuguan*

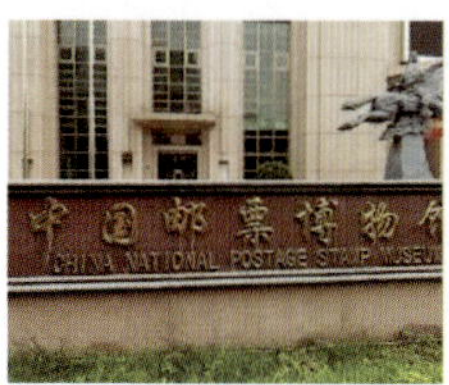

Building D, 6 Gongyuan West Street, Dongcheng District, Beijing
北京市东城区贡院西街六号D座
Tel: (010) 6521 3894
Open: 9.00–16.00 except Mon
www.cyzypm.com

The China National Post and Postage Stamp Museum is located in the centre of Beijing in a new building. The exhibit is spread out over three floors, with postage stamps exhibited on the first floor, the early history of communications and postal services introduced on the second floor, and China's modern postal system on the third floor. The stamp exhibition on the first floor, set in standing panels, covers the period from the Qing dynasty up to modern China. Stamps made in China up until the fall of the Nationalist government in 1949, which are against the wall on the left, have faded-looking inks and simple designs on cheap paper. It's only after 1949 that stamps become more colourful and themes begin to show a great deal of diversity.

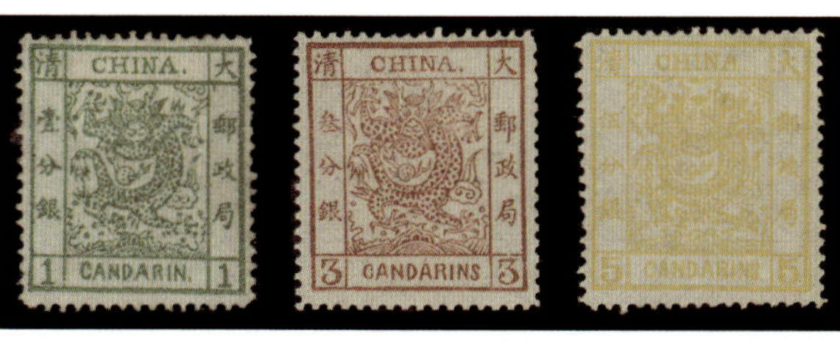

Rare set of China Candarins

The exhibition begins with Qing dynasty (1644–1911) in the 1800s. Prominent is the Dowager Jubilee, issued on 7 November 1894 to mark the 60th birthday celebration of the Empress Dowager Cixi. The stamp does not carry an image of the Empress Dowager, but rather a drawing of a dragon, possibly because it would have been considered improper to put the image of a member of the ruling family on a postage stamp.

The next period is the Republic of China (1912–49), featuring stamps with the image of Sun Yat-sen, the founder of the Nationalist Party that overthrew the Qing dynasty. Other stamps include Nationalist strongman Chiang Kai-shek, and sampans.

During the Revolutionary period, the 'People's Government', although not the official government of China, issued stamps in the areas under their control. A 1944 issue features Mao Zedong, then a guerrilla leader. There is also a workers' series issued in February 1949 showing an intellectual, soldier, postal worker and coal miner standing together in solidarity. The collection from this period also shows some actual envelopes bearing postage stamps and postal marks. A 1947 stamp celebrating the victory over the Japanese features Mao and Zhu De, in both perforated and unperforated editions, the latter for collectors.

The panels in the centre of the hall are devoted to stamps from around the world and modern China. This is a colourful collection, most of which is dedicated to Chinese culture. There are also stamps on folk dance, Chinese instruments, Peking opera, traditional paintings, Buddhism and temples and mosques. Of particular interest is the series on Peking opera, featuring famous opera stars, including the legendary Mei Lanfang, who performed the *huadan*, or female role, in opera before women were allowed to perform.

A room to the left of the main hall features special exhibits that are held for six months to a year, featuring special stamps from the museum's collection.

The second floor is dedicated to the history of communications in China, and the connection with postal services is not always clear. The exhibits here feature the use of drums, fire from beacon towers and the use of horseback couriers – much as in the old West in the United States – to communicate between the long distances that separated frontier fortresses in ancient China. In the Ming dynasty a rudimentary postal system begins to take shape, and by the Qing dynasty we have postal regulations and a management system governing the courier stations around China. There is an exhibit on the birth of the non-government commercial postal system in the fifteenth century, and the appearance of overseas mail offices in the nineteenth century, established so that overseas Chinese could send letters and financial remittances back home.

The exhibition traces the birth of the modern postal system in 1896 during the final years of the Qing dynasty, the advances under the postal system of the Republic of China, the Revolutionary period of secret communications instituted by the Communists, and the Red Post and Soviet Post during the Agrarian Revolution. On display here are black and white photos of early post offices, mail carrier uniforms, antique mailboxes, and other items related to the Chinese postal system.

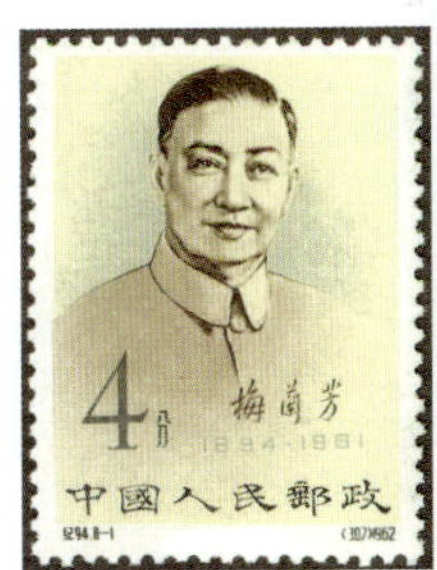

The third floor is dedicated to China's modern postal system. Of especial interest is a video programme about a postal worker in the mountains of Sichuan province. The carrier is seen leading a white horse carrying two large mail bags over a wooden saddle up mountain paths, sometimes across snow-covered trails, as he delivers mail to far-flung reaches of the province, sleeping in tents in the evening.

The highlight of the floor – and possibly the museum – is the dark room where the museum displays its most valuable stamps under special lights. The collection includes an original Penny Black stamp from the United Kingdom, said to be the first adhesive postage stamp to be issued in the world, on 1 May 1840. The stamp, considered a masterpiece of the engraver's art, displays a profile of young Queen Victoria, reminiscent of the cameos of rulers on coins, wearing a crown. The stamp is framed by the words Postage and One Penny.

Stamp celebrating
Mei Lanfang

China Printing Museum

中国印刷博物馆 *Zhongguo yinshua bowuguan*

18

25 Xinghua North Road, Huangcun Town, Daxing District, Beijing
北京市大兴区黄村兴华北路25号
Tel: (010) 6026 1237
Open: 8.00–16.30 except Mon

Although the museum building itself is rather unremarkable, its subject matter is not, for although it is common knowledge that Johannes Gutenberg fashioned the printing press in 1450, few know that he was neither the inventor of movable type, nor the creator of the first printed book. These firsts should actually be attributed to China. The exact dates of these inventions are rather murky. Probably as early as the seventh century, the Chinese were using carved wooden blocks to print Buddhist prayers on paper, although no examples to date survive. The oldest, extant printed scroll dates from between 704 and 751 and was found in a stupa at a Buddhist temple in Korea (written in Chinese characters). In China, the oldest printed book is said to be the Diamond Sutra scroll dating from 868 found in the Buddhist caves at Dunhuang. More recently, printed Buddhist charms (prayers known as *dharani* in Sanskrit rolled up and inserted into miniature pagodas) were discovered in a tomb in Sichuan, dating from around 757. It is certain that the Chinese developed the means to produce printed matter with the invention of writing 4,000 years ago and paper likely around the first century AD.

A further pioneering Chinese endeavour was recorded in the mid eleventh century by Shen Gua (who wrote on the history of Chinese science in his *Brush Talks from Dream Brook*) who credited the invention of clay moveable type (ready made characters which can be moved and reused) printing to the engraver, Bi Sheng – an innovation which would later find its way to the West and be used by Gutenberg to print the Bible. As visitors enter the museum, a large bronze statue of Bi Sheng holding moveable type takes centre stage, highlighting this printing milestone which made it possible to accelerate the production of books. Three main display halls and three special exhibition areas over the museum's four floors trace the origin and development of printing through pictures, explanatory text (some in English), original objects and

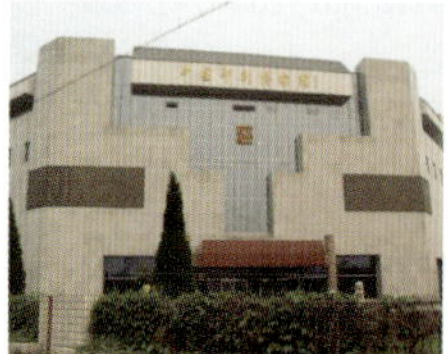

Bi Sheng, inventor of moveable type

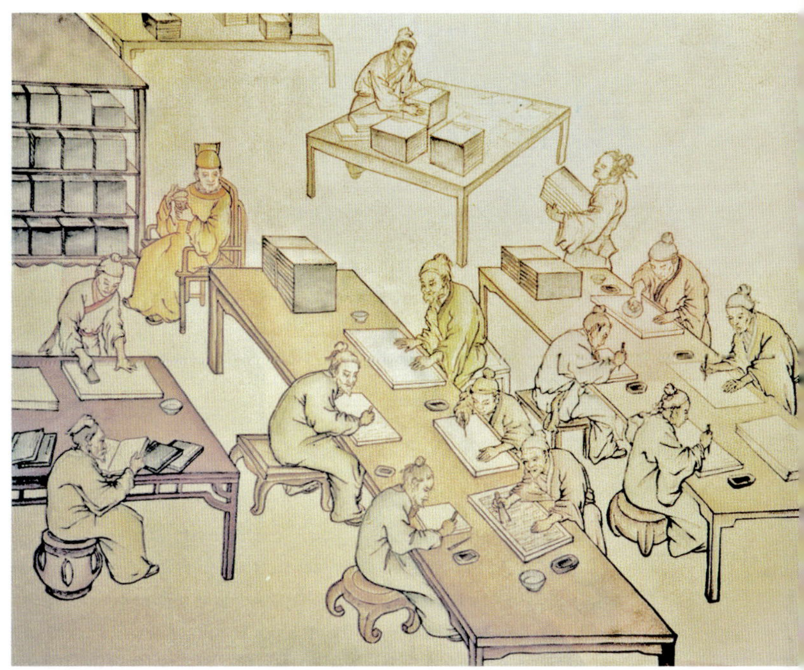

Workers at the 'Directorate of Ceremonies' printing the Classics

reproductions. Of these, the most fascinating exhibits relate to the invention of printing in China and elsewhere, from the earliest clay type to the later bronze used first in the Yuan dynasty for the printing of *The Imperial Examination Scripts*. Government as well as private printing were active during the Yuan with Hangzhou as the major centre in the south and Pingyang in the north, while during the Ming – known as the golden period of printing in China – the scale of printing grew exponentially, the quality improved and colour printing was invented. The second floor focuses on more recent printing advances such as planography (the technique of transferring ink to paper from a flat surface) and stencil printing and displays methods for specific types of printing, such as those used to print money (China was the first country to print a form of paper money known as 'exchange media' in the Southern Song) and stamps. The glamour of digital printing technology is touched upon on the first floor along with a concise history of printing in the West. An excellent publication entitled *An Illustrated History of Printing in Ancient China* (1998) chronicles this glorious history by means of excellent text and illustrations.

19

China Railway Museum

中国铁道博物馆 *Zhongguo tiedao bowuguan*

Dongjiao Branch:
North of the Loop Line, 1 Jiuxianqiao
North Road, Chaoyang District,
Beijing
北京市朝阳区酒仙桥北路1号院北侧
Tel: (010) 6438 1317
Open: 9.00–16.00 except Mon

Zhengyangmen Branch:
A2 Qianmenda Street, Dongcheng
District, Beijing

北京市东城区前门大街甲2号
Tel: (010) 6705 1638
Open: 9.00–17.00 except Mon

Zhan Tianyou Memorial
Museum:
Badaling District, Beijing

北京市八达岭特区
Tel: (010) 6912 1516
Open: 8.30–16.30 except Mon

www.china-rail.org   *English and Chinese audio guides   Kids*

Though somewhat difficult to find, this state-owned museum – China Railway Museum (Dongjiao Branch) is well worth the adventurous journey. Just off the Fifth Ring Road and only fifteen minutes from the hip contemporary art scene at Dashanzi, this is a must-see for train enthusiasts. Housed in a large hangar-like shed connected to the China Academy of Railway Sciences Test Loop, the collection of locomotives and cars illustrates the development of China's railways from the nineteenth century to the present. Opened in 2002, the eight tracks can accommodate between eighty and ninety locomotives and carriages; more than one hundred locomotives are on display, thirty of which were steam powered.

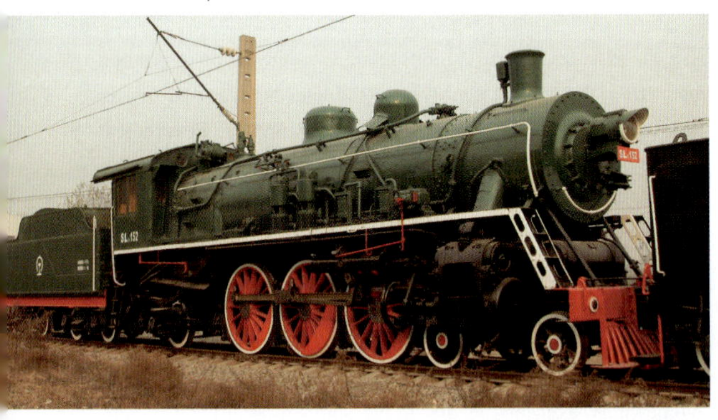

Japanese locomotive 'The Pacific'

The first railway line in China was built illegally in 1876 by a group of Englishmen associated with Jardine Matheson, the Hong Kong trading company. They built a narrow-gauge line from Shanghai to Wusong, a distance of 15km, to the mouth of the Huangpu River. This project was not approved by the Qing government, which purchased the railroad in 1877 and dismantled it. A standard-gauge railway was built by the English in 1881 from Tangshan to Xugezhuang for the purpose of transporting coal from the Tangshan mines. The first steam locomotive was constructed using the boiler and other parts of a portable steam winding engine borrowed from the colliery. This home-made 0-4-0

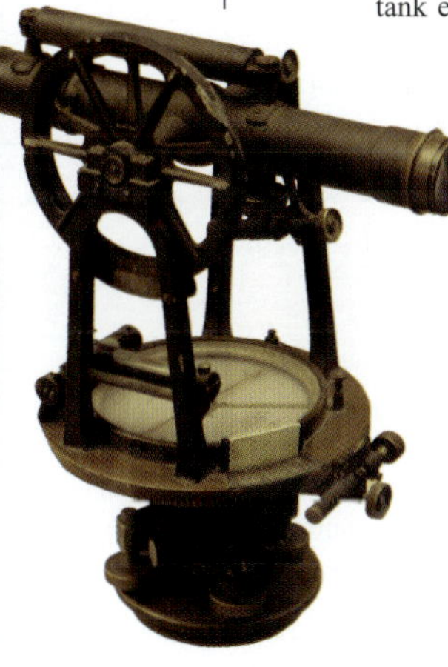

Theodolite used in
Jing–Sui Railway

tank engine was known as 'The Rocket of China', and it was so successful that two more were ordered from the well-known manufacturer Robert Stephenson & Co. of Newcastle, making them the first to be imported into China. An example of these, as well as the oldest steam locomotive in China (fully restored after the 1976 earthquake in Tangshan), can be found in the museum.

Following the defeat of China in the Sino-Japanese War of 1894–95, the Great Powers proceeded to 'carve up' China, building railways as a key element of their spheres of influence. Russia built a railway across the northern east of China, Germany built the Jiaoji Railway from Qingdao to Jinan, France built the Sino-Vietnamese Railway in the southwest, and the British built the Kowloon Canton Railway. This explains the extraordinary variety of rolling stock in the country.

Among the highlights of the collection are:

- Foreign locomotives used in Republican China, such as the 1947 US-built steam locomotive Class KD_7 534. This train, built by Bowen Locomotive Co. and used for freight as well as passengers, was among a batch donated by the United Nations to help with economic recovery after World War II. It was called the 'Union Style' and was at the time the most technologically advanced in production.

- The Class SL_3-152 Japanese locomotive known as 'The Pacific'. Produced in 1942 and made by Kawasaki, it was the main passenger car used throughout the north and east of China, retiring only in 1981.

- A Russian Class FD 1979 steam locomotive made in the Soviet Union in 1931 and brought to China in 1958, when the country had a shortage of railroad transport capacity. It was used extensively in central China.

- Zhou Enlai's official personal coach, Class GW 97336, built in 1936 in Manchuria at the Dalian Works. Premier Zhou used this as his office when travelling in the 1950s and '60s. Visitors can enter the cars and view his and his wife's bedrooms, including her fuchsia-coloured bathroom suite.

The museum's audio guide is quite helpful, though spiced with patriotic formulas and political sermonizing. Artefacts connected with train culture, such as uniforms, equipment, tools and models are also displayed. Besides Dongjiao Branch, China Railway Museum has another two branch museums: Zhengyangmen Branch and Zhan Tianyou Memorial Museum. Anyone interested in further exploring the railway history of China can also visit these two, especially the one dedicated to Zhan Tianyou, the engineer known as the father of China's railways.

20

Dabaotai Western Han Tomb Museum

大葆台西汉墓博物馆 *Dabaotai xihanmu bowuguan*

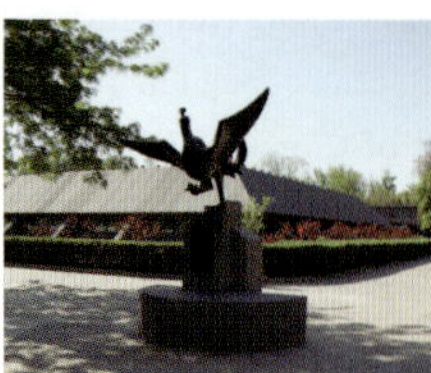

707 Fengbao Road, Fengtai District, Beijing
北京市丰台区丰葆路707号
Tel: (010) 8361 3073/2852
Open: 9.00–16.00 except Mon
Gift Shop

Archaeologists excavated the Dabaotai Western Han Tomb in 1975 but were unable to identify whose tomb it was. It's likely, however, that the person buried here was a prince of the Liu family who died sometime around 45 BC. Tombs like this were normally constructed for emperors and princesses during the Han dynasty.

Two tombs were located here when the site was excavated in 1975. Tomb No. 1 is an underground burial palace with wooden frames. It is 26.8 meters long and 21.2 meters wide. The inner coffin is made of Chinese catalpa, a tree with large heart-shaped leaves. It has three inner and outer wooden coffins enveloped by tens of thousands of large square beams, sealed with plaster to keep it dry, which may explain why the tomb is so well preserved. Some 400 funerary objects were uncovered, including ceramics, bronzes, and iron, jade and bone articles. The most striking items are the three lacquered chariots and eleven horses that were buried alive in a long, narrow passageway which opens at the entrance to the tomb.

Scale models of the chariots are on exhibit outside. There is also a small museum displaying several burial objects that were excavated in the tomb, such as jade carvings, miniature wooden burial figurines, bronze incense burners and a bronze door decoration resembling a beast. Tomb No. 2 once held the remains of the queen consort, but it was robbed and destroyed by fire in ancient times, and nothing remains.

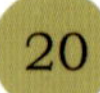

Jade *pei* with the pattern of *chi*-tiger (a mythical animal which combines dragon and tiger)

Forbidden City and the Palace Museum

紫禁城与故宫博物院 *Zijincheng yu Gugong bowuyuan*

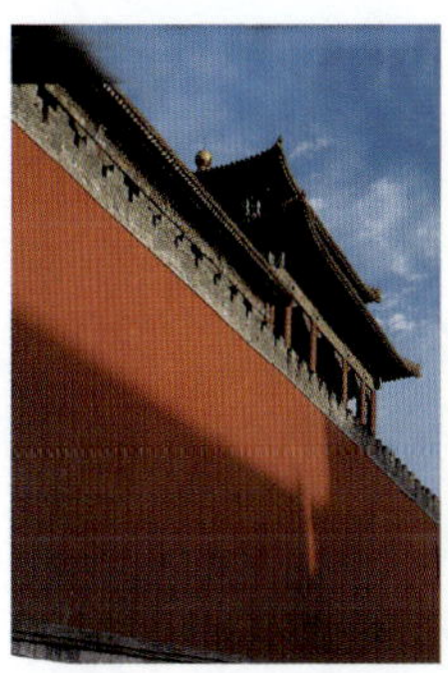

4 Jiangshanqian Street, Dongcheng District, Beijing (Entrance in South gate)
北京市东城区景山前街4号（南门入口）
Tel: (010) 8500 7421 / 7420
Open: 8.30–17.00, Apr 1–Oct 31; 8.30–16.30, Nov 1–Mar 31
Closed on Mon Afternoon except public holidays and summer vocation (July 1–Aug 31)
www.dpm.org.cn
Gift shop / book shop / museum guide available (written / audio) / restaurant / coffee shop / shops and cafés situated at intervals throughout the site   Kids

The Palace Museum, along with the Forbidden City in which it is housed, constitutes one of the three most famous, and most visited, sites of China (the others being the Great Wall and the Terracotta Warrior Army in Xi'an). Surrounded by moated walls, covering an area of 1,030,000 sq m (of which more than 400,000 sq m are open to the public), and with nearly 10,000,000 visitors a year, the nature and history of the site merit study before planning to visit.

The Forbidden City was the palace of the Emperors of the Ming and Qing dynasties. The overall impression is one of breadth, not height, with a procession of grand central palaces running from south to north. There is a balance between vast open courtyards, long walled thoroughfares, and more intimate palaces crowded together behind long purple walls away from the central courtyards. The purple walls and yellow and green tiles take on different hues at different times of year. In summer the brilliant white light flattens the effect; in winter the sunlight draws out the purple so that it almost glows – an effect

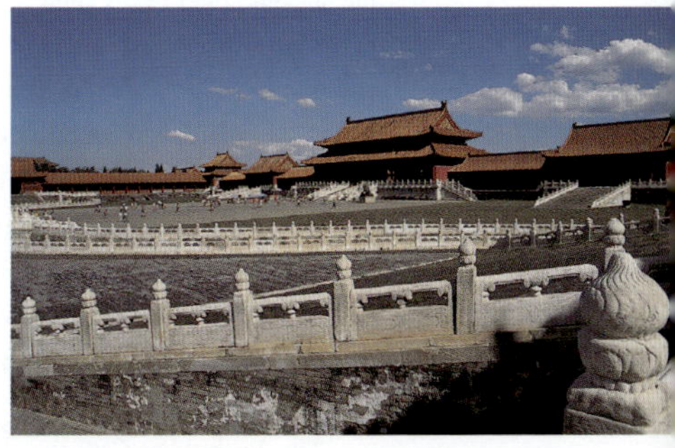

Gate of Supreme Harmony showing balustrades along the banks of the Golden Water River

much heightened during snow. The Forbidden City was also the administrative and bureaucratic hub of a vast empire; by the sixteenth century no other country in the world could boast a palace of such size, complexity and grandeur from which was controlled, with more or less success, the daily lives of more than 120 million people – more than the entire population of Europe at that date.

The Palace Museum is not only the most famous building in China, it also houses a significant part of the imperial collection of art and artefacts – in total the greatest of all the collections of Chinese art and civilization. At the fall of the empire in 1911, some 1,170,000 items were in the collection. A relatively small selection of these are

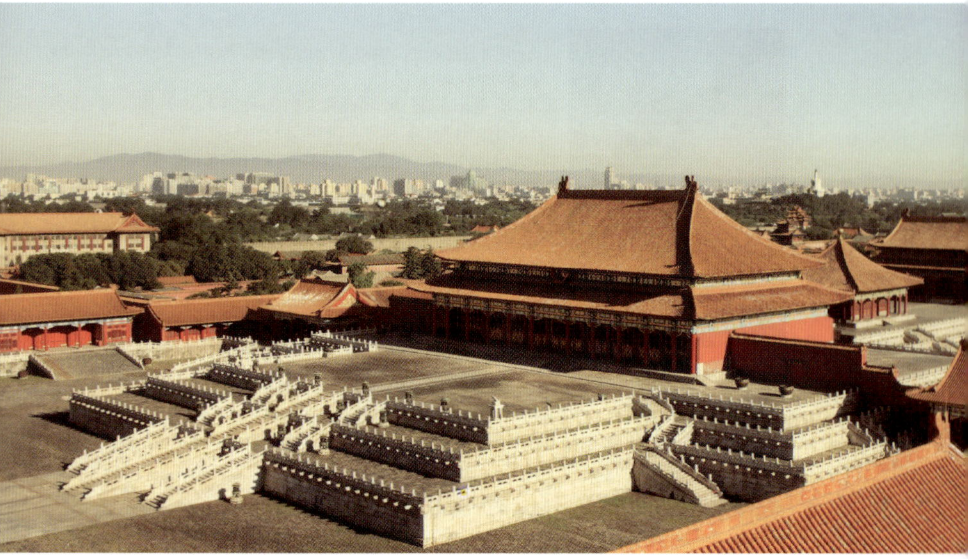

housed and displayed in galleries open to the public spread throughout the site.

This was truly a working palace. The Emperor was the Son of Heaven – not just the absolute ruler of his subjects on earth but the appointed link between them and the deity. He was both the supreme legislator and the chief executive of infinite power – and he controlled a vast, dedicated Confucian-trained bureaucracy to enforce his will and also to report back to him from the world outside. The largest country in the world was also the most centralized – the sheer volume of paperwork and opinion that came to the Emperor for appraisal would have overwhelmed the ruler of any modern state. It is no wonder that a conscientious Emperor like the eighteenth-century Qianlong, who rose every morning at 5.00 to cope with the workload, took early retirement and built for himself a special Retirement quarters – The Studio of Exhaustion from Diligent Reign – in the north-east corner of the city (restored and opened to the public in 2008).

The Forbidden City was built on an axis centred between the four imperial temples of Beijing. Its ground plan perfectly fulfilled the geomantic requirements of *feng shui*, while its predominantly purple colour referred by literary allusion to the Pole Star, and hence enforced the Emperor's pivotal role between heaven and earth.

Until 1911 the public knew nothing of the layout of the Forbidden City. Even ministers and civil servants had only strictly limited access to the outer courts, where the business of government was conducted, and no idea of what went on in the 9,000 rooms of the imperial residences at the eastern end. Those seeking access had to approach from the south through the Gate of Heavenly Peace (*Tiananmen*),

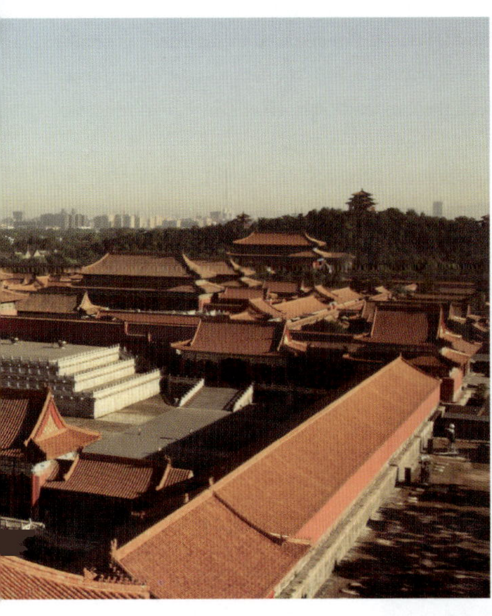

on the north side of Tiananmen Square. From the balcony of this gate in 1949 Chairman Mao proclaimed the birth of the People's Republic, saying 'that the Chinese people have stood up'.

This is still the best approach for the visitor today. After one more gateway, the Forbidden City proper is reached through the Meridian Gate (*Wumen*). Thirty-eight-metres high, it has a unique three-winged layout. The central gateway was for the exclusive use of the Emperor (with the exception of the Empress on her wedding day, and of the three examinees who passed top of the civil service examinations). It was where he reviewed his troops, where ministers who had failed were clubbed as punishment, and where officials with business within had to present themselves before daybreak.

The Qing dynasty was overthrown in the revolution of 1911, although the last Emperor, Puyi, was permitted to continue to live in the Inner Court – the imperial residence – until 1924. The Qing were Manchus from the northeast, and, after 1911, all their treasures from Chengde (originally Rehe) and Shenyang (originally Mukden) were brought down to Beijing and added to the imperial collection housed in the Forbidden City (although a significant number of Manchu relics were later sold off or pawned by Puyi himself).

A selection of the imperial collections was first shown to the public as the History Museum in 1914. The Palace Museum itself was opened, to great fanfare, in 1925. Its history was driven by the turbulent happenings in China during the War against Japan, World War II, and the Civil War. By 1933 the invading Japanese were about to capture Beijing, and the collection was evacuated for safety, first to Nanjing, then to Sichuan, then to Chongqing and finally, in 1947, back to Nanjing, headquarters of the Nationalists. When the Nationalists were evidently finally losing the Civil War, they shipped, in 1948–49, 2,972 crates of relics to Taipei. After Liberation in 1949, many of the remaining relics were returned from Nanjing to Beijing. The Palace Museum is therefore one of three museums housing the old imperial collection, the other two being the Nanjing Museum and the National Museum in Taipei. In Beijing only a fraction of the entire collection can be shown at any one time; a selection of works are exhibited in a number of buildings scattered throughout the palace.

The Forbidden City can also be entered from the Gate of Divine Prowess (*Shenwumen*) opposite Jingshan Hill in the north. However, entering via the Meridian Gate is recommended for a first visit, as walking from south to north gives a clearer picture of the palace's logical layout and follows the route taken by ministers, generals and civil servants and others with business at the court. The tunnel-vaulted entrance leads to a huge courtyard through which the Golden Water River (*Jinshuihe*) runs – it both feeds the moat and provided water for the palace complex.

Directly opposite is the Gate of Supreme Harmony (*Taihemen*), the gateway to the Outer Court, a vast 30,000-sq-m open space, with low, flanking buildings and a central route – the 'imperial road' – picked out in stone leading directly to the Hall of Supreme Harmony (*Taihedian*). From Ming times the *Taihedian* was the central ceremonial hall, the site of imperial coronations, the starting point for all of the major ceremonies that punctuated the court's annual round, as well as for the reception of successful candidates in the imperial scholars' civil service exams. This is where the Emperor would meet and address those of his subjects

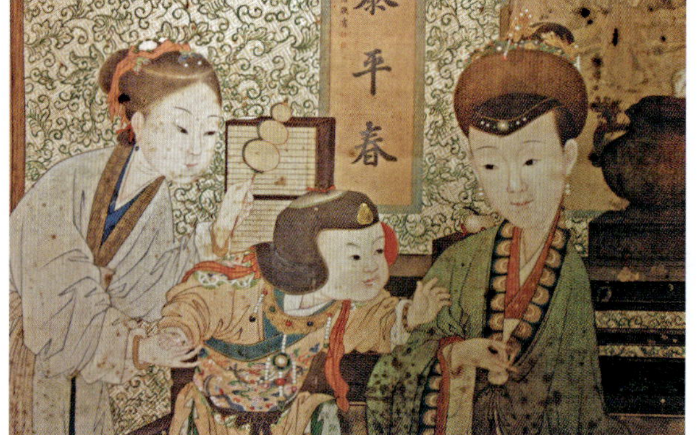

Wallpaper (*tielo*) detail in newly restored Jade Pavilion of Juanqinzhai

who had business with him, having himself progressed south down the 'imperial road' from his private quarters in the Inner Court.

Behind *Taihedian* is a smaller central building, the Hall of Central Harmony (*Zhonghedian*), where the Emperor would put on his robes. The next palace, marking the end of the Outer Court, was the Hall of Preserving Harmony (*Baohedian*), used by the Qing for banquets, concerts and the imperial exams. Passing through this, you descend three massive marble stairways into an open space that divides the Outer Court from the Inner Court – the private quarters of the Emperor, his family, concubines, eunuchs and maids. The Inner Court is reached through a relatively small but ornate Gate of Heavenly Purity (*Qianqingmen*), outside which

Hall of Supreme Harmony

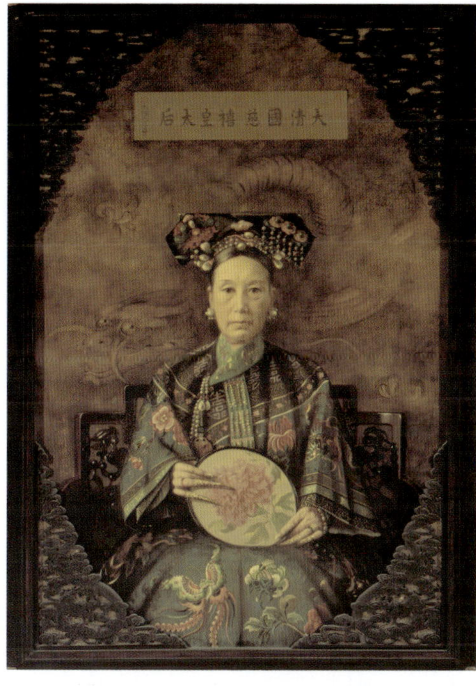

Portrait of Cixi

the Emperor would meet his ministers and supplicants and carry on the serious business of the day – more detailed and less ceremonial than that conducted in the Hall of Supreme Harmony. This was the northernmost point of his public functions.

Proceeding through the Inner Court, there are three more central palaces: the Palace of Heavenly Purity (*Qianqinggong*), the Hall of Union (*Jiaotaidian*) and the Palace of Earthly Tranquility (*Kunninggong*). The first doubled as throne room and imperial bedchamber; the second doubled as the seal room and the centre of the Empress' control of silk culture, and the third as shrine and imperial bridal chamber.

To the north of the Inner Court lie the beauties of the Imperial Garden – to the west and east lie a mass of smaller palaces and pavilions, each with a role in imperial life, all interconnected. One of the great joys of visiting the Forbidden City is to wander through these palaces and discover unexpected angles and delights. Be sure to allow enough time to do this. The exhibition halls of the permanent collection are scattered throughout. They can either be visited individually or, although of necessity too briefly, as part of a general tour. A museum guide is available. There are small shops and cafés situated at intervals throughout the site.

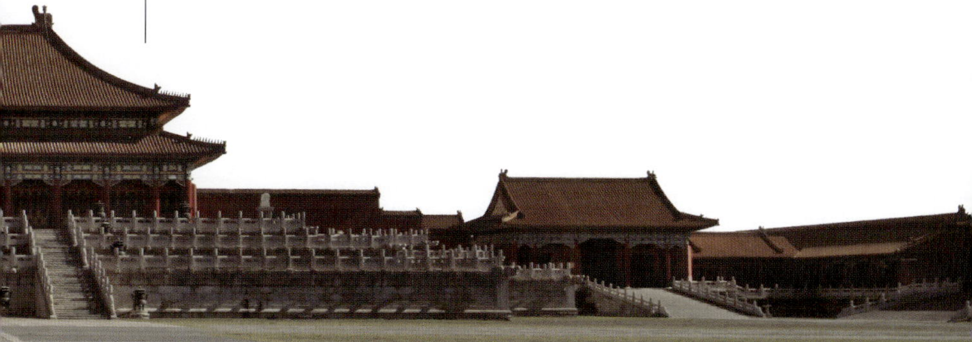

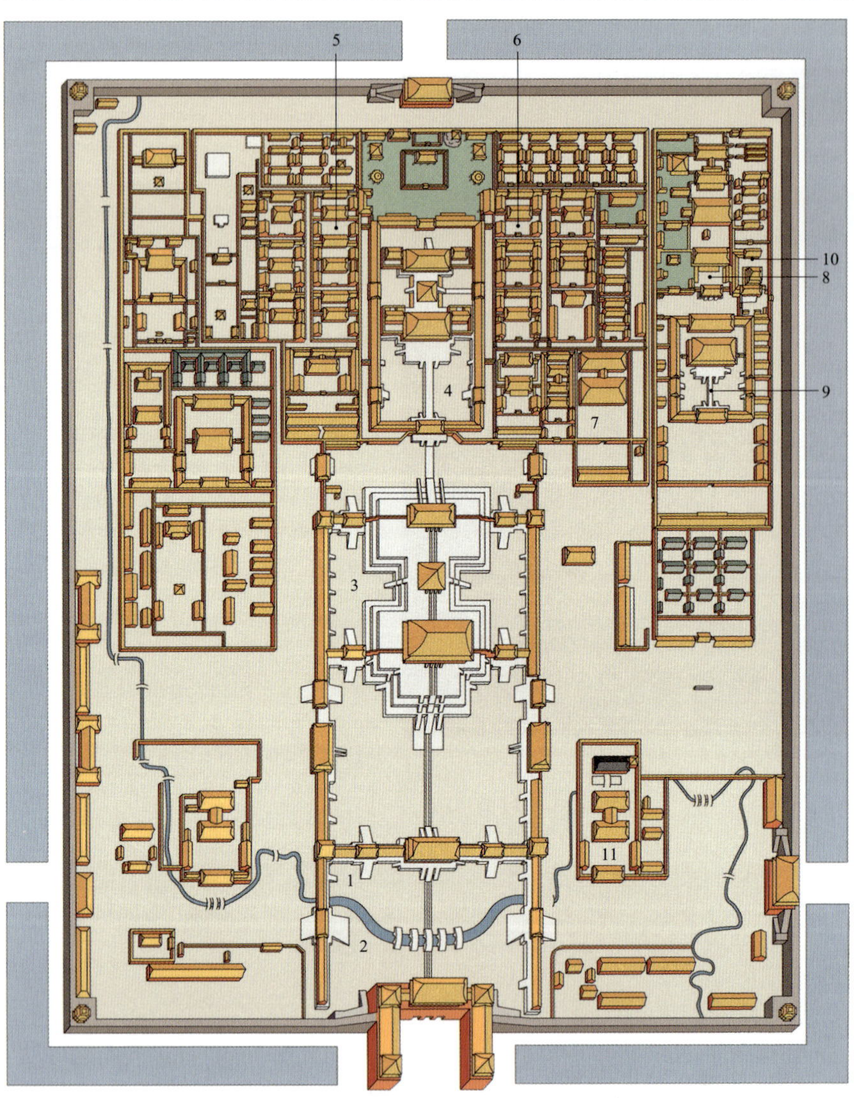

1. Qing Dynasty Court Insignia
2. Weapons of the Qing Dynasty
3. Long Live the Royal House: Treasures from the Qing Palace
4. The Qing Emperors' Grand Weddings
5. The Life of the Last Emperor, Puyi
6. Jade Carvings
7. Hall of Clocks
8. Imperial Treasures and Ornaments
9. The Stone Drums: Seal Script of the Qin Dynasty
10. Opera at the Qing Court
11. Chinese Ceramics

Permanent Exhibition Areas within the Forbidden City

Following are the permanent exhibition Areas within the Forbidden City.

Meridian Gate

1. Qing Dynasty Court Insignia
An exhibition of grand canopies, fans and insignia that were used in imperial ritual, housed in the corridors on the west side of the first courtyard after entering the Meridian Gate.

Outer Court

2. Weapons of the Qing Dynasty
The first corridor on the west side of the Outer Court.
The Qing were Manchus from the northeast for whom horsemanship was the basis of their culture. An exhibition of their horsemanship and archery; and, from the reign of Kangxi (1662–1722), of their firearms.

3. Long Live the Royal House: Treasures from the Qing Palace
The corridor on the west side running north, beginning opposite the Hall of Supreme Harmony (*Taihedian*).
An exhibition of selected paraphernalia of the Qing Court, including articles of daily use, scientific instruments and a look at the history of the palace in the post-1949 period.

Inner Court
Central Inner Court,
East side

4. The Qing Emperors' Grand Weddings
The east corridor of the Palace of Heavenly Purity (*Qianqinggong*).
An exhibition, including digital technology, of the rituals of betrothal, marriage, dowry and wedding presents, and the bridal chamber.

**Western Palaces of
the Inner Court**

5. The Life of the Last Emperor, Puyi
The back courtyard of the Palace of Preserved Elegance (*Chuxiugong*).
The sad story of Puyi, the last Emperor, who was allowed to remain in the Forbidden City until 1924, after which he was fatally compromised by the Japanese during the war period.

**Eastern Palaces of the
Inner Court**

6. Jade Carvings
The Palace of Accumulated Purity (*Zhongcuigong*).
An exhibition of jade from the Neolithic through the eighteenth century.

**East Side of the
Forbidden City**

7. Hall of Clocks
The Hall for Ancestral Worship (*Fengxiandian*).
An exhibition of the Qing collection of clocks and timepieces, many of them British and Swiss. On most days a selection of clocks' chimes are played at 11.00 and 14.00.

8. Imperial Treasures and Ornaments
Located in the corridors surrounding the Hall of Imperial Supremacy (*Huangjidian*), in the Hall of Cultivating Character (*Yangxindian*), in the Hall of Joyful Longevity (*Leshoutang*) and in the Belvedere of Well-Nourished Harmony (*Yihexuan*).

9. The Stone Drums: Seal Script of the Qin Dynasty

The eastern corridor of the Hall of Imperial Supremacy (*Huangjidian*). Drum-shaped stones carved with third-century BC script.

10. Opera at the Qing Court

The Pavilion of Pleasant Sounds (*Changyinge*) and the Hall for Viewing Opera (*Yueshi lou*).

An exhibition of costumes, masks, props and programmes from the resident opera companies at the Qing court.

Chinese Ceramics Gallery (Hall of Literary Brilliance)

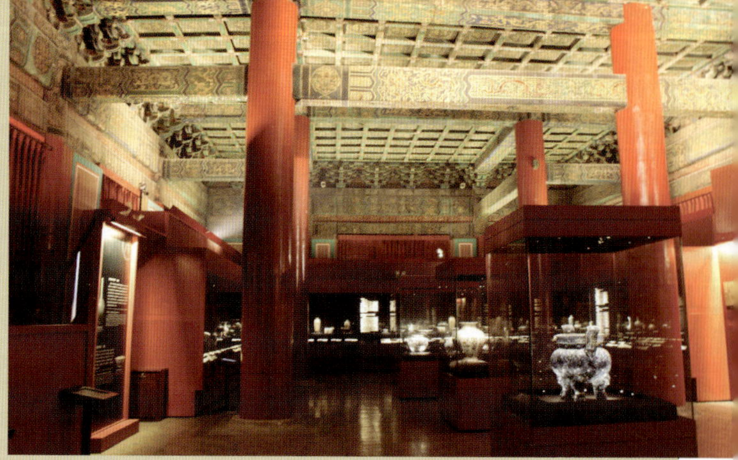

11. Chinese Ceramics

The Hall of Literary Brilliance (*Wenhuadian*).

This recently opened, splendid permanent display is a chronological survey based on the imperial wares and collection, generously supplemented by the objects that have come into the collection since the Palace Museum was founded.

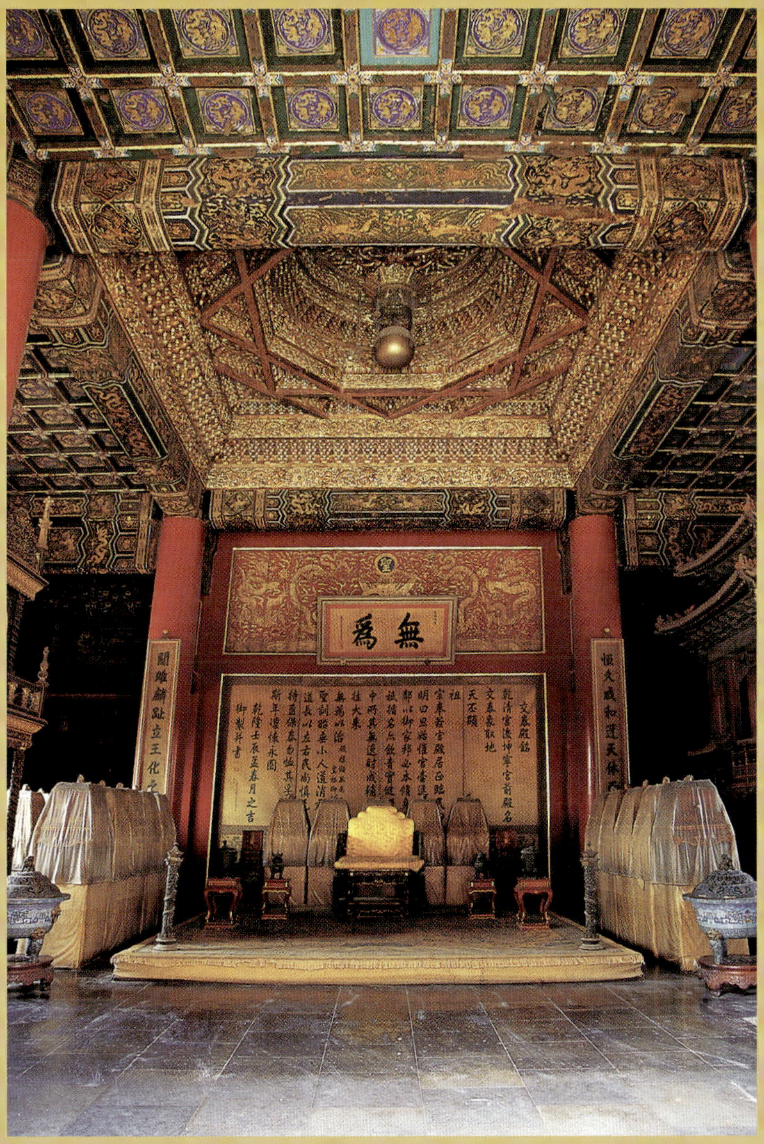

Geological Museum of China

中国地质博物馆 *Zhongguo dizhi bowuguan*

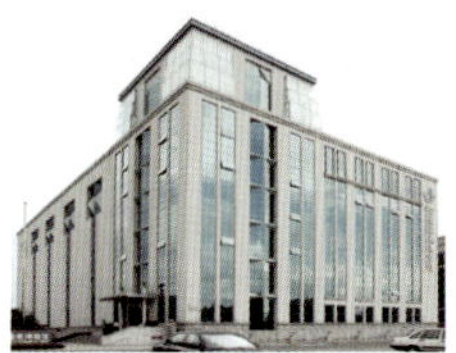

15 Yangrou Hutong, Xisi Street, Beijing
北京市西四羊肉胡同15号
Tel: (010) 6655 7858
Open: 9.00–16.30 except Mon
www.gmc.org.cn
English and Chinese audio guides　　Kids

There is something here for everyone who is fascinated by the marvels of geological science, from the truly stunning displays of diamonds, rubies and huge specimens of native gold in the Gemstone Gallery to the magnificent exhibits of rock-crystal geodes, a dramatic calcite druse intergrowth with fluorite crystals, and the rare blue aragonite on show in the Mineral and Rocks Gallery. But the real stars are the treasure trove of late Jurassic and early Cretaceous fossils unearthed from Liaoning Province. Dating from more than 128 million years ago, these rare specimens include dinosaur remains with evidence of proto-feathers – providing the evolutionary link between non-avian dinosaurs and living birds – as well as fossils of primitive aquatic and semi-aquatic animals with paddle-like limbs and, often, long, serpentine necks.

Although the first fossil feathers were discovered in 1861 in Germany on the 145-million-year-old bird *Archaeopteryx*, the first wingless feathered dinosaurs were unearthed in the early 1990s in Liaoning, just a day's drive from Beijing. Well preserved in what was once the marshy shore of a lake, the remains are incredibly fine and clear. Careful examination of the *Sinornithosaurus* specimen reveals its three different types of feathers: simple hair-like filaments, downy tufts and feathers in the modern sense. This fossil is the first evidence that animals other than birds had feather-like skins (not to help them to fly but probably to keep them warm). On display nearby is *Shenzhousaurus orientalis*, known as the Ostrich dinosaur because this species and related ones apparently behaved like modern ostriches. This bird-like creature had a beak with teeth.

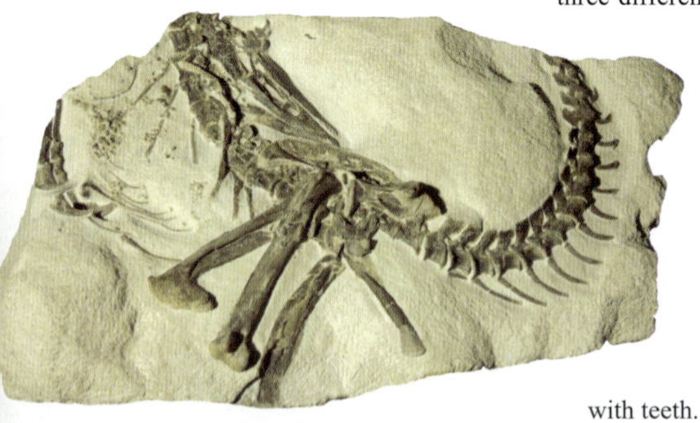

Ostrich dinosour

Very rare is the fossil species *Confuciusornis sanctus* – the holy Confucius bird – discovered by a farmer in Liaoning. The skull, wing, two feathered legs and pelvis were found in ancient lake-bed sediments. This bird, around the size of a rooster, had a long, feathered tail and claws on its forearms, probably for climbing trees. However, unlike previously found avian fossils, it was toothless, making it the earliest bird known to have abandoned the toothy jaws of its ancestors. Its discovery revised the texts on the evolution of birds.

Equally important is the fossil *Protarchaeopteryx robusta* found near Beipiao City in Liaoning, with its tail and body feathers. It was unable to fly, but with its short arms and long legs probably was a fast runner. The size of a modern-day turkey, it represents a stage in the evolution of birds from feathered, ground-living bipedal dinosaurs and closely resembled the meat-eating dinosaurs called theropods.

One of the most exciting pieces in the whole puzzle is that among more than a dozen wingless, feathered, dragon-like remains found in northeastern China is the forerunner of the daddy of all dinosaurs: *Tyrannosaurus rex*. The discovery of these creatures – land-bound but feathered – implies that these feathers were not full-blown flight feathers, but simpler ones that seem to have been the evolutionary precursors of bird plumage.

Also in this gallery are fossil finds recovered from what is known as the Chengjiang Fauna, a series of sites near Kunming in Yunnan Province where a large number of perfectly preserved fish and other soft-bodied fossils have been unearthed. The earliest examples date from the Lower Cambrian era, around 530 million years ago, extending the known time span of vertebrates back 50 million years and helping to solve the largest mystery of evolutionary biology – the origins of vertebrates. On this floor, displayed in well-lit and labelled cases, are stone implements and teeth drilled with holes – possibly indicating their use as ornaments – collected in 1933 from the famous cave site of Zhoukoudian, which has yielded the largest number of *Homo erectus* fossils in the world.

It's not surprising that this museum is visited by more than a million people a year – the modern cases (with excellent Chinese and English labelling) enhanced with digital imagery and covering all facets of geology (including the formation of the earth, volcanoes, gemmology and fossil history) making it a worthwhile visit for foreigners and a must for Chinese schoolchildren. There is a Specimen Care and Conservation Laboratory where you can watch specimens being cleaned and conserved, as well as have your own treasure – be it a fossil or mineral – identified by the museum's resident geologist.

Ongoing research within the museum and with various Chinese scientific bodies, including the National Natural Science Foundation of China and the Chinese Academy of Sciences, as well as numerous foreign institutions, make this a living museum where a stream of new finds and research are constantly challenging the enduring mysteries of the natural world.

Confuciusornis sanctus

23

Guanfu Museum

观复博物馆 *Guanfu bowuguan*

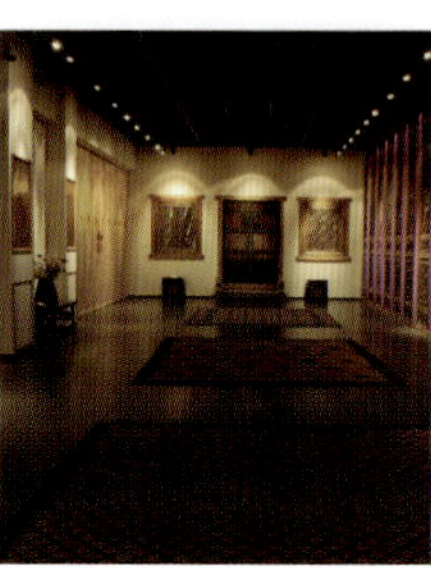

18 Jinnan Road, Zhangwanfen, Dashanzi, Chaoyang District, Beijing
北京市朝阳区大山子张万坟金南路18号
Tel: (010) 6433 8887
Open: 9.00–17.00, last entry 16.00, Tues–Sun; 9.00–16.00, last entry 15.00, Mon; closed on Spring Festival
www.guanfumuseum.org.cn
English guide available: no appointment necessary

According to the museum's own publicity materials, this was one of the first not-for-profit private museums in China. It houses, for the most part, the collection of Ma Weidu. Three other collectors are also contributors but less significantly. The collection has been housed in various places but now resides in this purpose-built museum in northeastern Beijing, not far from Caochangdi. It is somewhat tricky to find, so a telephone call in advance is recommended.

More and more museums are opening all over China exhibiting the collections of private art lovers who want to share their passion. This one is well worth your time. The objects are of the highest quality and are well displayed, and signage in English appears consistently alongside every object. The collection features porcelain, furniture, Qing dynasty windows and doors, lacquer, cloisonné, enamel ware and bronzes, modern paintings, sculpture and photographs. It also includes jade, but due to space problems, these objects are held in storage and are available for viewing only to scholars or students by appointment.

The museum tour begins in the ceramics gallery, in which you can see objects from the Tang to the Qing dynasties. Every object has a mirror beneath it so you can have a look at the bottom. Breathtaking examples from the major kilns are on display. Song dynasty celadon from the Ru, Guan, Ge and Jun Kilns is exhibited, as is porcelain from the Yuezhou, Longquan, Yaozhou, Cizhou, Dingzhou Kilns – and more. Note a Jingdezhen shadow-blue-glaze foliate-mouth vase from the Northern Song. The gorgeous lip of this vessel delicately falls open like a wilting leaf. Be sure to see the Cizhou white-glazed *meiping* painted with a floral design from the Northern Song. Standing on its own in a case is a large *famille rose* vase with six floral panels on a dark blue background. Each panel represents one of the seasons. Every object on display in this gallery is a feast for the eyes.

The museum continues with a furniture collection from the Ming and Qing periods.

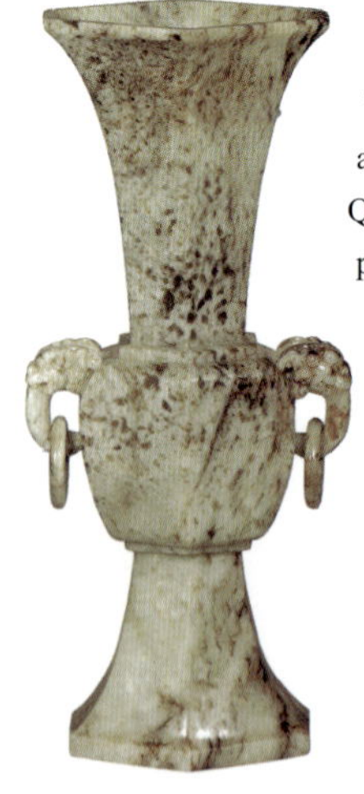

Ming dynasty *gu* with the shape of lion's ears

About 300 pieces are displayed, organized by type of wood – mahogany, *zitan* and *huanghuali* – and in addition there is a complete family room (mainly using mahogany) and study (mostly *huanghuali*).

Mahogany, or 'red wood', was used from the mid Qing period and was imported from Southeast Asia. From the Qianlong and Jiaqing periods it was frequently used for court furniture. The mahogany furniture on view includes tables, chairs, chests, cabinets and so on; notice especially a very graceful pair of eighteenth-century horseshoe-backed armchairs.

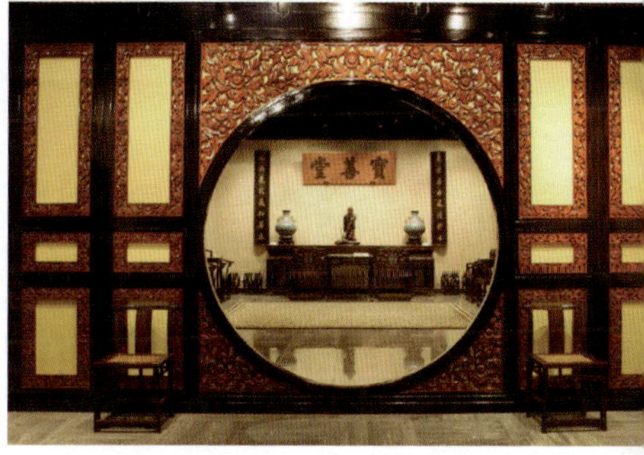

Zitan, or 'purple wood', was used during the Ming period but was most popular in the early Qing. The density and weight of this wood make it feel substantial, so it was equated with value and wealth. The trees grow slowly, and the wood is not always useable. These factors, along with its inevitable expense, contribute to its relative rarity. It carves well, so in the Qing it was often elaborately decorated, although Ming examples are simple and plain. Note the *zitan* painting table on display, dated to the Kangxi period or earlier. This is the largest known Qing painting table, with a width of 96 cm and length of 182 cm, and is ornately carved with dragon panels.

Huanghuali (yellow-flowering pear), exhibited in one large room, was most popular in the Ming dynasty, and the majority of examples here are from that period. Chests, screens, beds and chairs are on view. Note the late Ming southern official's chair whose back is inlaid with multicoloured jade decoration of a bird on flowering branches.

Next are the galleries entitled 'Works of Art'; these contain cloisonné, enamel, lacquer, bronzes, carved jade and wooden objects ranging from folk objects to imperial wares. The museum also has a collection of photographs, including historical images, landscapes and portraits of famous people.

Upstairs is a collection of windows and doors in four rooms, mainly from the Qing dynasty. The patterns, history and craftsmanship involved are explained on panels in the galleries. Many of the windows are finely carved with much detail. One series of eight depicts trees with delicate, multi-textured feathery leaves of varying species of trees. A magnifying glass is available for careful examination. Most of the doors and windows are from southern China, where such lattice and cut-out design was the style (the weather in the north would not allow this). There are also examples of heavier solid doors from the north.

There is a gallery of modern painting (not the collection of Ma Weidu) which includes three paintings by Chen Yifei.

The displays in the museum are rotated every one or two years.

24

Jiaozhuanghu Underground Tunnel War Remains Museum

焦庄户地道战遗址纪念馆 *Jiaozhuanghu didaozhanyizhi jinianguan*

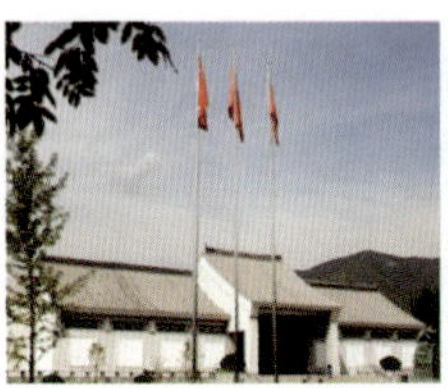

Jiaozhuanghu Village, Longwantun Town, Shunyi District, Beijing
北京市顺义区龙湾屯镇焦庄户村
Tel: (010) 6046 1906
Open: 8.30–16.30
www.bjjzhdd.com/zy.html (Chinese only)

During World War II the people in this tiny village dug an extensive interlocking series of tunnels linking up their houses and leading out to the countryside in an effort to resist the Japanese invaders. Entrances to the tunnels can be found in cupboards, stables, water-storage tanks, under beds and elsewhere.

By 1946 there were 23km of tunnels connecting the houses and even reaching nearby villages. According to the museum, from 1943 until 1948 the villagers fought more than 150 battles against the Japanese and the Nationalists, killing 130 and taking sixty prisoners.

Visitors to the site can go into some of the restored village houses and enter the 650 m of tunnel now open. The famous film made about this place called *Underground Tunnel Guerilla War* is sometimes shown at the museum and is available on DVD in the shop. There is also a small outdoor snack bar. Look for the sign reading 'Anti-Japanese Food' to find it!

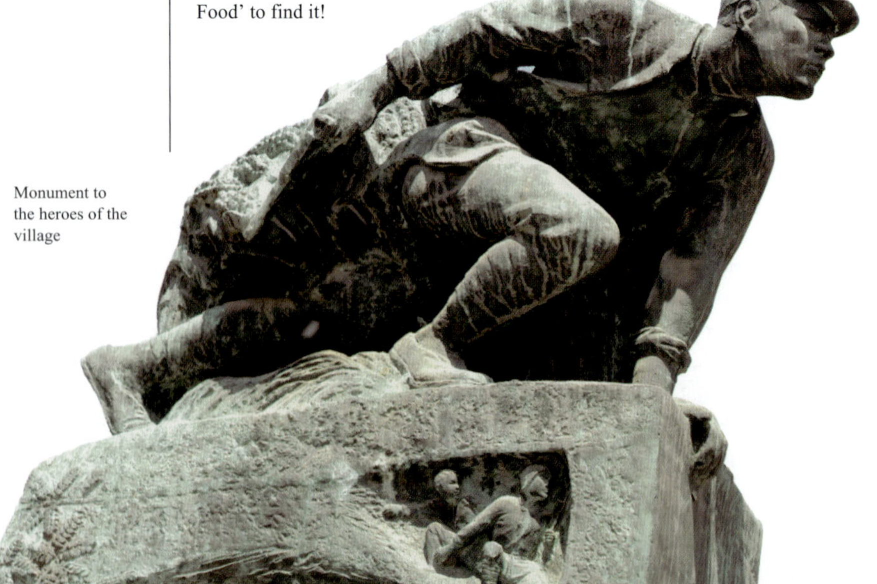

Monument to the heroes of the village

25

Lao She Museum

老舍纪念馆 *Laoshe jinianguan*

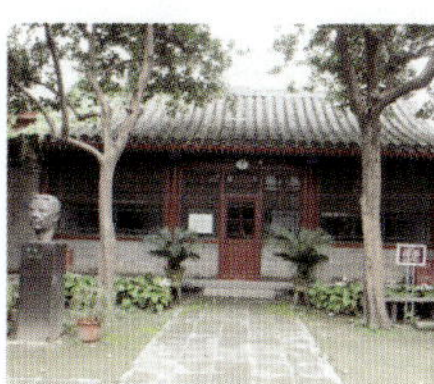

19 Fengfu Hutong, Dengshikou West Street, Dongcheng
District, Beijing
北京市东城区灯市口西街丰富胡同19号
Tel: (010) 6514 2612
Open: 9.00–17.00, last entry 16.30
www.bjlsjng.com (Chinese only)

This is one of the most charming of the courtyard residences and the home of one of China's best-loved writers, Lao She, from 1950 until his untimely death. This is a common siheyuan (a traditional Chinese courtyard) with 19 rooms, covering about 400 square meters. A five-colour wooden screen and a fish vat are standing in the front of the courtyard.

Lao She is best known

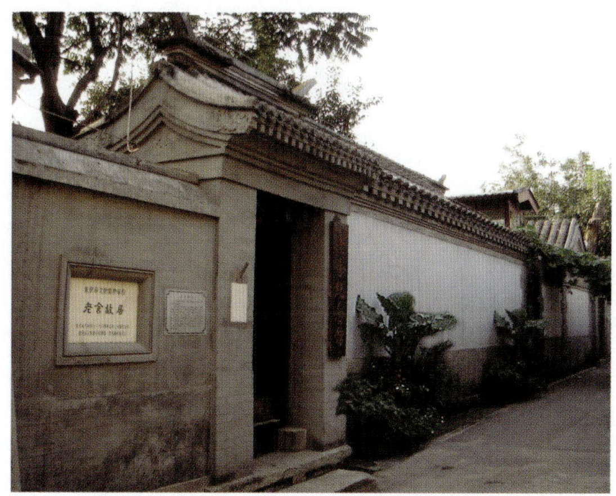

for his 1936 novel *Rickshaw Boy* (*Luotuo Xiangzi*), which depicts a Dickensian Beijing at the turn of the century. Exhibits detail his biography, and his study has been left intact. The two persimmon trees in the yard were personally planted by Lao She and his wife in the spring of 1953 and the couple therefore named the yard "Red Persimmon Yard". Every year there would be lots of flowers blooming in all seasons, especially chrysanthemums in the winter.

Lao She's former residence

anbeipian, Lao She's ng poem

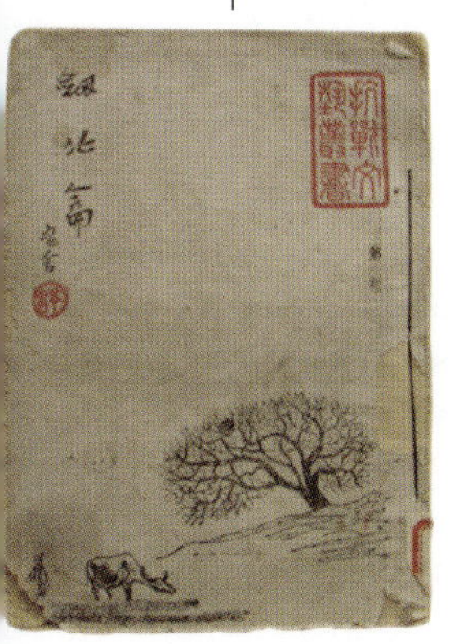

Lu Xun Museum Beijing

26

北京鲁迅博物馆 *Beijing Lu Xun bowuguan*

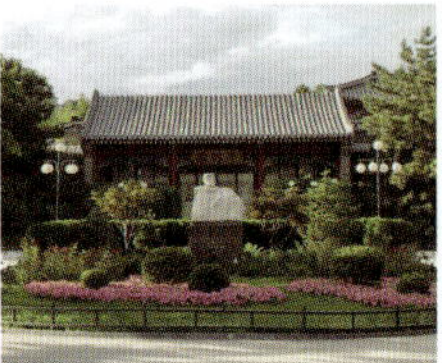

19 Gongmenkou Ertiao, Fuchengmennei Street,
Xicheng District, Beijing
北京市西城区阜城门内大街宫门口二条19号
Tel: (010) 6616 4080
Open: 9.00–16.00 except Mon
www.luxunmuseum.com.cn

Lu Xun

Lu Xun's
handwriting

Lu Xun (1881–1936) was one of China's most famous writers of the first half of the twentieth century. The museum consists of his house, in which he lived from 1924 to 1926, and, on its east side, a new museum, expanded and re-opened in 1994, dedicated to his work. The house, with its small courtyards, trees and simple furnishings, gives an authentic glimpse of a Beijing courtyard residence of the period – functional and modest yet attractive – which will appeal to any visitor. The new museum building is more for those interested in left-wing Chinese literature of the pre-war period.

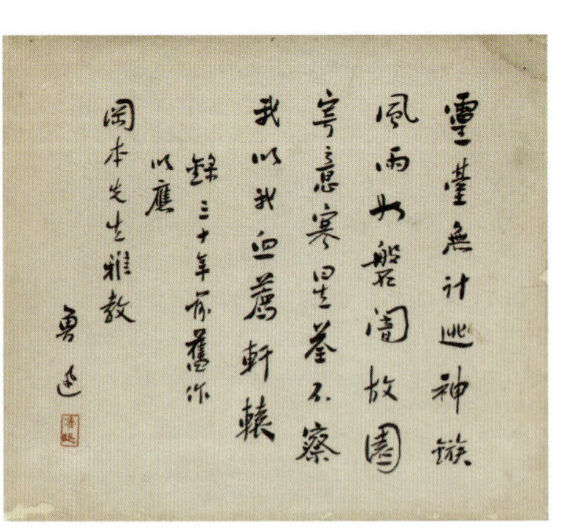

Lu Xun studied in Japan as a medical doctor until the oppression and poverty of Chinese society convinced him to change careers. He took part in the May 4th Movement and, although he became a leading socialist writer, he never became a Communist. Nevertheless he has been hailed since 1949 as one of the great modern novelists – he was one of Mao's favourite authors. Lu Xun was internationally known, both translating progressive Western works and himself reaching a Western audience. He specialized in short, sharp satirical novels such as *The True Story of Ah Q* (1921–22). The museum houses a wide range of literary relics of the period and some fascinating photographs (including one of George Bernard Shaw). There is excellent English signage throughout the museum.

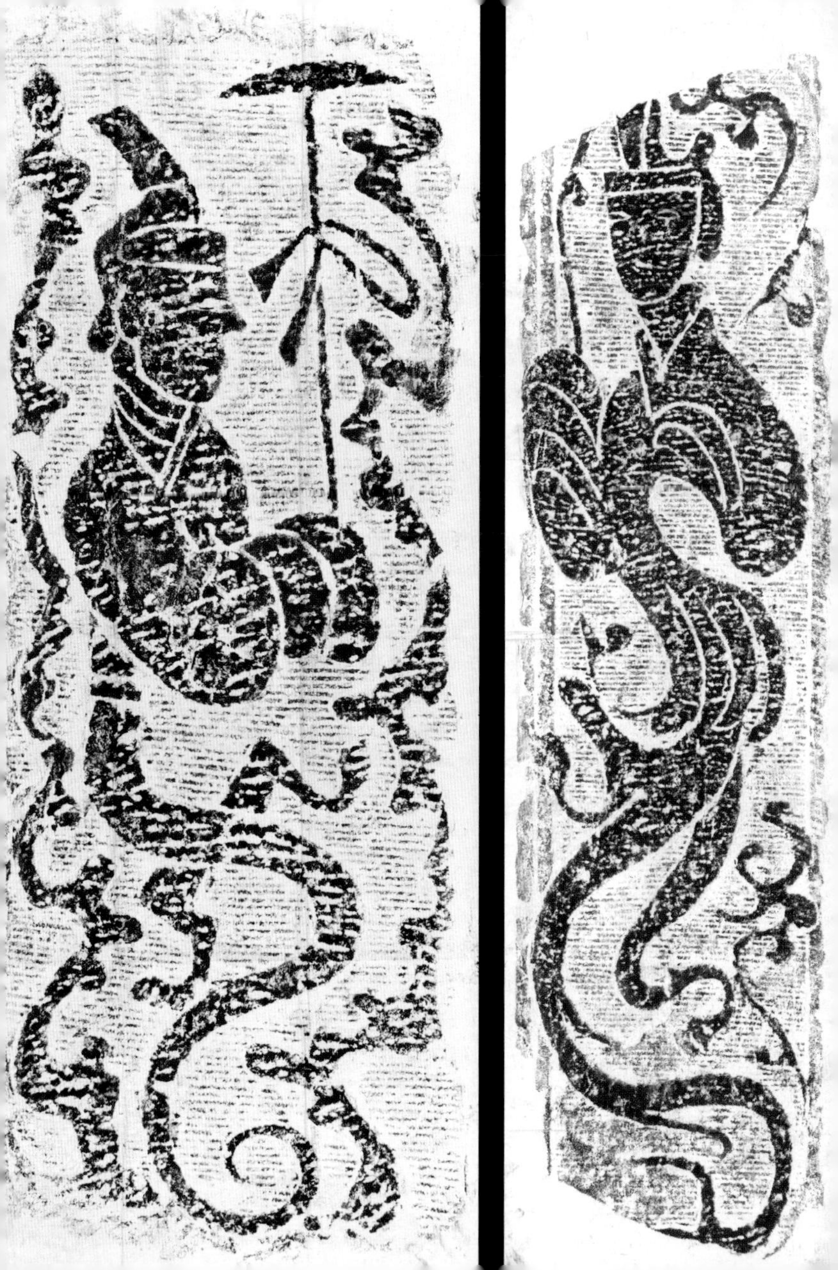

27

Mei Lanfang Memorial Museum

梅兰芳纪念馆 *Mei Lanfang jinianguan*

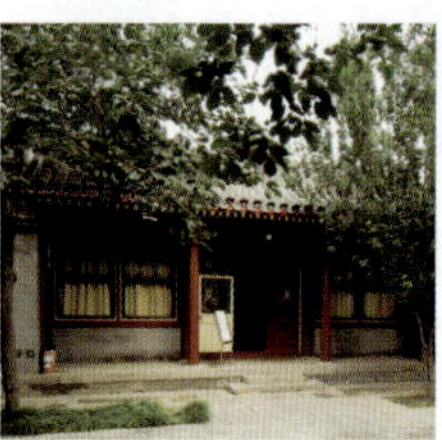

9 Huguosi Street, Xicheng District, Beijing
北京市西城区护国寺街9号
Tel: (010) 8322 3598
Open: 9.00–16.00 except Mon
www.meilanfang.com.cn/mlf/english.htm
Gift shop sells variety of books, DVDs and trinkets / illustrated
pamphlet with some English

Mei Lanfang (1894–1961), the legendary Beijing opera performer, excelled in his performance of the *huadan*, in which all female roles were played by male impersonators. His fame stretched as far as Europe and the US. Mei visited America in 1930, and despite the fact that the country was going through the Great Depression, he performed in front of packed-out, enthusiastic audiences. He won glowing reviews in the *New York World*, which said he was one of the most extraordinary actors ever seen in the city. The legendary star made an even bigger splash in Europe, where his performance in Berlin made a deep impression on the dramatist Bertolt Brecht; it's said that Brecht's acting method grew out of his experience of watching Mei.

Mei, of course, also made a major contribution to the theatre in China. He boosted the status of actors, created a new type of design for opera costumes, and, through his excellence as a performer, lifted the art form to a new level. And, even though he himself played female roles, he broke the theatrical gender barrier when he accepted the actress Xue Yanqin as his student in the 1930s. Prior to this, there

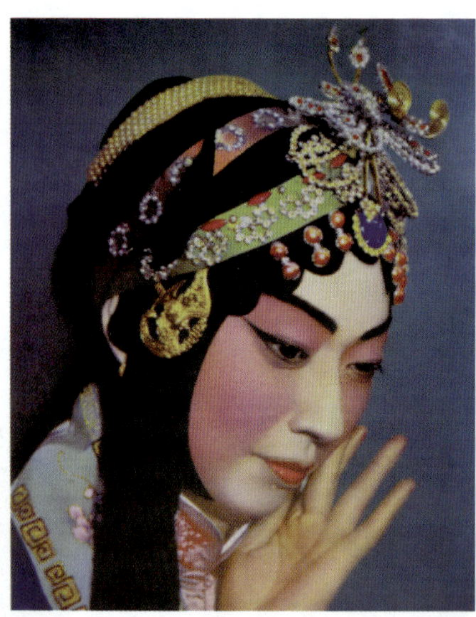

Mei Lanfang
in costume

were few mixed-gender troupes in Beijing opera, making female impersonation a key characteristic of the genre. Xue went on to become one of the opera's greatest performers.

Mei's traditional courtyard home, an excellent example of its type, is reason enough to visit here. At the end of the nineteenth century, it was part of a much larger mansion that belonged to a prince. The house had become quite run down, but was renovated for Mei and fitted with both Chinese and Western furniture and fixtures, blending old and modern elements. The star lived here from 1949 until he passed away in 1961. During the Cultural Revolution, Red Guards slapped posters on the outer walls accusing the actor of leading a 'bourgeois life'. His family decided to leave the house, which fell into ruin, remaining closed until 1986, when it was renovated.

The first rectangular building in this complex features wonderful black and white and colour photos from Mei's life and of his many performances. There are also the ornate costumes he wore on the stage. There is also a monitor here showing videos of some of his performances. In the rear courtyard are Mei's living quarters – his living room, study and bedroom – all with the original furniture. In one room there is a wonderful poster showing his delicate hands expressing dozens of different operatic gestures, each expressing a different emotion. In the warmer months, chairs would be moved out into the courtyard so the family could enjoy the fresh air.

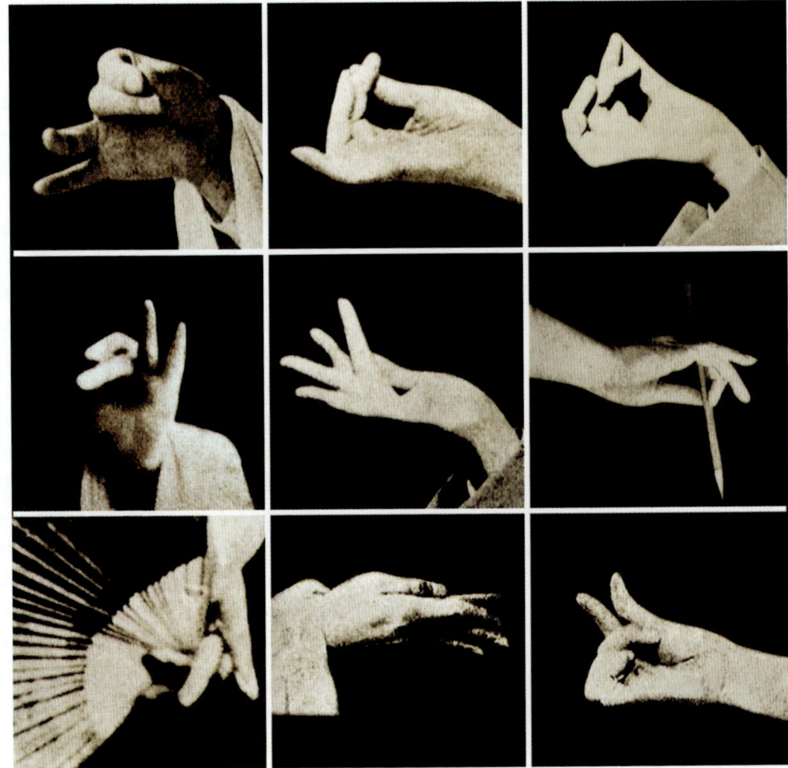

Hand positions in Chinese opera have specific meanings

Military Museum of the Chinese People's Revolution

28

中国人民革命军事博物馆 *Zhongguo renmin geming junshi bowuguan*

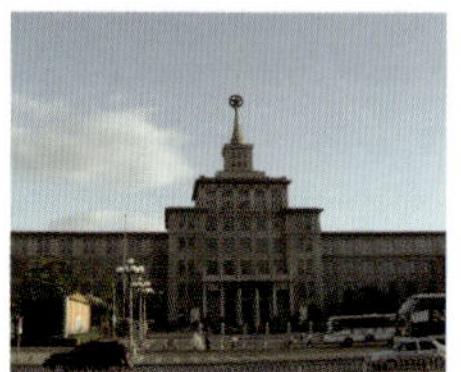

9 Fuxing Road, Haidian District, Beijing
北京市海淀区复兴路9号
Tel: (010) 6686 6114
Open: 8.30–17.00 Nov–Mar; 8.00–17.30 Apr–Oct
Gift shop / café
Kids

This is an enormous museum – 60,000 sq m – of great interest not only to lovers of guns and violence but also to those interested in Chinese history, especially the 5,000-year history of the Chinese military. The building is a huge, recently refurbished Soviet-style monolith built as one of the key construction projects in Beijing during the Great Leap Forward. Its central tower is crowned by a military star with the characters '8.1', denoting the date of the birth of the People's Liberation Army (PLA) during the Nanchang Uprising of 1 August 1928. It dominates the wide Fuxing Road just south of Yuyuantan Park and beside the Millennium Monument.

On the museum forecourt there are tanks, rockets and the Trident jet used by Zhou Enlai and other top leaders during the 1960s and 1970s.

The entrance hall is dominated by a huge white marble statue of Mao Zedong surrounded by mural-sized photos of Mao as well as Deng Xiaoping and Jiang Zemin, to provide political balance. In the large halls on the ground floor are tanks, missiles, and space rockets and capsules. The tank collection includes American tanks captured from the Nationalist forces during the Civil War and from US forces during the Korean War. One can pay extra to swivel round on an anti-aircraft gun or to sit in the driver's and gunner's seats of a modern Chinese heavy tank. Prominently placed as you enter are two limousines used by Zhu De and by Mao, the latter given to him by Stalin. Also on the first floor is the Hall of the Agrarian Revolution, illustrating Mao's theory on the role of the peasants.

On the upper floors one can view a large

Interior displays

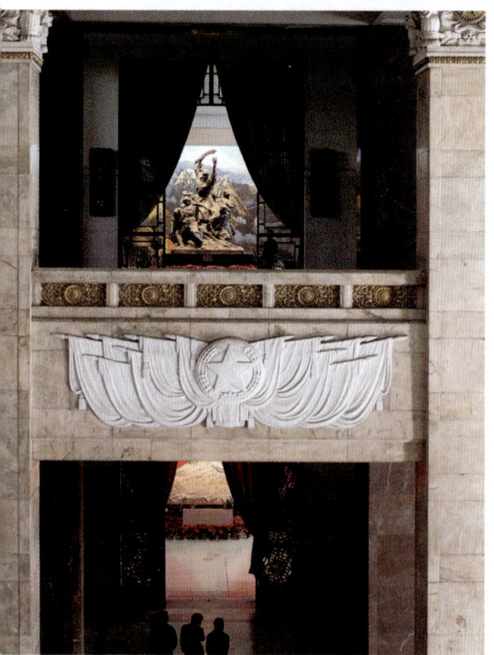

collection of pistols, rifles, machine guns, flamethrowers, torpedoes and bombs from all over the world. A sculpture hall features busts and statues of Chinese leaders and generals, as well as foreign luminaries such as Kim Il Sung. There is also a large collection of historical and archaeological material which deals with ancient Chinese warfare. In contrast to the other exhibits, there are plenty of English explanations in this exhibition. Ancient weaponry, both authentic and replica, is on display. A few of the famous Terracotta Warriors are exhibited, as well as paintings, models, a replica of a fortified city wall surrounded by a variety of siege weapons, and many other fascinating objects telling the history of Chinese warfare up to the Opium War with Britain. Of special interest are ancient grenades, bombs and rocket-born arrows, demonstrating how gunpowder, a Chinese invention, was put to use for military purposes.

Other halls feature the War against Japan (World War II), the Civil War (against the Nationalists) and the War of Resistance against US Aggression and Support Korea (the Korean War). There are guns, uniforms, objects, paintings, photographs, relics such as an oil lamp used by Mao, flags and letters, as well as other personal effects and originals of documents written by the revolutionary leaders.

Except for the Hall of Ancient Warfare, English signage is sporadic, but in many areas major themes, at least, are noted in English.

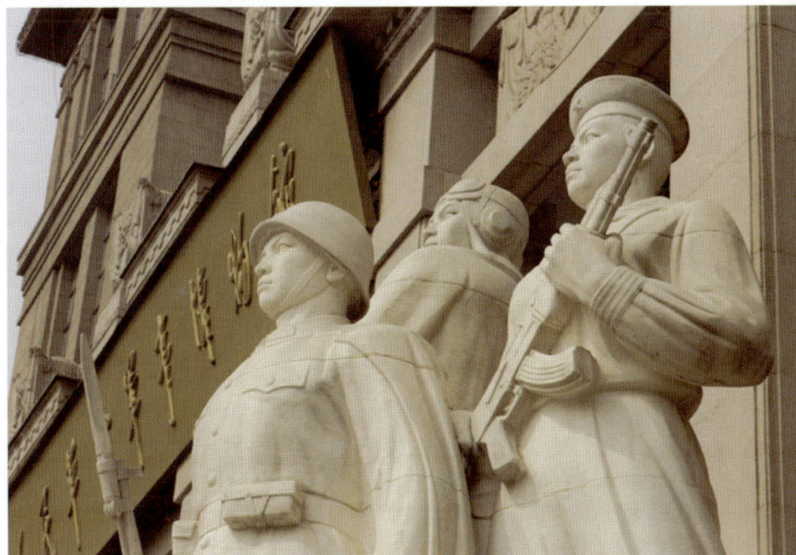

Sculptures at
the entrance

29

Ethnic Costumes Museum of BIFT

北京服装学院民族服饰博物馆 *Beijing fuzhuangxueyuan minzu fushi bowuguan*

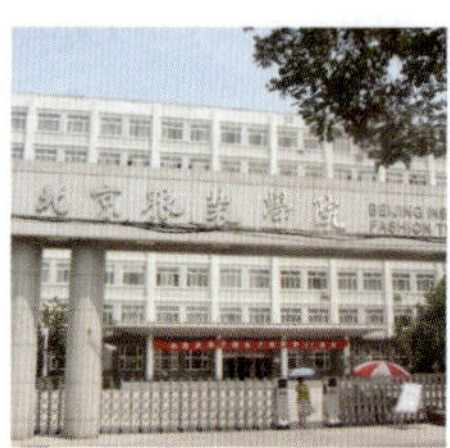

A2 Yinghua East Road, Chaoyang District, Beijing
北京市朝阳区樱花东街甲2号
Tel: (010) 6428 8067
Open: 8.30–11.30, Mon & Tues; 13.30–16.00, Thurs & Sat;
　　　closed on summer / winter vocations and holidays
http://bwg.bift.edu.cn

Eighteenth-century royal dragon robe

This utterly modern and fascinating museum with excellent English and some French signage is well worth the trouble to find if you're interested in Chinese textiles and costume history. The textiles are exhibited beautifully. Only 5 per cent of the collection of more than 100,000 items is on display and includes all manner of textiles and related accoutrements from both the Han and some of China's ethnic minorities, and from ancient to modern times. All are the finest examples of their type. The museum claims to hold the most comprehensive collection in China, amassed largely at the end of the 1980s before prices for such pieces became prohibitive. The Institute of Clothing Technology is continuing to collect with funds from the municipal government. The range of textiles displayed includes embroidery, batik, weaving, brocade and printing on cloth.

Featured are such items as a nineteenth-century Han jacket made of bamboo beads. These jackets, although unusual, can still be found in antique stores around Beijing. Similar to the waterproof fish-skin clothing made by Native Americans is a suit of the Hezhe people also made of fish skin. The nomadic Hezhe, one of the smallest of China's minority groups, come from the north, and their clothing is traditionally made of fish skin and deer hide. One of the star pieces in the collection is a royal dragon robe with a Manchu-style pattern dating to the late eighteenth century. This is woven in the now obsolete *kesi* style, meaning 'carved silk'– a technique developed in the Tang dynasty that reached its apex in the Song. It was used when weaving detailed pictures and intricate motifs to create raised decoration.

Walking through the galleries while reading the explanatory panels, you can learn about Chinese textiles in general as well as regional variations. For example, they explain that the clothing of the north tends to be heavier and richer, incorporating fur, felt, silk and satin, while that of the south tends to be made of cotton, flax or silk. Various types of trimming are displayed with explanations of the different stitches used.

By understanding textile traditions you can appreciate Chinese culture and ethnic minority culture more deeply. For example, the Miao people illustrate their history and oral traditions through textile decoration. They believe that the butterfly is the ancestor of everything on earth – thus the butterfly is a common batik motif. The museum's collection of Miao costumes is one of the most complete in China, from the exquisite festive costumes of the Miao women in Shidong (Guizhou Province) to the collarless coats and pleated skirts of the Miao of the Nandan area of Guangxi Zhuang Autonomous Region.

Scores of silver accessories and items of jewellery are also displayed with examples from about twenty branches of the Miao, as well as from the Tibetan, Mongolian, Jingpo, Dong, Dai, Yao and Hani peoples. These adornments include bracelets, earrings, combs, shoulder ornaments, necklaces and headdresses. Some incorporate inlay of pearls, jade, silver wire and gold. Amazing are the thick, twisted silver chokers of the Dong people and the horn-shaped headdresses with chiselled dragon designs of the Miao people of Shidong.

Especially noteworthy for its elegance is a magnificent early eighteenth-century Mongolian silver headdress which belonged to a princess of the Chahar tribe. The headdress, in two parts, includes a decoration for the princess' plait and is decorated with gold chain and inlaid with coral. It was obtained by the museum from a male descendant of the princess following difficult negotiations as he did not want his people to abandon their cultural property. Ultimately, however, he was convinced that many more people would be able to appreciate its beauty if it were displayed in a public gallery in China's capital.

One gallery is dedicated to a unique collection of photographs taken by the well-known photographer and ethnographer Zhuang Xueben in the early twentieth century. Of great anthropological interest, they record wedding ceremonies, holiday celebrations and even wars by the tribes in western Sichuan including the Tibetan and Qiang minorities. The photographs bring to life and give context to the costumes that you see as you walk through the galleries.

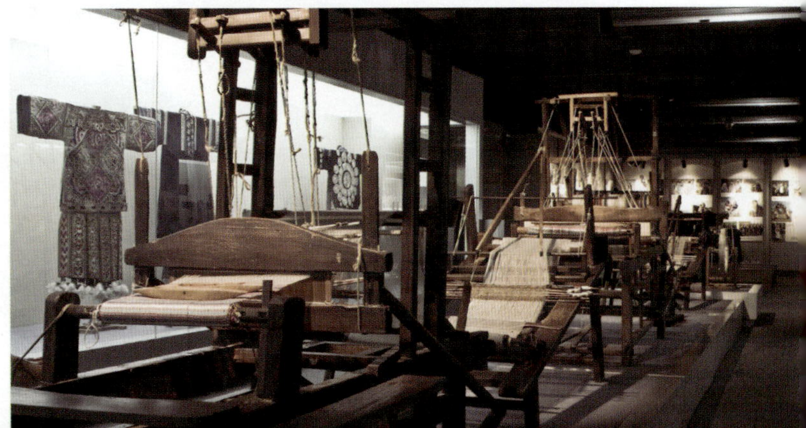

Selection of looms

National Art Museum of China (NAMOC)

中国美术馆 *Zhongguo meishuguan*

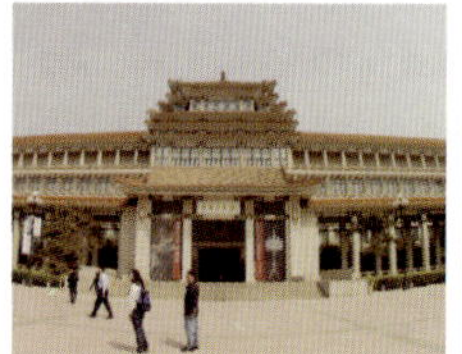

1 Wusida Street, Dongcheng District, Beijing
北京市东城区五四大街1号
Tel: (010) 6400 1476
Open: 9.00–17.00, last entry 16.00
www.namoc.org
Cafeteria at the back of the building

Beijing's museum of modern art, compared to those of other world capitals, has a long way to go. The museum was recently refurbished, but the results are highly disappointing. The collection includes modern and contemporary Chinese painting, folk art and crafts such as cut paper, kites and puppets, and sculpture, as well as a small collection of Western paintings donated by a couple from Germany. There is English signage in all of the galleries, but it is often garbled. The museum does have temporary shows and hosts visiting exhibitions. These can be of high quality. It is recommended that you check listings to see what is on while you're visiting.

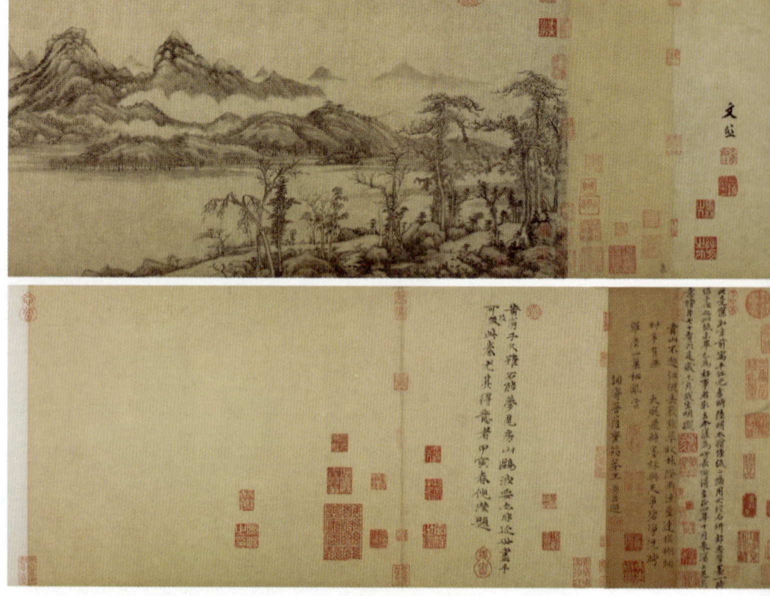

National Museum of China

中国国家博物馆 *Zhongguo guojia bowuguan*

31

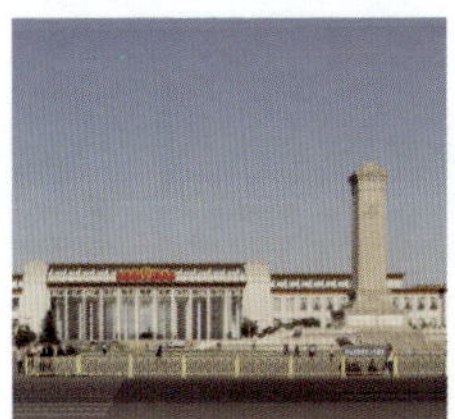

16 East Changan Street, Dongcheng District, Beijing (east of the Tiananmen Square)
北京市东城区东长安街16号 天安门广场东侧
Tel: (010) 6511 6188
Open: 9.00–17.00 except Mon, ticket box closed at 15.30
www.chnmuseum.cn
Gift shop / audio guides

The new National Museum of China was re-opened with much fanfare and celebration in March 2011. Consciously built to be the largest museum in the world, it aims successfully to illustrate with many masterpieces the entire history of Chinese civilization, from Yuanmou man (1,700,000 years old) through the overthrow of the Qing, the last dynasty, in 1911 to the revolution which culminated in 1949 in the founding of the People's Republic.

Hills and Water in the Rain by Huang Gongwang, Yuan dynasty

The new museum is the result of the merger of the original Museum of Chinese History, founded in 1912 and the National Museum of the Revolution founded in 1950. Both have undergone many changes, including the location of both museums in a complex of ten buildings on the East side of Tiananmen Square to commemorate the tenth anniversary of the founding of the Republic in 1959. These buildings have now been restructured by the German architects Gerkan, Marg and Partners with more than 28 new exhibition galleries, more than triple the original exhibition space, and state of the art facilities throughout. The iconic 1959 façade has been retained.

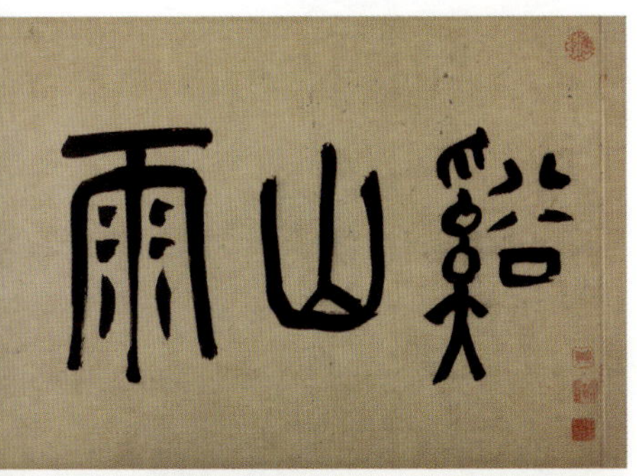

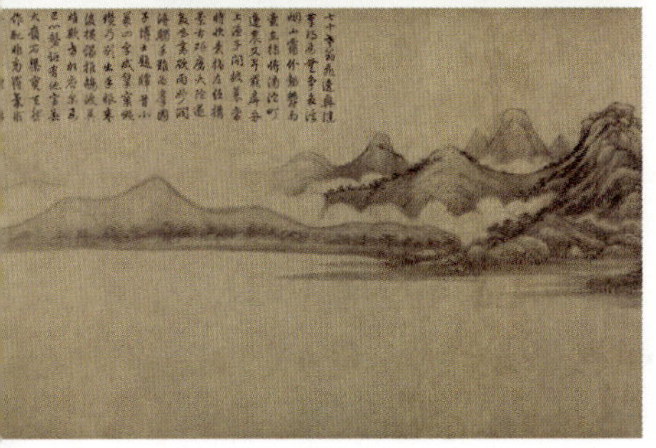

The collection of ancient bronzes is the finest and most comprehensive in China, including ritual vessels, musical instruments and everyday objects. Many have inscriptions that are crucial to the understanding of pre-Qin history. Among the most famous of the Shang bronzes is the so-called Houmuwu (the posthumous name of Fu Hao, consort of the Shang king Wu Ding) ding; the

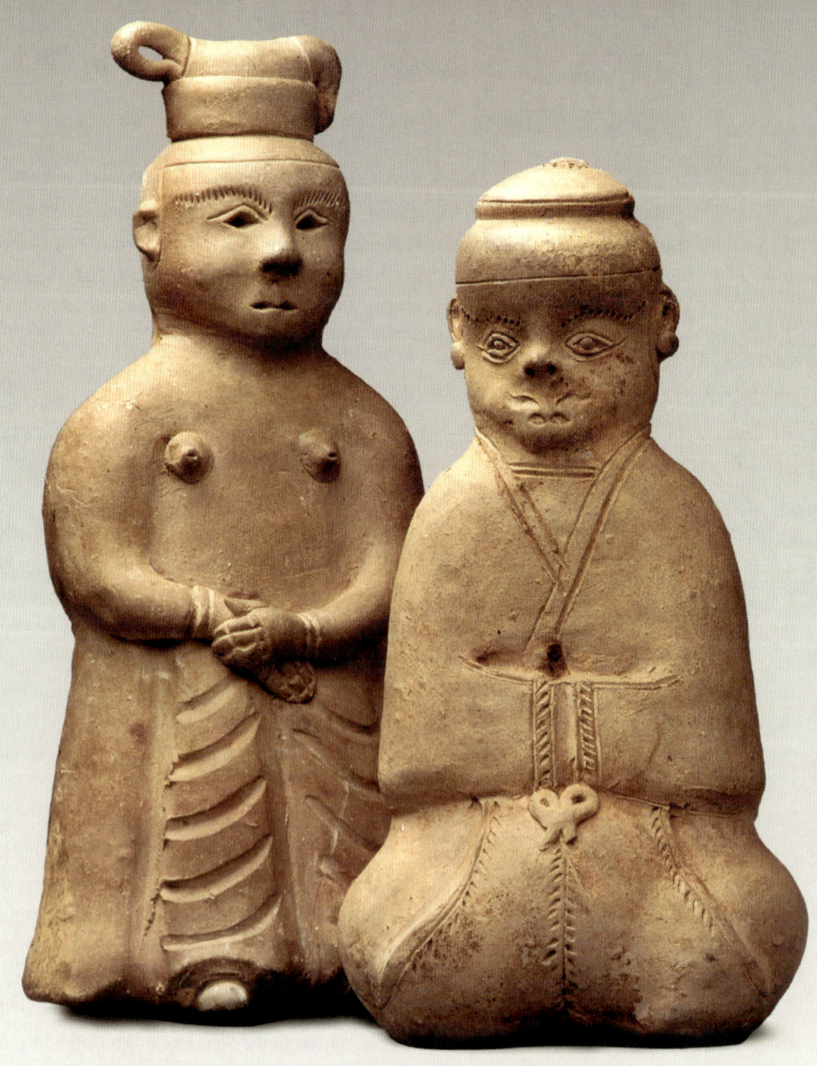

Porcelain male and female figurines, Western Jin dynasty
Unearthed at Banqiao, Nanjing, Jiangsu province, 1964

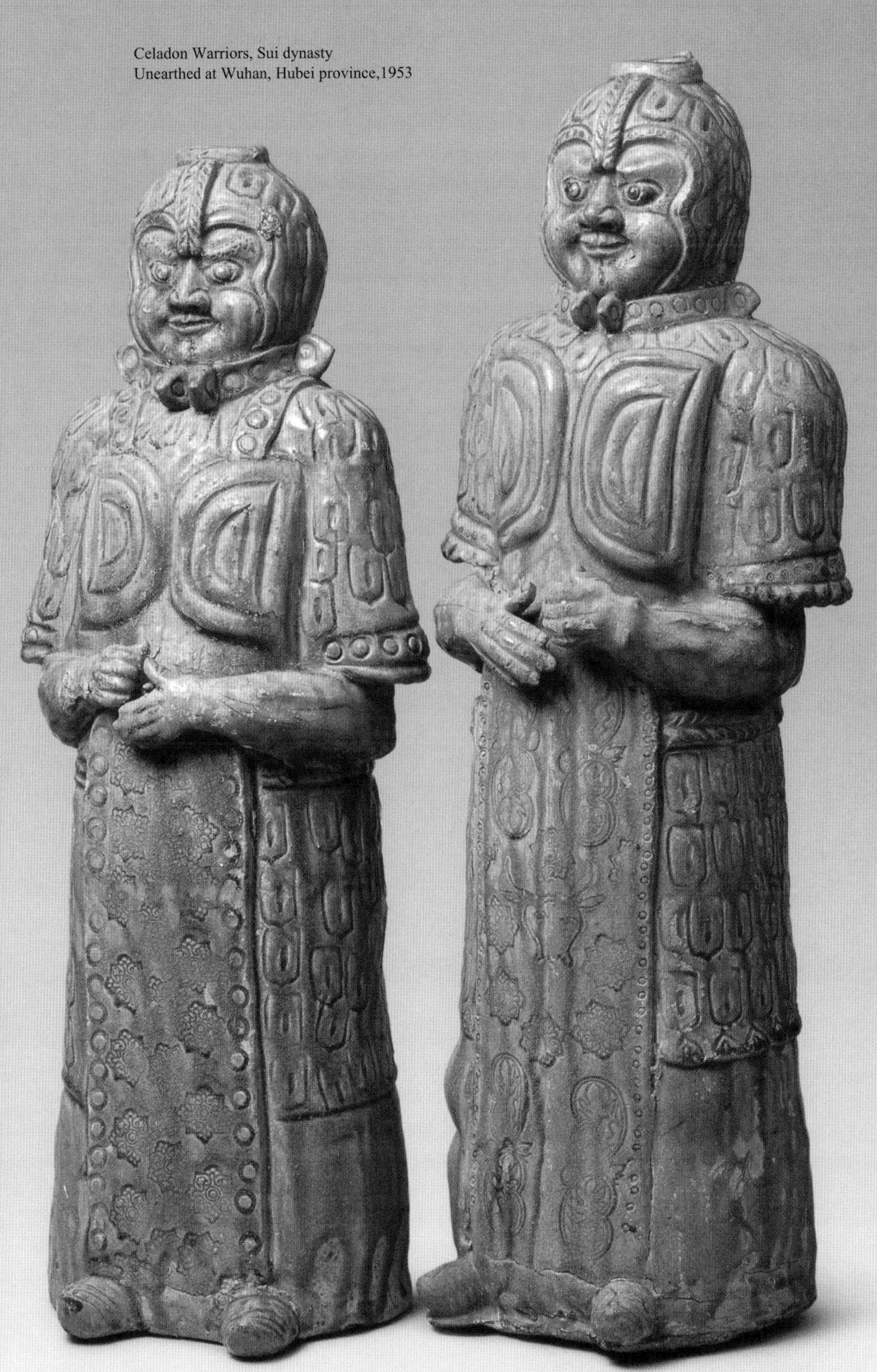

Celadon Warriors, Sui dynasty
Unearthed at Wuhan, Hubei province,1953

Western Zhou Da Yu cauldron with an inscription of 291 characters; and the Ji Zibai pan of the state of Guo which is the largest bronze water container from the Shang and Zhou periods, with an inscription of great importance for research into the politics, military affairs and tribal relations in the late   Western Zhou.

The ceramics rage from pieces with primitive patterns reflecting the life of the time, to ceramics from the Han to the Tang periods, and the tri-coloured glaze of the Tang to porcelain from the kilns of the Song, Yuan, Ming and Qing dynasties.

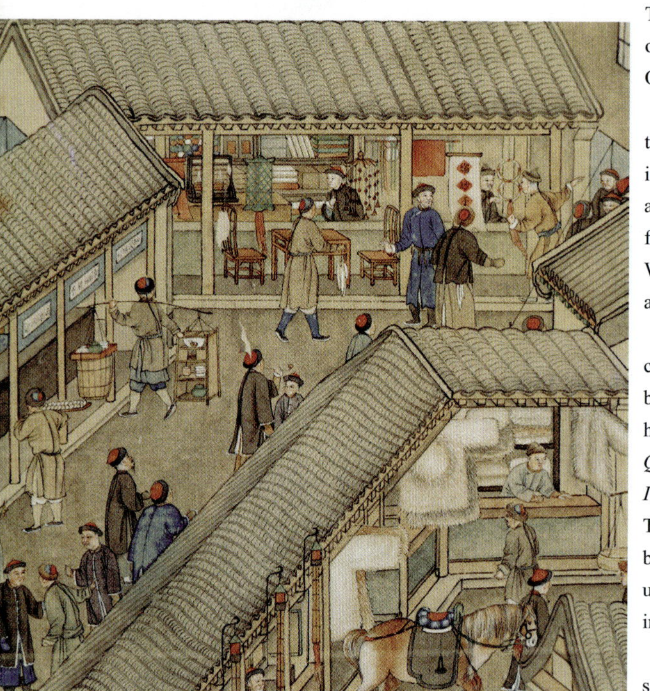

Jades form a major part of the collection, diverse and rich in form and type, ranging from a Hongshan Culture dragon from the tomb of Fu Hao, to the Western Han gold sewn jade suit and a Sui gold-rimmed jade cup.

There are paintings and calligraphy of great range and beauty and many of particular historical interest, such as *The Qianlong Emperor's Southern Inspection Tour*, a National Treasure of unsurpassed beauty and importance for the understanding of Chinese society in the 18th century.

Collections of gold and silver ware, coins and money, historical seals and pictorial bricks are all of the highest quality showing the range of craftsmanship, technology and aesthetics of the art and culture of the many peoples of China.

Elegantly laid out and displayed with ample space and perfect lighting, the collections of the new National Museum of China form an essential part of any programme for all visitors to Beijing.

National Museum of Modern Chinese Literature

中国现代文学馆 *Zhongguo xiandai wenxueguan*

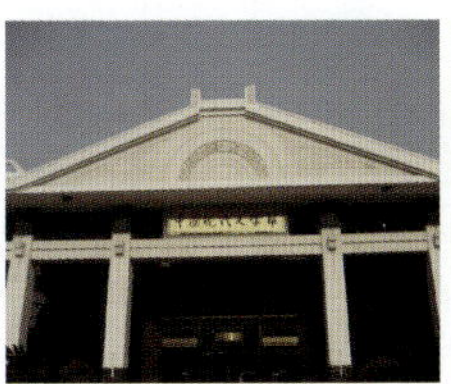

45 Wenxueguan Road, Shaoyaoju, Chaoyang District, Beijing
北京市朝阳区芍药居文学馆路45号
Tel: (010) 5731 1800
Open: 9.00–16.30 except Mon
www.wxg.org.cn

The museum defines modern literature as that of the twentieth century to the present and includes in its purview all works in Chinese including those from outside the mainland, i.e. Hong Kong, Macao and Taiwan as well as those written by overseas Chinese. The institution serves as a museum, library, archive and research institute and continually collects, conserves and organizes books, letters, videos, photographs, magazines, written reviews, mementoes – everything collectable relating to the works and lives of modern Chinese writers. They also publish a quarterly journal and host retrospective exhibitions.

The museum has reproduced the studies of selected writers such as Lu Xun, Ba Jin, Cao Yu and others using their personal effects. Their desks, lamps, reading glasses and teacups are laid out as if they had just momentarily stepped away.

Complete libraries of luminary Chinese authors are in the collection such as those of China's beloved female writer Bing Xin, the playwright and journalist Xia Yan, Yu Pingbo, the persecuted essayist and poet and many others. The museum actively seeks donations from authors and collectors.

Their archive is impressive: the library holds over 80,000 volumes, 110,000 books are available on disc and thousands of actual manuscripts are in the collection and available for scholarly research. The holdings are all in Chinese and the English descriptions are limited.

Ba Jin

New Culture Movement Memorial Museum

北京新文化运动纪念馆 *Beijing xinwenhuayundong jinianguan*

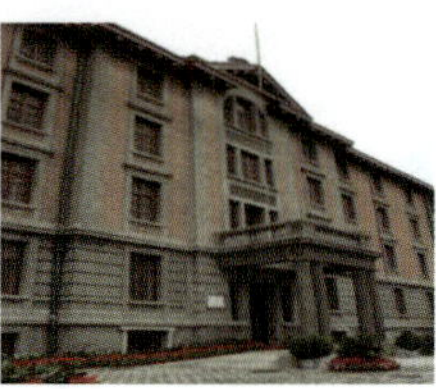

29 Wusida Street, Dongcheng District, Beijing
北京市东城区五四大街29号
Tel: (010) 6612 8596
Open: 9.00–16.00 except Mon, last entry 15.45
www.xwh.org.cn

The Museum covers both the New Culture Movement which began in 1915 and the May Fourth Movement of 1919. While reflecting different ideological trends these two movements were closely related and the location of the museum in the old red brick building of the original Beijing University is appropriate since it was the heart of the intellectual ferment that fuelled both of them.

In 1915, shortly after the establishment of the Republic, the New Culture Movement began spreading Western ideas such as science, liberal democracy and women's rights and denouncing Confucian culture. The leaders of the movement included Cai Yuanpei, who served briefly as the Republic's first Minister of Education and Chen Duxiu who established the influential *New Youth* magazine. The movement successfully promoted the Chinese vernacular as China's written language as a replacement for classical Chinese which had been used until then.

After World War 1, the Treaty of Versailles ceded the former German colonial territories in Shandong Province to the Japanese and did not return them to China.

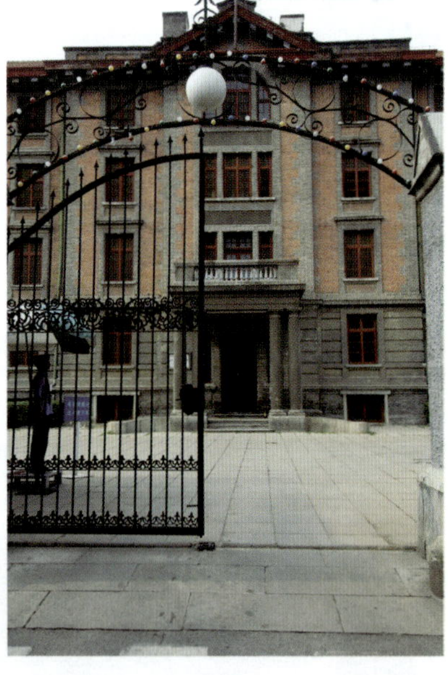

'Red Building' of the old Beijing University

On May 4, 1919 a student protest against this decision and the lack of action against it by the Chinese warlord government broke out in Beijing and spread to other cities such as Shanghai where asworkers joined the movement. A nationwide boycott of Japanese goods was organized. The actions of the Great Powers and President Wilson fundamentally discredited Western liberalism and the concept of national self-determination they espoused. Many Chinese radicals including Chen Duxiu turned to the ideals of the Russian October Revolution of 1917 and Chinese communism was born, with the Chinese Communist Party being established in 1921.

Poly Art Museum

保利艺术博物馆 *Baoli yishu bowuguan*

34

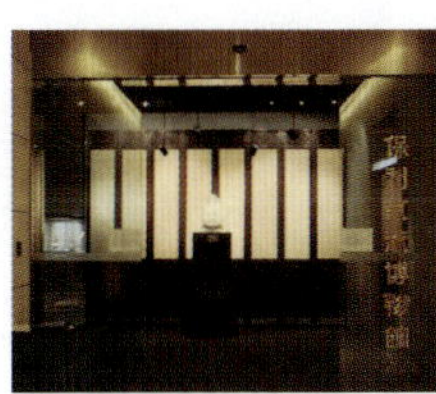

9F, Poly Plaza, Dongzhimen South Street, Dongcheng District, Beijing
北京市东城区东直门南大街14号保利大厦9楼
Tel: (010) 6500 8117
Open: 9.30–16.30 except Mon & national holidays
Bookshop / gift shop

The aim of the Poly Art Museum, owned by the Poly Corporation, is to bring Chinese art treasures looted in the past back to China. Their most publicized purchase took place in 2000 at an auction in Hong Kong. Three Qing dynasty bronze astrological animal heads – a monkey, a tiger and an ox – stolen by British troops in 1860 from the Old Summer Palace went on the block. Amid great publicity, the Poly Corporation paid US$4 million for them. They are now on display in the museum.

The Poly Museum, located in the Poly Corporation's gleaming headquarters, has a first class collection of art lushly displayed in modern cases with dramatic lighting. There is excellent English signage throughout the gallery, as well as useful placards with time-lines and visual explanations of the terminology used for Chinese pots and vessels. The collection mainly consists of bronzes dating from the Shang to the Tang period and Buddhist stone sculpture. These are separated into two galleries.

Some highlights of the bronzes include, from the Western Zhou, a set of eight bells and an oddly formed *gui* which is very organic in shape and looks as if it was modelled from clay. Also from this period is an extraordinary *you*, or wine vessel. The body and lid are in the form of a face with eyes, nose and smile; the top of the lid has scalloped 'hair' and a bird perched at the centre. There is a high looped handle with fantastical bird decoration and two side handles in the shape of a mythical animal: a goat's head with an elephant's trunk. A dragon writhes around the base. This splendid piece should not be missed.

Bronze weapons from the Warring States period are also exhibited such as a *yue*, or axe, and a sword with gold inlay. There are various examples of arms and armour from the Shang and Zhou dynasties such as a Shang helmet decorated with animal faces. From the Western Han is displayed a tall, stemmed lamp supported by kneeling human figures armed with knives. Finally there is a Tang dynasty *hu* with dragon handles.

In the second gallery can be seen some very fine examples of Buddhist sculpture of the Southern, Northern, Sui and Tang dynasties.

Bodhisattva in meditation, Northern Qi

35

Sino-Japanese War Memorial Museum / Marco Polo Bridge

中国人民抗日战争纪念馆 *Zhongguo renmin kangrizhanzheng jinianguan*

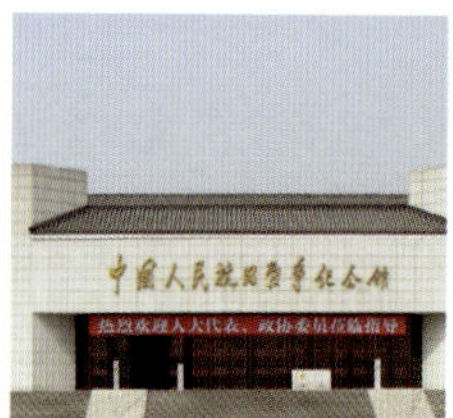

101 Chengnei Street, Wanping Town, Lugouqiao, Fengtai District, Beijing
北京市丰台区卢沟桥宛平城内街101号
Tel: (010) 8389 2355
Open: 9.30–16.30 except Mon, last entry 16.00
www.1937china.org.cn/enweb
Restaurants / souvenir shops

The location of this Memorial Museum is no coincidence as the 'Marco Polo Bridge Incident' is often cited as the beginning of the Sino-Japanese War. On 7 July 1937 tensions erupted into violence between Japanese troops stationed on one side of the bridge and the Chinese on the other. A prolonged battle ensued and after three days the Japanese ultimately took the bridge and the town of Wanping. From there they marched on to Beijing, seizing control on 29 July and Tianjin the day after.

The exhibits in the Memorial Hall are divided into three sections, focusing on Japanese atrocities, the war years and anti-Japanese heroes. Exhibits detail gruesome episodes during the Japanese occupation, including the use of germ warfare and the Rape of Nanjing. Some exhibits are quite graphic, including pictures of decapitated Chinese and implements of torture. While some exhibits include actual weapons (rusting swords, implements of torture and at least one skull, purportedly of a Nanjing massacre victim), most of the displays consist of photographs and original documents, with explanations of the most salient features in English and the rest in Chinese. This museum is not suitable for young children.

The *Lugou Qiao*, or Marco Polo Bridge as it is known in English, was built in 1192 and rebuilt in the seventeenth century by the Kangxi Emperor after it was washed away in a flood. There is no chance of such an incident repeating itself today as the Yongding River has been diverted to supply the needs of Beijing. The bridge gets its English name from the fact that Marco Polo saw the bridge during his time in China in the thirteenth century and waxed lyrical over it in his book *The Travels of Marco Polo*. The magnificent span of this handsome granite bridge, held up by eleven arches, now extends across dry brush or grass depending on the season. But the bridge is still a sight to behold. It measures 235 m and has 250 marble balustrades supporting 485 carved stone lions – none of which are identical or in the same position. Many of them have smaller lions crawling on them or resting between their paws. On either side of the bridge is a commemorative stele, one built by the Kangxi Emperor on its reconstruction, the other by his grandson, the Qianlong Emperor. Tradition has it that the bridge is best seen while viewing the moon during the Mid-Autumn Festival.

Soong Ching Ling's Former Residence

宋庆龄同志故居 *Song Qingling tongzhi guju*

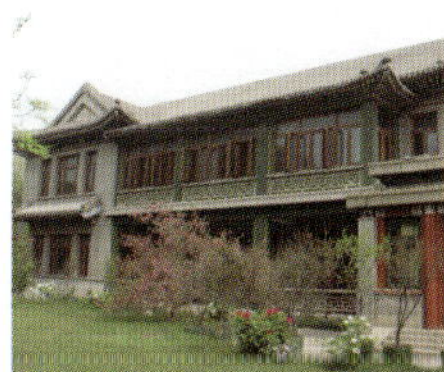

46 Houhai, Xicheng District, Beijing
北京市西城区后海46号
Tel: (010) 6404 4205
Open: 9.00–17.00 summer; 16.30 winter
www.sql.org.cn (Chinese only)

This is the Beijing residence of Soong Ching Ling (1893–1981), wife of Dr Sun Yat-Sen. The house, set among gardens on the north side of Houhai Lake, was her official residence and is basically unchanged since she occupied it.

Soong Ching Ling
at her desk

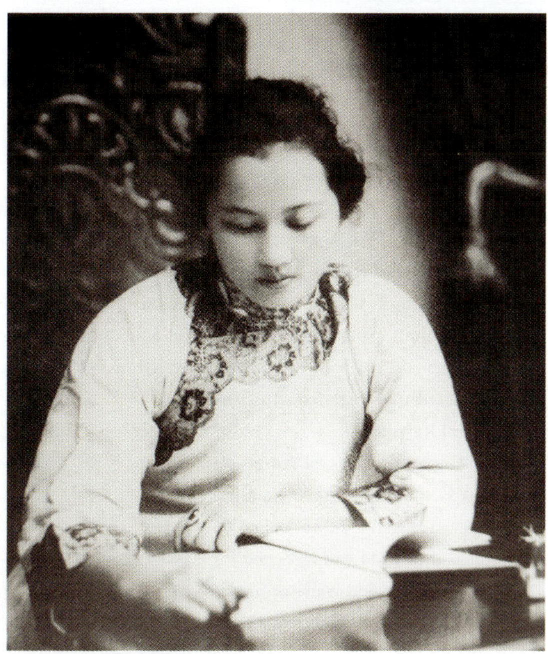

Exhibited are many photos and personal possessions of Soong Ching Ling from her childhood to the time of her death which document many of the historic events she lived through and took part in. There are also many mementos on display recording her associations with renowned figures of China's recent history.

37

Tank Museum

中国坦克博物馆 *Zhongguo tanke bowuguan*

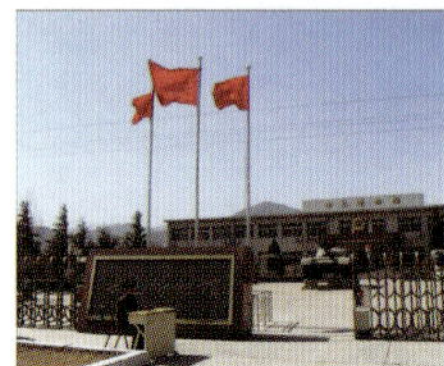

No.88372 Army Unit, Yangfang Town, Changping District, Beijing
北京市昌平区阳坊镇八八三七二部队
Tel: (010) 6675 9901
Open: 8.30–17.00 except Mon
Kids

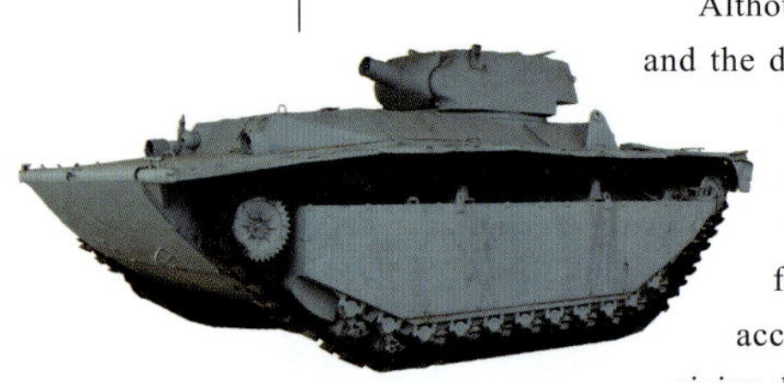

T-54 Medium Tank

Although the museum's building is somewhat dilapidated and the displays inside, consisting mainly of photos, do not elicit great excitement, a good selection of Chinese, American and Japanese tanks is displayed in the courtyard outside, making this a worthwhile stop for the tank enthusiast. Almost all of the displays are accompanied by good signage in Chinese and English giving detailed historical information as well as specifications. Plans are afoot to move some of the non-vehicle displays into a nearby building undergoing refurbishment.

Like other military equipment in the arsenal of the People's Liberation Army (PLA), many of the tanks are remakes of Soviet examples either licensed or purchased, including the Type 59 Medium Tank based on the Soviet T-54. Externally this tank was almost identical to its Soviet model, but its innards were made to Chinese specifications. Subsequent models with added improvements are also shown. The experimental 111 Heavy Tank was delivered in 1970 without its turret and was never completed due to the start of the Cultural Revolution.

Among the several American tanks is the amphibious Landing Vehicle Tracked LVT variant (A)-4 produced in 1944 and designed for use in areas around water or in rice fields (where the Americans used it during the Vietnam War). The museum's example would have been captured by the PLA from the Nationalists during the Civil War.

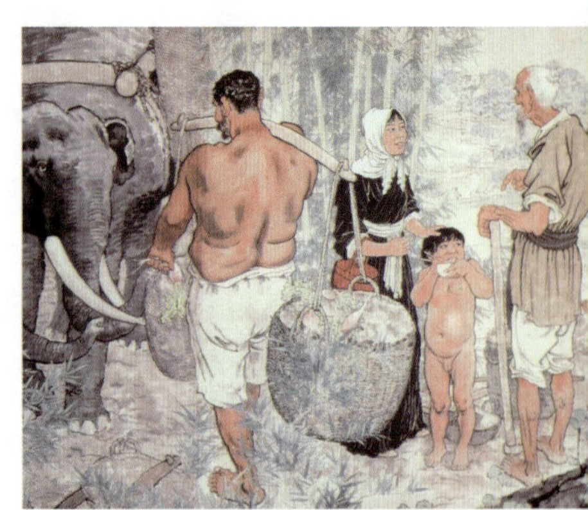

Xu Beihong Museum

徐悲鸿纪念馆 *Xu Beihong jinianguan*

38

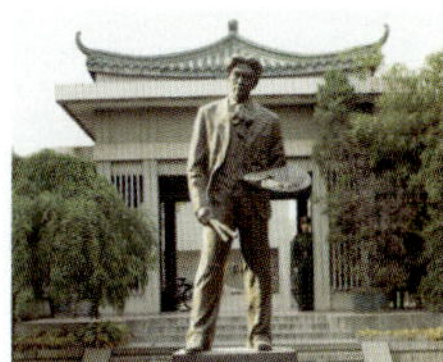

53 Xinjiekou North Street, Xicheng District, Beijing
北京市西城区新街口北大街53号
Tel: (010) 6225 2187
Open: 9.00–16.00 except Mon

Xu Beihong was one of China's most famous twentieth-century artists. Born in 1895 in Jiangsu Province, he was taught by his father and spent his youth with him as an itinerant portraitist. After his father's death, he went to Shanghai, where he worked and studied, soon becoming prominent in art circles. In 1917, he spent a year in Japan, then returned to China and taught at Beijing University. There he became politically involved, joining the revolutionary New Culture Movement. In 1919, Xu moved to Europe, studying and painting in Paris, Berlin and Brussels. By the time he returned to China in 1926, he was a well-known painter with a strong academic background and a solid technique in classical European-style drawing and oil painting. In 1927, he became the head of the Art department of the National Central University in Nanjing where he remained for the following ten years.

On his return to China, Xu began creating paintings combining classical Western realism with Chinese themes and contemporary political messages. Each message is spelled out for visitors by the curators of the Xu Beihong Museum.

During the 1930s and early 1940s, Xu continued to travel, returning to Europe as well as going to the Soviet Union and India, where he painted a portrait of Mahatma Gandhi which can be seen in the museum. During this period, he also finished one of his huge patriotic paintings, *Yu Gong Removes the Mountain*, an allegorical work which was one of Mao Zedong's favourite paintings as its message describes relentless struggle leading ultimately to success.

Xu died of a cerebral haemorrhage in 1953 after some years of poor health. The Xu Beihong Museum is situated in an older building next door to his original house and studio (no longer standing).

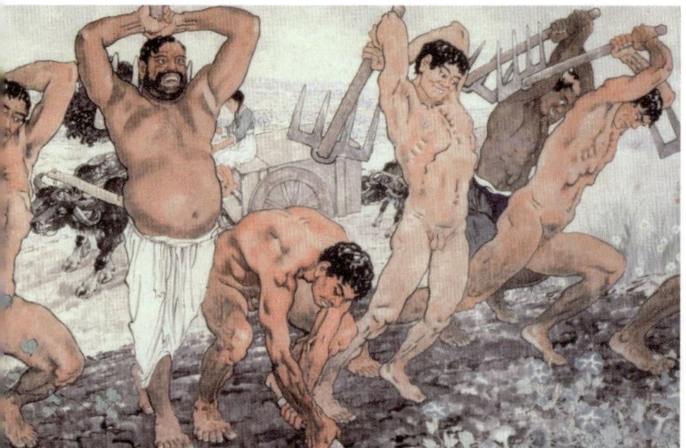

Yu Gong Removes the Mountain (1940)

Zhoukoudian Site Museum

周口店北京人遗址博物馆 *Zhoukoudian beijingren yizhi bowuguan*

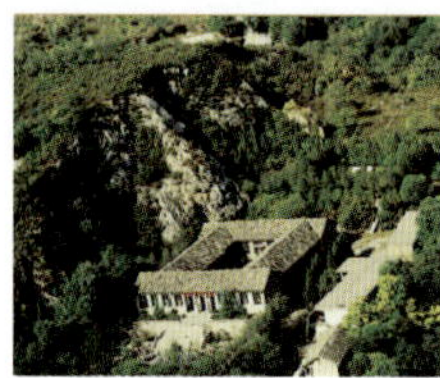

1 Zhoukoudian Street, Fangshan District, Beijing
北京市房山区周口店大街1号
Tel: (010) 6930 1080 / 1090
Open: 8.30–16.30, Apr–Oct; 8.30–16.00, Nov–Mar
www.zkd.cn
Bookshop

Cast of skull *Homo erectus pekinensis*

About fifty miles southwest of Beijing is the Palaeolithic site of Zhoukoudian. It was here that the first *Homo erectus pekinesis* skull cap was excavated in 1929, later known as 'Peking Man'. This discovery ranked alongside Africa's Olduvai Gorge as one of the greatest stories in archaeological history and remains one of the most widely known prehistoric sites in the world.

The story began in 1899 with the German doctor and fossil collector K. A. Harberer. While visiting China Harberer collected what were then known as 'dragon bones' but were actually fossil bones. These were ground up and sold in pharmacies to be used as a cure for every sort of medical problem. Harberer had them analyzed on his return to Germany and found that they were actually the remains of many different types of extinct mammals, including sabretooth tigers, antelopes and hyenas. He also had collected a molar that looked somewhat human and was estimated to be up to 2,000,000 years old.

The story picked up again in the 1920s with the Swedish scientist Johann Gunnar Anderson, who was searching for 'dragon bones' at a limestone quarry near Zhoukoudian, when he was directed by a local resident to a site known as 'Dragon Bone Hill'. There Anderson and his colleague found many mammalian fossils, as well as two teeth similar to those found earlier by Harberer. These molars, analyzed in 1927 by the Canadian Davidson Black, head of the Anatomy department of Peking Union Medical College, were identified as in fact belonging to a hominid and up to 2,000,000 years old. This caused an uproar in the archaeological community as the molars constituted the oldest known evidence of human fossils.

The site of Chou K'ou Tian (Zhoukoudian) became the focus of palaeontological research, with a large-scale excavation funded by the Rockefeller Foundation in America. Besides many fossilized animal bones of differing species, another similar molar was found, confirming Black's theory that these teeth came from a new and separate genus of hominid which he named *Sinanthropus pekinensis* – now classified as *Homo erectus pekinensis* – 'Peking Man'. Davidson Black became director of the excavation and – uniquely for his time – demanded that Chinese archaeologists working at the site be on equal footing with their European colleagues. He hired prominent Chinese scientists to work in the team, including Pei Wenzhong ,Yang Zhongjian and Bian Meinian.

At a dramatic moment at the very end of the 1929 season, in the midst of the Civil War, Pei Wenzhong, excavating a cave by candlelight, discovered a complete human skull cap. Between 1929 and 1937 several more skull caps were found, as

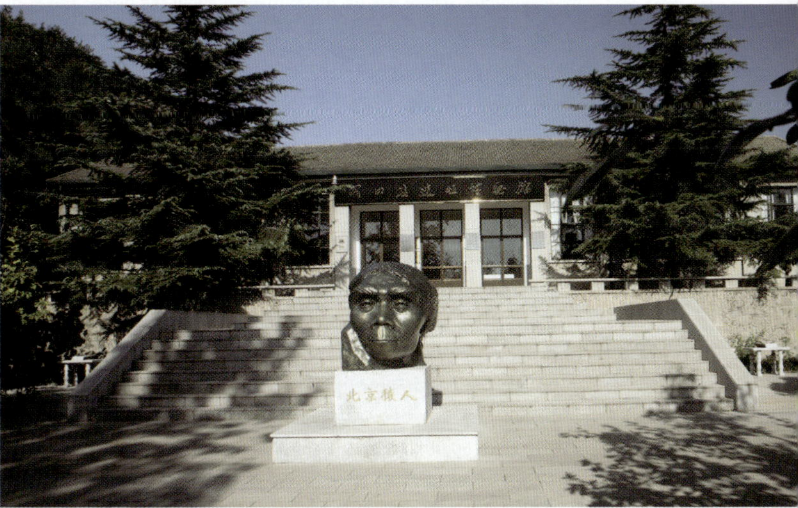

well as eleven mandibles, various facial bones and about 150 teeth. These fragments confirmed the existence of forty individuals, males and females of varying ages – still the largest known sample of *Homo erectus* fossils ever found. The fossil remains tell us that *H. erectus pekinensis* had a long, sloping forehead and thick brow ridge. The jaws and teeth were much bigger than ours, and there was no chin.

In July 1937, as work at the site was progressing so well, everything was suddenly stopped due to the Japanese invasion. The Japanese occupiers took a great interest in Zhoukoudian. In order to protect the fossils from them, they were stored at Peking Union Medical College, and casts were made. In 1941 the originals were packed up to be sent to the US for safekeeping. Somewhere along the way to the port city of Qinhuangdao they disappeared, never to be seen again. Some say they were stolen by the US Marines who were guarding the boxes; others think the Japanese took them; still others believe they remain hidden away in an American university somewhere. There is no evidence for any of these stories. Research had to continue using the plaster casts made in the 1930s.

Excavation at the site was resumed after the war. Two more skull fragments belonging to one individual were found, as well as many more tools from the Early-Late Palaeolithic. Pollen analysis yielded information about the diet of the individuals and about the species of fauna during this period. Late Cenozoic fish fossils have been found as has evidence of ninety other mammal species, including hyenas, deer, bears and tigers.

On the evidence of the many stone tools found at the site (more than 100,000 artefacts) and many quartz-flake tools, it seems that these individuals subsisted mainly by scavenging. There has been controversy about the use of fire at the site. Evidence of ash was thought to remain from hearth fires, but now some say that the ash was caused by lightning–induced spontaneous fires and had been washed into the soil by flooding. On the other hand, burned bone associated with stone tools has been found, which would in fact indicate a controlled use of fire.

Interestingly, some scientists now feel that the caves themselves were actually the dens of hyenas – not the homes of Peking Man. The hominid fossils found do not include many long bones, hands or feet – they are mainly teeth and skull fragments, many of which show puncture marks. The theory is that the very large Pleistocene cave hyena was using *H. erectus pekinensis* as a food source; they would have taken their prey back to their caves and eaten the extremities in their entirety. There is also evidence of the skulls being split open and the brain removed. This fits the hyena theory well, although some feel it is evidence of cannibalism.

Homo erectus pekinensis is now believed to have inhabited Zhoukoudian from 550,000 to 400,000 years ago until about 230,000 years ago, giving the species a very long survival rate. In 1987 Zhoukoudian became a UNESCO World Heritage Site. None of the human fossils on display are originals – all are casts. The animal and fish fossils are real, however. Also on exhibit are large-scale dioramas depicting Peking Man in his natural habitat, including stone tools and bone implements. There is as well a display of the geological history of the site in conjunction with human and animal evolution. Large posters tell the story of the discoveries with biographies of the archaeologists.

At the time of writing, the museum cases and display were quite musty and outdated. However, the material exhibited and history of the site are so important that the site is worth a visit for those with an interest in the subject. You can also wander round the park-like site and visit (from the outside) the limestone fissures in which Peking Man was found. There is not a lot to see, but the levels at which the finds were made are well marked. If you call a day or two ahead, you can hire an English-speaking guide – very helpful when it comes to navigating the excavation areas. The museum has some English signage.

40

Museum of Chinese Opera

天津戏剧博物馆 *Tianjin xiju bowuguan*

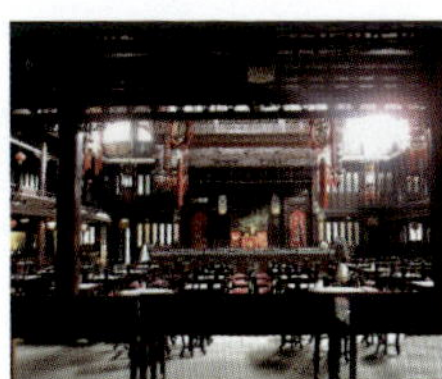

31 Nanmenli Street, Nankai District, Tianjin
天津市南开区南门里大街31号
Tel: (022) 2735 6475
Open: 9.00–11.20 & 14.00–16.30 except Sun

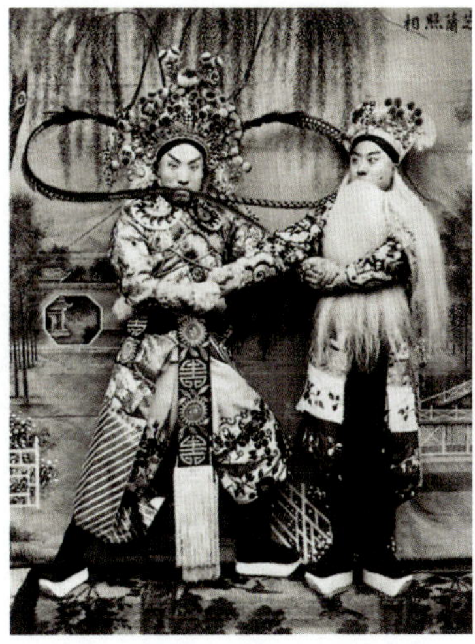

The Museum of Chinese Opera, located on the site of the former Guangdong Guildhall (built in 1907), includes a magnificent traditional wooden opera hall and display rooms in the eastern and western chambers which have exhibits on the history of Chinese opera, primarily black and white photographs of China's legendary opera greats, opera dolls and costumes. Surrounding the back and two sides of the opera hall are glass-encased dolls dressed in colourful outfits representing characters from China's most famous operas, including *Sun Wukong*, or the Monkey King.

Actors in the Beijing Opera *Lian Hua Hu* (Lotus Lake)

The Guangdong Guildhall served as a gathering place for businessmen coming to Tianjin from the provinces. The wonderful umbrella-shaped caisson which hangs above the centre of the stage is not merely decorative but also provides good acoustics, amplifying and transmitting the voices of the performers in a natural way without the need for a modern sound system. The centre of the opera hall has no columns–the beams being relegated to the sides – which means that there is nothing blocking the view of the audience. The windows at the top of the building allow natural light to penetrate so that no stage lights are needed for matinee performances.

The century-old grey-brick and wood structure with its courtyard is alone worth the visit. The design of the building is based on the style of buildings in Chaozhou in Guangdong Province.

There are no explanatory materials in English. Photography is allowed in the opera hall but not in the exhibition rooms.

Tianjin Academy of Fine Arts Gallery

41

天津美术学院美术馆 *Tianjin meishuxueyuan meishuguan*

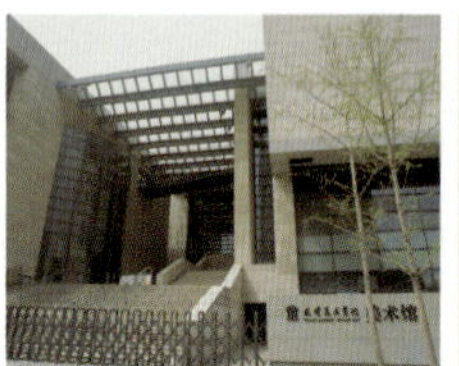

4 Tianwei Road, Hebei District, Tianjin
天津市河北区天纬路4号
Tel: (022) 2624 1542 /1540
Open: 9.30–17.00
www.tjarts.edu.cn

Although the city's contemporary art scene is not as effervescent as that of Beijing's, it has enormous potential, for not only is Tianjin just an hour by train from the capital, but it boasts the well-established Tianjin Academy of Fine Arts – founded in 1906, as well as Schools of Art, Design and Architecture. Many well-known Chinese artists are alumni and have returned to teach at the Academy; several have also displayed their work in the newly opened gallery. There are 10 galleries in this five-floor modern edifice, which built on a corner plot adjacent to Academy, houses temporary exhibitions of alumni and international artists' works ranging from contemporary and traditional painting, photography,

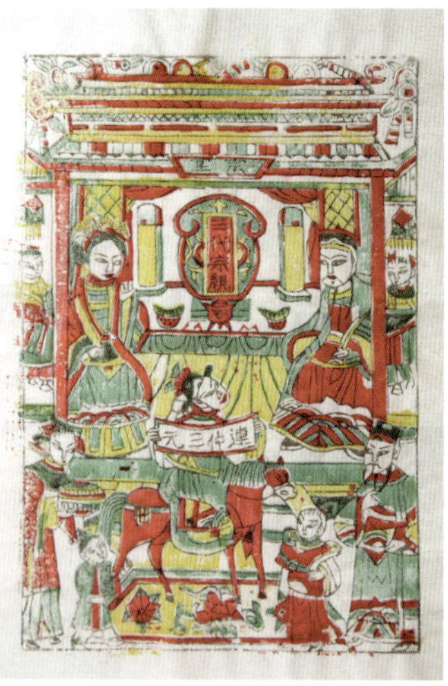

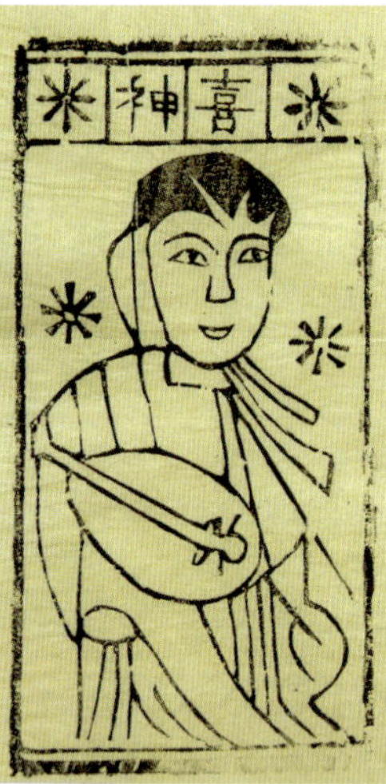

Lunar New Year door poster (*nianhua*) depicting ancestors (left) and God of Happiness (*xishen*, right)

sculpture and multimedia rotated several times throughout the year – while the other half comprises offices, conference spaces and artists' studios. New commercial contemporary galleries have also starting opening in the city. Those on the trail of the contemporary art scene in China should check local listings for upcoming shows at this gallery and the seemingly burgeoning commercial ones too.

42

Tianjin Museum

天津博物馆 *Tianjin bowuguan*

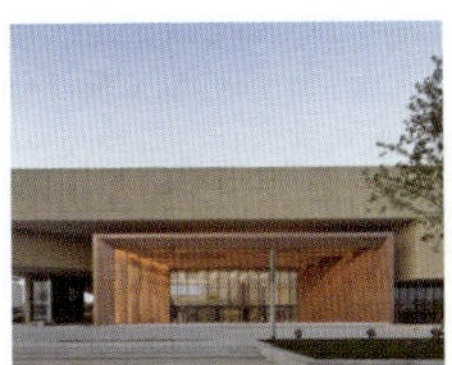

62 Pingjiang Road, Hexi District, Tianjin
天津市河西区平江道62号
Tel: (022) 8388 3000 / 3001
Open: 9.00–16.30 except Mon, last entry 16.00
www.tjbwg.com
Bookshop / restaurant

The present Tianjin Museum replaces an earlier museum established in 1918 that was ultimately housed in a French-style Art Deco mansion dating to the 1930s. Although quaint, space restrictions in the old building allowed only a small part of the collection to be exhibited. The new museum on a new site was designed by the Japanese architect Mamoru Kawaguchi to represent a swan with wings extended and ready to take flight, meant as an analogy to Tianjin's re-emergence as a city of major importance. The complex consists of the main building, a long walkway (the swan's neck) across a small lake and a garden surrounding the lake.

Tortoise-shaped box, Liao dynasty

The ground floor is mainly a large atrium housing an information counter, ticket office, bookstore and so on. The two upper floors house an impressive collection of ceramics, paintings, calligraphy, jades, bronzes, ink stones and oracle bones. On the top floor are a number of historically important Shang dynasty oracle bones dating from the Reign of Wu Ding. One of them, along with a divination regarding the weather, records the sacrifice of 500 people to ensure success in battle.

While viewing the jade collection, do not miss the Neolithic Hongshan material, notably a yellow-jade pig dragon, *hongshan huangyu zhulong*, with the head of a pig and the coiled body of a dragon. The Hongshan Culture, which stretched from Inner Mongolia to Liaoning and Hebei and which dates to *c.* 4700–2900 BC, is

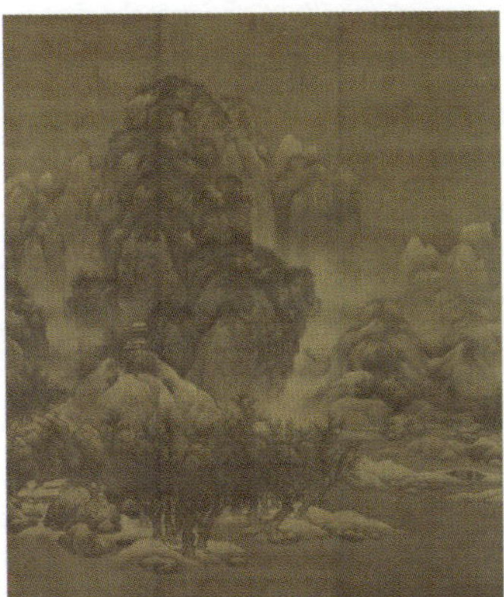

Snow-Covered Scene and Cold Forest, Song dynasty

renowned for its jade-carving techniques. Such items are related to Neolithic tombs and rituals.

Be sure to see the Qing dynasty jadeite leaf with two crickets and a mantis, *feicui guoguo baicai*. This beautifully carved object is made from a single piece of stone and varies in colour from yellow to bright green. The bronze collection also contains splendid items, including a Warring States *ding* known as the *Chu Wang Ding*. It has a loop and three stylized bird-shaped knots on the lid, with handles on each side. The three legs are in the shape of hooves at the bottom and animal masks at the top. A forty-six-character inscription near the rim records the story of producing this *ding*, which was made from the weapons seized by the Chu King to celebrate his victory in a particular battle. One of the great treasures of this museum is the *Tai Bao Ding* dating to the Reign of Emperor Zhou Kang. This *ding* is known for its fine casting and elaborate decoration consisting of crawling mythical animals and abstract designs on body and legs. Inside the *ding*, there is a three-character inscription recording its casting by Tai Bao.

The History Exhibition Hall has exhibits related to the foreign presence in Tianjin. There is the actual stone tablet erected in memory of an American captain serving with the US 9th Infantry Regiment who was killed fighting Chinese forces in the area, as well as weapons captured from the Eight Allied Army, made up of troops from eight countries whose citizens were under siege in the Beijing Legation Quarter by the Boxers. Other items include a Ming dynasty cannon, a model of the old city wall in Tianjin, China's first mini-submarine and 'The Rocket of China', China's first locomotive.

Yu hu chun vase,
Qing dynasty

The museum has a fine ceramic collection that covers China's entire history. Of special interest is the Qing period *famille rose* enamel vase, *yu hu chun*. This marvellous pot, decorated with birds and peonies and inscribed with a poem, was made for the Qianlong Emperor and painted by the court painter at the imperial workshop. It is considered one of the museum's prized possessions. Also note the Southern Song *guan* ware brush washer (*guanyao longwenxi*), a perfect example with its pale greenish-grey glaze and fine brown crackles. The pot is rimmed with bronze, providing a beautiful contrast with the colour of the glaze.

The museum also houses a fine collection of folk art, including woodblock prints, kites and masks.

Tianjin Natural History Museum

天津自然博物馆 *Tianjin ziran bowuguan*

43

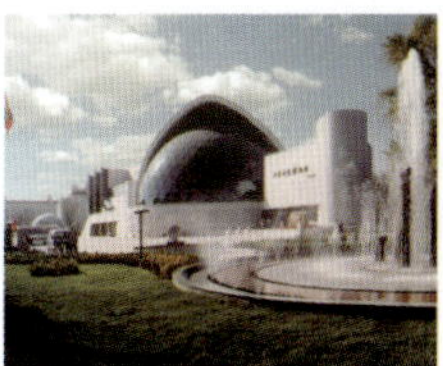

The museum has been closed since May 2, 2013. It will be moved to a new site and is scheduled to reopen at the end of 2013.

www.tjnhm.org

The museum was founded in 1914 by the French palaeontologist and Catholic priest, Émile Licent, who, together with his French Jesuit colleague Teilhard de Chardin (who participated on the Gobi Desert expedition with Roy Chapman Andrews), went to China during the early 1900s when it started to open to the West and a number of foreign-led expeditions – including those of Aurel Stein – fuelled interest in China's past. Although Licent went originally to work in China's educational institutions, during his twenty-five years in China from 1914 to 1939 he also began to train Chinese colleagues as archaeologists from his base in Tianjin. His grounding in palaeontology proved invaluable as he and Teilhard de Chardin conducted numerous expeditions across northern and central

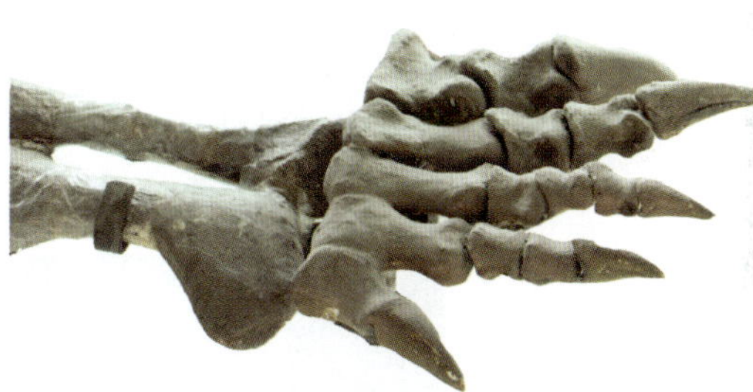

China, including at the important site of Salawusu in Inner Mongolia which contained early fragmentary human remains (*Ordos Man*) attributed to early modern humans or Neanderthals.

This museum is one of the oldest of its kind in China and Licent's accumulation of knowledge, specimens of plants and minerals, Quaternary mammal fossils, prehistoric human tools – not to mention his travelogues and scientific reports – firmly set the scientific foundations of this remarkable museum. Today it still prides itself on being home to several thousand of China's natural history treasures among its nearly 400,000 specimens and its reputation for continued research in the field collaborating with many of China's leading universities as well as those abroad.

The museum has moved several times during its long history. Now it is closed. The new one will open at the end of 2013.

Tianjin Science and Technology Museum

天津科学技术馆 *Tianjin kexuejishuguan*

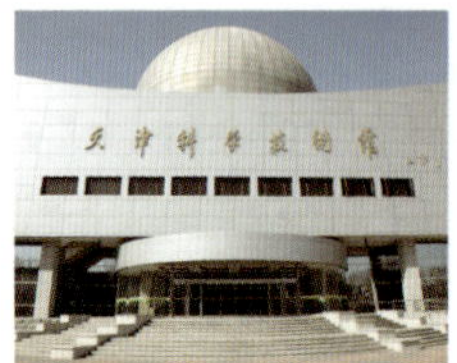

94 Longchang Road, Hexi District, Tianjin
天津市河西区隆昌路94号
Tel: (022) 2832 0315
Open: 9.00–16.30 except Mon & Tues
www.tjstm.org
Kids

The museum has many interactive exhibits and demonstrations at various times throughout the day, with fourteen sections and hundreds of items on display.

The exhibition hall is the main part of the museum which has 10,000 square meters. It consists of two floors with hundreds of exhibits. The first floor has exhibits on energy, communications and astronomy, and an area dedicated to famous scientists. The second floor offers a look at the human body, life sciences, mathematics, acoustics, optics, machinery and robotics. The space theatre on the third floor serves as a cinema and planetarium. It is equipped with dome screen film projector and Digistar II planetarium projector.

Photography is allowed.

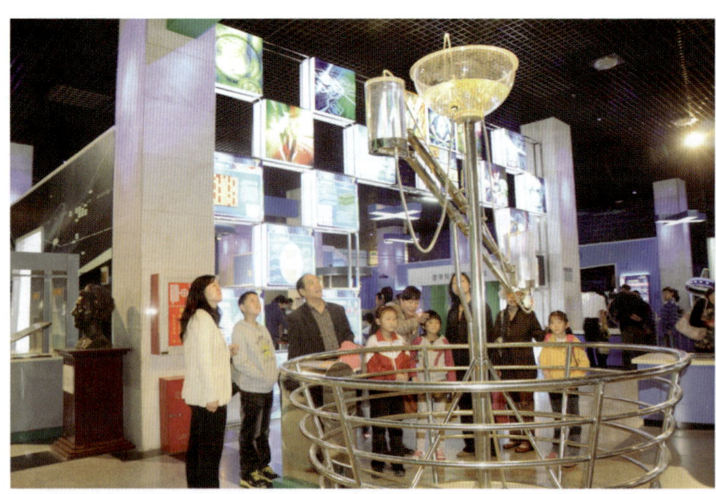

45

Hebei Provincial Museum

河北省博物馆 *Hebeisheng bowuguan*

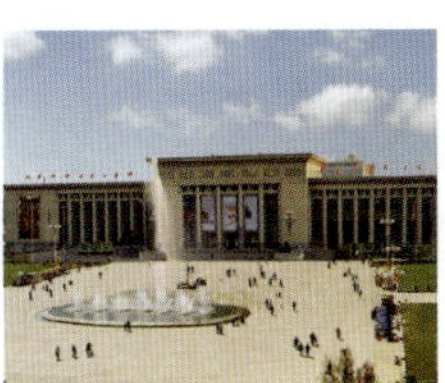

4 Dongda Street, Shijiazhuang, Hebei
河北省石家庄市东大街4号
Tel: (0311) 8604 9534
Open: 9.00–17.00 except Mon, last entry 16.00
www.hebeimuseum.org

The old building of Hebei Provincial Museum was a copy of Beijing's Great Hall of the People. It was constructed in 1968 for the purpose of displaying Chairman Mao's books, memorabilia and related artefacts. In 1986, the building became the Hebei Provincial Museum. The museum is now home to a superb collection of art, archaeological artefacts and documents from prehistory to modern times, and is well worth an admittedly long day trip to Shijiazhuang.

The objects in the Warring States and Han era galleries are the stars of the collection and some of the finest material from these periods to be seen in China. On view are objects excavated from the late fourth-century BC tombs of King Cheng and his son, King Cuo of the Zhongshan kingdom. The Zhongshan were non-Chinese nomads who assimilated into Chinese culture, as is evidenced by the artefacts and bronze inscriptions they left behind. Although the burial chamber of King Cuo was looted in antiquity, undisturbed material

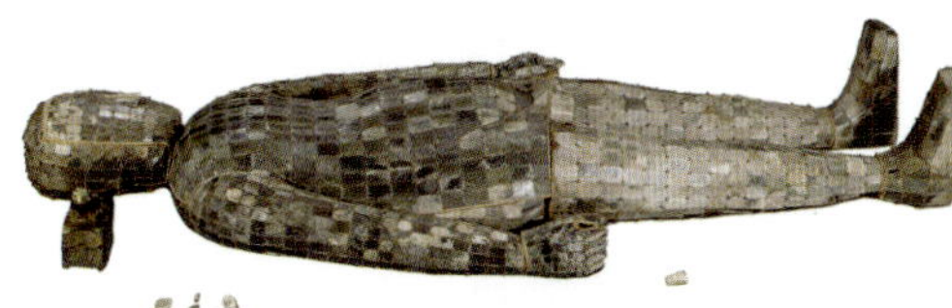

was discovered in associated rooms. Discovered in Tomb 1 and on exhibition here is a bronze 'map' (inlaid with gold and silver) of the tomb complex. Using this, archaeologists have reconstructed detailed plans of the royal tomb. This double-walled complex would have been built on a pounded-earth mound with the grave pit underneath. The mound would have had roofed wooden structures on top and probably looked very similar to the palace complex. According to the literature, these remains are the earliest evidence of monumental architecture in China. The bronze plan shows us that the King was meant to have two tombs built on either side of his own, housing his wives and consorts. There are also six more tombs presumably for retainers or family, as well as two horse-and-chariot pits. There were further pits for animals and a pit containing three boats and evidence of a canal which led out to the nearby Hutuo River.

Jade burial suit from the tomb of Liu Sheng, Western Han dynasty

The many bronzes found in the tombs include inscriptions describing historical events including a war in 312 BC against the Yan state to the north. There is a large tripod with cast-iron legs inscribed with 469 characters, and two bronze vessels listing the lineage of the Zhongshan kings. Don't miss the pair of bronze dragon-like beasts inlaid with silver from the tomb of King Cuo. These chimeras, known in traditional Chinese literature as *bixie*, meaning 'to ward off evil spirits', have claws, wings, horns, scaled skin and long forked tails. The purpose of these objects is not known, but they may have been weights to hold down mats for sitting on. It wasn't until the tenth century that chairs appeared in China.

Boshanlu censer from the tomb of Dou Wan, Han dynasty

Also not to be missed is the silver- and gold-inlaid bronze sculpture depicting a tiger trapping a deer in its jaws. Some scholars believe this illustrates the artistic traditions of the nomadic Di tribe which ruled the Zhongshan state. The Di may have brought with them the Animal Style art of the steppes. Again, what use these objects had can only be conjectured.

The objects found in the Zhongshan tombs differ from those of earlier periods in that they contain more objects of daily use. In addition, the tombs themselves are set up as a house for the dead with rooms for specific purposes, not just as a burial pit as in previous periods. Many scholars feel that at this time, people began to think of themselves as having souls – and the soul needed a place to live, eat and enjoy life just as the living did.

Gilt bronze figure of a maidservant holding a lamp from the tomb of Dou Wan, Han dynasty

The Hebei Provincial Museum is also known for its superb collection of objects from the tomb of the Western Han dynasty King Liu Sheng and his consort Dou Wan. These tombs, dug into a rocky hillside, contained an entrance room, a central room, two side rooms for storage and, in the rear, the room containing the coffin itself. More than 2,700 objects made of bronze, gold, silver, jade, iron, silk, lacquer and clay were found in Liu Sheng's tomb, ranging from the everyday to highly ornate and refined pieces. The most famous objects are the jade funeral shrouds, the finest examples, in terms of both quality and condition, ever found. These funerary suits are made up of jade plaques with small holes bored into the corners and sewn tightly together with gold wire. This tomb also yielded numerous smaller jade offerings, including the fine nephrite cicada (Western Han), probably placed in the mouth of the deceased. Jade was believed to have the power to preserve a corpse from decay, and besides being encased in jade suits, members of the royal family had their orifices plugged with small pieces of jade.

Don't leave the gallery without seeing the elegant gilt

bronze lamp in the form of a young kneeling woman holding a lantern. Her robe and long, flowing sleeves are carefully tucked under her legs, the backs of her feet so realistically cast! The lamp comes apart for cleaning; the light could be directed and adjusted, the smoke disappearing into the woman's sleeve. Another exceptionally beautiful object from this tomb is a pedestalled bronze censer inlaid with gold, the shape of which is known as *boshanlu*, or 'universal mountain'. Rising from the bowl, the censer assumes the shape of a storm-battered mountain peak populated with animal and human-like creatures. The *boshanlu* made its first appearance in the Han dynasty and is thought to symbolize the home of the Immortals. When lit, the smoke from the incense drifted out of the crags, creating a numinous mist.

Besides the fabulous tomb finds, there are several thousand bronze and stone Buddhist stelae and statues, including white marble and sandstone ones excavated in the 1950s at the Xiude Temple in Xiudesi, Quyang. Notable is the early eighth-century headless standing bodhisattva exquisitely carved with scarves looping across the body and draped over the legs, as well as the Northern Wei seated Maitreya stele in sandstone.

Hebei is noted for its ceramics, including the white Tang dynasty porcelain from the Xing Kiln. Many fine examples of Cizhou ware are on display, including a white-glazed vase decorated with peonies and pillows, one with a boy playing cards, another with a young boy fishing. Characteristic of this type of porcelain is the use of bold, brownish-black pigment on a background of heavy white slip. The collection of paintings and calligraphy is also noteworthy and includes masterpieces by such distinguished painters as Wen Zhengming and Zhu Da.

During the Japanese occupation, Hebei was a major area for Communist-led guerrilla warfare. The museum has a large collection of material dealing with the War against Japan, and many photographs, objects and documents are on display. There is also a model of the tunnels by the locals to fight the Japanese from underground. The museum has an exhibition of Hebei revolutionary history from the Opium Wars through to the Communist takeover. Finally, there are exhibition halls displaying artefacts from prehistory though the Song period.

The museum has recently been expanded.

Blue and white baluster jar, Yuan dynasty

Chengde Imperial Summer Resort Museum

承德避暑山庄博物馆 *Chengde bishushanzhuang bowuguan*

46

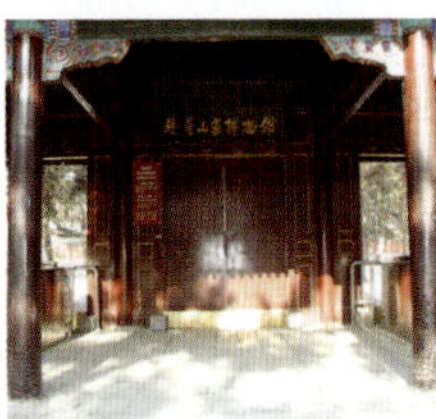

Lizheng Gate, Imperial Summer Resort, Shuangqiao District, Chengde, Hebei
河北省承德市双桥区避暑山庄丽正门
Tel: (0314)2050286
Open: 7.00–18.00 summer; 8.00–17.00 winter
www.bishushanzhuang.org
Gift shop

Chengde mountain resort was the summer seat of the Qing emperors where they escaped from the heat and dust of Beijing in summer, hunted and caroused, and administered the Empire in cool landscaped scenery with gardens, water, pavilions and winding corridors.

The Chengde Imperial Summer Resort Museum is a UNESCO Cultural Heritage site, among the world's top 500 museums listed by UNESCO. It comprises three complexes: the Main Palace, the Pine and Crane House, and the Pine Gullies. The major collections come from the imperial court of the Qing Dynasty and consist of some 30,000 pieces.

Ceramic bottle, Qing dynasty

The Main Palace

Completed in 1711 (the 50th year of Emperor Kangxi's reign), and renovated in 1754 (the 19th year of Emperor Qianlong's reign), it covers an area of over 10,000 square metres, with 219 palace buildings used for the imperial administration. Based on the ancient Chinese architectural convention of a 'nine-five pattern to keep the presence of the dragon and conserve the fortune of the nobility' and 'the nine heavenly blessings', the resort was designed to have nine courtyards divided into two parts: the front the administrative area and the rear the residential. The central axis runs through the Lizheng Gate, the Palace Gate, the Meridian Gate, the Danbojingcheng Hall (Hall of Simplicity and Sincerity), the Sizhi Library, the Wansui House, the Yanbozhishuang Hall (Hall of Refreshing Mists and Waves), the Cloud and Mountain Resort, and the Xiuyun Gate. Each gate contains halls, corridors, and verandas arranged in symmetrical patterns. The entire complex is laid out according to the rules of imperial architecture, yet each is intricate and

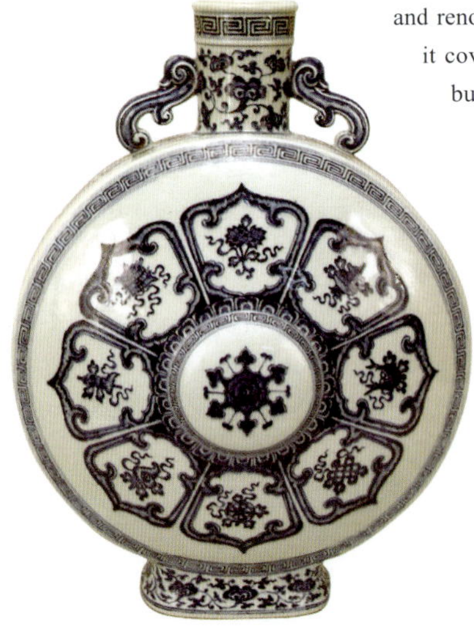

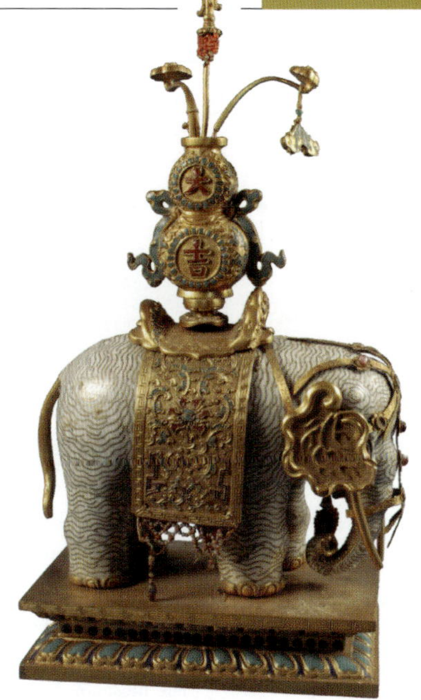

diversified, offering a garden-styled elegance with winding paths and tranquil scenery. Visitors can experience the ancient grandeur of the rituals of hunting, the prosperity of the reigns of the emperors Kangxi and Qianlong, and the wealth and ethnic diversity of Qing society.

The Pine and Crane House

Completed in 1749 (the 14th year of the Emperor Qianlong's reign), it is situated to the east of the Main Palace. Designed with eight courtyards, it was where Emperor Qianlong housed his mother, hoping that pines and cranes, symbols of longevity, could bring her relaxation and long life. The complex includes the Gate House, the Pine and Crane House, the Leshoutang (the Hall of Longevity), the Fifteen-room Courtyard, the Screen Door, the Jide Hall, and the Changyuan Pavilion. Jide Hall was where Emperor Jiaqing studied as a prince. Since the 20th year of Emperor Daoguang's reign (1832), this was where the portraits of the Qing Emperors were worshipped. The courtyards have towering ancient trees, dotted with flowers and rockeries, creating a serene and elegant atmosphere.

The Pine Gullies

This is the earliest complex in the Mountain Resort, with a high lakeside vantage point. It is surrounded by meandering covered corridors. The main building, the Pine Gullies Hall, faces north, while the other halls are arranged in a flexible and scattered layout, resembling the style of the private gardens of the Yangtze River Delta.

Henan Museum

河南博物院 *Henan bowuyuan*

47

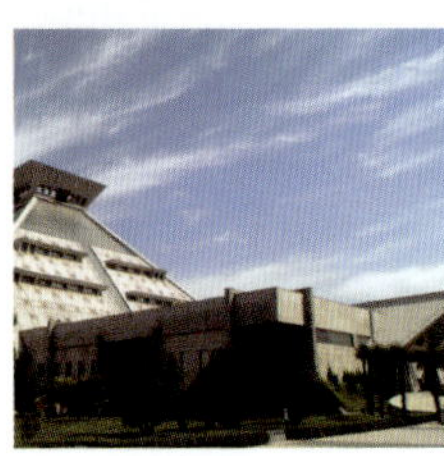

8 Nongye Road, Zhengzhou, Henan
河南省郑州市农业路8号
Tel: (0371) 6351 1237
Open: 9.00–17.30 except Mon, last entry 16.30;
        9.00–17.00 except Mon, last entry 16.00, winter
www.chnmus.net
English personal guides available / gift shop/bookshop

The Henan Museum was first established in 1927 in Kaifeng City which was then the capital of Henan Province. Due to its excellent collection it became one of the premier museums in the country and remains so to this day. In 1961, the provincial capital was moved to Zhengzhou and the Henan Museum followed. In May of 1998, a new and modern facility was built which is the present day Henan Museum.

The museum, built in a pyramidal shape, is on four floors. The entire museum collection contains approximately 130–140,000 objects, of which about 4,000 are on display at any one time. Every object in the museum is from Henan Province. The first and second floors comprise a chronologically displayed exhibition called 'The Most Brilliant Cultural Achievements in Ancient Henan'. The first hall contains an excellent selection of Palaeolithic and Neolithic artefacts. Of special interest are items of the Neolithic Peiligang Culture stone tools and pottery, including red pottery bowls, a *ding* with nipple pattern and a bone flute from Jiahu Village which is the earliest musical instrument ever found in China and the earliest musical instrument ever found with a complete scale of seven descending tones. Also displayed in this hall are objects from the Yangshao Culture. Among the artefacts to be noted is a pottery funeral urn from Zhengzhou which has been the subject of discussion as to whether it is a funeral urn or large drum.The exhibit moves on to objects of the Longshan Culture. Among the objects displayed are pottery drainage pipes from Pingliangtai City ruins and bits of copper slag, evidence of the transition from the Stone to the Bronze Age.

The second hall is entitled 'Three Splendid, Three Dynasties' and exhibits artefacts from the Xia, Shang and Zhou periods. Here we see in addition to an impressive collection of pottery and bronze vessels, a beautiful lead architectural piece decorated with an abstracted *taotie* (fierce animal) design, as well as Shang dynasty inscribed oracle bones. Take note of an especially important piece in this gallery, as it is the earliest porcelain in the museum – a proto-porcelain *zun* (wine vessel) from Zhengzhou, although, in fact, the

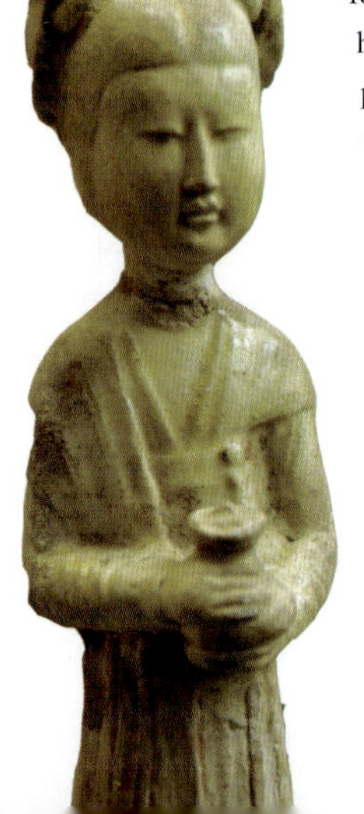

A Tang maiden

museum does have an even earlier example which was not on display. There is also a selection of objects from the burial site of Queen Fuhao, known as Houmuxin. She was the Shang dynasty consort of King Wu Ding and, incredibly, a general who took part in several successful campaigns. This tomb, dated c. 1250 bc is the only unlooted Shang tomb that has been found to date and contained 468 bronze objects as well as jade, stone, ivory, bone, pottery, cowry shells and many weapons and war implements.

Throughout the galleries there are signs in English as well as Chinese explaining the transitions between periods and explanations of how and why the material culture differs and evolved.

The next room is Eastern Zhou, Spring and Autumn period and Warring States period displays. Here are wonderful bronzes of all sorts, including nine large *dings* (bowls for meat) and *you* (wine vessels) excavated in 1997 from Xinzheng and a most elegant gilt bronze lamp in the form of a kneeling woman. Pride of place here and one of the jewels of the museum is an enormous bronze rectangular ewer (*fanghu*) with lotus and crane design. This was excavated from the tomb of Duke Zheng at Lijiayuan in Xinzheng County in 1923. This is one of a pair – the other, which is damaged, is in the basement of the Forbidden City. This piece is noteworthy, not only due to its beauty and complicated decoration, but because it has so much historical and spiritual meaning. The ewer rests on the backs of two dragons, ferocious animals inhabit its centre, writhing dragons are its handles and on the lotus petal lid stands a crane not in the traditional stance, but just about to take off with its wings spread for flight. This is a political analogy of strength, ferocity and finally at the top of the vessel, a sense of spirituality and hopefulness symbolized by the bird. There is also a visual demonstration of lost-wax casting and other various manufacturing techniques popular in the Warring States period such as stamping and inlaying with gold wire and stones.

'Incorporating the Diverse' is the title of the next hall. This includes the Western and Eastern Han, Wei, Jin and Southern and Northern dynasties and contains many large pottery funerary architectural models of houses and buildings of the Han period.

Dancers on a Han tomb brick

Yuan dynasty whistling man

These houses are thought to be actual representations of the houses of the dead. There is an especially impressive six-storey mansion found in Jiaozuo. Also here are smaller objects: tomb bricks, some with the original paint and a large mural painting of the Western Han depicting a blue dragon, white tiger, red bird and clouds. This painting is older than those at the Mogao Grottoes and is in superb condition.

The exhibition moves upstairs to the Han, Tang and Song Halls where the first gallery showcases objects from the Western and Eastern Han, Wei, Jin and Southern and Northern dynasties. Here there is a selection of ceramics, tomb bricks and models of buildings as well as Buddhist artefacts from the Gong Yi Grottoes. Of note here, Northern dynasty green ware and white-glazed pottery which is the precursor of Tang dynasty ceramics. The next hall is Sui–Tang where there is a large model of the imperial palace in Luoyang during the Tang dynasty along with pottery tiles and Tang dynasty guardians, horses and grooms, and camels. To be noted is a silver coin from the kingdom of Persia found at Luoyang and painted pottery seated musicians (*zuobuji*) and a lovely group of Tang 'fat ladies'. Also displayed are bronze mirrors, white wares, tri-colour pottery and of special note a white-glazed porcelain *weiqi* chessboard. Displays of Tang dynasty Buddhist stone heads and sculptures are worth seeing, as Henan was the major region in China for the diffusion of Buddhism during this period. Following is the hall displaying Northern Song, Jin and Yuan objects including copper coinage, Yuan dynasty ceramics, blue and white ware, Jun ware of various shapes, Song dynasty ceramics and descriptions of major scientific contributions of this period such as gunpowder, moveable type and the compass.

The Third Floor galleries include the 'Ming and Qing Dynasties Handicraft Articles Hall' consisting of gold and silver jewellery, Qing enamel ware, ivory, porcelain, bronze, lacquer ware, and embroidery. Most impressive is the 'Chu State Bronzes Art Hall'. These are bronzes from tombs of the Spring and Autumn period Chu State found in Longcheng. Of special note is a set of twenty-six very large Yong bells buried with royalty and aristocrats indicating their high social status. There are also Han dynasty ceramic architectural ancient jades from the Neolithic to the Qing, examples of Shang halberds (*ge*), battle-axes (*yue*), spears, knives.

Note a jade *huang* or pendant from the Shang tomb of Fuhao, a Warring States *bi* and some lovely Western Zhou jade jewellery and a pair of jade ornaments from the Spring and Autumn period found at the Baoxiang Temple, Guangshan carved with a face looking like an indigenous Central American. The fourth floor contains a natural history exhibition.

This museum is one of the finest museums in the country. It is full of gorgeous artefacts sensitively displayed with adequate English signage. A visit to this unforgettable museum will be one of the highlights of your visit to China.

Tang dynasty guardian

48

Kaifeng Museum

开封市博物馆 *Kaifengshi bowuguan*

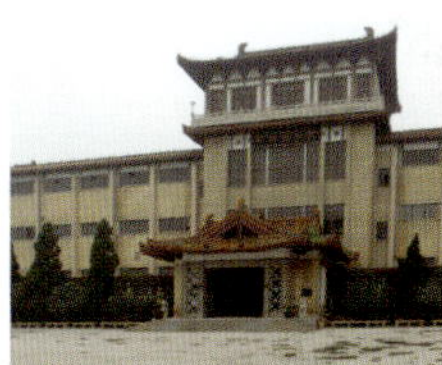

26 Yingbin Road, Kaifeng, Henan
河南省开封市迎宾路26号
Tel: (0378) 2178 8010
Open: 8.30–12.00 & 14.30–18.30 except Mon, summer
8.30–12.00 & 14.00–17.30 except Mon, winter

This museum is a bit dreary but does have in its collection a limestone stele dated to 1489 which records the history of Kaifeng's Jews. Unfortunately the characters are for the most part, worn and illegible, but rubbings made in the past are displayed alongside. On one side the stele recounts the rituals and stories of the Jews of Kaifeng. The inscription on the opposite side is dated to 1512 and describes the life of the Jews at the time, comparing Judaism to Confucianism. A reservation to view it is needed.

There was also a second stele, usually dated to 1663, which disappeared in 1912. Only a partial text had survived on the stone which honoured the Jews who were active in the community at the time and had restored the temple.

Jews of Kaifeng

Jews have a long and interesting tradition in this city. It is thought the first Jews came to China as traders on the Silk Road in the early eighth century during the Kaiyuan period of Emperor Tang Xuanzong. By the time of the Northern Song, the Jewish community here was well established. A synagogue was built in 1163 and during the Ming dynasty, the Jews were given permission to use seven Chinese surnames: Li, Zhao, Shi, Ai, Zhang, Gao and Jin. Marco Polo mentions meeting Jews in Kaifeng during his travels there in 1286. The stele tell us that in 1421, the Kaifeng Jews were given permission to take the civil service exam and enter government service, which was, no doubt, a large factor in their assimilation as they began to travel away from the core community. In 1605, Ai Tian, a Kaifeng Jew who had travelled to Beijing for the exam, met Matteo Ricci, the well-known Jesuit missionary. The records of his and other Jesuit missionaries' contacts with the community contribute greatly to the available information regarding the Jews in the city.

As the Jews began to intermarry with the Chinese population, they gradually lost their their knowledge of Hebrew and the rituals and traditions of Judaism. The synagogue in Kaifeng was repeatedly damaged by Yellow River flooding and destroyed by an earthquake in 1840. The synagogue no longer had a Torah and finally there were no more rabbis in the city.

Today there are, by some accounts, approximately 600 people who identify themselves as Jews descended from this ancient community. Nowadays, however, they neither practise nor know much about the religion except that they abstain from eating pork.

As the Chinese pass their heritage on through the father, and Jewish tradition is matrilinear, there is a technical problem for some (but not all) Jews to consider these people Jewish. There is, however, great interest in the Jewish community regarding this history and many Jews come to Kaifeng looking for any vestiges that might remain.

Disappointingly, there is now almost nothing of 'Jewish Kaifeng' to be seen. The site of the synagogue is now the Number Four Hospital and there are no traces of the Jewish Quarter or the now extinct Jewish community of Kaifeng.

49

Longmen Grottoes

龙门石窟 *Longmen shiku*

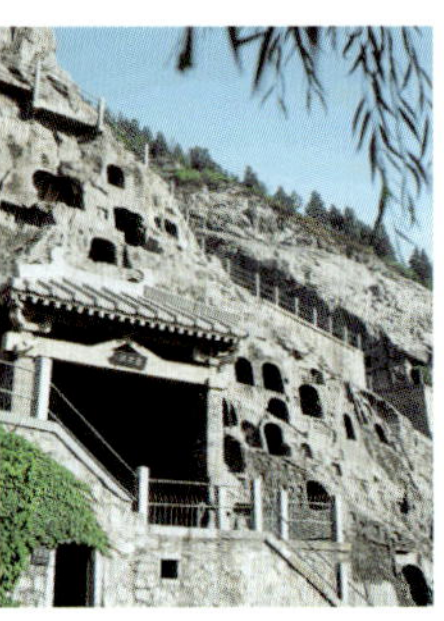

Approximately 13 km south of Luoyang, on the west bank of the Yi River, Henan
河南省洛阳市南郊13公里 伊河西岸
Tel: (0379) 6598 0216
Open: 8.00–18.00, last entry 17.00, spring;
      7.30–18.30, last entry 17.00, summer;
      7.30–18.00, last entry 17.00, autumn;
      8.00–17.30, last entry 16.00, winter
www.lmsk.cn/en
Kids

Following the break-up of the Han Empire and during the turmoil of the Sixteen Kingdoms, Buddhism became for a period the dominant religion of China. A tradition of cave temple sites developed. The first of the three great cave sites from this period was started in AD 366 at Mogao, Dunhuang. The other two major sites were at Yungang, near Datong (begun in AD 471) and at Longmen near Luoyang (begun c. AD 495). The latter two were the capital cities of the Northern Wei dynasty, Tuoba Turkic people who fiercely embraced Buddhism in opposition to Confucianism.

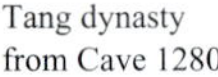

Tang dynasty
from Cave 1280

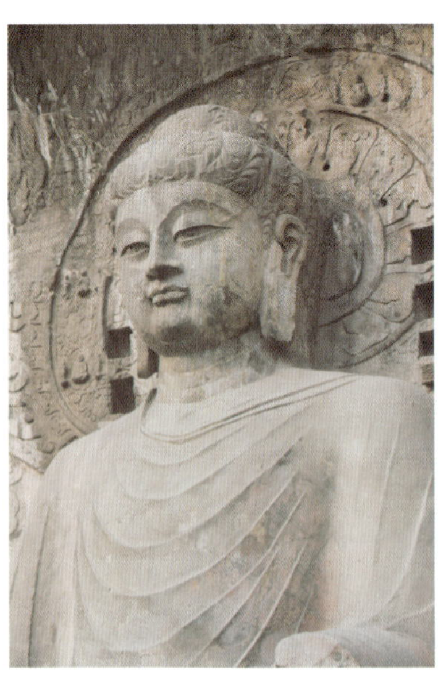

The Longmen site features more than 2,345 niches, 100,000 Buddha images and 2,800 stone carvings and tablets in a series of caves hollowed out of the rock over a 1 km stretch of the river. Production continued there for more than 400 years. Sadly many of the caves have suffered damage from the weather and theft by European and American collectors.

The entrance is at the north end. Moving from north to south, the caves of particular interest are: the Three Binyang Caves with some fine Northern Wei, Sui and Tang figures; the Tang dynasty Ten Thousand Buddha Cave, with little Buddhas, a giant Buddha and celestial dancers; the Northern Wei Lotus Flower Cave, with graceful *apsaras* flying among lotus flowers on the ceiling; the Tang Ancestor Worshipping Temple, the largest at Longmen, with the best works of art, including a large seated Maitreya; the tiny Medical Prescription Cave, the entrance of which is filled with sixth-century stelae; and finally the Carved Cave, full of intricate carvings of processions of the Northern Wei.

Luoyang Museum

洛阳博物馆 *Luoyang bowuguan*

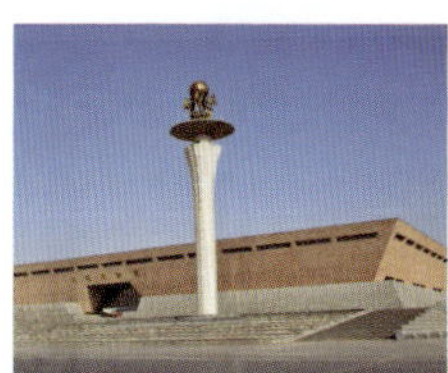

Nietai Road, Luolong District, Luoyang, Henan
河南省洛阳市洛龙区聂泰路
Tel: (0379) 6990 1020
Open: 9.00–17.00
www.lymuseum.com
Personal guides / gift shop / bookshop / café

Luoyang sits in a key geographical position at the heart of western Henan on the southern side of the middle reaches of the Yellow River. It was the capital city of nine dynasties from the Western Zhou stretching over more than 1,500 years. It was also the easternmost city on the principal section of the Silk Road, and during the Eastern Han, it was one of the most populated, flourishing cities in the ancient world. It continued to expand under the Northern Wei, who built the famous Buddhist caves at Longmen. As the eastern capital of the Tang, the western being Xi'an, it became one of the main production centres for tri-coloured glazed pottery *sancai*.

Although the museum is in need of refurbishment, it is certainly worth spending time to see this treasure house of finds unearthed in and around the city. Arranged over two floors are six galleries, including a temporary space that displays highlights from recently excavated sites and chance discoveries. All of the galleries have some English signage, though this too could be improved. It would be best to head first to the galleries showcasing ceramics, jade and bronzes and, if time permits, wander through the others.

One of the slightly better-lit galleries is devoted to Luoyang's pottery and porcelain. There are several simple, beautifully painted pots from the early Neolithic, including those from sites of the Yangshao Culture at Wangwan and Zhouli. Especially stunning are vessels from the Tumen site in Baiyuan with designs in black on a white ground. The apogee of pottery-making in the Xia is represented by finds from the Erlitou and Dongmagou sites located in the Yiluo basin. The Erlitou Culture built large palace sites with residential and workshop areas, and graves filled with

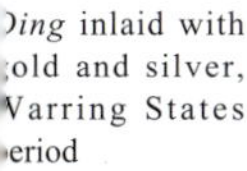

Ding inlaid with gold and silver, Warring States period

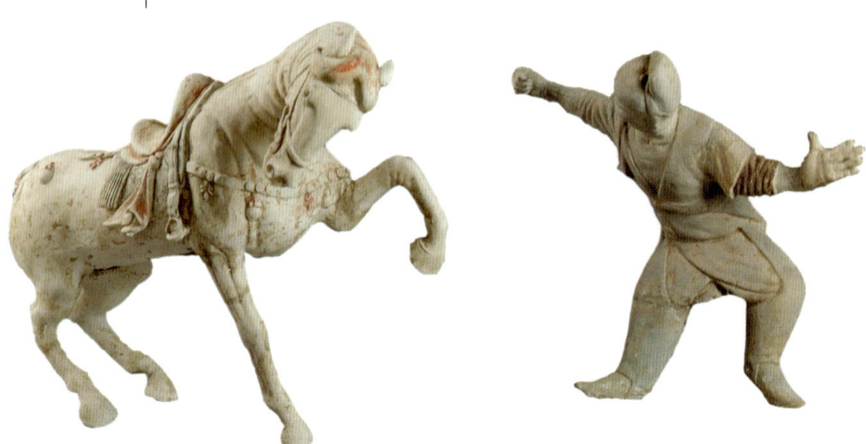

Tang dynasty horse and trainer from the tomb of Liukai in Yanshi

bronzes, ceramics and jade have been found over a broad region.

During the Western and Eastern Han periods, pottery-making at Luoyang was highly developed, with rich, bright colours like red and green in geometric patterns, spiralling clouds, and human and animal shapes. The vivid figures included depictions of farmers, acrobats, dancers and the like, as well as of domestic animals, and were buried in tombs to create for the dead a microcosm of the universe in the afterlife.

Evidence of a flourishing porcelain-making industry in the Sui and Tang periods can be seen here in great abundance. It was a period of economic boom, in particular throughout the Tang, when products made in Luoyang were highly sought after and traded along the Silk Route. By far the most popular was *sancai*. It has been found at tomb sites clustered in the suburbs, at the foot of the Mangshan Mountains and elsewhere. Besides practical vessel shapes like wine- and food-storage vessels, there were figures, toys and the glorious horses for which this period is so famous, including a rare black-glazed horse from Guanlin some 66.5cm in height. The tomb of Anpu and his wife in Longmen yielded more than fifty masterful examples, included a *hu* foreign-faced rider on a horse; a figure leading a white-glazed horse with a green blanket; tomb guardians; and camels in life-like poses laden with bags full of silk and other items. There is also a rarely seen, beautifully shaped glazed lamp from Jilin. Many privately run kilns such as Gongxian existed in the city. Excellent Song ceramics are also on view, including the tri-coloured porcelain pillow with peony designs (the peony has been a decorative motif for centuries, and Luoyang continues to be a centre of peony cultivation).

Bronzes in the collection excel; hundreds upon hundreds have been unearthed in large groups at sites in Luoyang and nearby. Superb examples have been found in burials at Erlitou and are among the earliest bronze vessels discovered in China. Among these are bronze *jue*, some decorated with nipple patterns. They were cast using multiple-piece clay moulds, a technique central to production in the later Chinese Bronze Age. Astonishing are bronzes found at this site with gold inlays and a turquoise-inlaid bronze plaque in the shape of a shield with an abstract animal face, discovered in a tomb at Yanshi and among the earliest inlaid objects anywhere in China.

To date, bronze finds from the Shang are sparser in Luoyang, most coming from Yanshi (an early Shang capital) and others from Yinchuan and Jianxi. One stellar example is a large square vessel with a roof-shaped lid, in fact a wine-storage vessel, from Pangjiagou at Beiyao, decorated with *taotie* and dragon patterns.

The ultimate highlights of this collection are the bronzes from the Western and Eastern Zhou periods. Not only have large assemblages of bronzes been found in the hundreds of tombs which have been excavated; a large-scaled bronze foundry not far from Beiyao indicates that there was local production. The tombs revealed spectacular examples like the *fangding* (a rectangular food vessel with legs) decorated on all four sides with *taotie* designs with bulging eyes – a rare example from this period.

More than a thousand Eastern Zhou tombs have been unearthed in and around Luoyang, including those from the Spring and Autumn period whose bronzes are characterized by very bold designs. One example is a large *yu* – the largest bronze found to date in Luoyang – with four dragon-shaped handles; it is believed to have been made as part of the trousseau offered by the Marquis of Qi to his second daughter Zhongjiang, who married the King of the Zhou.

The glory of Western Han dynasty bronze work can be seen in the gilded examples. Most unusual is a winged immortal with large ears and pointed nose who holds a container. Found in a brick tomb under a mound, this was one of the few objects left by ancient robbers in what must have been a noble or high-ranking person's burial. Large numbers of mirrors too (more than a thousand

Black-glazed *sancai* horse, Tang dynasty

to date) have been unearthed, including those from the late Eastern Han period covered with mythical figures and animals and cosmological symbols, and Tang ones burnished with gold and silver foil. Originally hung by a cord slotted through the central knob, mirrors were cast from bronze alloyed with a high percentage of tin, silver or lead to increase their reflectivity.

Although significant gold and silver objects have been found in Luoyang and nearby areas such as Yanshi, Yinchan and Mengjin, very few are on display. Among them are some from the Tang period plates, bowls and pots favoured by the high-ranking officials and elite living there.

Jade work from many of the tomb sites mentioned is also unsurpassed. Excellent examples have been found from the Xia and Shang periods at the Erlitou site, including knives like the one with seven holes in the shape of a trapezoid with double edges. Each side of the handle has toothed projections, and both are decorated with geometric patterns.At 65 cm in length it is one of the longest jade knives ever found. Spectacular too is the *zhang* blade also discovered there and similar to those found at Sanxingdui in Sichuan and other parts of China, suggesting communication between the Xia and other regional cultures at the time. Western Zhou jades from Beiyao include weapons and ornaments such as sheep, cicadas, fish and birds, while those from the Warring States period reflect the gradual decline of ritual jades in favour of garment hooks, spoons and beads. More jewels of the collection are found among the Han dynasty jades in the form of pendants with openwork designs. The Three Kingdom jade cup found in a tomb in the Jianxi district is a masterpiece. The inspiration for its tall, elegant shape no doubt came from glass imports from western Asia as trade between China and the West continued to expand.

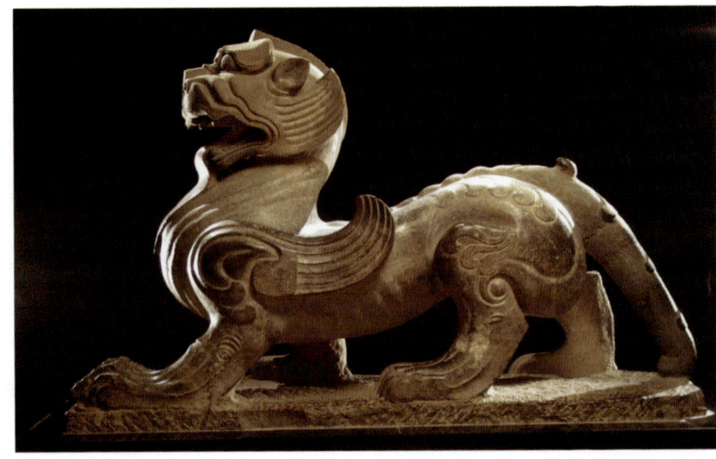

Eastern Han dynasty stone *Bixie*, a symbol of Luoyang for its long history as a capital city in ancient China

Luoyang Museum of Ancient Arts

51

洛阳古代艺术博物馆 *Luoyang gudai yishu bowuguan*

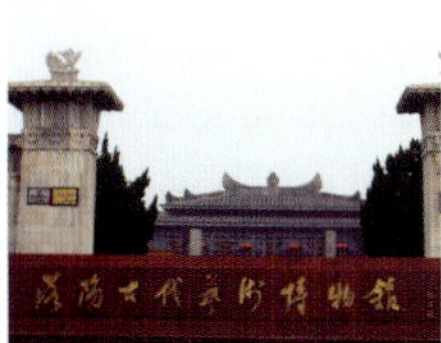

45 Jichang Road, Laocheng District, Luoyang, Henan
河南省洛阳市老城区机场路45号
Tel: (0379) 6226 5737
Open: 9.00–16.30 except Mon, summer;
 9.00–16.00 except Mon, winter
www.gumuguan.com

This museum (the former Luoyang Ancient Tombs Museum) was opened in 1987 and was the first of its kind in China. Its purpose is to exhibit and illustrate the evolution of tomb design over a period of more than a thousand years from the Han (206 BC–AD 220) to the Song dynasty (960–1279). A new separate museum – Museum of Henan Ancient Frescoes – was opened in 2011 to house the museum's collection of ancient tomb murals and frescoes.

One's first impression when entering the museum is not positive. It appears dark, dank and mouldy but don't be put off – if you have the opportunity to visit with an informed guide you will find this to be a fascinating and rewarding experience.

Twenty-one of the twenty-five tombs in the museum are on public view along four underground passageways radiating out from a central atrium. Both sides of the passageway from the museum entrance to this central area are lined with glass-fronted cases containing photos, pottery and other artefacts from the tombs. Some may be copies.

The halls are divided as follows: the Western and Eastern Han dynasties Hall, Wei and Jin dynasties Hall, the Tang and Song dynasties Hall and a separate hall to display artefacts.

The tombs, all from Luoyang excepting one from Jiaozuo, were taken apart brick by brick and reconstructed in the museum.

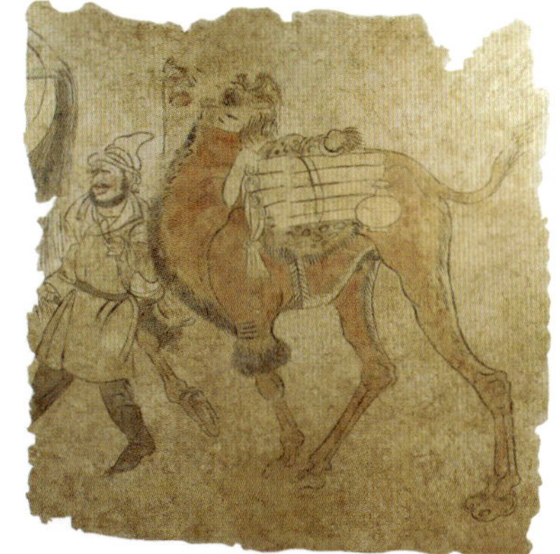

The tombs are organized in such a way to illustrate their development over time. For instance, the Western and Eastern Han tombs are contrasted. The early Western Han (206 BC–AD 9) tombs were quite simple and were built with hollow bricks. The ceilings are usually flat. In the Eastern Han (25–220),

Wall paintings, Tang dynasty

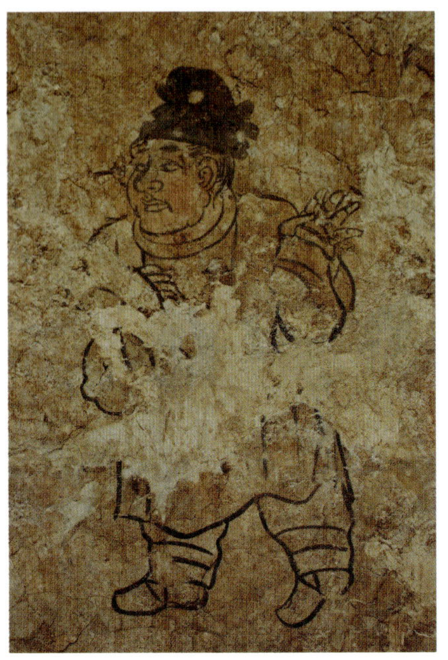

Wall paintings from Tang tombs

the bricks are often solid and much smaller than those of the Western Han, which allows for a vaulted ceiling. The tombs of the Eastern Han consist of four rooms, mirroring those in life: a sitting room, bedroom and two storage rooms. In both cases, the ceilings were painted to symbolize heaven. Clouds, divine celestial creatures and auspicious symbols are in abundance. Constellations and star charts can also be seen in the frescoes in many of the tombs here. Notably, on the ceiling of the tomb of Emperor Yuan and Emperor Cheng (49–7 BC) there is a star chart reputed to be the earliest ever found.

The objects found in the tombs are also different. The Western Han tend to have fewer and simpler vessels. Some of the pottery from the Eastern Han is foreign in shape indicating that there was trade from abroad.

By visiting the fresco tomb of the Xinmang dynasty one can observe the transition from Western to Eastern Han. The subject matter and composition of the painting here is closer to that of the Western Han while the painting style is closer to that of the Eastern Han.

Contrasting the tombs of the Jin and Northern Wei dynasties with those of the Eastern and Western Han, the former tend to be much simpler and not so well ordered. The people of the Jin and Wei did not seem to spend so much money on their tombs probably because it was a period of continuous war. There are two especially interesting Jin dynasty tombs. One is for a single woman. This is quite mysterious as it is highly unusual to have a person buried alone – especially a single woman. Another tomb is that of a family: grandmother, mother, father and adult daughter. In true Confucian style, grandmother gets the biggest room, mother and father the middle-sized and daughter the smallest.

Progressing along the time-line, we see in the Tang and Song Halls the continued trend towards complexity in design and structural detail. Notable amongst the Tang dynasty tombs is that of Anpu – a local military man – and his wife. Built to imitate a wooden-structured house it contained 129 objects, including fifty sancai glazed pottery pieces, excavated unlooted from the eastern mountain of Longmen Grottoes. This tomb also has beautiful wall paintings open to view.

Some of the tombs are on view with their wall paintings removed as conditions in the tomb were not safe for the fresco. Such is the case with a tomb from the Northern Wei. It contained a fresco illustrating a warrior leaning on his sword – the sleeves are especially well painted. This is the best preserved painting of the Northern Wei, and no doubt is on view in the new museum.

Luoyang was the logical location for this museum as it was repeatedly a capital city from the Zhou to the Tang and more than ninety ancient emperors were buried here. The museum is built on the grounds of the tomb of Emperor Xuanwu, the second Emperor of the Northern Wei who ruled for sixteen years (from AD 499 to 515) and who died at age thirty-three. This tomb was excavated in 1991 as the second stage of the opening of this museum. The rammed earth mound had a paved passage leading down to a stone door and a single brick square chamber six metres below ground. All the brick surfaces in the tomb were painted black. This was a period of frugality, hence there were no paintings or carvings in the tomb. At the time of excavation a stone head was found at the entrance to the tomb passage indicating that originally there were guardians at the front of mausoleum. It is the only Emperor's tomb in Luoyang open to the public.

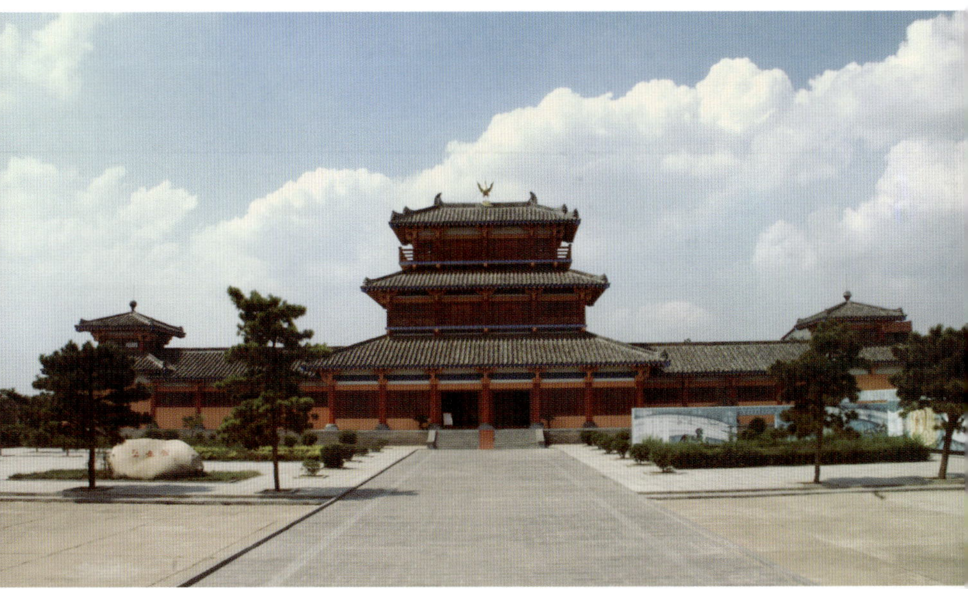

Museum of Zhou Capital and Royal Six-Horse Chariot

周王城天子驾六博物馆 *Zhouwangcheng tianzi jialiu bowuguan*

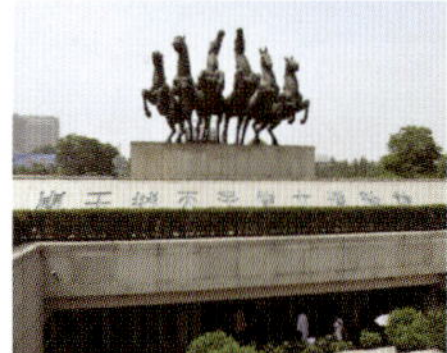

Wangcheng Plaza, Xigong District, Luoyang, Henan
河南省洛阳市西工区王城广场
Tel: (0379) 6391 2366
Open: 8.00–22.00 summer; 21.00 winter

A tussle between archaeologists and developers resulted in saving at least part of this site from being entombed forever under a shopping mall in the centre of Luoyang. Thankfully, visitors can now marvel at the large burial of Eastern Zhou dynasty horses, chariots and dog and human skeletons in the museum built above the site. It consists of two exhibition areas.

The first displays ritual bronzes, jade and pottery found at the site and presents a potted history of the Luoyang region when it served as an imperial capital over five dynasties.

The second hall displays two of the seventeen unearthed horse-and-chariot sacrificial pits, including the unique six-horse, two-wheeled chariot interred with its six skeletons and bronze axle pin. Ancient texts record 'the Son of Heaven (the ruler) riding six', suggesting that this chariot belonged to the ruler of the Eastern Zhou.

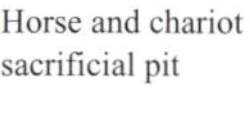

Horse and chariot sacrificial pit

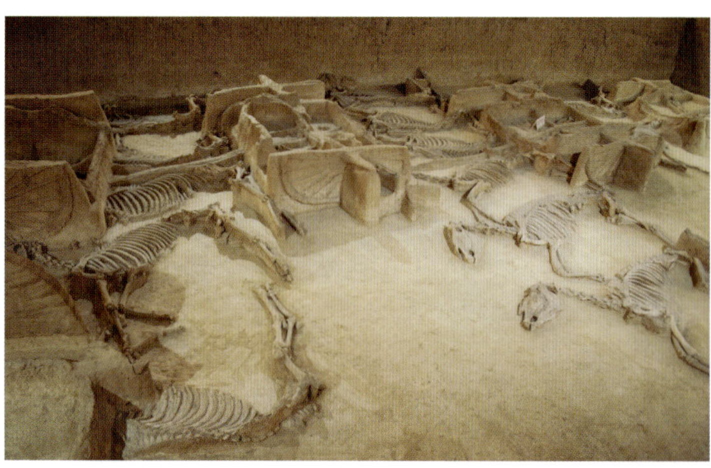

Yinxu Museum

殷墟博物馆 *Yinxu bowuguan*

53

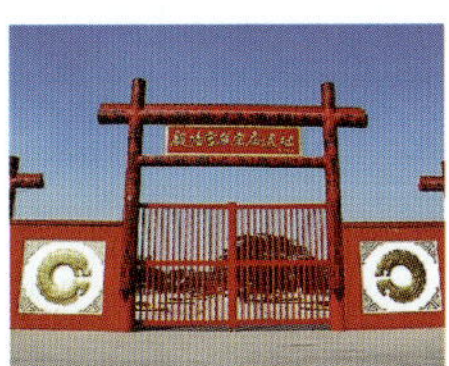

1 Yinxujian, Yindu District, Anyang, Henan
河南省安阳市殷都区殷墟践1号
Tel: (0372) 3161 002
Open: 8.00–18.00 summer; 8.00–17.00 winter
www.ayyx.com
English and Chinese tour guides / gift shop

Anyang was the last capital of the bellicose, long-lasting and highly influential Shang dynasty. There were at least five previous Shang capitals, but in 1,300 BC King Pan Geng moved it to Anyang, where it remained for 250 years.

Yinxu ('the ruins of Yin') is located on the southern bank of the River Huan and is called by some 'China's ancient Egypt' due to the splendid tombs of the Shang kings hidden underground and filled with valuable, extraordinarily beautiful objects, including famous bronzes. Aerial and satellite photos of the area displayed in the first gallery identify archaeological sites and royal tombs. Shang dynasty cities were complex and sophisticated. The streets were well planned, laid out on a north-south axis according to the rules of feng shui and incorporated drainage pipes. They were built around royal palaces and cemeteries, but there were also smaller outlying kinship settlements, as well as what seem to be 'industrial areas' for pottery, bone-carving, stone-cutting workshops and the like. The excavated material culture is rich and varied, permitting archaeologists and historians to understand much of the social organization of the Shang period as well as its infrastructure, culture, art and religion.

Shang dynasty soldier's skull with spearhead still embedded

The original finds at Yinxu were incised oracle bones. Up until the end of the nineteenth century, ancient incised animal bones and tortoise shells were thought to be dragons' bones. Highly prized, they were ground up and sold in apothecaries as a cure for many ailments. But at the beginning of the 1900s the markings on the bones were identified as an early form of writing. The oracle bones at Yinxu are unique in that they were often inscribed with questions, answers and results.

The museum at Yinxu, designed in 2005 by Cui Kai, one of China's leading modern architects, sits below ground level so that it merges into the surrounding landscape, thus evoking the underground tomb discovered on the site while maintaining its integrity.

The proportions of the rooms mirror the ruins of the palace found nearby, with objects thoughtfully displayed to present a coherent sense of the city's life and culture. The cases are well lit, with information in Chinese and English.

The museum is divided into five major galleries: Exhibition Hall of the Great Capital, Exhibition Hall of Bronzes, Exhibition Hall of Jades, Exhibition Hall of Oracle Bones and the Special Exhibition Hall.

You first enter the Great Capital Hall, where aerial and satellite photos show the layout and plan of the archaeological sites of Yinxu.

There is a model of a courtyard and simple dioramas which bring the aerial views to life. Pottery drainage pipes unearthed from the Baijiafen site are exhibited. Seeds and floral remains indicate that temperatures in Anyang were 2 to 3 degrees higher than today. The Huan often flooded, making the area very fertile. Millet and wheat seeds have been found, as well as boiled sheep and pig bones indicating the existence of animal husbandry. Bone ornaments, hairpins (both males and females had long hair), jewellery with turquoise inlay – even a ceramic loufa – are on exhibit. There are cowries used as currency originating from as far away as Taiwan and Hainan – indicating that the Shang people traded with other groups.

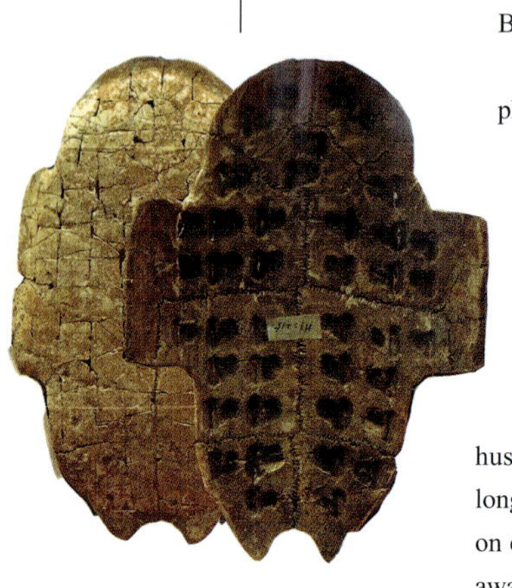
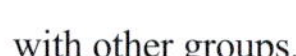

Turtle shell (plastron) with divination over cracked surface

Fourteen large-scale tombs with a few thousand sacrificial pits have been found here. Skeletons are also found along the foundations of houses. Some were beheaded and their heads buried separately. Some of these people were the King's servants; others were slaves or vanquished in war. In the museum can be seen a mass burial of as many as seventy young girls approximately fifteen years old. There is a bronze *yan* containing the remains of the boiled head of an enemy King, as well as a pottery vessel containing the squashed skeleton of a small child. Human and animal sacrifices as well as grain, alcohol and meat were offered to the gods and the royal ancestors, who controlled the weather, harvest and childbirth, war and illness. The living King needed their guidance and received it daily via the oracle bones.

The Oracle Bone Hall contains many examples of the incised ox bones and turtle shells used for divination. These are beautifully displayed with translations of the characters in both Chinese and English.

Bronze production in the Shang dynasty represents the technological pinnacle of the age. At Yinxu fantastic examples have been excavated, including the largest and heaviest sacrificial bronze vessel ever found: the spectacular *si mu wu fangding* (its current home is the National Museum in Beijing). Intricately designed bronzes were cast using pottery moulds, a process which could be quite complex when the object was large and the decoration complicated. Bronze objects were used mainly for military and ritual purposes; for agricultural and utilitarian purposes wood and bone continued to be utilized.

Many types of bronze vessels and weapons are on view here. Don't miss the fabulous bronze *yue* from Tomb M26 at Guojiazhuang or the skull of a Shang soldier with a spearhead through it.

One of the most spectacular finds at Yinxu was the undisturbed tomb of Princess Fu Hao. Discovered in 1976, this is the only intact Shang dynasty tomb excavated to date. Fu Hao was one of the consorts of King Wu Ding; oracle bones tell us she was a general who participated in military campaigns. This explains why her tomb, consisting of more than 1,500 objects, contains military bronzes as well as jades from the Liangzhu Culture, which would have been collected as antiques. Many of these objects can be seen in the Henan Museum in Zhengzhou.

The Shang are also known for their jade craftsmanship. Jade objects and ornaments were buried in many tombs. Many beautiful examples are on display.

Five excavated chariot pits are on display in a separate building within the park grounds.Each pit contains the skeletal remains of two horses ritually buried with their chariots. Many more chariots are known to exist but are yet to be excavated. A new chariot museum is planned.

This archaeological park was recently awarded inclusion on UNESCO's World Heritage List and is justly renowned for its archaeological richness and presentation.

Ox scapula with inscription

Oracle Bones and Divination

Shang Culture was driven by ritual, and the King was the intermediary between his people and the divine. The latter consisted of gods and nature spirits – the highest of whom was known as Di or Shang Di – as well as the King's ancestors. Both controlled all aspects of life and so required attention in the form of offerings and sacrifices, hence the large–scale use of human and animal oblations. Oracle bones made of ox scapulas and the bottom shells of turtles were used to ask specific questions – most often regarding rituals and sacrifice but also about weather forecasts, upcoming harvests, warfare, hunting and the like. Divinations were conducted by the King with the help of his diviner. Unique to Yinxu is that not only the question but also the answer was inscribed – and sometimes even the outcome.

After preparing the bone or shell to make a smooth surface, small hollows were carved in columns along the length of the bone, thus weakening its structure. A hot point was applied, causing cracks to appear. The angle, size and shape of the cracking all had meaning. These cracks were interpreted and the results inscribed and marked as favourable or unfavourable.

The inscriptions, which are the earliest form of Chinese writing we have, were created in logograms of which about 40 per cent have been identified. Some are pictographs and some paired symbols – one for meaning, the other for sound. This form of writing evolved into modern Chinese. The questions are written in a negative and positive manner – the harvest will be good; the harvest will be bad. Most of the inscriptions give the date of the divination, the name of the King doing the divining and the diviner. This amounts to a list of kings in chronological order, giving us a relative chronology which matches up to other historical sources, thus offering historians a wide range of information regarding Shang society.

54

Linzi Funerary Horse Pit Museum of the Eastern Zhou

东周殉马馆 *Dongzhou xunmaguan*

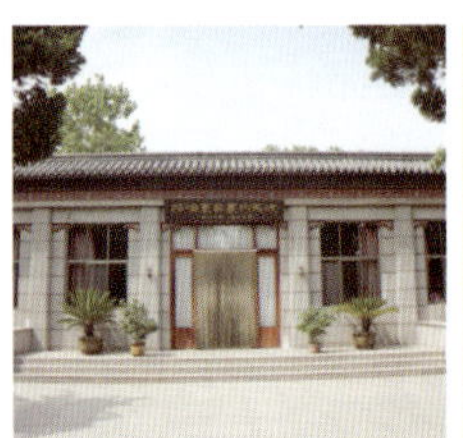

Heyatou Village, Qidu Town, Linzi District, Zibo, Shandong
山东省淄博市临淄区齐都镇河崖头村
Tel: (0533) 783 1008
Open: 8.00–17.00 (call to check opening hours and
for directions)
Chinese guides only
Kids

This extraordinary site museum is located down a dirt road in a small farming village near Linzi. Measuring 26.3m (length) × 23.35m (width) × 3.6m (depth), the partially excavated tomb is probably that of Jing Gong, ruler of the Qi dynasty. In the centre, still unexcavated, is the burial place of the King himself; surrounding him on three sides is a rectangular pit lined with the skeletons of 600 horses. Only 228 of these have been excavated – one side of the pit – as the museum currently does not have the resources to properly protect the site if it were fully excavated. Jing Gong is believed to have been a great lover of horses, so he was buried with this enormous number of animals to serve and protect him in the next life. The horses show no sign of struggle, and it is likely that they were given some type of herbal potion to drug them before being buried alive.

This excavation pit is an astonishing sight and should not be missed if you are in the area.

One side of the
rectangular pit
lined with
horse skeletons

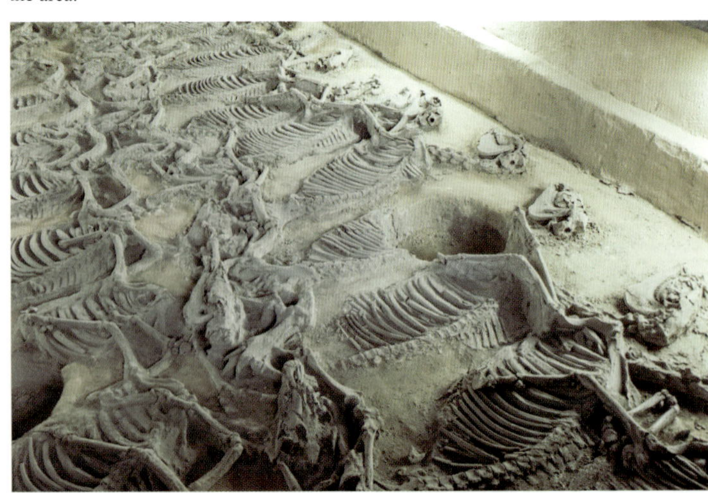

东周殉马馆 *Dongzhou xunmaguan*

Linzi Museum of Chinese Ancient Chariots

55

临淄中国古车博物馆 *Linzi zhongguo guche bowuguan*

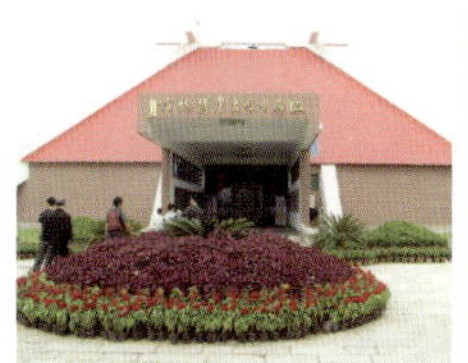

Qiling Town, Linzi District, Zibo, Shandong
山东省淄博市临淄区齐陵街道办事处
Tel: (0533) 708 3310
Open: 8.30–17.00
Kids

This beautifully preserved sacrificial horse pit dating to the middle of the Spring and Autumn period was discovered while excavating for the road. Indeed, cars on the motorway rattle the roof of the excavation site conserved just below it. The museum was completed in 1994 and is presented in two sections: the burial-pit area and a hall of chariot reproductions.

Two pits have been excavated. The first is 32 by 5 m and contains the remains of ten chariots and thirty-two horses; six of the chariots are associated with four horses, and four chariots were buried with two horses. The second pit is 8 by 3 m and contains three chariots and six horses. The wood of the chariot frame has decayed, but its impression remains in the loess. Traces of bronze beads, large bronze buttons and cowrie shells sewn on to fabric in a circular pattern can still be seen on the horses' skulls, along with some of the surviving tack, permit the whole arrangement to be revealed. The chariots are mostly about 3 m long and between 2.5 and 2.7 m wide. They are all single-axle. The wheels have a diameter of between 50 cm and 1.4 m. The chariots are of two types: smaller two-horse ones (war chariots) and larger four-horse ones (for transportation of goods). In the first pit, the horses and chariots are lined up in an orderly fashion. In the second pit, three chariots are buried beneath and the six horses above.

This museum also has a large collection of ancient Chinese chariot reproductions on display along with an exhibition case devoted to the development of the stirrup in China. To the north of the chariot museum lie the ancient walls of the Qi state, while to the south are the striking pyramid-shaped tombs of four Qi kings from which the museum borrowed its pyramidal design.

Impression of chariot wheel recorded in clay

56

Sino-Japanese War (1894–1895) Museum

甲午战争博物馆 *Jiawuzhanzheng bowuguan*

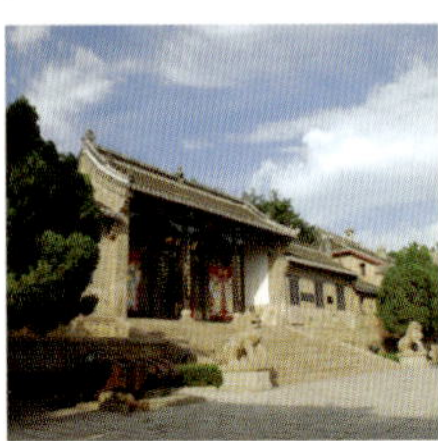

Liugong Island, Weihai, Shandong
山东省威海市刘公岛
Tel: (0631) 5324 184 / 5226 357
Open: 8.30–16.30 busy season, last entry 16.00;
        7.30–18.00 off season, last entry 17.30
www.jiawuzhanzheng.org
Gift shop

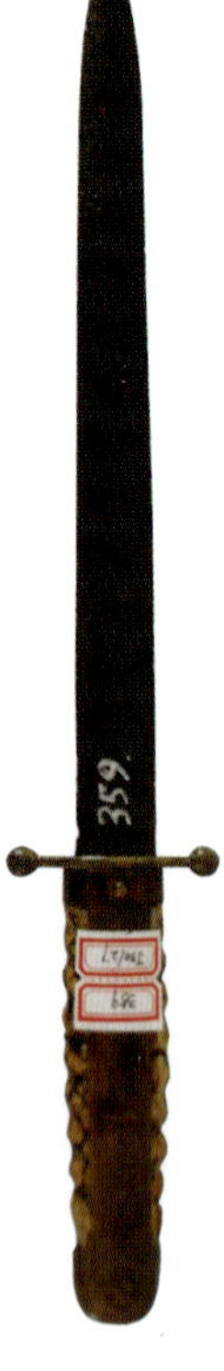

Dagger of Ding Ruchang, the commander of Northern Navy

The Sino-Japanese War of 1894–1895 marked the failure of the Qing dynasty's "self-strengthening" movement which included efforts to develop a modern navy to defend China. The humiliating defeat by Japan, another Asian nation, fuelled demands for political reform and ultimately the overthrow of the dynasty.

Weihai (then called Weihaiwei) was the site of the final major battle of the war in early 1895. Located on the northeastern tip of the Shandong peninsula, Weihai commanded the approaches to the Gulf of Bohai and access to Beijing. The natural harbour was the home base of the Qing's Northern (Beiyang) Navy. In the battle, after a siege lasting 23 days, Japanese troops took the land defenses and then proceeded to sink key vessels of the Chinese fleet using torpedo boats. The Chinese defeat was complete and the Admiral of the Northern Navy, Ding Ruchang, committed suicide in his office at the fleet's headquarters on Liugong Island, by eating an overdose of opium.

The war ended shortly afterwards with the Treaty of Shimonoseki in which China was forced to cede Taiwan to Japan and to pay a war indemnity.

The Museum's location is spectacular, on Weihai's scenic Liugong Island in buildings that housed the Northern Navy's offices. One can gaze out into the broad bay where the battleships from the fleet still lie under the water.

The museum incorporates both the well preserved buildings and objects from the Northern Navy's base and instructs the visitors about the broader history of the Sino-Japanese War.

One can see Admiral Ding's Offices, the only such admiral's headquarters from the Qing Dynasty preserved in China, as well as Admiral Ding's residence, a naval academy, theatre, temples, and three forts. On display are the huge pair of Krupp 210 mm calibre front guns – each weighing 20 tonnes – from the German-built Chinese cruiser Jiyuan.

The section devoted to the history of the Sino-Japanese War of 1894–1895 is well presented with explanations in English as well as in Chinese. This is a rich collection of photographs, paintings, ship models and sculptures of historical figures all enhanced by the use of high tech multimedia. The dramatic story of the rise and destruction of the Northern Navy is vividly conveyed. Late-Qing navy leaders who died such as Ding Ruchang and Deng Shichang are singled out as "martyrs" who sought to defend China's "national integrity." The museum conveys a strong patriotic message.

Though Weihai and the Museum are somewhat off the main tourist routes, a visit can be combined with visits to other places in Shandong. Weihai is also of interest in that after the Japanese left in 1898 it became a British colony until 1930.

Weihai is located in a wonderful setting and has some of the best seafood in China.

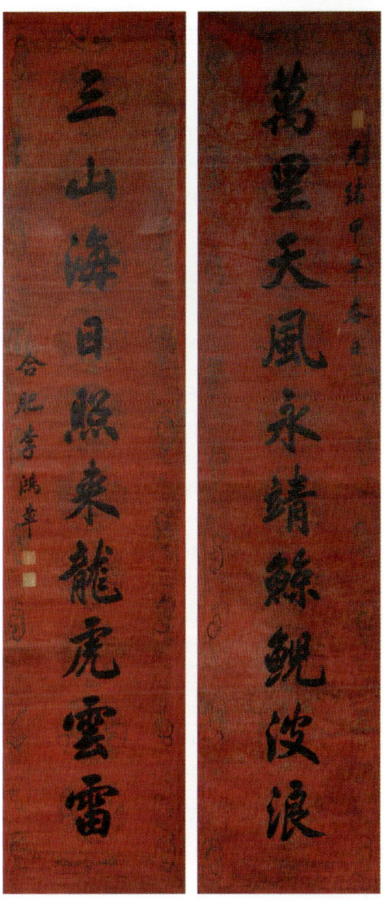

Li Hongzhang's couplet for Beiyang Navy

57

Qi State History Museum

齐国历史博物馆 *Qiguo lishi bowuguan*

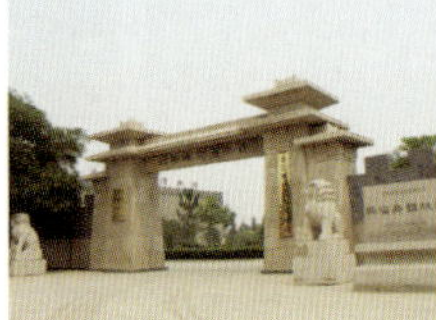

7 Zhanghuang Road, Linzi District, Zibo, Shandong
山东省淄博市临淄区张皇路7号
Tel: (0533) 7830 229
Open: 8.00–17.30 summer; 8.00–17.00 winter
Gift shop / bookshop

The Qi State Museum in Linzi, a district of the modern city of Zibo, and the nearby sites of the Ancient Chariot Museum and the Funerary Horse Pit of Eastern Zhou dynasty can all be seen in one day and make a neat unit. Ancient Linzi was the capital of the Qi State of the Eastern Zhou (770–221 BC). This period is divided by historians into two separate subdivisions, namely the Spring and Autumn period (770–450 BC) and the Warring States period (450–221 BC). Although an era of instability, war and confusion it was, conversely, also an age of great developments in culture and civilization.

At the end of the period preceding this, the Western Zhou, smaller vassal states began to gain in power and confidence and desiring autonomy, broke off from the centralized Zhou State. In addition, nomadic groups were invading from the West causing the Zhou King to move his capital eastwards to Luoyang.

From this point, the military power of the Zhou kings continued to diminish and the smaller states – now in effect independent – began fighting amongst themselves for influence and hegemony. This period of decentralization, violence and unstable alliances is known as the Eastern Zhou, which continued until 221 BC with the complete victory of the Qin.

From the Spring and Autumn period the Qi state, with its capital in Linzi, gained in prominence mainly due to the successful leadership of Duke Huan of Qi in the mid fifth century BC. The Qi State became very prosperous and powerful – so much so that they were able to keep the formidable Chu and Qin states at bay but ultimately they could not resist domination by the Qin in 221 BC. The walled city, believed to have been highly populated, was built on a north-south axis and was surrounded by a moat. It had a functioning water and drainage system, a royal palace, roads, market places

Qi State period bronze *zun*

and workshops. Iron tools and pottery were produced on a large scale, bronze-casting technology advanced, coins were cast, textiles such as silk, hemp and linen were produced and salt production was a local industry.

The museum, built in 1985, displays over 300 objects in a modern museum environment. Oracle bones, bronzes, silver, ceramics and royal burial material from the Han Qi tomb of Dawu, are displayed. There is also an ancient technology hall, exhibition hall of musical instruments and an exhibit about the Qi State's invention of football.

The specific highlights of the collection include:

- Western Zhou incised oracle bones and turtle shells.
- A very large bronze *yu* with two handles in the shape of dragons.
- A wonderful bronze *zun* in the shape of a stocky ox-like mythical animal with its head facing upward expressively, its ears erect and a delicately formed tail. It is inlaid with gold and silver in an abstract cloud pattern.

Another prized object in the museum is a very large bronze mirror with a dragon-incised pattern excavated from the Han Qi tomb at Dawu.

There is a set of fourteen bronze bells exhibited. The music of these bells can be heard playing in the background in this gallery.

Many Qi pottery roof tiles from tombs decorated with patterns and characters are presented. Each of the several hundred roof tiles found is different. They are often decorated with trees accompanied by wild animals, birds, eyes, circles and other decorative motifs. Some are inscribed with inscriptions such as '10,000 autumns, 10,000 years' meaning 'long life'.

The Ancient Technology Exhibit shows how pottery-making in the Qi went from handicraft to production line. There is also a display of the development of bronze-casting technology in the Qi State as well as a presentation on the casting of coinage including the inscribed knife-shaped currency of the Warring States period.

The game of football has been officially recognized as originating in Linzi. In 2004, FIFA acknowledged that the ancient game called *cuju*, played as early as the Spring and Autumn period and depicted on a Song dynasty mirror displayed in the museum, is the origin of the modern game. The museum also exhibits FIFA's certificate attesting to this assertion.

The ancient game of *cuju*

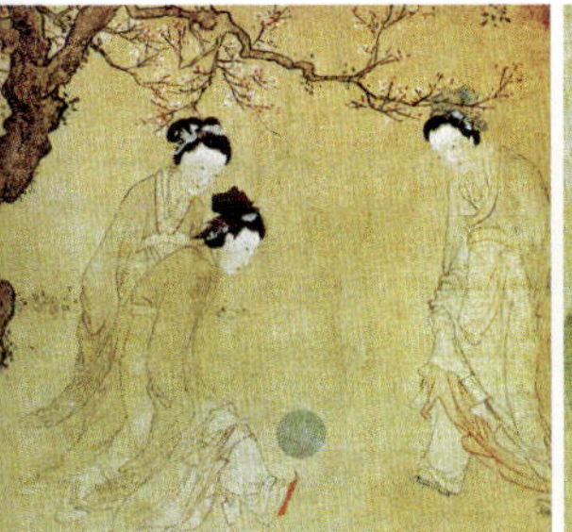
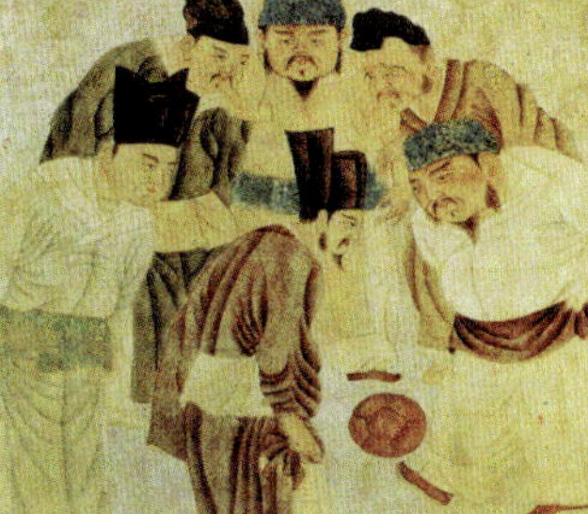

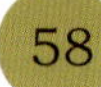

58

Shandong Museum

山东博物馆 *Shandong bowuguan*

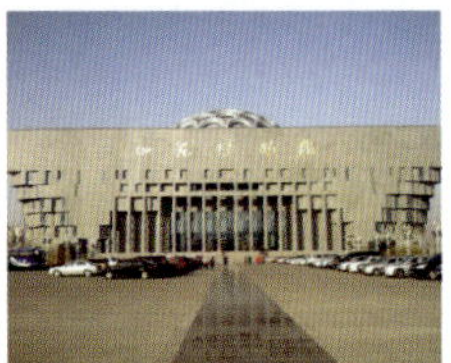

East of Jingshi Road, Jinan, Shandong
山东省济南市经十路东段
Tel: (0531) 8296 7179
Open: 9.00–17.00 except Mon, last entry 16.00
www.sdmuseum.com

This museum has undergone several incarnations – not surprisingly, as it was among the earliest museums in China. It was established in two parts, the first part by the British Baptist missionary J. S. Whitewright in 1904, with natural-history specimens which he used to attract crowds to hear his Christian sermons; the second part in 1942 by a religious society. The two were amalgamated in 1954 to form the kernel of today's museum and expanded with donations from the city library, the Committee of Cultural Relics, private donors from the 1950s onwards, and the vast number of archaeological excavations in the province. When they moved again in 1992 to their purpose-built home at the foot of Qianfo Mountain, the collections numbered more than 200,000 items, a true amalgam of natural and man-made artefacts.

After a 3-year construction project, Shandong museum moved to its new site and re-opened on November 16, 2010. The new building combines a square and circle, reflecting the ancient Chinese conception of the earth as square and the circle symbolizing heaven. There are eight galleries and four halls. The new galleries encompass all the aspects expected of a provincial museum, from the history of Shandong to folklore, ancient transportation, archaeology and natural history. The four halls consist of spaces for temporary loans, a conference hall, an education centre and a special exhibition gallery.

Shandong is one of China's political, economic and cultural hubs, situated east of the Taihang Mountains on the lower reaches of the Yellow River. A large, agricultural province, it is rich in natural resources including coal and oil, and with its large eastern coastline reaches out to countries over the sea. It is known for its numerous early Neolithic sites and was ruled by the Shang and, later, the powerful Zhou until the Eastern Zhou period, when the rulers fled eastwards and it was split between the Qi and the Lu. The Qin defeated the Qi, and during the Han dynasty the region was split between areas north sand south of the Yellow River. Jinan, the present-day capital, was

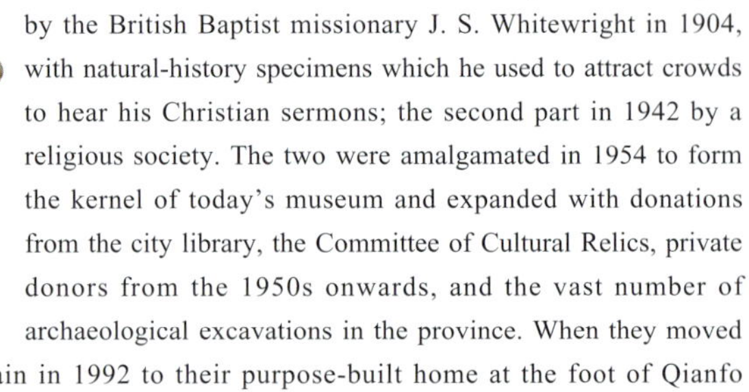

Neolithic food container, early phase of Dawenkou Culture

a military outpost and trading centre in the fourth century, and during the Ming became a walled city (no longer visible; its original position is defined by the remaining moats).

The museum's core holdings range from the important Neolithic sites of the Dawenkou and Longshan Cultures, to bronzes from the Shang and Zhou, to bamboo slips from the Han, to Buddhist and other stone carvings and tablets, and finally to natural-history material from the Palaeolithic to the more recent past.

Grave deposits from the early to the middle Neolithic Dawenkou Culture site of Tai'an on the lower reaches of the Yellow River were excavated by the museum and yielded a vast array of goods, including jades, painted pots and inscribed turtle shells (plastrons), indicating that the inhabitants were skilled craftsmen and that the materials they used pointed to interactions with outlying communities. Holdings include a stemmed food container decorated with octagonal designs (possibly symbolizing a cosmological system); a red-clay zoomorphic jar with holes at both the tail and head end, the back one for water coming into the container and front for it to pour out; and distinctive white-clay tripod vessels for heating food. A rare item is the *hu* jar painted with black and white net designs. Jade comes in a bewildering range of shapes and colours from a light yellow shovel to a necklace consisting of eleven pieces including rings and a turquoise pendant. Special funerary objects on display include a hook made from roe-deer teeth with a bone handle found in the hands of the deceased and a bone tube with turquoise inlays. Artefacts from Longshan sites yielded distinctly different pottery, black with incised designs – like the spectacular 'egg-shell' *bei* cup with a long stem.

The collection of ceramics continues with superb examples from the Shang right through to the Qing. Visitors can select from a green-glazed Eastern Han figure chopping food at a table (likely to be a chef); a double-fish-shaped tri-coloured vase from the Tang; a Song celadon covered vase with six tubes extending from the neck and decorated with flowers; a Ming gourd-shaped vase with its lower belly decorated with auspicious animals; and another in the same shape from the Qianlong period decorated with red bats, green leaves and yellow gourds. Double gourds were associated with abundance and fertility and also the double structure of the universe – heaven and earth – while the red bats are a rebus, or visual pun, signifying good fortune.

Not to be missed is one of the defining objects of the museum: a *yue*, or ceremonial axe, with a vicious human face with bulging eyes and clenched teeth

Long-stemmed 'egg-shell' *bei* (cup), Longshan Culture

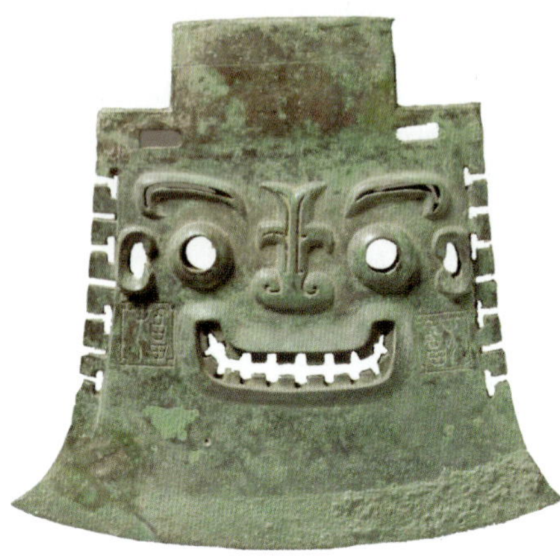

Yue, with Yachou inscription, late Shang

pierced into the bronze. Unearthed at the Shang site of Yidu, Sufutun in Qingzhou, it was used to behead humans and animals for sacrifices. It is similar to a *taotie,* though all parts of the face are human. Another stunning object from this site is the bronze *he* with a tubular spout and animal-head handle. Unearthed at the Xiaotun site in Changqing is a square *ding* with *kui*-dragon motif under the rim and cicada designs on all four legs. Remarkable are several bronzes from the Xiaowangshuang site, including a bronze *hu* with a rope design, handles in the shape of an elephant's trunk, and a thirteen-character inscription stating that it is from the Chen state (today's eastern Henan). Several splendid mirrors and plates from the Warring States period are inlaid with turquoise, gold and silver.

Objects excavated from the tomb of Zhu Tan, Prince of Lu in the fourteenth century and the tenth son of the founding Emperor of the Ming, yielded around 400 painted wooden figures of musicians, attendants and military figures along with other personal possessions like his crown of wood and jade beads, gold buckle, several jade blades wrapped in gold, a wooden zither and a red-lacquer box with gold-inlaid clouds and dragons.

The holdings of stone sculpture here are outstanding. Among them are Eastern Han stone pictorial carvings with intricately carved scenes of everyday life or life imagined after death. One from Xihukou has seven bands carved with various scenes, among them animals with human faces, men holding weapons, and carriages with servants. Another from the Longyangdian site, carved in relief, shows people spinning and weaving as well as travelling in horse-drawn chariots. Scenes of merriment with musicians, dancers and acrobats occupy one side of another carving found in Jiaxiang County while on the other side the audience is shown eating and drinking.

Among scores of other objects is the Yuan warship (20 m in length) uncovered at the site of the Ming naval base in Penglai (former Dengzhou). The Emperors of the Yuan were keen to strengthen their sea power and ordered thousands of warships to be built. The collections also excel in their holdings of paintings, hand scrolls and calligraphy, as well as fossils,

Ming dynasty gold buckle

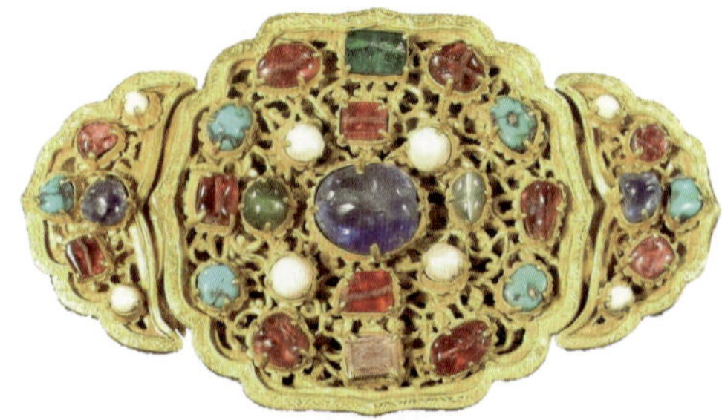

dinosaurs and other natural-history specimens. The province has several major fossil sites, including the Laiyang Formation (Lower Cretaceous) in the Shandong Peninsula, which have revealed numerous fossil insects, while the coal mines of the Wutu Basin east of Jinan, dating from the Early Eocene, have revealed numerous mammal and plant fossils. One of the richest assemblages of plant and animal remains in the province is located in the Shanwang National Geological Park. During the Middle Miocene the humid and warm climate was host to hundreds of species. Remains from here include beautifully preserved skeletons of deer and mice, as well as fish, insects, amphibians, birds, mammals and fossil pollens.

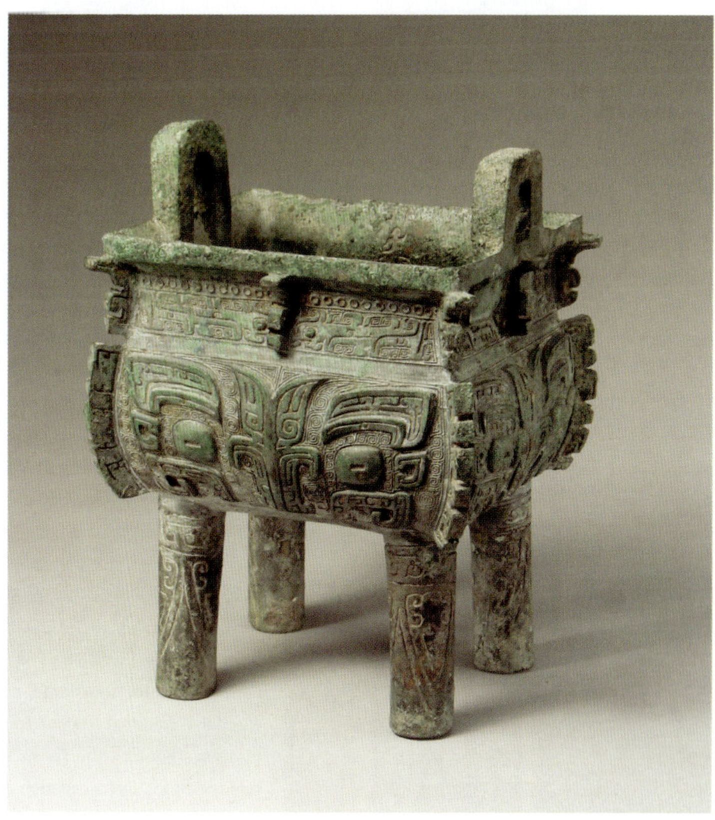

fang ding

59

Qingdao Municipal Museum

青岛市博物馆 *Qingdaoshi bowuguan*

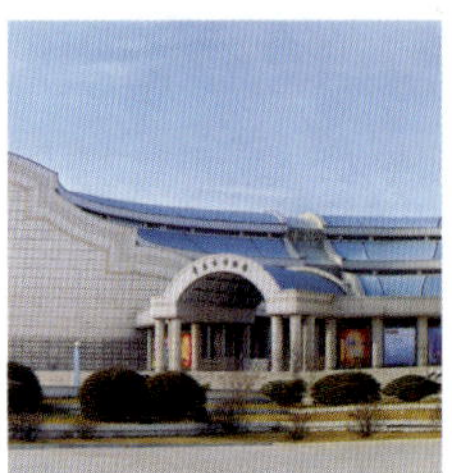

51 Meiling East Road, Laoshan District, Qingdao, Shandong
山东省青岛市崂山区梅岭东路51号
Tel: (0532) 8889 6286
www.qingdaomuseum.com
Open: 9.00–17.00 except Mon, last entry 16.00, May–Oct;
        9.00–16.30 except Mon, last entry 15.30, Nov–Apr
Gift shop / bookshop / coffee shop

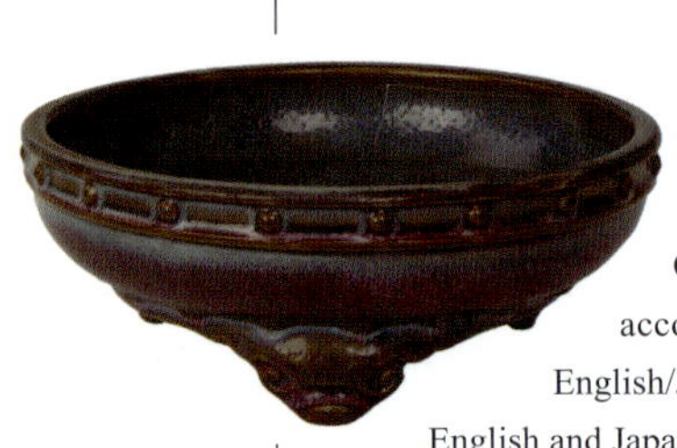

Drum-Shaped
Brush Washer with
a Nipple Pattern of
the Jun Kiln, Song
Dynasty

Daoist scriptures
(*Daozang*) from
Wanli Period of the
Ming Dynasty

Founded in 1965, Qingdao Municipal Museum is a comprehensive museum focusing on history and arts. The six permanent galleries once have had a makeover to take advantage of the waves of visitors attending the 2008 Olympic sailing competitions at the city's new facility. To accommodate foreign visitors, the museum has introduced new English/Japanese/Korean audio guides, along with signage in Chinese, English and Japanese.

The collection is a real mixed bag of treasures; among the best galleries are those of Ming and Qing dynasties porcelain, numismatics from the Xia and Shang dynasties to the Republican period, and calligraphy and paintings ranging from works by the well-known Ming painter Xie Shichen to the Qing dynasty Buddhist monk Zhu Da and Qingdao-born painter Gao Fenghan, one of the 'Eight Eccentrics of Yangzhou' known for his paintings of flowers and landscapes. There is also a gallery of ancient Chinese crafts containing lacquer wares, bamboo and ivory carvings, enamels and implements such as brushes and ink slabs. Another room offers a chronological overview of Qingdao's development up to its establishment as a municipality in 1891. The climax of the collection is the four large, elegantly carved Buddhist limestone statues from the Northern Qi dynasty which the Japanese attempted to remove during the occupation of Shandong.

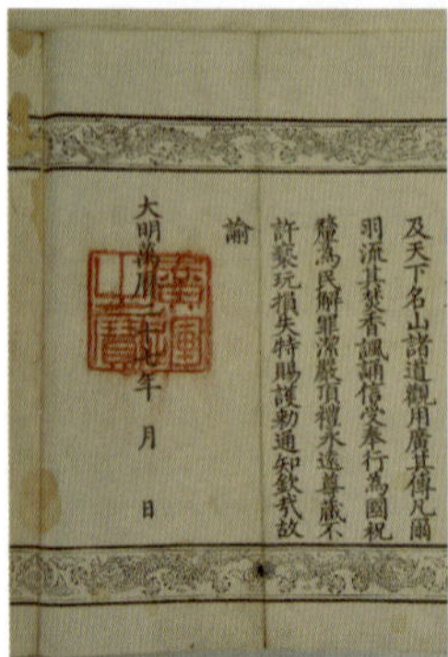

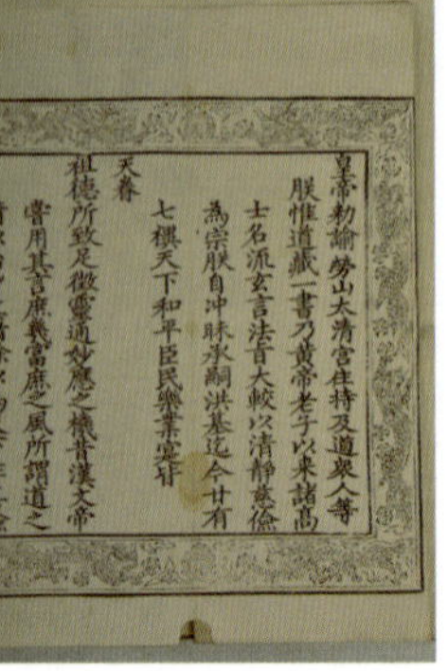

60

Qingdao Naval Museum

青岛海军博物馆 *Qingdao haijun bowuguan*

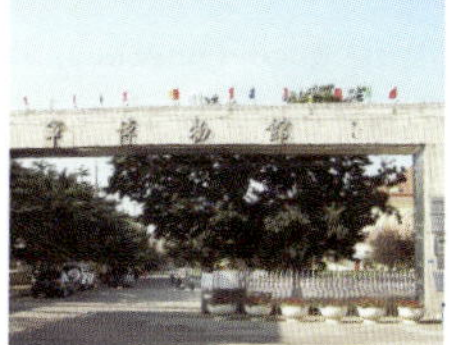

8 Laiyang Road, Qingdao, Shandong
山东省青岛市莱阳路8号
Tel: (0532) 8286 6784 / 8287 4786
Open: 8.00–18.00, Apr–Oct; 8.30–17.00, Nov–Mar
Extensive shop offers a mixed selection of gifts
Kids

This specialist museum founded by the Chinese People's Liberation Army Navy (PLAN) faces the sea at the now defunct naval base on the edge of scenic Lu Xun Park. Opened in 1989 to showcase China's naval history, it consists of two parts: an enclosed exhibition space and a sprawling open-air area which extends to an assortment of piers.

A brief wander through the hall provides visitors with an overview of the PLAN's history told through exhibits of uniforms, historic images and insignia from 1949, the year PLAN was founded, to the present day. Among the highlights is the dress uniform of the first commander of PLAN, Gen. Xiao Jingguang. More than 300 gifts given by foreign armies to PLAN are also displayed, including a sword presented by the Soviet Vice National Defence Minister to Gen. Xiao in 1957.

A rare treat is in store outside, where open access allows visitors to get up close to all sorts of weapons and equipment, including aircraft, missiles, artillery, torpedoes, radar and submarines. The accelerated development of China's naval radar and electronic-warfare systems came in 1953, when Russia agreed to assist with aid and licenses to manufacture this equipment; therefore much of what is seen was either directly purchased from the Soviets or bears a close resemblance to Russian counterparts. Highlights include the wooden-hulled torpedo boat that carried Chairman Mao and Zhou Enlai in 1957 when they reviewed PLAN in Qingdao; a Y-14 aircraft which was a make favoured by Mao; a Chinese-developed Hongqi-2 surface-to-air missile based on the Russian S-75; and a row of MiGs or Soviet fighter airplanes and their Chinese variants, F-5 etc. In the port you can enter many decommissioned vessels, including an Anshan-class destroyer – the first destroyers of China which were modified ex-Soviet destroyers from WWII; a Romeo-class 229 submarine copied by the Chinese with six torpedo tubes at the front; and the 90-m long Chinese-built Nanchong launched in 1968.

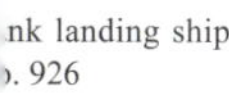

nk landing ship,
. 926

61

Qingzhou Municipal Museum

青州博物馆 *Qingzhou bowuguan*

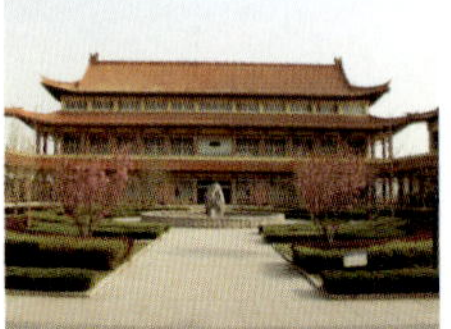

1 Fangongting West Road, Qingzhou, Shandong
山东省青州市范公亭西路1号
Tel: (0536) 3266 200
Open: 9.00–17.00
www.qzbowuguan.com

At first glance, the museum does not appear particularly inviting. However, for within the museum's galleries, which are set around a courtyard, is one of the most astounding collections of Buddhist statues ever to be unearthed in China. Startled construction workers making way for a sports complex chanced upon this cache of nearly 400 Buddhist sculptures in 1996. Several years ago they went on a world tour, which was hailed as one of the great Asian shows of recent years and resulted in a wonderful catalogue entitled *Return of the Buddha: The Qingzhou Discoveries*.

Found near the former site of the city's Longxing Temple in a bare earth rectangular pit, the fragmented figures of Buddha and his attendants (*bodhisattvas*) were arranged in three layers with their heads around the pit walls, with the most complete ones in the centre. Most are carved from local bluish-grey limestone and date from a period which spans 600 years, from the late Northern Wei dynasty (386–534) to the Northern Song (960–1126), with the core dating from the sixth century, providing scholars with a unique historical continuum of Buddhist sculpture in China. Some are gilded and painted in a range of natural blue, green and black pigments, the majority are incomplete and noticeably restored with their jigsaw-puzzle pieces stuck together. Why they were buried and left, no one really knows. Perhaps they were buried during a period when rulers persecuted followers of Buddhism and they were in danger of confiscation.

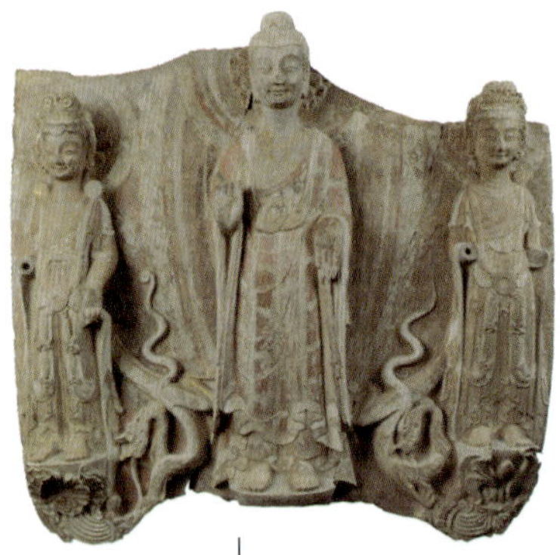

Bodhisattva, Eastern Wei period

Triad with mandorla, Eastern Wei period

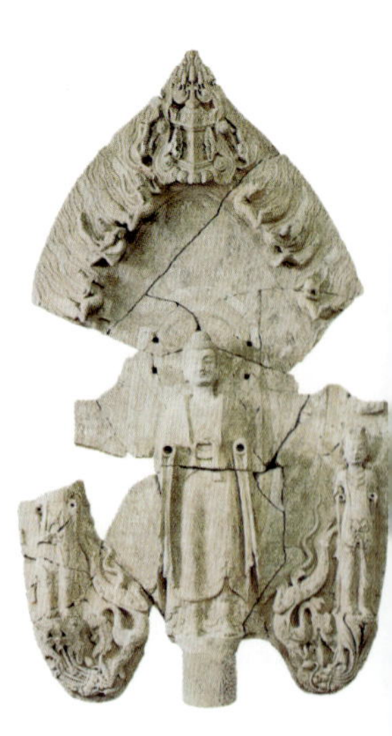

Bodhisattva, Eastern Wei period

Central to this collection is the fifty-year period between 529 and 577, when two main stylistic differences were evident as Buddhism spread along the trade routes and blended with Chinese qualities. Those from the Northern (386–534) and Eastern (534–550) Wei dynasties embraced all things Chinese and so designed their figures in typical Chinese monastic robes concealing the body, with stiff faces bearing benign smiles, elongated earlobes and Buddhas with prominent *usnisa* (protuberances on the head representing wisdom). The Northern Qi (550–577), on the other hand, who disliked all things Chinese, turned to Gupta India, adopting close-fitting, light garments revealing the body's contours, with fuller faces bearing perfectly formed sensuous lips. These, along with other recently unearthed hoards, add greatly to our knowledge of Chinese Buddhist art. In 2005, 400 Ming dynasty stone Buddha statues were uncovered in Chongqing during a survey of a ruined Ming temple in Liangping county, and a cache of Buddhist statuary consisting of 324 pieces was discovered in 2006 in Houdigecun village, Nangong, Hebei, dating from the Northern dynasties through to the Tang.

Besides these wondrous sculptures, there are galleries on the Neolithic Cultures of Longshan and Dawenkou, displays of Warring States period bronzes and Eastern Han dynasty pottery, including, among other pieces, a wonderful glazed model of a pottery store.

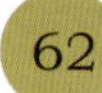

Coal Museum of China

中国煤炭博物馆 *Zhongguo meitan bowuguan*

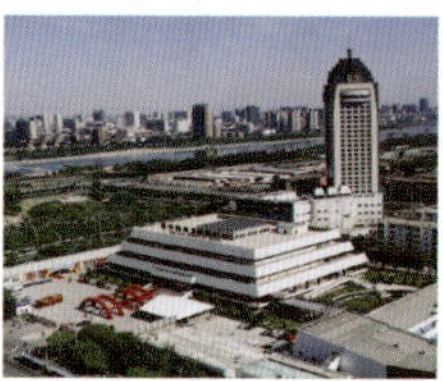

2 Yingze West Street, Taiyuan, Shanxi
山西省太原市迎泽西大街2号
Tel: (0351) 6040 885 / 6180 108
Open: 8:00–18:00
www.coalmus.org.cn
Gift shop

It comes as no surprise to find China's coal museum in Taiyuan, the capital of Shanxi Province.

Parts of Shanxi, Inner Mongolia and Shaanxi Provinces share the Ordos Basin, famous for its abundant thick seams of coal laid down in the Early and Middle Jurassic

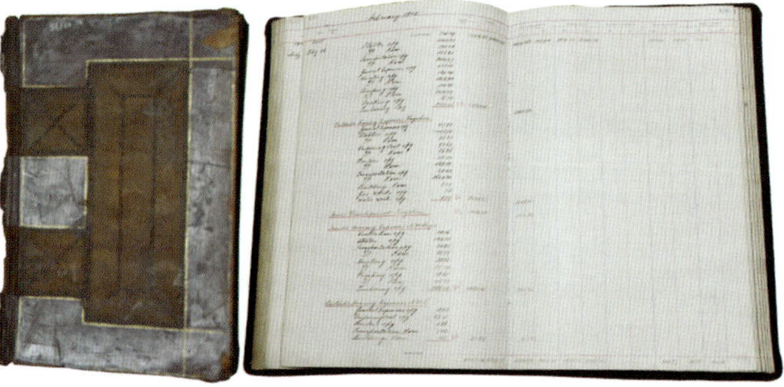

Ledgers from the Kailuan Mine

periods. These three provinces account for about 65% of the coal reserves in China.

The mountain-shaped museum with three distinct tiered levels looms out of the hazy-grey sky along the west bank of Fen River. Venture here only if you need to learn more about China's coal production or have a business interest, as although its coverage of the subject is comprehensive its main function is as a showcase and communication centre for the state-owned industry.

Inside there are eight easy to follow halls telling the story of coal in China – from its formation to the history of mining it, as well as the future role of coal as an energy source, using many of the thirty thousand objects the museum has collected. The last of these spaces is the most enjoyable. Here you don a hard hat and enter a simulated mine touted to be the largest of its kind in Asia. Technological wizardry allows you to visit an ancient mine, discover how blast-hole mining is employed, watch how coal is mechanically sourced and learn about the development of coal mining through time.

Of particularly interest at the mine entrance is a tool dating from the Ming dynasty used for hoisting coal out of the mines known as a windlass. Consisting of a crank, support structure and a rope with two baskets attached on either side, when the crank was wound the rope on one side would lift the coal-filled basket while simultaneously lowering the empty one on the opposite side. Known in China as a longba, this example was excavated in Shanxi. Today, mine hoists are still used to handle almost all transport requirements in underground mines, but are technologically more advanced.

Although not much is known about the discovery of coal and its initial usage as an energy source, it is believed that China was one of the first countries to mine coal starting in the Han dynasty. Today, China is the largest coal producer and consumer in the world – almost half the global total. It is however, not all doom and fumes. Over the last decade, China has been closing down coal plants and investment in mining has decreased; instead it has been put into renewables with wind leading the way.

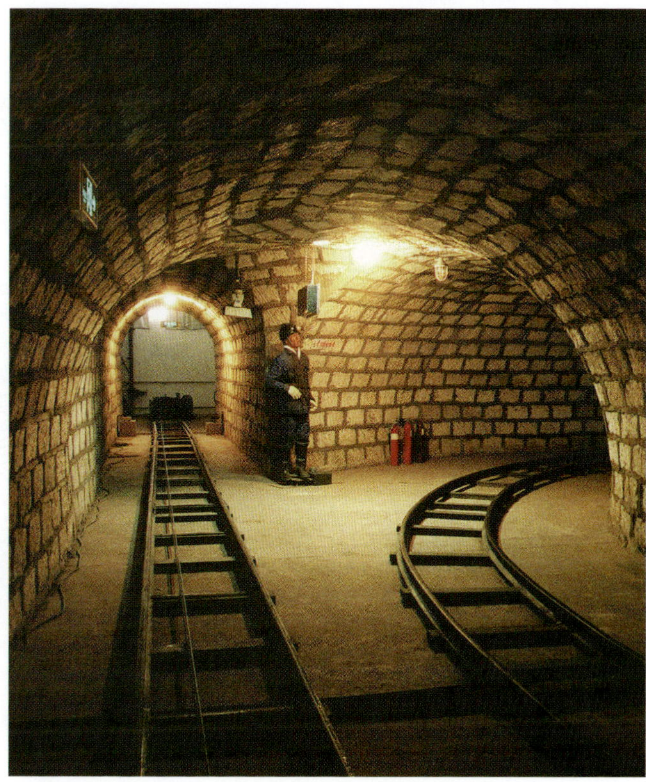

Pingyao Confucius Temple Museum

平遥文庙学宫博物院 *Pingyao wenmiao xuegong bowuyuan*

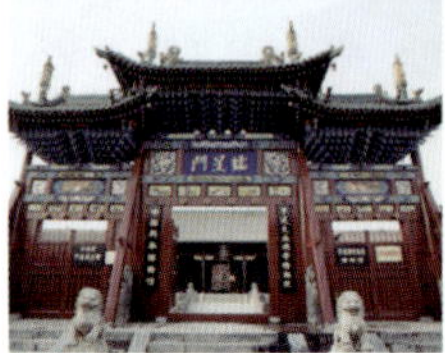

19 Wenmiao Street, Pingyao, Shanxi
山西省平遥县城内文庙街19号
Tel: (0354) 5685 466
Open: 8.00–19.00

The main building of this temple, Dacheng Hall, was built in 1163, 248 years earlier than the Confucius Temple in Beijing and 317 years earlier than that in Qufu, the hometown of Confucius. In the temple are eighty-seven sculptures of Confucius and his disciples, and an exhibition surveying the history of the ancient imperial examination system.

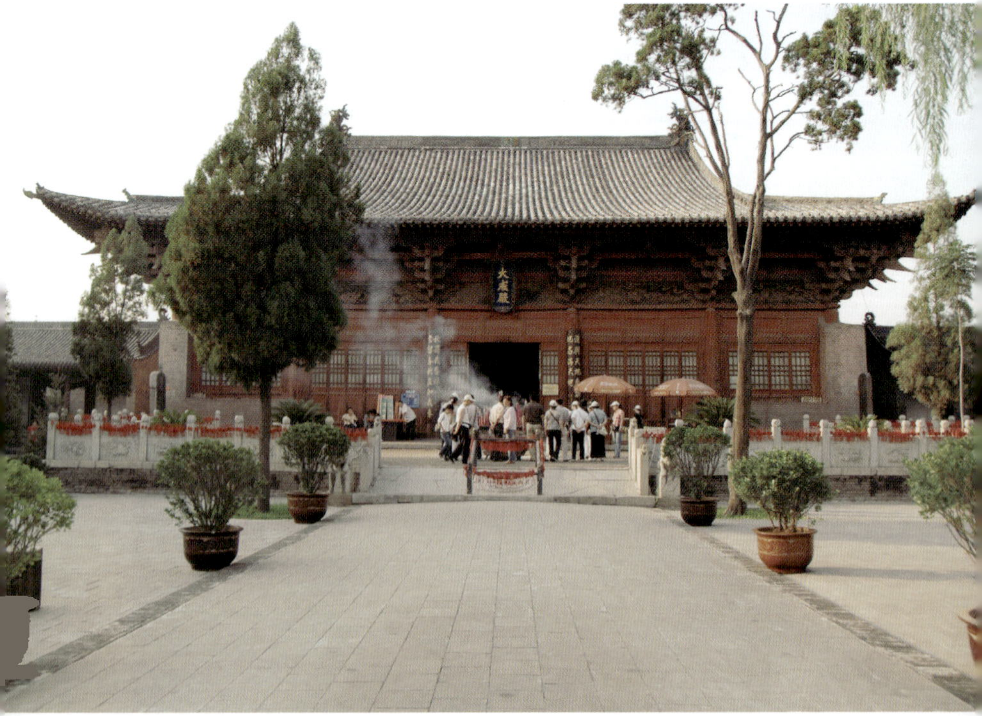

Also in the complex is the Pingyao International Photography Museum. Picturesque Pingyao, with the best-preserved city walls in China, is an outstanding example of a Han Chinese city of the Ming and Qing dynasties and is always buzzing with shutterbugs. Since 2001, it has hosted an annual international photography festival, providing a window onto China's burgeoning photography scene. The collection includes photos by the well-known documentarians of the revolution, Sha Fei and Wu Yinxian, as well some work by Western photographers.

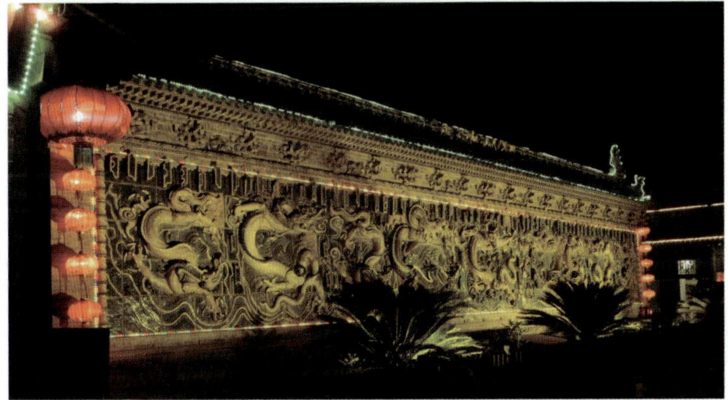

Pingyao Museum (Qingxu Temple)

平遥县博物馆(清虚观) *Pingyaoxian bowuguan (qingxuguan)*

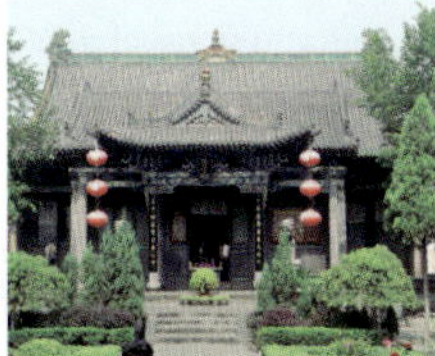

109 Dong Street, Pingyao, Shanxi
山西省平遥县城东大街109号
Tel: (0354) 5685 851
Open: 8.00–19.00

This Tang dynasty Daoist temple is also home to the Pingyao Museum in which there are exhibits of Daoist civilization, the history of Pingyao and a small collection of local artefacts.

Shanxi Museum

山西博物院 *Shanxi bowuyuan*

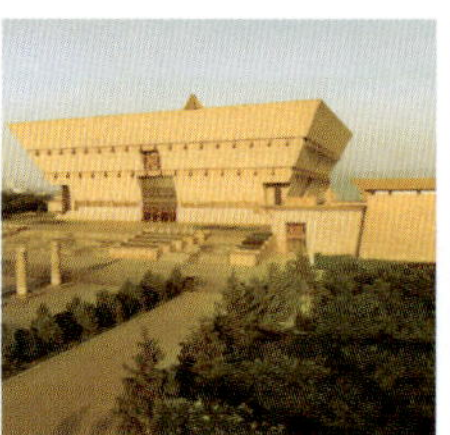

13 Binhe West Road, Taiyuan, Shanxi
山西省太原市滨河西路13号
Tel: (0351) 8789 555
Open: 9.00–17.00 except Mon, last entry 16.00
www.shanximuseum.com.cn
Gift shop / bookshop / café / restaurant
Excellent publications

This remarkably shaped museum looming large on the bank of the Fen River emerges between nests of high-rise buildings like a spaceship that has just landed on some alien planet. Its central rhomboid is the result of combining two shapes, that of a *dou* – a measure for dry grain – and that of a *ding* – a round-bodied three-legged vessel for food – the former symbolizing a healthy harvest, the latter, stability. Added to this are four smaller buildings resembling outstretched wings, so embodying the ancient Chinese association of the free spirit with flying birds. Walk inside and you enter a double-height atrium mimicking the unique shape of the wooden Sakyamuni pagoda, built 950 years ago. Walk further in and the granite-and-glass interiors open up to reveal twelve exhibition halls over four floors, seven devoted to ancient history, the remaining five a combination of fine art and themed galleries.

As the main repository of cultural relics from this rich province, it is the largest and most prestigious, housing research and conservation facilities, temporary exhibition spaces, conference halls, a library and all the usual services including a canteen. Like so many museums, a small percentage of its massive collection of more than 400,000 items is displayed; the majority are authentic. All the displays are beautifully lit with comprehensive labels in English augmented by excellent images, dioramas, maps and interactive computer displays. The collections have been amassed since 1919, originally as part of the Shanxi library, then moved to two locations (a Confucian monastery and a former palace) until being reincarnated in their latest form. It opened in 2005.

A panel in the entrance atrium illustrates numerous ways of depicting the character for the word *jin* – the shortened name for Shanxi. Located in the centre of the county, it is embraced by the nurturing Yellow River as well as the Fen, which runs

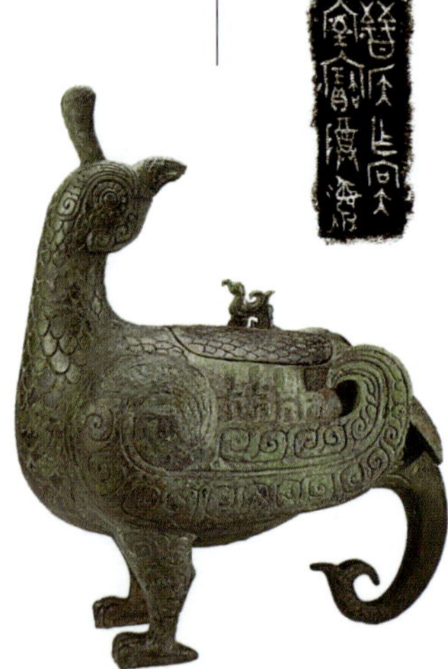

A *zun* unearthed from the tomb of Xiefu; its shape looks like a standing phoenix turning its head backward; its tail is curved and shaped like a trunk of an elephant

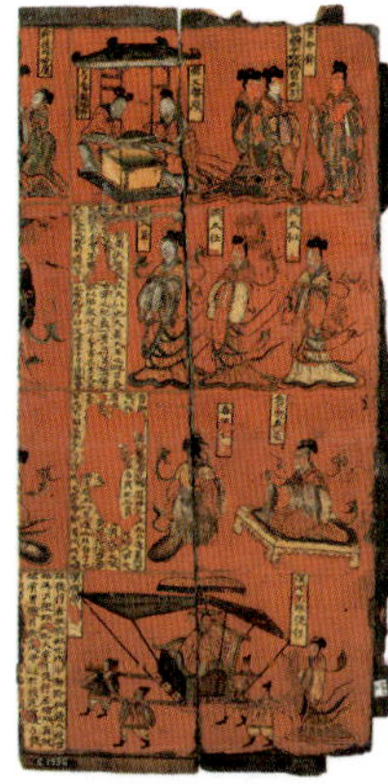
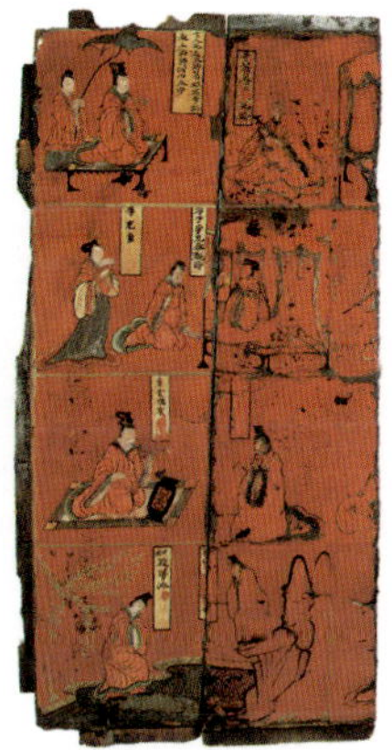

Wooden lacquer paintings, Northern Wei Dynasty, unearthed in the Tomb of Sima Jinlong

across the loess plateau. To east and west it is bounded by mountains which protected it from the invading minorities of the north. Over the centuries, though, cultural interactions and exchanges took place to create this rich cradle of civilization. As you weave your way through the chronologically laid-out galleries, you start on the ground floor with numerous dioramas and a selection of artefacts discovered from the hundreds of Palaeolithic sites located in Shanxi. Interactive models, didactic explanations and comparisons with finds of similar dates in other parts of the world put the finds in context.

The second floor is home to the museum's teahouse, as well as exhibits on the later Neolithic Cultures of north-central China, including the site of Taosi (2300 BC) in the southern part of the province (an offshoot of the Central Plain Longshan Culture). This extensive site with houses and kilns is defined by its large cemetery containing thousands of burials, several with outstanding contents indicating social stratification. Besides brown earthenware with red painting on a black ground, the site also contained wooden furniture and jade objects. Laid out in the centre of the gallery is a female skeleton of high rank (judging by the outstanding quality of the jade found with her, much of which is jewellery). Surrounding cases display superb examples of jade artefacts including axes, rings and a single-tiered jade *cong* with a hole through the middle.

Displays continue with the rich seam of finds from the Xia and Shang dynasties in Shanxi, including outstanding examples of Xia period pottery such as the large steamer (*yan*) excavated at the Erlitou site in Dongxiafeng. Objects that will blow your socks off include the high-quality ritual bronzes from the Shang; many unusual shapes are on display. Among these is the owl-shaped *you* excavated from Erlangpo in Shilou County and, from nearby, a dragon-shaped *gong* excavated from Taohuazhe, as well as one of the museum's national treasures, an imaginary animal-shaped *gong* excavated at Jinjie in Lingshi County. All

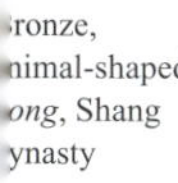

Bronze, animal-shaped *gong*, Shang Dynasty

are elaborately decorated and likely to have been used to make wine offerings. Superb here too are the three-dimensional animal-and bird-shaped carved jades.

Gallery 3 highlights the achievements of the Jin kingdom and the splendour of the bronzes of the Western Zhou. When the Zhou overthrew the Shang and established their capital near present-day Xi'an, relatives of their kings ruled small city-states. One of these was the vassal state of Jin. Among their most stellar objects are their ritual bronzes, including a *zun* and *you* with animal faces (*taotie*) – a decorative element they borrowed from the Shang – as well as inscribed pig and bird-shaped *zuns*. Other bronzes are displayed from the royal cemeteries of the marquises of Jin discovered in the 1990s. Tombs M63 and M31 revealed exotic bronzes including a *hu* with a bird-shaped lid and human feet. Besides the stunning *dings* and other bronzes there are a large number of jades of the highest class. Among the most spectacular of these are sets used as facial coverings during burials and as ornaments. Body ornaments consisted of *huangs* (arch-shaped ornaments) and beads; the longer they were, the higher the wearer's status.

The collections are so varied that it's worth spending time admiring the workmanship and their whimsical forms. A bronze worth special mention was found in the Jin cemetery site at Shangguo in Wenxi, a miniature carriage or chariot box with a hinged cover. Rectangular and decorated on top and sides with birds, lions, monkeys and tigers, it has six wheels. At the door stands a guardian or slave with his left foot amputated for having committed a serious crime; his job was to guard the royal zoo.

Jade disc
with dragon
design,
Western Zhou
dynasty

Dazzling bronzes from the Jin tombs of the Spring and Autumn period should not be missed, as the quality is astounding. Many were probably produced at the large foundry site at Houma, where refined, complex bronzes have been found along with the clay moulds and models used to produce them. Among these are a *ding* with openwork interlace designs, a bird-shaped *zun* with a tiger handle, and a set of bells with handles in the shape of creatures with wings and claws like Central Asian griffins – illustrating the outside influences on this local industry. Also found at several sites around Houma were tablets of jade and stone with brush-written red-ink inscriptions recording rituals of covenant and curses buried in sacrificial pits. From the Warring States period are bronzes including a *hu* with scenes of people picking mulberries, and a highly decorated ox with a man springing from its back holding a circular plate stand.

Collections of stone carving also stand out and cover more than 2,000 years from the Western Han dynasty onwards. Among the highlights is the Han dynasty crouching tiger from Yuncheng and the finely modelled stone coffin found in the tomb of Emperor Shaozu of the Song dynasty. Composed of hundreds of pieces, the coffin provides a rare insight into the architecture of the Northern Wei period. Another jewel is the marble outer coffin from the 1,400-year-old tomb of Yu Hong of the Sui dynasty (uncovered in Taiyuan) with exquisite relief carvings of people with European traits such as straight noses and deep-set eyes. Evidence points to Yu Hong having been of European origin (his DNA has been analyzed). He probably married a local woman and became leader of the Central Asian people who settled here at that time. He belongs to one of the oldest known genetic groups from western Eurasia.

The richness of Buddhist statues from the province is brought home not only by those on display but also by a diagram listing and illustrating those which have been lost to leading overseas museums. Shanxi is famous for it numerous temples, and of course for the Han dynasty Buddhist caves at Yungang. At the museum there is a wide range of examples dating from the Northern dynasties to the Tang and found at sites in Qinxian and elsewhere. Among the beauties on display is a white-marble head of Buddha Sakyamuni from the sixth century found in Huata in Taiyuan.

The collections of pottery are equally noteworthy, from the early Yangshao Cultures, to the dancing figures of the Northern Qi, to the amazing brick carvings illustrating festive performances and figures of eight immortals from the Jin period tombs of southern Shanxi. The most distinctive pieces of porcelain are those made in the north. From the Song onwards, Shanxi entered a golden age of porcelain-making with numerous kilns all over the province characterized by superb workmanship.

The gallery displaying a selection of the thousands of paintings and calligraphy scrolls housed in the museum dating from the Yuan to the Qing dynasties should not be missed, nor should that devoted to ancient currency. There's so much to see that you won't be able to take it all in on one visit.

lief carving on
ite marble,
dynasty

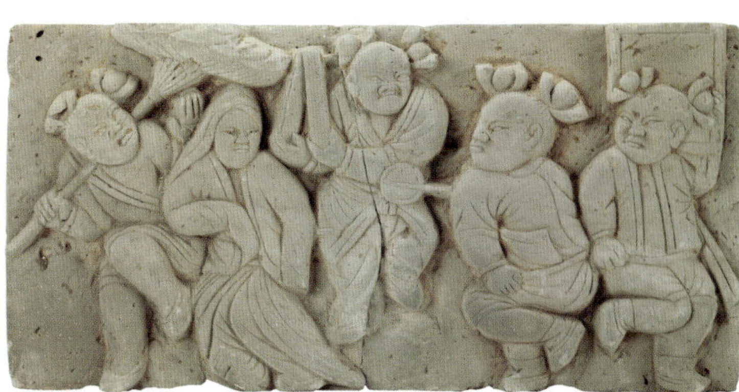

CHINESE MUSEUMS ASSOCIATION GUIDE

BEIJING AND THE NORTH

THE NORTHEAST

SHANGHAI AND EAST CHINA

THE YANGTZE

THE SOUTH

THE SILK ROAD AND THE NORTHWEST

TIBET

HONG KONG, MACAO, TAIWAN

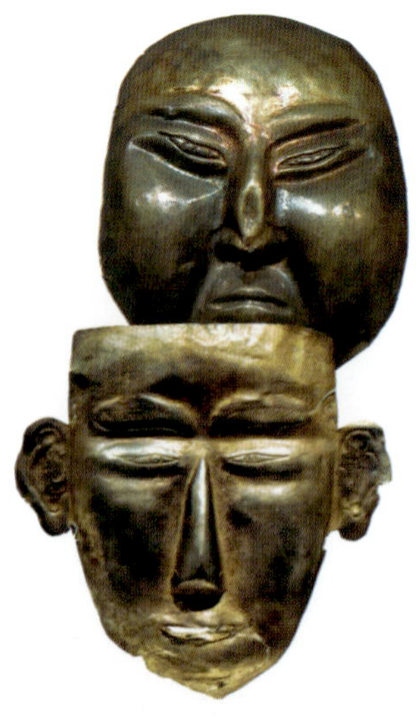

东北

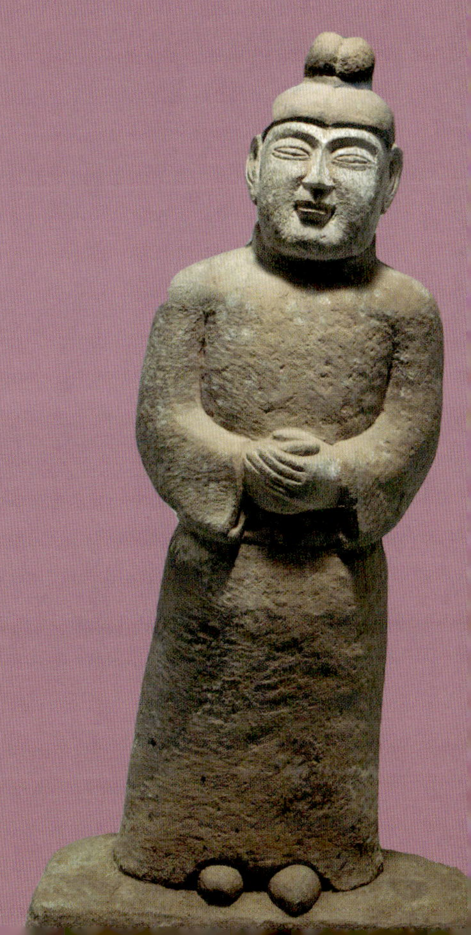

66

Aihui History Museum

瑷珲历史陈列馆 *Aihui lishi chenlieguan*

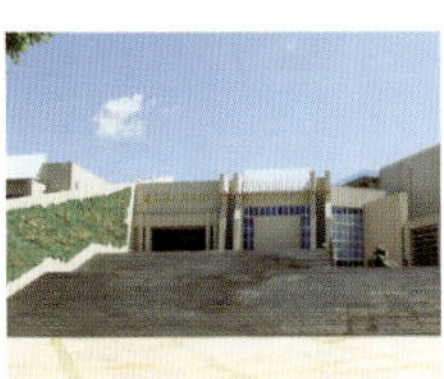

Aihui Town, Heihe, Heilongjiang
黑龙江省黑河市爱辉镇
Tel: (0456)8211007-8013
Open: 9.00–14.00 except Mon
www.aihuihistorymuseum.com
Gift shop / restaurant

The Aihui History Museum is the only museum in China that comprehensively displays the history of the relationship between the eastern parts of China and Russia.

Built in 1975, the museum was expanded and re-opened in 2002, and again in 2011. The displays resonate with patriotic education and show that the Heilongjiang River and its watershed is the heartland of the many ethnic groups in northern China.

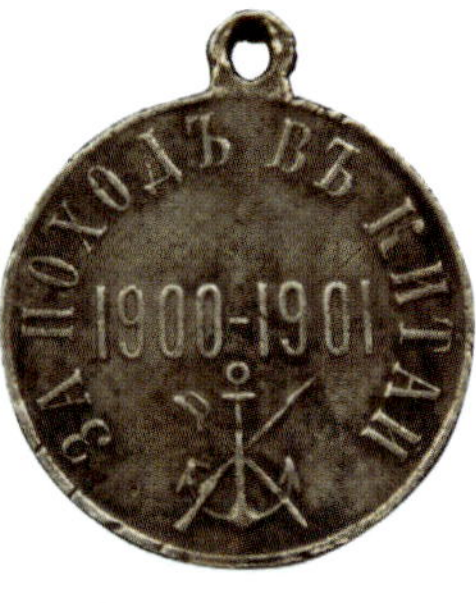
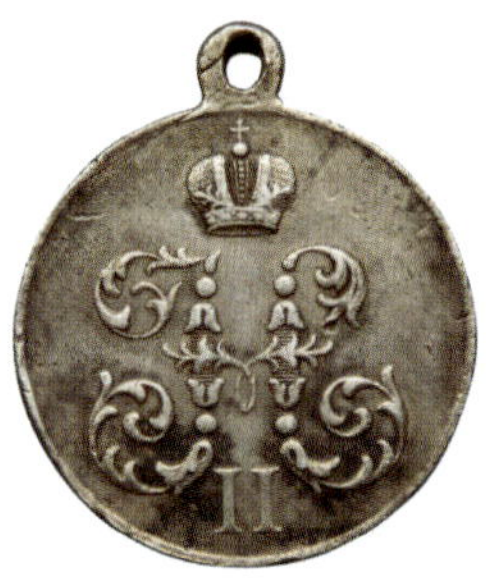

The Eight-Power Allied Forces invaded China in 1900. After the war, the eight countries cast medals and awarded them to their soldiers who served in China. This was a silver medal awarded by Russia

But by the middle of the 17th century, the Russian Cossacks had invaded the area. In 1683 the Qing Emperor Kangxi ordered the construction of Aihui City as the centre of resistance to the Russians, and the garrison town for the Heilongjiang Military Governor and deputy administrator. After the two Yakesa campaigns between 1685 and 1687, the Qing administration and the Russia government signed the Treaty of Nerchinsk, which clearly stated that the region on the south of the Stanovoy Range, as far as the eastern coast, including the island of Sakhalin, belongs to China.

However, with the decline in Chinese imperial power over the next century, the Qing administration in 1858 was forced to sign the Treaty of Aihui, ratified in 1860 at the Convention of Peking between China and Russia, which surrendered to Russia the territory on the south of the Stanovoy Range, to the north of the Heilongjiang River, and to the east of the Ussuri River, including the island of Sakhalin, altogether over one million square kilometers. In 1900, Russia sent troops to Northeast China on the ground of protecting the railway, and the Russian troops perpetrated the Blagoveshchensk Massacre and Massacre in Sixty-Four Villages East of the River, drowning unarmed civilians in the Heilongjiang River, shooting and stabbing the women and children to death. The Russian invaders captured and burned Aihui, an ancient city with a history of more than 300 years.

Harbin Architectural Museum

哈尔滨市建筑艺术馆 *Haerbinshi jianzhu yishuguan*

67

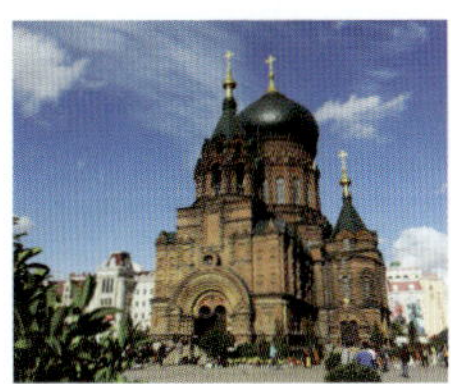

88 Toulong Street, Daoli District, Harbin, Heilongjiang
黑龙江省哈尔滨市道里区透笼街88号
Tel: (0451) 8468 4170
Open: 8.30–17.00
www.sofia.com.cn

The museum is situated inside the impressive and unmistakable former Orthodox Church of St. Sophia, constructed from 1923 to 1935 on the site of an earlier church built in 1907. Located in the heart of Harbin's historic district, this institution forms the centrepiece of the city's world-renowned architectural ensemble, largely designed and constructed by the Russians in the early twentieth century. The museum's inception formed an integral part of the regeneration of Harbin's architectural heritage by the Municipality in the 1990s and included the complete renovation of St. Sophia itself, which had been used as a warehouse for many years. Exhibits include audio-visual displays of the city's architectural history, which boasts a rich and diverse character influenced heavily by Art Nouveau.

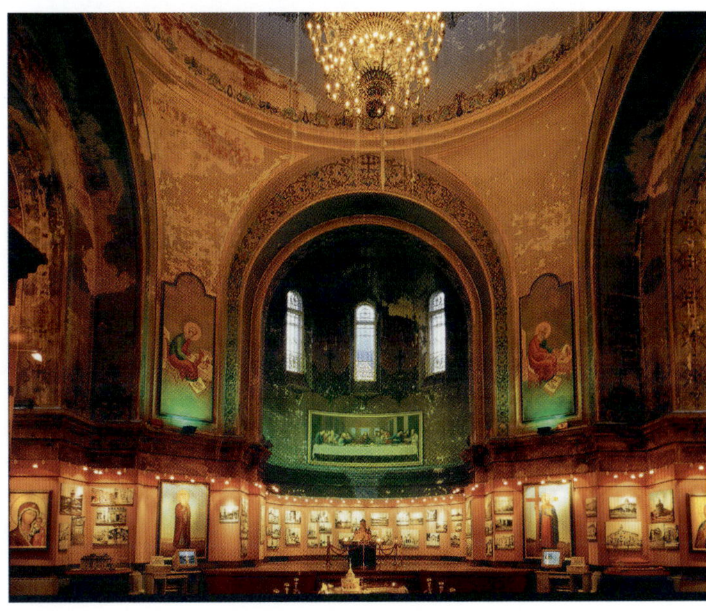

Church of
St. Sophia, interior

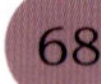

Heilongjiang Provincial Museum

黑龙江省博物馆 *Heilongjiangsheng bowuguan*

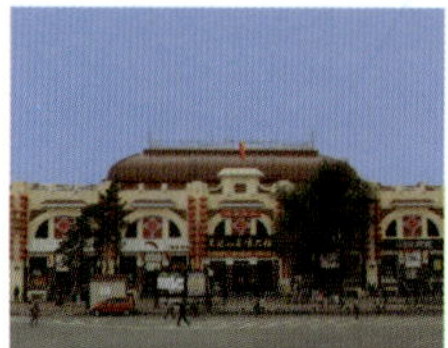

50 Hongjun Street, Harbin, Heilongjiang
黑龙江省哈尔滨市红军街50号
Tel: (0451) 5364 4151
Open: 9.00–16.00 except Mon, summer;
    9.00–17.00 except Mon, winter

The museum is housed in the old 'Moscow Emporium', built in 1904 near the centre of Harbin. The site is one of the large open civic spaces that form a key component of the city's original urban plan as laid out by the Russians at the turn of

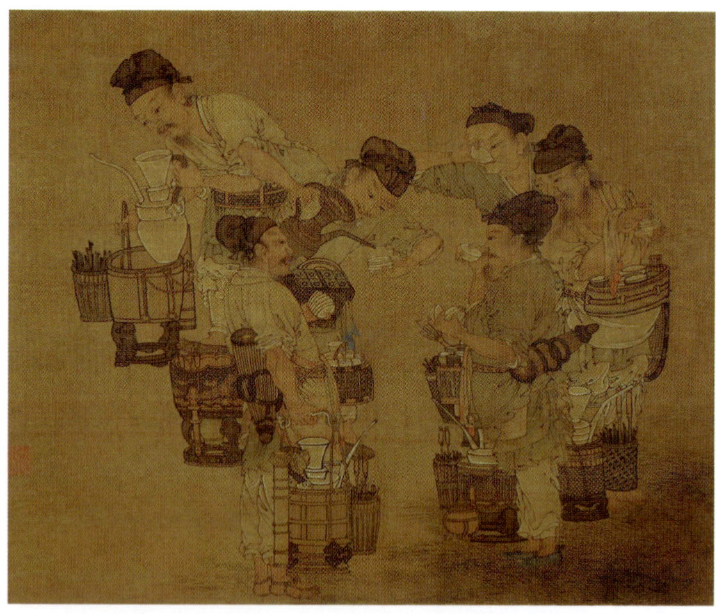

Painting,
Song dynasty

the early twentieth century. The building became a museum in 1922 and officially the Heilongjiang Provincial Museum in 1954.

The uninspiring collection numbers over 113,441 objects including stuffed animals and dinosaur fossils, and there is an aquarium in the basement. Perhaps of greatest interest is the archaeological and ethnographic material displayed upstairs, including silks and jade from the Jin dynasty (1115–1234), which had its first capital

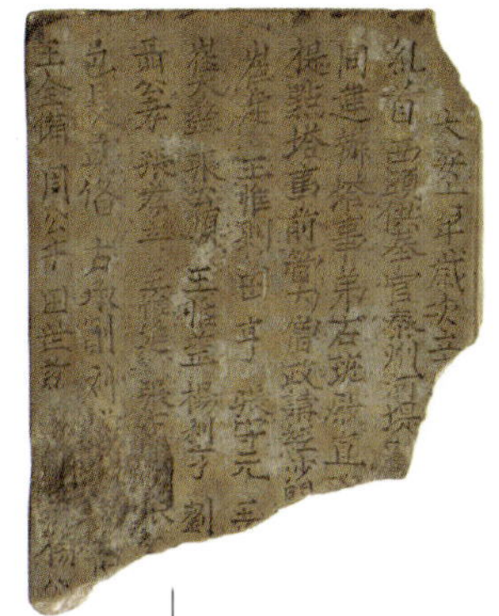

Stone carvings,
Liao dynasty

just outside of Harbin, as well as textiles and artefacts from the Hezhe minority of Heilongjiang. Among highlights of the several thousand historical documents are the 'Painting of Silk Weaving' and a historical map of the west of China from the Qing dynasty. English signage is sparse.

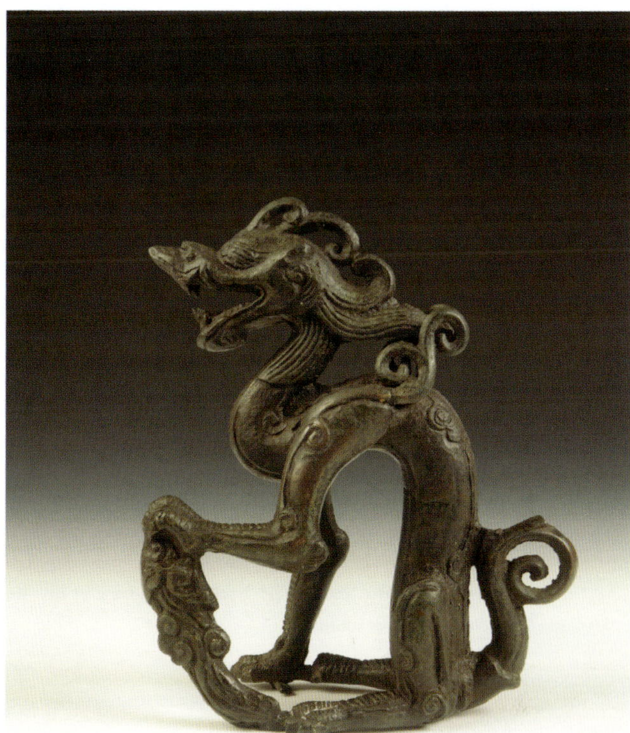

Bronze dragon,
Jin dynasty

69

Japanese Germ Warfare Museum Unit 731

侵华日军第731部队罪证陈列馆 *Qinhua rijun diqisanyaobudui zuizheng chenlieguan*

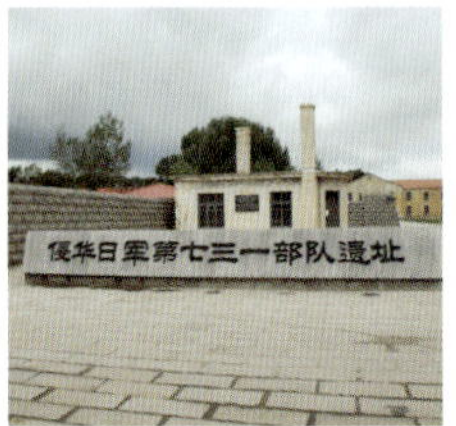

47 Xinjiang Street, Pingfang District, Harbin, Heilongjiang
黑龙江省哈尔滨市平房区新疆大街47号
Tel:(0451) 8710 8731
Open: 9.00–11.00 & 13.00–15.30 except Mon
www.731museum.org.cn
Bookshop / café

This infamous establishment, Unit 731, located in the village of Pingfang, 30 km from central Harbin, was where Japan conducted extensive research and testing of biological warfare agents and established the biological warfare command during World War II. Between 1939 and 1945, the Japanese performed unspeakably horrific acts on mainly Chinese prisoners of war and civilians but also on Soviet, Korean, British and Mongolian prisoners. More than 3,000 souls perished as victims of grisly experiments including vivisection. These people, whom the Japanese referred to as 'logs', were injected with viruses and diseases, left out in the cold to freeze, cut open and dissected – and on and on. There is a long list of unimaginable acts of barbarity.

Following Japan's defeat in 1945, the site was bombed by the Japanese and remaining prisoners killed in an effort to hide what went on there. Today, only a few original structures survive, all of which are incorporated into the museum, which remains a pertinent reminder of the most gruesome aspects of the Japanese occupation of China during World War II.

The museum itself is located in Unit 731's only fully intact structure, the former main office. Actual historical artefacts are sparse but there are photographs and tableaux with wax figures illustrating the site's gruesome past. At the end of the tour, and most affecting, is a video showing former Japanese soldiers, now repentant, speaking bluntly about their work here and the events that took place. The video includes English subtitles.

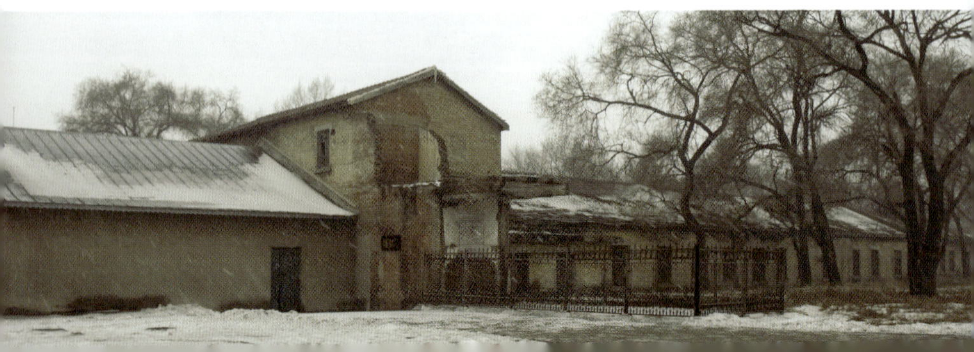

Northeast China Revolutionary Martyrs Memorial Hall

70

东北烈士纪念馆 *Dongbei lieshi jinianguan*

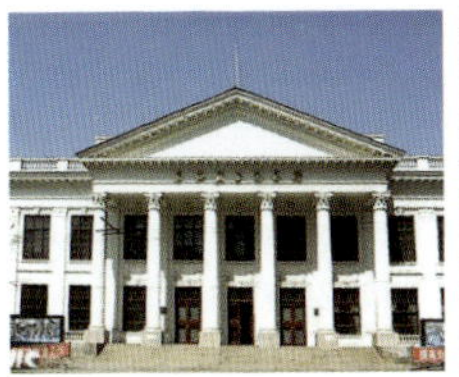

241 Yiman Street, Nangang District, Harbin, Heilongjiang
黑龙江省哈尔滨市南岗区一曼街241号
Tel: (0451) 5364 3712
Open: 9.00–16.30 except Mon, last entry 16.00

In 1931 Japan began its aggression against China by invading China's northeast provinces and establishing a puppet state called Manchukuo. However Chinese guerrillas continued to fight back against the invaders. This museum commemorates those who gave their lives in this struggle.

Construction of the building which now houses the museum was begun in 1928, to a design by the Russian Ridanov, in a neo-classical European style with 6 huge and impressive Corinthian columns. Completed in 1931, its original purpose, as a library, was short lived since in 1933 it was taken over by the Harbin Police Department, part of the Japanese puppet government.

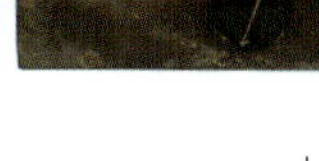

Transceiver used in the war time

Countless communist party members and other patriots were imprisoned in this building. One of the most revered is Zhao Yiman. Born in Sichuan, she joined the communist party in 1926 and studied in Moscow. After Japan's invasion of the North East she was sent there to engage in guerrilla warfare. She was captured by the Japanese in 1936, tortured and executed.

After the end of the war with Japan in 1945, the building was designated as a memorial to the revolutionary martyrs who had perished during the war with Japan and in the subsequent War of Liberation (China's civil war). It was opened to the public in 1948. The documents and objects illustrating this tragic history cover two main themes. Firstly it highlights the courage and sacrifice of the martyrs themselves including Zhao Yiman, Yang Jingyu, Zhao Shangzhi, Li Zhaolin and others. Secondly it lays bare the savage cruelty of the puppet police force in Harbin.

As it is a memorial hall, the exhibits have a strong didactic flavour. Local school children visit the museum to ensure that the new generation does not forget the sacrifices that were made. It is also an important site for Chinese who engage in Red Tourism.

American POW Memorial Museum – Mukden Prison Camp

沈阳二战盟军战俘营旧址纪念馆

Shenyang erzhan mengjun zhanfuying jiuzhi jinianguan

71

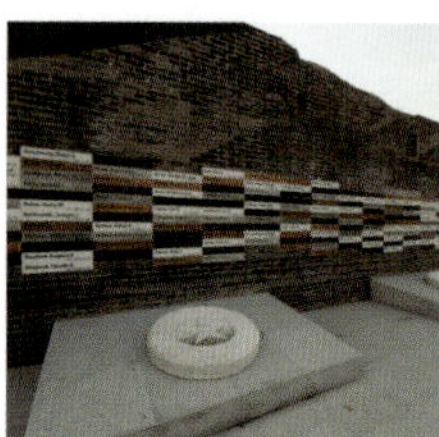

30-3 Ditan Street, Dadong District, Shenyang, Liaoning
辽宁省沈阳市大东区地坛街30-3号
Tel: (024) 8859 0530
Open: 9.00–16.00 except Mon, last entry 15.00, summer;
9.00–17.00 except Mon, last entry 16.00, winter
Bookshop

As many as 1,500 allied troops – mainly Americans and British – were held at any one time as slave labourers at Mukden Camp from 1942 to 1945. The total number throughout the war totalled 2,027, many of whom had survived the Battles of Bataan and Corregidor, as well as the infamous 'Bataan Death March'. They were then shipped by the Japanese to China in the holds of 'Hell Ships', named for the horrendous conditions in which the prisoners were kept. At first they were taken to a camp in Shenyang, then a few months later moved to this site, about 3km away, which became a Japanese showcase camp as it had barracks made of bricks. When

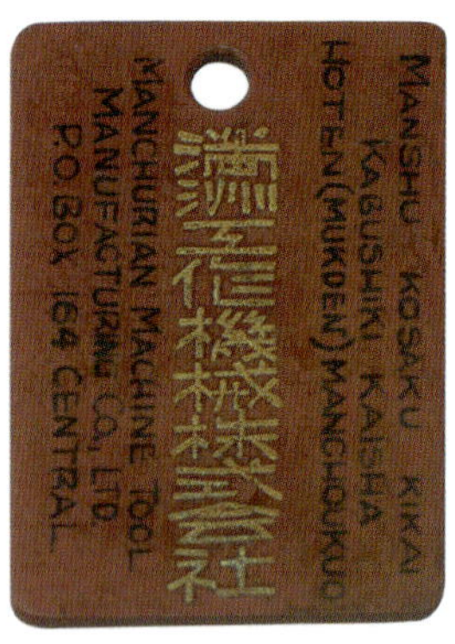

Identification tag

visitors and UN inspectors came, the prisoners' conditions were temporarily improved, in a masquerade of adherence to the Geneva Convention. In fact, the men were used as slaves at a heavy machinery plant (which they continuously sabotaged), a tannery, a canvas-weaving factory and other work places. While in detention they were routinely beaten, tortured and starved. Between November 1942 and March 1943 alone – the first winter at Mukden Camp – 206 prisoners of war died.

Perhaps most egregiously, many have also testified that they were used as guinea pigs for medical and germ warfare experiments.

Displays include photos, uniforms, dog tags, letters and other documentation, as well as DVDs of ex-prisoners recounting their experiences here. The museum continues to actively seek contact with and donations from survivors and their families.

72

Chinese Memorial Hall of the War to Resist US Aggression and Aid Korea

抗美援朝纪念馆

Kangmeiyuanchao jinianguan

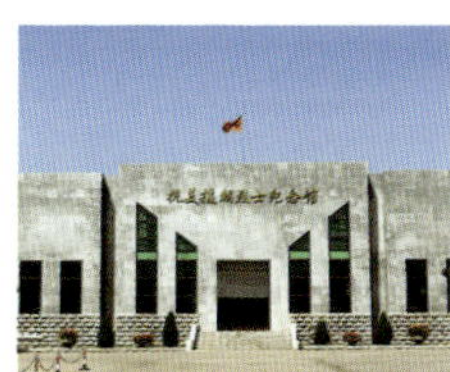

7 Shanshang Street, Zhenxing District, Dandong, Liaoning
辽宁省丹东市振兴区山上街7号
Tel: (0415) 3876 318
Open: 9.00–16.00 except Mon
www.kmycjng.com
Gift shop / bookshop

In China, the Korean War (1950–53) is referred to as the War to Resist US Aggression and Aid Korea. In June 1950, shortly after the establishment of the People's Republic, when U.S. troops got close to the Chinese border, China entered the war. The Chinese People's Volunteer Army crossed the border to support the north. In the war approximately 400,000 Chinese troops died and a similar number were wounded.

Appropriately the memorial hall is in Dandong, Liaoning Province, on a hill just across the Yalu River from North Korea. In its current form it was opened to the public in 1993. In front of the hall there is a 53 metre high monument to the war, inscribed with Deng Xiaoping's handwriting.

The memorial hall itself is enormous. Its centrepiece is a room with statues of Mao Zedong and Peng Dehuai, the commander of the People's Volunteer Army. The exhibitions cover all aspects of the war with 600 photographs and 700 objects from the period. Happily, signage includes clear English. Not to be missed is the Panorama Gallery, a diorama set against a panoramic painting depicting the Battle on the Qingchuan River Bank which is 132 metres in circumference and 16 metres in height!

Outside the hall in the open air is a treat for those who are interested in the weapons of the period. The fascinating collection from the war includes J6 and MiG-15 fighters, Tu-2 bombers, Soviet Katyusha rocket launchers, Soviet T34 tanks, 122 mm howitzers and 100 mm anti-aircraft guns.

This is a memorial hall designed to tell a political story. Some foreign visitors from the U.S. have felt uneasy about the strong message it conveys. But it is useful for an understanding of the Chinese point of view.

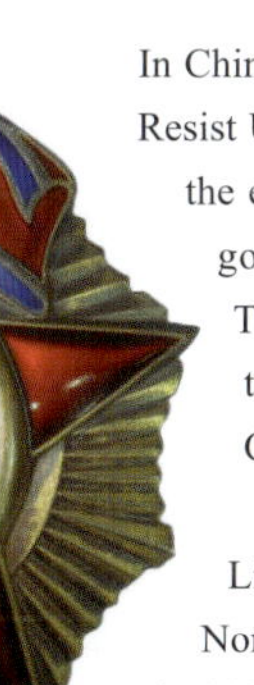

The medal of the Chinese People's Volunteer Army

Inscribed shell case, gift from the North Korean army to the Chinese People's Volunteer Army

73

Liaoning Provincial Museum

辽宁省博物馆 *Liaoningsheng bowuguan*

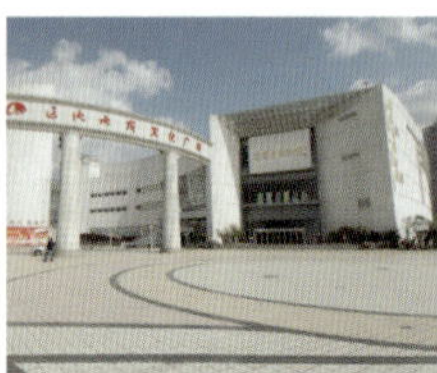

363 Shifu Road, Shenhe District, Shenyang, Liaoning
辽宁省沈阳市沈河区市府大路363号
Tel: (024) 2274 1193
Open: 9.00–17.00 except Mon
English guidebook & audio guide

The Liaoning Provincial Museum was one of only three major 'national museums' planned by the Republican government between the end of the war in 1945 and the establishment of the People's Republic in 1949 – the others being the Palace Museum and the Nanjing Museum. It was originally called the Dongbei Museum (the Northeast Museum).

The original collections were based on the art and archaeology of the northeast. The archaeological collections have been hugely expanded by nearly fifty years of excavation in the region. However, many of the finest of the other treasures come from the old imperial collections housed in the Forbidden City – in common with the Palace Museum in the Forbidden City, which houses the parts of the original collection that never left Beijing, and the Nanjing Museum and the National Museum in Taipei. However, unlike Nanjing and Taipei, which owe their collections to the wanderings, and eventual flight and defeat of Chiang Kai-shek and the Nationalist army, the story of the Liaoning collection goes back earlier to the Reign of Puyi, the last Qing

A Tang dynasty painting, Court Ladies Adorning their Hair with Flowers

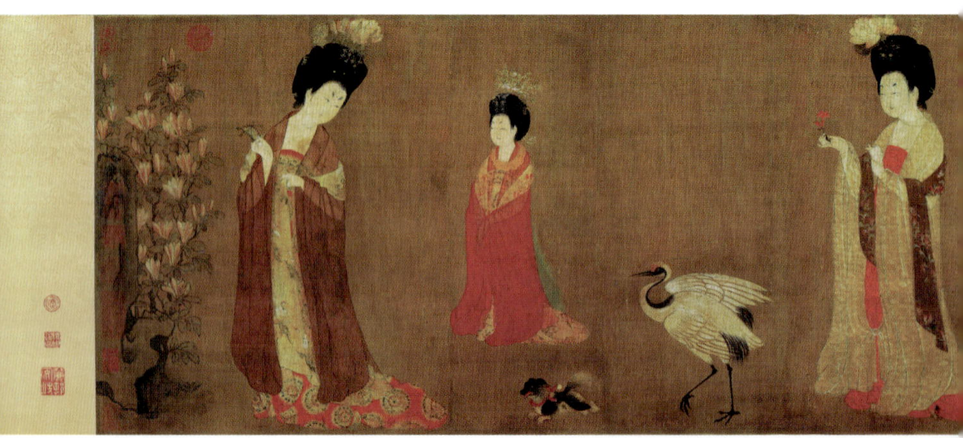

Emperor. On the founding of the Republic in 1911, Puyi was allowed to live on in the Forbidden City – until his eventual expulsion in 1924, after which he first lived in Tianjin and eventually moved to the northeast where in 1932 he became the puppet Emperor of the Japan-established Manchukuo. He probably started selling works from the collection shortly after 1911, and, on his final departure from Beijing, he took with him a number of important works to sell, or to barter with the Japanese. These treasures had been gradually dispersed throughout Manchuria by 1949, and it is to the huge credit of the Liaoning Museum that so many were tracked down and have come to be housed in Shenyang. Only some of these had been fully documented, and it is possible that yet more may still come to light. Even as they stand, they represent one of the finest collections of Tang and Song calligraphy and painting in the world, making the collection of this museum one of the key destinations for the visitor to China.

The museum was renamed the Liaoning Provincial Museum in 1959. In 2004, a new three-storey 16,000 sq m purpose-built museum was opened to house the collections. It is an imposing building constructed to international museum standards, which provides a base not only for exhibition and storage but also as a centre for the continuing province-wide programme of excavation.

The centre of the archaeological exhibit is a permanent display of Liaoning's ancient history, in particular of the distinctive regional cultures found along the Daling

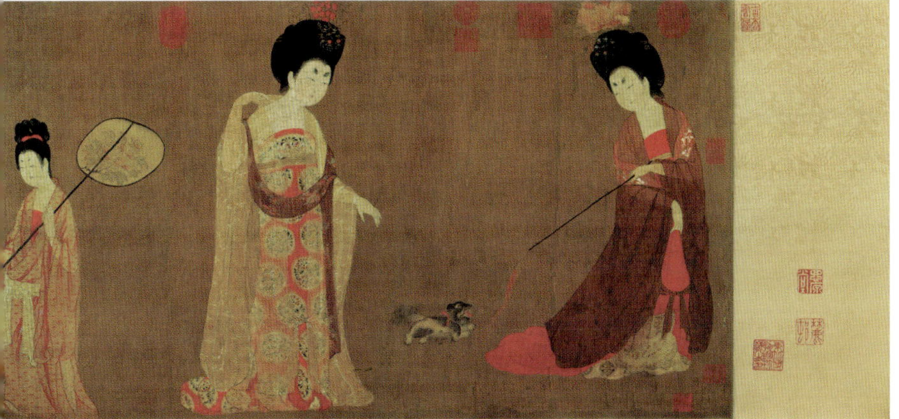

River and the Liao River, and along the shores of the Yellow and the Bohai seas. Other galleries, radiating off a central well area near the entrance to the building, show well-displayed and instructively arranged collections of historical artefacts, and of the major Liaoning archaeological sites. There are impressive tableaux of the life of the early peoples of the province, and a gallery devoted to Chinese history. The most important

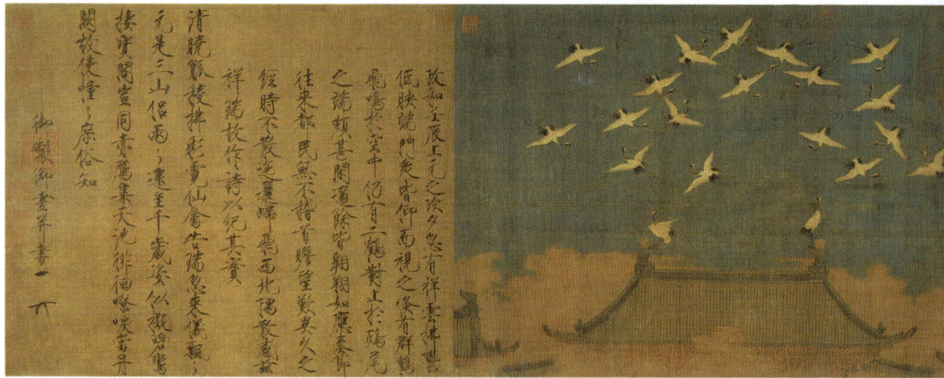

A Song dynasty painting, *Auspicious Cranes*

and impressive of the excavated objects are the bronzes from the sites at Machanggou, Beidong and Shanwanzi, Kazuo County.

The calligraphy collection contains masterpieces such as a Tang dynasty copy of a work by Wang Xizhi, and works by Ouyang Xun and Zhang Xu, amongst many others. The painting collection contains works by Zhou Fang, Dong Yuan and the Song dynasty Emperor, Huizong.

There is a spectacular collection of tapestry and embroidery beginning with a Five Dynasties embroidered Buddhist sutra, and examples of *kesi* work from the Northern Song, the Southern Song and the Ming dynasties. The most impressive of the Northern Song examples come from the private collection of Zhang Xueliang, one of the most powerful of the warlords who carved little kingdoms for themselves in the northeast during the Republican and the Civil War periods.

There is also a fine exhibition of the history and achievement of Liao ware ceramics, and a collection of maps and topographical studies including very rare works by Xu Lun and the Jesuit priest, Matteo Ricci.

Lüshun Museum

旅顺博物馆 *Lüshun bowuguan*

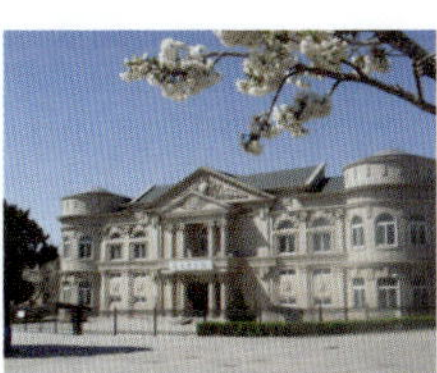

42 Liening Street, Lüshunkou District, Dalian, Liaoning
辽宁省大连市旅顺口区列宁街42号
Tel: (0411) 8638 2378
Open: 9.00–16.00 except Mon
www.lvshunmuseum.org
Gift shop / bookshop

The deep-water port of Lüshun, in what is today called Dalian, is located strategically at the southern point of Liaodong Peninsula in Liaoning Province and was much fought over by the Great Powers. The port along with peninsula were seized by Japan during Sino-Japanese War (1894–95). Later Russia took control of the port and linked it to Harbin through a railway line. After Russia was defeated by Japan during the Russo-Japanese war (1904–05) Japan regained control of the port and ruled it for the next 40 years. At the end World War II, the Soviet's liberated North East China from the Japanese. China, a strong ally of the Soviet Union at that time provided them with a lease to the Lüshun Port and Dalian which lasted until 1955 when China took it back.

The museum has had many incarnations and is one of China's earliest museums. It was built in 1915 in European style during the Japanese colonial period to exhibit Mongolian products and in 1918 it was rebuilt as a museum hall. In 2001 it was expanded to provide space for its growing collection. Since the museum reverted to Chinese control in 1951, decades of archaeological excavations and extensive collecting has expanded its holdings to more than 60,000 objects and 200,000 archival documents.

The scope is correspondingly broad, ranging from natural history specimens to Japanese calligraphy, Japanese and Korean ceramics and archaeological finds from Dalian. Among the highlights of the museum are mummies from Xinjiang, part of the collection of Count Ōtani Kōzui (1876–1948), a Japanese Buddhist priest who financed three archaeological expeditions between 1902–14 to Buddhist sites in Central Asia. Today many of his other finds are spread between several countries and various museums, including The National Museum of China in Beijing and in libraries and university collections in China. The Lüshun Museum once held a significant number of Dunhuang manuscripts but today only a handful is left, since the majority have been transferred to the National Library of China.

September 18 History Museum

75

"九·一八" 历史博物馆 *Jiuyiba lishi bowuguan*

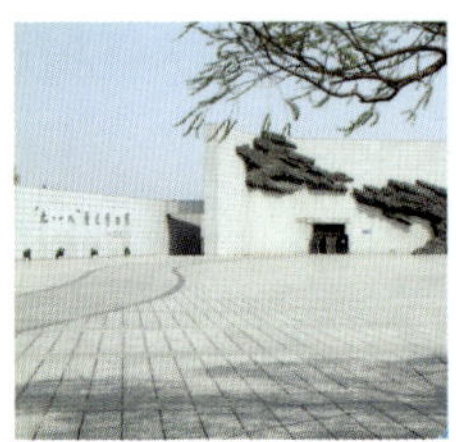

46 Wanghua South Street, Dadong District, Shenyang, Liaoning
辽宁省沈阳市大东区望花南街46号
Open: 9.00–17.00 except Mon, last entry 16.00, summer;
9.00–16.30 except Mon, last entry 15.30, winter
Gift and bookshop / museum guide in English

This memorial museum is built on the actual site of the September 18th Incident, known in the West as the Manchurian Incident, or the Mukden Incident (Mukden being the Manchu name for Shenyang). This date in 1931 marked one of the key events leading to the total Japanese occupation of Manchuria and the foundation of the puppet state of Manchukuo in February 1932.

The Japanese had occupied part of Manchuria since the war of 1894–95, and it was alleged that Chinese forces had carried out a bombing raid on September 18 on a Japanese-operated bridge and railway crossing just north of Shenyang. This gave the Japanese army the excuse to capture Shenyang, to occupy Liaoning, Jilin and Heilongjiang, and to create the puppet state of Manchukuo in 1932.

The date of 18 September 1931, even more than that of the Nanjing Massacre, has come to be regarded as one of the defining moments of modern Chinese history–known to every twenty-first-century Chinese schoolchild. The museum memorializes the brutality of the attack on Shenyang and the savage oppression of the Chinese population of the whole of Manchuria until 1945. Opened in 1999, the museum, set on a huge 31,000 sq m site, is housed in dramatic and unusual buildings resonating with symbolism. The exhibition area shows reconstructions – some life-size, some models – of scenes of destruction and acts of heroism. The total impact is horrifyingly impressive. There are also instruments of torture on display and a life-size reconstruction of a medical team shown dissecting patients (who would have been still alive), and experimenting with bacteriological weapons – with the claim that 2.7 million Chinese soldiers were killed in this way.

Many of the captions are in Chinese, but there is enough English information for the visitor to get the point of this monument to a particularly nasty and brutish war of occupation.

Shenyang Imperial Palace Museum

沈阳故宫博物院 *Shenyang gugong bowuyuan*

76

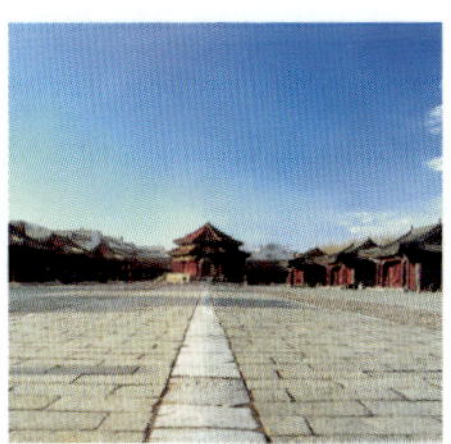

171 Shenyang Road, Shenhe District, Shenyang, Liaoning
辽宁省沈阳市沈河区沈阳路171号
Tel: (024) 2484 3819
Open: 8.30–17.30, last entry 16.45, Apr 15–Oct 15;
      9.00–16.30, last entry 15.45, Nov 16–Apr 14
Bookshop / café / English-speaking guides

The Qing Emperors (1644–1911) were Manchus, tribesmen from the northeast. In 1626, their leader Nurhaci united the tribes against the corrupt rule of the Ming and began to build the Shenyang Imperial Palace from which to rule and administer their realm.

The Manchu were horsemen, who, as a result of years of gripping their stirrups, evolved to grow a second little toe.

The palace was modelled on the Forbidden City in Beijing – partly because it was the imperial palace model to hand, and partly to reflect the growing ambitions of China itself. Partially completed by 1636, it was laid out in three sections and based on Ming style, with colour and decoration subtly altered to reflect Manchu taste. The earliest and most interesting section was the Eastern Wing, a rectangular open space with the Dazheng Hall of the Emperor at the north point and eight pavilions, four ranged on

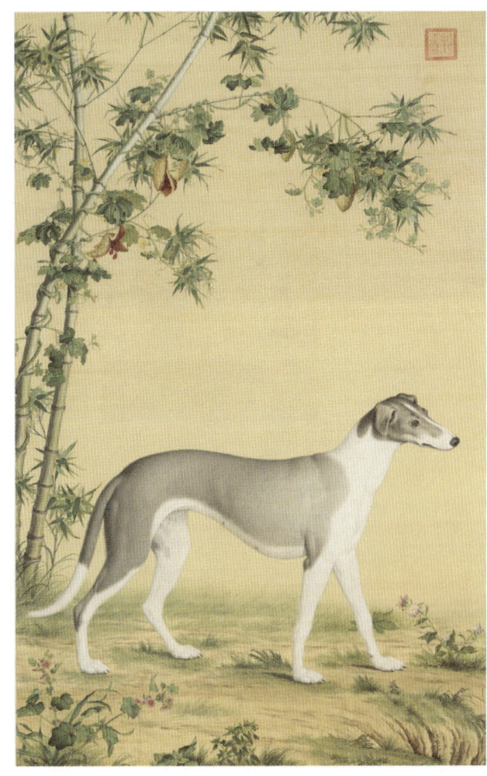

painting by Giuseppe Castiglione, Italian court painter of the Qianlong Emperor.

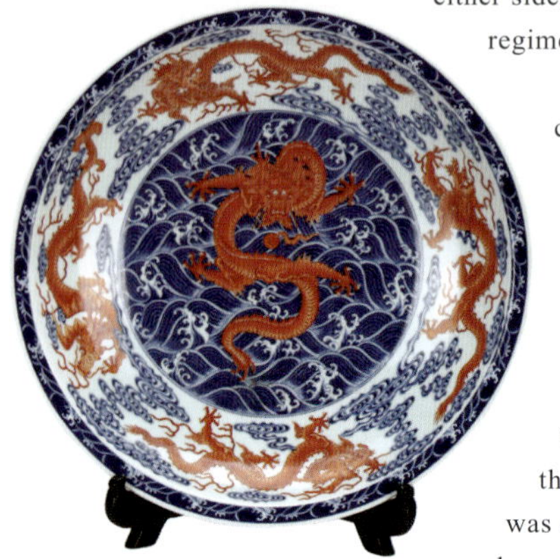

Red dragon
ceramic tray,
Qing dynasty

either side, for his kings – who became his banner men, his elite regiments of fearsome cavalry.

The layout of these pavilions was like a military camp, reflecting the power and structure of Manchu rule. It was from here that the Emperor Shunzhi ordered his troops to sweep across the plains, capture Beijing and overthrow the Ming Empire in 1644.

After the transfer of government to Beijing in 1644, the Shenyang Imperial Palace remained the centre of Manchu power in their homeland, and thereafter both their cultural and their power base. It was embellished and enlarged by Qianlong (1736–1795), and now has 300 halls and covers 60,000 sq m.

Any visitor interested in Chinese history, or in Qing art and architecture, must visit this well-preserved and intact site. It is interesting to see it after a visit to the Forbidden City in Beijing.

Jilin Provincial Museum

77

吉林省博物院 *Jilinsheng bowuyuan*

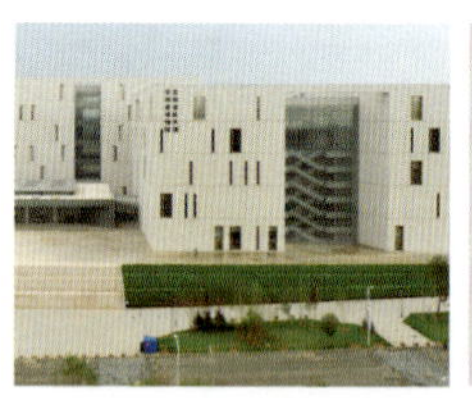

3188 Renmin Street, Changchun, Jilin
吉林省长春市人民大街3188号
Tel: (0431)8891 7353
Open: 9.00–16.00 except Mon, last entry 15.30
www.jlmuseum.org
Gift shop

The site of this museum has moved several times. At one point it was located in the former palace of Puyi, the last emperor of the Qing dynasty, where he lived as the 'puppet emperor of Manchukuo' during the Sino-Japanese War.

The museum is now in modern premises, opened in 2007, and is a combination of the original Jilin Museum and the Jilin Museum of Contemporary and Modern History. The museum houses the largest cultural collection of the province and is responsible for the preservation, conservation and research of its own collections.

Like most provincial museums in China, its collection

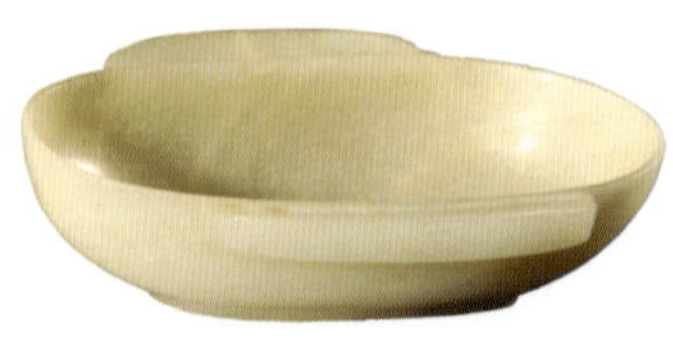

White jade ear cup,
Han dynasty

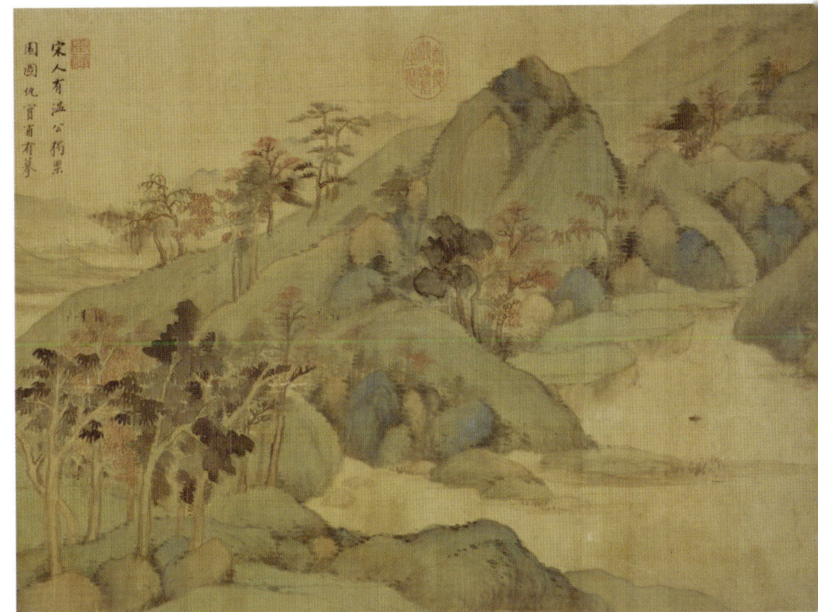

...inting by
...ong Qichang,
...ing dynasty

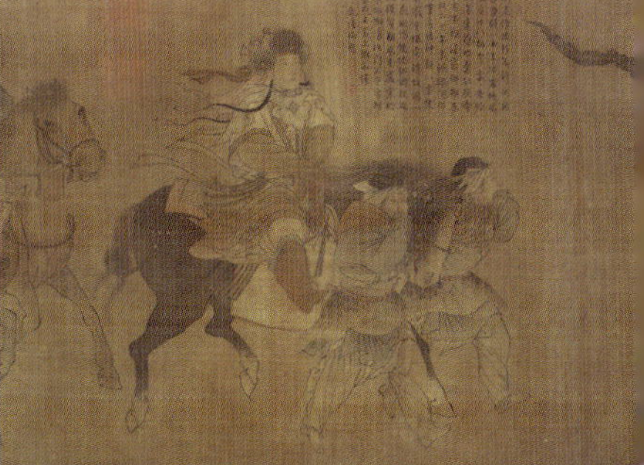

...inting by
...ang Yu,
...en Ji's Return
...Han,
...dynasty

of over 100,00 objects ranges from the Paleolithic to the Qing. The museum prides itself on its calligraphy and paintings collection as well as its artefacts from the Gaogouli, Bohai and Manchu ethnic groups from this region. Its prize objects include a white jade ear cup (wine vessel) from Han dynasty Goguryeo and an octagonal bronze mirror engraved with Khitan scripts from the Liao and Jin Dynasty. Other treasures include *Wen Ji's Return to Han* which is one of the few surviving paintings from the Jin Dynasty and *Hundred Flowers* by the Southern Song Dynasty painter, Yang Jieyu, one of China's earliest works by a female painter.

Finally, if you have a special interest or curiosity about Puyi, China's last emperor, while in Changchun you can visit The Museum of the Imperial Palace of the Manchu State mentioned above. This walled complex, designed as a miniature Forbidden City, consisting of several buildings, gardens, swimming pool, tennis court and even a race track, was the living quarters of the emperor and his family as well as the offices of state during the period of the Manchukuo government.

CHINESE MUSEUMS ASSOCIATION GUIDE

BEIJING AND THE NORTH

THE NORTHEAST

SHANGHAI AND EAST CHINA

THE YANGTZE

THE SOUTH

THE SILK ROAD AND THE NORTHWEST

TIBET

HONG KONG, MACAO, TAIWAN

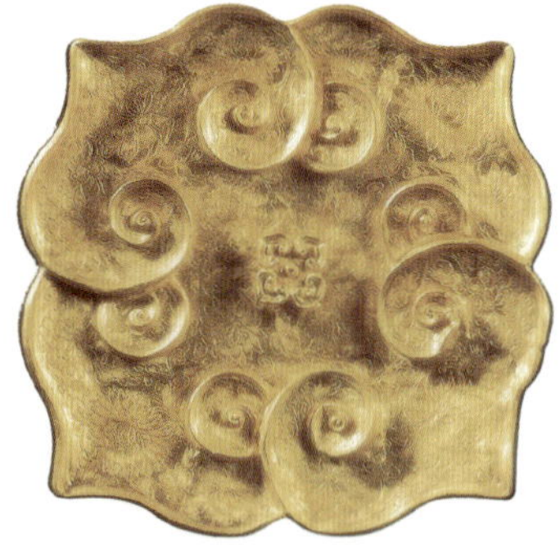

上海与华东

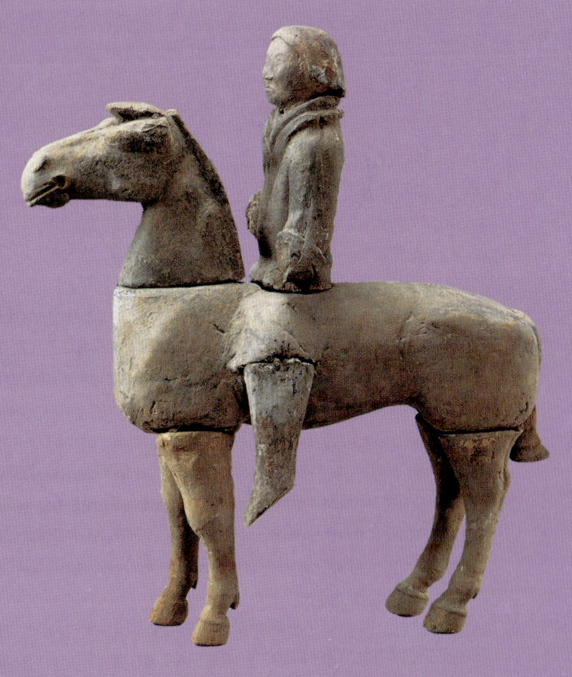

78

China Art Museum

中华艺术宫 *Zhonghua yishugong*

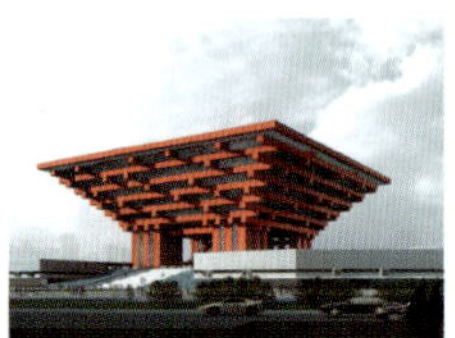

205 Shangnan Road, Pudong District, Shanghai
上海市浦东新区上南路205号
Tel: (021) 2025 2018
Open: 9.00–17.00 except Mon, last entry 16.00
www.sh-artmuseum.org.cn

In October 2012 the Shanghai Art Museum was moved from Nanjing Road West across the river to the site of Shanghai Expo 2010, and re-named the China Art Museum. The old museum had been founded in 1956 and housed in the old Shanghai Race Club building, an imposing structure built of granite with a tinge of purple and an impressive clock tower. It overlooked People's Park and People's Square, adjacent to City Hall, the Opera House and the Shanghai Museum. It was an exhibition centre, with no permanent collection, placing particular emphasis on contemporary and international art, thus for the next fifty years remedying the absence of these in the more traditional museums of China. In 1996 it became the first home of the Shanghai Biennale, an event intended to reflect the international, cosmopolitan and creative nature of Shanghai City itself. The Shanghai Art Museum was finally closed in 2013.

The China Art Museum is the cultural legacy of Shanghai Expo 2010, housed in the very distinguished China Pavilion, designed in the shape of a traditional Chinese roof support. Housed in huge galleries, the same size in total as the Museum of Modern Art, New York, it is worth a visit for its top attraction – exhibited at Expo and retained for the new museum, a huge animated mural version of an ancient Chinese scroll *Along the River during Qingming Festival* which gives a detailed and entertaining picture of life during the Song Dynasty (960–1279). It is the length of a football pitch and two stories high, and its animation brings to life figures as they wander across an arched bridge or launch barges into the river.

As with the old Shanghai Art Museum there is no permanent collection, but rather an increasingly ambitious programme of international loans and loan exhibitions from great western museums such as the British Museum, the Rijksmuseum, the Whitney Museum of American Art and the Musée d'Orsay – a programme which aims to bring to Shanghai an increasing knowledge and understanding of western art both historic and modern.

79

China Tobacco Museum

中国烟草博物馆   *Zhongguo yancao bowuguan*

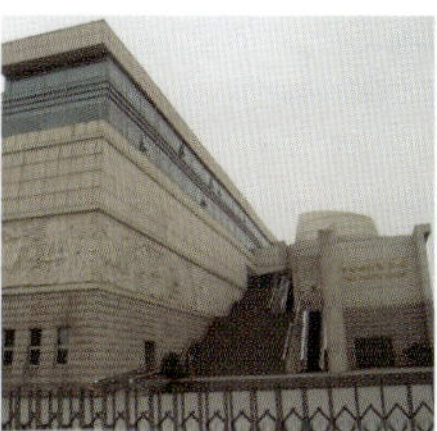

728 Changyang Road, Shanghai
上海市长阳路728号
Tel: (021) 6547 1135
Open: 9.00–16.00 on Tues / Thur / Sat
www.tobaccomuseum.com.cn
English audio guide / gift shop

This is the largest tobacco museum in the world (appropriately enough, as China is the world's largest tobacco producer), housing over 150,000 artefacts tracing the history of tobacco agriculture, industry, economy and trade in China over the past 400 years. The museum is state-owned and situated in a purpose-built modern edifice in the Yangpu District. The collection is divided into eight sections: Development Course of Tobacco, Tobacco Agriculture, Tobacco Industry, Tobacco Economy and Trade, Tobacco Administration, Smoking and Smoking Control, Tobacco Culture and Tobacco Literature.

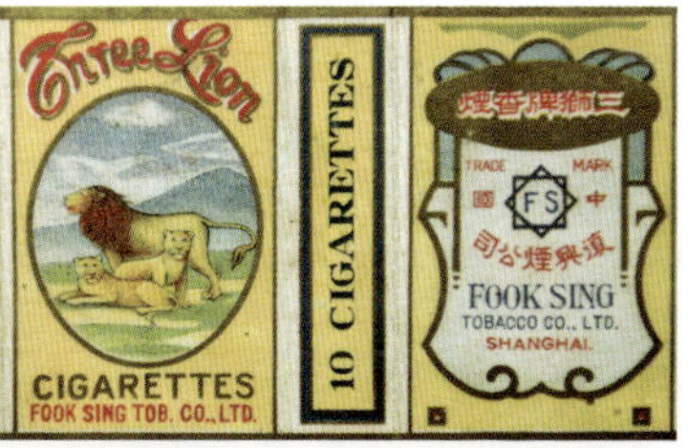

d cigarette packet
bels

Historical information is presented on well-lit panels indicating the route by which tobacco was introduced to China, the rapid development of its influence through the Qing dynasty, the industry's prosperity during the anti-imperialism movement and the subsequent struggle against the imperial tobacco monopoly. There is also documentation on the tobacco workers' movement, with information about the Shanghai Tobacco Trade Union, established in 1921 in the wake of the cigarette workers' anti-imperialism strike of 1919. Smoking-related paraphernalia is also on display, including ornate water pipes from the 1800s, snuff containers, matchboxes and agricultural tools. The collection includes smoking equipment belonging to famous Chinese people, such as an ashtray of Mao Zedong and a cigarette case used by Mao's friend, Madame Soong Ching Ling. The museum also houses tobacco processing machines and several engaging, life-size dioramas of tobacco farmers and cigarette factory workers. The sixth section presents information on the detrimental effects of smoking on health. This is particularly relevant in China, where the death rates due to smoking-related diseases are very high.

Himalayas Art Museum

上海喜马拉雅美术馆 *Shanghai ximalaya meishuguan*

80

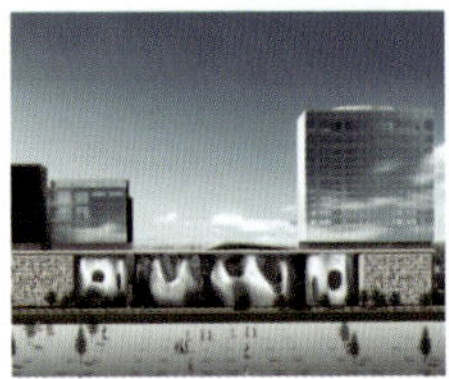

3F, Zone A, 869 Yinghua Road, Shanghai
上海市浦东新区樱花路869号A区3楼
Tel: (021) 5033 9801
Open: 10.00–18.00 Tues–Fri & Sun, last entry 17.30
      10.00–21.30 Sat, last entry 21.00 (free on Wed)
www.himalayasart.cn

Formerly known as the Shanghai Zendai Museum of Modern Art, this museum is on the top floor of an extraordinary building designed by the Japanese superstar architect, Arata Isozaki.

The building, which will also include a shopping mall, hotel and other facilities, is the project of Shanghai property developer and billionaire, Dai Zhikang, whose collection the museum exhibits.

From its inception, this non-profit institution has had an ambitious and energetic mission to bring cutting-edge contemporary art to the attention of the public and to engage them by offering many different activities city-wide as well as internationally.

Focusing on promoting emerging Asian artists and giving them exhibition space, its stated goals also include collaboration with the international contemporary art world and exposing the public to contemporary trends in all sorts of media.

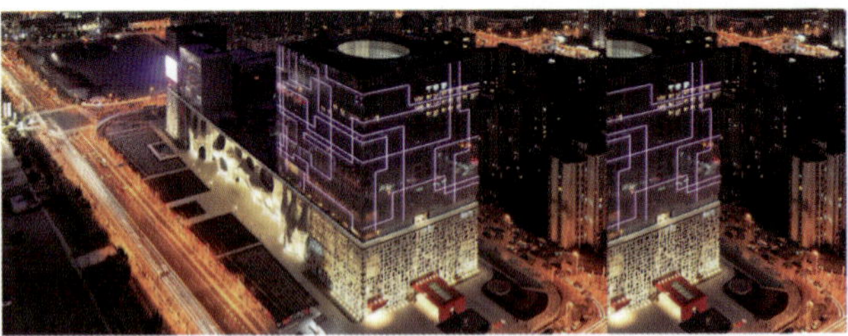

The museum attaches great importance to their outreach efforts and has an energetic education department as well as a library open to the public.

The museum has two branches in addition to the the Pudong location. There is an artist in residence programme associated with their Zhujiajiao location, a picturesque suburb of Shanghai, and another gallery in Wuwei Creative Park in northeast Shanghai.

This is surely one of the most exciting new galleries to open amongst the many emerging in Shanghai at this time.

MoCA Shanghai

81

上海当代艺术馆 *Shanghai dangdai yishuguan*

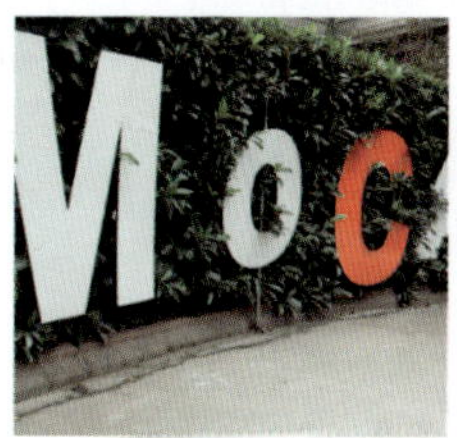

231 Nanjing West Road (People Park), Shanghai
上海市南京西路231号人民公园
Tel: (021) 6327 9900
Open: 10.00–21.30
www.mocashanghai.org
Kids

Set in Shanghai's central park, a stone's throw from the Shanghai Art Museum and close to the Shanghai Museum, is this greenhouse-turned-contemporary art space. The brainchild of Samuel Kung, a Hong Kong jewellery designer, it must have been the most innovative proposal put to Shanghai's officials when they were looking for an alternative use for this largely glass-walled space. Add a sweeping ramp, several enclosed exhibition spaces and a roof-top café and you have an impressive contemporary museum with an income stream attached.

Groundbreaking when it opened in 2005, it was hailed, along with the city's other privately funded contemporary space, the Zendai Museum of Modern Art, as Shanghai's answer to New York's MOMA, or at least a smaller version of it. Hiring Victoria Lu, the funky, energetic founding board member of the Taipei Contemporary Art Museum, as its creative director, launched the museum on its mission to promote Chinese contemporary art and bring quality international contemporary art and design to China. This was achieved with great aplomb, with Ms. Lu hosting a variety of powerful, adventurous shows at the moment when China was positioning itself as a world centre for contemporary art and riding the wave of success set by the establishment of the Shanghai Biennale in 1994.

Ms. Lu has departed – although she still curates the odd show–and adequate funding is now a problem. A re-think of the space has resulted in a smaller café and a new area which will host installations, performance art and lectures by well-known artists and photographers. In this way, it hopes to draw in visitors on a more regular basis. Check local listings for exhibition schedules, special events and lectures.

82

Memorial Hall of First National Congress of Communist Party of China

中国共产党第一次全国代表大会会址纪念馆

Zhongguo gongchandang diyici quanguo daibiaodahui huizhi jinianguan

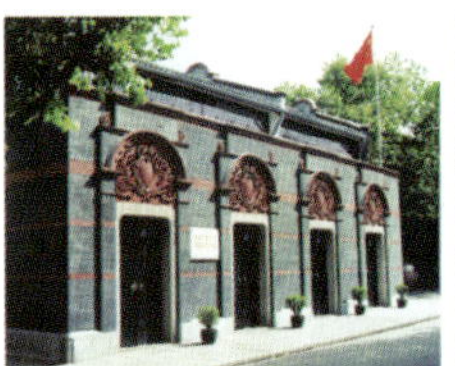

374 Huangpi South Road, Huangpu District, Shanghai
上海市黄浦区黄陂南路374号
Tel: (021)5383 2171–111
Open: 9.00–17.00
www.zgyd1921.com

On July 23, 1921 the Communist Party of China opened its first National Congress in Shanghai at 106 Rue Wantz (today 76 Xingye Road) in what was then the French Concession. Interrupted due to a search by the Concession's police, the congress was completed some days later on a boat on a lake in nearby Zhejiang Province. Representing the only 53 party members at that time were 13 delegates including Mao Zedong, Dong Biwu and Zhang Guotao and two brothers who owned the house. Also attending were two non-voting representatives from the Comintern, a Dutchman and a Russian.

The congress adopted the party's strategy and guidelines, and elected its Central Bureau, with Chen Duxiu as its first Secretary General, even though he was unable to attend the congress. This was an historic event that marked the official birth of the Party that went on to become the nation's ruling party with over 80 million members today.

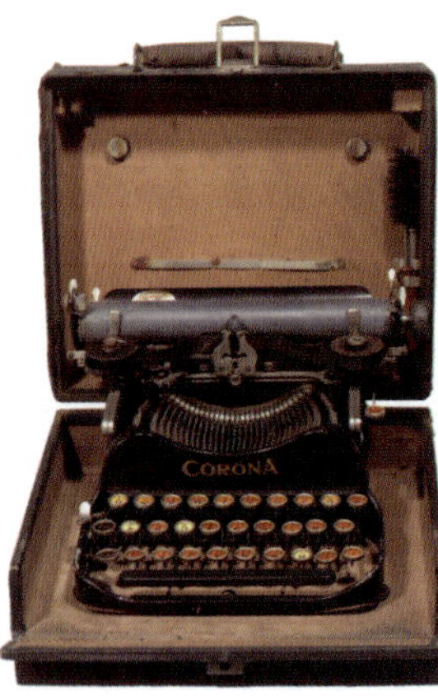

Li Dazhao's typewriter (1925)

The building was heavily restored and reopened in 1999, but retains the simple appearance it had in 1921. The exhibits include life-size wax figures of the 13 delegates, with Mao Zedong addressing the gathering.

In light of its revolutionary significance, the Memorial Hall is essentially a Party shrine. It is very much an icon of the official view of the Party history. Given the Memorial Hall's compact size, a visit need not take more than 30 minutes, leaving plenty of time to visit the excellent restaurants and boutiques in the Xintiandi district in which it is located.

The Communist Manifesto, the first Chinese version (1920)

Museum of Oriental Musical Instruments

83

东方乐器博物馆 *Dongfang yueqi bowuguan*

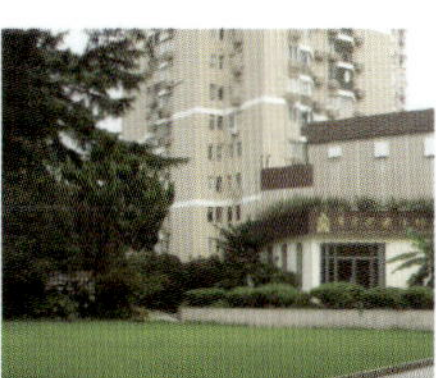

20 Fenyang Road, Shanghai
上海市汾阳路20号
Tel: (021) 6437 0137 ex 2134 / 2132
Open: 9.00–16.00
www.shcmusic.edu.cn/html/dongfangleqibowuguan

This museum was previously housed in the Shanghai Conservatory of Music.

The collection numbers over 400 instruments, including a selection of unusual examples from China's ethnic minorities. Ancient instruments are displayed, some of them very rare, such as an 8,000-year-old Neolithic flute found near Shanghai and a Tang dynasty five-stringed *pipa*. Also known as the Chinese lute, the *pipa* is played by plucking and has a pear-shaped wooden body. Modern Chinese pieces are on view, as well as folk instruments from foreign countries.

ang funerary
ottery
gurines
om a tomb
Xi'an

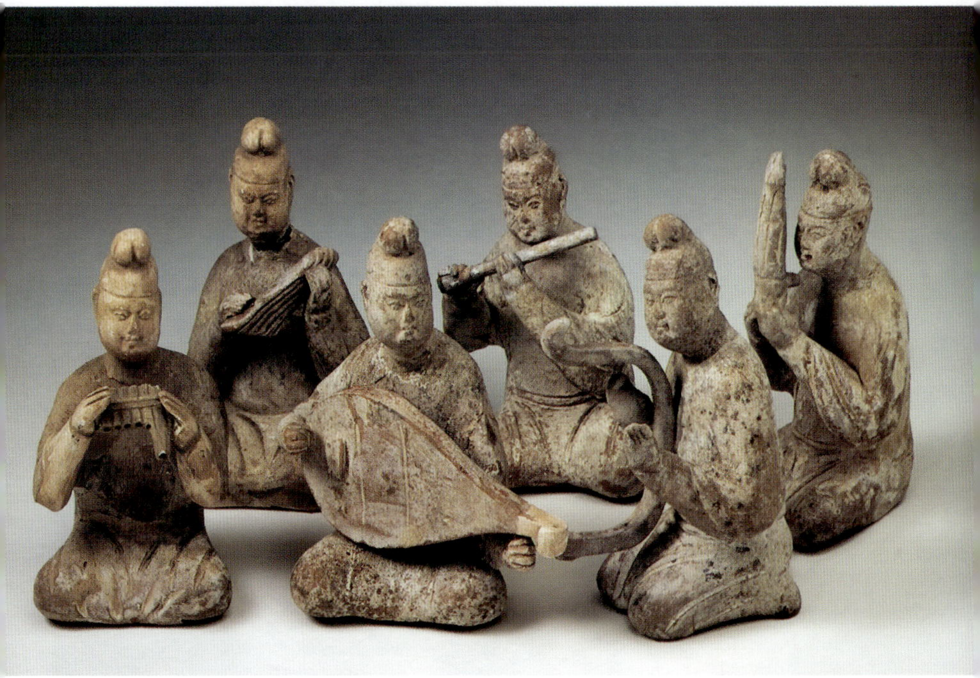

Shanghai Auto Museum

84

上海汽车博物馆 *Shanghai qiche bowuguan*

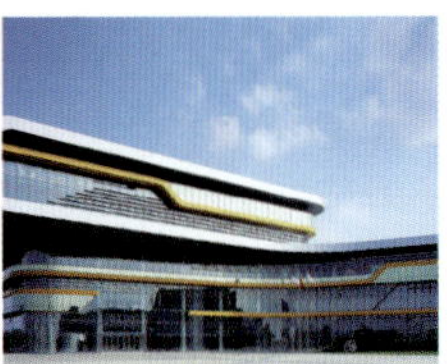

7565 Boyuan Road, Anting Town, Jiading District, Shanghai
上海市嘉定区安亭博园路7565号
Tel: (021) 6955 0055
Open: 9.30–16.30 except Mon, last entry 15.30
www.shautomuseum.gov.cn
English audio guide / gift shop / bookshop　　Kids

Next to the USA, China has the world's largest car market – more than ten million cars made and sold in 2008 alone. Despite horrific pollution levels and gridlocked traffic, the Chinese public is mad for cars and car culture. This museum is a vehicle lover's dream.

Located in the Auto Expo Park of the Shanghai International Automobile City, the innovative museum design by Stuttgart's Atelier Brckner is based on the concept of an urban landscape. The layout of the exhibition is arranged as a street, complete with road markings that guide you through a time line of automobile history and innovation. The galleries and cases are sleek and smooth, mimicking an atmosphere of speed and aerodynamic design.

At the time of writing four pavilions were open: the Antique Car Pavilion, the History Pavilion, the Exploring Centre and the New Energy Center.

In the Antique Car Pavilion are cars from France, Germany, Italy, Britain and the USA dating from 1904 to 1972 and including elegant classics such as a 1967 Jaguar XKE convertible, a 1923 Rolls Royce Ghost Phaeton and a 1936 BMW Cabriolet.

The galleries in the History Pavilion are divided by subject (mass production, racing and speed, energy saving etc.) and the design of each gallery reflects its subject. Appropriate cars are on display, so you will see a 1913 Model T Ford in the mass production gallery and a 1939 Lincoln Zephyr in the aerodynamic gallery.

There is also an exhibition of the fifty-year history of the Chinese auto industry. There you will see some of China's classics, including a 1959 Red Flag (*Hongqi*) CA72 and a 1964 Shanghai SH760.

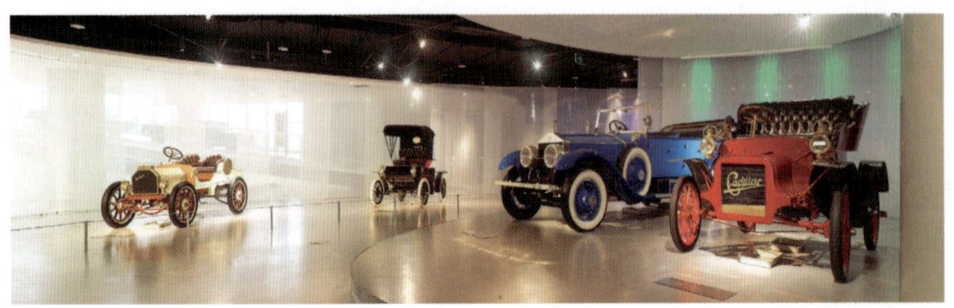

Shanghai Bank Museum

上海市银行博物馆 *Shanghaishi yinhang bowuguan*

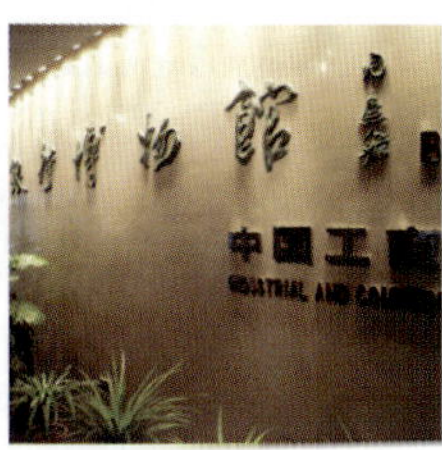

7F, 9 Pudong Avenue, Shanghai
上海市浦东大道9号7楼
Tel: (021) 5878 8743
Open: 9.00–11.30 & 13.00–16.00, Mon–Fri,
by appointment only to groups; open to individual visitors
13.00–16.00; best to ring ahead to confirm opening hours

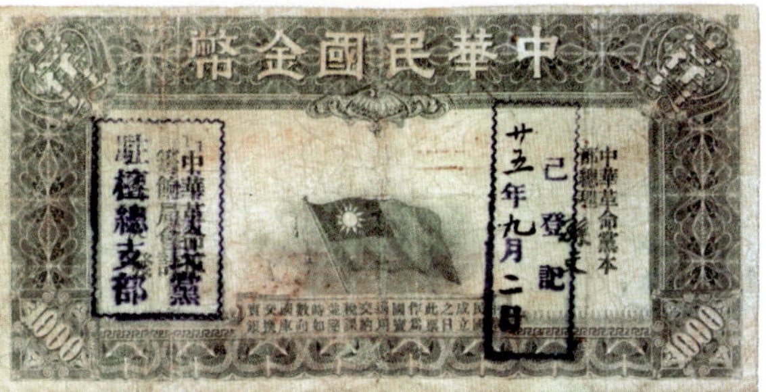

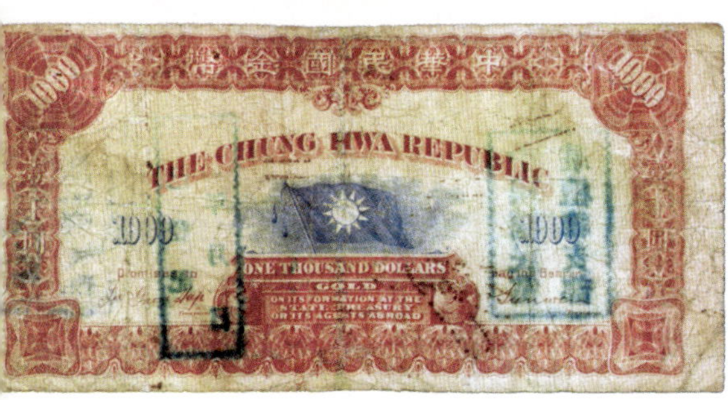

1,000-yuan gold certificate issued in 1911 by Sun Yat-sen to raise funds in San Francisco to overthrow the Manchu government

Housed in the Industrial and Commercial Bank of China (ICBC) building in Pudong is this first-rate collection documenting the financial history of China. It's a fitting tribute to the role finance has played in Shanghai's transformation from a fishing village to an international financial hub: now, Shanghai and Hong Kong are China's most advanced financial centres. The exhibition, displaying several thousand artefacts, is divided into three sections, the first two encompassing the development of Chinese banking and the history of Chinese currency, and the third set aside for temporary exhibits. The collection was amassed through purchases and donations such as those by the well-known Shanghai-based freelance photographer and collector extraordinaire Deke Erh, who understood the historical value of artefacts like the first published foreign bank share certificate issued in 1852 by the then named Oriental Bank Corporation and military bonds of the Republic of China, issued in 1912 when Sun Yat-sen was sworn in as the Provisional President of the Republic of China for the purpose of raising capital.

A cylindrical gold ingot from the Western Han dynasty measuring just 6 cm in diameter, examples of which would have been used as royal awards to high officials or as a means for payment, are shown alongside spade-shaped bronze coins used in the Spring and Autumn period, a knife-shaped *jincuodao* coin inlaid with gold from the Xin dynasty and a coin tree of the Qing dynasty showing the coins minted but not yet cut from the stalk; the twenty-one coins flanking both sides were not for general circulation but served as commemorative awards to high officials. Several hundred examples of paper money are on view, along with documents and photographs tracing the opening of Shanghai to foreign trade in 1843, accompanied by the establishment of British-funded banks, the first of which was the Oriental Bank Corporation in 1847. Major events in China's financial history are highlighted, such as the gold certificate issued in 1911 by Sun Yat-sen who sought to raise funds in San Francisco for his campaign to overthrow the Manchu government. Issued in three denominations of 10, 100 and 1,000 yuan, after the Revolution he redeemed most of them, and others were either destroyed in public or kept as mementoes – hence today they are extremely rare.

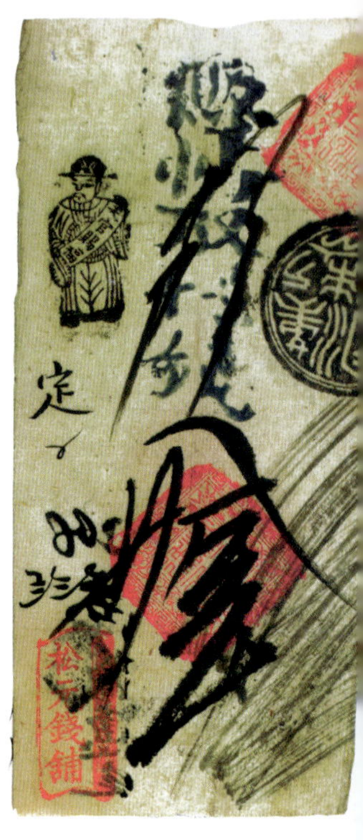

Among the museum's treasures is the only volume in existence of Chinese specimens of bank notes published by the American Bank Note Company, recording successive issues of Chinese paper currencies between 1905 and 1949. It includes 1,113 specimens as ordered by fifty-four financial institutions, including Chinese banks, foreign banks and joint ventures, documenting each, with details such as the issuing bank, par value and printing date of each note. Associated equipment and instruments, such as a first-generation note-packaging machine dating from the 1950s, reminds us of the former time-consuming and demanding task of manual packaging of paper notes, while the first auto-teller machine installed in Shanghai in 1988 demonstrates how far the industry had come by then.

86

Shanghai Kids' Museum

上海儿童博物馆 *Shanghai ertong bowuguan*

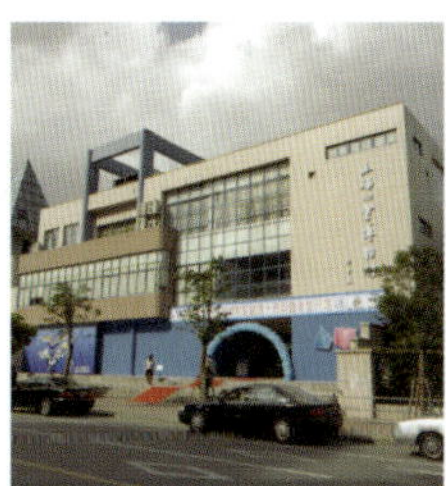

61 Songyuan Road, Changning District, Shanghai
上海市长宁区宋园路61号
Tel: (021) 6278 3130
www.shetbwg.com (Chinese only)
Open: 8.45–16.45 except Mon, last entry 15.30
Shop / publications/brochure in Chinese with a map of the museum with main points of interest identified in English Kids

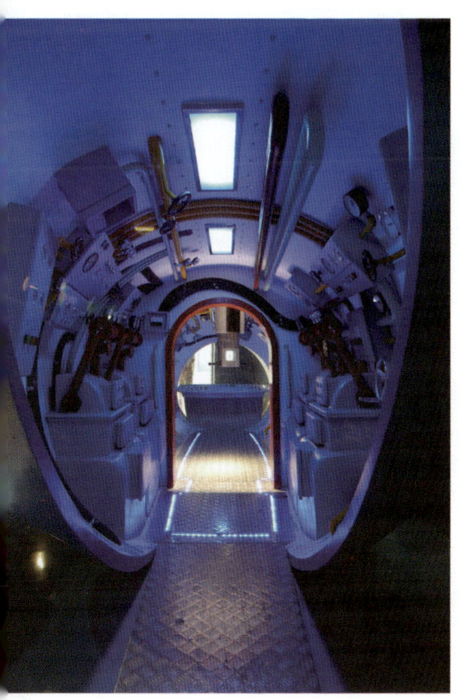

The interior of the submarine model

The Shanghai Kids' Museum has a hands-on approach to learning that encourages children to not only look but also to touch just about everything in sight. There are few explanations in English, but the museum's focus on interactive exhibits means language is not really a problem.

The first floor includes the Space Hall, Nautical Hall and Planetarium, which has a ceiling video screen. The Nautical Hall has a toy submarine for children to play in, a large screen that allows users to choose a boat – from a selection of old Chinese sampans to modern-day container ships – which they can then steer through large waves that break against the ship. There is also a good collection of model boats from different periods of history. The Space Hall contains a series of Chinese space ships, training equipment for astronauts and other exhibits.

On the second floor is the Interactive Exploration Area, with interactive screens and a robotic arm children can play with. The costume room and stage allows children to dress up and perform, and they can record themselves with a camera as well as control the lighting and sound effects. There is also a mock grocery shop, doctor's office, beauty salon and dentist's office to play in. In addition to a computer room there is a reading room with weekly storytelling in Chinese and English. The museum has astronomy and satellite demonstrations five times a day.

87

Shanghai Lu Xun Memorial Hall (Final Residence / The Tomb of Lu Xun)

上海鲁迅纪念馆 (鲁迅故居/鲁迅墓)

Shanghai Lu Xun jinianguan (Lu Xun guju / Lu Xun mu)

Museum:
200 Tian'ai Road, Hongkou
District, Shanghai
上海市虹口区甜爱路200号

Residence:
9 Shanyin Road, Lane 2,
Shanghai
上海市山阴路2弄9号

Tomb:
2288 Sichuan North
Road, Shanghai
上海市四川北路2288号

Tel: (021) 6540 2288; 5666 2608 (residence)
Open: 9.00–17.00, last entry 16.00 (museum); 9.00–16.00 (residence)
www.luxunmuseum.com
Bookshop / English-speaking guide available at the house only

Lu Xun (1881–1936) was a famous left-wing Chinese writer of the first half of the twentieth century. In October 1927, he left Beijing for Shanghai, where he spent the last decade of his life.

The museum was originally housed in Lu Xun's final home in Shanyin Road, where he lived from 1933 until his death – in a very interesting new-style experimental housing development called Continental Terrace, which was completed in 1932. Now, the house contains little more than some simple furniture, a few objects and the respirator that he used during his final illness, but it has a certain charm which, combined with its literary associations and the unusual building, definitely

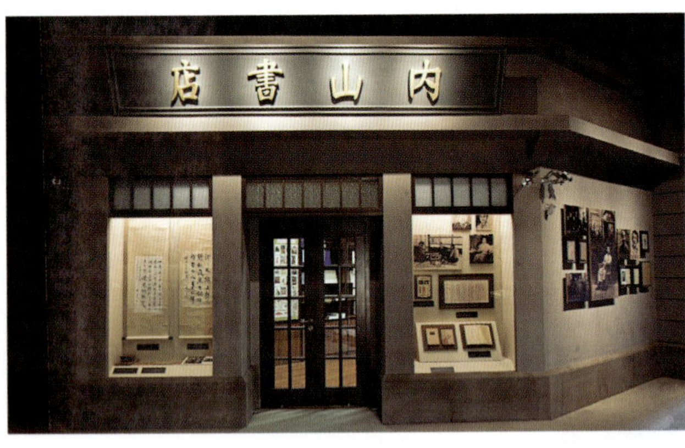

makes it worth a visit.

Uchiyama Bookstore: Uchiyama Kanzo was one of Lu Xun's best friends

The museum was moved in 1956 to the nearby park, now named after Lu Xun, which also contains his monumental tomb. A new building was opened in 1999, which is rather too grand and appears somewhat overblown in comparison with the simplicity of the house. It contains a thorough pictorial record of Lu Xun's life, his studies in Japan, his role in the New Culture Movement and his membership of the League of Leftist Writers. It is revealing that he insisted on the translation and publication of Western writers in Chinese. There is also a good collection of woodcut illustrations, contemporary magazines and books, and historic photographs – and some rather startling waxwork recreations of Lu Xun and his colleagues. The English signage is unreliable and the visitors should preferably have an interest in twentieth-century Chinese writing.

The introduction states that 'The Museum is the National Exemplary Base for Patriotism Education, and is one of the dedicated places for the Red Tour of Shanghai which is to help travellers learn about our history and understand patriotism education.' More prosaically, however, the New Culture Movement, which is well documented in the museum, made a great contribution to Chinese communist culture, introducing the thoughts of the early German philosophers, and the likes of John Dewey and Bertrand Russell, as well as the Russians and the Marxists.

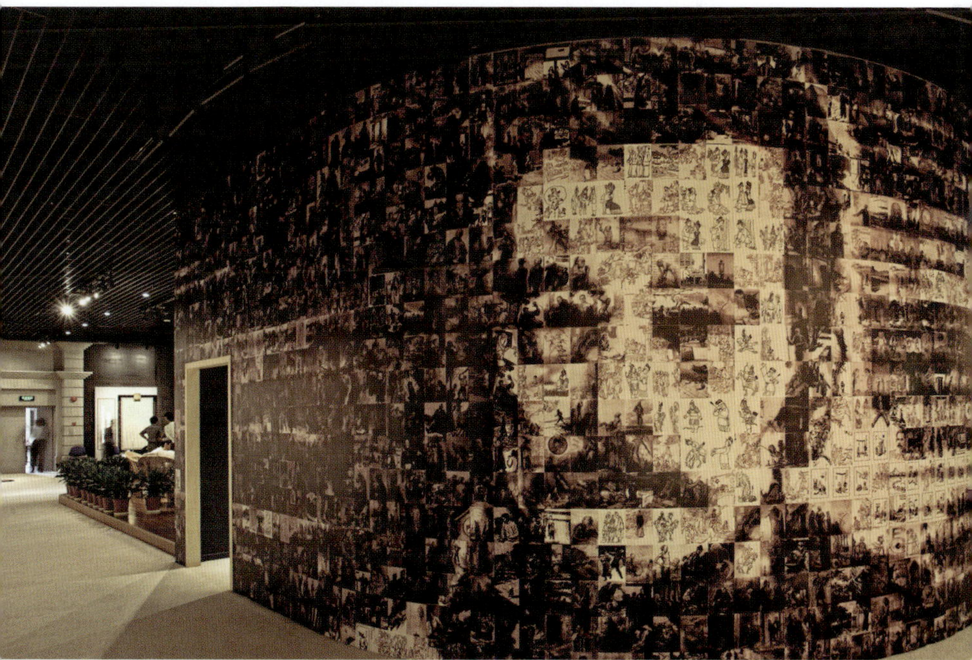

Portrait of Lu Xun inside the Memorial Hall

Shanghai Museum

上海博物馆 *Shanghai bowuguan*

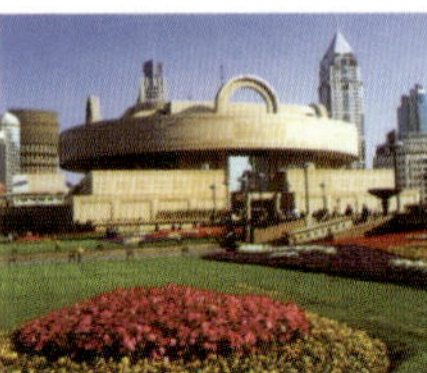

201 Renmin Avenue (People Square), Shanghai
上海市人民大道201号 (人民广场)
Tel: (021) 6372 3500
Open: 9.00–17.00, last entry 16.00
www.shanghaimuseum.net
Bookshop / gift shop / restaurant

The Shanghai Museum was the first museum of modern China of outstanding international quality – in terms of wealth of collection, display and architecture.

Originally built in 1952 on the site of the old racecourse, it re-opened in 1996 in a startling new building in People Square in the heart of central Shanghai. Designed by the architect Xing Tonghe, the building has a circular top on a square base, reflecting the Chinese cosmological belief in a square earth under a round sky. It also resembles a *ding*, one of the most important forms of the ancient funerary bronzes that are among the glories of the collection. The design of the building is thus a wholly modern exercise on an ancient Chinese form, with a cosmological reference tying it to one of the fundamentals of Chinese philosophy.

The museum is situated opposite the new City Hall and the new Opera House. It provides an iconic symbol of the staggering new wealth, power and taste of the city of Shanghai, which was, already by the early 1990s, as it has remained, the most potent engine driving the startling recent economic renaissance of China today.

The building was financed largely by the Shanghai City government. The collections have been hugely enhanced by a large number of gifts from outside China, many from prominent overseas Chinese collectors.

There are nine major collections, all important and representative, with items of the highest quality: the ancient Bronze Collection is unique. The Ceramics Collection and the Painting and Calligraphy Collection are also of outstanding national importance. Other galleries are devoted to seals, jades, Ming and Qing furniture, coins, and the arts and crafts of the minority nationalities.

On the ground floor, the first gallery is devoted to the whole of the history and art of the ancient Chinese bronze from the eighteenth to the seventh century BC.

Early bronzes were intimately linked with the religious and

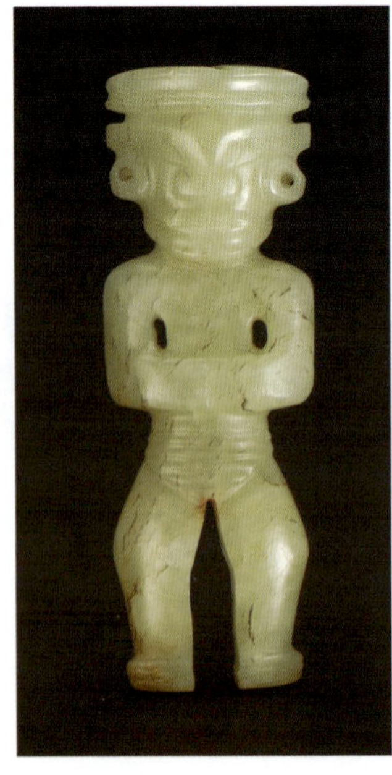

Jade figurine,
Shijiahe Culture
(2500–2000 BC)

political structures of their time as, aside from weapons, they were designed and made for sacrificial and other ritual ceremonies. They are cast in bronze to an astonishing degree of skill; their colours, shapes and very presence give an air of ancient mystery which in this display is perfectly brought out by the presentation and lighting. A visit to the bronzes in the Shanghai Museum is one of the great experiences to be enjoyed by the visitor to the museums of China. There are many national treasures, such as the famous *Da Ke Ding*.

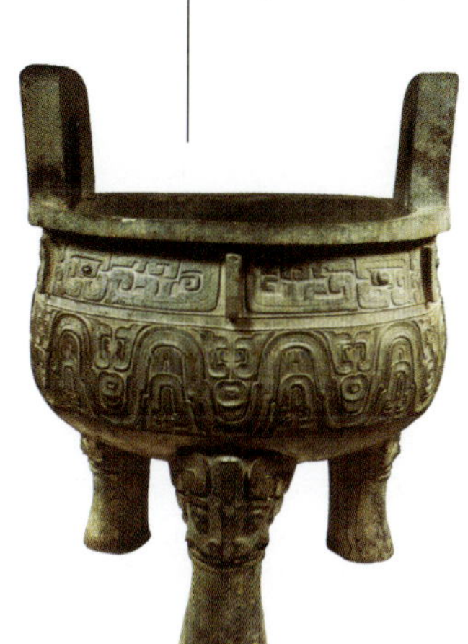

The famous
Da Ke Ding

Also on the ground floor is the sculpture collection, filled with masterpieces of all types and periods. From tomb figurines and carved stones, to Buddhist cave and temple sculptures, the collection also contains representational pieces from all periods from the Warring States period to the Qing.

The first floor is entirely devoted to porcelain and ceramics, with masterpieces from all the major kilns – from the exquisitely carved earthenware of Liangzhu Neolithic Culture, through stoneware and then porcelain from the Tang and Song periods, to the products of Jingdezhen imperial kiln in the Ming and Qing periods. The collection covers the complete history of Chinese ceramics.

The calligraphy and painting collections exhibited on the second floor are said to comprise half the total collection from southern China. The calligraphic masterpieces include the *Yatouwan Letter* by Wang Xianzhi; the *Kusun Letter* by Huai Su; the Tang period *Thousand Character Classic*, in cursive script, by Gao Xian; and the Song period *Landscape after a Poem by Du Fu*, by Zhao Kui.

The Ming and Qing painting and calligraphy collections represent a comprehensive history of this period. Paintings such as Sun Wei's *Hermits* and Liang Kai's *Eight Eminent Monks* are world treasures, while the Ming and Qing painting collection is unsurpassed. There are earlier works such as *Retreat in the Blue Bian Mountains* by Wang Meng of the Yuan. The Shanghai Museum also has more works than any other Chinese museum of the so-called 'The Ming Masters' and 'The Four Wangs of the Qing'.

There is also a fascinating collection of the oldest writing discovered in China, which was found inscribed on oracle bones from the Shang period site of Yinxu. These inscriptions were carved on tortoise plastrons and animal bones and provide a record of the history of the Shang dynasty 3,000 years ago. And there is a collection of early pre-Han books made from wooden or bamboo strips inscribed with one or more lines of writing and strung together to form a continuous text.

Also on the second floor is the Chinese seal gallery. Chinese seals combine the arts of calligraphy and carving, and are praised in Chinese as showing 'thousands of variations within a square inch'. Shanghai Museum's seal collection, comprising around 13,000 items, is special as it is comprehensive and representative of Chinese seal history.

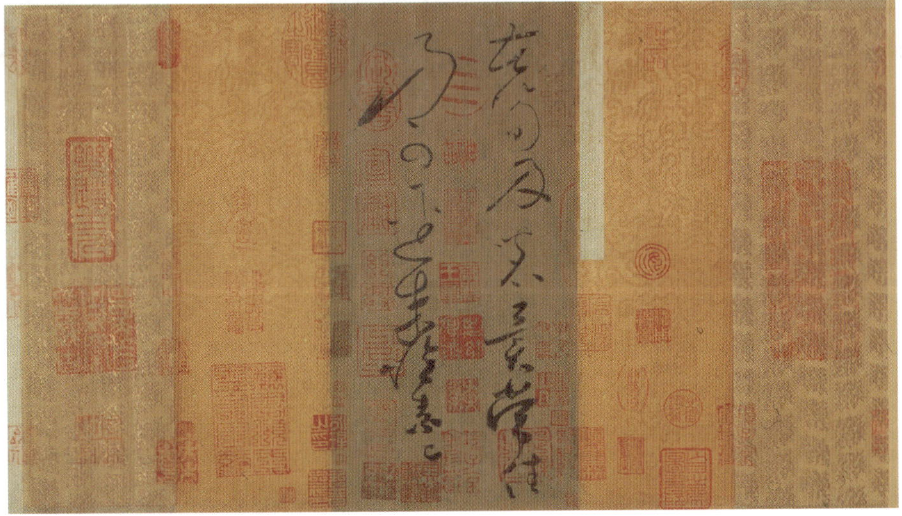

The *Kusun Letter* by Huai Su

On the third floor there are galleries dedicated to jades, Ming and Qing furniture, the art of the minority peoples and to Chinese coins.

Jade plays a key role in Chinese civilization. China was not only the first culture in the world to carve jade, and the stone was also linked from the earliest times with religious, ritual and political influence. Not only did it have a decorative function, it was also used as a symbol of wealth and power, for talismans by rulers making offerings to heaven and earth, for instruments of communication with the ancestors and for charms for the dead to fend off evil spirits.

The furniture gallery contains pieces from two great masters, Wang Shixiang and Chen Mengjia.

The exhibition of the art of the minority cultures of China includes works of art, religious art, folk art and items for everyday use, including jewellery, clothes and textiles.

The Shanghai Museum coin collection has one million items, and is renowned for its quality.

In addition to all of the above, the museum has a fine collection of lacquer ware, tapestry and embroidery, and bamboo, wood, ivory and rhinoceros horn carvings.

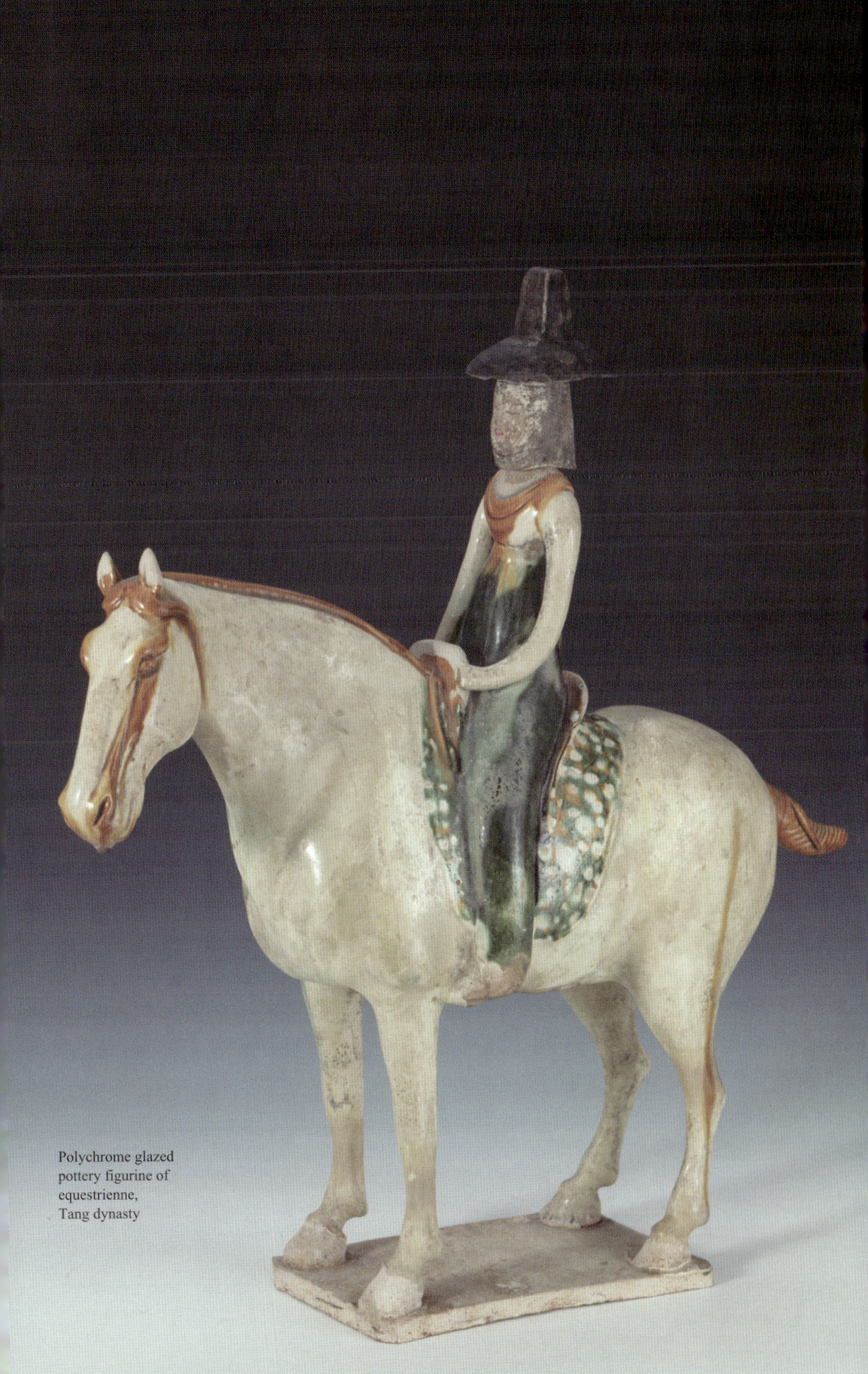

Polychrome glazed
pottery figurine of
equestrienne,
Tang dynasty

Shanghai Museum of Public Security

上海公安博物馆 *Shanghai gongan bowuguan*

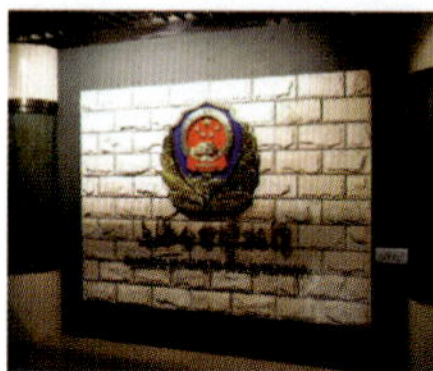

518 Ruijin South Road, Shanghai
上海市瑞金南路518号
Tel: (021) 6472 0256
Open: 9.00–16.30 Mon–Fri, last entry 16.00
http://bwg.police.sh.cn/gabwg/

This museum traces the history of the police force in Shanghai, from the establishment of the city's first police department in 1854 to the People's Republic of China. The collection of 3,000 items is arranged over the second, third and fourth floors. There is a description in English at the entrance to each floor but unfortunately none of the items on display have English descriptions. In fact, many speak for themselves and need no introduction.

The old city of Shanghai had an infamous reputation as a centre for drug selling, gambling and prostitution, populated with gangsters such as Pockmarked Huang (Huang Jinrong) and Big-eared Du (Du Yuesheng, he sent coffins to the establishments of potential clients), and this museum provides some interesting illustrations of the bad old days.

The second floor of the museum draws you immediately into the past. The first exhibit is a reconstructed old Shanghai Street, complete with cobblestones and antique iron manhole covers emblazoned with the word 'England' and the cryptic letters 'S.M.C.' and 'P.W.D.'. There are life-sized wax statues of red-turbaned, bearded Sikh policemen standing beside pith-helmeted British police officers, part of the international force that once patrolled the old International Settlement. Nearby, an old fire hydrant stands along the sidewalk. According to the sign, the Kuomintang (KMT), or Nationalist, police used water from the fire hydrant to 'suppress mass protests' before liberation in 1949.

There is also a beautiful selection of pistols on display: a small one neatly hidden away in a musical instrument box in true gangster style, an elaborately engraved pistol once owned by Sun Yat-sen and a small pistol with a folding gold handle that was once deftly hidden up the sleeve of 1930s crime boss Pockmarked Huang. Huang had little to worry about in any case: he also served as the chief detective for the French Sûreté.

A display case exhibits a book with the centre of its pages neatly cut out to hide secret documents or paraphernalia. Two stuffed pigeons, used for secret communication in the 1950s, sit in another glass case. A Minox spy camera, no longer than an index finger, was used by an unnamed Chinese operative; no details are provided.

The third floor introduces criminology, including gruesome photos and descriptions of some of the most famous crimes in the city. There is the bloody '*qiaotou an*' or 'knock on the head case' in which a serial killer terrified Shanghai's female population by beating women on the head with an axe. Rumour had it that the murderer had a penchant for women with long hair, a rumour that is said to have given the local hair-cutting business a significant economic boost.

The museum offers a detailed description of the city's first bank robbery, which was carried out by a modern-day Bonnie and Clyde in the early 1980s. The police killed him, and she served a prison term, later becoming a popular singer after her release. And there is the 1996 case of best-selling author Dai Houying, who was mysteriously murdered in her home along with her niece by a robber.

There is a model prison cell and an authentic day-by-day prison menu, which included green peppers and shredded meat, pickled vegetable and egg drop soup. There's even a special chair used for police interrogations, which has a wooden plank running across the lap to keep suspects securely in place during questioning, and the actual form used by Shanghai university students to apply for permission to hold demonstrations following the NATO bombing of the Chinese Embassy in Belgrade in 1999.

The fourth floor is dedicated to firefighters and firefighting equipment, hero police officers, police uniforms and equipment, and a large selection of guns and rifles.

The display of old firefighting equipment includes an antiquated manual pumping tank, complete with hoses and wooden buckets, much like the ones seen in films set at the turn of the twentieth century. In addition, there are straw conical hats once worn by firefighters, and more modern metal firemen's helmets with the city districts written on them in Chinese. There is also a wonderful collection of replicas of classic old fire trucks. The collection of captured weapons includes pistols, rifles, shot guns and machine guns.

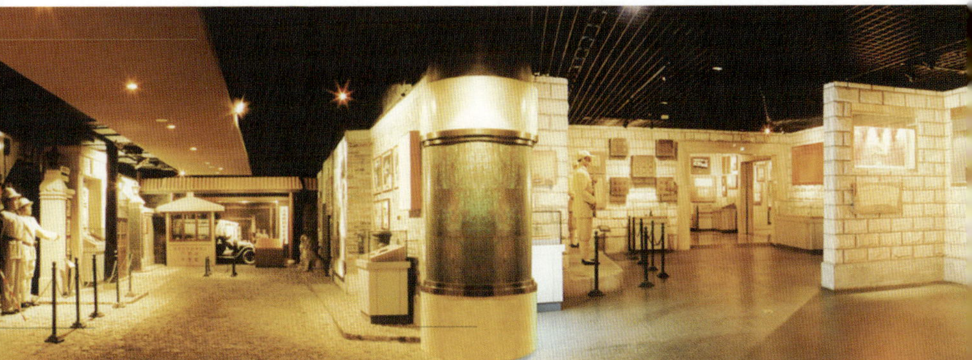

90

Shikumen Open House Museum

石库门博物馆 *Shikumen bowuguan*

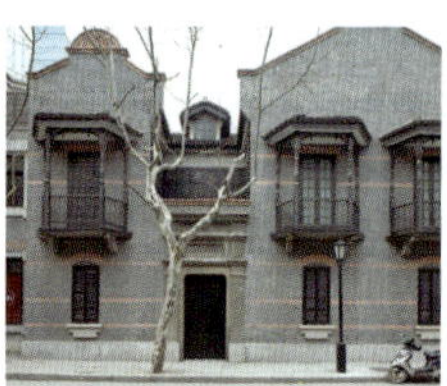

25 Lane 181, Taicang Road, Shanghai
上海市太仓路181弄25号
Tel: (021) 3307 0337
Open: 10.30–22.30 Sun–Thurs;
11.00–23.00 Fri & Sat

Located in the heart of Shanghai's Xintiandi District – a complex of reconfigured heritage buildings redeveloped into luxury boutiques, bars and restaurants – is a museum of the city's unique and once ubiquitous Shikumen or lane houses.

The origin of Shikumen buildings can be traced to the 1860s, when the Taiping Rebellion led to a surge in the refugee population in Shanghai and an increased need for housing. Due to the scarcity of available land, many of the houses were constructed close together in rows of the Shikumen style, which was a mixture of

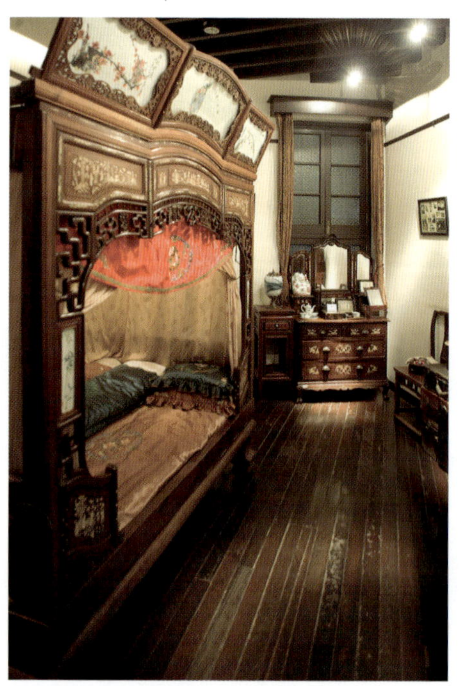

Chinese and foreign styles of architecture. At their peak, Shikumen-style housing accounted for 60 per cent of the total housing in Shanghai. This remained the case until the city's economic resurgence, beginning in the 1990s, which resulted in the demolition of tens of thousands of these houses. As with the destruction of the *hutongs* in Beijing, the whole character of Shanghai has changed with the destruction of the Shikumen neigbourhoods.

This museum offers an opportunity to see how the Shanghainese lived when the Shikumen was in its prime in the early twentieth century. Arranged over two floors, the museum comprises two separate parts: a restored Shi Ku Men unit sumptuously furnished with authentic period pieces from the 1920s and 1930s, and a modern exhibition space. Entry into the museum is not through the original stone doorway (or Shikumen, from which the building type derives its name), but via a side entrance. Beyond the small ticket hall visitors pass through the reception hall, living room, downstairs bedroom and rear kitchen before climbing the stairs to the second floor and passing the celebrated *tingzijian* – a small and inhospitable room often rented to artists and writers. Mao Dun, Lu Xun, Ding Ling and others lived in such rooms, and their writings of this period are known as '*tingzijian* literature'. Upstairs is the study and two master bedrooms. Next to the study, which overlooks the small courtyard at the front of the building, is an exhibition space illustrating the history of the Shikumen and the development of Xintiandi.

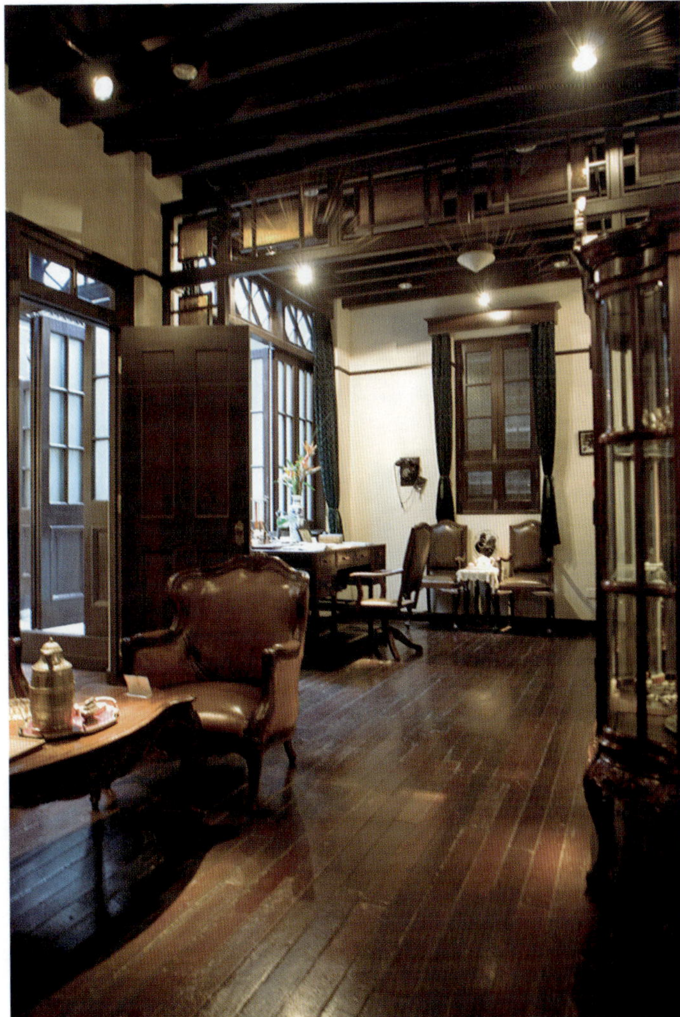

Living Room in the Shikumen Open House Museum

91

Soong Ching Ling Memorial Residence in Shanghai / Soong Ching Ling Mausoleum

宋庆龄故居纪念馆/宋庆龄陵园

Song Qingling guju jinianguan / Song Qingling lingyuan

Main building
of Soong Ching
Ling Memorial
Residence

Residence:
1843 Huaihaizhong Road, Shanghai
上海市淮海中路1843号
Tel: (021) 6474 7183
Open: 9.00–16.30
www.shsoong-chingling.com

Mausoleum:
21 Songyuan Road, Changning
District, Shanghai
上海市长宁区宋园路21号
Tel: (021) 6278 3104
Open: 8.30–17.00

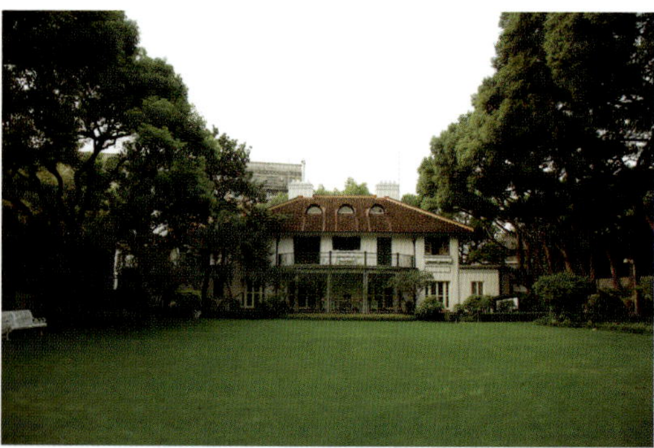

Soong Ching Ling (Song Qingling), the wife of Sun Yat-sen, once lived here from 1949. She passed away in Beijing in 1981 at the age of ninety. In front of her tomb, where she is buried alongside her parents and a former maid, is a white marble statue of her surrounded by her favourite camphor trees. The adjoining International Cemetery contains the graves of some 600 famous foreigners who lived in the city prior to 1949, including

The Soong Sisters

The three Soong sisters, Ching Ling, Mei Ling and Ai Ling played an enormous role in the Chinese Republic (1911–1949) as influential and charismatic wives of its leaders. Born to a wealthy banker called Charlie Soong, who was a Christian, their life paths were to lead in very diverse directions. There is a glib saying which nonetheless sheds light on their roles and their marriages: Mei Ling 'loved power'. She married Nationalist Party (KMT) strong man Chiang Kai-shek, who converted to Christianity. She was very much the power behind the throne in the National Government and even after the KMT's flight to Taiwan she continued to espouse the anti-Communist cause in Washington.

Ai Ling 'loved money'. She married H. H. Kung, the enormously wealthy Minister of Finance at the heart of the party's business interests.

'But Ching Ling loved China' (this is the Communist punch-line to this saying). She married Sun Yat-sen, first President of the Republic. After her husband's death in 1925, her politics took a leftist, pro-Soviet direction, with her leading a split in the KMT and ultimately aligning herself with the Communist Party and becoming a prominent 'non-Communist' figure in the post-1949 government.

members of the well-known Kadoorie and Sassoon families.

A small museum beside the tomb houses a collection of hundreds of black and white photographs documenting Mme Soong's life, as well as some of her personal effects, including memorabilia from Wesleyan Female College where she studied in the USA.

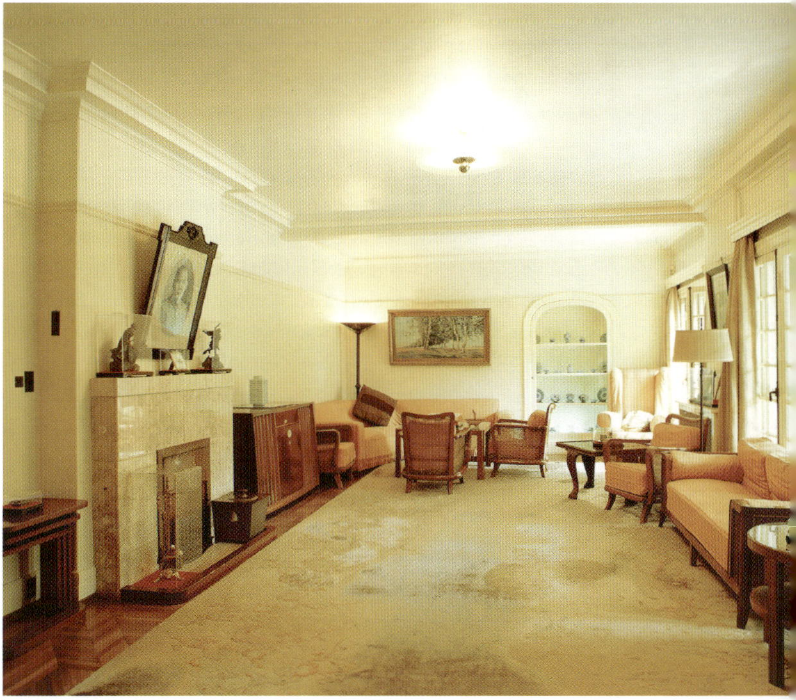

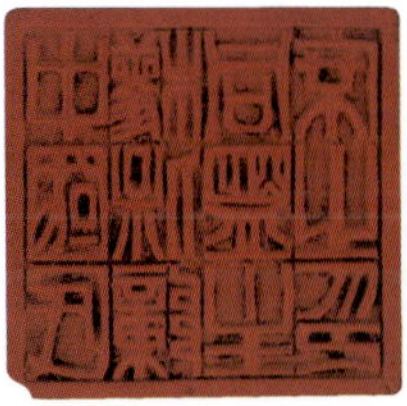

The sitting room of
Soong Ching
Ling's residence

Sun Yat-sen's Former Residence and Museum in Shanghai

92

上海孙中山故居纪念馆 *Shanghai Sun Zhongshan guju jinianguan*

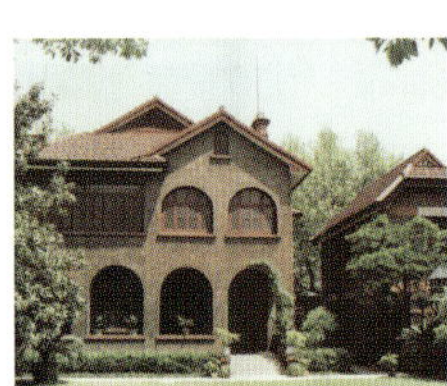

7 Xiangshan Road, Shanghai
上海市香山路7号
Tel: (021) 5306 3361
Open: 9.00–16.00
www.sh-sunyat-sen.org

Sun Yat-sen is considered the father of Republican China and, as such, is one of the most important figures in modern Chinese history. He and his wife, Soong Ching Ling, a prominent Chinese stateswoman in her own right, lived in this well-preserved European building in the old French Concession from 1918 to 1924 (Ching Ling continued to live here after her husband's death until the Japanese occupation of Shanghai in 1937). It was while he was here that Sun Yat-sen wrote some of his most important political works. It is also where the Suns entertained the famous people of their day, including George Bernard Shaw, Lu Xun and Ho Chi Minh. This complex contains two British-style structures that date back close to a century, one their former residence and another building which was turned into a museum in 2006.

On arrival, you will see a large statue of a seated Sun Yat-sen at the front of the two buildings. The structure on the right is the museum, where the exhibits all have good English descriptions. On the first floor is an old sword and various pistols 'used by foreign invaders'. Some of Sun Yat-sen's personal effects are also on display: his medical tools in a leather case, a faded Republican flag used during an uprising and daily items used by the Suns. On the second floor there are TV screens in each room showing archival footage from the turn of the twentieth century. There is also a Chinese suit worn by Sun Yat-sen, his cane, a fur-lined jacket, a stethoscope, a sphygmomanometer and a blue polka dot *qipao* worn by his wife. The third floor is devoted to a collection of calligraphy seals.

Proceed next door through the charming garden to the former home of the Suns,

Dr. Sun Yat-sen's sword

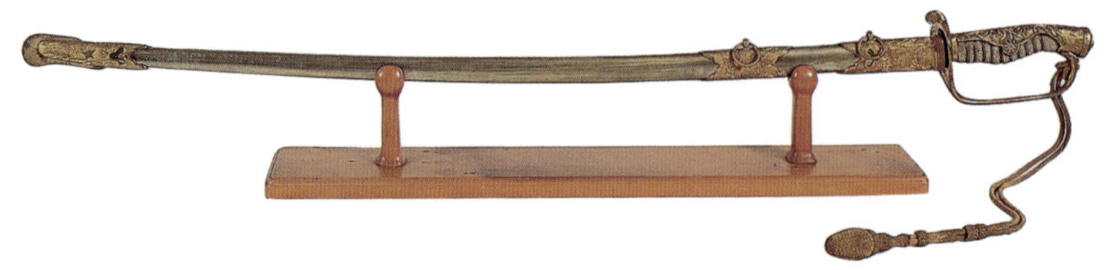

where the rooms still contain original furniture. When you enter here you must put plastic bags over your shoes to protect the floor. The first item on view is an old black, heavy metal oven, *c.* 1920s. On the first floor is the dining room where it is explained that the Suns lived a simple life, spending just 2 yuan a day on food. On the second floor is a small sitting room, a bedroom and a large number of books neatly stacked in a glass-covered bookcase – a closer look reveals that they are actually photocopies of the bookbindings.

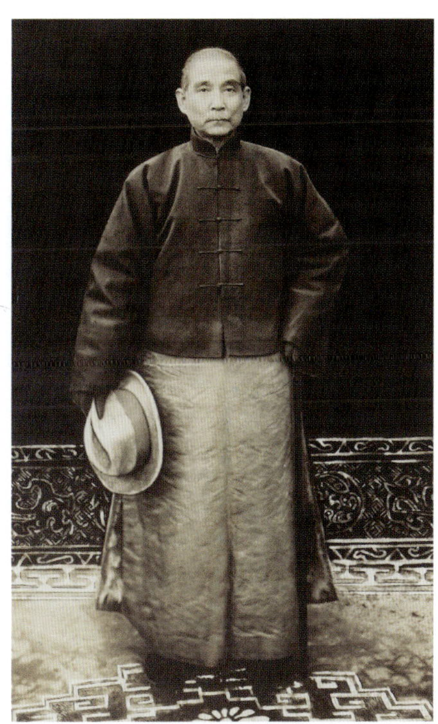

Dr. Sun Yat-sen

Sun Yat-sen (1866–1925)

Sun Yat-sen is celebrated in China today as the 'father of the nation', revered in equal measure in Beijing and in Taipei as a great nationalist revolutionary and the first President of the Republic after the overthrow of the Qing dynasty. It is difficult to get an idea of the real person through the mythology that has grown up around him; the historical view of him has been generous and tends to gloss over his deficiencies as a leader and a thinker.

In the face of what was seen as China's impending dismemberment by the great powers, Sun threw himself into revolutionary politics, organizing a series of uprisings against the Manchus, all of which failed. Having spent time as a teenager with relatives in Honolulu, he now engaged in fundraising and organization among Chinese communities from Hawaii to Japan to England. In 1896 his kidnap by the Chinese embassy in London, and his eventual release before he could be shipped back to China for execution, gave him instant fame overseas, which contrasted with his low profile in China. Having established a unified coalition of anti-Qing dynasty groups in Japan in 1905, the 1911 revolution was actually triggered, ironically, by an uprising of troops in Wuchang, working independently of Sun. However, he returned to form the first government of the Republic of China, which can be seen as the high point of his career. The Republic soon fell victim to warlords who seized power and broke up China. Sun's Nationalist Party eventually came to learn from Soviet advisors and created its own military force to reunite the country. But it was left to Sun's successor, Chiang Kai-shek, to complete that reunification process.

93

The Memorial Hall to the Victims in the Nanjing Massacre by Japanese Invaders

侵华日军南京大屠杀遇难同胞纪念馆

Qinhua rijun Nanjingdatusha yunantongbao jinianguan

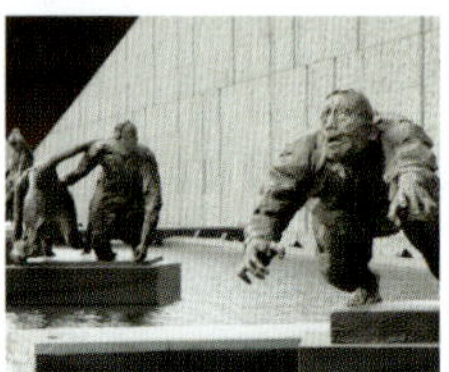

418 Shuiximen Street, Nanjing, Jiangsu
江苏省南京市水西门大街418号
Tel: (025) 8661 2230
Open: 8.30–16.30 except Mon
www.nj1937.org

The Nanjing Massacre was one of the most appalling events of the brutally cruel Japanese War. Nanjing, capital of the Republic of China, fell to the Japanese invading forces on 13 December 1937, the start of two months of murder, rape and looting. Chinese estimates put the death toll at 300,000 – with 20,000 rapes. The Japanese, who have never fully accepted the scale of the atrocity, put it as low as 40,000. A wartime tribunal gave a figure of 142,000.

Whatever the truth of the numbers, there is no argument, attested by Westerners as well as Chinese, that a third of the city was destroyed, shops and private homes were looted, and for weeks corpses littered the streets. It is also accepted that the Japanese have never fully acknowledged or taken clear responsibility for the scale of the atrocity. Japanese history books have played the event down, souring relations between the two countries still today.

The memorial is a moving tribute to relatives, friends and fellow citizens. One need only see the faces of some of the elderly people here, or the schoolchildren writing and leaving cards, to comprehend the nature of the loss and sorrow.

The new memorial hall, opened on 13 December 2007 – the seventieth anniversary of the start of the massacre – is on a par with the holocaust museums of Europe, and with Hiroshima and Nagasaki.

The hall stands on the site of the Jiangdong Gate, on a mass grave of 10,000 corpses. It is designed like a ship, with a huge prow rising to the heavens. The approach along a sloping wall is reminiscent of Washington's Vietnam Memorial. Inside, a room shows, behind glass, corpses packed into the burial pit. In the next room, the public can leave mementoes, tokens and cards with messages. Following this are darkened rooms with memorial lights, multimedia exhibits, survivors'accounts, dioramas of bombed-out buildings, and accounts of the history of Sino-Japanese conflict dating back to the 1890s.

Statues outside the hall pay silent tribute to the dead

Nanjing Cloud Brocade Museum and Research Institute

94

南京云锦博物馆与云锦研究所
Nanjing yunjin bowuguan yu yunjin yanjiusuo

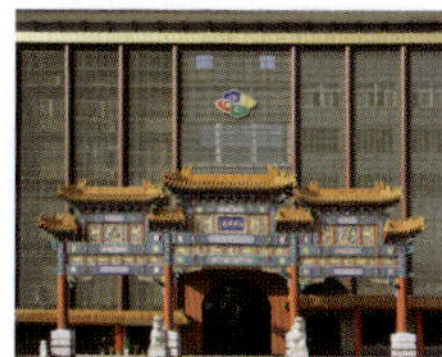

240 Chating East Road, Nanjing, Jiangsu
江苏省南京市茶亭东街240号
Tel: (025) 8656 3710
Open: 9.00–17.00
www.njyunjin.com
Kids

The historical importance of Nanjing (it served as the capital of China during several earlier periods) is reflected in the richness of the collections showcased in the city's museums and this one, focusing on *yunjin* – or cloud-pattern brocade – is no exception. During the Yuan, Ming and Qing dynasties, tens of thousands of looms wove this highly prized, exquisite textile exclusively to make dragon robes (*longpao*) and official garments for the Emperor, other members of the imperial household and his courtiers. Official fabric bureaus were set up by the rulers to administer and control its production in the city. By 1949, however, only four looms remained, and this unique handicraft was dying out. Today, this 'living museum' and its associated research institute are working hard to revive this unparalleled textile tradition, with teams of expert artisans weaving away on over a dozen reproduction wooden looms, producing traditional silk brocades for sale here and elsewhere in the city.

The most fascinating part of the visit is watching the weavers in action on the first floor. The process requires two weavers; the one at the top of the loom controls the pattern and the bottom weaver manipulates vertical frames of thread with a series of pedals, while feeding numerous shuttles of various coloured silk strands under and over these threads. In the past, these might also have included gold or silver supplementary weft threads, interwoven to produce shimmering pattern silks with designs of brightly coloured peacocks, dragons, flowers and clouds for exclusive use by the Emperor.

In 2009, Nanjing brocade was been selected into the list of the oral and intangible heritage of humans at UNESCO.

Detail from a cloud-pattern brocade (*yunjin*) dragon robe

95

Nanjing Museum

南京博物院 *Nanjing bowuyuan*

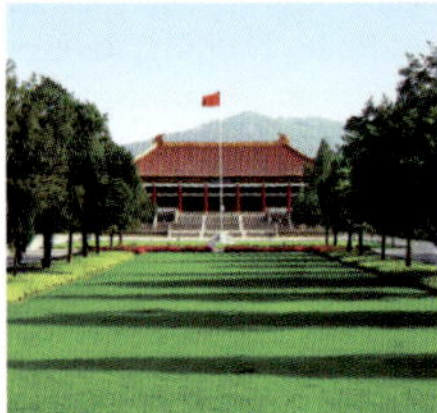

321 Zhongshan East Road, Nanjing, Jiangsu
江苏省南京市中山东路321号
Tel: (025) 8480 7923
Open: 9.00–16.30
www.njmuseum.com
Book and gift shop / English audio guide / delightful tea shop

The Nanjing Museum is one of the most beautiful modern museums in China and its collection is rivalled only by those at the museums of Beijing and Taipei. It is on no account to be missed.

It is both the provincial museum of Jiangsu Province, as well as a national museum. It was founded in 1933 (making it one of the oldest museums in China) by Cai Yuanpei (1868–1940), the educator and prominent scholar who had been Minister of Education in Sun Yat-sen's government. Cai was also the founding director.

Gold cicada and jade leaf

Built in the form of a Liao dynasty palace, the museum is sited on a fine 83,000 sq m estate, near the Zhongshan Gate to the east of the city. From its foundation it was dedicated to achieving the highest international standards in conservation, research, pedagogy and display.

From the outset it showed not only the arts, but also the crafts, both of the Han as well as the minority cultures of China; and aimed to show these within the context of the natural world.

The Civil War and the invading Japanese had a profound effect on the city and, in turn, the fortunes of the museum.

Nanjing had been the capital city of China from the third to the sixth centuries, and again briefly during the Ming dynasty. It was in Nanjing that the new republic was officially proclaimed on 1 January 1912. After Chiang Kai-shek abandoned Beijing to the Japanese, it again became the Chinese capital during the 'Nanjing Decade', from 1928 to 1937. Then, it too fell to the Japanese and suffered the appalling Nanjing Massacre in December 1937, during which some 300,000 of its people were murdered. Although the Kuomintang had to move their headquarters to Chongqing until the end of the War against Japan, they were back in 1945. Nanjing remained the capital until 1949.

Therefore, at the time of its foundation, the museum was a leading institution of the Chinese capital, active in scholarship, publication and excavation. It is telling that, during this period, the Beijing History Museum was a branch of the museum at Nanjing. Some 300,000 pieces, including six of national importance, had been collected by 1949, despite the turbulent history that accompanied the early years of its growth.

When the Ming Emperor, Yongle, moved the capital northwards to Beijing in 1420, he took the whole of the great imperial art collection with him, which continued to grow during the rest of the Ming dynasty, and again, spectacularly, during the Qing. Until 1949, the imperial collection in the Forbidden City in Beijing was the only national collection of Chinese art – one of incomparable wealth both in terms of quality and quantity. Understandably, however, there was no proper inventory of the collection, and with the increasing weakness of the Qing, objects from the collection probably began to disappear as early as the nineteenth century. In 1911, at the fall of the empire, the last Emperor, Puyi (1906–1967), was allowed to remain in residence temporarily in the Forbidden City, during which time, according to official estimates,

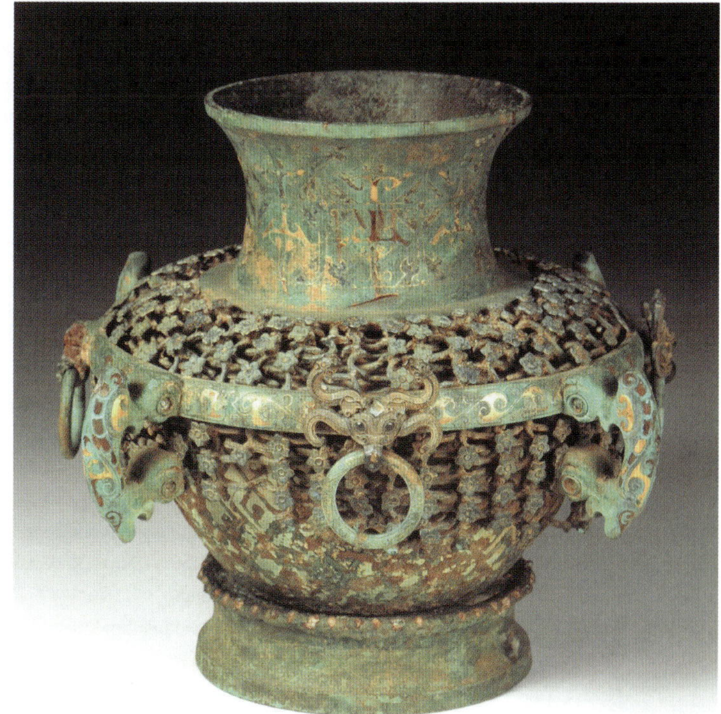

Gold and silver inlaid *hu*, Warring States period

he sold at least 1,200 items from the collection.

Then, in 1927, Chiang Kai-shek packed up at least two-thirds of the collection rather than leave it to the Japanese. These objects were transported first to Nanjing, then to Chongqing, and in 1945 back to Nanjing again. In 1949, when it was evident that Kuomintang power was on the brink of collapse, the nationalists collected up works of art from all over China and intended to take all of it, including the entire imperial collection, with them to Taipei. The speed of their demise was such, however, that at least half of the objects were left in Nanjing where they now form the cream of the collection. The imperial collection is therefore shared between the Palace Museum in Beijing, the National Museum in Taipei and the Nanjing Museum. It is even possible that some items still remain hidden in Nanjing.

Thus, the Nanjing Museum now holds some 420,000 items, of which more than 2,000 are national treasures. Many are acquisitions made after 1949, and there are many stupendous, recently excavated treasures. The museum has over 300,000 manuscripts and books.

Tapestry portrait of Jesus Christ by Shen Shou

A second and beautifully appointed building, in the same Liao style as the original, was opened in 1999, the same year in which the museum was upgraded to the rank of national museum.

The collection in the building is laid out over two floors, ground and lower, with galleries devoted to Folk Art, Bronzes, Porcelain, Treasure, Pottery, Textiles and Embroideries, Jades, Calligraphy and Painting, Lacquer, and Costumes and Accessories. It also has a gallery for temporary exhibitions of modern art. The objects are beautifully presented, and there are instructive and attractive reconstructions of pottery kilns and factories, and of weaving and embroidery techniques.

With a collection of such wealth it is almost invidious to single out individual items for the visitor's attention, but the following pieces will guarantee satisfaction, ensure that all the main galleries are visited and hence lead to a host of other treasures:

- Small Bronze Seated Deer with the most elegant antlers, from the Warring States period (excavated at Lianshui, Jiangsu)
- Qing Gold Boddhisattva made in the Imperial Palace Workshops
- Jade *Pei* Pectoral – fourteen pierced jade plaques from a Dawenkou Culture tomb (*c.* 2500 BC) excavated in Jiangsu
- Grey Pottery Brick with a Design of a Winged Immortal, Southern dynasties (317–589), from Xinyi, Jiangsu
- Peach Bloom Water Pot with Incised Dragon Design, Qing dynasty
- Carved Lacquer Barbed Dish, Qing dynasty, illustrating the story of 'The

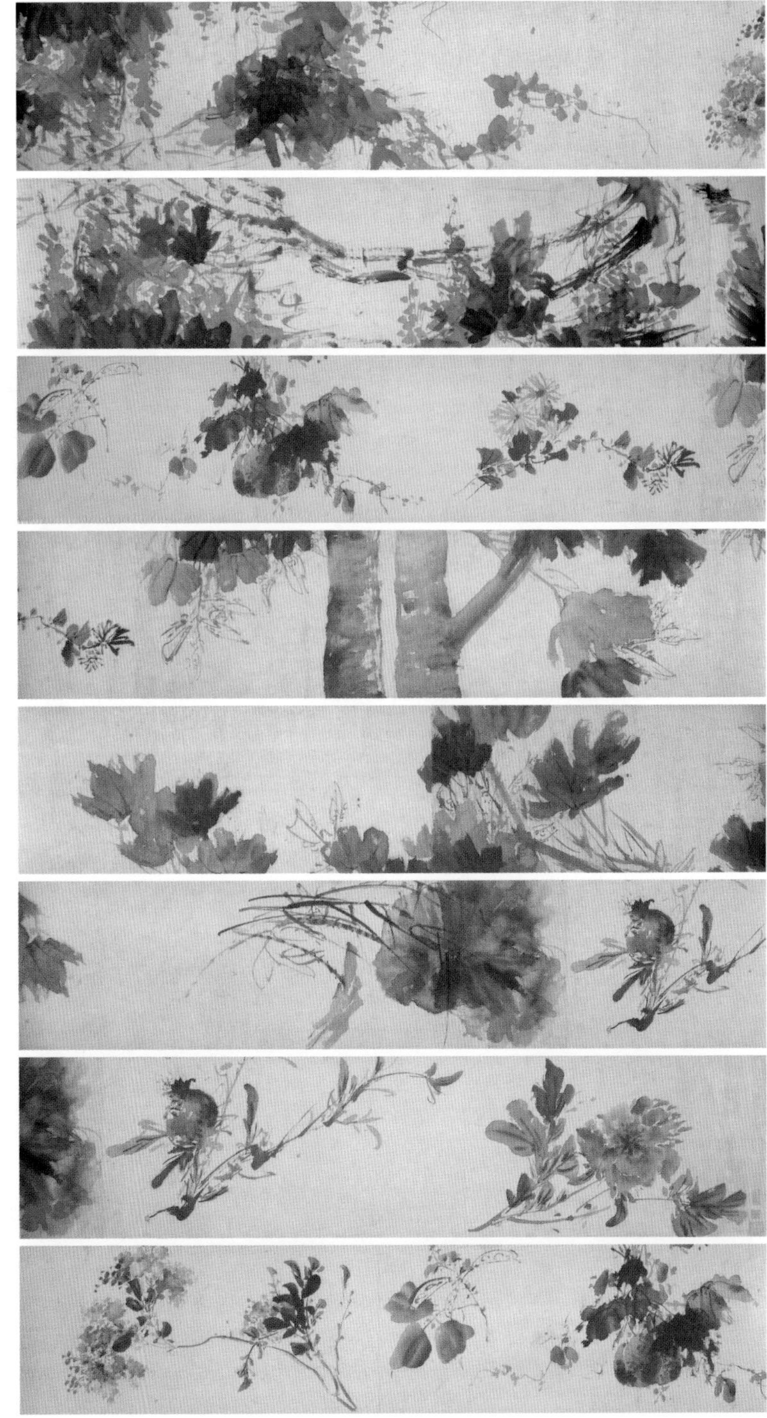

Flowers
by Xu Wei,
Ming dynasty

Bronze ox lamp
with cloud pattern,
Han dynasty

Cowherd and the Weaving Maid'

- Bamboo Carving of a Fisherman, Ming dynasty
- Imperial Painting of Birds by the Song dynasty Emperor Huizong (r. 1101–1125)
- Embroidered Portrait of Guanyin by Guan Zhongji (1261–1319), Yuan dynasty. Guan Zhongji was the wife of Zhao Mengfu, a famous Yuan dynasty artist.

Apart from its permanent exhibitions, the museum organizes frequent special events, including international exhibitions and exchange projects with foreign museums, including Japan, Germany, Egypt, Mexico, Spain, Russia, Belgium, South Korea and Australia.

The Nanjing Museum is the only Chinese museum with developed ethnic and folklore research, most recently on the Han ethnic group of the Tai Lake region.

A stroll in the sculpture garden after your visit will be an added pleasure.

In 2013, after a four-year expansion project, Nanjing Museum will re-open with six galleries: the History Pavilion, the Arts Pavilion, the Special Exhibition Pavilion, the *Minguo* (1912–1949) Pavilion and the Intangible Cultural Heritage and the Digital Pavilion, displaying more than 50,000 amazing collections.

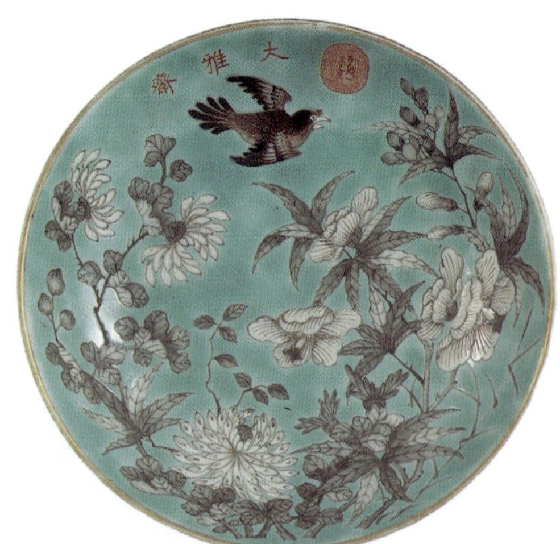

Porcelain plates,
Qing dynasty

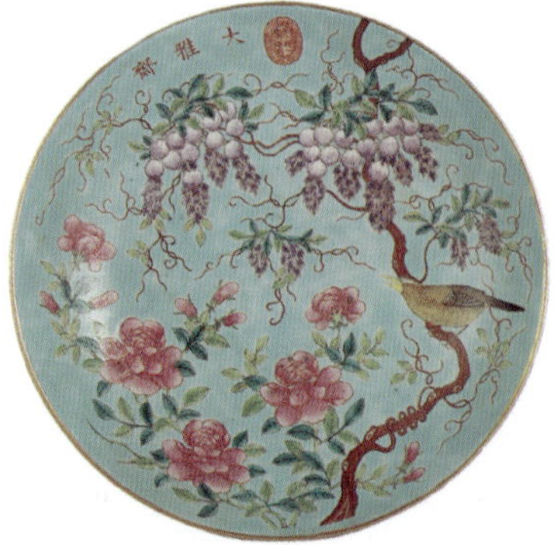

Taiping Heavenly Kingdom Historical Museum

96

太平天国历史博物馆 *Taiping tianguo lishi bowuguan*

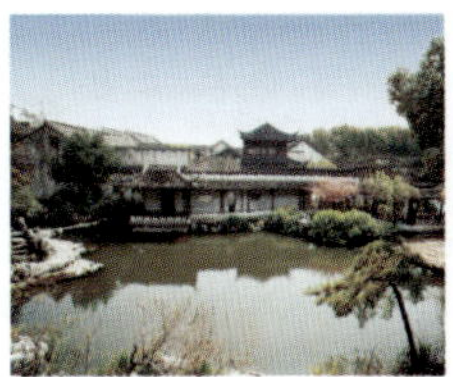

128 Zhanyuan Road, Nanjing, Jiangsu
江苏省南京市瞻园路128号
Tel: (025) 8661 2230
Open: 8.00–18.00
www.njtptglsbwg.com
Café in garden

The Museum is situated in the Zhanyuan Garden, a Ming garden of 18,000 sq m – one of the finest of the Suzhou-style gardens in China. In 1853, the garden was made the seat of the East kingdom of the Taiping rebels, but was destroyed in 1864 when the rebel regime was crushed. It has subsequently been recreated and is worth a visit in its own right.

The Taiping Rebellion was the greatest of the popular uprisings against the Manchu Qing dynasty in the nineteenth century. Led predominantly by the Hakka and Zhuang minority peoples, it was driven by the unorthodox Christianity of its leader, Hong Xiuquan, who believed he was the younger brother of Jesus.

From 1850 to 1864, the Taiping kingdom ruled a large portion of southern China, with a population of some thirty million and its capital in Nanjing. This fascinating museum gives a full picture of this extraordinary regime – its organization based on imperial China; its revolutionary social ideas on the one hand, and its obscurantism on the other. For instance, women played a role in public life for the first time in Chinese society, even becoming generals in the army. Foot binding, one of the great social evils, was abolished (although it has to be said that few working women bound their feet, and this was a predominantly working-class movement). There was strict segregation of the sexes – even amongst married couples. Land was socialized and, in theory, dispossessed. Private trade was also, in theory, suppressed. Confucianism as the dominant philosophy and regulator of Chinese life was replaced by a form of Christianity. Simplified Chinese characters were introduced by the regime a century earlier than their eventual acceptance. Poetry books were written for the education and edification of peasant children. Examples of all of these can be seen in the museum.

Unsurprisingly, all this radical and inflammatory policy drew the condemnation of landowners, merchants and foreign powers, who helped the Qing government to destroy it. Probably 30 million people died, many of starvation. Mao viewed the Taiping as early anti-feudal revolutionaries. Today, the verdict on their temporary success and the destruction they wrought may be more open. See for yourself in this fascinating museum who they were, what they achieved and why they failed. The English signage is not particularly good – but the graphics are fine.

97

Nantong Abacus Museum

南通中国珠算博物馆 *Nantong zhongguo zhusuan bowuguan*

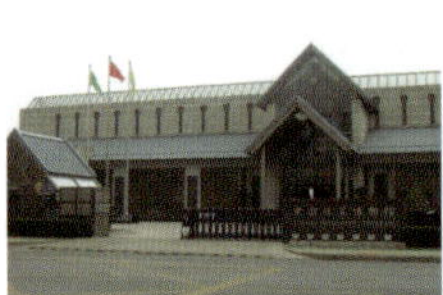

58 Haobei Road, Nantong, Jiangsu
江苏省南通市濠北路58号
Tel: (0513) 8505 3103
Open: 9.00–11.30 & 14.00–16.30 except Mon
Shop and leaflets in Chinese, English, Japanese & Korean

Believed to have been invented in China, the abacus (*suan pan*), as most of us know it, is a wooden-framed counting device with beads sliding freely on fixed rods. A visit to this museum, however, will confirm that abaci have been made from many other materials too: gold, silver, brass, agate, ivory and even ceramic (which requires that it is made all in one piece when fired). They come in a myriad of shapes and sizes, and in Chinese banks they are still the preferred tool for calculation, often placed next to the tellers. In fact, Chinese bank employees and certified

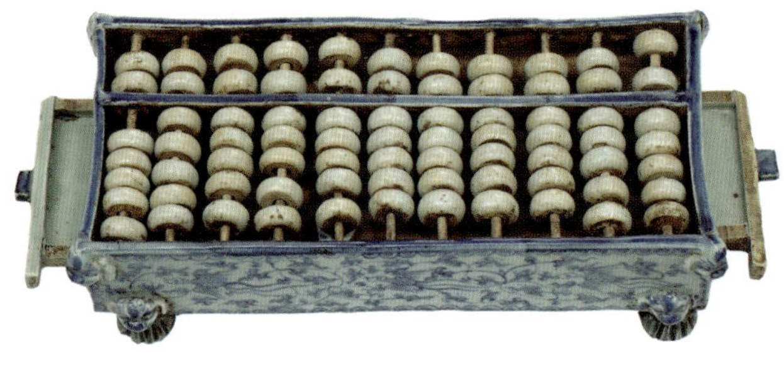

Blue and white porcelain abacus

accountants are required to pass an exam using only an abacus, and many claim they can calculate faster with one than with a calculator.

The sweeping galleries on the ground floor take visitors through the instrument's history. On display is a whole range of simple counting devices such as calculating sticks and boards with moveable counters that were in use as early as the Spring and Autumn period, according to an early work on the subject. Diagrams, pictures of important books on calculations and the men who wrote them attempt to take you through the complicated history of Chinese mathematics, which, unlike other forms of mathematics, developed out of the need to solve problems to do with land measurement, architecture and the like. Few early documents have been found which offer any real insights; however, it is clear that early astronomy texts showing how to measure the positions of the heavenly bodies played an important role in the development of the subject. The most famous is the Han dynasty book, *Nine Chapters on the Mathematical Art*, which solves 246 practical problems over nine chapters and which dominated Chinese mathematics for hundreds of years. Several of these ancient texts, including Sun Zi's manual on mathematics (*c.* 460) also includes instructions on how to use counting rods to add, subtract, multiply, divide and perform square roots.

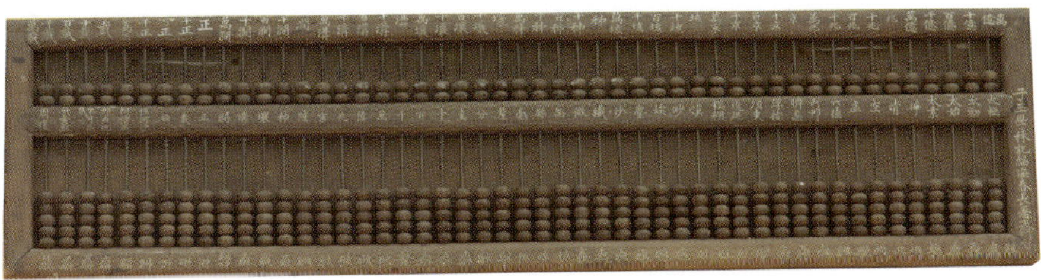

Yu Abacus

When the abacus finally came into use in China is debatable; however, it seems that it may have appeared as early as the eleventh century.

Other galleries highlight the role abaci have played in modern Chinese history. On display is a replica of an abacus used by Chinese physicists at the secret department at Beijing University, where they were studying the theory of nuclear reactors later used to produce the plutonium isotope for China's first atomic bomb in the 1960s. The physicists' biggest problem was a numerical calculation for which they lacked any kind of computer device and which they used abaci to solve instead. A bronze bust of Cheng Dawei, the influential sixteenth-century Chinese mathematician who published the *Suanfa tong zong* (General source of computational methods), takes pride of place. His treatise contained 600 computational problems, many applicable to everyday business and commerce. Displayed at the end of the gallery is a bust of Hua Yinchun (1896–1990), who spent most of his life on the systematic study of the abacus, producing the definitive text on the subject at the age of ninety, entitled *1000 Years of Abacus History*.

The second floor showcases dozens of abaci collected by the Chinese Association . Many have been purchased; others are donated often after visitors have been to the museum. Most on show are original, or are labelled when reproductions. They range from a 4-m-long abacus from 1949, which was used in a medical herbal factory, to a modern ivory one measuring 6 × 4 mm, which you view through a magnifying lens. The reproduction Qing dynasty abacus made for officers building the first iron warship in China is equally remarkable. Called the Zi Yu Abacus, it was needed for large number calculations and had forty-nine crosspieces with two beads on the upper deck and five on the lower (referred to as a 2/5 abacus). The last cases feature the ubiquitous plastic abaci, which can still be found throughout Asia, and the various combinations of calculators and abaci still being produced.

Nantong Kite Museum

南通风筝博物馆 *Nantong fengzheng bowuguan*

98

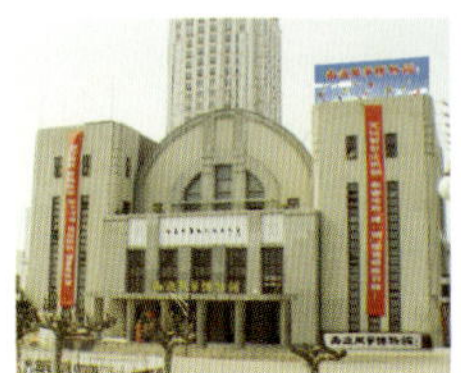

Jingye Temple, Beihaoqiaodong Village, Nantong, Jiangsu
江苏省南通市北濠桥东村静业庵内
Tel: (0513) 8558 0858
Open: 8.30–11.30 & 13.30–16.30
Kids

This museum is plastered from top to bottom with kites of all shapes, sizes and colours; even the ceiling is draped with distinctive examples. Display panels divide the space into sections, with diagrams, images and maps used to celebrate the origins and artistic achievements of this remarkable folk craft in China. The collection focuses on the whimsical creations known as whistle kites, made exclusively in Nantong for hundreds of years.

The art of making these unique kites still thrives in Nantong and you can visit workshops in the area and view generations of kite makers producing these works of art. The process consists of three steps, each executed by an artisan who specializes in a particular stage. Only very few makers are considered 'perfect masters' – able to do all three. Using thin strips of bamboo (different types are used depending on the size of the kite), the pieces are flexed into various shapes to produce the frame of the kite. Unique to these kites is the use of squares and rectangles, which are placed on top of one another to produce a hexagonal shape. The most basic kite is the 'one-star form', with one large square turned at an angle and laid over a similarly sized rectangle to form a star or semi-hexangular shape. One of the largest on display has 271 'stars' sewn together. The frame is covered with either ordinary or specially prepared paper and then painted with vivid geometric designs, animals or with images from legends, often with auspicious meanings. Lashed to the bamboo frame in various formations are rows of whistles of various sizes and either cylindrical or orb shaped. The cylindrical ones are fashioned out of very thin bamboo and are paper-thin to reduce weight and increase their vibration capacity in the wind. The orbs are made from dried, hollowed-out gourds with slotted tops carved from wood, which allow the wind to enter. Each of these 'whistles' is painted, usually in red

Large whistle of the whistling kite, Qing dynasty

and green, and lacquered. The whistles can also be made from other hollow shapes, from silkworm cocoons to the egg shells of chickens or quail. A large late Qing dynasty whistle, made from a gourd and beautifully painted, is on display. Acquired by the museum from a local family, the top is carved from a special tree native to the area. Some of the kites on display have dozens of whistles attached (the largest has over one hundred), but even larger ones have been known to have up to 300. The smallest whistles are at the top of the kite in rows of descending sizes, ending with the largest at the back so that the 'wind is not stolen'. When flown, each whistle produces a musical tone which together creates a 'symphony

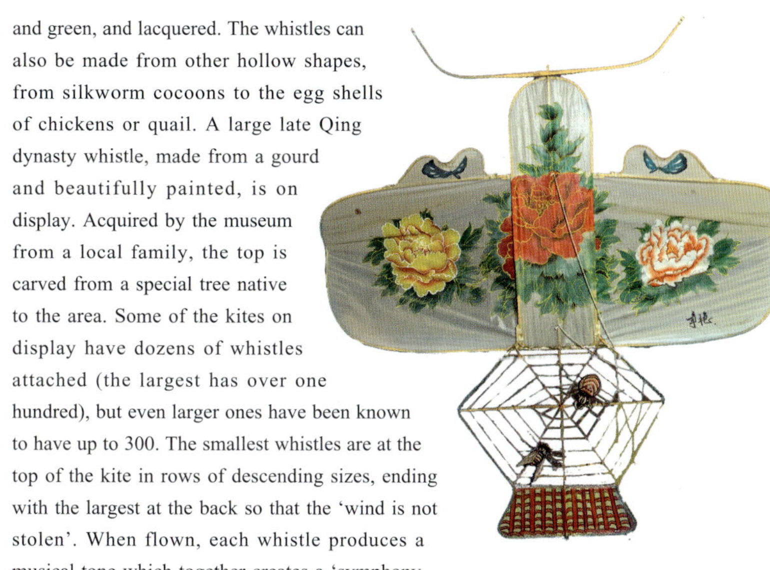

in the sky'. By slackening the line and pulling it in, the flier can generate a variety of rhythms and sounds.

The invention and early history of kites can only be surmised from legends, which suggest they were in existence 3,000 years ago in China and perhaps Malaysia. There is, however, evidence which points to them being flown in China back in 200 BC, used as a tool during the Chu-Han War and later spreading west to Japan and Korea and then eastwards via the South China Sea and overland via the Silk Route. Other uses through the ages have been to scare birds from crops and to lift fireworks into the air. During World War II, whistle kites were used in Nantong to warn locals that the Japanese were invading, and in ancient times to predict the weather. Strong winds would mean rain and storms were on their way and the resulting louder whistling sound would warn fishermen and those drying salt.

Besides Nantong, there are other areas in China famous for kites, including Beijing, Weifang in Shandong Province, and Tianjin. Weifang is famous for its annual International Kite Festival, when the air swarms with ingeniously designed examples, and there is also a kite museum there. There are numerous other kite festivals, clubs and kite competitions throughout the country and, besides being a popular pastime for families, the Chinese believe that flying a kite is very therapeutic and allowing it to fly away even healthier, as it will take your illness away with it.

Nantong Museum

99

南通博物苑 *Nantong bowuyuan*

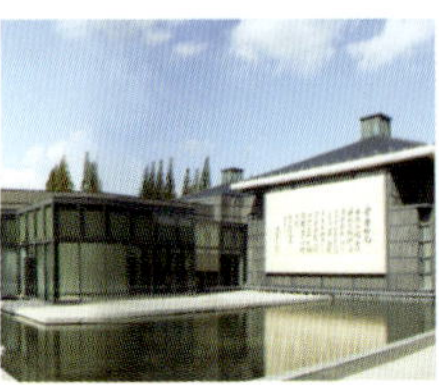

19 Haonan Road, Chongchuan District, Nantong, Jiangsu
江苏省南通市崇川区濠南路19号
Tel: (0513) 8506 2518/2528
Open: 9.00–17.00 except Mon, last entry 16.30
www.ntmuseum.com
Book and gift shop

The Nantong Museum is seated on the bank of the pretty Haohe River, founded by Zhang Jian, forerunner of Chinese modernism in 1905. It is the earliest museum in China. The original collection included natural history, history, fine art and education, much of it outdoors. There were trees and grasses, birds and animals to parallel the indoor exhibits. This garden style offered an exquisite, elegant and light atmosphere.

The idea of the garden museum was an original idea of Zhang Jian (1853–1926). As Number One Scholar in the late Qing Dynasty, he served in the Imperial Academy. He was also an industrialist and shipping magnate and a visionary educationalist and philanthropist. After the downfall of the Qing Dynasty, he was Minister of Industry and Minister of Agriculture and Commerce in the Republican government. To make China bigger and the people richer, Zhang Jian carried out his plans in his hometown, Nantong. The founding of the Nantong Museum is one of his patriotic ideas put into practice.

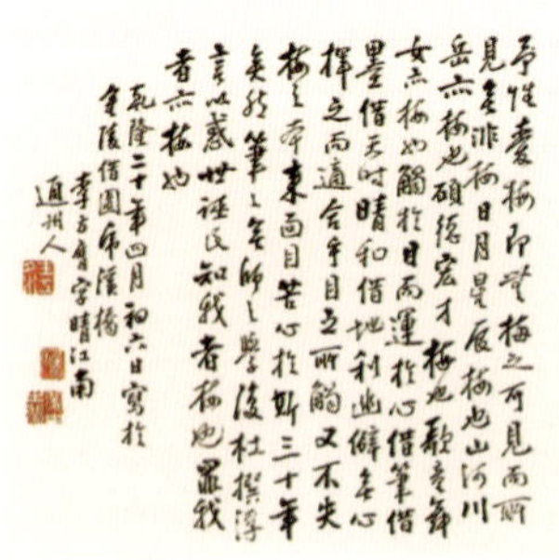

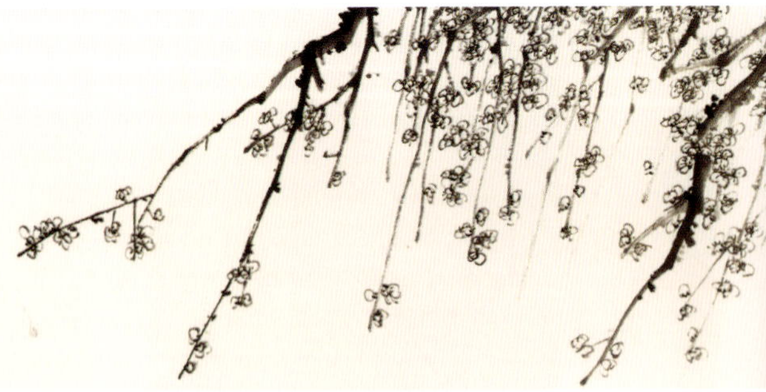

Plum blossom
By Li Fangying,
Qing dynasty

Zhang Jian combined Chinese traditional culture with western ideas on the construction of the museum, setting up a museum mixed with gardens. Nowadays, people still deeply respect Zhang Jian's theory of museums.

During the Japanese War the Nantong Museum in 1938 was turned into a stable by the Japanese invaders and greatly damaged. Most of the exhibits were stolen or destroyed. It was not until the founding of new China that the museum began to be reconstructed.

By 2005, at its centenary, the museum had been rapidly redeveloped. It has a new aspect. In the northern section, many parts have been restored to their original appearance. The southwestern section is newly built with new exhibits. The planned eastern section will be a comprehensive cultural gallery and the southern section will be a new ecological region. Within the museum there is once again a harmonious air with buildings old and new, an atmosphere of culture and an environment of beautiful gardens. The connection of exhibition buildings with gardens, indoor display with outdoor show, quiet articles with living things, embodies the link of science and culture. The original scenes and buildings offer an elegant place for study and tourism. It manifests both history and contemporary colour.

The new collection once again combines historical relics and natural specimens. The historical relics tell the story of the local people from the Neolithic Age to the revolutionary era of the first half of the twentieth century, and also the modern world. The natural specimens tell of the vast variety of flora and fauna of the Nantong area, in addition to specimens from other parts of the country.

The museum pays much attention to the educational and scientific ideas of Zhang

Porcelain hu from Yue kiln, late Tang dynasty

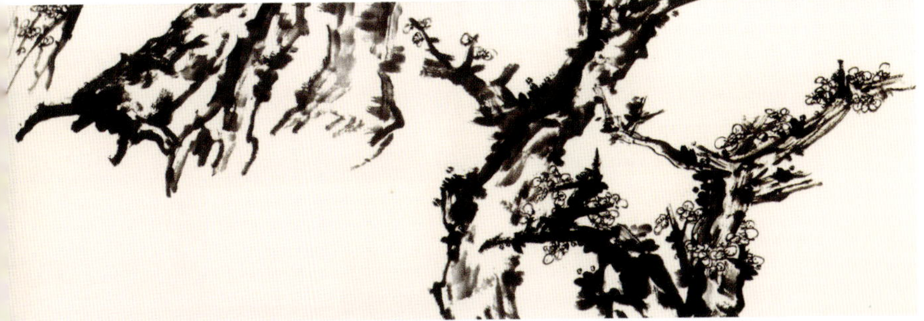

Jian. It organizes diverse exhibitions in communities and schools. It was made the moral education centre of Jiangsu Province. As Zhang Jian wrote in a poem: 'Green is the garden on the south of the Haohe River, and flourishing, faster and prettier is everything here growing.'

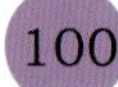

100

Nantong Textile Museum

南通纺织博物馆 *Nantong fangzhi bowuguan*

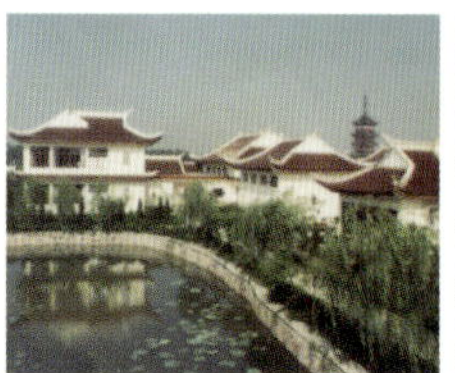

4 Wenfeng Road, Chuongchuan District, Nantong, Jiangsu
江苏省南通市崇川区文峰路4号
Tel: (0513) 8559 7740
Open: 9.00–16.30 except Mon
Gift shop

The semi-tropical monsoon climate in eastern Jiangsu Province is perfect for growing cotton, which has been a thriving industry here since the Song dynasty. It is not surprising, therefore, that the area has a rich tradition of textile design.

This old-fashioned but charming museum displays examples of a variety of ethnic textiles besides the local Nantong blue calico. In addition to the large collection of woven fabrics and clothing, other aspects of traditional life are illustrated, for example through demonstrations showing the old techniques such as hand weaving on traditional looms and basket weaving. There are also reconstructions of an old-fashioned kitchen and shop, making this as much a folk museum as a textile gallery. All sorts of paraphernalia and tools involved in textile production, from ancient to modern times, are exhibited. Historical contracts, bills and paperwork regarding transactions of local textile mills are also on view.

A detailed understanding of a number of the displays may be difficult as English signage is quite limited but the collection is well worth seeing, and the spacious rooms and pleasant gardens make for an enjoyable visit.

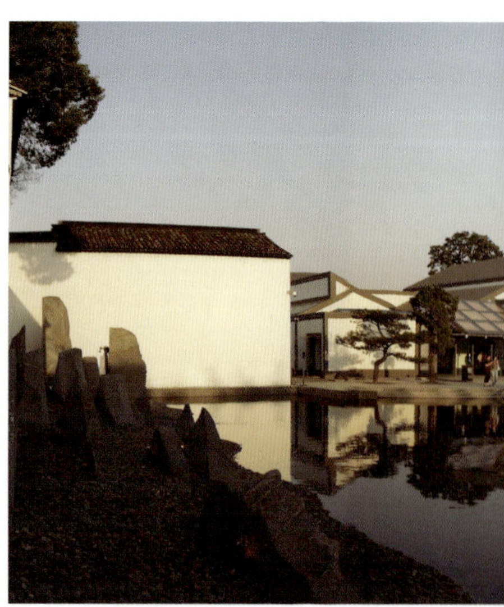

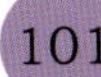

Suzhou Museum

苏州博物馆 *Suzhou bowuguan*

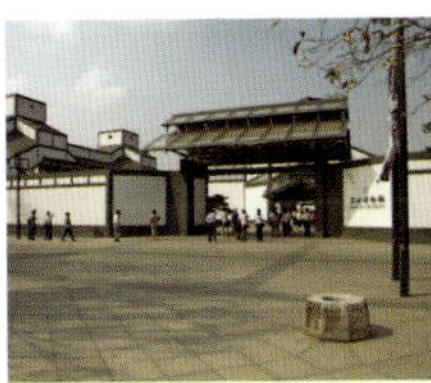

204 Dongbei Street, Suzhou, Jiangsu
江苏省苏州市东北街204号
Tel: (0512) 6757 5666
Open: 9.00–17.00 except Mon, last entry 16.00
www.szmuseum.com
Gift shop / bookstore / café

The new museum in Suzhou looks set to become an iconic building that will do for Suzhou what the Guggenheim has done for Bilbao, the difference here being that the collection itself is of more intrinsic interest than Bilbao. Suzhou is one of the most famous and beautiful cities in China, and the building is the last work of one of the city's most internationally famous native sons.

I. M. Pei's ancestors were of a noble Suzhou family. As a child, he lived in the Pei family house in the Lion Forest Garden, one of the great gardens of Suzhou, close to the site of the new museum. He emigrated in the 1930s and studied architecture at MIT and Harvard. He has undertaken many high-profile building commissions world-wide, including the Louvre pyramid, the Miho Museum near Kyoto and the Museum of Islamic Art in Doha. In 1999, he was commissioned to build this new museum for Suzhou, which opened in 2006.

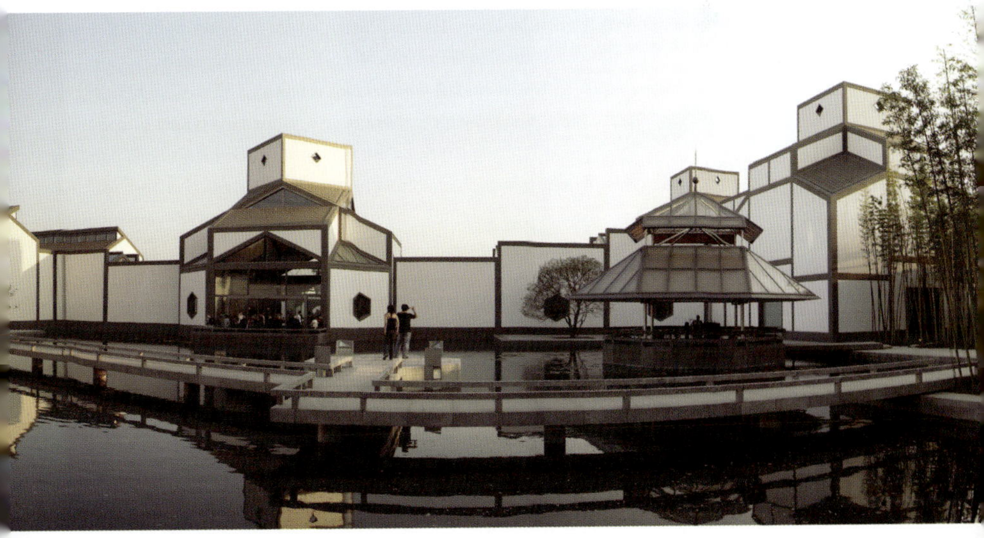

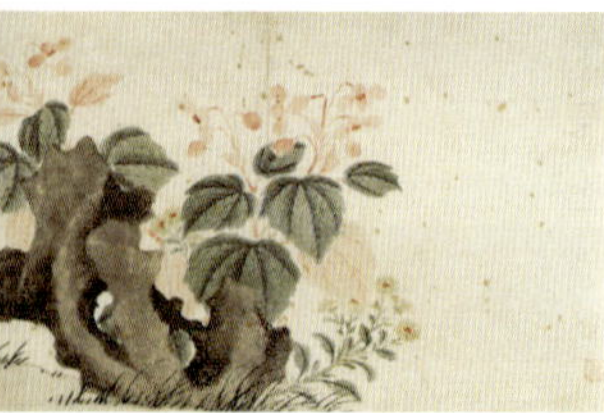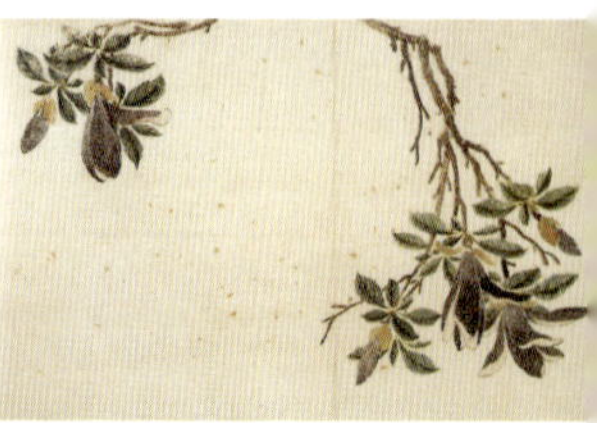

Flowers and birds
by Shen Zhou

Suzhou must not be missed. Situated on the lower Yangtze and the shores of Tai Lake, its garden and water culture are one of the great achievements of China. It is the capital of a land of tea, rice, fish and silk, with a recorded history of 2,500 years. In the Warring States period, it was the cradle of Wu culture, a highpoint of early Chinese civilization. Marco Polo called it 'the Venice of the East'; the Chinese called it 'Heaven on earth' (with Hangzhou).

Since 1949, the economy of the city has grown steadily, and it has sought to blend its new commercial wealth with the historic and pivotal role it has played in the taste and culture of southern China.

The original Suzhou Museum was opened in 1960 and housed in the Palace of Zhong Wangfu – a memorial to the history of the Taiping Rebellion. The new museum, of 10,700 sq m, is attached to Zhong Wangfu. It abuts the Humble Administrator's Garden, a high point of Suzhou's garden design. Situated on the corner of Dong Da Jie, it is thus at the heart of old Suzhou.

The building combines Pei's distinctive modern style with classical Suzhou style. Pei uses modern materials to recreate traditional structures; the steel and glass roof recreates the character of the seemingly random mixture of movement and structure found in traditional Suzhou building. The traditional pattern of white walls with black tiles is recreated in the white walls with grey-black granite.

The traditional wooden roof is replaced by steel and glass with metal louvres with wooden covers, allowing daylight to permeate the building and thereby minimizing the need for artificial lighting. Breaking with the tradition of large sloped roofs, Pei has created a complex of carefully integrated directional lines in harmony with the slopes of surrounding buildings.

The museum is centred on a garden with several smaller courtyards. The trees of the Humble Administrator's Garden provide the backdrop; there are staggered white walls, and a range of miniature mountains of slabs of sheet stone. There is a large water area with a cobbled bottom, a rockery, a zigzag bridge, an octagonal pavilion, bamboo groves and a stunning selection of trees. This modern Suzhou garden is worth a visit in itself.

Olive-green
celadon lotus-
shaped bowl and
saucer

The collections are housed in galleries which encircle the central garden, each one

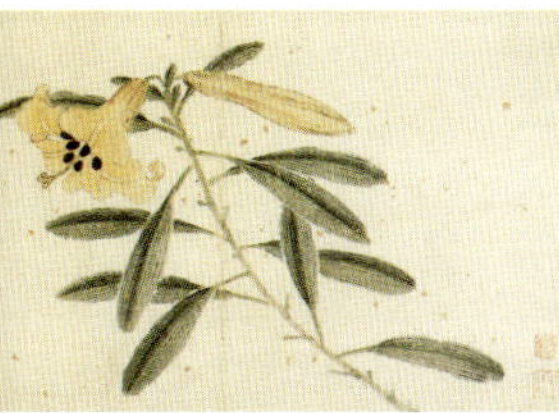 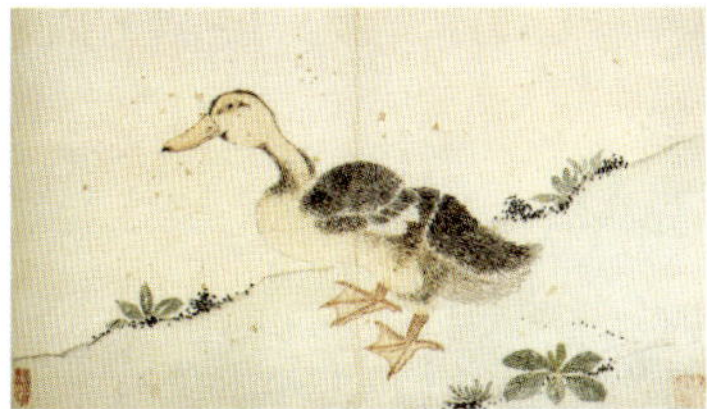 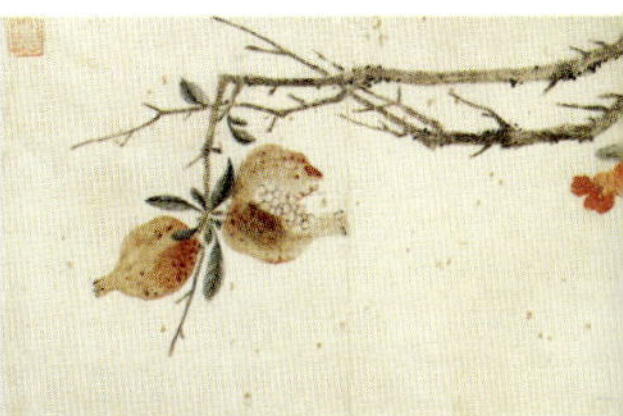

having its own shape and character appropriate to the nature of its contents – with a logical layout combined with constant glimpses of water, white walls, grey granite and a pattern of sloping roofs.

The treasures range from the Neolithic to the Qing. The tomb of King Helu of Wu has yielded agricultural implements, weapons and ritual bronzes. Another Wu tomb at Zhenshan has revealed a set of splendid jade objects with specifically local features from the Warring States period. Two excavations from the Five Dynasties and the Northern Song have enriched the collection; the former with an exquisite olive-green celadon lotus-shaped bowl and saucer; the latter with a pearl shrine for Buddhist relics, 122 cm tall, uniquely designed and superbly made.

The collection contains many treasures from the Tang and the Song dynasties, and a collection of painting and calligraphy from the Ming and the Qing.

A visit to the Suzhou Museum combines the pleasures of a most beautiful city, a landmark modern museum with a beautiful garden, and an interesting and varied collection.

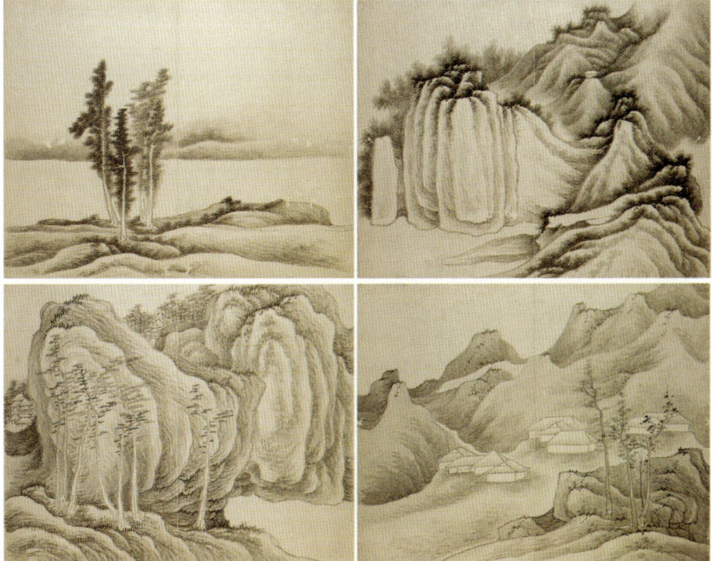

A Qing dynasty painting by Gong Xian

Suzhou Opera Museum

102

苏州戏曲博物馆 *Suzhou xiqu bowuguan*

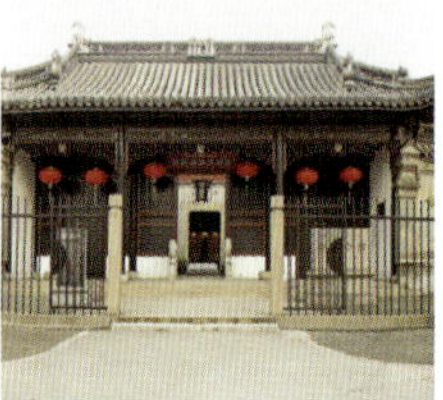

14 Zhongzhangjia Lane, Pingjiang District, Suzhou, Jiangsu
苏州市平江区中张家巷14号
Tel: (0512) 6727 5338 / 3334
Open: 8.30–16.30
Tea house decorated with scenes from famous operas

Suzhou Opera Museum – along with its two affiliated museums, China Kunqu Museum and Suzhou Pingtan Museum – is a place no opera buff should miss, for Kunqu opera is a cultural institution like no other. One of the oldest surviving operas in China, along with the famed Peking Opera, it is one of the best known forms among over 300 varieties. It originated in Kunshan, near Suzhou, during the Yuan and early Ming dynasties and is characterized by a classical form that focuses more on music and poetic wording than acrobatics. Librettos cover a range of topics and themes, including the intrigues of emperors and gods, love stories and comedies. The stories combine Chinese folklore, symbolism and drama, and include dancers, clowns and acrobats, as well as singers. The result is an extremely stylized spectacle that attempts to portray the full spectrum of life and beauty through crystallized choreography, make-up and costumes. Common actions such as laughing, crying, sleeping and opening doors are all precisely choreographed. The accompaniment usually consists of six instrumentalists led by the clapper, and includes the vertical flute and the *pipa* (lute) players, as well as other percussion players. Kunqu opera is a remarkable sight, but can be an acquired taste on account of its guttural, high-pitched singing style that differs so drastically from that of Western opera.

Being listed by UNESCO in 2001 as one of the Masterpieces of Oral and Intangible Cultural Heritage has led to government funding for the collection of traditional librettos, to support public performances and to train professionals. As a result, performances of updated versions of classic operas have been playing to large audiences around China, as well as abroad, with the Suzhou Kunqu Opera Company touring Europe and the USA with one of the classic plays

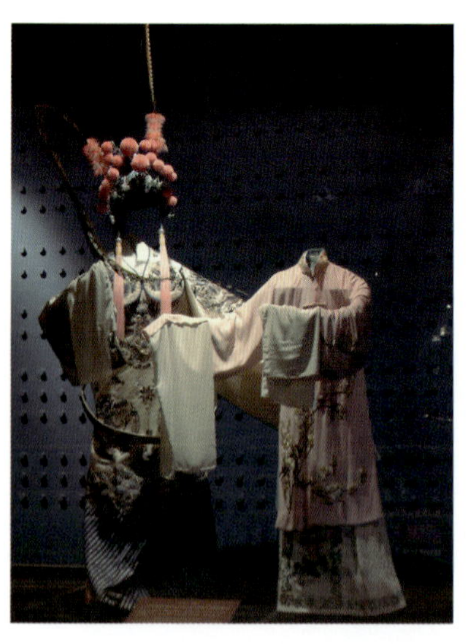

Opera costumes on display inside the theatre

of the Kunqu opera, *The Peony Pavilion*, written during the Ming dynasty and first performed in 1598.

Beautiful wooden doors flank the entrance of this recently restored venue, built by a Shanxi businessman during the Qing dynasty and opened as a museum in 2003. Visitors are greeted by a wooden sculpture of Wei Liangfu, a Ming musician who worked on developing southern opera to bring it up to par with that from the north, eventually producing rules for the singing of Kunqu. Music fills the air in the courtyard, giving a flavour of the artistic and dramatic power of watching a performance in the main building with its classical stage covered by a saddle-shaped roof and decorative well-shaped ceiling (caisson). Collections of costumes, scripts, masks, instruments, photographs, historical documents and miniature models are displayed in the exhibition areas offering a concise introduction to Kunqu, although with limited English explanations.

Very few historic Kunqu stages survive, so the displays of scaled wooden models of reconstructed stages are the best way to learn about the development and variety of opera venues. Performances took place in playhouses in the city, but also in private gardens (including Suzhou's Humble Administrator's Garden) and residences, guildhalls, government offices, teahouses and even in fields and temples. The Kangxi and Qianlong Emperors, on their tours south to the city, had their provisional palaces fitted out with stages and make-up rooms. Performances were played out on red carpets, hence the association of the phrase 'red carpet' with centre stage. Suzhou's profusion of waterways meant performances were also often staged on the bow of boats, with the cabins used as make-up rooms, while spectators watched seated on the boat or from boats nearby. Impromptu venues were replaced by more permanent playhouses, many of them refurbished old teahouses equipped with stages, pits and electric lighting. Besides a 1:25 scale model of the first lit stage in Suzhou, fashioned from stone and wood, there is a model of a mobile stage which originally would have been made of wood and bamboo so that it could easily be disassembled and moved to another venue. A replica stage boat is also on display.

Several traditionally dressed characters from celebrated Kunqu operas give visitors some idea of the complexity and sophistication of the headpieces and costumes, many richly embroidered and all with long sleeves extending well beyond the hands, used to great effect when executing a movement. A range of musical instruments used in Kunqu are displayed, along with an assortment of books about Chinese opera (all in Chinese) and works by the famous painter of Kunqu characters, Gao Made. This is a research venue for Kunqu opera, although performances for small groups can be arranged if booked in advance. A DVD (in Chinese and English) is also available, providing information on the history and practice of Kunqu opera.

Actors in the Kunqu opera *Yu Zan Ji* (Story of Jade Hair Clasp)

Xuzhou Museum

徐州博物馆 *Xuzhou bowuguan*

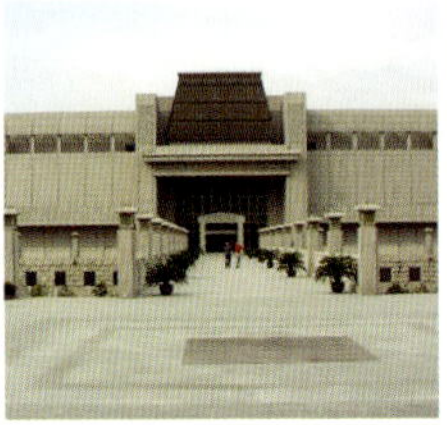

101 Heping Road, Xuzhou, Jiangsu
江苏省徐州市和平路101号
Tel: (0516) 8380 4412
Open: 9.00–17.00 except Mon, last entry 16.30
www.xzmuseum.com/index2.asp
Gift shop / bookshop

Although not considered a tourist hot spot, Xuzhou (previously known as Pengcheng) was the capital of the vassal state of Chu in the early periods of the Western Han dynasty (206 BC–AD 9) and in recent years has demonstrated how significant a place it was by the astounding finds excavated from a number of tombs among hundreds scattered throughout the eastern part of the city and in nearby locations. Many of the tombs are open for viewing, including the rock cut tomb at Shizishan (Lion Hill) built for the King of the Western Han dynasty Chu state, Liu Wu (174–154 BC), that of the third Prince of Chu and the Guishan (Turtle Hill) tomb of Liu Zhu (128–116 BC), the sixth Prince of Chu.

The tomb and mausoleum of Liu Wu and his wife were excavated in 1994–1995 and, besides the numerous miniature terracotta warriors and horses (25–60 cm in height) buried in pits around the tomb, it yielded thousands of stunning finds. A selection of these, plus several items from the other tombs are on display in the second floor galleries. They include finely fashioned jades, gold plaques, bronzes, seals, gilt belt buckles, coins and lutes, giving visitors an idea of the lavish lifestyle of the princes and an insight into their burial practices. Liu Wu's tomb, cut deep into the rock face of the mountain, includes a 117-m long vaulted passage connecting to a burial chamber with a nearby courtyard. That of Liu Zhu and his wife was rather more elaborate, with two connected coffin chambers and ancillary rooms including a stable, two chariot and horse rooms, an armoury and even a lavatory. They had complicated bathing rituals which included using silver basins and bronze mirrors and granting their officials holidays to take baths. A silver seal with a tortoise-shaped knob found in the tomb identifies its occupants. Like the Pharaohs of ancient Egypt, they believed in an afterlife and prepared for it by surrounding themselves with all the paraphernalia believed to be necessary for a luxurious life after death.

Liu Wu was entombed within a coffin consisting of three layers: the outer rock mausoleum, a jade and red lacquered wooden coffin and a jade burial suit stitched together with gold thread (which has been replaced because the thread was stolen by ancient grave robbers). The exceptional burial suit, a national treasure, is also on display. Constructed of over 4,200 pieces, it covered every part of the body, including the head and feet. There was even a jade mask for his face made from some twenty-eight geometrically shaped pieces. The ancient Chinese believed jade would help preserve the body and therefore also their spirits.

Other highlights among the finds from the Western Han tombs are some lovely terracotta figurines, in particular a collection of dancers and musicians, as well as a selection of notable jade artefacts including a jade dragon and ceremonial *bi* that exemplify the skills of the ancient craftsmen who fashioned such quality objects. The first floor contains a collection of pottery and jade pieces dating from the Neolithic Qingliangang Culture to the Qin dynasty. The third floor focuses on porcelain, with representative examples from the Tang to the Qing dynasties, including a large selection of Tang *sancai*-glazed pottery and figurines. There are English labels on most of the exhibits and some introductory signs are in English, but little else in the way of supplementary information. However, the beauty of many of the items on display speaks for itself.

Jade burial suits displayed on either side of a jade coffin, second century BC, Western Han dynasty

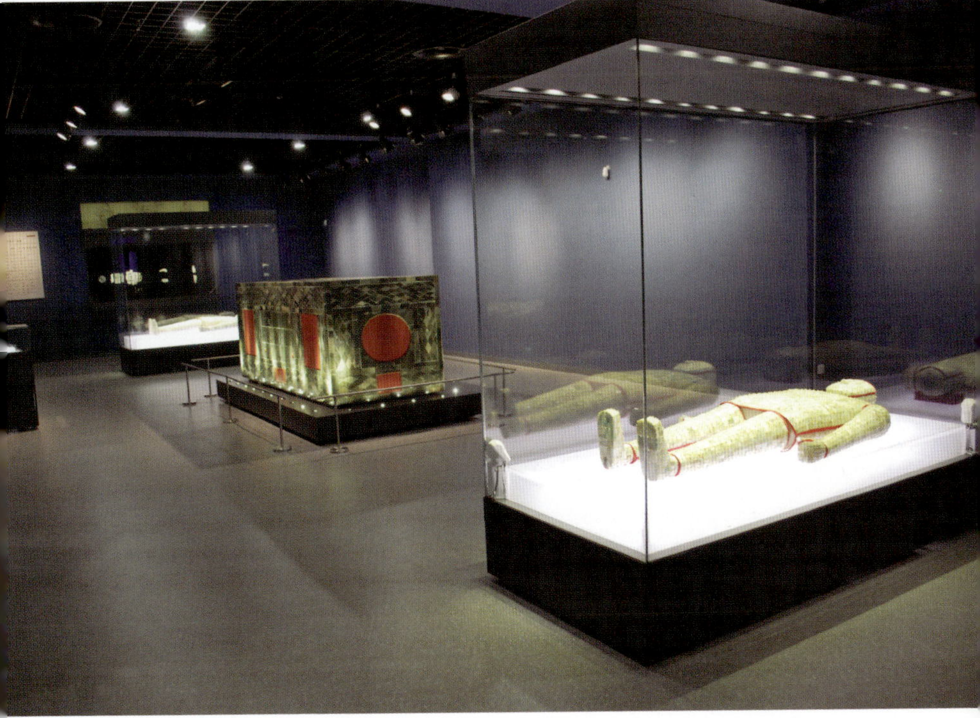

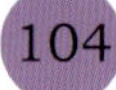

Yangzhou Museum / China Block-printing Museum

扬州博物馆/中国雕版印刷博物馆

Yangzhou bowuguan / zhongguo diaobanyinshua bowuguan

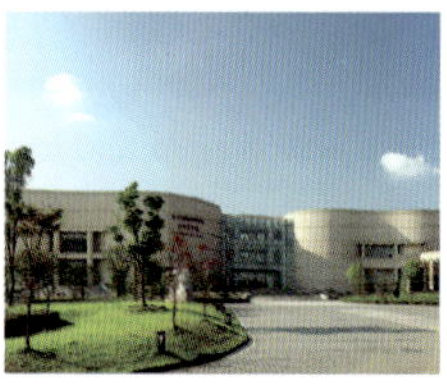

468 Wenchang West Road, Yangzhou, Jiangsu
江苏省扬州市文昌西路468号
Tel: (0514) 8522 8001 / 8522 8003
Open: 9.00–17.00 except Mon
www.yzmuseum.com
Gift shop / restaurant

Yangzhou's old city is a charming place with part of the original moat still surviving and dotted with lakes and and canals. On the west side of the poetically named 'Mingyue' or Bright Moon Lake, stands The China Block Printing Museum and Yangzhou Museum, known locally as the Twin Museum.

The Yangzhou museum showcases a variety of Chinese art from the Neolithic to the late Qing Dynasty. Originally housed in the 1500 year old Tianning Temple and after several moves, it has now moved into a more modern building to accommodate its growing collection. In 2003, the museum acquired over 3 million antique block-printed books and thus the newly created China Block Printing Museum was joined to the Yangzhou Museum.

The Yangzhou Museum collection covers Yangzhou's history from the Neolithic to the Qing but specializes in objects from the Han Dynasty, Sui, Tang, and Qing. Many objects displayed have been recently excavated from sites in the area.

Yangzhou was a flourishing city from the Ming to the Qing. It was a distribution centre for salt, silk and rice.

During the Tang dynasty, the city had one of the largest harbours in China and so Yangzhou's commerce flourished alongside the fine workmanship of its artisans. A magnificent and huge dragon boat made of beautiful nanmu sits in the centre of the museum.

It is said that during the Yuan Dynasty, Marco Polo lived and worked in Yangzhou. To the west of the museum building stands a statue of the explorer.

There are six permanent exhibition halls and one temporary gallery. These are divided into Yangzhou History, Ancient Chinese Sculptures, Paintings and Calligraphy of Yangzhou, National Treasures, Chinese Block Printing and Yangzhou Block Printing.

The Paintings exhibition includes work from the famous "Eight Eccentrics of Yangzhou". Their names were Jin Nong, Huang Shen, Zheng Xie (Zheng Banqiao), Li Shan, Li Fangying, Wang Shishen, Gao Xiang and Luo Pin. These were a group of artists from

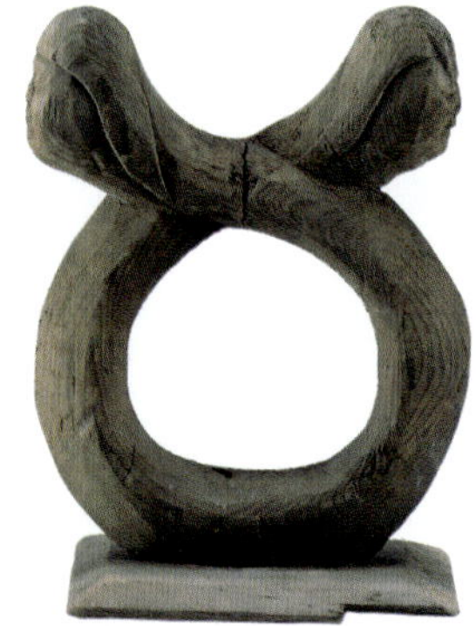

Wooden figurine in the shape of double-heads and snake's body

the early part of the Qing Dynasty, during the Qianglong Reign. They are called 'eccentric' as they spurned traditional painting methods and preferred a more creative approach. Their work influenced many of China's later painters and calligraphers including Qi Baishi and Wu Changshuo.

History tells us that during the Tang dynasty, Yangzhou had a large population of Arab merchants. Artefacts from the time of their residence in the city are displayed in the museum – pottery, texts and everyday utensils.

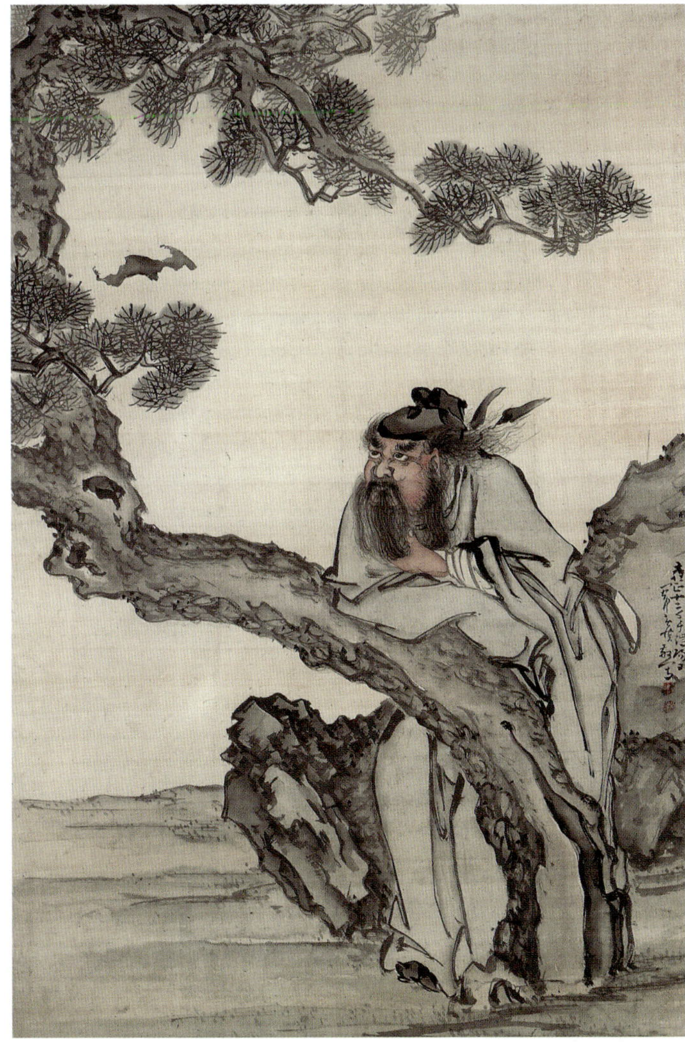

Zhong Kui by Huang Shen. Zhong Kui is a figure of Chinese mythology who is able to command demons

105

China Grand Canal Museum

中国京杭大运河博物馆 *Zhongguo jinghang dayunhe bowuguan*

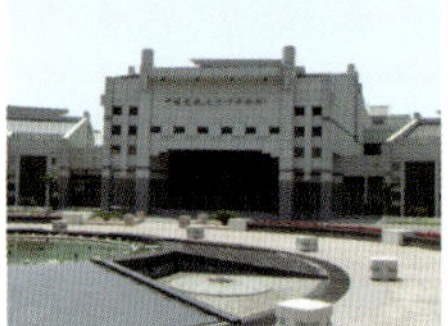

1 Grand Canal Culture Square, Gongshu District, Hangzhou, Zhejiang
浙江省杭州市拱墅区运河文化广场1号
Tel: (0571) 8816 2058/2018
Open: 9.00–16.30 Wed–Sun
www.canal-museum.cn
English audio guide and brochure

Completed in the Sui dynasty (581–618), the Grand Canal laid the foundation for the economic development of the Tang and subsequent dynasties. This major engineering feat, which stretches 1,800 km from south to north, was designed to serve as a transport channel, providing an economic and cultural conduit through the heart of China.

Little more than half of the original Grand Canal is still a functional transport channel, but it's still a bustling and important channel and a historical site. Triple the amount of goods is transported along the canal each year than is moved by railways between Beijing and Shanghai. Furthermore, the industrial output of the eighteen key cities straddling the canal accounts for one-fifth of the country's total industrial output. Unfortunately, parts of the canal, primarily in the north, have gone dry, making it impossible for boats to pass through.

This interesting and well-organized museum is divided into five halls, each dedicated to a different topic, and with limited English explanations. The Introductory Hall focuses on canals around the world and China's own Grand Canal. The First Hall and Second Hall are devoted to technical issues regarding the Grand Canal, the Third Hall tells the story of cities along the canal, and the Fourth Hall describes canal culture.

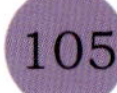

Han dynasty celadon, one of the many objects found along the canal between Hangzhou and Jiaxing

The exhibits are quite interesting, and include the following: a 3D movie theater, cartoons, interactive screens, boat replicas, a mock canal dock, old black and white photos of towns and life on the canal, and artefacts discovered along the canal, from buckets to pottery. In one large room, a glass-covered replica of the Grand Canal runs underfoot from Hangzhou to Beijing, winding its way along the floor past houses, bridges and other recognizable landmarks.

One of the highlights of the Grand Canal Museum is that just to the west of the entrance is the ancient Gongchen Bridge, which spans the Grand Canal. Walk out the entrance and turn left and walk through the square until you reach the sharply arched bridge. When you get to the top, you can sit there and watch the barges going up and down the canal as they have for centuries.

106

China National Silk Museum

中国丝绸博物馆 *Zhongguo sichou bowuguan*

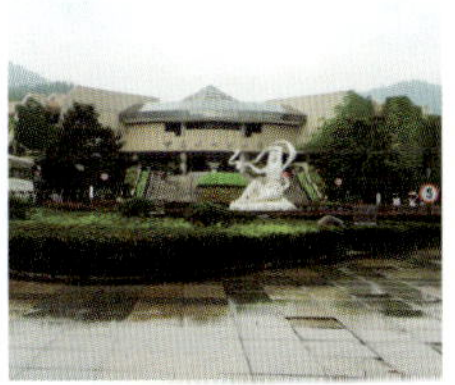

73-1 Yuhuangshan Road, Hangzhou, Zhejiang
浙江省杭州市玉皇山路73-1号
Tel: (0571) 8703 5223 / 5150
Open: 9.00–17.00 except 9.00–12.00 Mon and holidays
www.chinasilkmuseum.com
English and Chinese audio guide/small guide book / gift shop
/ shop selling silk items/tea house   Kids

No textile enthusiast would miss this superlative storehouse of cultural wonders covering all aspects of silk history, from sericulture (silk production) and the origins of silk weaving and trade, to displays of twentieth-century fashion. Known as the 'queen of fibres', silk has been produced in China from around 2700 BC and since it became a major commodity in the Western Han under the reign of Emperor Wu-ti (140–87 BC), it has played a significant part in the economic and social development of the country. Located near the city's scenic West Lake, the museum opened in 1992 and is one of the largest showcases for silk history in China. Daily fashion shows, as well as educational   activities and a textile conservation, research and identification facility make this a truly vibrant museum.

Over three floors there are eight galleries with displays in well-lit, modern showcases augmented with excellent and more than adequate English and Chinese signage. Although the lighting may seem dim in some galleries this is because textiles are highly sensitive to light and explains why they are also regularly rotated. Besides drawing from the museum's core collection, much of which has been donated by private collectors, some objects are on loan from the Palace Museum and other institutions.

A silk costume from Ming dynasty

A good place to start is in the entry hall on the first floor, where an illustrated, comprehensive timeline on the history of silk sweeps across a curved wall. In another hall, a large map shows the three major Silk Roads: the one through the grasslands of the north, the one via the desert to the west and the maritime route. For those interested in weaving technology, head to the ground floor's Dyeing and Weaving Gallery and Weaving Workshop. The first section uses objects and reproduction images of Chinese women processing silk to demonstrate the steps required in silk dyeing and thread production. Unwinding the cocoons is done by 'reeling' women. Once the pupae in the cocoon are killed by heating, they are placed in hot water to soften the gum that binds the filaments together. The reeling women find the loose end of the cocoon and, with great skill, several filaments at a time are reeled onto a bobbin to make one long thread. The more filaments wound together the thicker the thread and, when woven, the heavier the cloth. Two large model looms illustrate the processes of shedding and patterning in weaving. Shedding is one of several complex steps used in loom weaving and is the point where the warp (or vertical) yarn is raised to form a 'shed' through which the shuttle carrying the filler yarn is passed. Models of ancient looms from China and elsewhere are on display. Particularly fascinating are the numerous replica working looms manned by first-rate weavers producing an array of silk cloths. They range from a drawloom operated by two people and used to weave complicated figured fabrics like brocade and samite, to a balance treadle loom popular in the Qing and a multi-heddle loom developed in the Han for the production of *jin* silk (complex warp-faced polychrome woven silks).

The first floor includes the Textile Gallery, which explores the origins, production and trade of silk, and features displays of different types of woven silks, and dyed and printed textiles. There is also the Costume Gallery and a delightful gallery devoted to sericulture, which children will enjoy.

Understanding the lifecycle of the silk moth is crucial to appreciating the mystery of silk and its considerable value in China and elsewhere for centuries. Interactive displays and enlarged models of the silk worms and cocoons bring to life the four stages of the blind, flightless moth, *Bombyx mori*. The moth lays hundreds of eggs (approx 500 eggs will produce 10 kg of silk) which hatch into worms (larva) that munch away on a diet of mulberry leaves until they are bursting and ready to spin their cocoon of silk filaments from a substance in their silk glands. Several days later they produce a white fluffy cocoon–home for the pupa. Eight days after that, they are baked to kill the pupas, placed in hot water and the silk filaments unwound.

The textile galleries are the highlight of the museum, displaying samples of rare silks discovered in tomb sites and along the Silk Road; decorative textiles-woven, printed, tie-dyed, clamp-resist dyed and embroidered-imperial robes and accoutrements, and garments such as the delicate gauze pants and coat dating from the Southern Song. Here, not only does it start to become clear how important a role silk has played in China on many levels, including economically and politically, but also the sheer artistic magnificence of the creations on display is breathtaking in itself. These galleries offer a wealth of information on this fascinating art form, including the technological advances that made possible the weaving of symbols and complicated

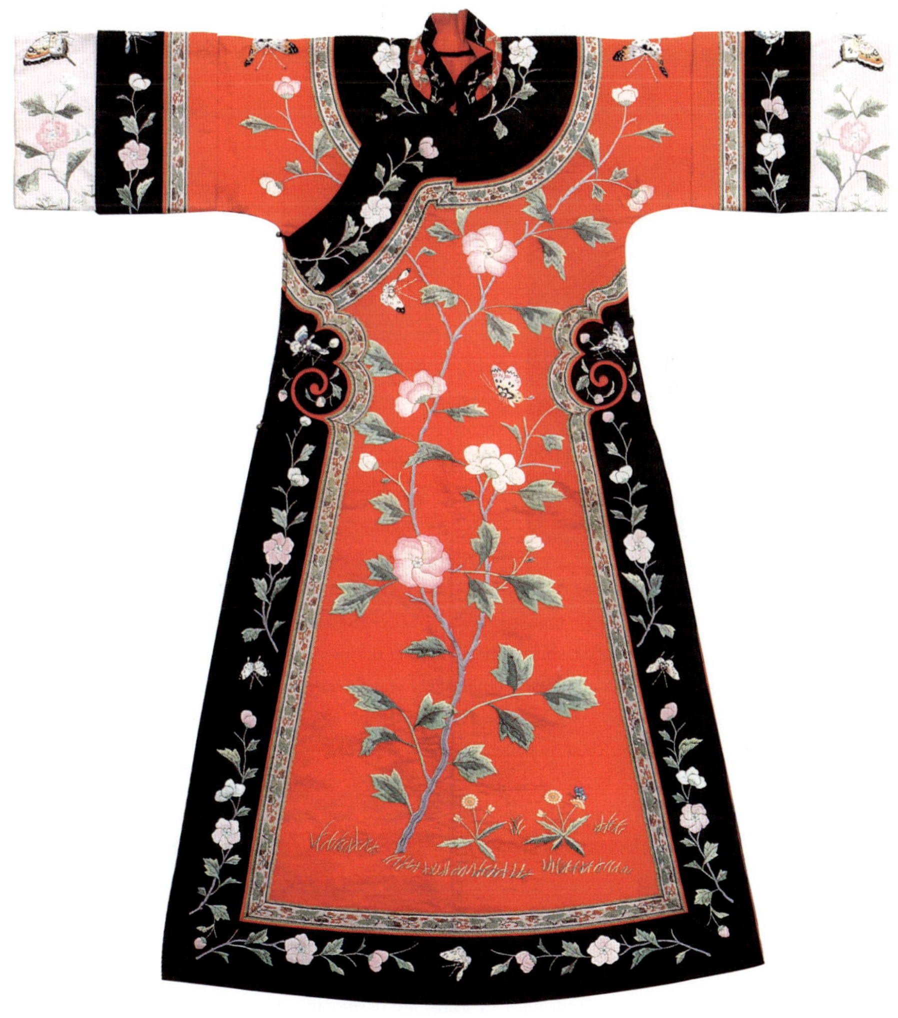

Qipao with flower and butterfly pattern, Qing dynasty

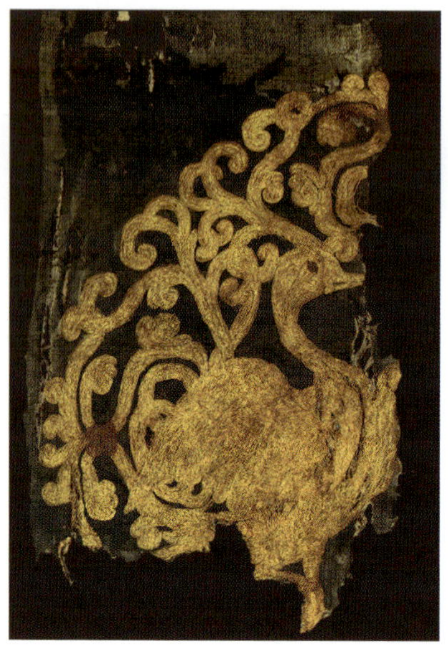

Golden decorative pattern from Liao dynasty

designs into colourful, patterned fabrics to make garments which had deep meaning and were visually stunning. One of the items is a silk ribbon dating from 2750 BC, which was discovered in 1958 at the Qianshanyang site of the Neolithic Liangzhu Culture. One of the earliest silk finds in the Yangtze River basin, this small, seemingly insignificant group of threads represented a historical milestone. It was here, from this small beginning in the Yangtze Delta, that silk production originated and where later, in the Ming dynasty, ten major weaving and dyeing workshops were established. By the Qing dynasty, there were three official imperial silk workshops located here, in Jiangning (present day Nanjing), Suzhou and Hangzhou. During the Qing, passports were issued for the silks produced by these private imperial looms, allowing them permission to travel to the imperial workshops for fashioning into garments, or as gifts for the Emperor to bestow on dignitaries or high-ranking officials.

An entire gallery is dedicated to the various classifications that categorize woven textiles, from silk tabby, plan gauze and twill damask to *kesi* or tapestry weave. Magnified sections of samples illustrate the complexity of their construction. Starting during the Shang dynasty we learn that the dominant stitch of Chinese embroidery was the chain stitch, which was later replaced in the Tang dynasty by the plain and coaching stitches. The Han and Tang silks from the Silk Road and the Liao and Yuan examples from the northern grasslands are especially beautiful. Samples of *jin* silk, with dragon and phoenix designs dating from the Warring States period are a must see, as are later examples woven with musicians, hunters and animals from the Northern dynasties (AD 386–581). The Liao (916–1125) examples include brocaded twills with designs of birds and flowers, and gauze embroidered with animals. Among the rows of cases displaying costumes are marvellous Yuan robes punctuated with thick waistbands, looking like contemporary garments with their simple designs and muted colours; and the Qing brocade four-clawed dragon robes, some of which are decorated with Taoist emblems and clouds, reflecting the importance of ceremony and ritual.

The second floor displays more recent textiles from the late Qing dynasty to the present day – there are excellent examples of *qipaos*, and Western-style jackets and shirts dating from 1912 to 1949, some fur lined, others quilted. The *qipaos* from the 1930s reveal how Western influences transformed these once loose garments into closer-fitting dresses with side slits. Using imported and Shanghai Art Deco designed fabrics made them fashionable even abroad.

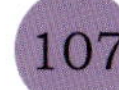

107

China National Tea Museum

中国茶叶博物馆 *Zhongguo chaye bowuguan*

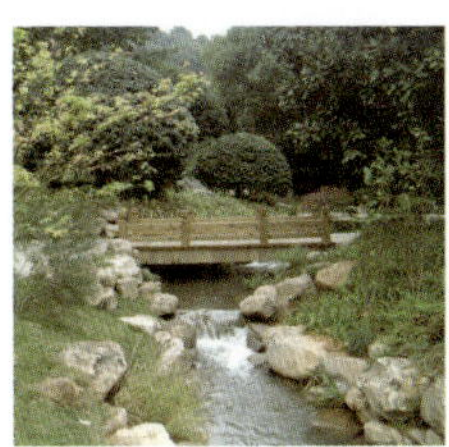

88 Longjing Road, Hangzhou, Zhejiang
浙江省杭州市龙井路88号
Tel: (0571) 8796 4221
Open: 9.00–17.00 except Mon, May 1–Oct 7;
　　　8.30–16.30 except Mon, Oct 8–Apr 30
www.english.teamuseum.cn
Tea house / shop

It's worth being dropped off at the end of the road which leads up to the museum and walking up, as the surrounding sea of green leaves being plucked from the low lying tea plants by women young and old wearing cone-shaped strawhats, each with a basket strapped to their backs, is well worth savouring. Nestled amongst these rolling mounds covered with Hangzhou's famous Longjing (or Dragon Well) green tea, are four separate buildings comprising this complex. The main two-storey building contains six halls covering every aspect of tea, from its cultural significance and its bewildering varieties, to tea customs, the art of the tea ceremony and the role tea has played in the world's economy. The other buildings are used for educational purposes, tea ceremonies, receptions and academic conferences and there is a tea house, restaurant and shop where you can sip infusions of steely coloured balls of Gunflower tea, or the flat leaves of the local Dragon Well tea or else purchase a tea pot from a dizzying selection.

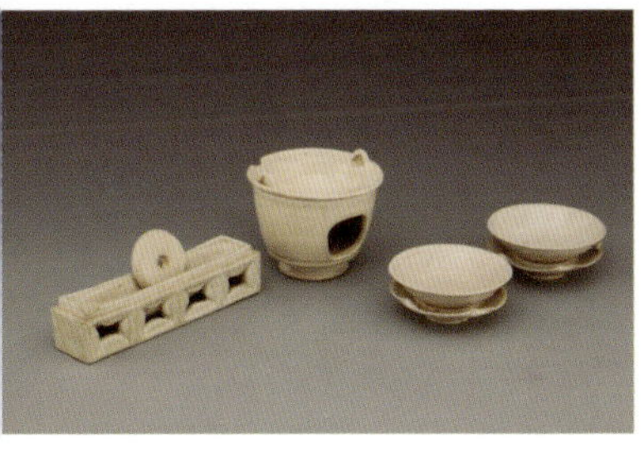

White glazed tea set, Tang dynasty

Statues of Lu Yu, the Tang scholar cum tea sage, greet you both inside and outside the main exhibition building. Revered as a saint in China, he wrote the *cha jing* or 'Classic of Tea', a three-volume discourse covering every aspect of tea, from growing and brewing it to a description of a formal tea ceremony using dozens of tea utensils. During the Song tea tasting became an intellectual enjoyment and a means of cultivating one's moral character. It was seen to be in harmony with other arts such as poetry and painting.

Artefacts such as a Han dynasty model pottery stove and tea cups and saucers from the Southern dynasty among other items in the first galleries attempt to shed some light on the question of where tea-drinking began or how the wild tea bush, *Camellia sinensis* (a strain of camellia, but with duller flowers) arrived in China. It is thought that it was first brought in the Han dynasty from India with Buddhism via Sichuan, which today remains a main tea-growing region. Then it was most probably used for medicinal purposes. Certainly by the Tang, tea was being drunk for pleasure and had become a popular activity in the imperial court. At this time tea also started being traded for horses along the ancient 'tea-horse road' stretching from Sichuan and Yunnan provinces to the Tibetan Plateau. *Pu-erh* tea named after the area in Yunnan where it is produced became sought after by the Tibetans (they mixed it with yak butter) and for ease of transport was steamed and compressed into various shapes, including square blocks or bricks. Examples of those displayed include ones imprinted with patterns or designs and which were also used as a form of currency in China and Central Asia.

Tea-processing methods, which produce an intricate variety of specialities from black tea, white tea, green tea and Oolong tea etc. are demonstrated through images, diagrams and models. Green tea remains the most popular tea in China. Around 70 per cent of the world's trade is produced here made from unfermented leaves that are heated or steamed, rubbed, dried and rolled into a variety of shapes. Black tea is allowed to wither in the sun, then kneaded and allow to oxidize and finally dry roasted to stop the oxidation. The process of preparing infusions is also explained. Making a cup of Longjing tea is not a matter of just pouring boiling water on the leaves. Instead, two grams are placed in a transparent glass and infused with around a quarter of a cup of 80-degree centigrade water and left for 40 seconds before more hot water is poured in with three nods of the kettle until it is 70 per cent full. The filling action helps the leaves to 'dance' up and down and evens out the concentration between the layers, while filling it to just 70 per cent leaves 30 per cent for affection!

The second floor is split into two galleries and shows several hundred top class tea implements, including kettles, cups, trays and bowls from the glazed ceramic beauties of the Song dynasty, to an under-glazed blue tea vase from the Qing. Objects include imperial pieces on loan from the Palace Museum and others from Korea and Japan. The Customs Hall describes the five main tea-drinking regions of China and their variations through recreated displays of their furnishings and sets of tea implements. Included is a bamboo pavilion from an area called the Xishuangbanna in southern Yunnan where the Dai and other ethnic groups grow the well-known *Pu-erh* tea in the tropical forests of this region, to the serene setting of Sichuan where green tea infused with jasmine blossoms is sipped from porcelain tea bowls complete with a lid and saucer.

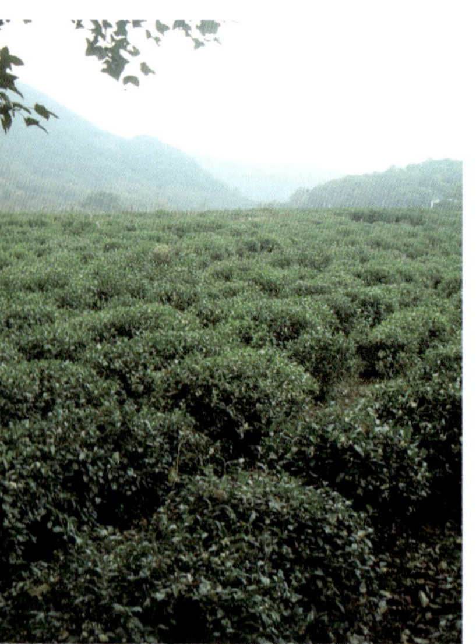

Tea plantation outside the museum

Hu Qingyu Tang Traditional Chinese Medicine Museum

胡庆余堂中药博物馆 *Huqingyutang zhongyao bowuguan*

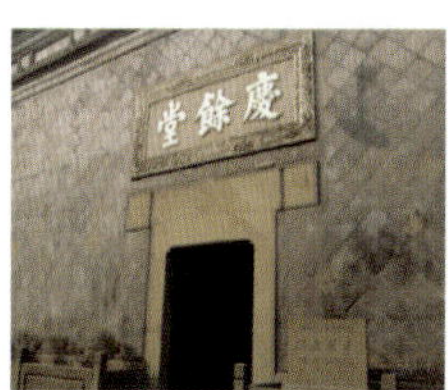

95 Daijing Lane, Hangzhou, Zhejiang
浙江省杭州市大井巷95号
Tel: (0571) 8783 9108
Open: 8.30–17.30
Chinese medicine pharmacy

'Collect bulging caterpillar fungi... dry them in the dark... take five *bai* (grain-like plant), two *mendong* (drug from plants in the genus Liriope), and one *fuling* (pine truffle). Pestle them together... soak in water... press to obtain liquid ... drink a three-fingered pinch in one half cup of... 'Although this sounds like the witches' brew from Shakespeare's *Macbeth*, it was written 1800 years earlier in a medical manual, entitled 'Recipes for Nurturing Life' unearthed in Tomb 3 at the famous Western Han dynasty site of Mawangdui in Hunan Province. It was one of eighty-seven detailed concoctions recorded in medical manuscripts written on silk. Today this 'curative' and other traditional Chinese herbal medical literature and plants are being screened for new drugs by powerful Western drug companies in the hope of discovering new cures for cancers, malaria and other ailments. Step through the austere entrance of this museum cum working pharmacy and you'll be staring in awe at a rare original Qing period pharmacy and come face to face with jars and cabinets piled high with all kinds of weird and wonderful substances, from dried geckos to *Hippocampus* (sea horses) and behind the polished wooden counters, row upon row of small wooden drawers and mounds of paper-wrapped parcels filled with remedies. The only hint of the present are the dispensing staff dressed in white lab coats. Even if you don't buy into traditional Chinese medicine (TCM), this place is a must, and you will come away with a broad sense of its philosophy; the desire to treat the body, mind and spirit as one system using a combination of herbs, diet and exercise.

The pharmacy was established in 1874 by the well-known Qing businessman, Hu Xueyan who besides dealing in silk and tea became known for his astute running of this successful medical dispensary. Since 1991 it also opened as a museum with displays presenting a general overview on the history and development of TCM with good English signage throughout. Included is an area demonstrating how pills were shaped and coated with wax and herbs were cut. There is a separate building where medicines were prepared and behind it what was once a deer farm. Their antlers were a common ingredient in many preparations and it was necessary to have a fresh supply always on hand. Ground up and mixed together with tortoise shell and ginseng they produced a remedy to replenish the *yin*, tone the *qi* (the body's energy) and strengthen the *yang* (the opposite of the *yin* and in Chinese medicine the two must be in balance for a healthy body). They were also widely used in a tonic produced in pill form – one to nourish the right kidney (*yang*), the other the left (*yin*).

Further displays consist of tools used for external treatments, such as bell-shaped cupping jars used in cupping, which treats pain in various ailments, mortars and pestles in all shapes and sizes for mixing, numerous books on concocting medicines, methods of processing, including stewing and fermenting, copper ladles, brushes, and a mussel shell cutter for slicing pills. There are sections describing medicines used by the various minorities. Fascinating is the current obsession and collecting methods of the parasitic fungus that grows on a caterpillar mentioned in the recipe above. Native to the Tibetan plateau, this rare and very expensive fungi known as *Cordyceps* is considered a wonder drug, curing a whole range of ailments from hepatitis to sexual dysfunction and today can be found served at select restaurants in China and in Western skin creams and energy drinks.

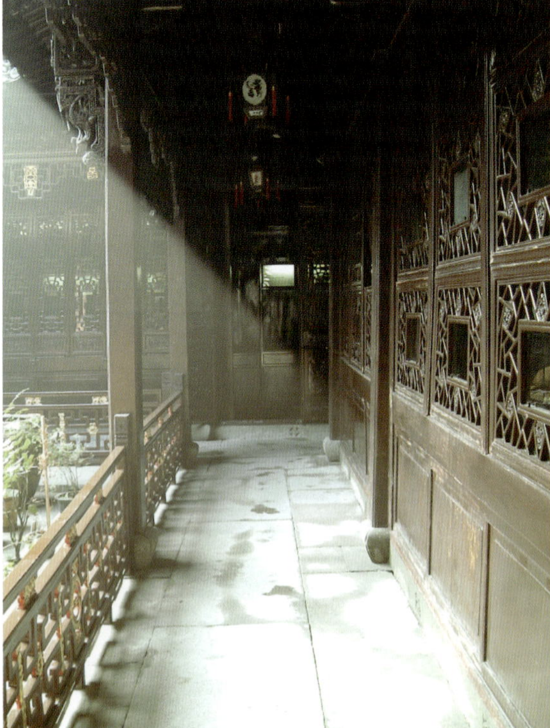

Exhibition areas inside the courtyard of the pharmacy

Pan Tianshou Memorial Hall

潘天寿纪念馆 *Pantianshou jinianguan*

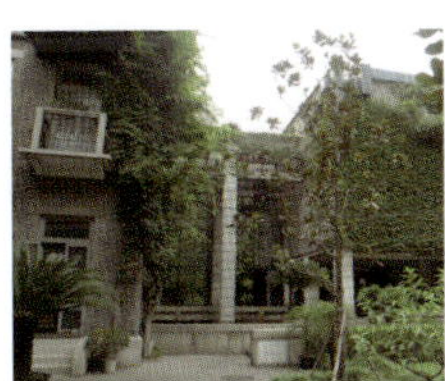

212 Nanshan Road, Hangzhou, Zhejiang
浙江省杭州市南山路212号
Tel: (0571) 8791 2845
Open: 9.00–16.30 except Mon & Fri afternoons
Shop with books on the artist, mostly in Chinese

Pan Tianshou (1897–1971), one of the most important traditional Chinese painters of the twentieth century, is admired for his landscape, bird-and-flower and occasional figure painting and his calligraphy. Although he came from a small mountain village, his father sent him to a private village school as a young boy, where he studied literature, painting and calligraphy. When he was nineteen, he enrolled in the Zhejiang Provincial Teachers' College in Hangzhou, where he began to formally study painting. In 1923, Pan moved to Shanghai, where he was greatly influenced by the powerful calligraphy and fruit-and-flower painting style of the eighty-year-old master Wu Changshuo. In 1928, he was appointed to teach Chinese painting at the newly established National Academy of Art in Hangzhou, later becoming the president of the academy. It was not until the 1940s, however, that Pan began to develop his own unique style, but he did not fully mature as an artist for at least another decade. Pan came under harsh attack at the start of the Cultural Revolution (1966–1976), and continued to be persecuted right up until his death in 1971.

The Pan Tianshou Memorial Hall is divided into two parts, a residence and a gallery. Only the first floor of Pan's former home, where he spent his last years, is open to the public. Visitors

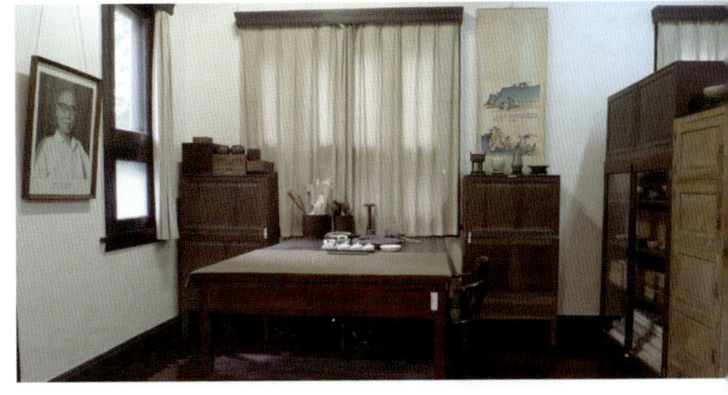

can see his furnished studio, study and a limited display of his personal effects. The gallery, in an adjoining building in this complex, exhibits a collection of some of his finest works.

Pan's desk and painting table

Southern Song Dynasty Guan Kiln Museum in Hangzhou

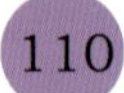

110

杭州南宋官窑博物馆 *Hangzhou nansong guanyao bowuguan*

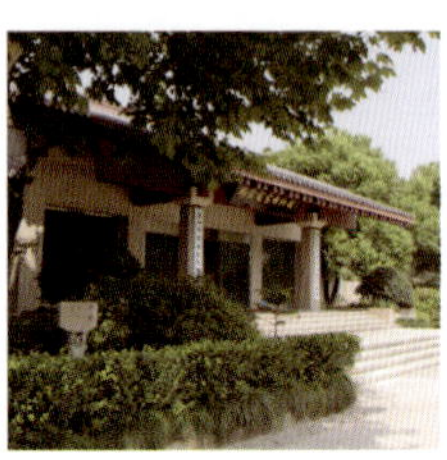

42 Shijiashan Nanfu Road, Shangcheng District,
Hangzhou, Zhejiang
浙江省杭州市上城区南复路施家山42号
Tel: (0571) 8608 2071
Open: 8.30–16.00 except Mon & official holidays
www.ssikiln.com

The word 'guan' means 'official', and Guan Kilns were set up to make porcelain exclusively for imperial use in both the Northern and Southern Song dynasties. The Song dynasty originally had its capital in Kaifeng (Henan Province) until Tartar invaders from the north forced them to flee southwards in 1127. Emperor Gaozong established a new capital in present day Hangzhou, then known as Lin'an, where it remained until the end of the dynasty in 1279. Thus, the Song is divided into the Northern and Southern Song periods.

Porcelain hu from Guan Kilns

Two Guan Kilns were set up at Hangzhou, one near the Xiuneisi (the government department in charge of maintenance of imperial buildings, including kilns) and one at Jiaotan (the Altar of Heaven). The location of the Xiuneisi Kiln was a great mystery until it was finally discovered in excavations undertaken between 1996 and 2001 at the Tiger Cave Kiln site located near the north wall of the imperial city. The Jiaotanxia Kiln (the site of this museum) was first excavated in 1930 and then again in the 1980s and is located at the foot of Tortoise Hill on the south edge of West Lake.

Guan ware of the Southern Song is considered one of the finest of the period and is famous for its celadon glaze which is light green, grey or yellow in colour. The body of the vessels is thin, with either a thick or thin glaze, but the best pieces are those with the thickest glaze – applied in many layers often thicker than the body itself. The rich, smooth and bright glaze is deliberately crackled, with names such as 'iron thread' for the black cracks and 'silk thread' for the yellow. Another characteristic is what is known as 'violet mouth and iron foot' which refers to a purplish colour on the upper rim caused by a separation of the glaze with the iron-rich clay left unglazed and exposed on the foot.

The modern museum galleries include ceramic examples in well-designed cases from the Neolithic to the Qing dynasty, as well as displays and signage in Chinese and English explaining the history and development of the Southern Song Guan kilns.

During the Southern Song, guan kiln celadon was used for ritual ware, replacing shapes used in earlier Shang and Zhou dynasties bronze vessels. This is effectively illustrated in using photographs of the earlier bronzes which hang above the porcelain objects on display.

Another part of the museum is the ancient kiln workshop site, with reproduction architectural features. It is hard to get a sense of the production process they attempt to describe from the sanitized and strangely bare excavation area, even though each feature is labelled. There is also a resident potter here and it is possible to try your hand at the craft, something particularly popular with visiting schoolchildren.

Porcelain stove from Guan Kilns

The highlight here, however, is the remains of the dragon kiln itself, which stretches upwards for over 40 m. Stairs have been added along the sides so you can walk along the length of the kiln, with the remnants of the firebox at the lower end visible. There were two main benefits to this type of kiln. Firstly, thousands of pots could be fired at once and secondly, the length and slope of the design, along with side stoking, allowed for a rapid rise to extremely high temperatures, followed by a quick fall. This was particularly advantageous in terms of the chemistry of the clay and glazes in use here, as the clay could be prevented from distorting or cracking during firing, allowing for a bright, clear finish to the glaze.

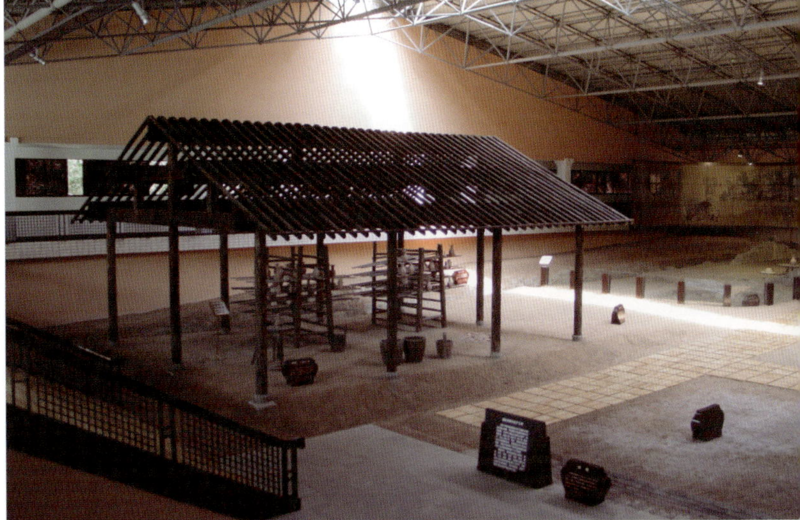

Remains of the ancient kiln workshop

Zhejiang Museum of Natural History

111

浙江自然博物馆 *Zhejiang ziran bowuguan*

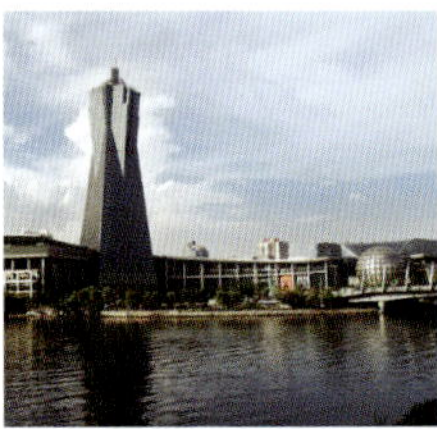

6 West Lake Square, Hangzhou, Zhejiang
浙江省杭州市西湖文化广场6号
Tel: (0751) 8805 0941 / 8821 2712
Open: 9.00–17.00 except Mon, last entry 16.00
www.zmnh.com
Gift shop

Zhejiang Museum of Natural History is one of the few provincial museums of natural history in China. Originally the collections were part of the Zhejiang West Lake Museum established in 1929, however later its name was changed and the natural history items were separated from the main collections to form the museum you see today, opened in 2009.

Sitting within the much-visited West Lake Cultural Plaza in Hangzhou, the museum has over 1 million visitors a year and is home over 130,000 specimens taking visitors on journeys through various subjects, such as the formation of the solar system, the origins of life on earth and evolution. It also showcases modern revolutionary history, and intangible culture, but for the foreign visitor, it is the natural history collections which are full of delights and should be the main focus of any visit.

Set up mostly to entertain and for educational purposes, the highlights include the endless displays of dinosaurs – and if you can get to see them, the vast collection of Chinese dinosaur eggs in the basement storeroom – approximately 3,000. Most have no provenance, but are currently being studied and reported on in scientific journals and at symposia, including the International Symposium on Dinosaur Eggs and Babies, the last of which was held in Hangzhou at the museum. If you are fascinated by clutches of fossilized eggs, or eggs with embryos exposed inside, this is the place to visit.

Among the ranks of dinosaurs on display are those from the dinosaur rich areas of Zhejiang Province, many of which are from the Cretaceous period (100 million years ago). Based on paleo-geographical evidence it seems that there are areas within the province near rivers and lakes where various dinosaurs lived and nested. When seasonal flooding occurred these were submerged and sealed up in the mud. There are several dinosaur skeletons visitors should not to miss. They are: *Yueosaurus Tiantaiensis*, an ornithopod unearthed in Tiantai Country and rare in Asia, as they are mostly found in the Americas and a new species of nodosaurid which is an armoured dinosaur named after the area where it was found – *Zhejiangosaurus linshuiensis*.

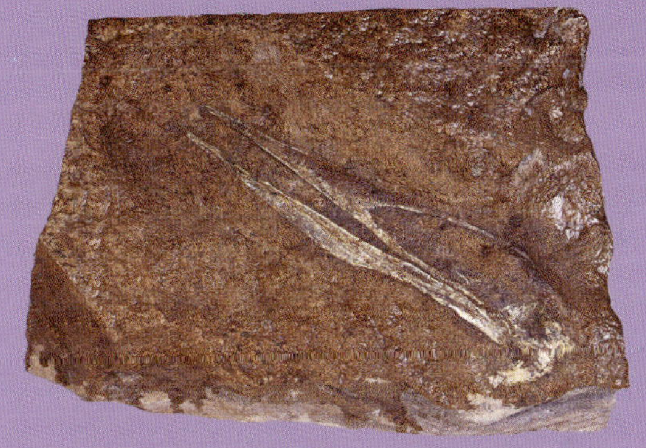

The fossil of *Zhejiangosaurus linshuiensis*

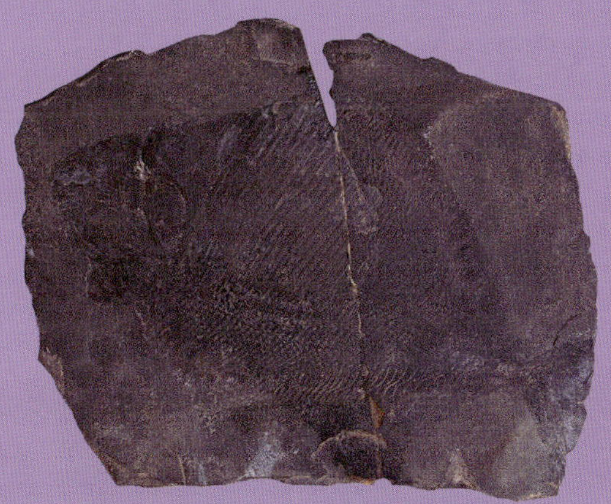

A *Platysomus* fossil

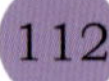

112

Zhejiang Provincial Museum

浙江省博物馆 *Zhejiangsheng bowuguan*

Gushan Branch:
25 Gushan Road, Hangzhou, Zhejiang

浙江省杭州市孤山路25号

Wulin Branch:
29 West Lake Culture Square, Xiacheng District, Hangzhou, Zhejiang

浙江省杭州市下城区西湖文化广场29号

Tel: (0517) 8797 0017   Open: 12.00–17.00 except Mon, last entry 16.30
www.zhejiangmuseum.com   *Gift shop*

The Gushan Branch of the museum is set on the shore of Hangzhou's sublimely picturesque West Lake. The design of the museum is characteristic of Southern Yangtze River construction in that the building and its gardens seamlessly flow into one another. The serene lake in front and the green hills behind the building complete its perfect 'feng shui'.

In 1993 the museum was reconstructed and expanded. The complex consists of a main building with three floors and numerous additional gallery spaces – some of which are connected to the main building by covered walkways meandering through landscaped gardens.

The collection of over 100,000 objects come mainly from Zhejiang Province and exhibited objects are regularly rotated. Most of the galleries have labelling in both

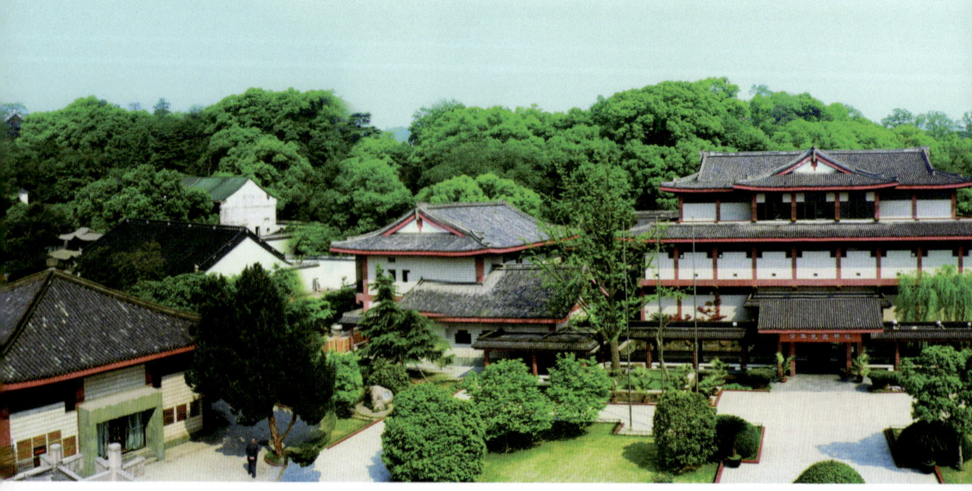

Chinese and English.

On the ground floor of the main building are two galleries dedicated to the Neolithic Hemudu and Liangzhu Cultures. This museum, like many in China, sometimes displays replicas of particularly valuable pieces which may not be labelled as copies. Note the (unmarked) replica of a lacquer beaker

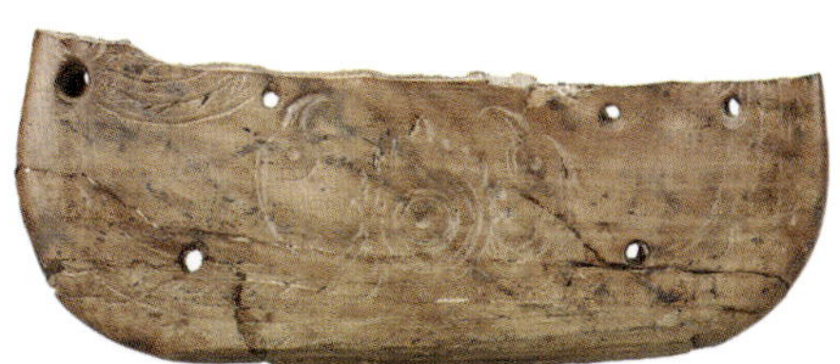

believed to be the earliest known example of Chinese lacquer ware from the Neolithic Hemudu Culture. From the third millennium BC Liangzhu Culture, be sure to see the jade battle axe excavated at Jaoshan, the jade *cong* (ritual object) with *taotie* decoration and an exceptional black pottery *ding* excavated in Huzhou. Also significant is a large stone plough head indicating the beginnings of agriculture and the possible of the use of animal labour. The second floor exhibits many artefacts from the Yue kingdom of the Spring and Autumn period. From Tomb no. 306 of the Yue kingdom Cemetery near Shaoxing, there are many fine examples of pottery, bronzes and weaponry. Don't miss the exceptional bronze tripod vessel with dragon spout, hoof-shaped feet and a lid adorned with animals.

In another room on this floor, objects from the kingdoms of Wu and Yue are on view. During this time, known as the Five Dynasties and Ten Kingdoms period, the Wu and Yue kingdoms were united under the Emperor Qian Liu. This was a prosperous period in which there was much patronage of Buddhist art and architecture, hence the preponderance of Buddhist art in these galleries. Note the silver tablets

Carved ivory artefacts in the shape of birds, Hemudu Culture

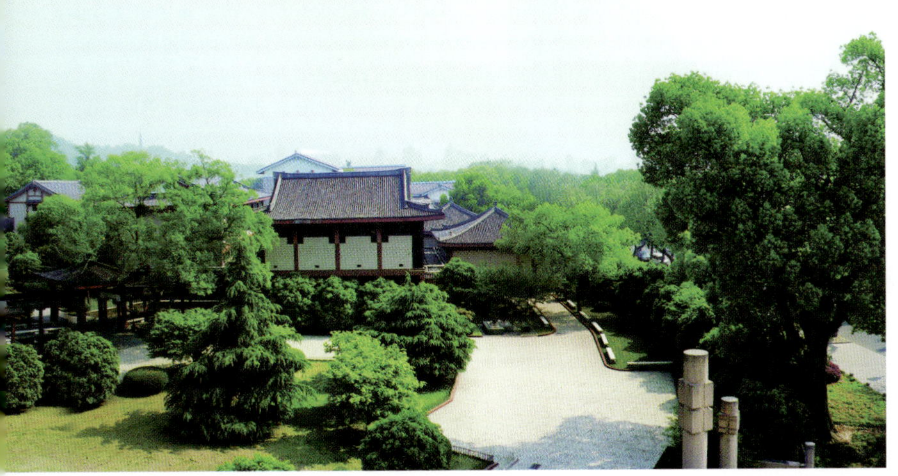

inscribed with a prayer for good weather, which was thrown into the West Lake by King Qian Liu and found at the bottom of the lake, the white porcelain ware for use by the Emperor alone and a small bronze pagoda from the tomb of Qian Liu's parents.

Finally on this floor is the Northern Song Gallery. As Hangzhou was a capital during this period there are many fine Buddhist pieces in the collection including a model for the rebuilding of a pagoda. During the Song, models were often made of buildings before construction.

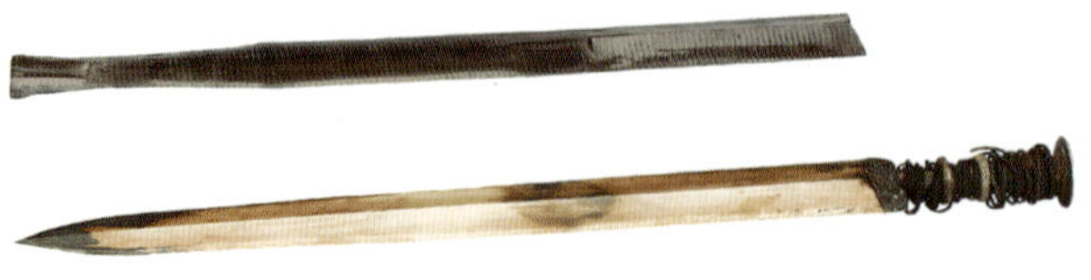

Bronze musical house, Spring and Autumn Period

Also note a lovely small blue *sarira* glass vase with engraved decoration. Although glass was imported into China from the Han period, it was first made in China during the Song dynasty. *Sarira* are bead-like relics found in the ashes from the cremation of the Buddha. The *sarira* is placed in reliquaries which in turn are placed in a pagoda along with other offerings.

The third floor of the main building is dedicated to Zhejiang's history from the Opium War to 1949. Artefacts, photos and documents are presented.

One of the historical figures featured is Qiu Jin (1875–1907), a poet, orator and early leader of the Chinese women's movement. She was a collegue of many of the forward-thinking intellectuals of the time, including Cai Yuanpei and Sun Yat-sen. An ardent feminist, she fought for women's rights including the abolishment of foot binding and forced marriage and was co-founder of the 1906 journal 'Chinese Women'. Because of her revolutionary activity and following her involvement in an uprising in Shaoxing, she was tortured and then executed in July 1907.

As noted above there are many adjacent buildings in the museum. The gallery known as the Gem Gallery is not for viewing valuable stones, but rather to exhibit the very best, 'the gems' of the collection and of visiting collections. At the time of the author's visit this gallery had

Ancient sword of the Yue Kingdom

an exceptionally fine exhibition which was presented in a contemporary manner with well-lit cases but no English signage.

There are several galleries dedicated to individual Zhejiang painters. One of them is devoted to the paintings and drawings of the modern painter, Chang Shuhong (1904–

1994) who was born in Hangzhou. Returning from France in 1936 where he was studying painting, Chang became very worried about the possible fate of the Mogao Grottoes (see no. 180) in Dunhuang during the Japanese invasion. Taking his family with him, he moved to the site in order to protect and conserve this world treasure. He spent the rest of his life dedicated to the preservation of these incomparable wall paintings and was appointed Director of the Dunhuang Cultural Relics Research Institute in 1950.

The Ming and Qing furniture gallery is sparse. At the time of writing, the display was dusty and poorly lit with no English signage.

The Celadon Gallery exhibits examples of ceramics from the famous kilns of Zhejiang – the Yue, Wuzhou, Ou, Deqing, Southern Song Guan and the Longquan. The objects are displayed to illustrate the evolution of pottery to porcelain and the rise and fall of the various kilns.

The museum also has galleries dedicated to the exhibition of currency, gifts presented to the Province of Zhejiang by foreign countries, specialty crafts of the province such as lacquer ware, bamboo ware and ivory work and a painting and calligraphy gallery.

Wulin branch of the museum located in downtown Hangzhou was opened in 2009. Its galleries are entitled History and Culture of Zhejiang, Modern History of Revolutions in Zhejiang, Folk Art, and Paintings.

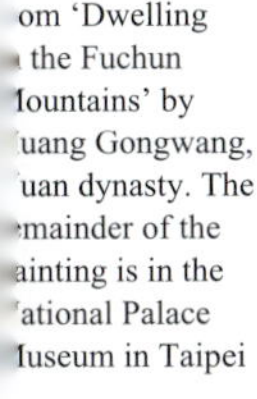

A fragment from 'Dwelling in the Fuchun Mountains' by Huang Gongwang, Yuan dynasty. The remainder of the painting is in the National Palace Museum in Taipei

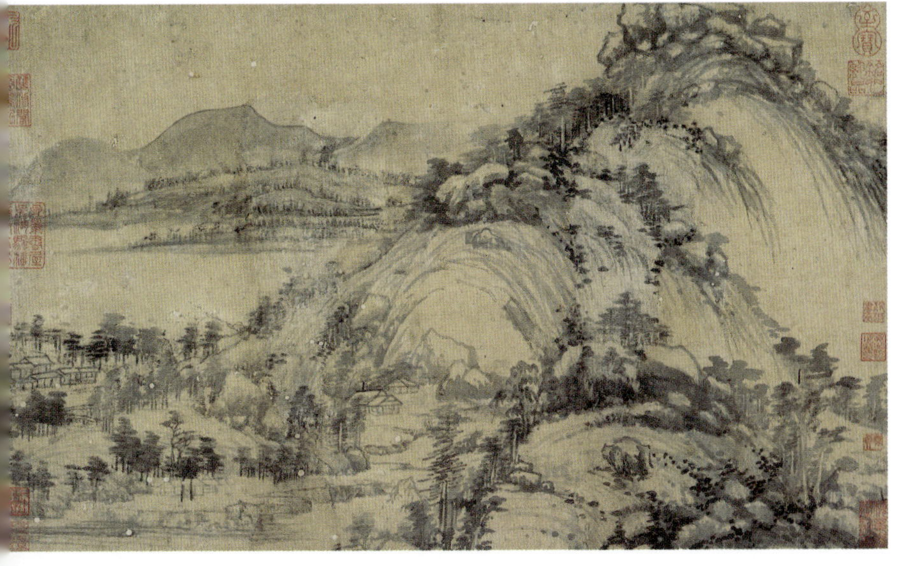

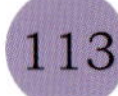

113

Ningbo Museum

宁波博物馆 *Ningbo bowuguan*

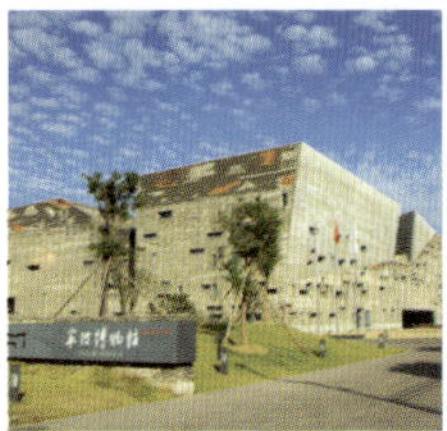

1000 Shounanzhong Road, Yinzhou District, Ningbo, Zhejiang
浙江省宁波市鄞州区首南中路1000号
Tel: (0574)82815588
Open: 9.00–17.00 except Mon, last entry 16.00
www.nbmuseum.cn
Gift shop / bookshop / café

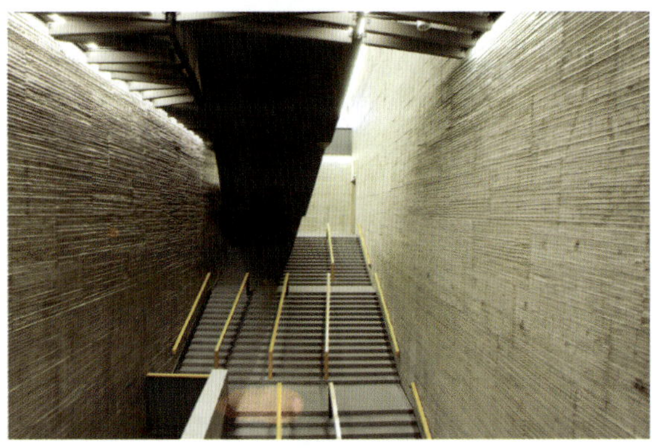

Ningbo, situated in northeast Zhejiang Province, is one of the oldest cities in China, dating back to the Hemudu Culture of 4,800 BC. Already powerful during the Tang, situated on the East China Sea and with good canal connections, it became the major seaport of China during the Ming. Its importance as a port was later gradually eclipsed by Shanghai. Ningbo is also the port for the outlying island of Putuo Shan, one of China's four Buddhist sacred mountains, still a popular pilgrimage centre, and one of the most delightful places to visit in the whole of eastern China.

The Ningbo Museum, situated in Yinzhou district was opened in 2008 and built by Wang Shu, a Pritzker Prize-winning architect. Designed as a museum of local culture and history, its shape reflects the mountains, waters and ocean; and incorporates features of the local domestic architectural style. A part of the interior tilts like a boat, reflecting the maritime connections of the city.

The main exhibits illustrate the history and progress of local Ningbo culture from the Hemudu period to the Republic.

Blue and white porcelain vase, Ming dynasty

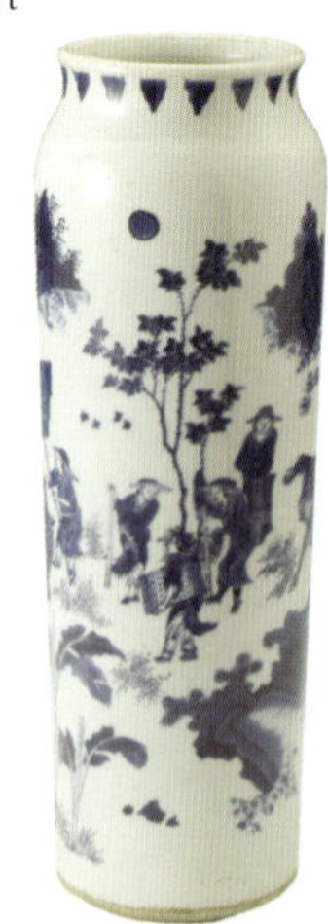

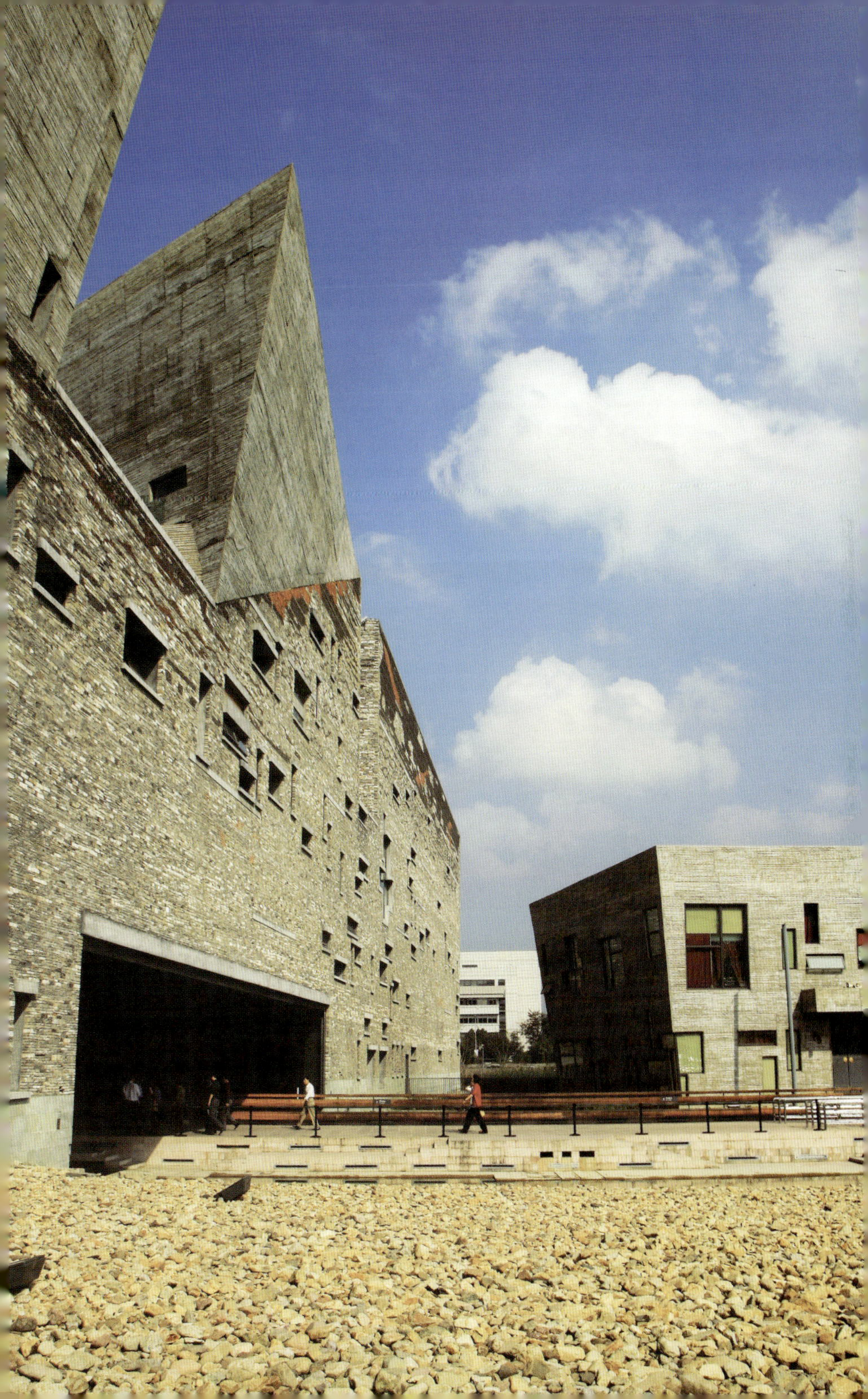

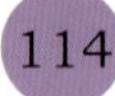

The Museum of Hemudu Site

河姆渡遗址博物馆 *Hemudu yizhi bowuguan*

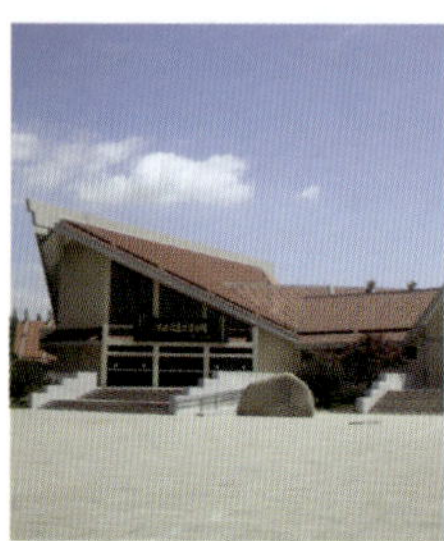

Hemudu Township, Yuyao, Zhejiang
浙江省余姚市河姆渡镇
Tel: (0574) 6296 3731 / 3732
Open: 8.30–17.00, last entry 16.30, Apr–Oct;
       8.30–16.30, last entry 16.00, Nov–Mar
www.hemudusite.com
*A 20-minute video in Chinese, English or Japanese is available
for viewing*
English guide available / gift shop / restaurant

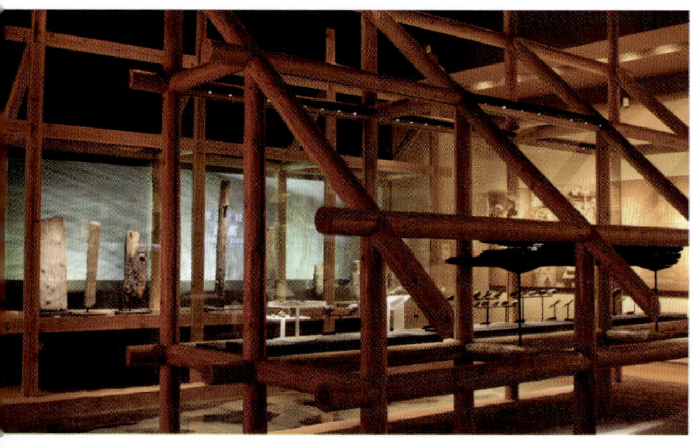

The site contains a museum, an open excavation site, and a model village representing local life and customs during the Neolithic period. The Hemudu site has been carbon dated to between 7,000 and 4,700 years ago. The exhibits are from local excavations and tombs and include many items of daily use, including pottery and bone and wood tools such as needles and knives. In addition there are toys and decorative objects such as carved stone animals and ivory, jade and shell jewellery. Important information about the local Neolithic Culture can be gleaned from the artefacts unearthed at Hemudu, including the content of their diet and the centrality of rice, which is evidenced in pottery with rice designs and vessels that were found containing remnants of the grain. The model village contains buildings constructed using Hemudu architectural styles and materials, and has various scenes of typical Neolithic life, including clothing, weaving and cooking methods.

Pottery statue in the shape of animal, unearthed in Hemudu site in 1977

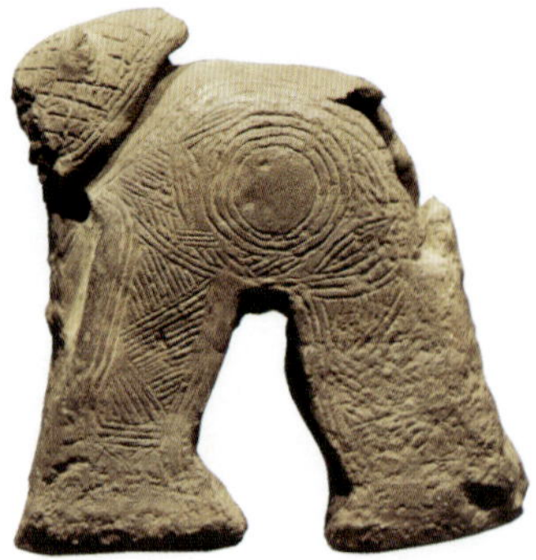

Liangzhu Museum

良渚博物院 *Liangzhu bowuyuan*

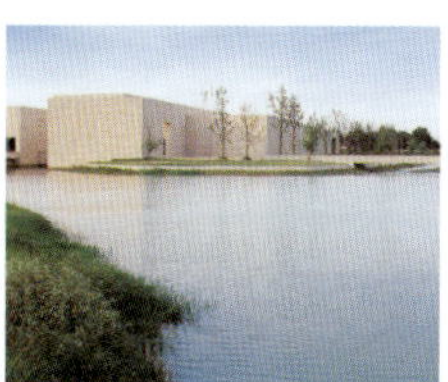

1 Meilizhou Road, Liangzhu Street, Yuhang District, Hangzhou, Zhejiang
浙江省杭州市余杭区良渚街道美丽洲路1号
Tel: (0571) 8877 3875
Open: 9.00–17.00 except Mon, last entry 16.30
www.lzmuseum.cn

Liangzhu Museum – the former Liangzhu Culture Museum – is the first museum in China by one of England's celebrated architects, David Chipperfield. Built of cream and tan Iranian travertine, inspired by the colour of the jade artefacts for which the Liangzhu Culture is so famous, the glorious structure surrounded on three sides by water is set in charming new cultural parkland. Composed of four rectangular volumes of different heights, it rises out of the landscape like a sculptural form. A bridge leads to the entrance where visitors can choose to view either the permanent collection or the temporary exhibitions. Internal courtyards link the indoor galleries, allowing natural light to enter and provide visitors with the experience of taking a journey through time. A second bridge in the rear of the building brings you to an island and the museum's outdoor exhibition area, as well as a view of the surrounding rolling landscape under which the artefacts from this Neolithic Culture emerged. Opened in 2008, it replaces the original Liangzhu Culture Museum built in 1994. It not only has more excavated objects on display, but also engages visitors through the use of interactive displays that explore the material and spiritual life of the Liangzhu.

The Liangzhu Culture (*c.* 3500–2500 BC), named after one of China's most important archaeological sites, is defined by its well-developed rice and silk agriculture (sections of silk looms were found), black-burnished pottery, lacquer ware and most of all by its quantity of stupendous jade artefacts found at sites located northwest of Hangzhou embraced by the Tianmu Mountains and two rivers. Several of this Culture's best-known sites, among more than 135 scattered across the area, are those of Fanshan, Yaoshan, Huiguanshan, Mojiaoshan and Tangshan. The site of Fanshan revealed burial grounds with graves for people of high rank, at Yaoshan there was a cemetery as well as earthen altar, while at the other sites defensive works and workshops were discovered. Among the objects displayed is a selection from the many thousands

Black-glazed pottery jar, Liangzhu Culture

of jade objects found in the graves; at Fanshan alone around 3,200 were recovered. The jades are of outstanding craftsmanship and include the distinctive *cong* cylinder, *bi* disc and *yue* battle-axe shapes, as well as plaques incised with human-like faces with large bulging eyes often found alongside beads, indicating that they may have been personal adornments or associated with shamans. Certain shapes probably indicated status, power and sex of their owners, therefore indicating a stratified society. The *cong* (square in shape with a circular bore in the centre) found at Fanshan is the largest and most distinctive found to date in China. Milky-white in colour, it is decorated with pairs of faces, bird-like figures and human figures with large headdresses and must have belonged to someone important; however, their use remains a mystery. Visitors will leave having not only seen an amazing collection of artefacts, but knowing more about the possible uses and significance of the jade objects in the life of this Culture, as well as the methods of production.

Besides the display areas, there is an educational space where children can reconstruct a Liangzhu house, produce pottery, or enjoy multimedia programmes.

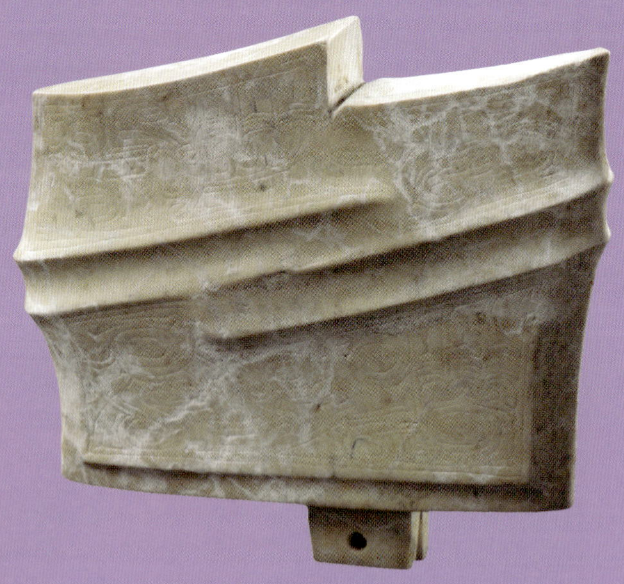

Yue battle-axe shapes, Liangzhu Culture

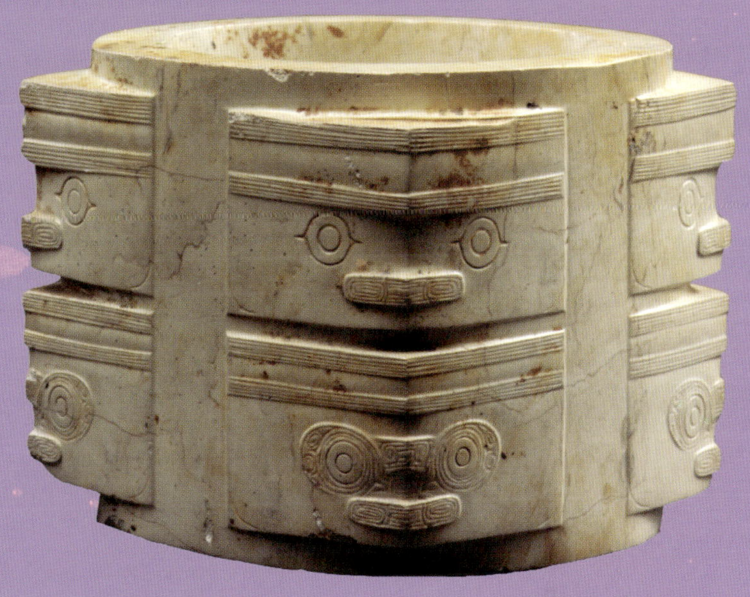

The distinctive *cong* cylinder, Liangzhu Culture

Beijing and the North

The Northeast

Shanghai and East China

The Yangtze

The South

The Silk Road and the Northwest

Tibet

Hong Kong, Macao, Taiwan

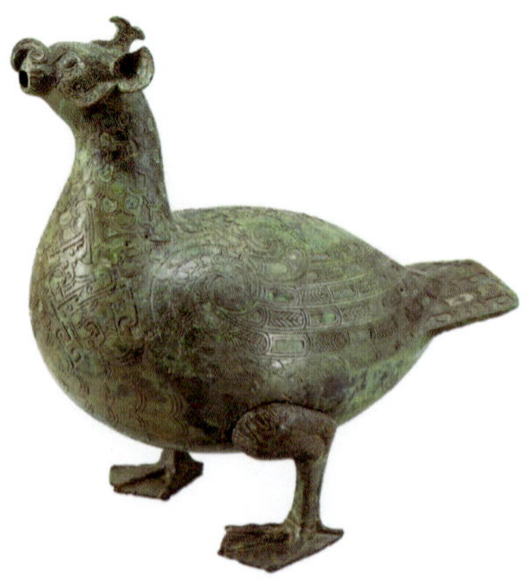

长江流域

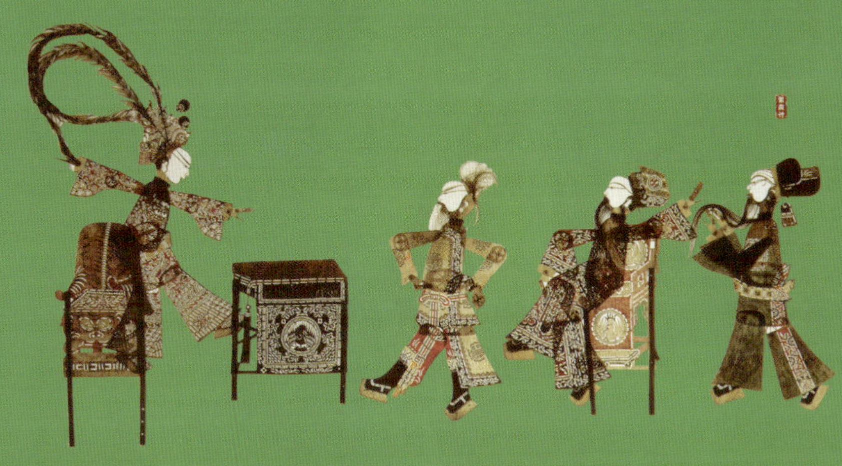

Anhui Museum

安徽博物院 *Anhui bowuyuan*

116

The Old Museum: 268 Anqing Road, Hefei, Anhui 安徽省合肥市安庆路268号	The New Museum: 268 Huaining Road, Hefei, Anhui 安徽省合肥市怀宁路268号

Tel: (0551) 6373 6658
Open: 9.00–17.00 except Mon, last entry 16.00
www.ahm.cn
English audio guide / gift shops   Kids

The School of Architecture at the South China University of Technology in Guangzhou secured the coveted job of designing the new museum, which was completed in 2011. Today, it is the city's cultural landmark.

Set over seven floors – six above ground and one below – and comprising nearly 41,000 sq m, the galleries are showcasing objects dating from the Palaeolithic to the present, finally affording this vast and varied collection the space it deserves.

The exhibitions are well worth seeing should you happen to be in Hefei. There are superb collections of bronzes, pottery, porcelain, jade, ancient coins, paintings, fossils and natural history specimens, as well as displays of architecture and the 'Four Treasures of the Scholar's Study': writing brushes, ink sticks, ink slabs and paper. Highlights include the Anhui bronze treasures, with a number of exceptional ritual bronzes from the Shang dynasty, the vassal state of Cai (Spring and Autumn period) and the state of Chu (Warring States period). These include the most admired artefact in the museum: a large bronze *ding* from Chu weighing 400 kg, the largest extant one of its kind. On seeing it, Chairman Mao was said to have remarked that 'it was big enough to cook an ox in'. Equally exceptional are the Spring and Autumn period bronze vessels from the tomb of the Marquis of Cai, discovered in 1955 during a major construction project to harness the power of the Huaihe River.

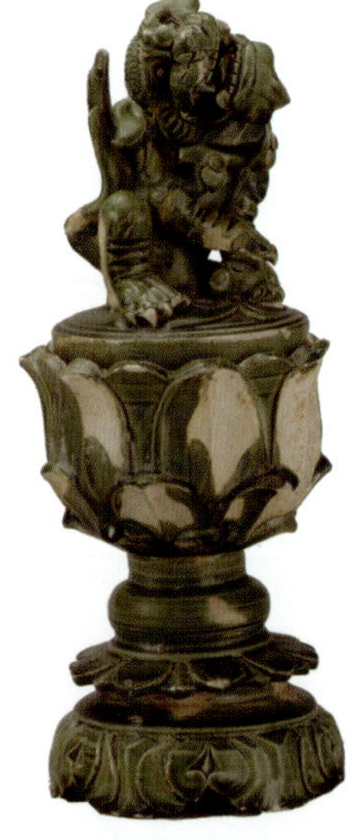

Green-glazed incense burner, Northern Song dynasty

Scenic villages in the surrounding countryside are a popular tourist attraction and the basis for an award-winning exhibit on Huizhou vernacular architecture. The audio accompanying the exhibit is excellent, providing commentary on cultural history and beliefs. Such architecture is admired for it beauty and elegance, embodying as it does the aesthetic values of the region such as harmony and symmetry.

The museum's fine collection of ceramics extends from the Western Zhou to the Qing dynasties, and contains many unusual pieces, especially dating from the Western Zhou, Jin, Tang and Song periods. Notable among these are the Song dynasty celadon, including the rare bowl unearthed from a tomb of the Northern Song dynasty.

The first-floor galleries are devoted to travelling exhibitions, from contemporary Chinese paintings to documentary photography.

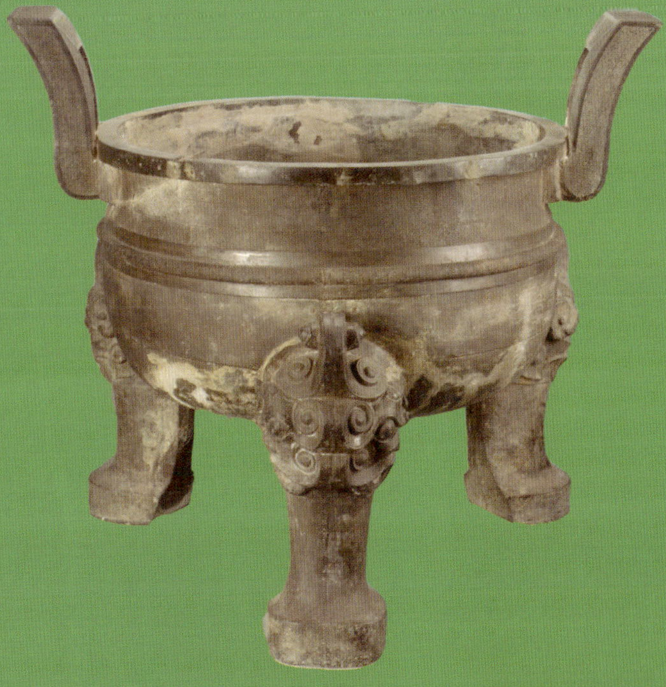

Chu Da Ding, the large bronze *ding* from Chu

117

Hubei Provincial Museum

湖北省博物馆 *Hubeisheng bowuguan*

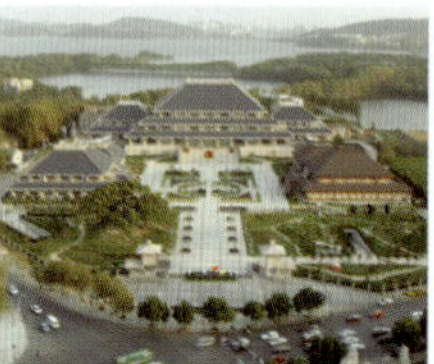

160 Donghu Road, Wuchang District, Wuhan, Hubei
湖北省武汉市武昌区东湖路160号
Tel: (027) 8679 4127
Open: 9.00–17.00 except Mon, last entry 16.00
www.hbww.org
English audio guide / gift shop / bookshop / restaurant

The Hubei Provincial Museum, which houses more than 200,000 cultural relics, is located on the banks of the beautiful East Lake. Some 1,000 items are considered to be national treasures. The museum is divided into three sections: the Chu Culture Exhibition Hall, the newly opened Comprehensive Exhibition Building, and the Chime Bells Exhibition Hall. It is one of the best provincial museums in China. There are good English descriptions on the displays.

The Chu Culture Exhibition Hall, the first building on your left after you enter the grounds, features the regional culture of the state of Chu, which dates back to the Spring and Autumn period (770–476 BC). The cultural relics exhibited in this hall are primarily bronze vessels, lacquer ware, bamboo and wooden artefacts, and silk products. Some of the highlights include ancient weapons such as the sword of Gou Jian (King of the Yue state in the Spring and Autumn period) and the shaft of Fu Chai (King of the Wu state), both still in excellent condition. The sword is as legendary in China as King Arthur's sword is in the West. On the blade near the handle are eight seal characters that proclaim: 'This sword belongs to Goujian, the King of the Yue State'. Other ancient weapons include a crossbow, a bronze dagger axe and a lacquer shield, all from the Warring States period. There is also a large model of the ancient capital of Chu, later known as Ji'nancheng, and exhibits showing smelting and casting.

In 2002, archaeologists discovered the remains of chariots and horses from the Chu era. Some of the chariots and skeletons were painstakingly excavated and are displayed in this hall. There are two pits here, one real, the other a replica. This room also displays chariot parts, including fittings for bridles and decorative bronze axle caps.

The museum's central structure, the Comprehensive Exhibition Building, opened in September 2007. On the second floor are exhibits of lacquer ware, including ear bowls (so named because

Sword of Gou Jian

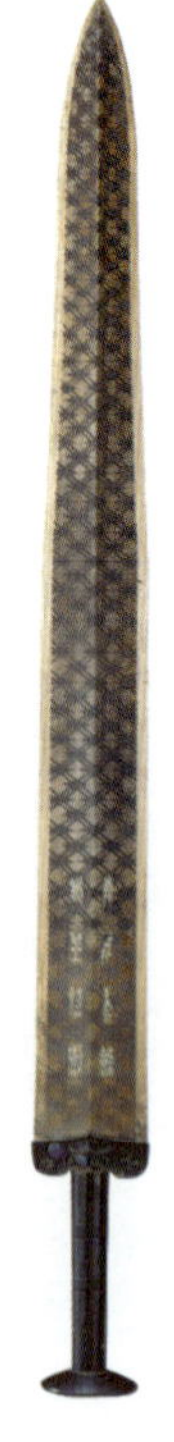

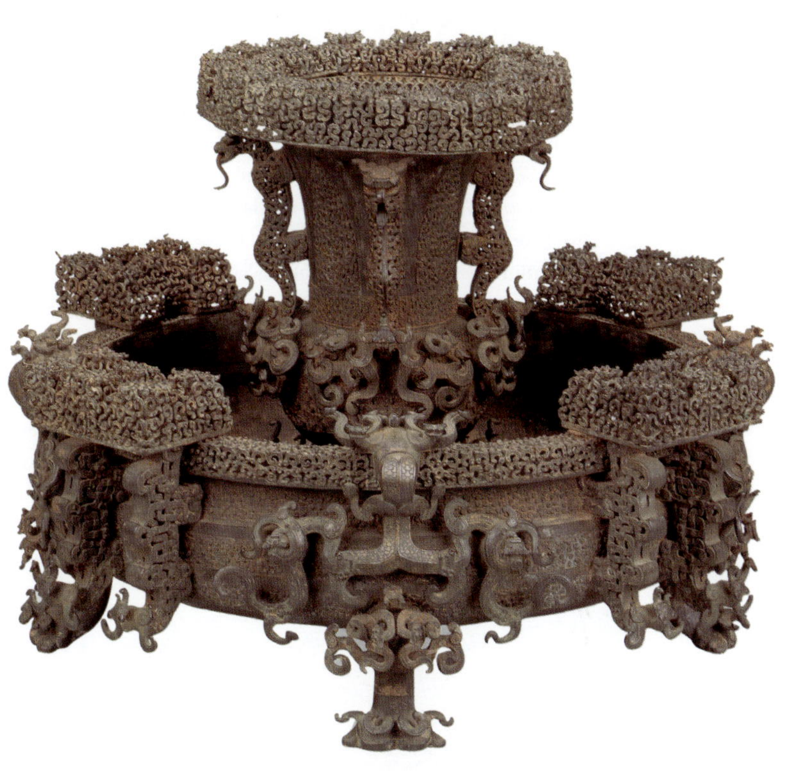

Marquis Yi of Zeng *Zun* and *Pan* with highly elaborate decoration

they look like ears) and jade, as well as displays explaining ancient customs such as hairstyles, clothing, headgear styles and forms of recreation.

The third floor has several exhibits. 'The Art of Earth and Fire' displays ancient porcelain such as celadon, blue and white and official kiln porcelain. The Lacquer Hall exhibits bowls, ear cups, pitchers and wine vessels. There's also a section on the history of writing on bamboo. One of the main items of interest is Prince Liang Zhuang's tomb. This room has a selection of beautiful items made from gold: teapots, buttons, ear picks, coins, belts, hair pins, head ornaments, bracelets and so on. In the Yunxian Man Exhibition Hall there are examples of fossils from the Palaeolithic period. Archaeologists say that two skulls on exhibit are fossils of *Homo erectus* dating back a million years. Their facial features are similar to that of palaeo-anthropological fossils that have been excavated in other parts of China.

The fourth floor features exhibits of modern paintings and photos of Hubei's favourite sons from the past century. There's also a gift shop, a café and an area outside from which you can see the city.

The Chinese Bells Exhibition Hall is on your left as you walk back towards the gate. In 1978, 15,000 items were excavated from the tomb of Marquis Zeng, King of the Zeng state in the Warring States period. Discovered in Suizhou, these included bronze ritual vessels and weapons, horses and carts, items made of bamboo, lacquer, gold and jade, coffins and musical instruments. The highlight of the excavation is the sixty-five bronze chimes hanging on a three-tiered rack weighing more than 2,000 kg. Although the bells date back more than a thousand years, their tone quality is still

Bell stand hung with sixty-five bronze chimes on three tiers from the tomb of the Marquis Yi of Zeng; the bells are ornamented with knots and held in place with clasps in the shape of tigers

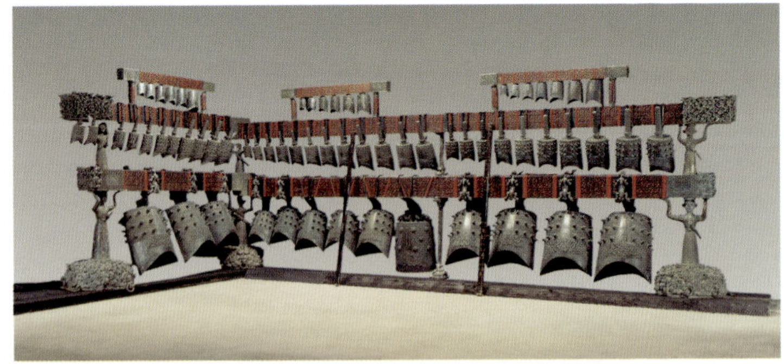

excellent. The chimes are believed to be the biggest and oldest bells in existence. Of various sizes, they play a range of tones on the musical scale. Some 3,000 ancient gilt Chinese characters are inscribed on the bells and hooks, providing us with the oldest known details about musicology. Several times a day, musicians dress up in ancient costumes and perform on a replica set. Bell performances last twenty minutes.

118

Memorial Hall of Wuchang Uprising of 1911 Revolution

辛亥革命武昌起义纪念馆 *Xinhaigeming Wuchangqiyi jinianguan*

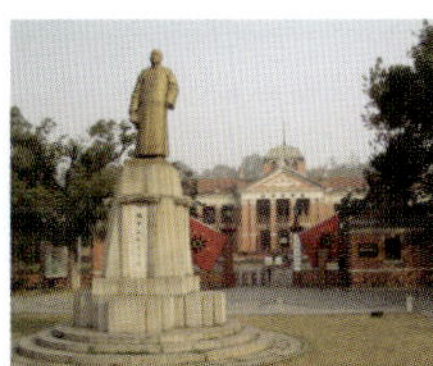

1 Wuluo Road, Wuchang District, Wuhan, Hubei
湖北省武汉市武昌区武珞路1号
Tel: (027) 8887 5305
Open: 9:00–17:00 except Mon
www.1911museum.com
Gift shop

The Wuchang Uprising which occurred on October 11, 1911 in the city of Wuchang (now part of the city of Wuhan) in Hubei Province triggered the end of imperial rule in China and the founding of the Republic of China.

Since 1894, Sun Yat-sen, living in exile, had organized a series of uprisings against the Qing Dynasty but without success. As it turned out the end of the dynasty came from within. The Qing's New Army, established in 1901, had become imbued with revolutionary ideas and on that day in 1911 the Hubei section of the army seized power after a bomb exploded by accident in the city. The rebellion spread across China, the Xuantong Emperor ('Last Emperor' Puyi) abdicated and Sun Yat-sen returned to be appointed the Republic's first President.

The Museum is located in a large and imposing red brick building (known as the 'Red Mansion') built in 1910, in which the victorious rebel Hubei troops established their headquarters. In front of its gates there is statue of Sun Yat-sen. The museum contains a rich collection of photographs, documents, weapons and other relics from the period relating not just to the Wuchang Uprising but also to the entire revolutionary movement.

This museum is one of key sites for visitors to Wuhan. For many tourists this is the starting point for a Yangtze River cruise up the Three Gorges to Chongqing.

A notice by Britain, Russia, France, Germany and Japan, declaring that they would 'strictly observe neutrality' after the Wuchang Uprising

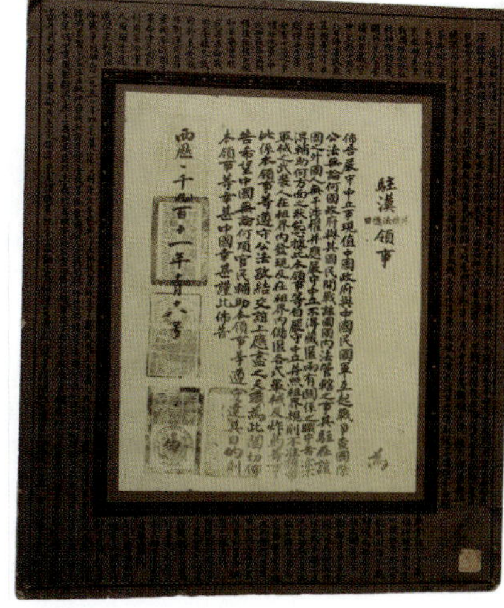

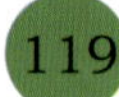

119

Tonglushan Ancient Metallurgy Museum

铜绿山古铜矿遗址博物馆 *Tonglüshan gutongkuangyizhi bowuguan*

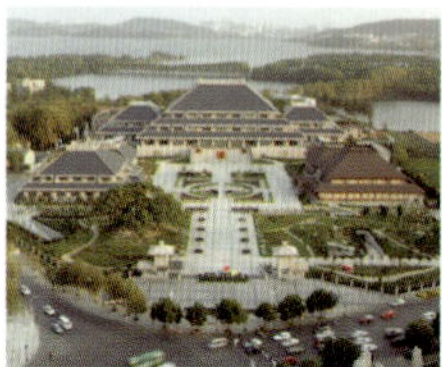

30 km southwest of Tonglushan, Daye County, Huangshi, Hubei
湖北省黄石市大冶县铜绿山矿区西南30公里
Open: 8.00–17.00

This is the largest and most important ancient copper-mining site in China; it was in use in ancient China for more than a thousand years, from the early Western Zhou to the Han dynasties. Discovered in 1965, later excavations revealed a number of techniques from drift mines (tunnels dug horizontally into the side of the mountain) to mines that slanted upwards. Wooden tunnel supports were constructed to prevent the walls from collapsing, and wooden lifting devices were used in the Warring States period and perhaps earlier to send baskets full of material up and, once emptied, back down again to be refilled. Tools used to process the ore – bronze, iron, bamboo and stone axes, adzes and picks – have been found along with tons of slag left over from the production of what is estimated to have been around 40,000 or more tons of copper.

The museum is built over part of the site so that numerous shafts can be viewed from the large central hall. Displays along the surrounding walls illustrate the techniques used to mine copper, which, when alloyed with tin and lead, produced the bronze used to cast the magnificent ritual vessels that can be seen in collections in China and elsewhere. The importance of this site has been recognized by an injection of funds, allowing the museum to update its facilities, adding interactive touch screens to assist in understanding the processes of extracting and smelting copper ore. Future plans include opening up other parts of the site, including the ancient copper smelting furnaces.

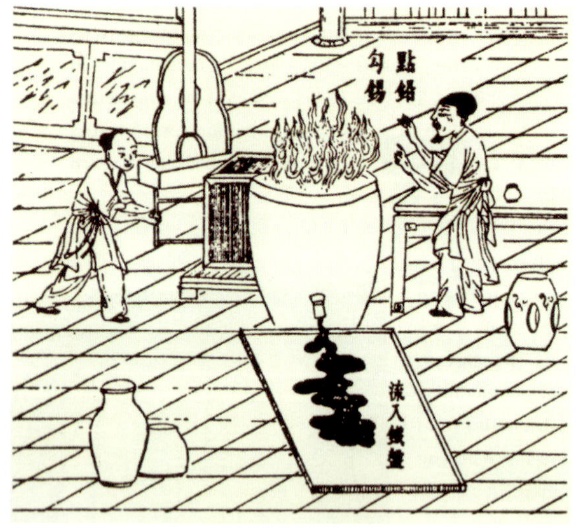

Woodcut illustrating the smelting of tin with lead, which, combined with copper, produced bronze for casting artefacts

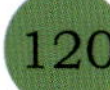

China Lantern Museum

中国彩灯博物馆 *Zhongguo caideng bowuguan*

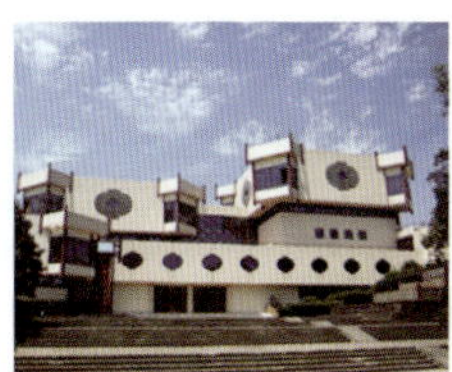

6 Gongyuan Road, Zigong, Sichuan
四川省自贡市公园路6号
Tel: (0813) 2305 061
Open: 9.00–16.30
www.lantern-museum.com
Guides are available but must be arranged in advanced

Zigong is hailed as the 'Capital of Lanterns' and over the past several decades has taken what was once a folk-craft industry built around small groups of artisans and made it into a major industry. Today there are more than ninety lantern-making companies in the city, which have revitalized the local economy and put Zigong on the cultural map. Such is the success of Zigong's festivals that groups of local lantern-makers now stage similar events in cities around China and abroad. The craft has gone from the simple bamboo and coloured-paper lanterns first fashioned in the Han dynasty to complicated three-dimensional lanterns, often larger than life, representing well-known characters from cartoons or legends fitted with electronic chips to control moving parts.

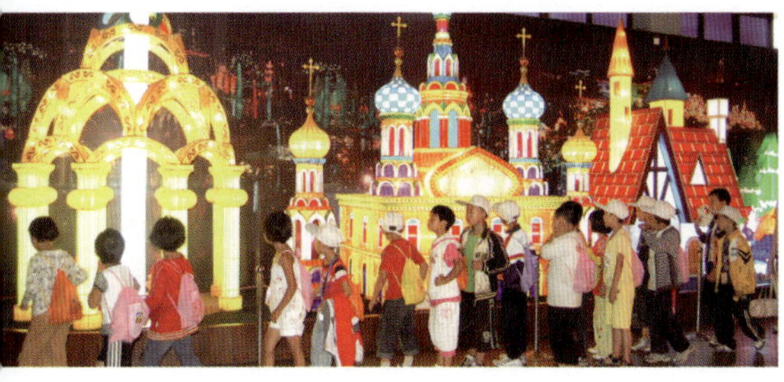

Over five floors and eight exhibition halls, displays of historic and modern examples supported by interactive screens tell the origin of lanterns, the history of their construction from the Warring States period to the present day, explain modern methods of fashioning lanterns, describe the various festivals in Zigong and elsewhere, and show the best examples created for the annual festivals. These masterpieces are ingenious creations, from the dragon-and-phoenix lantern made by stringing together thousands of china plates to the flying-dragon realized from numerous silk cocoons. Displays of lanterns from other provinces, countries and across time surprise by their diversity. Finer lanterns were fashioned with frames of carved wood covered in silk and glass, others from slices of sheep horn moulded and shaped, or painted with flowers or birds and dangling with tassels. There are lanterns that float on water (popular in Guizhou and Yunnan), ice lanterns from Harbin, and those festooned with braided beads from Wanzhou. There is even a workshop where you can try your hand at fabricating your own lantern from a myriad of materials!

Lantern Festivals

Lanterns in Chinese culture are usually connected with two main festivals. The first is the Lantern Festival held on the fifteenth day of the first month of the Chinese lunar calendar and marks not only the end of the fifteen-day celebration of Chinese New Year but also the first full moon in the lunar New Year. The origins of this festival are many but were always marked by displays of lanterns in limitless shapes and sizes from gates, overhangs and even trees. Celebrations extend to composing poetry, parading lanterns around town and eating tangyuan. These balls of sticky rice with various fillings symbolize important family values such as unity. The second celebration, the Mid-Autumn Festival, highlights the fullest moon of the year and takes place on the fifteenth day of the eighth month in the lunar calendar. This marks the end of the harvest and, like harvest festivals elsewhere, is celebrated with food offerings, the eating of special foods — such as moon cakes or round cakes made with various fillings either sweet or salty, and the staging of lantern shows.

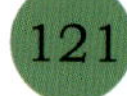

Chengdu City Museum

成都市博物馆 *Chengdushi bowuguan*

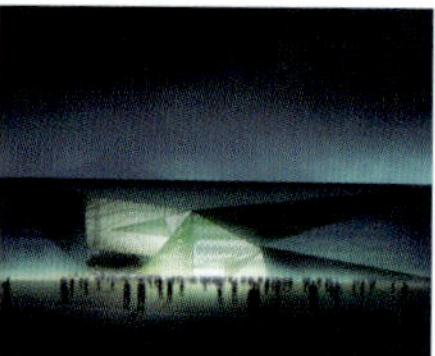

West of Tianfu Square, Chengdu, Sichuan
四川省成都市天府广场西侧
Scheduled to open at the end of 2013

The Edinburgh-based architects Sutherland Hussey won first prize in the international competition to design this new museum in the heart of Chengdu. It will sit along one edge of Tianfu Square as part of a plan to create pedestrian routes through the site. These 'shortcuts' will allow people respite from the hustle and bustle of the square and the surrounding road traffic. It will also give them the opportunity to engage momentarily with the displays or events taking place in the museum. A monumental opening through the south-western part of the building will become a covered outdoor space where people can mingle, events can be held, or market stalls can be installed.

Collaborating with Pansolution International Design, the architects designed a dramatic structure with a glazed south façade and a large roof light which allows natural light to pour into and through the interior. The exterior will be covered in patinated brass-alloyed panels wrapped around a perforated mesh, resulting in a structure which has an intense gold colour by day and a golden glow at night, alluding to the gold artefacts of the province's ancient Shu Culture and to the Sichuan tradition of the shadow-play.

Over six storeys of exhibition space, natural history objects, folk art, history collections and shadow puppets will be displayed.

Chengdu Shu Brocade and Embroidery Museum

122

成都蜀锦织绣博物馆 *Chengdu shujinzhixiu bowuguan*

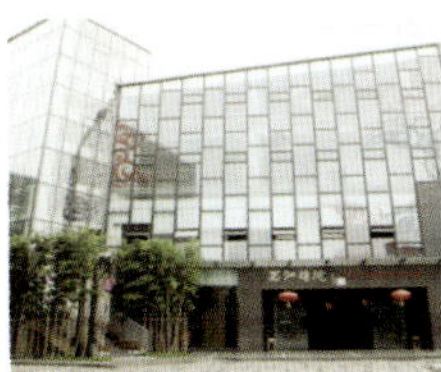

2 Caotang East Road, Chengdu, Sichuan
四川省成都市草堂东路2号
Tel: (028) 8733 7990
Open: 8.00–18.00
www.cdbem.cn
English guides available upon request   *Gift shop*

It was fitting that Chengdu hosted the first International Festival for Intangible Culture to promote and protect 'living cultures' world-wide, as the city is home to a whole assortment of China's endangered 'living skills', including traditional Shu (the ancient name for Sichuan) brocade weaving and embroidery. Since the Han dynasty, Chengdu has been known as the 'brocade city'; Sichuan was one of the cradles of the Chinese silk industry, beginning some 4,000 years ago. As far back as the Warring States period silk Shu brocade was traded along the Southern Silk Road, through southwestern China to India and Central Asia. It became such an important trade item that during the Western Han dynasty a *jin guan*, or Brocade Officer, was appointed by the government to supervise the lucrative growing industry across both the Northern and Southern Silk routes. At that time there would have been more than 20,000 looms weaving the highly prized, elaborately designed silk brocade. Today there are at most twenty people capable of operating the looms.

Over two floors the Shu brocade museum presents all facets of its subject, from its ancient history and the role it played in trade, to the development of the wooden looms used to weave it. Besides displaying examples of Shu brocade, silk embroidery and silk tapestry from the Tang dynasty to the present day, photographs, books illustrating the craft, and Qing dynasty brocade costumes, the Institute has enrolled the services of several retired master weavers from the Shu Brocade Factory to teach young interns with the aim of saving the ancient craft from extinction.

At the museum's heart is an exhibition hall with five Shu brocade platform jacquard looms (known as *dahualou*) from the Qing dynasty (one is original, the others replicas) at which visitors can watch weavers at work. A complicated and highly skilled craft, Shu brocade requires more than a dozen preparation steps before weaving can begin, and these take up to six months for each motif. They include pattern designing, colour matching, basic weaving and pattern transfer. A loom, 6 m long by 5 m high and 1.5 m wide, requires two people to operate, a task undertaken more frequently by men than women, although there are woman weavers. Weavers train for more than two years just to learn the basic skills, and several more to become proficient and earn the title of 'master weaver'.

Watching the weavers in action is like seeing a well-choreographed dance. As the top weaver is pulling up the silk warps and separating them, the weaver seated at the bottom pushes the shuttles with the silk weft through them while controlling the shafts by a series of peddles called treadles. To produce brocade you have the addition of a supplementary weft, usually of a material different to that of the ground weft. These supplementary weft threads are often gold or silver, which catch the light and add a subtle shimmer to the final fabric. It takes good rhythm and perfect timing, with the top weaver controlling the pattern and the one below the colours and the speed at which it is woven. To produce 1cm of brocade takes 160 shuttle movements, producing on average only 7cm of fabric per day depending upon the design.

The heyday of Shu brocade production lasted for about a thousand years from the Western Han dynasty through to the Song. It was particularly prized by the imperial family of the Northern Song dynasty because of its elaborate patterns and colours. Borrowing from the techniques of Shu brocade, three other schools of brocades were established, including Song brocade of Suzhou in Jiangsu Province; *Yun* (or Cloud) brocade of Nanjing, also in Jiangsu Province; and Zhuang brocade in Guangxi Zhuang Autonomous Region.

In an effort to keep this craft alive, the museum complex has a large shop specializing in fashionably designed products produced using old methods of embroidery. In 2006, Shu brocade weaving was listed as one of 'China's Intangible Cultural Heritages' by the Ministry of Culture.

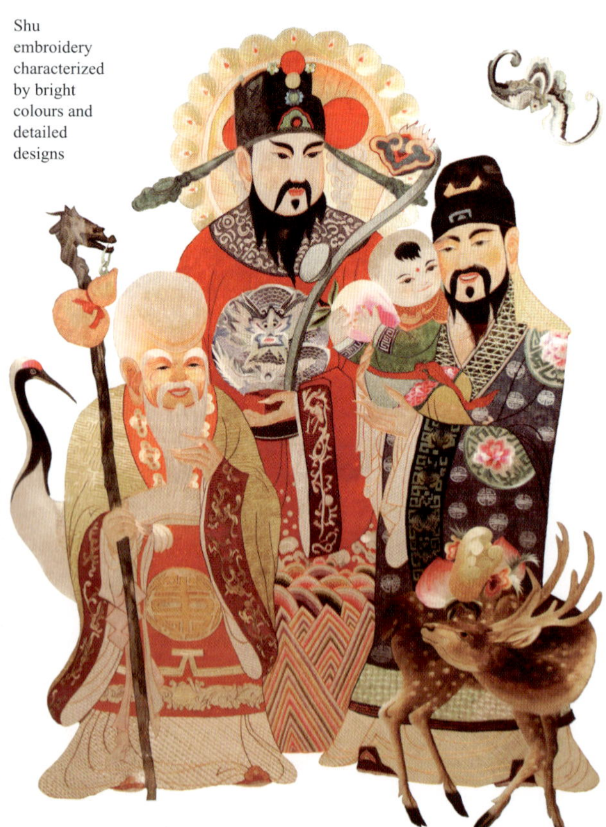

Shu embroidery characterized by bright colours and detailed designs

Chengdu Wuhou Shrine Museum

123

成都武侯祠博物馆 *Chengdu wuhouci bowuguan*

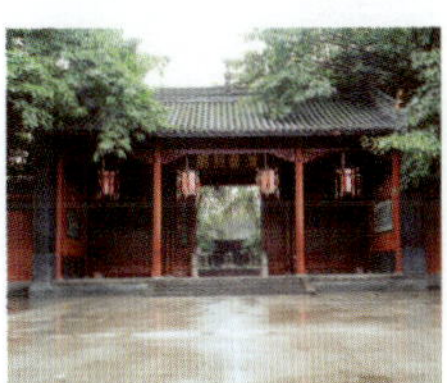

231 Wuhouci Street, Chengdu, Sichuan
四川省成都市武侯祠大街231号
Tel: (028)8556 8685/8555 2397
Open: 8.30–18.00
www.wuhouci.net.cn
Gift shop / bookshop / café

The Wuhou Shrine Museum, situated south of the Jin River on the outskirts of Chengdu, consists of a temple area, a display dedicated to *The Romance of the Three Kingdoms*, the 14th-century historical novel, and the Jinli Folk Area. The temple area was restored in 1672 by the Qing Emperor Kangxi. It will provide the visitor with information and insight into the history of the Three Kingdoms, one of the most important periods for the long term development of the structure of the Chinese nation – and also of the classic stories of Chinese literature.

The earliest building in the temple complex is the Hui Mausoleum of 223AD which houses the tomb of Liu Bei, the first emperor of the Shu Kingdom – the predecessor of modern Sichuan. Liu Bei and his Prime Minister Zhuge Liang both feature largely in *The Romance of the Three Kingdoms*.

Zhuge Liang is buried in a Tang Temple (now heavily restored) also within the museum area. These two and other heroes of the Three Kingdoms period are all featured in the Three Kingdoms Museum, the largest such memorial in the world. There are 50 heroic statues, including Liu Bei and Zhuge Liang, with inscriptions and famous couplets. The museum also has thousands

A stone tablet named *Tablet of Zhuge Wuhou Shrine*. It was drafted by Prime Minister Pei Du in 809 in Tang Dynasty, written by the famous calligrapher Liu Gongchuo and engraved by eminent craftsman Lu Jian

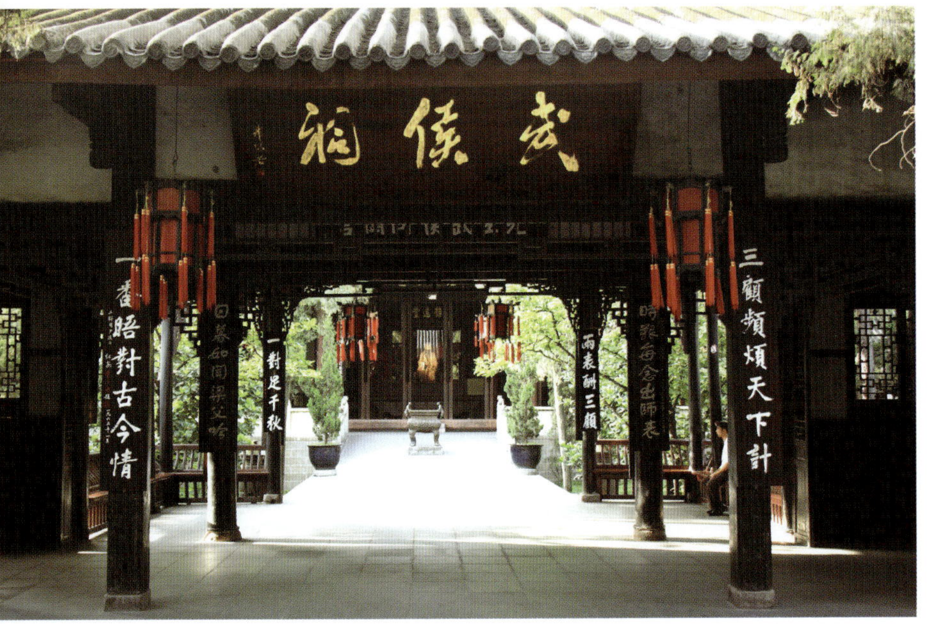

of clocks, drums, tripods, calligraphies and paintings as well as tens of thousands of items illustrating the Three Kingdoms period.

During Qin and Han Dynasty and the Three Kingdoms period, Jinli was an old street producing and selling brocades in Chengdu. There are many records about Jinli in historical documents. Jinli Old Street has been re-created according to these sources by the Wuhou Shrine Museum over a large area in the local Sichuan style of the Ming and Qing. It combines Three Kingdoms' and traditional Sichuan folk art and culture with an extensive shopping area.

Dayi Liu Family Estate Museum / Rent Collection Courtyard

124

大邑刘氏庄园博物馆 *Dayi liushi zhuangyuan bowuguan*

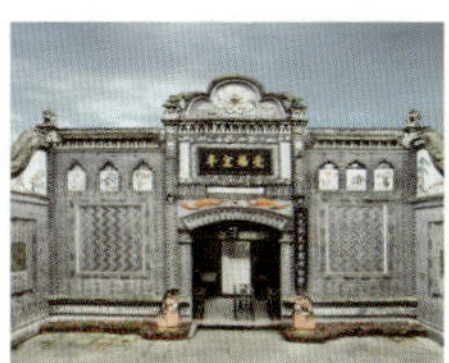

15 Jingui Street, Anren Township, Dayi County, Sichuan
四川省大邑县安仁镇金桂街15号
Tel: (028) 8831 5113
Open: 9.00–17.00

A tour of the typical Qing dynasty home of the landlord Liu Wencai is only of moderate interest. The complex, home to Liu's extended family, was originally built in 1931. It had twenty-seven courtyards, three gardens decorated in both Western and Chinese style, and about 180 rooms. An addition was completed in 1938 with a further 170 rooms and three courtyards. Besides an opium warehouse and tennis court, there are various outbuildings. Visitors led by a guide can peek into some of the living quarters fitted out with fusty furniture and accoutrements. Liu's old car is displayed behind glass, and exhibition halls feature rosewood furniture, wedding paraphernalia and other Qing artefacts. The most pleasant part of the visit, though, is wandering through the gardens.

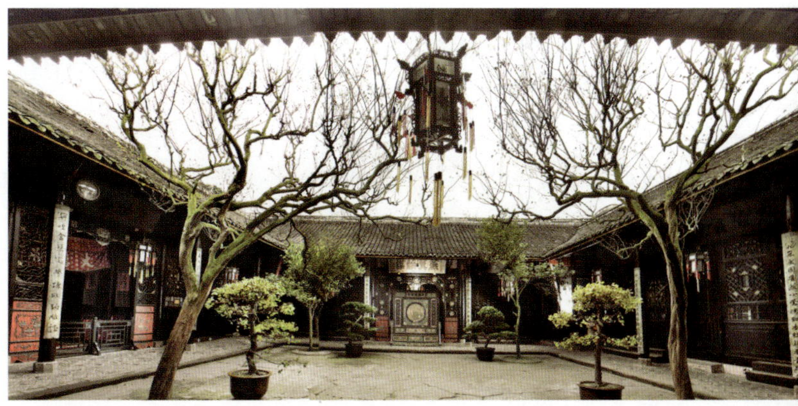

Dayi Liu Family Estate Museum / Rent Collection Courtyard

The Qing dynasty home of the landlord Liu Wencai served as the backdrop to one of the most emblematic works of Mao era art — *The Rent Collection Courtyard*. Still in situ, it is a collection of 114 life-sized clay figures in a series of scenes depicting the heinous deeds of a pre-revolutionary landlord. These figures, combined with props such as brooms, hoes, baskets and other agrarian implements, form twenty-six tableaux of misery and despair. Starving, beaten and abused peasants are exploited and assaulted as they come to pay their rent, the grain is measured and so on.

This political work, meant to stir the emotions, instil revolutionary fervour and highlight class struggle, was created a year before the beginning of the Cultural Revolution by a group from the Sichuan Art Academy whose names were kept anonymous in keeping with the revolution's collective ideals. The piece soon became famous, a model sculpture and favourite of Jiang Qing, Mao's wife. Adaptations and revisions were made, and it travelled around the country and abroad.

In 1999, at the Venice Biennale, the celebrated artist Cai Guo-Qiang won a prize for a work entitled *Venice's Rent Collection Courtyard* which re-created some of the original figures. As they were fired, the sculptures cracked and then disintegrated, revealing the armatures around which they'd been constructed. This work of part conceptual part performance art caused outrage in China and started a huge debate about the place and value of contemporary art. Cai, the Biennale and its director were threatened by a lawsuit brought by the Sichuan Academy of Fine Arts and some of the original artists for copyright infringement — an irony considering that when the original work was created, it would have been unthinkable for individuals to take credit for it. Cai has since made another version, *New York Rent Collection Courtyard*, which was shown at the Guggenheim Museum in New York in 2008.

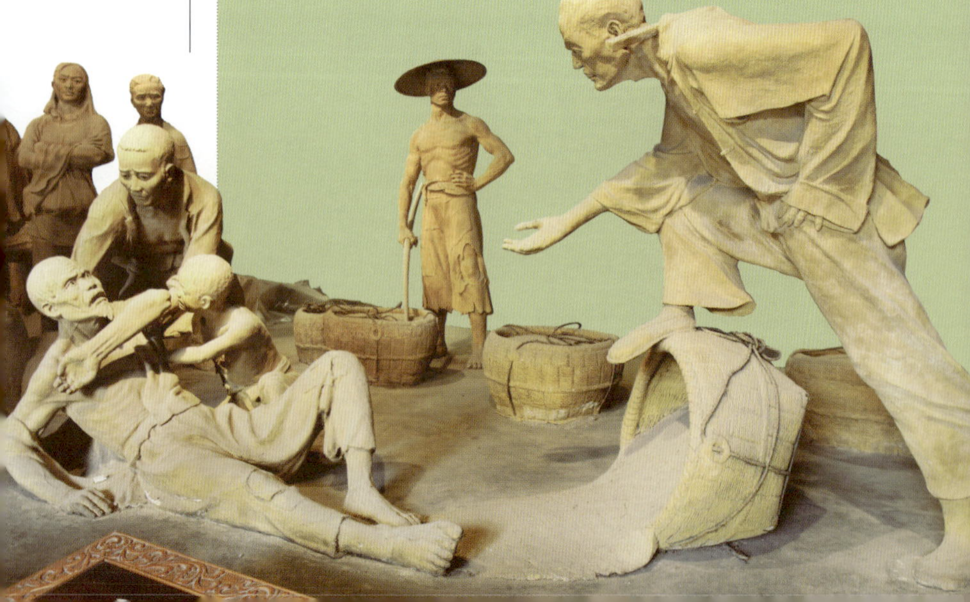

Jianchuan Museum Cluster

建川博物馆聚落 *Jianchuan bowuguan juluo*

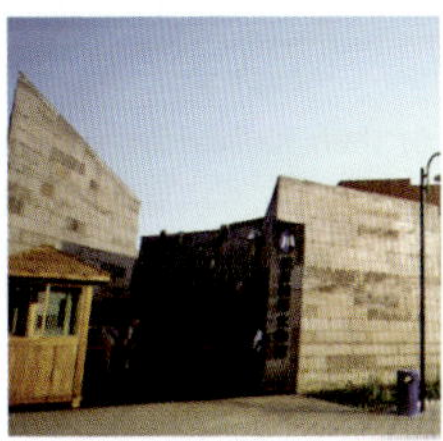

Anren Township, Dayi County, Sichuan
四川省大邑县安仁镇
Tel: (028) 8831 8000
Open: 9.00–17.30 except Spring Festival Eve
www.jc-museum.cn
English and Chinese audio guides
Hotel / restaurant on the premises

Hold on to your hats – this is one of the most impressive museum experiences you will ever have. Fan Jianchuan, the owner of this private complex, has personally built it, with his own money, a half billion RMB at last count, to house his collection of more than 8,000,000 (yes, EIGHT MILLION) artefacts dealing primarily with the Cultural Revolution and the War against Japan. This charismatic powerhouse of a man is not a materialist gone mad; his museums are an expression of his wish to expose man's inhumanity to man, and to show that although the Japanese behaved savagely to the Chinese during the war, the Chinese did the same to their own people during the Cultural Revolution. He wants us to remember, to learn, to honour the heroes of these struggles and to admit to the many shameful acts of the times. The fact that this museum even exists in China is reason enough to visit. As one walks through the exhibitions, the message is clear: Never forget.

What is displayed is only the tiny tip of the iceberg – much is stored away. Documents, photos, diaries and letters must wait for their creators to die before they go on view.

The grounds are set round a lake, and you travel from museum to museum either by walking down the tree-shaded lanes or by hitching a ride from one of the golf carts cruising the complex. All of the museums have a social or political aspect – even the 'folk art' museums, including The Hall of Mirrors, The Three-Inch Shoe Museum, and the Gallery of Furniture from Private Houses, which features a set of furniture from the Sichuan State Guest House used by China's leaders from the 1960s through to the 1980s. The experience in each one is unique. For instance, when one enters the Three-Inch Shoe Museum (Bound Feet Shoe Museum), at first it seems as if you're entering a brothel – the walls are pink, beaded curtains divide the space, the lights are low. Looking up, you are faced with big posters showing photographs of unwrapped 'lotus feet' and a description of the mutilation young girls were forced to undergo. As you walk through the gallery looking at all the paraphernalia of female repression, humiliation and sexual exploitation, you find yourself tripping and losing your balance on the uneven floor – and you realize the intention: this is what it is like to walk when your feet have been broken and bound.

The POW museum is built as a prison – a razor of light streaming in from the high window above, bleak grey walls, bars and cells all are deeply affecting, as are the accompanying period letters, artefacts and uniforms. Lining the walls are stark images of the Japanese committing atrocities against Chinese prisoners. As the Japanese have still not acknowledged the full extent of their barbarism, this gallery is deeply moving. Rather shaken, you pass out of the gallery through the barred gates and find yourself walking alongside a peaceful pond. On the wall is a plaque with the smiling photo of one POW, Cheng Penghua, reminding us that war is all about the sacrifice of individuals.

Each of the anti-Japanese-war museums focuses on a single theme. These include the Hall of the Resistance, Hall of the Conventional Battlefront, Hall of the Sichuan Army, Chinese Prisoner of War Museum and Flying Tiger Museum. As you walk through this incredible village of museums, open-air exhibits are also displayed such as the Chinese Heroes Statue Plaza and Veterans of the Anti-Japanese War Handprints Plaza.

The Chinese Heroes Plaza is filled with life-size bronze statues of historical figures from the Civil War – both KMT and Communists – standing side by side. The arrangement invites you to walk between and around each one contemplating their past acts. Set in another plaza nearby is a display of large vertically mounted sheets of glass covered with orange handprints of Chinese veterans from the Anti-Japanese War inscribed with their names. It is a moving memorial.

The Chinese
Heroes Plaza

There are now 26 museums open and many more projected. Among the most recent are three which commemorate all those who died in the 2008 Wenchuan earthquake.

To see the entire museum complex and leave time for contemplation you'll need at least two days. It's possible to stay in one of the two small guesthouses on the site or in the larger hotel. Reservations are essential.

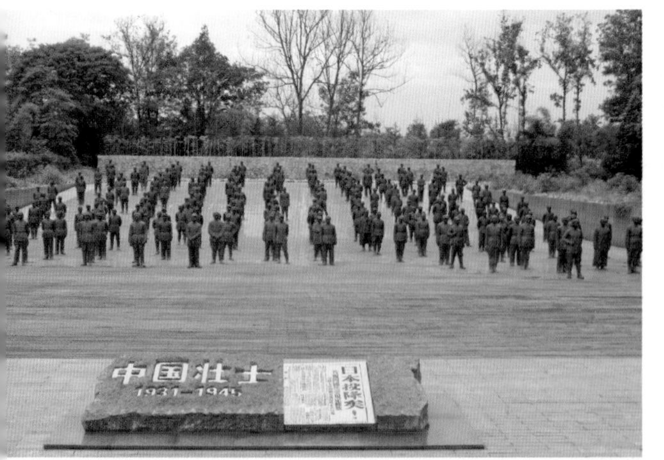

Jinsha Archaeological Site Museum

金沙遗址博物馆 *Jinsha yizhi bowuguan*

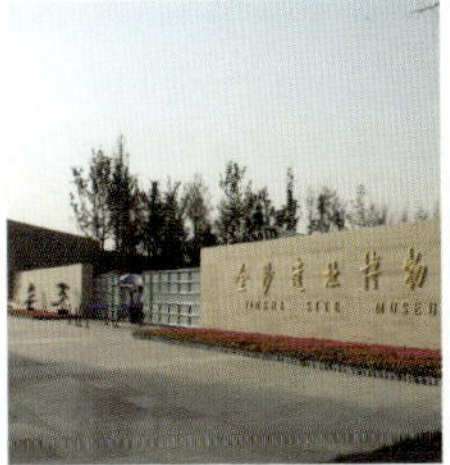

2 Jinshayizhi Road, Chengdu, Sichuan
四川省成都市金沙遗址路 2 号
Tel: (028) 8730 3522
Open: 8.00–17.30
www.jinshasitemuseum.com
English and other language guides / English and Chinese audio guides
Book / gift shops

In February 2001 construction for new housing in the village of Jinsha near Chengdu was halted as a trove of gold, bronze, jade, stone and ivory artefacts was unearthed. This site became known as one of the most exciting archaeological discoveries in Chinese history. Many of the objects bear a close relationship to those found at nearby Sanxingdui, helping to create a timeline for the mysterious ancient Shu kingdom.

Archaeologists then realized that a site discovered in a village near Jinsha was a part of that ancient city. So the two were combined into what is now a single site covering 5 sq km. Within it, archaeologists have identified a large building or palace zone, a residential zone, a graveyard and a sacrificial zone along the banks of an ancient river. Other smaller sites nearby have been identified as Shu kingdom sites, but Jinsha is by far the largest and has the most valuable artefacts and largest structures and so is believed to have been the capital city. It is now thought that when Sanxingdui was abandoned, the Shu capital moved to Jinsha until its mysterious decline around 600 BC.

The archaeology tells us that the history of Jinsha can be broken into three distinct phases. Phase I dates to the late Shang period. The objects found in this phase are mainly ivory and stone. One sacrificial pit included fifteen ivory tusks in addition to other ivory objects. The longest one, on display in the museum encased in silicon, measures a whopping 8.5 m! Whether or not this ivory comes from wild elephants living in the area has been debated. Scientists now think they did live here as inscriptions from the Shang in the central plains speak of kings hunting them and of their use in battle. As the climate at the time was warmer than today and the Chengdu Plain was forested, it is not unlikely that elephants thrived here.

Phase II is equivalent to the late Shang to mid Western Zhou and marks the high

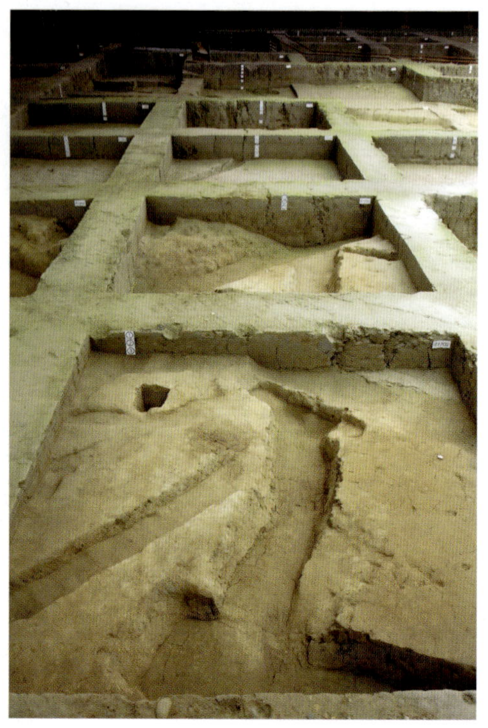

The excavation at the sacrificial zone

point of Jinsha Culture. This is when we find beautiful bronzes, gold and jade, as well as some ivory. Phase III (late Western Zhou and early Spring and Autumn period) was a time of decline. Many fewer bronze and ivory artefacts have been found, though tortoise shells used for divination feature in this era. They were burned and cracked but carry no inscriptions. It is hard to believe that a culture as advanced as the Shu had no system of writing.

More than 2,000 graves have been discovered at Jinsha, all with a chamber running northwest to southeast. The bodies lie face up with their hands on their chests. There are single, group and couple burials. Some contain funerary objects; most are humble, but a few contain jade and bronze artefacts.

The finest objects at Jinsha were found in the sacrificial pits, and these trenches are open to public view. The quality and quantity of the gold and gilt objects here exceed any other pre-Qin site in China. So far, more than 200 gold artefacts have been unearthed, mostly gold foils attached to bronze objects. Now famous and the symbol of China Cultural Heritage is the circular 'Sun and Bird Gold Foil'. Cut out from the foil is the image of the sun with its rays swirling out in curves. Encircling the rays are four stylized divine birds. This iconography, not unusual in ancient China, was connected with sun worship.

Bronze objects at Jinsha also show a close similarity to those at Sanxingdui. More than 1,200 bronze items have been excavated. It is interesting to see how our knowledge of the Shu kingdom is enhanced by comparing and contrasting the material culture of Sanxingdui and the Jinsha. For example, a small standing bronze figure was excavated at Jinsha which looks very much like the very large figure at Sanxingdui that originally held something in its cupped hands. Exactly what was being held is debated – a stick, a jade blade, something ceremonial? The hands of the small Jinsha figure are curved and look as if they could have been holding an ivory tusk. This theory is backed up by another object on display, a jade blade, finely and delicately etched, showing a man carrying a tusk over his shoulder.

Jade objects were also made with excellent craftsmanship and plentifully; more than 2,000 had been excavated by 2007. These include vessels, chisels, dagger-axes

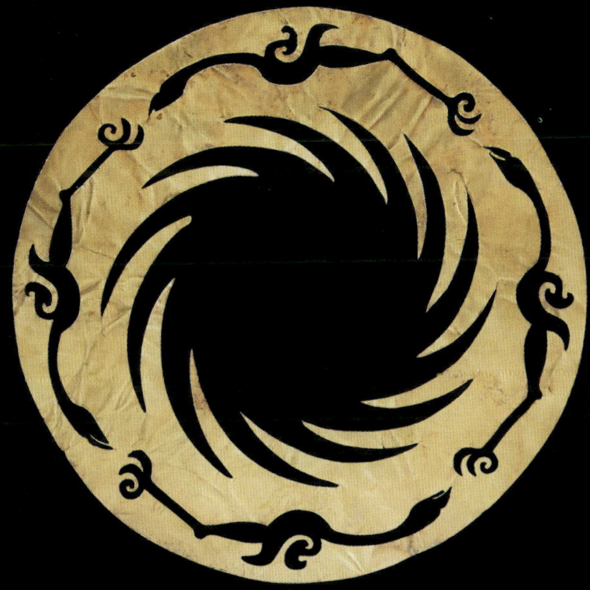

Sun and bird gold foil, cut-out diameter 12.5 cm

and other items. Most of the stone was locally sourced and includes hopfnerite, nefrite and marble. Be sure to see the ten-section jade *cong* identified as a 'national treasure'. It was brought into Jinsha from outside as it predates the Culture by a thousand years. Perhaps it came from the Liangzhu Culture in Zhejiang.

A tremendous amount of pottery has been found at Jinsha. Many typical forms are found; however, there are some unique shapes including certain types of cups and jars with pointed bottoms. These are all displayed in the museum.

This site should be visited in conjunction with a visit to Sanxingdui to give you an understanding of the Shu kingdom and ancient Sichuan. The basement gallery at Jinsha offers a lot of comparative material and posters explaining the history of the place and its relationship to other cultures in Sichuan, China and the rest of the ancient world.

127

Liangshan Yi Ethnic Group's Slavery Museum

凉山彝族奴隶社会博物馆 *Liangshan yizu nulishehui bowuguan*

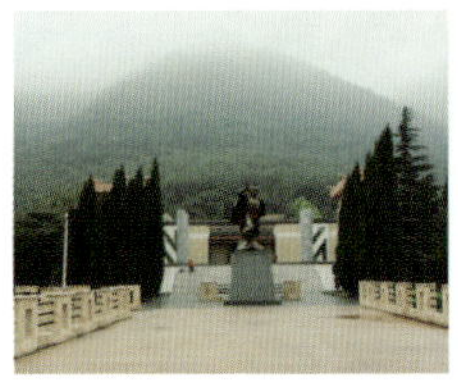

6 Lushan Road, Lushan park, Xichang, Sichuan
四川省西昌市泸山风景区泸山路6号
Tel: (0834) 3223 150
Open: 8.30–16.00
Gift shop / bookshop / tea room

The Museum is located on beautiful Lushan Mountain facing Qionghai Lake, in Xichang City, in the Liangshan Yi Autonomous Prefecture of Sichuan Province. The Yi people with their own language and customs are one of China's largest non-Han ethnic groups, totalling approximatelly 8 million of which 2 million are in Sichuan.

According to Marxist theory, society moves through a series of stages: primitive, slave, feudal, capitalist and socialist on the way to communism. The slave-owning society of the Liangshan Yi ethnic group reached its peak during the 8th–9th centuries AD, much later than in other parts of China. This museum is the only one in China dedicated to the theme of slave society.

The Museum, which was opened in 1985, is laid out in a garden style with traditional Yi buildings set in a wooded landscape. The permanent exhibition covers all aspects of the Yi's slave period – political, economic, military (including slave uprisings), religious, social customs and laws. Of specialist interest is the mysterious culture of the Bimo – shamans who practiced animism and magic rituals. The superb Yi art, which ranges from diverse ethnic costumes to exquisite hand-painted lacquer and silver, is well presented.

Do not be put off by the theme of the museum. The collection contains fine and fascinating objects. Additionally, your visit to Xichang can be combined with a visit to Qionghai Lake (and its fish restaurants) and a trip to the Xichang Space Centre where China launches its spacecraft.

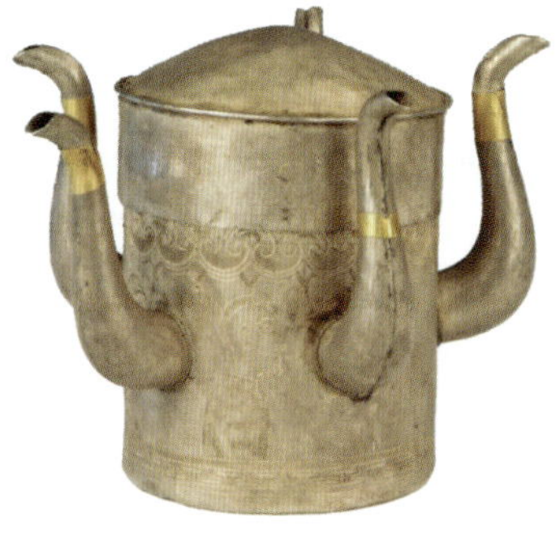

Silver wine vessel used by Yi nobles, Ming dynasty

Wooden wine cup in the shape of eagle's claw and painted with unique Yi pattern, Qing dynasty

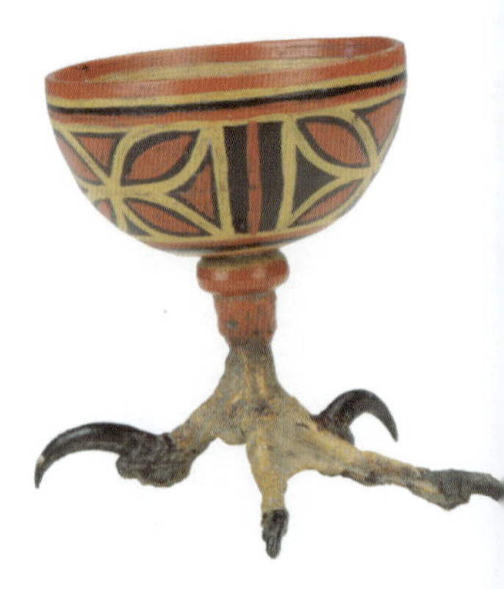

Sanxingdui Museum

三星堆博物馆 *Sanxingdui bowuguan*

128

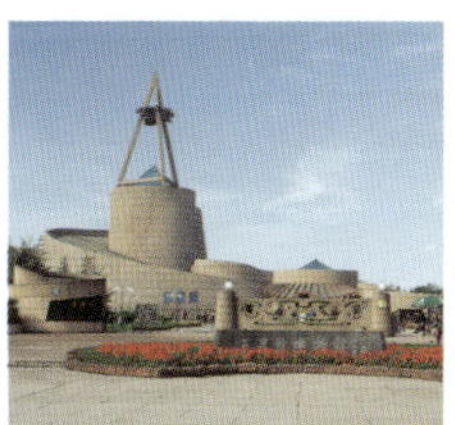

133 Xi'an Road, Guanghan, Sichuan
四川省广汉市西安路133号
Tel: (0838) 5651 526
Gallery 1: Open: 8.30–18.00, last entry 17.00
Gallery 2: Open:8.30–18.30, last entry 17.00
www.sxd.cn

Sanxingdui is one of the great museum destinations in China, rivalling the Terracotta Warriors in Xi'an. If you find yourself in Sichuan, do not pass up the opportunity to see the museum.

The Shu Culture (Shu is the ancient name for the area now known as Sichuan – a large, fertile region surrounded by mountains and known as the Red Basin) was wrapped in mystery until the discovery of this site. Although the archaeological evidence shows that it existed from the Late Neolithic (equivalent to the Longshan Culture in the northern plains) through to the Eastern Zhou, very little mention is made of it in the historical record before the Spring and Autumn period, and to date no written records exist. In fact, no system of writing has been found, with the exception of seven glyphs.

The first breakthrough came in 1929 when a Sichuan farmer digging on his land found a pit containing several hundred jade and stone artefacts. Subsequent archaeological investigations uncovered more objects and structures. Then in 1986 two Shang dynasty sacrificial pits were found. Pit I contained bronzes, jade, gold, elephant tusks, and burnt bones and associated objects, some of which are spectacular, such as a life-size bronze human head, a gold mask and a dragon-shaped bronze column. Breaking and burning were common practices for sacrificial offerings at the time.

Pit II, some metres away, contained objects even more dazzling. They too had been burnt and broken before burial, but no bones were found here. The objects were neatly organized: on the top, sixty-seven elephant tusks, then bronzes, gold, jade ware, turquoise ornaments, stone implements and seashells. Some of the finds are of the sort common in Xia and Shang burials, but others are exquisite and unique artefacts such as a 2.6-m-high bronze statue of a human, a divine tree made of bronze nearly

etail from Shu
ulture bronze,
garded as the
asterpiece of the
llection, in a pose
at suggests he
exercising magic
a mystic
remony (note the
ystic band on his
oulder decorated
th rectangular
otifs)

4m high, a 1.9-m-wide bronze mask with bulging eyes, and a bronze human head with a gilded mask. The purpose of these pits is debated – it is thought there is a hundred-year difference in their ages. Whether they are themselves a tomb, subordinate to a tomb or a storehouse is not clear.

The site of Sanxingdui covers an area of approximately 26 sq km. Only the museum is open to the public. The archaeological evidence reveals an ambitious scale of city planning including traces of a wall, roads, a palace site, residences, workshops and sacrificial sites.

Many of the objects are of spectacular workmanship and unsurpassed beauty. The bronze figures differ in visage, dress, hairstyle and stance, and seem to portray different classes of society. Most have large almond-shaped eyes. The eye motif, prevalent in Shu Culture, seems to have had some association with supernatural power, perhaps due to the eye's connection with the image of the sun and to light. Another theory involves an early chronicle of the Shu kingdom which states that the Shu people's ancestral deity and earliest king, Cancong, had 'protruding eyes'. Bronze eyes or rhomboid objects (which look like beautiful pieces of contemporary sculpture) were also discovered, further indicating some concept of ocular divinity.

Bronze animal masks and animals, vessels, decorations and spears also abound.

Small ritual items made of pounded gold foil were also found at the site. The craftsmanship is sophisticated and technically advanced. The gold wares were exclusively for ritual purposes; no gold for personal adornment has been discovered.

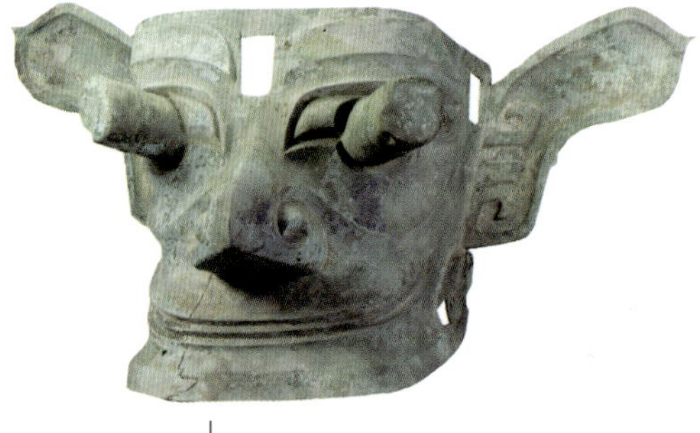

Bronze mask with protruding eyes

The 'divine tree' found in Pit II is the largest ancient bronze artefact ever found in China. The elaborate decoration includes a pedestal, and coming off the main trunk are branches bearing fruit with crested birds perched on the ends. Scholars do not agree on the purpose of this object, but it does have many references to cosmology, a common feature of ancient religions. The excavations have uncovered about a thousand jade and stone artefacts, again made to an exquisite standard. They include shapes such as the *zhang*, *bi*, *yuan*, *cong* and *ge*. Many ritual tools and weapons were found, giving credence to the theory that the Shu kingdom had a large and active ritual system. Interestingly, no actual weapons were found here, nor is there any other evidence of conflict, unlike for other Shang groups. Finally, a great deal of earthenware was excavated here, some types of which are rare at other sites: small, flat-based, high-stemmed bowls and ladles with bird-headed handles.

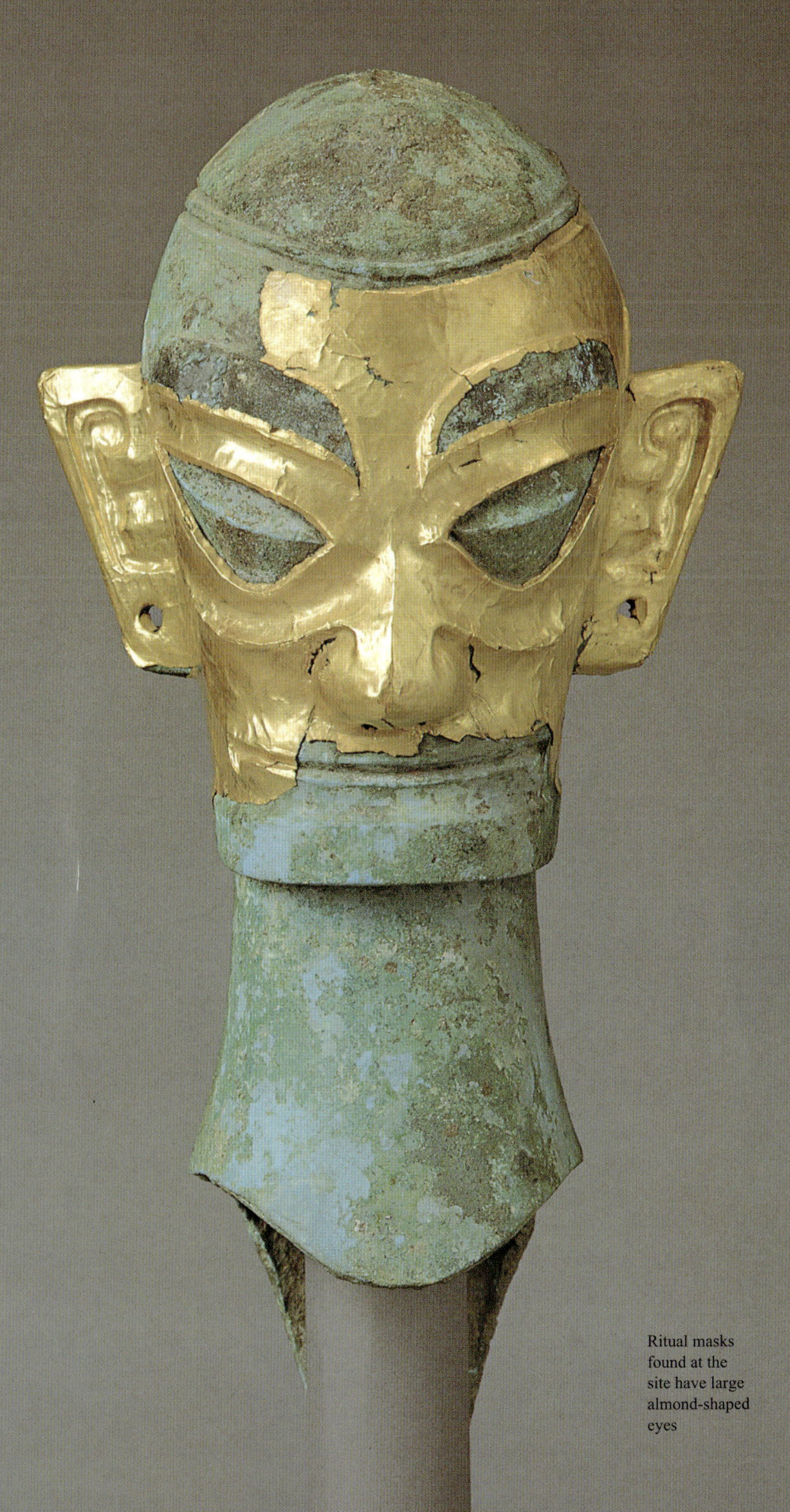

Ritual masks
found at the
site have large
almond-shaped
eyes

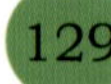

Sichuan Museum

四川博物院 *Sichuan bowuyuan*

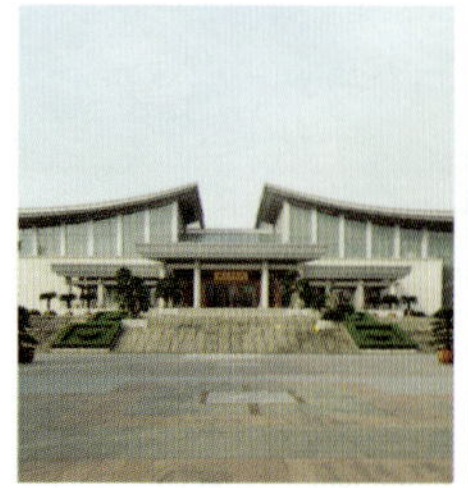

251 Huanhua South Road, Qingyang District,
Chengdu, Sichuan
四川省成都市青羊区浣花南路251号
Tel: (028) 8522 6723
Open: 9.00–17.00 except Mon
www.scmuseum.cn
Audio guides in all major languages and personal guides
Restaurant / fast-food café / bookshop / hotel

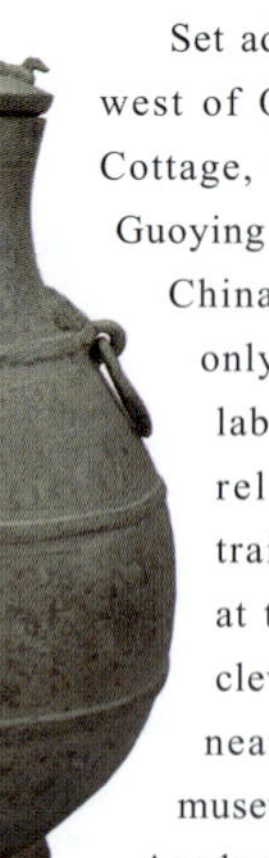

Bronze *Hu* (wine vessel) with inlaid battle design, Warring States period

Set adjacent to the splendid Huanhuaxi Park a couple of kilometres west of Qingyang on the edge of Chengdu near Du Fu's Thatched Cottage, this new museum designed by the Chinese architect Zheng Guoying is a real jewel. It is the largest provincial museum in southwest China. Spread over 12,000 sq m, the main building contains not only ten galleries but also four auxiliary centres: a conservation laboratory, an international cultural exchange-office, a cultural relics examination unit for authentication and another for training personnel for Sichuan's various museums (a hundred at the latest count and growing). Additionally, the museum has cleverly tapped into the growing tourism boom and opened a hotel nearby, providing an additional revenue stream. Although the museum keeps standard opening hours, the restaurant, as well as the Academic Hall, which seats close to 400 and can be used either as a conference centre or a performance space, stays open into the evening.

Started in 1941, the collection has grown exponentially as dozens of new sites have been discovered and excavated, and is now home to more than 260,000 cultural relics. Combine one of the seven best collections of artefacts in China with some of the most advanced multimedia tools in the museum tool box and a large investment from the city, and you get an intoxicating experience symbolic of the Sichuan Basin's rich cultural past. Exhibition areas feature: bronzes from the Ba and Shu Cultures; sculpture and tomb bricks from the Han dynasty; porcelain from the primitive to the Qing dynasty (in two parts: material from Sichuan and material from Song dynasty sites); ancient calligraphy; a gallery dedicated to Zhang Daqian, the renowned twentieth-century artist (400 paintings); cultural relics from the fourteen minorities in the province, including textiles; Southern dynasty Buddhist sculpture and costumes; Tibetan and Buddhist objects; arts and crafts, such as bamboo-carving, Shu textiles and lacquer; a modern history gallery covering events including the Red Army's Long March, most of which took place here; and two galleries for travelling exhibitions. Exhibits will be updated periodically, enabling the museum's massive collection to be seen in turns.

The holdings are particularly strong in Ba and Shu Warring States period bronzes, in particular vessels, weapons and ritual objects unearthed from the tomb at Xindu Majiaxiang in the territory of the ancient Shu kingdom; Han pottery figures and bricks; Liang and Tang dynasties Buddhist sculpture, including magnificent stele; Song dynasty Shu brocade; a large number of Tibetan objects and embroidery; Longquan celadon porcelain and a dizzying array of material culture from the fourteen ethnic minorities in Sichuan.

The superb Warring States bronzes clearly show that although several distinct cultures originated in Sichuan they did not develop in isolation. Exchanges occurred not only among them but also with neighbouring cultures and even beyond. The tomb at Xindu Majiaxiang is the richest burial known to be from later Bronze Age Sichuan, possibly belonging to the King of Shu. More than sixty bronze weapons were found in the *yaokeng*, or waste pit, of the tomb, among them five rare swords of two types, which, at the beginning of the fifth century, became the classic forms most widely used in the Yangtze region and beyond. When they were excavated several were found in their original black-lacquered wooden scabbards. Most likely they were made in the state of Chu.

Equally delightful are the pictorial decorations carved on tomb bricks from the Eastern Han, the most impressive of which came from rock-cut tombs in cliff faces, the tomb type most commonly found in Sichuan. These pictures, along with pottery figurines and models also found in the tombs, provided the deceased with everything they needed in the afterlife. The tombs in Sichuan are famous for their depiction of farming scenes, salt production and entertainers, including one excavated from Pang Xian Taipingchang showing acrobats and jugglers. These along with the pottery figures of a squatting drummer, seated musician, dancing lady, kneeling woman and peasant soldier protected and entertained rich landowners and merchants in the afterlife.

Buddhist sculptures in Sichuan

Eastern Han brick with chariot and horsemen crossing a bridge

tended to be of the 'southern' as distinct from the 'northern' style and were mostly freestanding stone images and stele. A large body of Liang dynasty examples from Wanfosi, Chengdu and, more recently, the Xi'an Road in Chengdu are wonderful examples of this style, which favours realism and often includes exotic elements from India or Southeast Asia. The Wanfosi Shakyamuni is an example of such an indianized style. Particularly handsome is a fragmentary stele with bodhisattvas standing on lotuses on the front and landscape scenes on the back exhibiting distinctly Sichuanese innovations including spatial perspective.

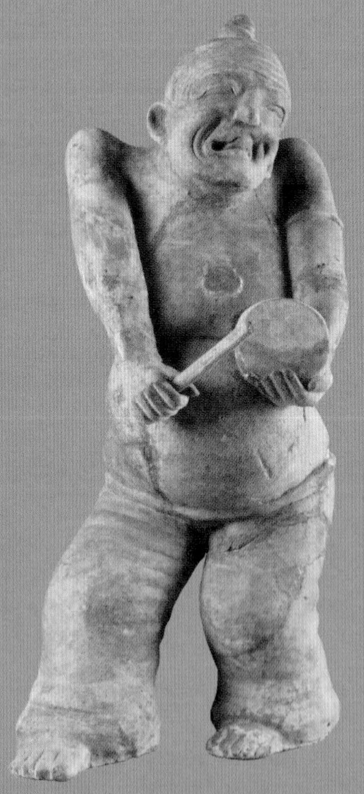

Pottery story-teller
beating a drum

Sichuan University Museum

四川大学博物馆 *Sichuan daxue bowuguan*

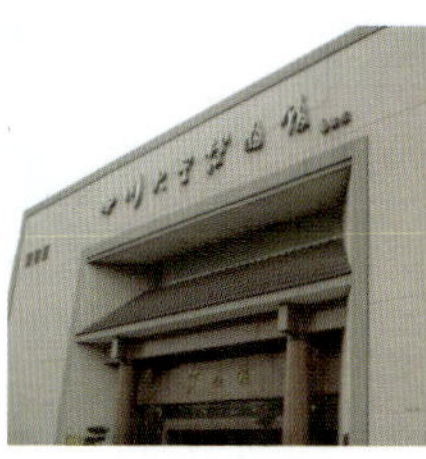

29 Wangjiang Road, Chengdu, Sichuan
四川省成都市望江路29号
Tel: (028) 8541 2543
Open: 9.00–17.00
Guides are available but must be arranged in advance
Shop sells craft items from ethnic minorities.

This museum is one of the earliest established in the southwest of China. Originally known as the West China Union University Museum, it was founded by the American Daniel S. Dye, who taught there from 1910 to 1949, serving under the American Baptist Foreign Missionary Society. During his spare time he documented the designs used in West China window latticework, woven belts and pottery. Dye, like so many of his colleagues, contributed much of what they collected to the museum. During the war archaeologists from the east also came here and added to the collection. The University offers degrees in archaeology. Many of the country's famous sites have been excavated by scholars trained here, including Sanxingdui. The University also has a Centre for Tibetan Studies and for South Asian Studies.

Today the collection stands at some 40,000 items and ranges from folk art, embroideries, porcelain and bronzes to ethnography and traditional arts. At any one time there is a selection of objects displayed in one of the seven halls arranged over four floors. Good lighting, proper display cases and labels in English and Chinese make this a pleasurable place to visit. The Tibetan collection and those of other minorities such as the Yi are considered among the best in China, with an impressive collection of ethnic costumes, and shaman's tools and exceptional painted *thangkas*. Equally outstanding are the Eastern Han dynasty tomb tiles, including one depicting Xiwangmu, the goddess of immortality, flanked by a tiger (east) and a dragon (west) and others illustrating an afterlife of fishing and harvesting.

There is a new room devoted to shadow puppets dating from the Qing dynasty (1644–1911) cut from paper-thin leather hide of donkey, cow or sheep delightfully painted on both sides with vegetable dyes in a kaleidoscope of colours. Made in sections, those depicting humans were usually composed of at least eleven parts with silk or cotton string holding the parts together. The heads were usually not attached permanently allowing the character to change persona during the performance. The application of tung oil made from the seeds of a fruit grown in China was applied to the leather to add to its translucency. Wires with bamboo handles were attached to

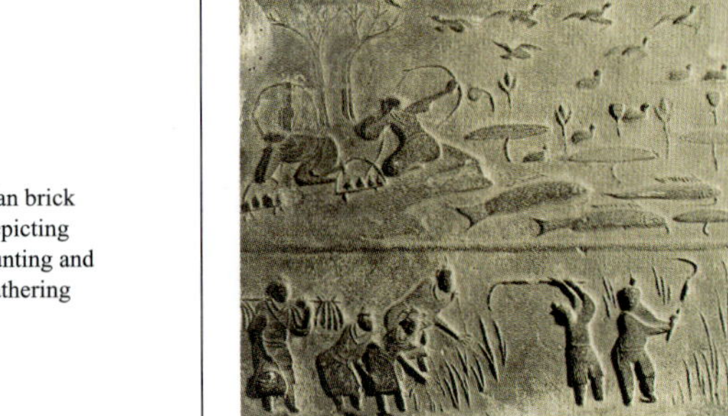

manipulate the figures in front of a light source projecting their stained-glass coloured shadows onto a translucent screen. A selection of specialized chisels and knives used to cut the intricate designs into the leather are also displayed.

Zigong Dinosaur Museum

自贡恐龙博物馆 *Zigong konglong bowuguan*

131

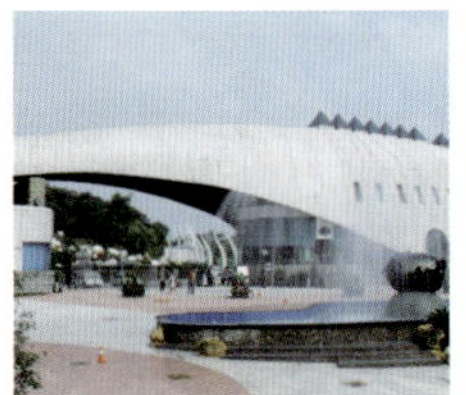

238 Dashanpu Township, Da'an District, Zigong, Sichuan
四川省自贡市大安区大山铺镇238号
Tel: (0813) 580 1235
Open: 8.30–17.30, last entry 17.00
www.zdm.cn
Café / shop selling books, salt, and all things related to dinosaurs
Kids

Jurassic Park fans will feel like they've died and gone to heaven upon entering this amazing museum built at the dinosaur burial site of Dashanpu, for this is the greatest concentration of Middle Jurassic (180–154 million years ago) dinosaur finds anywhere in the world. Covering a huge area – 66,000 sq m), it is also one of the world's three largest dinosaur museums built in situ. Although your heart might sink when upon arrival you are greeted by a dinosaur-shaped visitor's centre, don't let this deaden your enthusiasm, as young and old will love this truly magnificent park. Modelled on dinosaur museums in North America, it has a slight Disney feel with dinosaurs you can ride and fountains with bronzes of baby dinosaurs emerging from eggs. These delights aside, it has been designed to the highest level with first-rate information panels and labels throughout. Leave at least two hours to view it properly, as there is a fair bit of walking between the exhibition halls and the open pits where you can see excavations in progress.

When the dinosaurs roamed the area around Zigong, it was even more lush and fertile than it is today, resulting in river, lake and floodplain deposits over four strata, or layers – the most perfect environment for dinosaurs, bony fish and marine reptiles imaginable. This explains the mother lode of finds that have been excavated here since the first hint of a 'dinosaur graveyard' was discovered by China's greatest dinosaur hunter, Dong Zhiming, in the 1970s. After fighting off an oil-and-gas company that was already bulldozing the site, Dong rallied officials and got permission to excavate. When the museum complex opened in 1987, a selection of the 40 tons of fossils and tens of thousands of bones was put on display or placed in store for palaeontologists from abroad and China's universities to examine.

After picking up a map of the park in the visitor's centre and a walking stick, umbrella or pushchair, make your way outside and walk behind the building to the right towards the main exhibition building. Along the way you will pass a large, raised circular grassy area containing large-scale dinosaur models. Further on there is a living garden planted with Mesozoic trees, ferns, gingkoes and cypresses, very like the flora that would have existed at the time in the lush forests. Ahead is a rather massive, sandstone-coloured building – the heart of the museum-park complex – containing two floors of displays and an exposed section of the original excavated site.

Upon entering, your eyes will be drawn to the breathtaking display of eighteen dinosaur skeletons in the Dinosaur World exhibition space. It is, however, worth taking a moment to first study the nearby world-distribution map of dinosaur bones covering the Triassic, Jurassic and Cretaceous periods and having a look at the images of the skeletons being excavated. There are too many highlights to list, but do be sure to see an extremely well-preserved specimen of the herbivore *Huayangosaurus* (160 million years old), one of the most primitive of the stegosauruses. Around 4.5 m in length, it had two sets of huge bony plates running the length of its spine with spikes at the end of its tail, most likely for protection. Look also at the *Yangchuanosaurus*, a carnivorous monster from the Upper Jurassic period extending 10 m and to date the largest and best-preserved meat-eater found in Asia.

Best not to linger too long in the main hall, as there's lot more to see. Around the corner in the central hall you can look down onto ten dinosaur skeletons piled upon one another, perhaps caught in the swirl of the waters during a flood. Stop here too if you'd like to envision yourself thirty million years ago in the darkest depths of the Jurassic period – for you can step inside a simulated composition and have yourself filmed and take home a DVD to show your friends. Waiting on the other side of this central area is the 2,800-sq-m dinosaur graveyard exposing more than a hundred individual bones and fossils such as turtles. You are able to walk not only around the entire preserved site but also down into it via stairs and a viewing platform.

slice of earth
exposing the
Xiashaximiao
formation of the
Middle Jurassic

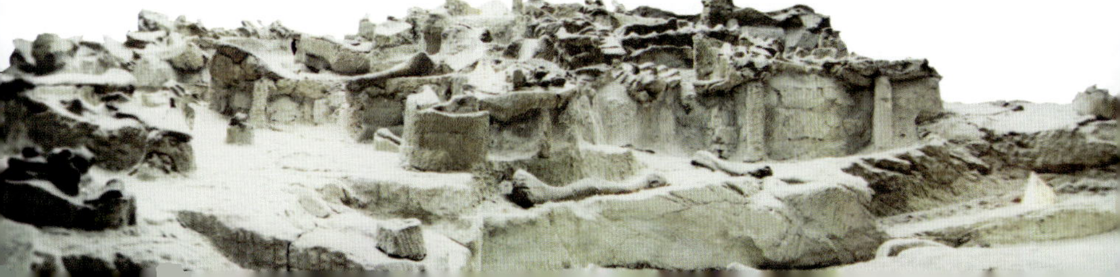

The second floor contains the gallery devoted to the Mesozoic (250–65 million years ago) fauna and flora – this was the true 'Age of the Dinosaurs'. Displayed here are specimens of crocodiles, fishes, early birds, mammals, and flora of all types which existed alongside the dinosaurs over the Triassic, Jurassic and Cretaceous periods. Particularly spectacular are the well-preserved fossils of turtles from Liaoxi (west of Liaoning Province), as well as the aquatic reptile *Hyphalosaurus lingyuanensis*, with paddle-like limbs and a long serpentine neck, and the fish-shaped reptile with four fin-shaped limbs known as an ichthyosaur.

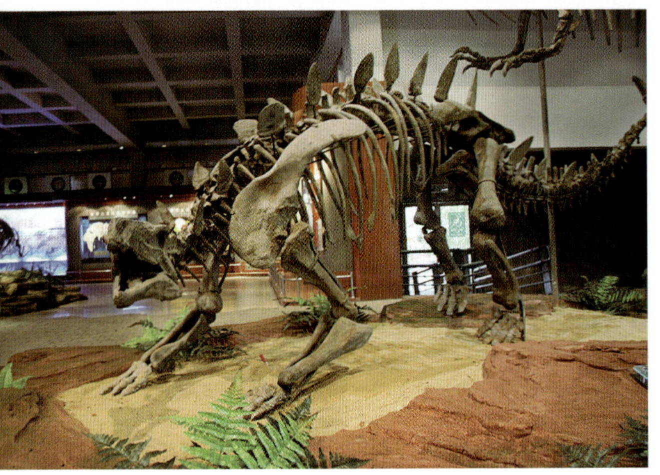

Huayangosaurus Taibaii

The Treasure Hall in the next gallery is a must, for here are some of the prizes of the museum rightly displayed on red velvet in specially lit glass cases. Sadly not all of these are original as security demands that the real ones are kept in store. The beauties include the best-preserved fossil of *Agilisaurus louderbacki* (named after the American geologist Dr. Louderback, who first recognized dinosaur fossils from Sichuan Province in 1915), the small dinosaur which looks like a lizard lying curled up. It was found 90 per cent complete and adds tremendously to our evolutionary knowledge of this genus. The skull of the *Shunosaurus*, the best-preserved specimen known is sensational, as almost 100 per cent of it was found, and in the next case is a fossil of its club-shaped tail, the first discovery of this type anywhere. The skin impression of the *Mamenchisaurus youngi* covered in polygonal scales was the first example of such a find from a sauropod in China.

Finally, outside and a bit of a walk from the main museum is a slice of earth exposing the Xiashaximiao formation of the Middle Jurassic, which covers a wide area of the Sichuan Basin. Composed of several large sedimentary rhythms, it contains the most diverse dinosaur fauna before the Late Jurassic and is best known for its sauropods, including the one here in view, the *Omisauraus*, the long-necked herbivore that stretched to over 20 m in length.

Zigong Salt History Museum

自贡市盐业历史博物馆 *Zigongshi yanye lishi bowuguan*

132

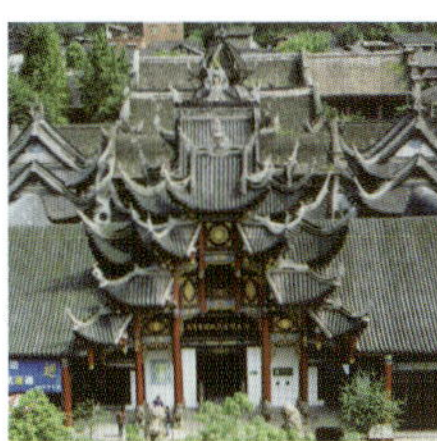

107 Jiefang Road, Ziliujing District, Zigong, Sichuan
四川省自贡市自流井区解放路107号
Tel: (0813) 220 2083
Open: 8.30–17.30 except Spring Festival Eve
English-speaking guide available without booking

Not only was Zigong one of the Sichuan Basin's centres for inland salt production, but it is credited with an array of spectacular technological breakthroughs which have had lasting impact world-wide. The most impressive has to be the invention of deep drilling in the mid eleventh century AD, listed by the famous historian of technology Joseph Needham in his summary of twenty of China's most important inventions to have entered Europe. Later, this technique would be instrumental in the advance of drilling technology for the oil and gas industries. If that were not enough, the area around Zigong saw the drilling of the first-ever wells to a depth of more than 1,000 m (in the early nineteenth century), and goes down in history as using coal and natural gas as fuel for salt production for the first time.

Salt has been one of the most traded commodities, whether for food preservation or as a condiment, at least since Neolithic times. As in many parts of the world, archaeological evidence points to salt being produced in Zigong by the evaporation of briny water in wide-mouthed shallow wells, or by using pottery vessels and boiling away the water content. Here in the Sichuan Basin, around 2,250 years ago, the first salt well was recorded in China, exploiting the thick, black salt-brine layers formed hundreds of metres below the surface during the Jurassic and Cretaceous periods.

Over time, drilling technology developed, and so did salt production. During the Tang dynasty a well reached a depth of 250 m, but it was not until the invention of a new cable-drilling method between 1041 and 1048 that production took off. This, coupled with the discovery of natural gas in the Zigong area in the early seventeenth century and, later, new gas-production techniques, moved production on to a different level, producing sufficient heat for more than 700 salt pans. By the middle of the nineteenth century, the industry was employing tens of thousands, dozens of wooden derricks (tall wooden

Tool used to repair and drill wells

structures made of hundreds of fir trees bundled together) could be seen across the landscape, and the Fuxi River was crowded with salt boats exporting some 150,000 tons of edible salt. Zigong City became the salt-production capital of southwestern China, its name the combination of two famous salt-production areas, Ziliujing and Gongjing.

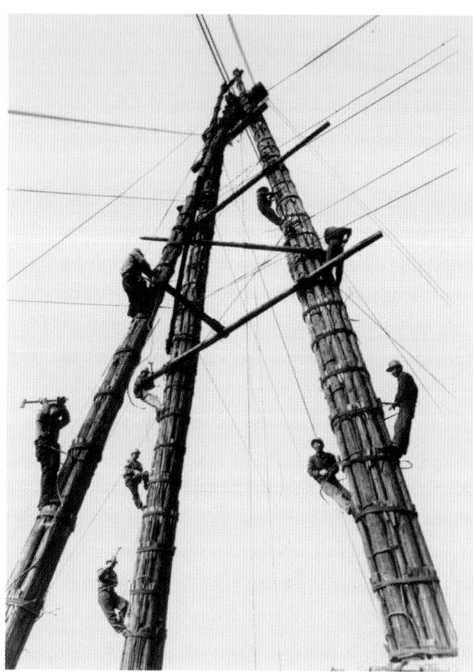

A 1982 photo of derrick workers repairing a 'Heaven Cart', which could reach more than 100 m in height

This fascinating history of salt-well production and its cultural, economic and environmental impact is told in chronological order over two floors in the completely original Shanxi Guildhall, built from 1736 to 1752 by the rich Shanxi merchants who were active in the salt industry in the Ziliujing area. Displayed are cases filled with scores of tools for opening the well-heads and drilling the wells. Numerous models allow visitors to work a lever or press a button and watch how various tools removed mud and stones from the bore-hole, or corrected deviations to ensure the well-bore was vertical. Others show how dozens of tools perfected for fishing out objects which fell into the bore-holes were used. Fallen chisels would be retrieved using the 'king of fishing tools', the Fixture. Its bamboo shell would be manoeuvred until the chisel shaft slid into the narrow section of the shell.

Illustrations from *The Annals of Salt Law of Sichuan Province* show the elaborate but advanced method of cable drilling, which with the help of gravity drove an iron chisel at the bottom of the hole, thus deepening the well and cutting the time needed to drill one down from ten to between three and five years. Others demonstrate how wooden columns were made and mud was lifted from the wells as they were dug. Equally informative are the historic images showing the forest of wooden derricks or tall wooden structures used for drilling and brine-lifting, which, in the 1950s covered the Zigong saltern, nineteen of which can still be seen today dotting the landscape. The collection extends to salt-industry contracts, marketing accounts and records of well-digging. Huang Jian, associate professor and curator of the museum, has made the history of salt production in this region his life's work and is worth speaking to if you have a translator. The Shenhai Well, the first to exceed 1,000 m in depth, can be visited in the nearby Da'an District of Zigong.

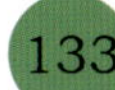

Baiheliang Underwater Museum

白鹤梁水下博物馆 *Baiheliang shuixia bowuguan*

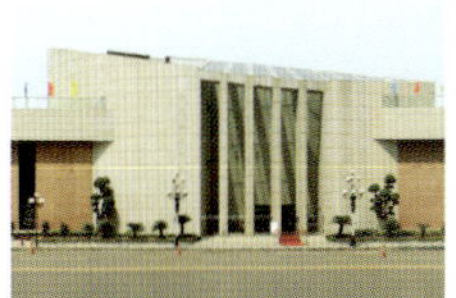

185 Section 2 Binjiang Road, Fuling District, Chongqing
重庆市涪陵区滨江大道二段185号
Open: 9.00–17.00 except Mon
www.cqbhl.com.cn

When the Three Gorges Dam project was announced, not only were the environmentalists up in arms along with the 1.5 million people who had to be relocated, but so were the archaeologists. The flooding of the Yangtze valley meant the loss of thousands of important sites, many related to the ancient Ba people. Archaeologists scrambled to save and record as many sites as they could before they were submerged forever. Baiheliang, although it will eventually lie under around 40m of water, has had a reprieve. Opened in 2009, the museum makes part of this unique site accessible to visitors.

Located along the river north of the Fuling District, Baiheliang, or White Crane Ridge, is covered with carp-shaped carvings and inscriptions dating back to the Tang dynasty. This ledge, 1,600 m long and 15 m wide, is an ancient record of changes in the river's water levels, knowledge essential for predicting availability for a good harvest. Only during the winter and early spring when the water table was low would

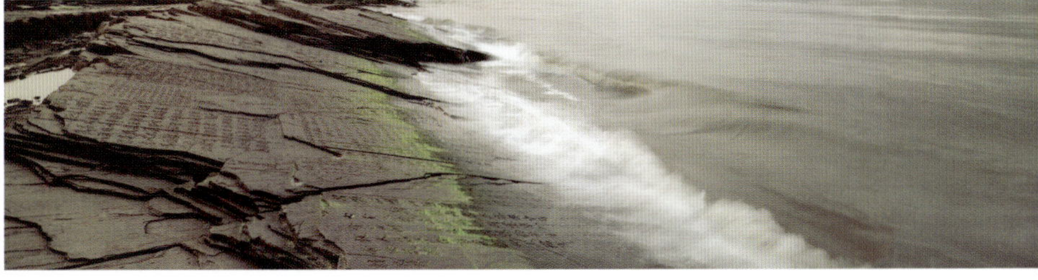

Carvings and inscriptions on the ledge show old water levels

the ledge have been visible; then it also was useful as a marker to navigators. What remains is 1,200 years of hydrological data enlivened by poetic descriptions of the landscape carved in the rock faces over various dynasties. The most impressive section of the ridge, including a pair of spectacularly carved carp, is covered by a glass dome. This, together with two underwater channels extending out from the riverbank, allows visitors to view the inscriptions and carvings lit with underwater lighting.

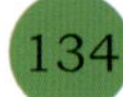

Chongqing Huguang Guildhall Complex

重庆湖广会馆 *Chongqing huguang huiguan*

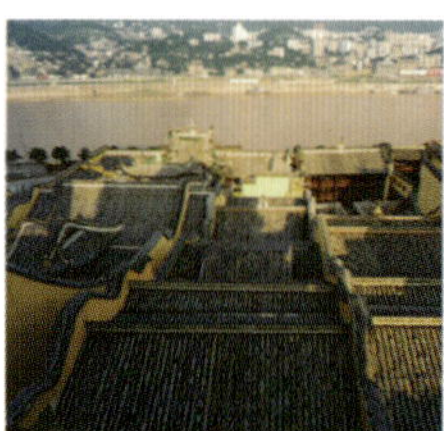

1 Bajiaoyuan, Yuzhong District, Chongqing
重庆市渝中区芭蕉园1号
Tel: (023) 6393 0287
Open: 8.30–18.00, last entry 17.30
www.cqhghg.com
Audio guides in English and Chinese for all parts of the complex

The end of the Ming dynasty and beginning of the Qing saw Manchu troops enter Sichuan and raze the area to the ground. To repopulate the province, the new rulers ordered millions of residents from Guangdong, Guangxi, Jiangxi, Hunan and Hubei to relocate. These immigrants needed a place to meet, conduct business and be entertained. What is known today as the Huguang Guildhall is in fact a series of halls built by merchants from the various provinces with these purposes in mind. Taking pride of place is the main hall with its various rooms, platforms and courtyard. The beams, window frames and door surrounds are decorated with vividly carved animals, plants and people. There is also a temple where people would pray for good fortune.

This complex is home to a museum documenting the migration, as well as an outstanding museum of traditional carved and decorated boards (right wing of the main hall). Suspended above the lintels of halls, pavilions or gardens, they were fashioned from wood of various kinds and carved with two, three or four characters. Some are signed and dated. Simple looking at first glance, they were in fact the product of skilled artisans. Often one person would do the carving of the characters and another would apply the gold leaf. The calligraphy was considered the 'soul' of the board, and their making a prestigious career for an artisan. The actual sayings were considered an art in themselves and reflected the writing ability of their authors.

This collection was amassed by the father and son team, Liu Shaolin and Liu Guangrui, both well-known local doctors of traditional Chinese medicine. Obsessed with saving these boards from being used as firewood, they set about collecting them from all over Sichuan. Currently there are over 300 examples from the Ming and Qing dynasties, as well as later examples from the Republic of China; however, the collection is still growing. Displayed are around seventy examples covering five types, from those praising excellence and encouraging business and study, to messages of congratulation on birthdays and those used to identify buildings or residences. To eulogize someone's success or character, it might say 'being honest in performing official duties' and could be presented by a person at a lower level to someone more senior. These were often hung inside the central living space to flaunt the person's status. Those crafted as a present to a newly opened shop were very carefully created as they became the public 'face' of a business.

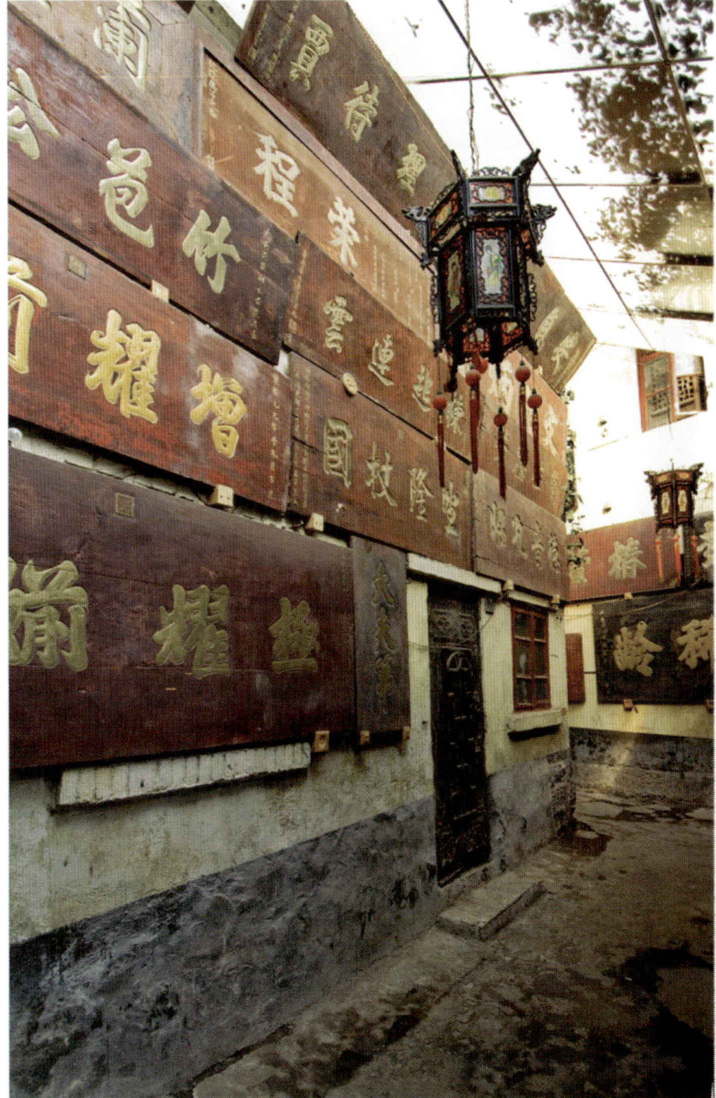

Wooden signs
in the home of
collector
Liu Shaolin

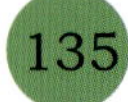

Chongqing Three Gorges Museum

重庆中国三峡博物馆 *Chongqing zhongguo sanxia bowuguan*

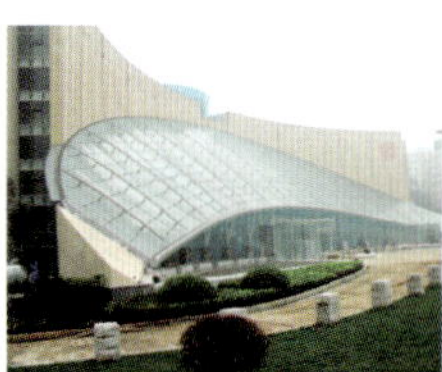

236 Renmin Road, Yuzhong District, Chongqing
重庆市渝中区人民路236号
Tel: (023) 6367 9066
Open: 9.00–17.00, last entry 16.00
www.3gmuseum.cn

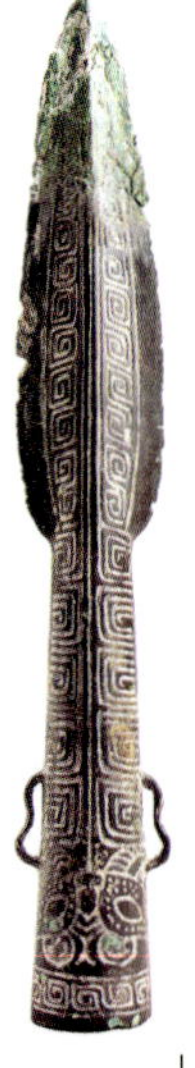

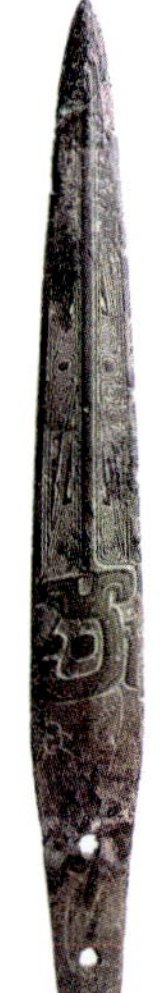

A bronze spear incised with abstract designs

A bronze sword with animal mask designs, Ba-Shu State

It promised to provide hydro-electric power, flood control and enhanced navigation, but the world's largest dam, known as the Three Gorges project, has also displaced millions, flooded some of the best agricultural land in the area, destroyed natural wonders and lost to the world thousands of important ancient sites. Hundreds of archaeologists scrambled to save as many sites as possible before they disappeared. A large part of what they were able to rescue has now been deposited, together with objects from the old Chongqing Museum, in this massive new museum. Opened in 2005 and stretching one whole side of a pedestrian plaza, this nondescript concrete-and-glass refuge displays at any one time around 17,000 objects over four floors. Despite getting carried away with one too many lengthy galleries hosting interactive dioramas and floor-to-ceiling photographic panoramas of the Three Gorges (which consists of the Qutang, Wuxia and Xiling Gorges along the 200 km stretch of the Yangtze), the museum displays many exceptional items and offers a good overview of the area's rich ancient civilization and equally important plant and animal life.

The first galleries are reconstructions of historic scenes – coolies pulling boats along rugged shorelines and models of boat-shaped coffins used in Ba kingdom burials. Also displayed are a selection of mounted specimens from the hundreds of known species of fish and animals living in the Three Gorges, from golden eagles, porcupines and mountain goats to the now extinct White Fin Dolphin and currently protected White Sturgeon. Further on is a cursory mention of the towns lost and people displaced when the dam was built.

The third floor galleries display the treasure trove of Palaeolithic finds from the Three Gorges area. Among the most spectacular are those from the Longgupo Site in Wushan, which have caused China's history to be rewritten. These are fossilized remains of a primitive human species dating to about two million years BC. Pictures and replicas of some of the more than 230 finds include a lower jawbone fragment and stone tools. Excavations of caves such as Xinglongdong Cave in Fengjie County produced a human tooth, mammalian fossils, stone artefacts and an ivory Stegodon tusk engraved with abstract patterns – the earliest known engravings by humans. This site dates to 120,000–150,000 years ago. Fengdu is home to the important Palaeolithic sites of Jingshuiwan, Yandunbao and Ranjialukou in nearby Gaojia, the most spectacular of which is Jingshuiwan, dating from the middle phase of the Palaeolithic (around 100,000 years ago) where stone tools including cores, flakes and scrapers were found as well as animal fossils. This is the earliest and only site in the Three Gorges area where tools have been found.

This floor also showcases spectacular objects from the Ba Culture dating from the Shang, Spring and Autumn and Warring States periods (Zhou dynasty) displayed by theme. These include a large bronze bell, or *chunyu*, with a suspension loop in the form of a tiger, its long, curled tail extended and mouth open. This curious creature might have been a symbol of the ancient Ba people. (The decoration also includes

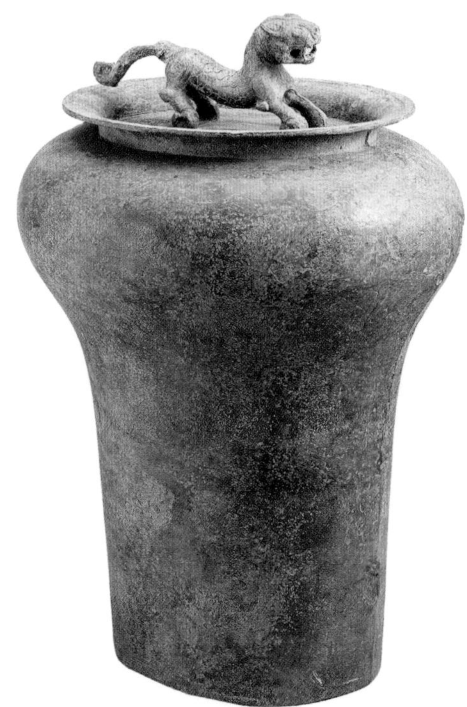

Bronze *chunyu* or bell with suspension hook in the shape of a tiger

small designs and graphics which might have been the Ba's set of characters.) Here too is a bronze *zhong*, or hand bell, also used for signalling; wonderful bronze dagger axes known as *ge*, some triangular in shape, others decorated with a deer motif or cloud designs; and spearheads with silver inlays and animal-mask designs. Notice the excellent craftsmanship of the weapons. Another superb bronze item relating to war is the rare undecorated conical bronze helmet. Many of these were unearthed at Xiaotianxi Village in Fuling, built on a mound near the Wujiang River. Numerous tombs of what are believed by some to be former Ba kings who stayed on the land after the Ba kingdom was conquered by the Qin state, have been excavated since its discovery in 1972 and likely to date from the middle and late Warring States period. Other highlights include the very large Shang dynasty *zun* with its flaring undecorated mouth and sheep sitting on its shoulder, decorated with a single-horned dragon. Found at Dachang in Wushan, this is one of the oldest vessels discovered in the area. One of the small tombs at Xiaotianxi yielded yet another prized item, a bird-shaped *zun* with duck's feet and decorated with feather designs, some of which still exhibit their original turquoise inlays.

A large display of small round-bottomed pots discovered by the hundreds at the Zhongba Site near the Yangtze are displayed hanging on poles. Although this is not how they were found, this might have been how they were used, for this site, with a sequence from the late Neolithic to the Shang, was also once home to the Ba and a source of salt water. Could these pots have held brine and been left in the sun to harvest salt? Note also the long boat-shaped coffins (here 4.7m, but they were often longer) hollowed out from single logs where the Bronze Age Ba and Shu buried their dead, along with artefacts placed at both head and feet. Unique to eastern Sichuan, this type of burial had never been found elsewhere in China and survived a bit longer in Ba than in Shu.

The fourth floor galleries host a great display of Han dynasty pottery, and although there is little English signage, the objects speak for themselves, among them wonderful figurines dancing, playing a zither and drumming, all placed in the tombs of their patrons to entertain them in the afterlife. Cases display fearsome grave guardians, a bird-shaped pedestal, a pottery horse with inscriptions down its back leg and bricks with impressions illustrating the region's industries.

The final floor features a selection of works donated by Li Chuli, a native of Jiangjin in Chongqing (Li and his wife donated 600 items to the museum). Notable among them are paintings by renowned artists of the Ming and Qing periods. The porcelain galleries exhibit pieces in exceptionally well-lit cases and with English signage. Featured are ceramics from local kilns, including those from the Qiong or Qionglai site, identifiable by their opaque green glazes, and the Longquan Kiln, reknowned for its celadon jars and vases. There is also a gallery devoted to the history of Chongqing during the War against Japan.

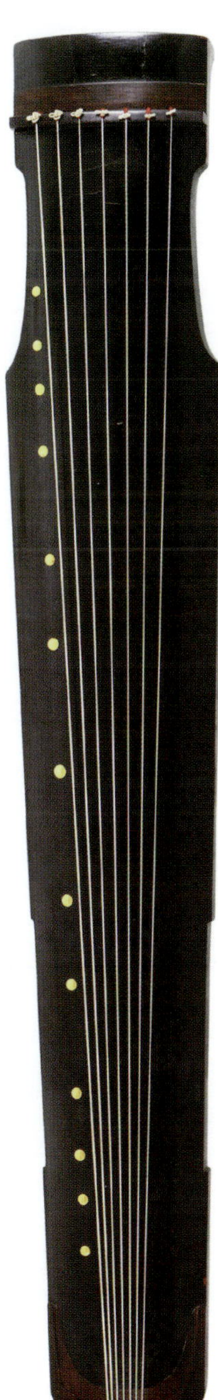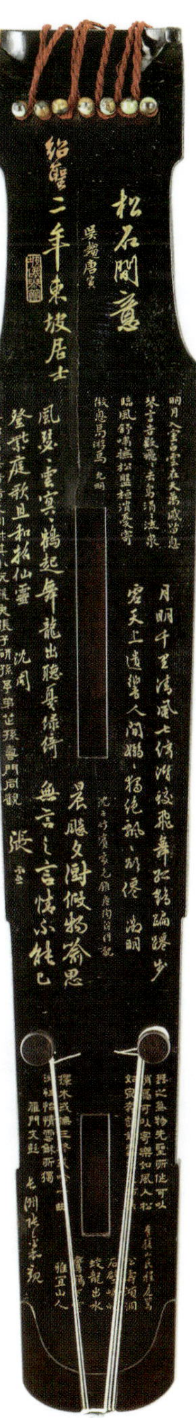

Pine and stone *guqin* (a plucked seven-strong Chinese musical instrument) with inscriptions by well-known calligraphers and artists

CHINESE MUSEUMS ASSOCIATION GUIDE

BEIJING AND THE NORTH

THE NORTHEAST

SHANGHAI AND EAST CHINA

THE YANGTZE

THE SOUTH

THE SILK ROAD AND THE NORTHWEST

TIBET

HONG KONG, MACAO, TAIWAN

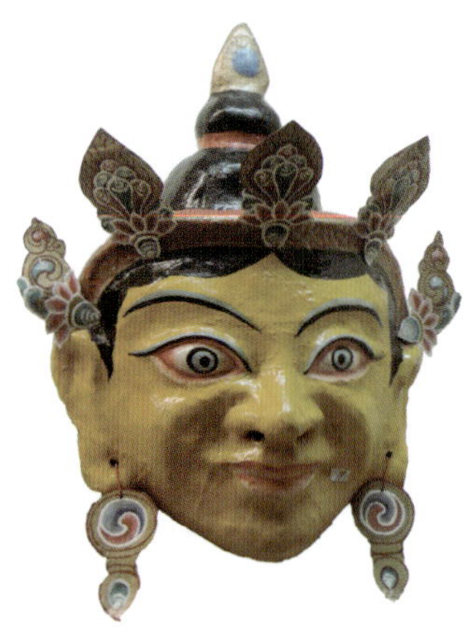

华南

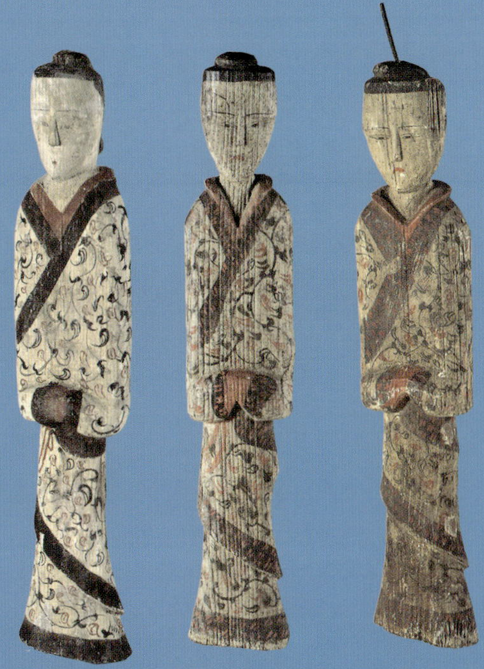

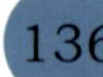

Overseas Chinese Museum

华侨博物院 *Huaqiao bowuyuan*

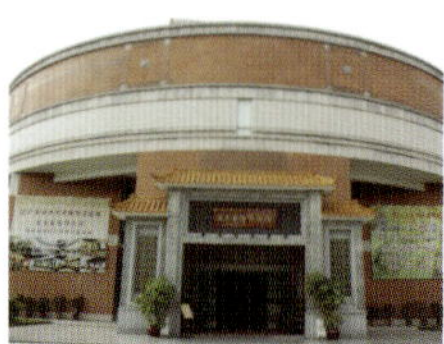

493 Siming South Road, Xiamen, Fujian
福建省厦门市思明南路493号
Tel: (0592) 208 4028
Open: 9.30–16.30 except Mon
www.hqbwy.org.cn

The Overseas Chinese Museum tells the story of the native sons of Fujian who left here in search of their fortune a century or longer ago. The museum was built with funding from Chen Jiageng, an overseas Chinese philanthropist, and it opened in 1959. The museum is organized into three sections: one explores the Chinese overseas, the second displays Chen Jiageng's private collection and the third is the Natural Science Museum.

At the heart of this museum is the Hall of Overseas Chinese, which tells the story of Chinese emigrants through photographs, art and bronze reproductions demonstrating how life was lived by the early waves of Chinese people who travelled abroad. In the main hall there are several wooden boats, models of the types that took the Chinese to Southeast Asia and other neighbouring parts of the world. There is a mock of a ship's hold, with life-like models of people sitting on the floor of the boat, complemented by paintings on the wall. Other models include a Chinese school, a tailor's shop and a printer's, as well as a gold miner and a rickshaw puller. On the second floor there are scenes of the Chinese people who helped to build the US railroad, and of rubber harvesting from rubber trees in Malaysia.

The Hall of Relics, on the third floor, displays thousands of artefacts, most of which were collected by Mr Chen, including pottery, bronze ware, sculpture and art. The Natural Science Museum, on the second floor, has displays of rare animals, plants, aquatic life and the skeleton of a large whale.

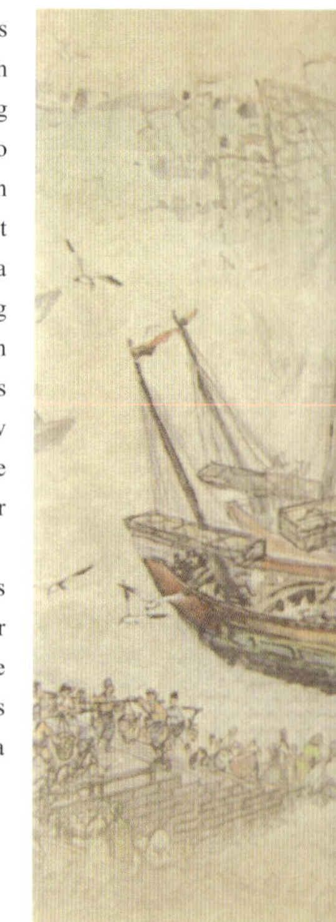

Quanzhou Maritime Museum

泉州海外交通史博物馆 *Quanzhou haiwaijiaotongshi bowuguan*

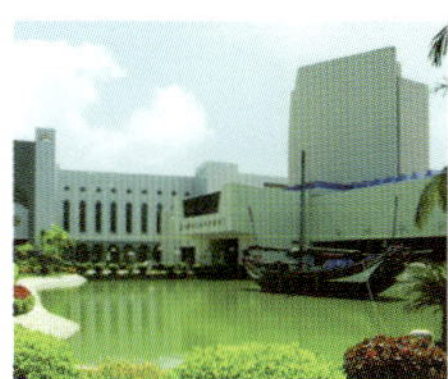

425 Donghu Street, Fengze District, Quanzhou, Fujian
福建省泉州市丰泽区东湖街425号
Tel: (0595) 2210 0561
Open: 8:30–17:00
www.qzhjg.com
Gift shop / bookshop

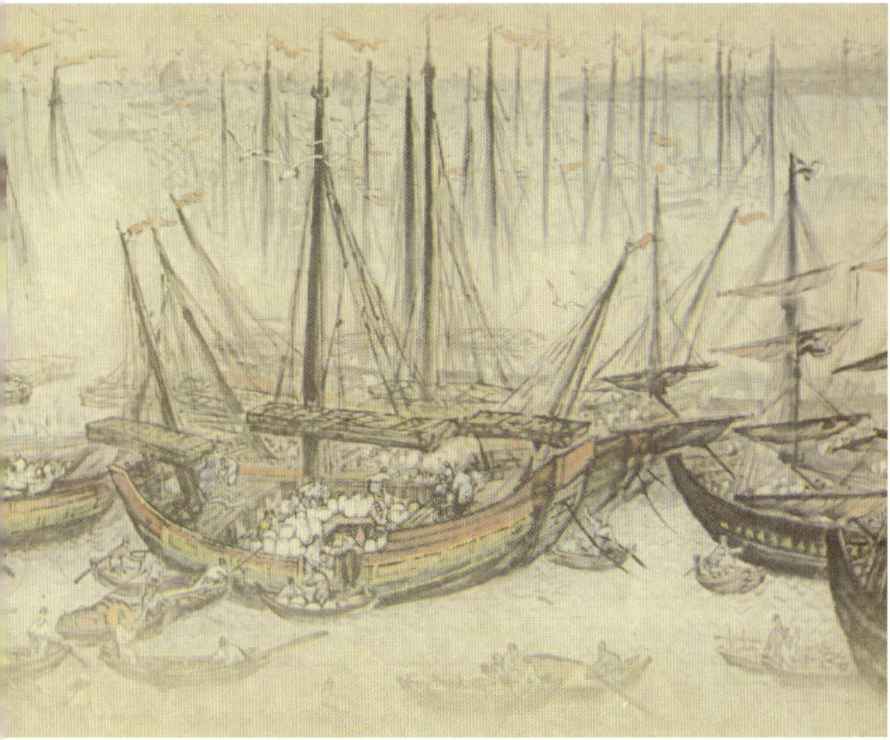

Quanzhou, a coastal city in Fujian province, became an international trading port in the 12th to the 15th centuries, and during the Song and Yuan dynasties was one of the world's largest seaports with a sizeable foreign community, mainly Arabs, but also Persians, Indians and other nationalities. Quanzhou was the main port from which satin was traded and was known as Zayton, derived from the Arabic name for the silk exported from there. Marco Polo is said to have sailed home from Quanzhou and in his book *The Travels of Marco Polo*, he described it as the busiest port in the world – 'the Alexandria of the East.'

Established in 1959, Quanzhou Maritime Museum was originally located at the east side of Quanzhou Kaiyuan Temple with a special space showcasing boats found locally. However, in 1991 the current museum opened on the scenic East Lake. With over seven permanent thematic exhibition halls, including those entitled Quanzhou Religious Stone Inscriptions and Arabic-Persians in Quanzhou, this museum introduces the maritime history of Quanzhou through its rich collection of artefacts related to trade, shipping, boats and religion, including Catholic, Islamic and Nestorian tombstones as well as Hindu and Manichean pieces.

When you enter the museum you'll see an exhibit of several boat models. A nearby room features a map showing various sea trading routes, including the Marine Silk Road, which started from the port of Quanzhou, more model boats, earthenware, tomb bricks, sails made of bamboo and a bust of Marco Polo. Exhibits here focus on the Quanzhou Harbor in the Tang dynasty, the rapid rise of the city, a picture of the Grand Ashab Mosque, which was built in 1009 (although most of what is seen at the mosque today in Quanzhou dates from 1310), local pottery, Japanese piracy in the Ming dynasty, and the migration of the Chinese to other countries.

In a second room, there is a display of different knots on the wall and models of boats that once plied the Yellow and Yangzi Rivers. Just outside the room on the left are two ropes and instructions on how to tie four different kinds of knots. Exhibitions here focus on ocean-going ships, maritime activities, explanations of different parts of boats, navigation tools and maps using the location of stars, the sun and the moon to determine position, a model on boat building, warships through the ages, and a reproduction of a battle fought by Zheng Chenggong, better known in the West as Koxinga, the Ming dynasty loyalist who forced the Dutch out of Taiwan.

A highlight of the collections is the remains of a Song dynasty sailing junk discovered near Quanzhou in 1973 while a canal was dredged. Among the cargo excavated from the hull were copper and iron coins, thousands of cowrie shells and incense wood, indicating trade along the silk route and with China's neighbours. Significant too, is the hall featuring a large display of the tombstones and grave monuments mostly collected by Wu Wenliang, a local teacher who spent years searching the city and amassing them. A large number of them are Islamic, though Christian, Hindu, Buddhist and Daoist among others are also in evidence, reflecting the diverse religious communities that resided in the city.

While in Quanzhou you might like to also visit the Kaiyuan Temple, first built in the Tang Dynasty, as it is one of Fujian's most important. By 1285 it covered thousands of acres and had 3,000 monks in residence, a vast library of Buddhist scriptures and the tallest twin stone pagodas in China.

Guangdong Marine Silk Road Museum

广东海上丝绸之路博物馆 *Guangdong haishang sichouzhilu bowuguan*

138

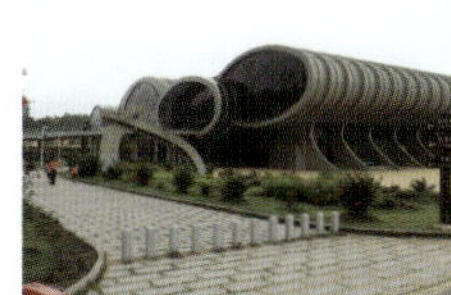

Shiliyintan Beach, Hailing Island, Yangjiang, Guangdong
广东省阳江市海陵岛十里银滩
Open: 9.00–17.30, last entry 17.00 except Spring Festival
www.msrmuseum.com
Kids

It was not until treasure hunters started finding Chinese merchant shipwrecks in the South China Sea full to the gunnels with cargos of eighteenth-century porcelain that archaeologists realized China had set up marine trading routes 200 years before those of the Spanish, Portuguese and British. Wrecks like the Tang dynasty *Batu Hitam* provided evidence that over 1,200 years ago the Chinese began trading by sea as an alternative to the famous overland Silk Road. The Marine Silk Road took porcelain, tea and silk from the southern ports in Guangdong and Fujian for export to countries in the Middle East, India and Europe.

This enormous, purpose-built museum on the beach on Hailing Island adjacent to Yangjiang city tells the story of China's success and the wealth it accumulated while trading with the world via its marine routes in the Tang and Song dynasties. The building overlooks the ancient waterways that were once the start of the Marine Silk Road and

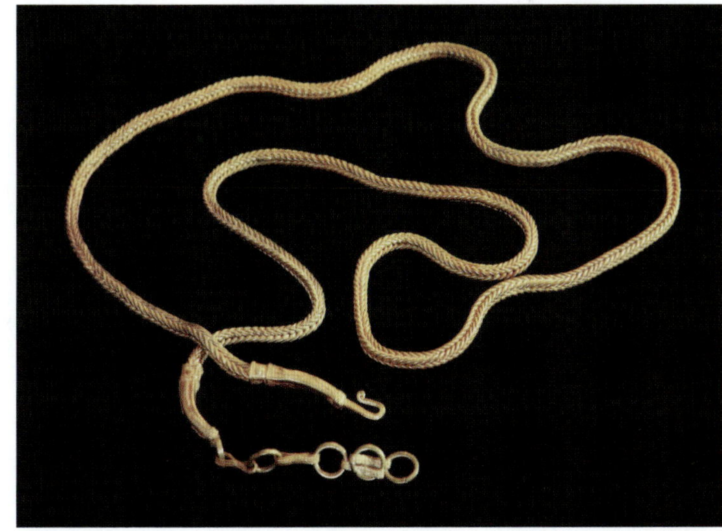

Gold chain recovered from the Nanhai No. 1 shipwreck

some of the busiest sea lanes in ancient times. Consisting of five interlinking ellipse-shaped halls, the structure bears a resemblance to a seagull in flight.

The museum's star attraction undoubtedly is the Nanhai No. 1 (South China Sea No. 1) shipwreck, which is displayed in 'Crystal Palace', the largest of the halls. Dating from the early Southern Song dynasty, it was found lying upright in silt off the coast of Guangdong. Its fine state of preservation, complete with a stunning cargo of mostly export porcelain produced at China's southern kilns, gold and silver containers and jewellery, urged archaeologists to consider raising it as a whole so it could be excavated in controlled conditions. After years of planning, a huge steel cage was engineered to raise the wreck and its tens of thousands of artefacts to the surface. It is in the museum's giant sealed salt-water aquarium, where it is stored underwater in conditions that mimic those where it lay on the seabed. Visitors have been able to watch underwater archaeologists measure, draw and photograph the vessel as it was being excavated. Thousands of objects that have been recovered can now be seen on display in the museum.

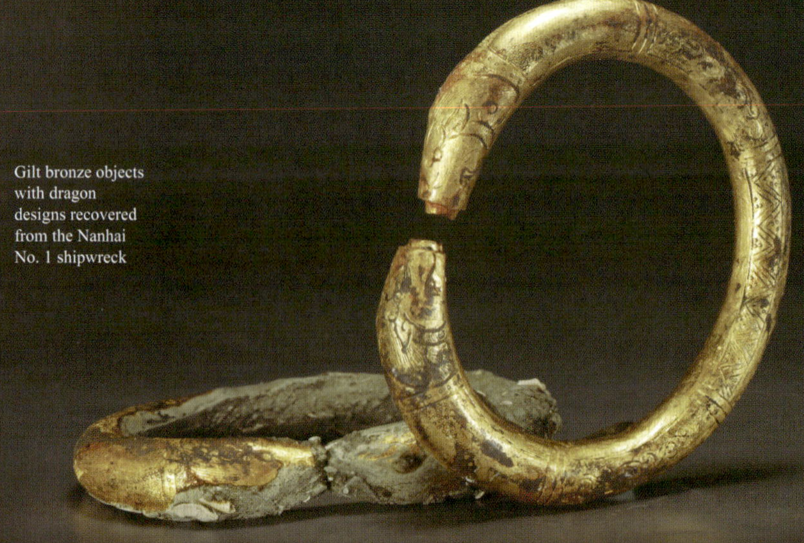

Gilt bronze objects
with dragon
designs recovered
from the Nanhai
No. 1 shipwreck

Guangzhou Museum of Art

广州艺术博物院 *Guangzhou yishu bowuyuan*

139

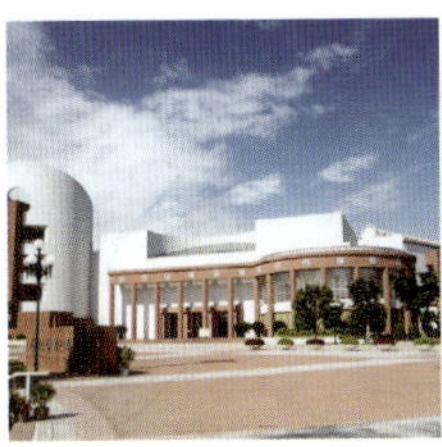

13 Luhu Road, Guangzhou, Guangdong
广东省广州市麓湖路13号
Tel: (020) 8365 9202
Open: 9.00–17.00 except Mon;
 9.30–16.30 weekends and holidays
www.gzam.com.cn
English audio guide / multimedia information screens / bookshop

The Guangzhou Museum of Art is one of the biggest and best art museums in southern China, known for its diverse range of ancient and contemporary pieces created by artists from the region. The collection includes paintings, calligraphy, woodblock prints, watercolours, gouache, powder paintings, cartoons, sculpture, *thangkas*, Tibetan religious tapestry and ceramics.

Both permanent and special exhibitions are housed over the three floors of this sprawling museum. Particularly good is a special collection of Liao Bingxiong's political cartoons and drawings of people, such as opera performers. The Zhao Tailai Collection Hall features a varied, private antique collection, including an ivory fan with an embroidered peacock from the Qing dynasty, a pearly sphere vase from France, Tibetan religious items, bamboo and ivory carvings, jade and bronzes. Wonderful pieces of sculpture are scattered throughout the museum. You will need at least half a day to view all that's on display here.

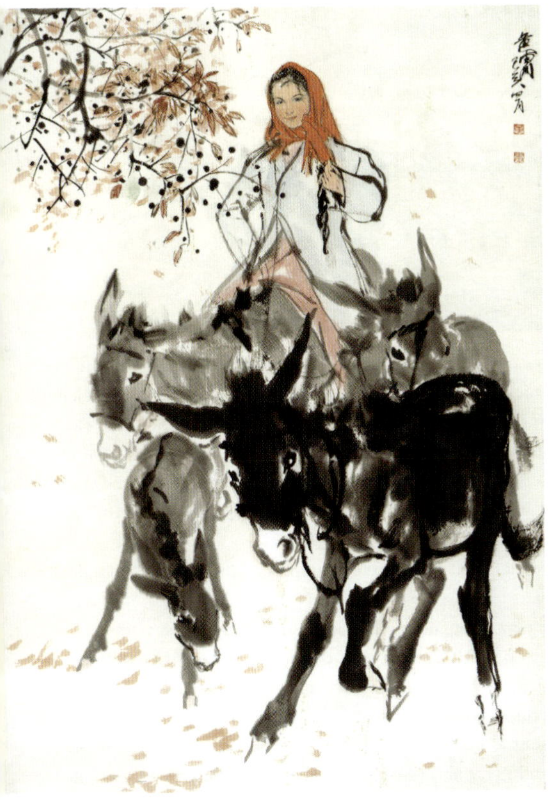

Watercolour by
Huang Zhou

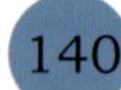

Guangdong Provincial Museum

广东省博物馆 *Guangdongsheng bowuguan*

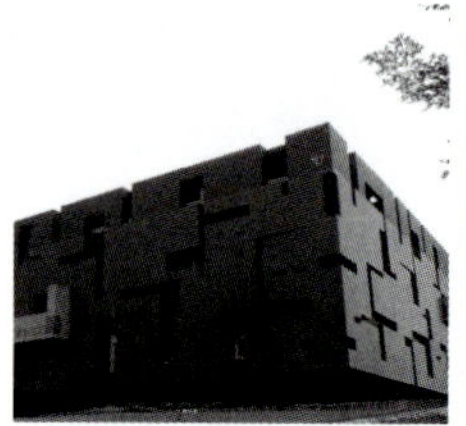

2 Zhujiang East Road, Tianhe District, Guangzhou, Guangdong
广东省广州市天河区珠江东路2号
Tel: (020) 3804 6886
Open: 9.00–17.00 except Mon
www.gdmuseum.com
English audio guide / multimedia information screens

The highlight of the museum is its wonderful collection of Chaozhou wood carvings and furniture, Chaozhou being one of the oldest and most famous schools of woodcarving in China. The elaborately carved gold window lattice and panels depicting ancient Chinese tales are especially fine.

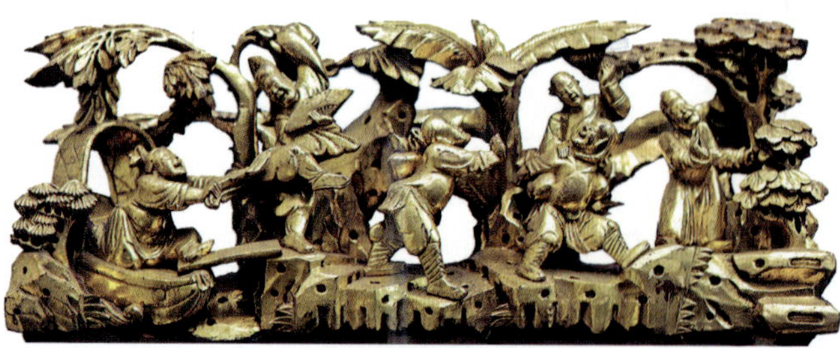

Detail of Qing carved wood

There are also displays on Guangdong history, ceramics, calligraphy, paintings and handicrafts. The ceramics collection includes pieces from many famous ancient kilns, and the calligraphy exhibition contains sutras written in the Sui and Tang dynasties, and pieces created by some of China's most famous calligraphers. On the second floor is a section dedicated to the history of Guangzhou city, from prehistoric to modern times, including ancient bronzes and clay figurines. Especially interesting is a Han dynasty clay reproduction of a banquet scene.

There is also a Nature Hall that has simple examples of the natural ecological environment of Guangdong.

On May 18, 2010, the new Guangdong Museum started to welcome visitors. The new building covers an area of 41,027 sq m with construction area of 66,980 sq m and display area of 21,000 sq m. It looks like a delicate ancient openwork container of treasures. Permanent exhibitions in terms of 'Guangdong History and Culture', 'Guangdong Natural Resource and Arts' (such as the Duan inkstone, Chaozhou Woodcarving and Pottery and Porcelain) as well as temporary exhibitions are exhibited in it.

Guangzhou City Museum

广州博物馆 *Guangzhou bowuguan*

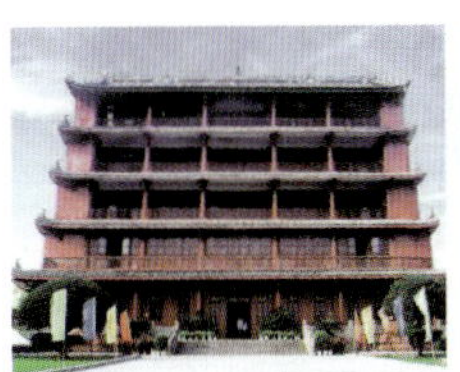

Zhenhai Tower, inside Yuexiu Park, Guangzhou, Guangdong
广东省广州市越秀公园内镇海楼
Tel: (020) 8365 0627
Open: 9.00–17.30, last entry 17.00 (Gallery closed on Mon)
www.guangzhoumuseum.cn
English audio guide / multimedia information screens

The Guangzhou Museum is located in the historic Zhenhai Tower (or Tower Controlling the Sea), which was first built here on a hill in Yuexiu Park in 1380 by Zhu Liangzu, a general of the Ming dynasty, and was rebuilt a total of five times after that.

The museum focuses on the history of the Guangzhou area, with 1,000 exhibits covering 2,000 years of history spread out over its five floors. On the first floor there is simply a large map of the city and an old anchor dating back to the Ming dynasty. The second floor displays items from the Han dynasty, including two statues of Persian men – ancient visitors to the region. The third and fourth floors focus on the city's role as a trading centre in the nineteenth century and the Western influence on Guangzhou. The fifth floor has a gift shop and a balcony with excellent views of the city.

Just outside the museum is a collection of steles, several old cannons from the Opium War and a large wooden tomb.

Guangdong Museum of Art

广东美术馆 *Guangdong meishuguan*

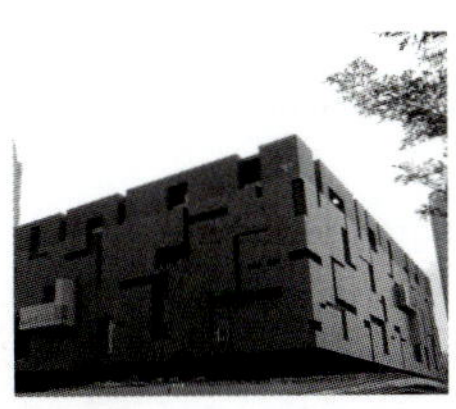

38 Yanyu Road, Ersha Island, Guangzhou, Guangdong
广东省广州市二沙岛烟雨路38号
Tel: (020) 8735 1468
Open: 9.00–17.00 except Mon
www.gdmoa.org
English audio guide / multimedia information screens

This contemporary art museum, located on Ersha Island in the centre of the Pearl River, has twelve exhibition halls featuring both permanent and temporary exhibitions, and an outdoor sculpture garden. Each year, the museum hosts a large exhibition of its permanent collection of sculpture, painting and ceramics, which includes contemporary artistic works of the coastal areas of China and Guangdong Province, as well as work by overseas Chinese artists. The museum also hosts exhibitions of artwork from various countries around the world.

The Museum of the Mausoleum of the Nanyue King of the Western Han Dynasty

143

西汉南越王博物馆 *Xihan nanyuewang bowuguan*

867 Jiefang North Road, Guangzhou, Guangdong
广东省广州市解放北路867号
Tel: (020) 3618 2920
Open: 9.00–17.30 except Feb 28 & Aug 31
www.gznywmuseum.org
English audio guide / multimedia information screens

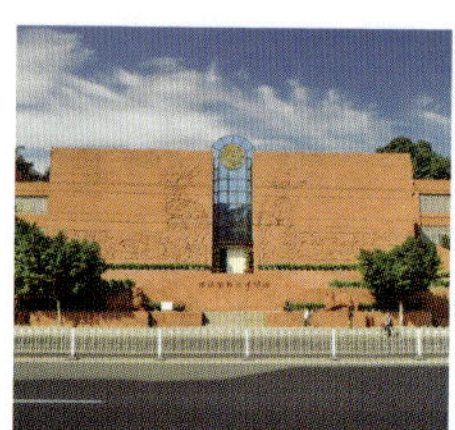

Jade ornament with dragon and phoenix pattern found on the King's right eye

This museum is located in a modern building situated against Xianggang Hill, which was the original site of the tomb of the second Nanyue King (the Nanyue kingdom was established in 203 BC). Enter the museum building and proceed to the third floor, where you exit outside to the site of the tomb, which has seven underground chambers guarded by heavy stone slab doors. The tomb, which was discovered by accident in 1983, had fortunately never been plundered and so was intact when opened, making it one of the largest and best protected tombs of its kind found in southern China. In the middle of the burial room once stood the inner and outer coffins, which have disintegrated. The vestiges of the king's corpse remained when found, the body dressed in a jade shroud made of 2,291 pieces of jade sewn with silk thread. At the time of the death of the king, it was believed that jade could prevent the body from decaying. At the time of excavation, the body had disintegrated and the jade pieces of the shroud lay scattered around the burial chamber. It took archaeologists three years to restore the shroud. The king's body had ten iron swords at his waist, and his head rested on a pearl-embroidered pillow.

The collection contains over 10,000 relics, including the gold seal of Emperor Wen, one of the earliest imperial seals ever discovered. The seal, which has a dragon-shaped handle, is evidence that the inhabitant of the tomb is the second Nanyue King, Zhao Mo. Fifteen sacrificial victims were also found buried in the tomb with the late Emperor. In the Western Chamber seven more sacrificial victims were found buried without coffins; these included cooks and servants. Four concubines were buried in the Eastern Chamber. Each of them was buried with a seal identifying

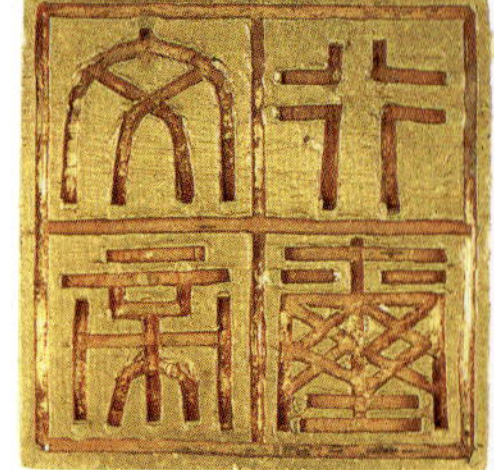

Gold seal with ornamental dragon knob, Western Han dynasty

who they were. In the Rear Storeroom, 155 large cooking vessels were found, along with food for the deceased royal family, including remains of fruit, fish-bones, rice, birds, domestic animals and shells. Seals found here bear the inscription 'Officer Tai', who was the director in charge of the kitchen. It's believed that Officer Tai, one of the sacrificial victims found in the Western Chamber, placed these items here before the burial.

After visiting the tomb, proceed to the exhibition halls where many of the excavated items are on display. In the first exhibition room is a reproduction of the jade shroud that covered the body of the king, as well as his dragon seal and many other pieces of jade unearthed from the tomb.

The museum also houses a collection of over 400 ceramic pillows, 200 of which were donated by Mr. and Mrs. Yueng Wing Tak, prominent Hong Kong collectors. The pillows date from the Tang dynasty to modern times, but the majority are from the Song and Jin dynasties. As they were produced by different provincial kilns at different times, their shapes and motifs reflect the designs that were favoured when they were made.

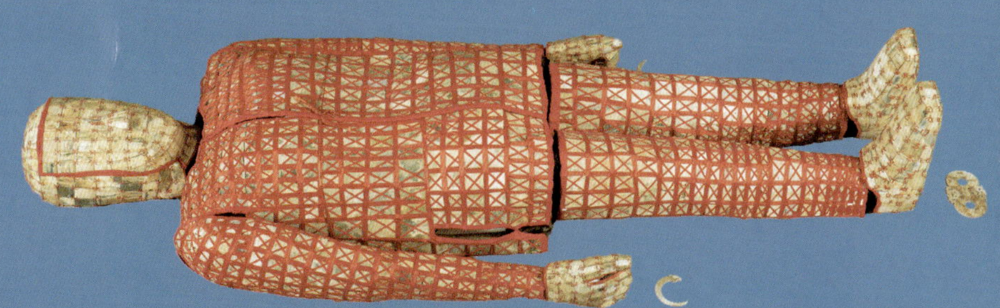

Jade shroud fastened with silk threads

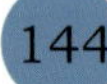

The Museum of Dr. Sun Yat-Sen

孙中山故居纪念馆 *Sun Zhongshan guju jinianguan*

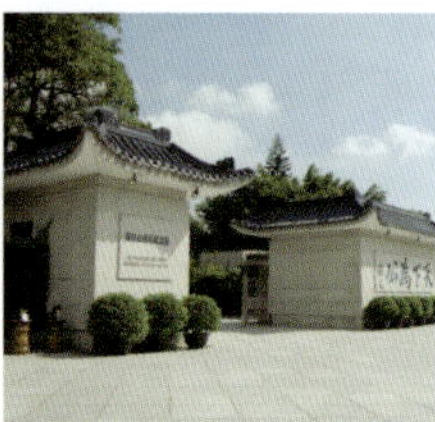

Cuiheng Village, Zhongshan, Guangdong
广东省中山市翠亨村
Tel: (0760) 2815 8366
Open: 9.00–17.00, last entry 16.30
www.sunyat-sen.org
Gift shop / bookshop

Dr. Sun Yat-sen, Chinese revolutionary and first President of the Republic of China was born in Cuiheng Village in 1866. Cuiheng, located in Guangdong close to Zhuhai and Macao, remains a peaceful rural setting protected from the tide of industrialization that has swept across the Pearl River Delta since China's reforms and opening up. The museum was established in 1956 next to the house where Dr. Sun lived as a child.

Of interest to tourists and researchers alike, the museum's Sun Yat-sen library houses historical objects, archives, books and other traditional literature and modern electronic data (about 15,000 gigabytes at present) to form the Sun Yat-sen Research and Information Centre. The Museum's Sun Yat-sen Research Institute engages in the study of Dr. Sun's historical role and his political theories.

In addition, the Museum has set up the Zhongshan Folklore Museum to carry out research on the folk culture of Cuiheng Village as well as of the Pearl River Delta. The collection includes artefacts illustrating everyday life and folk customs of that region.

Cuiheng is accessible as a day trip from Guangzhou or from Hong Kong (by boat) and makes a pleasant change of pace from the big cities.

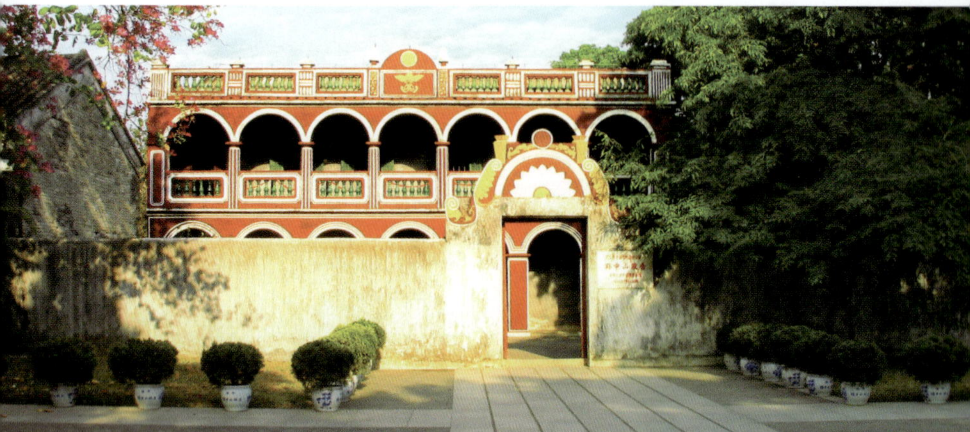

Opium War Museum

145

鸦片战争博物馆 *Yapian zhanzheng bowuguan*

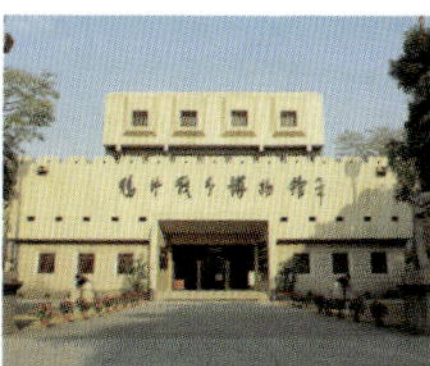

88 Jiefang Road, Humen Town, Dongguan, Guangdong
广东省东莞市虎门镇解放路88号
Tel: (0769) 8551 2065
Open: 8.30–17.00

Lin Zexu was an imperial commissioner in the Qing court. In 1838, he was sent to Guangdong to deal with the illegal importation of opium from India into China by

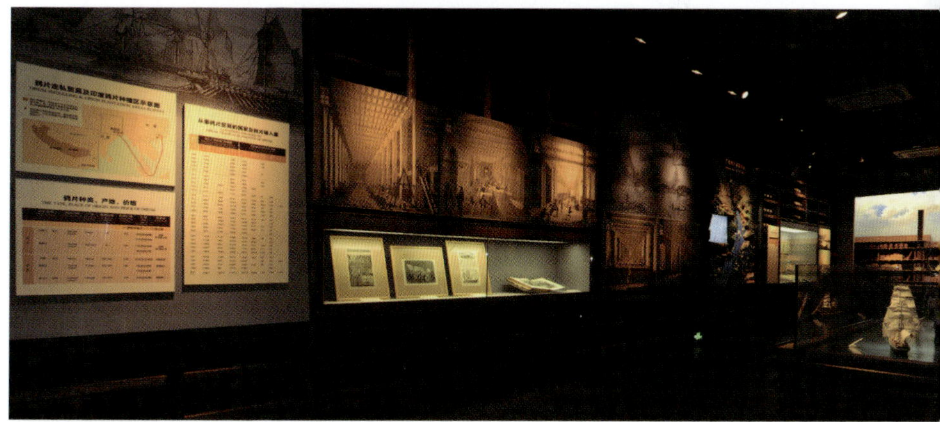

the British. Not only was opium addiction sapping the energy of the population, it was also undermining the economy, as silver was sucked out to pay for the growing trade. He ultimately rid Guangzhou of over one million kilos of opium, which he had burnt in pits in Humen. Lin is well known for writing a letter to Queen Victoria in which he asks her to stop the trade in opium on moral grounds. He is now regarded as the quintessential 'patriotic' official. In fact, his destruction of the opium actually drove the price of it up, thus benefiting the British. It also provided the excuse to the British for starting the First Opium War.

On display are cannons, cannonballs and other weapons of the Chinese, British and Americans. These are complemented by documents, photos and illustrations. Some displays are interactive but in Chinese only.

Besides the museum building, it is possible to visit the pits in which Lin burnt the opium and several old batteries along the coastline constructed during the Opium Wars.

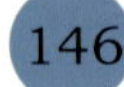

Shenzhen Museum

深圳博物馆 *Shenzhen bowuguan*

Historical and Folk Culture Gallery:	Ancient Arts Gallery:
Zone A, Citizen's Centre, Fuzhong Road,	6 Tongxin Road, Futian District,
Futian District, Shenzhen, Guangdong	Shenzhen, Guangdong
广东省深圳市福田区福中路市民中心	广东省深圳市福田区同心路6号
A区	Open: 9.30–17.30
Open: 10.00–18.00	

Tel: (0755)8210 5482　　www.shenzhenmuseum.com.cn　　*Gift shop / tea bar / restaur*

Shenzhen is the major city of China's special economic zone located in Guangdong Province near Hong Kong. The museum's collection includes objects which illustrate the breadth of China's past as well as that of the city's extraordinary contemporary urban development. The museum is split between two separate sites: the original building is located near the Mix City Shopping Mall and the new building in the eastern part of the Citizen's Centre.

The old Shenzhen Museum, known as the Shenzhen Museum of Art and Natural History has a collection of 20,000 antiquities including jade, porcelain and bronze artefacts. Painting and calligraphy as well as textiles are also exhibited.

Particular treasures include a Song dynasty green-glazed pot from the Yaozhou Kiln and calligraphy by the well-known late Qing dynasty politician, Li Hung Chang.

The new Shenzhen Museum concentrates on the history, folk culture and

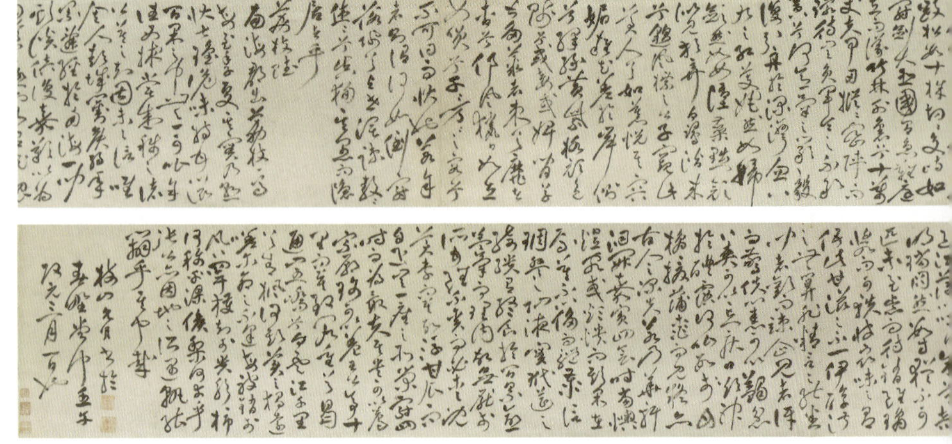

contemporary life of Shenzhen. The city's history is told chronologically using period rooms and wax figures. These tableaux portray Shenzhen's political development and reforms as well as scenes from the working life of a typical Chinese family, the life of border guards between Shenzhen and Hong Kong and other aspects of daily life.

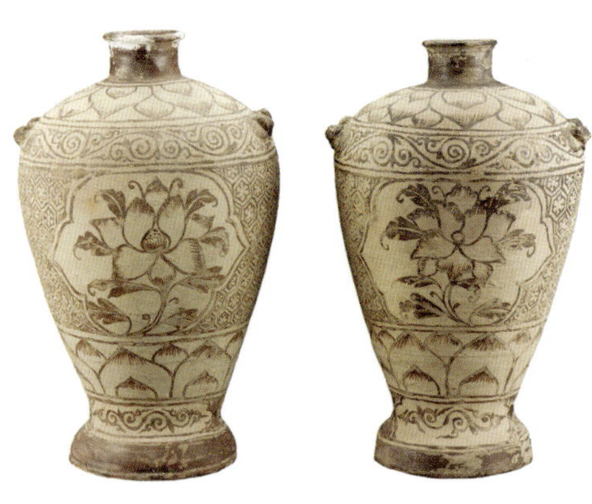

A pair of Yuan Dynasty iron rust vases

Archaeological material, including biological fossils, from sites in the area are displayed. The most significant objects in the museum are a pair of Yuan Dynasty iron rust vases found in the Nanshan district of Shenzhen. Each vase, a masterpiece of Canton pottery, is elegant in shape and painted with plum blossoms, lotus petals and curly grass. The plum blossom pattern symbolises courage and hope, as it withstands the inclement and cold weather of winter. Its five petals symbolise the 'five blessings'. These blessings refer to longevity, wealth, health, composure, and virtue.

A splendid calligraphic works by Zhu Yunming

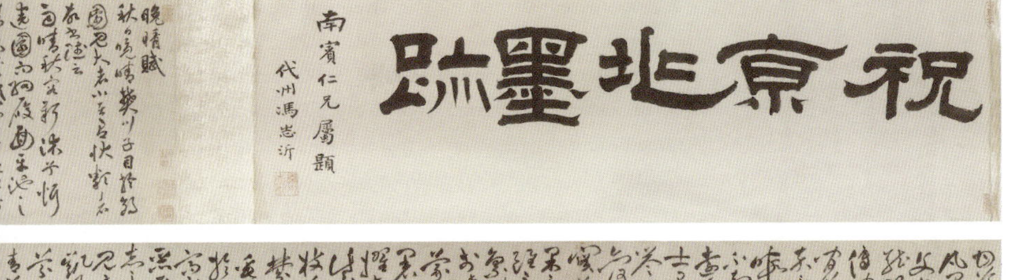

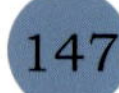

147

Hunan Provincial Museum

湖南省博物馆 *Hunansheng bowuguan*

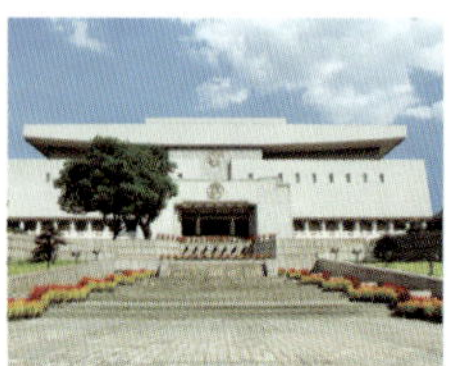

50 Dongfeng Road, Changsha, Hunan
湖南省长沙市东风路50号
Tel: (0731) 8451 4630
www.hnmuseum.com/hnmuseum/eng
Scheduled to open in 2015

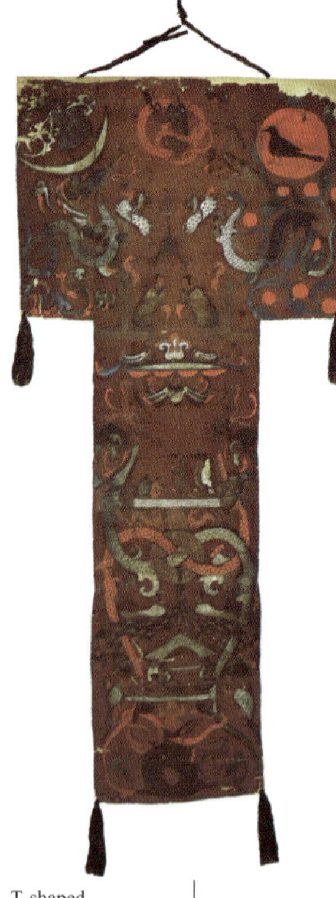

T-shaped
painting on
silk banner
carried in
funeral
procession,
from
Tomb No. 1
Mawangdui

The Hunan Provincial Museum first opened in Changsha, the capital of Hunan Province, in 1956. The discovery and excavation of the Mawangdui Han Tombs (the tomb of Marquise Dai's family in the Western Han dynasty) in 1972–74 was of major significance for the Provincial Museum, adding to its collection thousands of precious relics and the well-preserved corpse of a female member of the Dai family. In order to display the enlarged and valuable collection properly, a new exhibition hall was opened in 1973. Then, around 2000, a state-of-the-art exhibition centre was added, with excellent displays and brief descriptions in English. A new reconstruction and expansion project had been done since 2012, and the new Hunan Provincial Museum is scheduled to be completed in 2015.

The collections of the Mawangdui Han Tombs – including more than 3,000 cultural relics taken from three tombs – is the major attraction here, representing, as it does, one of the most significant archaeological discoveries in twentieth-century China. The most important piece is the well-preserved corpse of a female member of the family of Marquise Dai. Around 2,000 years old, it rests in a glass coffin and can be viewed from overhead. The cultural relics include three beautiful gauze gowns that the museum describes as 'thin as a cicada's wing', and a selection of silk robes. There are also wonderful wooden figurines of singers, dancers and musicians, some colourfully painted or wearing silk clothing. In addition, there is well-preserved lacquer ware, silk embroidery, socks and shoes, as well as paintings on silk and brightly painted inner coffins.

The collections of Shang and Zhou Bronzes include the earliest bronzes found in Hunan, some dating back around 3,500 years. The museum's fine collection of ceramics (from famous kilns in Hunan) are among the earliest ever found in China. In addition, there are calligraphy and paintings from the Ming and Qing dynasties.

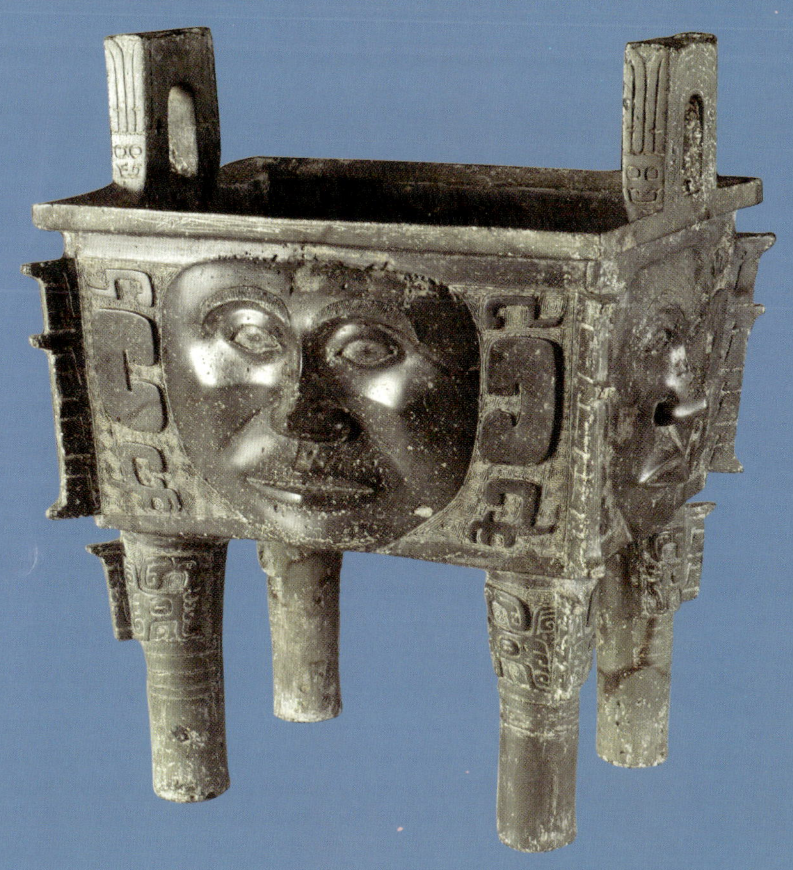

Bronze *ding* with human face design,
Shang dynasty

148

Shaoshan Mao Zedong Memorial Museum

韶山毛泽东同志纪念馆 *Shaoshan Mao Zedong tongzhi jinianguan*

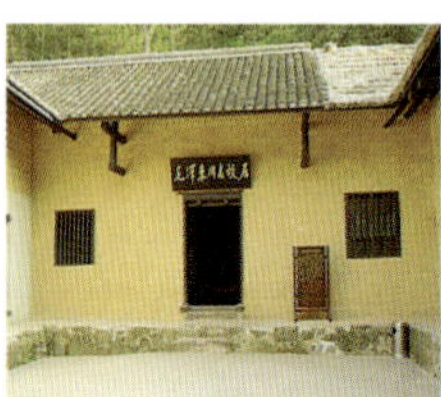

Shangwuchang, Tudichong, Shaoshan, Hunan
湖南省韶山市韶山乡土地冲上屋场
Tel: (0732) 5568 5157
Open: 9.00–17.00 except Mon
www.ssmzd.com
Gift shop at museum / English and Japanese guides available at house / refreshments

Tray dating back to the Cultural Revolution celebrating Mao's birthplace at Shaoshan

Shaoshan, located in the countryside approximately 100 km southwest of Changsha, was the birthplace of Mao Zedong and, while it may no longer be the pilgrimage site that it once was, it continues to attract a few million visitors per year. The 'Great Helmsman' was born here on 26 December 1893 to a relatively wealthy peasant family. The thirteen-room farmhouse is spacious and sparsely furnished with purportedly original furniture, and there are a few photographs of Mao as a young man, as well as his parents and his brother. Here, there is not the sense of voyeurism that permeates Xikou, Chiang Kai-shek's hometown, but rather a thoughtful solemnity, as if we might somehow wrap our minds – Chinese and Western alike – around the contradictory elements of Mao's legacy. It is clear that Mao did not like returning to his home, only visiting a handful of times during the decades after his rise to power, yet his political understandings and core beliefs were indelibly shaped by this humble rustic setting.

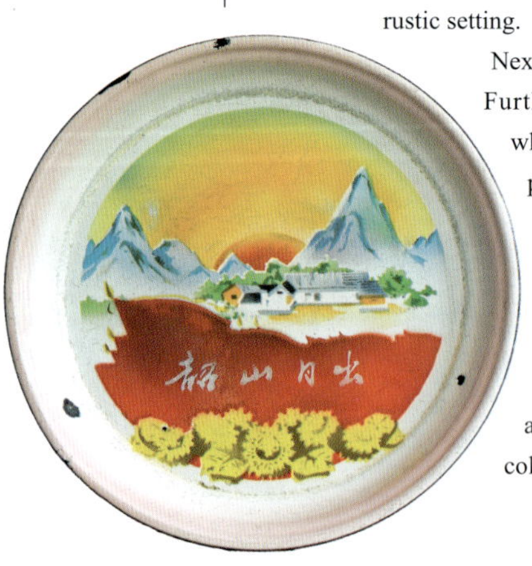

Next door to the house is the primary school that Mao attended. Further down the road is Comrade Mao's Memorial Hall, which was empty on the day of the author's visit. Despite the photographs, examples of his calligraphy and some books he read, the exhibits do not really illuminate this man who was to dominate Chinese politics for so many decades. Passing by Mao's shaving kit, bathrobe and slippers, and an enormous pair of swimming trunks, one cannot help but be struck by the contrast between these ordinary items and the god-like marble statue posed in front of a rainbow-coloured China in the grand foyer.

Jingdezhen Folk Kiln Museum (Hutian Kiln Site)

149

景德镇民窑博物馆（湖田窑址）*Jingdezhen minyao bowuguan (Hutian yaozhi)*

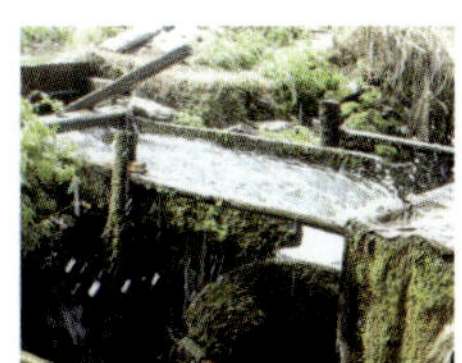

18, Hangkong Avenue, Jingdezhen, Jiangxi
江西省景德镇市航空大道18号
Tel: (0798) 8463 336
Open: 8.30–16.30 except Mon

The Hutian Kiln produced pottery here for over 700 years, from 907 to 1644. It was not an imperial kiln but it did produce porcelain for the court, most notably the thin-walled *qingbai* wares of the Northern Song.

The site includes a small museum with a few objects and limited English signage. The collection includes some very early celadon pieces from the Five Dynasties period, and Northern Song wares such as bowls, pillows, cups and jars. Note the especially elegant and simple pale celadon carved and impressed *qingbai* glazed ewer. There is also a lovely *qingbai* Guanyin fragment in the position known as 'Royal Ease', often seen during the Song dynasty. Yuan dynasty porcelain and examples of Ming dynasty blue and white porcelain are also on display.

The kiln excavations are on view and the excavated levels are marked as Song, Yuan and Ming.

porcelain Chinese
chess pieces,
Song dynasty

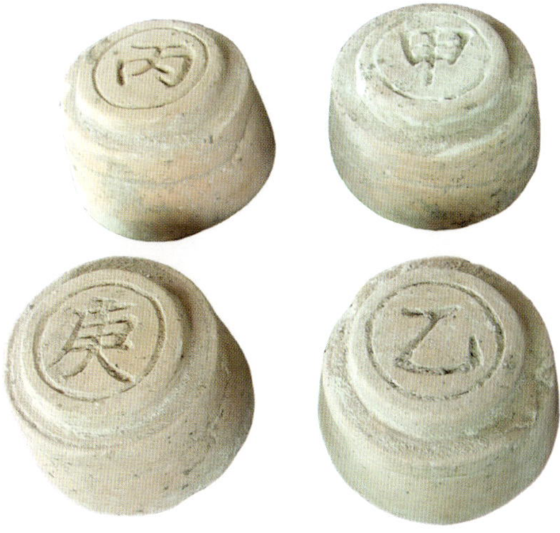

Jingdezhen Porcelain

The environmental conditions in the area surrounding Jingdezhen make it ideal for the development of its ceramic culture which has been synonymous with high-quality porcelain production and innovation for over 1,000 years.

The region is rich in porcelain stone and kaolin clay – the two ingredients essential to create the delicate and translucent final product. The surrounding mountains and forests provide plentiful wood to feed the kilns. In earlier times, the Changjiang River and its tributaries allowed for convenient transportation of both raw materials and finished products. Before the Song dynasty, the town was known as Changnan (south of the Chang), referring to its position on the river. Some believe that the English word 'china' is, in fact, a garbled pronunciation of Changnan. During the Jingde Reign of the Song dynasty, the name of the town was changed to Jingdezhen and from this time through the Yuan, Ming and Qing dynasties, Jingdezhen became the centre of imperial porcelain production. During the Yuan, the famous 'blue and white' porcelain appeared, using cobalt sourced from western Asia as trade increased with Mongol rule.

As orders for imperial porcelain increased, production was expanded beyond the official imperial kilns and outsourced to family workshops and kilns in the area. A governmental agency – the Porcelain Office – was set up to ensure quality control at kilns. The porcelain business became global: by the seventeenth century, more than 10,000 craftsmen were working in Jingdezhen, creating elaborate porcelains using sophisticated techniques and exporting them beyond the domestic market to Southeast Asia, Europe and the New World. A highly efficient system of mass production was developed, in which each step of the process was handled by a separate individual. It has been reported that as many as seventy people could be involved in the creation of a single item.

Today, the art and craft of porcelain production still oozes from the pores of the city. 'Biscuit carriers' haul unfinished wares in carts or on pallets to kilns or decoration houses. Porcelain shops line the road and stacks of colourfully glazed pots in every conceivable shape fill the street markets. Trucks and scooters are piled high with pots wrapped traditionally in rice straw packing. Even the lampposts are porcelain. Wander through the narrow hilly streets and you will find small family workshops, some many generations old, still creating porcelain ware according to traditions begun centuries ago.

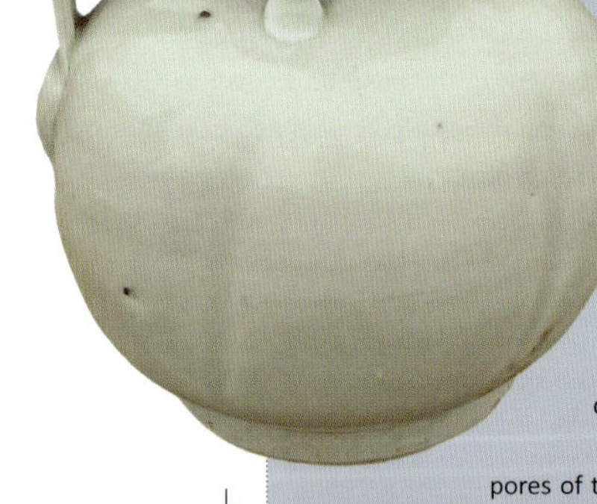

Qingbai-glazed *hu*,
Song dynasty

Jingdezhen Imperial Porcelain Museum

150

景德镇御窑博物馆 *Jingdezhen yuyao bowuguan*

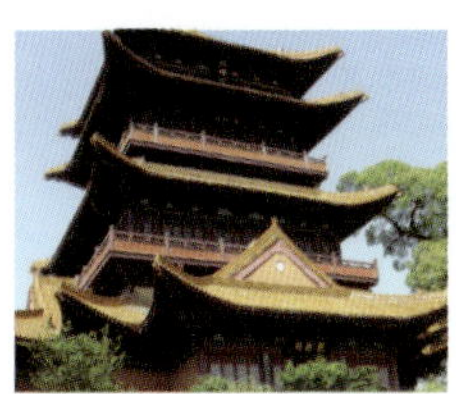

187 Zhushanzhong Road, Jingdezhen, Jiangxi
江西省景德镇市珠山中路187号
Tel: (0798) 8221 390
Open: 8.00–17.00 except Mon

This re-creation of the original Tang dynasty pagoda that once stood on this spot was built in the late 1980s and opened in 1990.

The objects in the museum date primarily from the Ming dynasty and were all excavated in the centre of Jingdezhen. These ceramics, usually found smashed and buried, were rejects due to misfiring or poor colour, failed experiments or over-supply. In large part, the pottery excavated in Jingdezhen had been thrown out (had the objects been perfect, they would have been shipped out for imperial use). Some of the shards carry reign seals and, interestingly, some of these depict a previous reign, i.e. they are fake old.

The collection holds shards and conserved objects from many periods. There is a blue and white ritual *jue* and dish decorated with dragons and clouds from the Yongle period, which is of special interest because in earlier times, bronze was generally used for ritual vessels, but at this time ceramics begin to be used for imperial rituals.

The crane-neck bottle from the Chenghua Reign (1447–87) is also of note. Made for the Korean ambassador as a gift, the vessel was created in a traditional Korean shape as a gesture.

The top floor holds objects that have recently been excavated, including many examples of red glazes. Some of these shards are from rejected vessels intended for ritual use in the Temple of Heaven in Beijing.

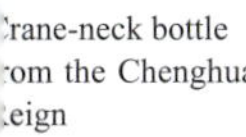

Crane-neck bottle from the Chenghua Reign

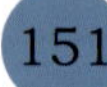

Jingdezhen Porcelain Museum

景德镇陶瓷馆 *Jingdezhen taociguan*

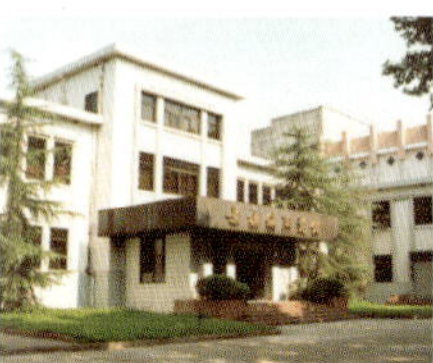

169 Lianshe North Road, Jingdezhen, Jiangxi
江西省景德镇市莲社北路169号
Tel: (0798) 822 9784
Open: 8.30–17.00
Shop selling reproduction Jingdezhen wares and books on all aspects of ceramics

The Jingdezhen Porcelain Museum first opened in 1954. There are about 20,000 objects in its inventory and, of these, about 2,000 have come from the collection of the Palace Museum in Beijing. As Jingdezhen was the centre of imperial porcelain production during the Song dynasty, most of the objects produced here were sent out of the city. Therefore, the finest examples of Jingdezhen porcelain cannot be seen in the place of its manufacture.

The oldest pieces from the collection are displayed on the ground floor and date from the first century BC. A Song dynasty bisque porcelain jar with a square lid is an important piece as it is unglazed, which is unusual for this period. In the same room is a Yuan dynasty blue and white jar decorated in a flower and plant pattern – the earliest example of cobalt blue with pale celadon in the museum. Most experts agree that blue and white ware, although most prevalent in the Ming, originated in the Yuan dynasty, with the cobalt mainly imported from Persia.

Blue and white porcelain *meiping* with fruit patterns, Yongle period

There is a Ming dynasty blue and white lidded pot from the Wanli Reign (1573–1620) decorated with a five-clawed dragon and phoenix pattern (a five-clawed dragon denotes imperial use). Also on display is a jar decorated with beautiful girls from the Chongzhen Reign (1628–44). Chongzhen was the last Ming Emperor and during this period of the collapse of the dynasty, potters were turning to popular production as they no longer had the patronage of the court.

Blue and white porcelain *zun* with phoenix patterns, Kangxi period

Upstairs, Qing dynasty ware is exhibited. The number of pieces on view is not very large but examples from most reigns are represented. Be sure to see the extraordinary Lang Kiln red ware, or ox blood, vase. This glaze, first made in the Kangxi Reign, is very unstable and tends to roll and gather at the foot of the pot. Therefore these vessels usually have a lip at the bottom to catch the glaze. They also often have tiny little spots where gaps are left in the glaze.

There is a charming blue and white plate showing a scene from the romantic play, *Xi Xiang Ji*. The image depicts a girl and her nurse craning their necks to hear the music her lover is playing on the opposite side of the wall.

During the Qianlong Reign (1736–95) in Jingdezhen, wares from many different areas were copied, such as Jun ware and Ru ware. Examples of these pots are also on display.

Finally, Republican period and post-1949 period pottery is also represented at the museum. At the end of the Opium Wars many painters came to Jingdezhen and painting became a major feature of ceramic production – a tradition that continues today.

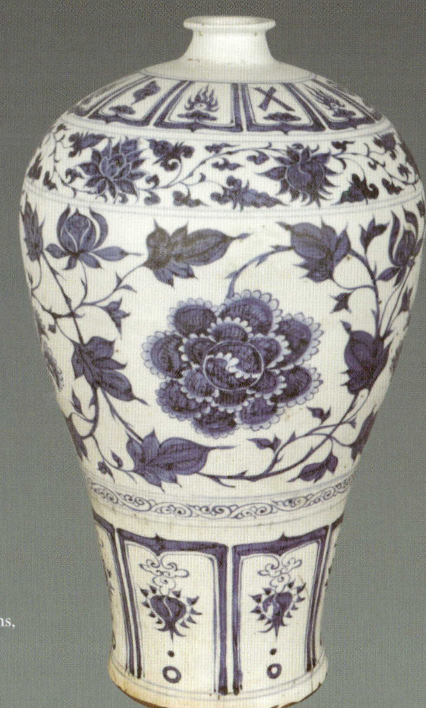

Blue and white
porcelain *meiping*
with peony patterns,
Yuan dynasty

152

Lushan Conference Site Memorial Museum

庐山会议旧址纪念馆 *Lushanhuiyi jiuzhi jinianguan*

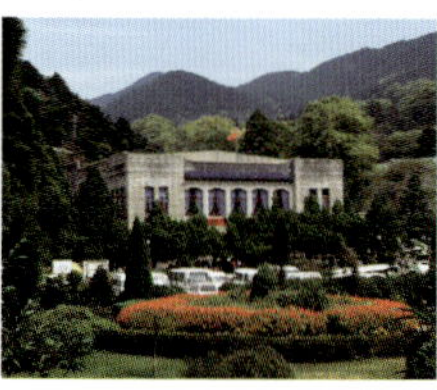

504 Hexi Road, Guling Town, Lushan, Jiujiang, Jiangxi
江西省九江市庐山牯岭镇河西路504号
Tel: (0792) 828 2584
Open: 8.15–15.15
Giftshop / bookshop

Beginning in 1957, the Great Leap Forward was promoted by Mao Zedong to acceler-
China's development as a leading industrial nation and to cement the Communist revoluti-
through collectivization and the establishment of People's Communes. This utopian drea
turned into a nightmare as the central leadership grew increasingly out of touch with reali-
By 1958, Mao revised his earlier estimate for China to overtake Britain in steel producti-
from fifteen years, insisting that it should be done in one. Peasants were mobilized to sm-
iron and steel, building backyard furnaces and neglecting crops in the fields, and within a f-
short months, widespread food shortages were already in evidence. Party officials were afr-
to report the truth, however, for fear of being labelled a rightist and 'spraying cold water on-
enthusiasm of the masses'.

The Lushan Conference took place from 2 July to 16 August and consisted of an enlarg-
meeting of the Central Committee Political Bureau. At first, the main topic of discussion w-

Jingdezhen
porcelain ashtray
used in the Lushan
Conference

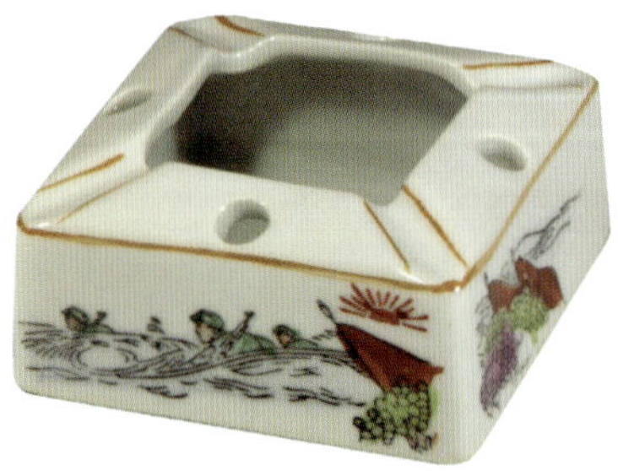

how to correct leftist errors in the Great Leap Forward. Howev-
Peng Dehuai, vice-premier and Minister of National Defen-
handed Mao a letter criticizing aspects of the Great Leap, su-
as 'the wind of boastfulness' that overestimated the agricultu-
production, the wasteful steel campaign, the lack of truth as ba-
for policy-making and the dangers of political belief clouding-
'scientific rule of economy'. Mao saw this letter as an attack-
his leadership, and Peng Dehuai, along with others who shar-
his views, were criticized, demoted and imprisoned. This was-
beginning of a rift in the communist leadership that culminated-
the Cultural Revolution. Scholars have estimated that somewh-
between 16.5 million and 40 million people died before the experiment came to an end in 19-
making the Great Leap famine the largest in world history. By 1961, Mao was forced to ad-
that the Great Leap Forward had been a failure.

Lushan Museum

153

庐山博物馆 *Lushan bowugan*

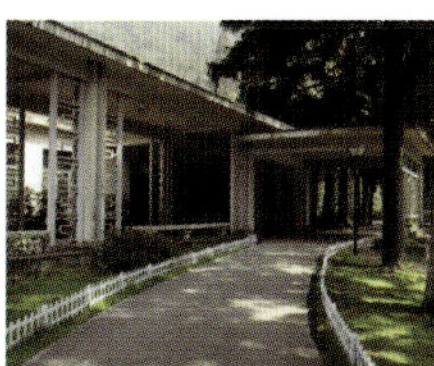

1 Lulin Road, Lushan, Jiujiang, Jiangxi
江西省九江市庐山庐林路1号
Tel: (0792) 828 1331
Open: 8.30–17.00
Gift shop

The museum is Mao Zedong's former residence here and his living quarters are preserved. There is a small collection of antiquities, numerous examples of Mao's calligraphy and a long photo gallery illustrating diplomatic and political events. Mao's living quarters include a plastic shrouded bedroom and a very large Western-style bathroom, but there is nothing more personal than the pictures of Mao shaking hands with various world leaders. There is also a small exhibit detailing features of the geological park.

Other villas scattered around the village include Villa 359, where Zhu De stayed during meetings of the Central Committee of the Communist Party of China, and Villa 286, where Deng Xiaoping and Dong Biwu stayed. Gen. Marshall stayed in Villa 442 a number of times, as did Zhou Enlai and Deng Yingchao during Party meetings.

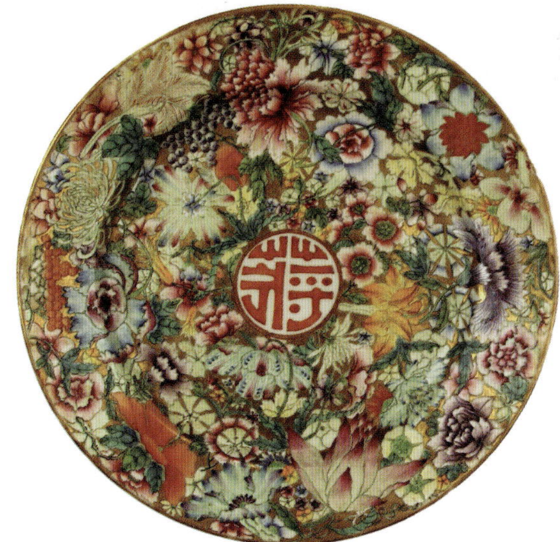

colorful plate
ith 'Chiang'
esign

Bada Shanren Memorial Hall

八大山人纪念馆 *Bada shanren jinianguan*

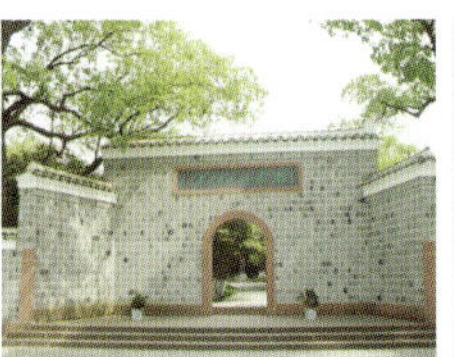

259 Qingyun Road, Nanchang, Jiangxi
江西省南昌市青云路259号
Tel: (0791) 8527 3565
Open: 8.30–17.00 except Mon
Gift shop

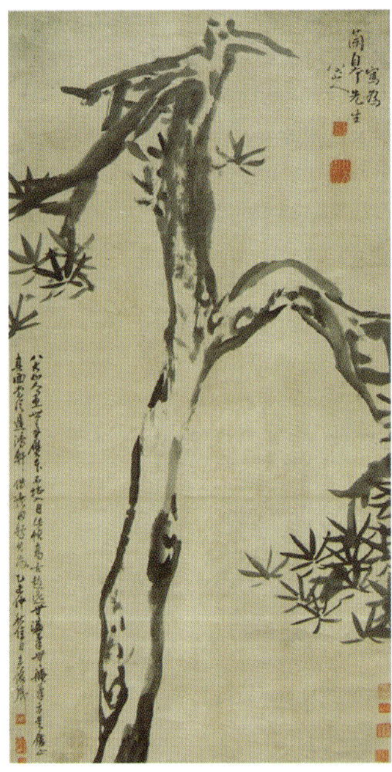

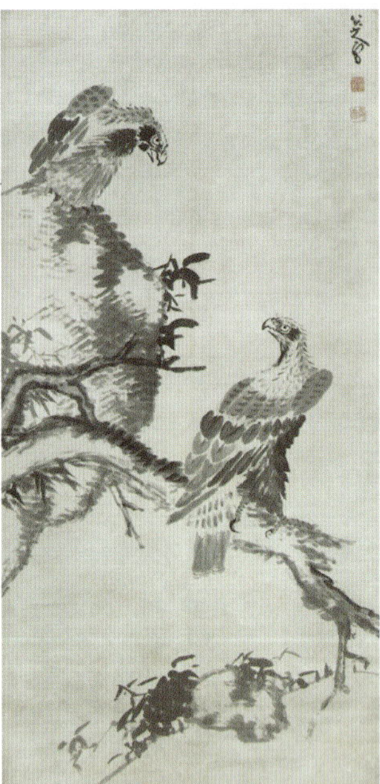

The museum is located in the Qingyun Pu Pavilion, a tranquil 2,500-year-old Taoist temple that was the artist's home and studio in his later years. Legend has it that Qiao, son of King Ling of the Eastern Zhou dynasty (700–221 BC), came here seeking immortality. Bada Shanren (1626–1705), as he is usually referred to, was a descendant of the imperial Zhu family of the Ming dynasty and an influential Chinese painter and poet of the early Qing. His distinctive calligraphic style was influential both in China and Japan, and his early extant work is in the National Palace Museum in Taipei. In addition to the calligraphy and paintings by Bada Shanren and Niu Shihui, there are works by later famous artists inspired by Bada Shanren's style of freehand brushwork, including Qi Baishi and Wu Changshuo.

Ink and colour paintings by Bada Shanren: *Pine* (left) and *Eagles*

Nanchang Bayi (August 1st) Uprising Museum

南昌八一起义纪念馆 *Nanchang bayi qiyi jinianguan*

155

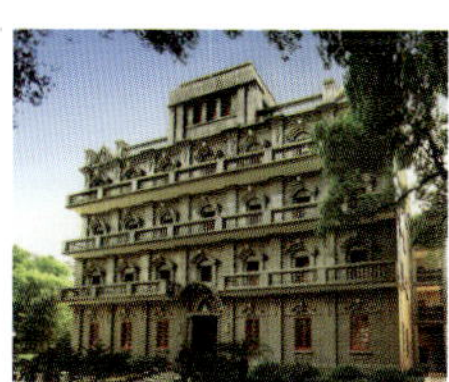

380 Zhongshan Road, Nanchang, Jiangxi
江西省南昌市中山路380号
Tel: (0791) 8661 3323
Open: 9.00–17.00 except Mon
English audio guide / gift shop/bookshop

In 1927, Chiang Kai-shek announced that the Communists were the enemies of the Nationalists and should be denied any say in the political future of China. This prompted the Bayi, or August 1st Uprising, during which the Communists captured and briefly held Nanchang. Despite the failure of the CCP to hold Nanchang, it was a pivotal historical development marking the beginning of hostilities between the Communists and the Kuomintang (KMT), and the growing ideological conviction among the Communists that they should focus on a peasant revolution rather than the Soviet model of a revolution of the workers.

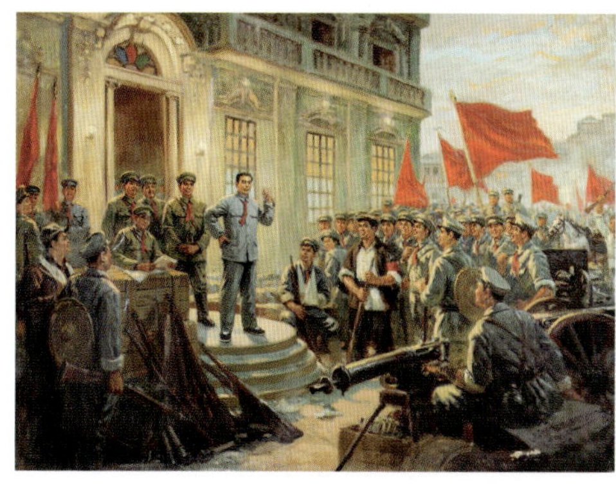

The Nanchang Bayi uprising was a pivotal historical development

Previously, the museum was housed in what had been the Communist headquarters during the Uprising, but a new museum was built next door in June 2007 and the old headquarters are undergoing renovation. The English audio, which provides interesting background details, including revolutionary songs, is recommended, as there is only limited English signage.

The exhibits detail events surrounding the Bayi Uprising and subsequent historical events, up to the founding of the People's Republic of China in 1949, using a variety of state-of-the-art techniques. As with the Huaihai Memorial Museum in Xuzhou, the People's Liberation Army is attempting to retell, and, in subtle ways, rebalance views of recent history. The standard story on the hostilities between the Communists and the KMT and the development of a split within the Party is presented, but the role of Mao Zedong in the 1930s has been adjusted to more realistic proportions, with the roles of other figures such as Zhu De and Zhou Enlai made more of, presenting a more nuanced view than has been previously available.

Jiangxi Provincial Museum

江西省博物馆 *Jiangxisheng bowuguan*

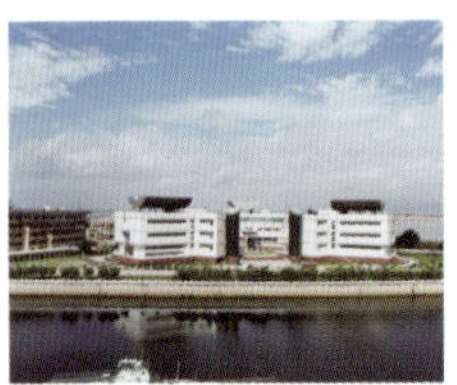

2 Xinzhou Road, Nanchang, Jiangxi
江西省南昌市新洲路2号
Tel: (0791) 8659 2509
Open: 9.00–17.00 except Mon and holidays
www.jxmuseum.cn
Kids

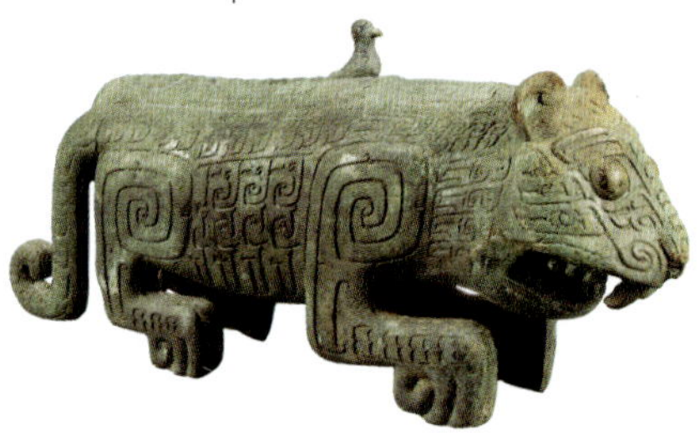

Bronze tiger with resting bird from Dayangzhou

This museum is housed in a new building opened in 1999, located on a sand bar between the Gan and Fu Rivers. It is divided into three parts: historic, revolutionary and natural history, and the value of the collection makes the museum well worth seeing.

The Provincial Revolutionary Museum has exhibits on the history of the Communist Party and local revolutionary events. These are in Chinese only. The Natural History hall contains an assortment of Paleozoic fossils, dinosaur skeletons – notably a 2.2-m-high ichthyosaurus – a minerals display, marine animals, insects and information about local topography. And there is an ethnographic exhibition concentrating on the Hakka minority, a prevalent peoples in southern Jiangxi.

The museum has a fine collection of Jiangxi ceramics exhibited in a timeline from the Neolithic to the late Qing, including examples from the Tang dynasty Hongzhou Kiln and of course, Ming and Qing examples from Jingdezhen, Jiangxi's premier porcelain centre.

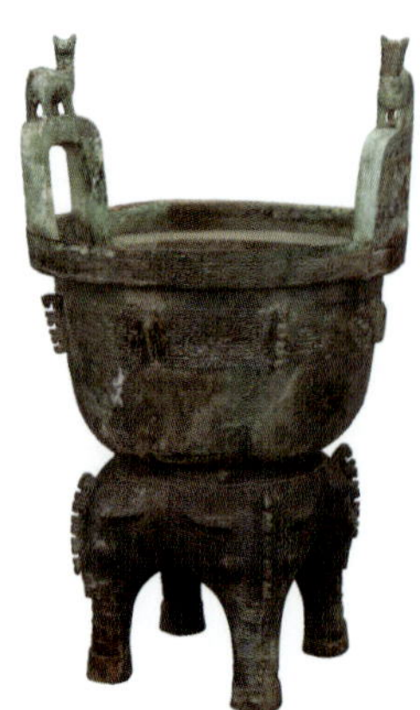

The most compelling reason to visit this museum, however, is to see the artefacts found at Dayangzhou, south of Nanchang. In September 1989, farmers found some bronze objects while digging on a construction site, which led to the excavation of a large royal burial chamber containing approximately 1,300 magnificently crafted bronzes, jades and ceramics dating from the period between *c*. 1200 BC and 1046 BC.

During the Shang dynasty, with its capitals at Zhengzhou and then Anyang on the Yellow River,

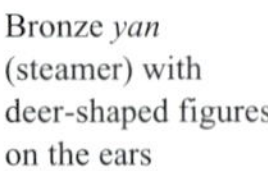

Bronze *yan* (steamer) with deer-shaped figures on the ears

Bronze Age civilization in China was at its height. It was previously believed that during this period the southern Yangtze River Valley was underdeveloped and uncivilized compared to the great capitals to the north, but discoveries at Sanxingdui, Jinsha and Dayangzhou have belied this assumption and proven that Bronze Age civilization in China was much more complex than was previously thought, and that other highly developed centres did indeed co-exist with the Shang kingdoms.

The marvellous and intricately patterned bronzes from Dayangzhou include sacrificial vessels, weapons, tools, cooking vessels and bells. Unique to this area, the tiger motif can be seen on many of the bronze and jade objects. Flat-legged vessels common here are rare at other Chinese sites. Don't miss the bronze, two-tailed tiger with a bird calmly resting on his back or the bronze double-faced mask with bulging eyes, reminiscent of those found at Sanxingdui. Ceramics and jade artefacts from the site arc also on display.

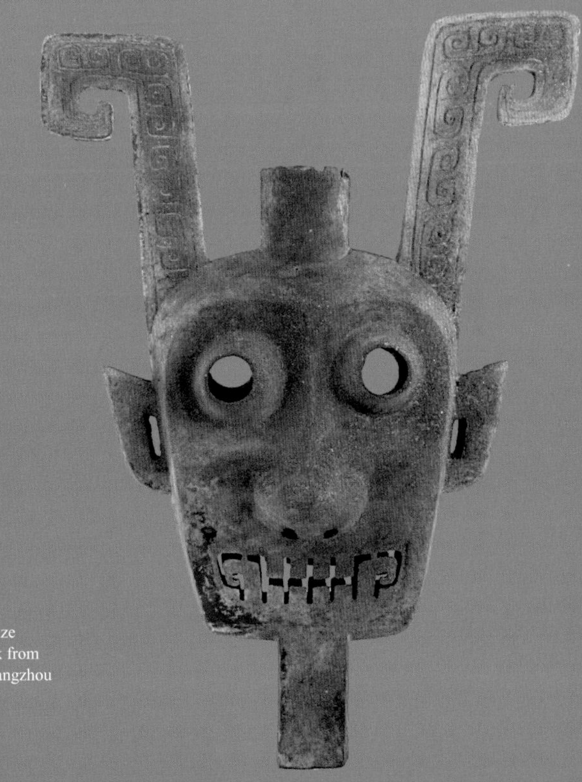

Bronze
mask from
Dayangzhou

Kunming City Museum

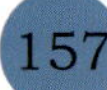

157

昆明市博物馆 *Kunmingshi bowuguan*

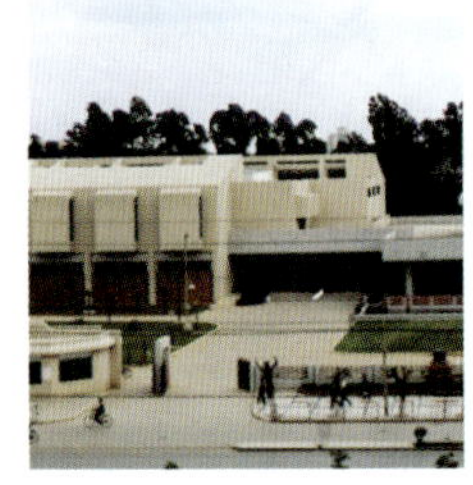

93 Tuodong Road, Kunming, Yunnan
云南省昆明市拓东路93号
Tel: (0871) 6315 3359
Open: 9.30–17.00
www.kmmuseum.com

A large and somewhat idiosyncratic 'folk collection/shop' displays the usual jade, porcelain and furniture (only some of which is for sale-ask the assistant) / Green tea is free to visitors

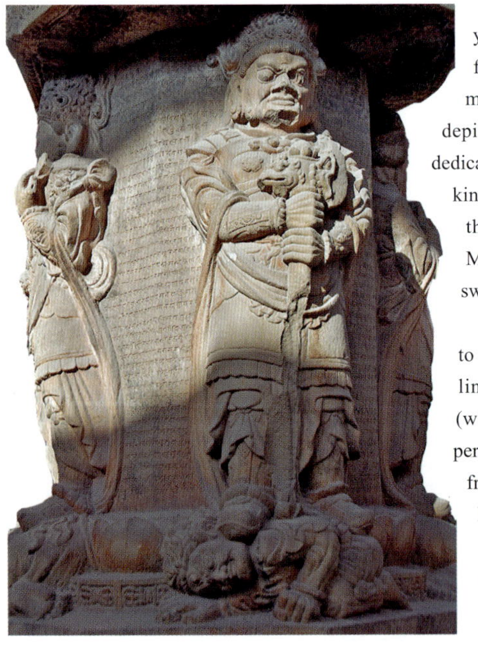

Sutra stone from the Dali kingdom

An attractive model of old Kunming greets you in the entrance hall of this museum, allowing for an interesting comparison between the modern metropolis of today and the walled Ming city as depicted in the model. To the left is a dimly lit hall dedicated to the ancient bronze and ironware of the Dian kingdom; many pieces are in fact reconstructions of the best pieces housed in the Yunnan Provincial Museum, but there are some beautiful daggers, swords, bronze bulls' heads and gold ornaments.

On the first floor is an exhibition room devoted to dinosaurs discovered in Yunnan – five skeletons line up for inspection, four of which are replicas (with the real bones under glass around the room's periphery) but the fifth, *Dilophosaurus*, is constructed from real bones. Sadly, there is not much written in English but this is not the case in the auditorium on the ground floor to the right of the entrance, where an impressive 6.6 m octagonal Sutra Stone Pillar stands alone, dating back to the kingdom of Dali (937–1253) and covered with Buddhist images and rare scriptures, as well as a good caption in English.

158

Yunnan Nationalities Museum

云南民族博物馆 *Yunnan minzu bowuguan*

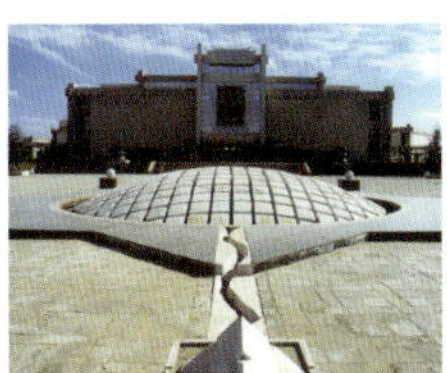

1503 Dianchi Road, Xishan District, Kunming, Yunnan
云南省昆明市西山区滇池路1503号
Tel: (0871) 6431 2091
Open: 9.00–16.30 except Mon
www.ynnmuseum.com
Bookshop / coffee shop in inner quadrangle

Opened in 1995 near the northern shore of Dianchi Lake, this museum is set around a green quadrangle and comprises seven exhibition halls that together house over 10,000 exhibits detailing the history and everyday life of Yunnan's twenty-two ethnic nationalities. Room 1 focuses on clothing and textiles, and is filled with a plethora of fantastically coloured traditional dress, weaving machines and examples of dyeing, appliqué and cross-stitching techniques. Other rooms exhibit musical instruments, minerals and precious stones, folk masks and ancient documents – twenty-three written languages exist in this province alone and the Tibetan scrolls and Naxi Dongba pictograph scripts are excellent. There are halls illustrating the diverse architecture and differing lifestyles of the various ethnic groups according to geographical location, from tropical hunting and fishing to mountain terrace agriculture.

Throughout the museum, large pictures on the walls behind the objects illustrate the objects being used in real-life situations, revealing a genuine connection between the exhibits and the modern world. Well worth at least half a day's exploration.

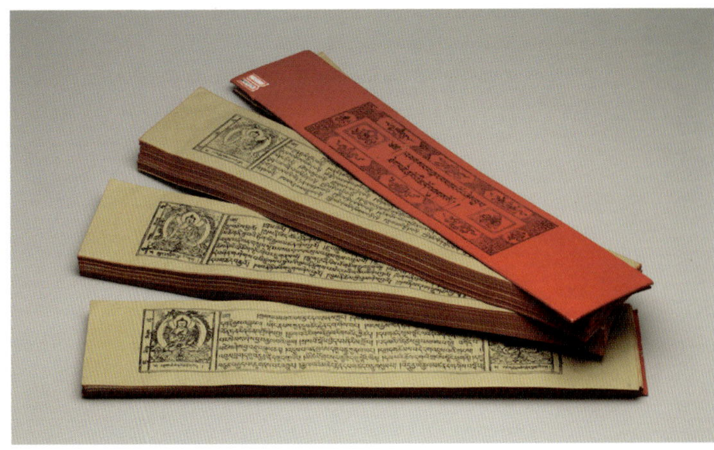

Tibetan scrolls

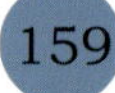

159

Yunnan Provincial Museum

云南省博物馆 *Yunnansheng bowuguan*

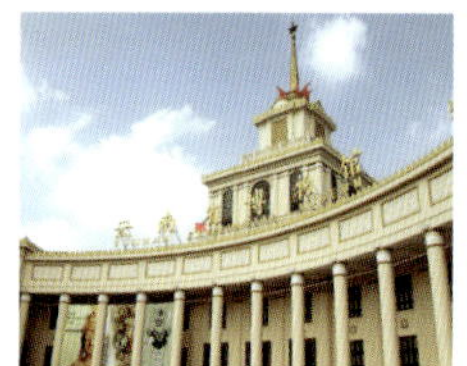

118 Wuyi Road, Kunming, Yunnan
云南省昆明市五一路118号
Tel: (0871) 6617 9536
Open 9.00–17.00 except Mon, last entry 16.30
www.ynbwg.cn

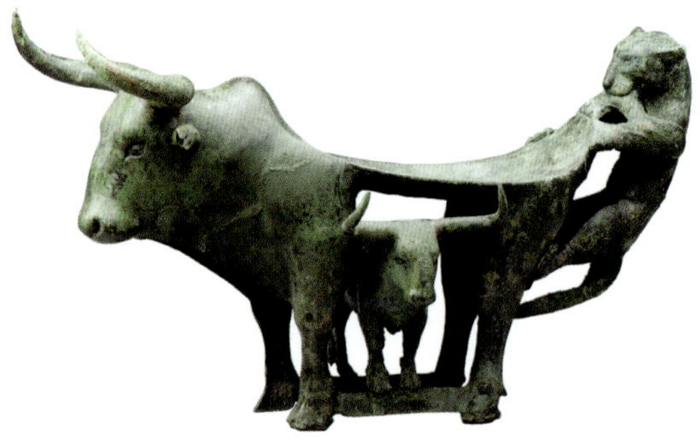

Bronze table with tiger and oxen figurines, Warring States period

Situated in central Kunming and newly renovated, the excellent Yunnan Provincial Museum focuses on the mysterious Bronze Age kingdom of Dian and the later Nanzhao kingdom (649–1253) centred around Erhai Lake and Dali, which flourished during the Tang and Song dynasties. The white-walled, brightly lit first floor 'Yunnan Bronze Civilization' gallery is packed full of interesting artefacts dating from the eighth century BC through to the end of the Han dynasty in the third century AD. Prize exhibits include huge bronze drums, cowrie shell containers with intricate lids and superb bronze and gold work illustrating how technologically advanced the Dian were.

On the second floor, the 'Regimes Illuminating Buddha's Light' gallery is moodily lit, with religious statues, scripts and pottery ranging from the seventh-century heyday of the Buddhist Nanzhao kingdom through to the Ming and Qing periods. Also on the second floor is a room titled simply 'Treasures', and it lives up to its name, being full of exquisite decorative and religious pieces made from all manner of materials, from gold and silver to ivory, bamboo, rhino horn, amber and sandalwood.

Inlaid Jewel Gold cap, Ming dynasty

The Dian Kingdom

The Dian reigned in southwest China (current day Yunnan) for around 500 years from the Warring States period to the Western Han, before being absorbed by the Eastern Han. It was not until excavations began in the 1950s of Dian burial sites located on and around Lake Dian (near Kunming) that more was discovered about this mystical kingdom, as they had no written language and only a few historical records referred to them. The most opulent and famous site is the cemetery of Shizhaishan where the Dian buried their kings and elite members of their kingdom. Among the forty-eight burials unearthed was one containing a rich range of offerings placed around the coffin, including beads, gold, bronze mirrors and weapons, as well as a gold seal bearing an inscription which reads 'The seal of the King of Dian'. Spectacular bronzes, which the Dian are renowned for, were also found in this grave and many of the others. They included drums and drum-shaped bronze vessels containing cowries (possibly to indicate status rather than for use as currency), their tops decorated with detailed scenes of miniature figures of humans and animals hunting, conducting sacrifices or at war. Bronze models of houses provide a unique opportunity to learn about the domestic life and architecture of the Dian, while other bronze objects such as plaques and weapons engraved with motifs confirm they primarily hunted, but were also agriculturally quite advanced. The bronze tableaux and engravings provide further visual clues to the Dian people's absorption of surrounding cultural influences from Central and Southeast Asia, south China and beyond.

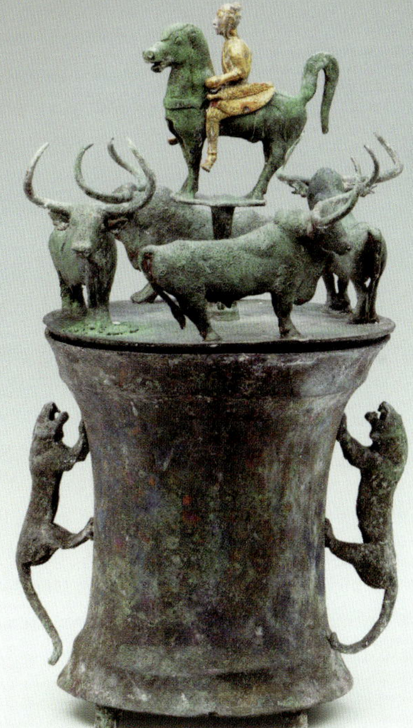

Cowrie container
with four oxen and
a gilt horseman,
Western Han
dynasty

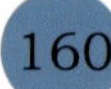

Lijiang Municipal Museum

丽江市博物院 *Lijiangshi bowuyuan*

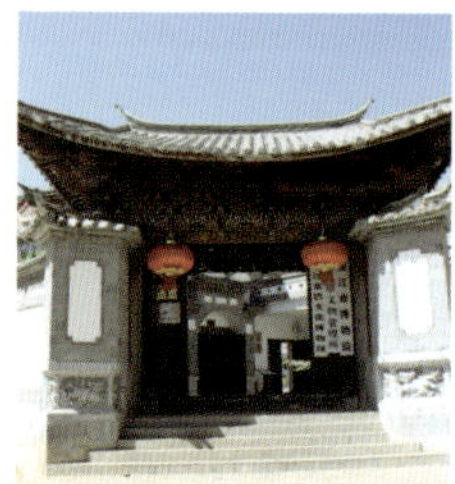

North entrance of Black Dragon Pool Park,
Lijiang, Yunnan
云南省丽江市黑龙潭公园北端入口
Tel: (0888) 3103 593
Open: 8.30–17.00 (closed on 1st and 3rd Mon of each month)
www.museumlj.cn
English-speaking guides are free of charge
Book / gift shop serves free Pu'er tea to visitors

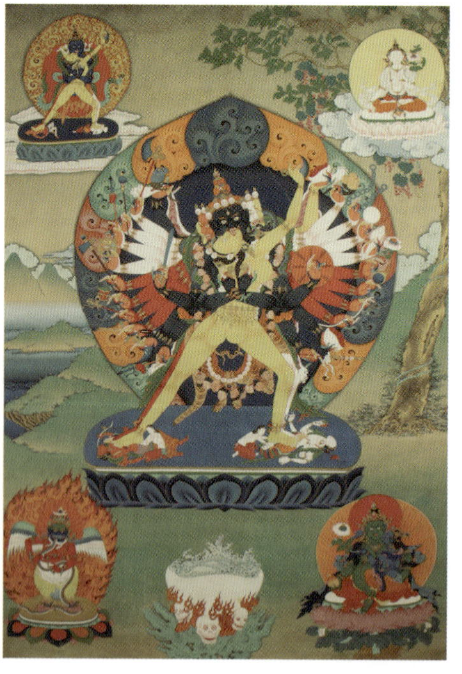

Exquisite
thangkas
on display

Originally called the Museum of Naxi Dongba Culture, in 2004 a new building was inaugurated at the same picturesque site, sporting a different name but still dedicated to the celebration of the unique Naxi Culture and, in particular, the Dongba religion that was brought to the world's attention by Joseph Rock in the early twentieth century.

The rectangular museum constitutes four halls set around an inner courtyard: the 'First Exhibition Hall' contains a huge 3D map of the mountainous region surrounding Lijiang, as well as detailed notice boards (in good English), photographs and bronze and clothing items that reveal the early history of the region dating from the Warring States period. The 'Life Rite Exhibition Hall' explains the importance of the shaman-like *Dongba*, or 'educated one', in Naxi Culture, and the divination techniques and religious instruments he uses.

The 'Dongba Manuscripts Exhibition Hall' and the 'Dongba Art Exhibition Hall' are filled with superb examples of how tree-bark paper is made, interesting comparisons between Babylonian and Egyptian pictographic alphabets and the Dongba system (the sole remaining pictographic writing system still in use today), and wood, paper and cloth panels and books (up to 1,500 years old) illustrating this rich and fascinating culture. Not to be missed.

Joseph Rock

Joseph Rock (1884-1962) was a botanist, adventurer, ethnographer, photographer, cartographer, linguist and journalist – in short a renaissance man. Born in Vienna in 1884, he emigrated to the USA at age 21. While working in Hawaii as a botanist, he was sent to China by

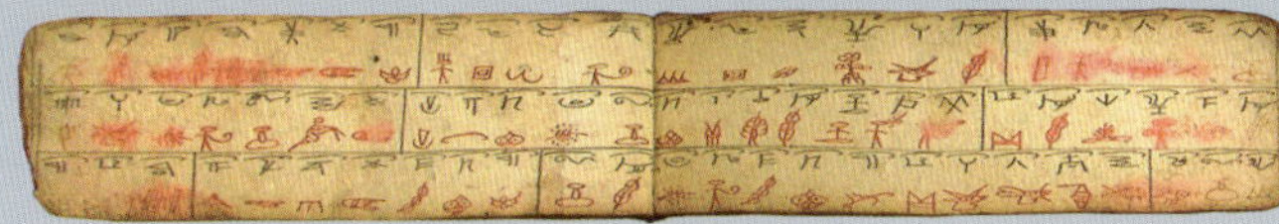

the US State Department to collect seeds used in the treatment of leprosy. This led to a lifetime dedicated to travel and discovery in Asia. Through his life, he collected and studied flora and fauna for various American universities and institutions, including the Museum of Comparative Zoology and the Arnold Arboretum of Harvard University and the Smithsonian. Besides his work in the field of biology and zoology, National Geographic Magazine regularly published reports and photos of his extensive travels through southwest China and Tibet. He died in Hawaii in 1962.

Rock's ethnographic studies and photographs of the various minority groups in Tibet, Yunnan, Gansu and Sichuan, as well as in Vietnam and Cambodia, remain an invaluable resource to this day. Perhaps his greatest legacy, however, is his collection and translations of thousands of volumes of Naxi literature and religious texts, as well as his Naxi dictionary published posthumously.

The Naxi language is a subset of the Tibeto-Burman language family and was spoken predominantly in Yunnan, especially in Lijiang, but also by Naxi in parts of Sichuan and Tibet. Today, only a small number of people can understand it. The Naxi Dongba script ('Dongba' refers to the religion, priests and written language of the Naxi), mostly comprising pictograms, was used by Dongba priests in religious ceremonies and rituals.

Just outside of Lijiang, on the slopes of the gorgeous Jade Dragon Snow Mountain, is Yuhu village, where you can visit Rock's house. There is also a small museum containing photographs and some of his belongings.

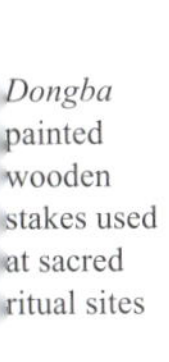

Naxi Dongba pictographic script is the only living pictographic script in the world

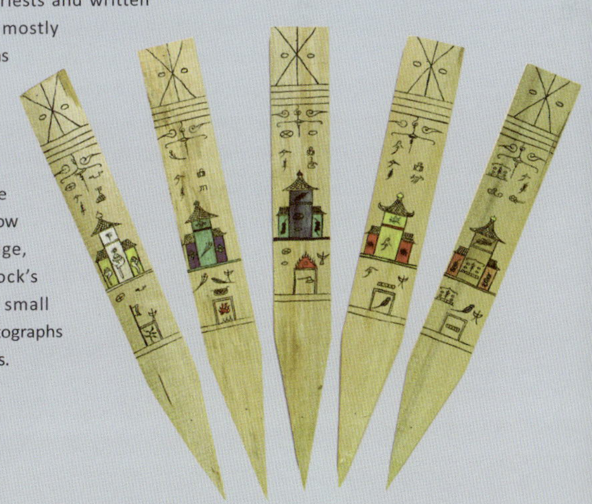

Dongba painted wooden stakes used at sacred ritual sites

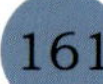

161

Guizhou Provincial Museum

贵州省博物馆 *Guizhousheng bowuguan*

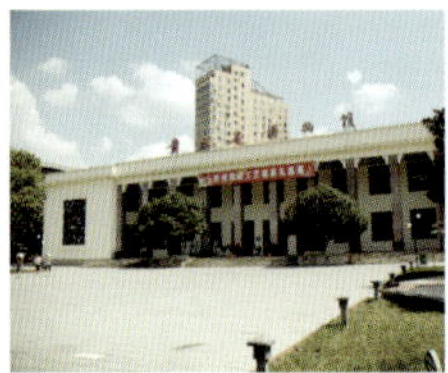

168 Beijing Road, Guiyang, Guizhou
贵州省贵阳市北京路168号
Tel: (0851) 6822 762
Open: 9.00–17.00 except Mon, last entry 16.30
www.gzmuseum.com
Gift shop

Guizhou is a mountainous province in southwestern China, with a humid subtropical climate. It is home to eleven different minority peoples, in particular the Miao, who occupy more than half the region. It is an area of great beauty with a wealth of flora and fauna – one of the most bio-diverse regions of China.

The Guizhou Provincial Museum, opened in 1958, is situated in the capital Guiyang. It has four departments displaying natural history, historical artefacts, minority peoples' folk art and modern art. It is the only museum to cover the geography, history, art and diverse culture of Guizhou and all its peoples. A new museum is being planned which will open in 2015.

The natural specimens give a fascinating insight into the plant and animal and bird life of the province.

The prehistoric collection is one of the most important in China and definitely worth a visit. It is rich in prehistoric fossils of extinct mammals, stone and bone artefacts, the teeth of the Tongzi Ape-Man, the jaw and thigh bones of the Xingyi Man, and the skull of the Chuandong Man.

From later periods the museum has representative collections from the Warring States Period, and a wealth of work excavated from the Han Dynasty tombs found throughout the province.

The ethnographic and folk art collections are particularly rich in the costume, trappings and silver ornaments of the Miao ethnic group.

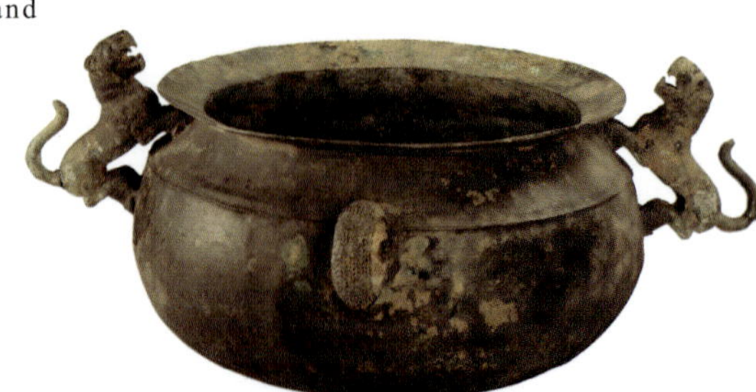

Bronze *fu* (boiler) with tiger design, Western Han dynasty

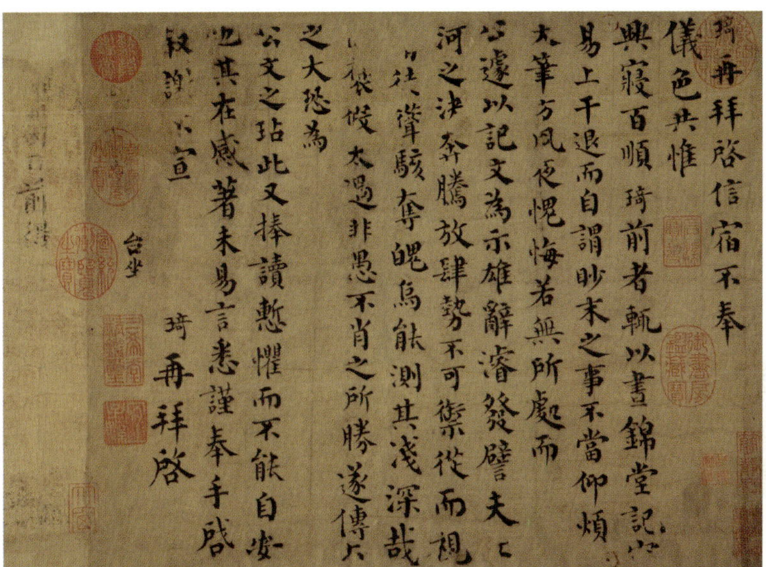

Detail from a Northern Song dynasty stroll

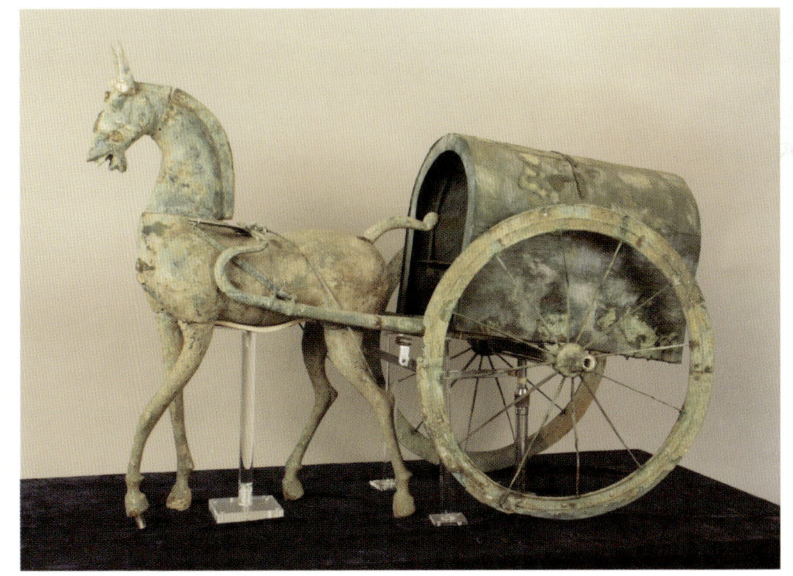

Bronze chariot, Eastern Han dynasty

162

The Memorial of Zunyi Meeting

遵义会议纪念馆 *Zunyihuiyi jinianguan*

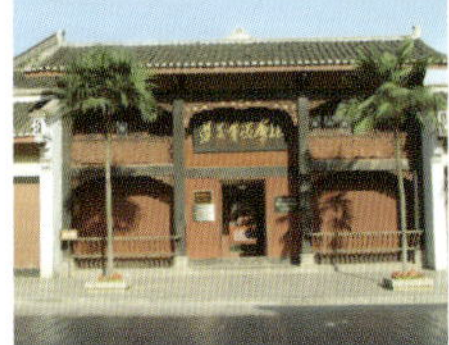

Ziyin Road, Honghuagang District, Zunyi, Guizhou
贵州省遵义市红花岗区子尹路
Tel: (0852)8222 052
Open: 8.30–17.00
Gift shop / bookshop

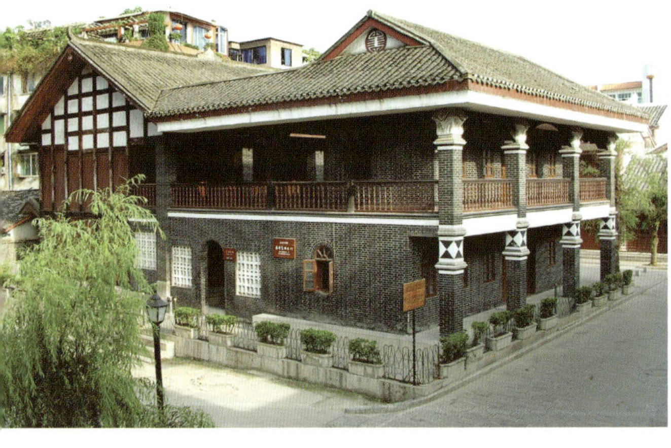

Former residence of Bo Gu

The Zunyi Meeting of the Chinese Communist Party's Politburo was held in January 1935 at Zunyi, in the hills of Guizhou, southwest China. The Party and its Red Army was on the Long March having made a strategic withdrawal from the Jiangxi bases. It was a turning point on the road to power not only for the Party but also for Mao Zedong. At the meeting, he for the first time won control of the armed forces and was elected top leader of the Party, winning a struggle against a group of party members more aligned to the Soviet Union and the Comintern. After Zunyi, the re-vitalized Party successfully established itself in a base in Yan'an in Shaanxi Province.

In addition to an exhibition including the actual table used during the conference, visitors can also visit the residences used by various leaders including not only Mao Zedong and Zhang Wentian but that of Bo Gu, the Politburo member who lost out to Mao, and Bo's German advisor from the Comintern, Otto Braun.

The Zunyi Meeting is of great symbolic importance in the history of the Party and is one of the most visited Red Tourism sites in China. Those wishing to retrace the footsteps of the Red Army during the heroic Long March can combine Zunyi with a visit to the nearby Loushan Pass where the Red Army scored its first major victory over the Guomindang, an event celebrated in a poem by Mao.

The Museum of Guangxi Zhuang Autonomous Region

163

广西壮族自治区博物馆 *Guangxi zhuangzuzizhiqu bowuguan*

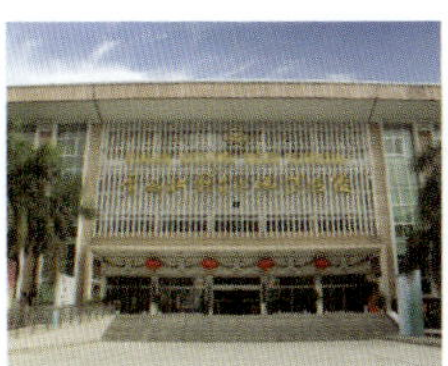

34 Minzu Avenue, Nanning, Guangxi
广西南宁市民族大道34号
Tel: (0771)2847055
Open:9:00–17.00 except Mon, last entry 16.00
www.gxmuseum.com
Gift shop / bookshop

Guangxi Zhuang Autonomous Region is situated at the extreme southwestern edge of China on the Vietnamese border – an area of wild, mountainous terrain at the very edges of the Chinese world. Inhabited by at least eleven different minority peoples, including most notably the Zhuang, their local customs and culture did not begin to interact with the Chinese until around the Shang and Zhou periods when social, political and economic contact with the Central Plains region began to influence life in the region.

Most visitors to Guangxi Zhuang will head for the breathless scenery of the Li River at Guilin near Lijiang in the northeast of the province, but those who also visit the museum in the capital Nanning will be richly rewarded by the insight they will gain into the customs, culture and art of many of China's most important minority societies.

The museum has a major collection of prehistoric fossils and remains, most notably the fossil of 'Liujiang Man', the earliest hominid fossil found to date in China – or anywhere else in Southeast Asia.

There are Neolithic remains from the many excavations in mountains, hills and caves throughout the province, in particular a large (66.4 cms in length) shovel-shaped ceremonial object which is polished to a spectacularly high degree demonstrating highly developed technical skill.

Guangxi developed at a very early date its own bronze culture. Unique to this region was the tradition of bronze drums, of which the museum has a collection of more than 300 pieces. These are displayed to show the eight main kinds of drum developed from as early as the Spring and Autumn period down to the time of the Qing. Chronological development, usage, and distribution are all explained.

Bronze horse,
Han dynasty

The collection also shows local pottery, celadon, glass, lacquer eared cups and bamboo flutes.And the customs, costume and folk art of the eleven minority peoples are all attractively displayed, together with an outdoor garden with reconstructions of local tribal domestic architecture.

Bronze drum with flying egret pattern, Western Han dynasty

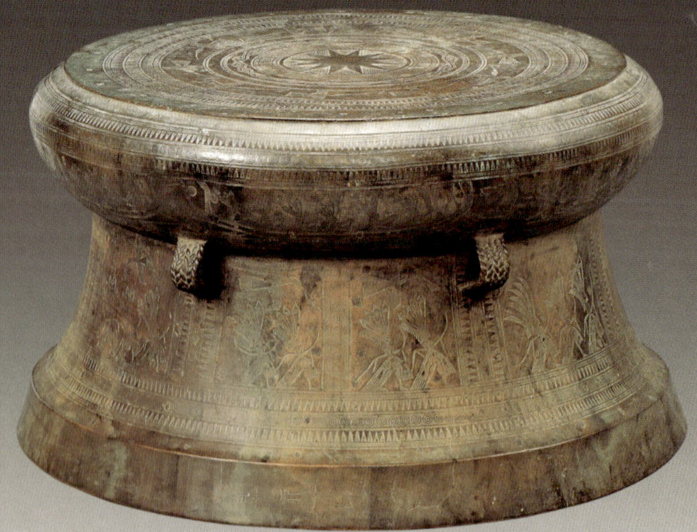

Guangxi Museum of Natural History

广西自然博物馆 *Guangxi ziran bowuguan*

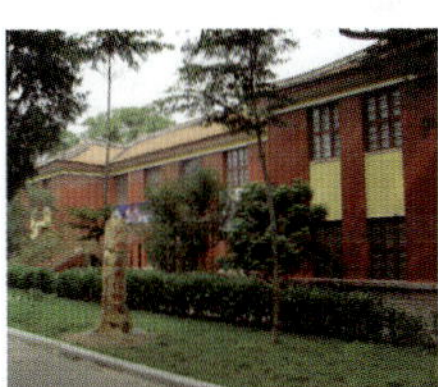

1-1 Renmin East Road, Nanning, Guangxi
广西南宁市人民东路1-1号
Tel: (0771)2820 502
Open: 9.00–16.30 except Mon
Gift shop

The Natural History Museum of Guangxi is located in Nanning, the capital of Guangxi autonomous region in southern China. Situated on the east side of Bailong Lake, it also looks out onto the beautiful Nanning People's Park.

Since its founding in 1988 it has amassed more than 50,000 specimens ranging from plants, animals and fossils, to the usual rocks and minerals that you might find in any museum on the subject. There are two main pavilions. The first, with dinosaur skeletons, tells the history of life on Earth. The second, which is more interesting, displays specimens of rare animals and marine life from the Beibu Gulf.

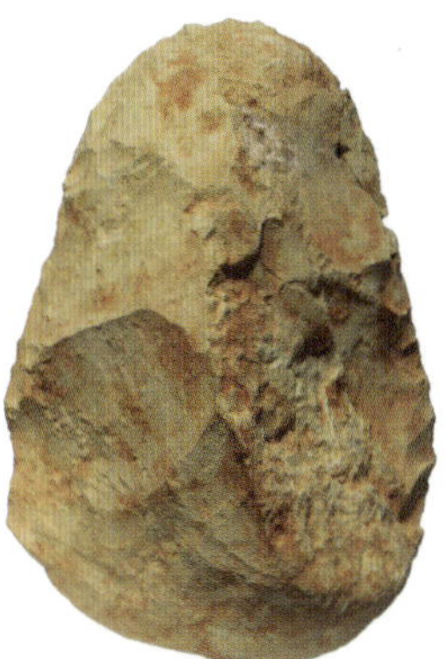
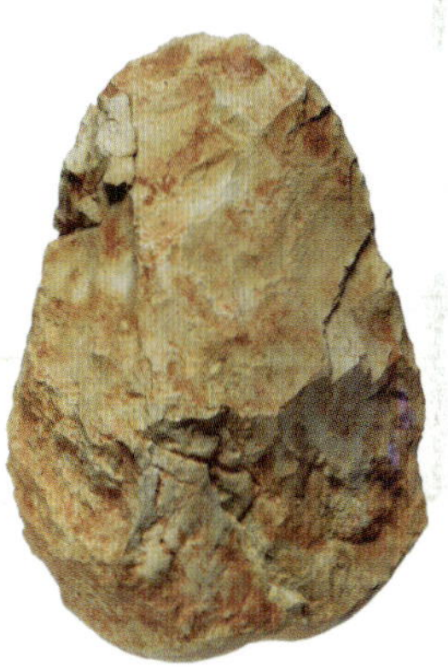

aise axe,
eolithic period

Teeming with marine life from numerous shellfish to large kelps and beautiful coral reefs, the Beibu Gulf is a semi-enclosed sea touching the boarders of China and Vietnam and China's Hainan Island. Also known as the Gulf of Tonkin, it is home to rare and endangered sea life, among the most famous of which is the Chinese White Dolphin. Generally white in colour or light grey, they can also have a pinkish tint to them, especially older ones. Besides nature's predators such as sharks, the biggest threat to the Chinese White Dolphin is mankind. Pollution and poaching, along with coastal development, have had a major impact on their survival.

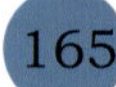

Hainan Museum

海南省博物馆 *Hainansheng bowuguan*

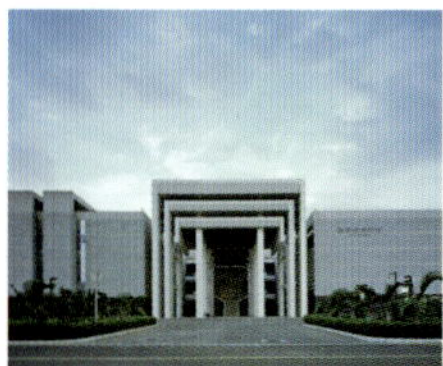

68 Guoxing Avenue, Haikou, Hainan
海南省海口市国兴大道68号
Tel: (0898)6523 8891
Open: 9.00–17.00 except Mon
www.hainanmuseum.org
Gift shop / bookshop / café

Hainan Museum was officially opened in 2008 in the Hainan Cultural Park in Haikou, the provincial capital. It is the successor of the original Hainan Museum founded in 1984. It occupies a vast site which is being developed with ambitious plans to illustrate the history and culture of Hainan.

Hainan did not become a province until 1988. It is China's southernmost province made up of more than 200 islands of which Hainan Island itself is by far the largest. In recent years, with its wealth of beaches and its tropical climate, it has become a hugely popular tourist centre – and a visit to the museum will round off the visitor's experience by providing insights into the unusual and fascinating history and culture of this maritime province.

The monsoon climate has resulted in large areas of tropical rain forest with over 4,600 kinds of plant and 570 species of animal.

The original inhabitants were the Li people, possibly the descendants of the ancient Yue tribes of China, who first settled the island more than 7,000 years ago. Hainan was not fully incorporated into China until the Song Dynasty and gradually over the years the Han people migrating from Fujian Province pushed the Li into the southern highlands. The Li revolted in the eighteenth century and the government responded by bringing in mercenaries from the Miao people of Guizhou. Both the Li and the Miao today represent the largest resident groups of minority peoples. Their history art and culture are shown in the museum in galleries dedicated to the Minority Nationalities of Hainan.

Situated in the South China Sea the region was part of the Maritime Silk Road. The museum is planning new space to exhibit the restored Huaguangjiao One wreck, together with 10,000 pieces of porcelain and other relics from the history of the South China Sea and its maritime trade.

During the Tang, Song and Yuan dynasties, a large number of Muslims lived in the southeast coast of Hainan Island. An Islamic coral tombstone of the Tang Dynasty was unearthed in Zhen Fu Bay, Lingshui in 1984. The tombstone was 66 cms high, 47 cms wide and 10 cms thick, on which are some Koranic inscriptions in Arabic and the name and the date of the tomb. It is decorated with a round moon, cirrus clouds, flowers, trees and other patterns which are all distinctively Islamic.

In modern times Hainan was for decades one of the strongest centres of communist guerrilla activity against the Guomindang led by Chiang Kai-shek and historical relics of this period are on display.

The museum has ambitious plans for growth to expand its presentation of the island's diverse and ever-changing history and culture.

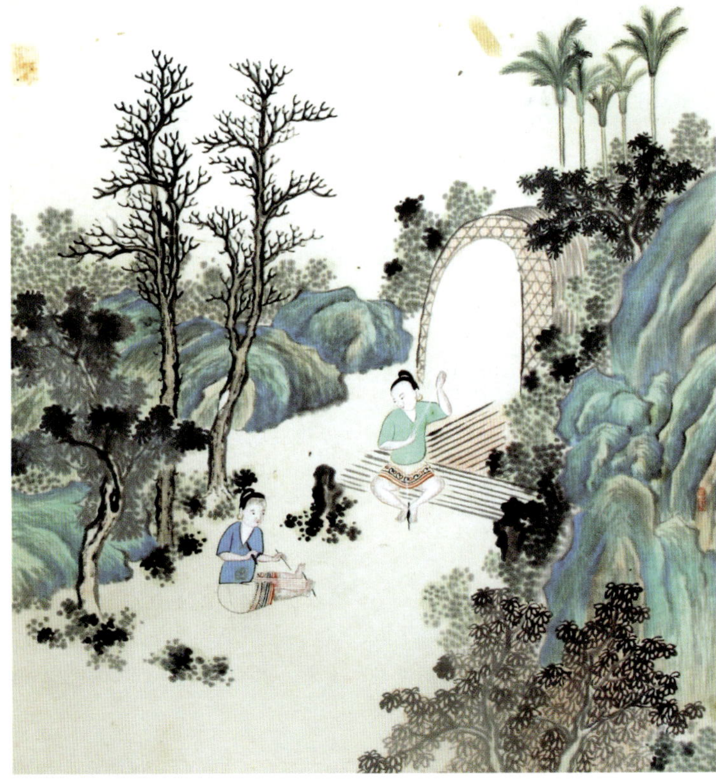

painting about stoms of Li ople

CHINESE MUSEUMS ASSOCIATION GUIDE

BEIJING AND THE NORTH

THE NORTHEAST

SHANGHAI AND EAST CHINA

THE YANGTZE

THE SOUTH

THE SILK ROAD AND THE NORTHWEST

TIBET

HONG KONG, MACAO, TAIWAN

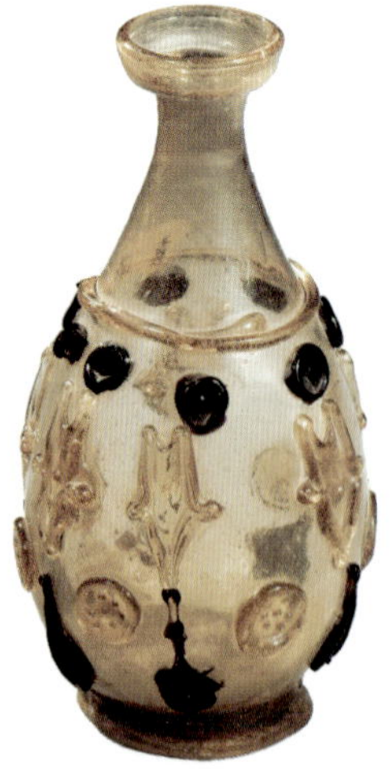

西北与
丝绸之路

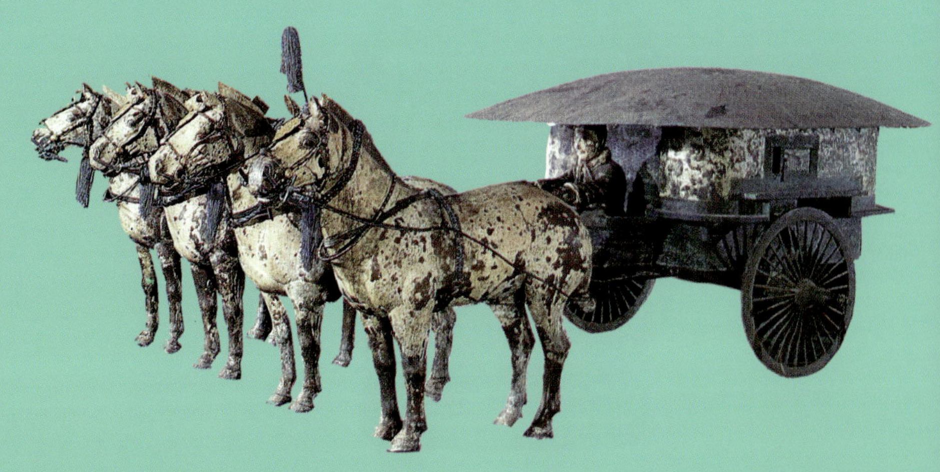

Baoji Bronze Museum

宝鸡青铜器博物馆 *Baoji qingtongqi bowuguan*

166

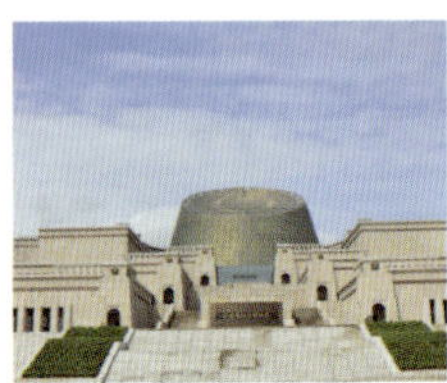

China Shigu Park, Binhe Avenue, Baoji, Shaanxi
陕西省宝鸡市滨河大道中华石鼓园
Tel: (0917) 2769 016
Open: 9.00–17.00 except Mon
www.bjqtqbwy.com (Chinese only)

The small city of Baoji sits on the western edge of the Guanzhong Plain, which was the birthplace of the Zhou and Qin dynasties. Chinese archaeologists have excavated a large quantity of bronze ware of the Western Zhou dynasty in this area, and many of these pieces are on display in this little-known museum. The first floor houses the museum's collection of bronze ware; on the second floor, there is an exhibition on ancient Chinese calligraphy and on the use of knotting for record keeping in the selling and buying of land. The museum is just 40 minutes southwest of the Famen Temple, and can be combined with a visit to the temple.

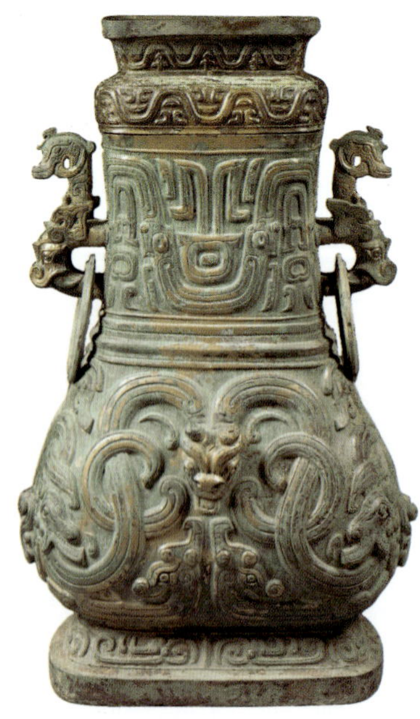

Bronze *hu*, one of the numerous bronzes on display from the Western Zhou dynasty

Emperor Qinshihuang's Terracotta Warriors and Horses and Mausoleum Site Museum

秦始皇帝陵博物院 *Qinshihuang diling bowuyuan*

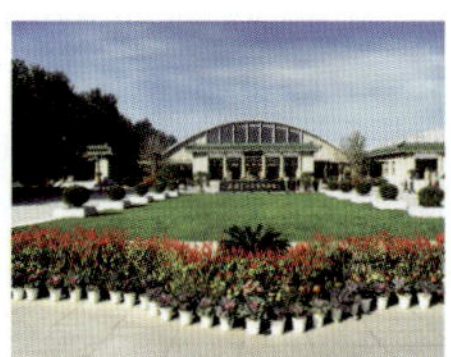

Lintong District, 30 km east of Xi'an, Shaanxi
陕西省西安市临潼区, 距西安以东30公里
Tel: (029) 839 4462 / 2542
Open: 8.30–19.00
www.bmy.com.cn

In 1974, some farmers were digging a well at Lintong, 35 km east of Xi'an, when they stumbled upon one of the greatest archaeological discoveries of history: the buried army of Emperor Qinshihuang.

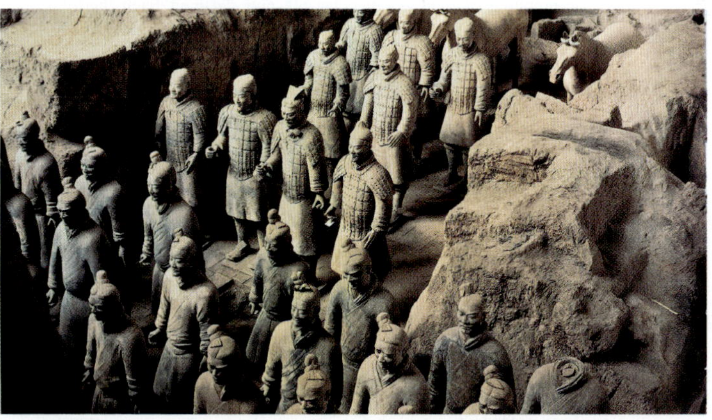

The larger-than-life-size terracotta figures were found in a vault 5 m (16 ft) below the surface, 1.5 km (less than a mile) east of the Emperor's tomb itself. The positions of the three pits discovered correspond to the prescribed military formation of a battle-ready army during the Warring States period and Qin dynasty times. The museum opened in 1979, and the area was declared a UNESCO World Heritage Site in 1987.

The terracotta soldiers are remarkably realistic pieces of sculpture. Each soldier's face has individual features, prompting speculation that they were based on living models. They have square faces with broad foreheads and large, thick-lipped mouths; they wear neat moustaches, and a number have beards; some of them have their hair in a topknot. The figures stand between 1.72 and 2 m (nearly 5 ft 8 in. and 6 ft 7 in.) tall.

There is a 360-degree cinema behind Pit No. 1 showing dramatizations of scenes from Emperor Qinshihuang's conquering of the six independent states, the construction of his mausoleum, the making of the terracotta figures and their eventual destruction by soldiers of the rebel general Xiang Yu. It is useful to see this film before visiting the museum, as it provides a background to what is on display.

Pit No. 1 is the first of the three pits to be discovered and forms the main exhibition hall. Extensive excavation in the eastern half of the pit uncovered 1,087 warriors, thirty-two horses and the traces of eight chariots. The display consists of infantry and charioteers arranged in battle formation. So far, over 1,000 soldiers have been restored to standing position on the original brick floor, in columns four abreast. At the head, facing east, is the vanguard, consisting of three rows of seventy archers each. They are followed by thirty-eight columns of more heavily armoured infantry interspersed with some forty war chariots, of which only the pottery horses remain. The south and north flanks are defended by a single column of spearmen facing outwards, some in armour and holding weapons, while more warriors on the west flank form the rearguard. In the centre of the formation, the warriors are lined up in nine columns, and among them are interspersed impressions of eight wooden chariots, now decayed. Each chariot is drawn by four horses and would have borne a driver and two warriors.

The entrance to the vault is through the west door, and from there one heads north. At the foot of a staircase, the spot is marked where the original discovery was made back in the drought-stricken spring of 1974. Proceeding down the northern flank of the vault you cross the excavations on an elevated walkway which affords views of both the wholly excavated area looking west and the partially excavated area to the eastern end of the vault. The grooves across the tops of the walls separating the corridors are the marks left by the decayed wooden beams.

At the unexcavated western end of the pit stand many half-reconstructed soldiers. As each piece is unearthed, it is coded, marking where it was found and to which statue it might belong. Archaeologists have estimated that, if completely excavated, the pit would yield more than 6,000 warriors, 160 horses and forty chariots.

Pit No. 2 is 20 m (65 ft) south of Pit No. 1. This L-shaped pit was discovered in 1976 after

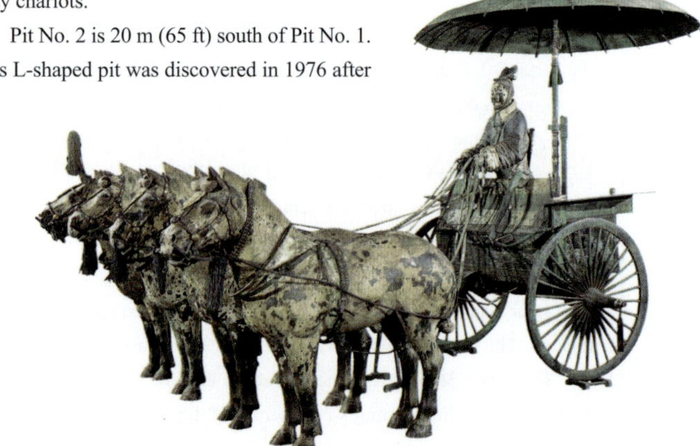

Bronze chariot excavated from Pit No. 1

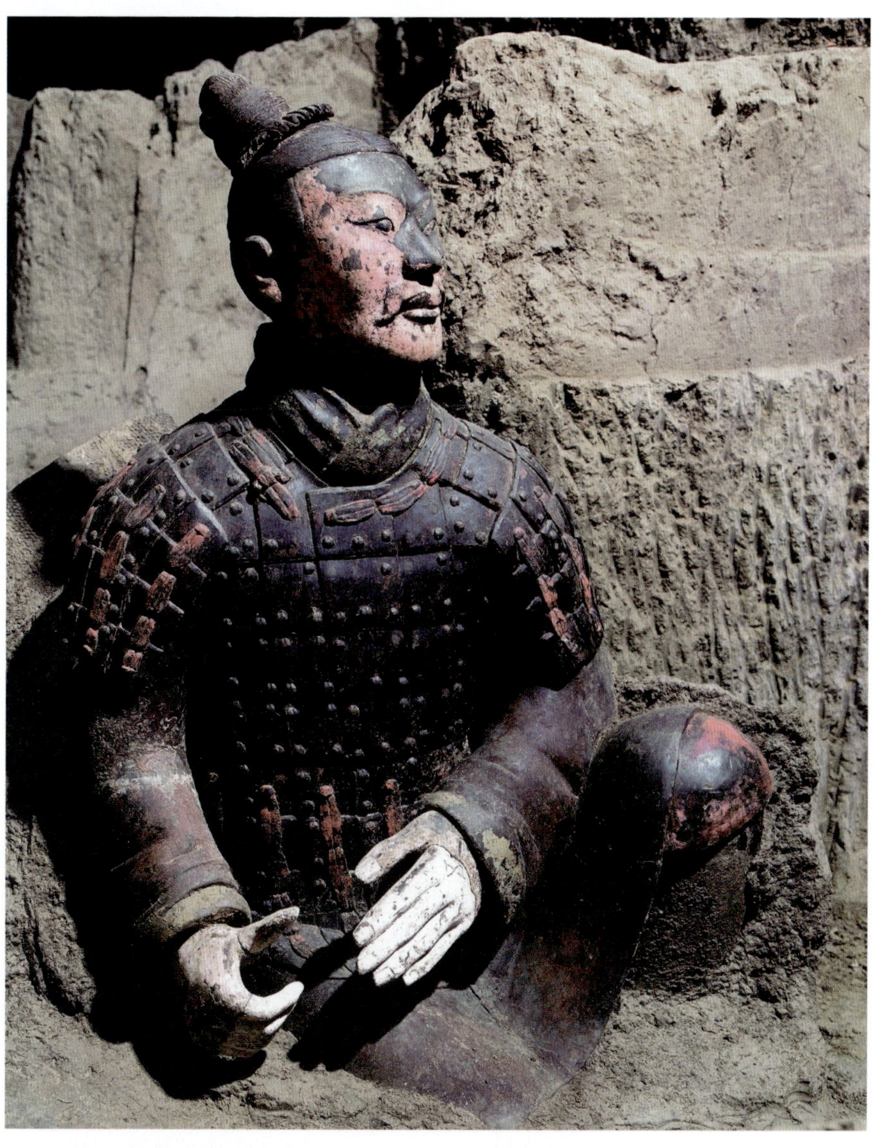

Painted kneeling archer excavated from Pit No. 2. His facial expression and hair, nails, shoe are all vivid, and the original polychrome cultural relics are preserved in excellent condition.

extensive test drilling, although the official excavation did not begin until March 1994. Pit No. 2 houses around 900 soldiers, including kneeling and standing archers, infantrymen and charioteers, together with some 350 chariot horses, 116 cavalry horses and the remains of eighty-nine wooden chariots.

The pit, which is only partially excavated, is contained in a modern building that allows visitors to walk around it and observe the ongoing excavations. The collection of figures here includes a higher number with vestiges of their original colouring. This pit has eleven sloping entrances, down which the terracotta warriors are believed to have been carried. Trial digging at several places unearthed seventy archers, some kneeling, others standing. Some fifty-two horses were also discovered. On the north side of the building, examples of some of the warriors unearthed in this pit are on display in glass cases. A stairway leads to a second-floor exhibition hall where more exhibits are on display, including some of the more than 30,000 pieces of Qin weaponry discovered in the three pits.

Archaeologists say the military formation of Pit No. 2 is far more complex than that in Pit No. 1. The larger quantity of archers, chariots and cavalry suggests that in the battles of the day those troops in Pit No. 2 would have been engaged in launching offensives and breaking up the enemy ranks. Once the enemy troops were on the run the cavalry would have given chase.

Pit No. 3 is the smallest of the three, strategically the most important since the command of the entire terracotta army was based here. Excavation of this battle headquarters has revealed the traces of a chariot, four horses and sixty-eight warriors. The four horses pulling the chariot and the four warriors behind it are in good condition, but many of the pit's other figures are headless or smashed completely. Numerous bronze weapons, and fragments of deer horn and animal bone have also been found. Animal sacrifice was probably part of the rites performed by commanders of a real army, who would have prayed to the gods for victory before a battle.

Pit No. 3 is housed within a modern building. Terracotta warriors, mainly headless, and the four draught horses of a chariot, stand upon a Qin brick floor. Within the pit, rammed earth walls form chambers housing small detachments. Timber once completed this subterranean vault structure, but these collapsed and damaged the warriors beneath.

Every figure is different. Their facial features and clothing reveal differences in age, function and rank; however, collectively, the figures do exhibit some general racial characteristics: they have squarish faces, wide foreheads, thick lips, moustaches and beards.

The figures are all fairly tall, with generals and commanders being the tallest and most portly. Apart from their larger size, generals can be clearly identified by their double-tailed headgear, longer tunics falling to below the knee, and minimal fish-scale-pattern armour on their midriff, which hangs in an inverted V-shape a little below the waist. On the chest and neck they have bow-like decorations, while their feet are shod

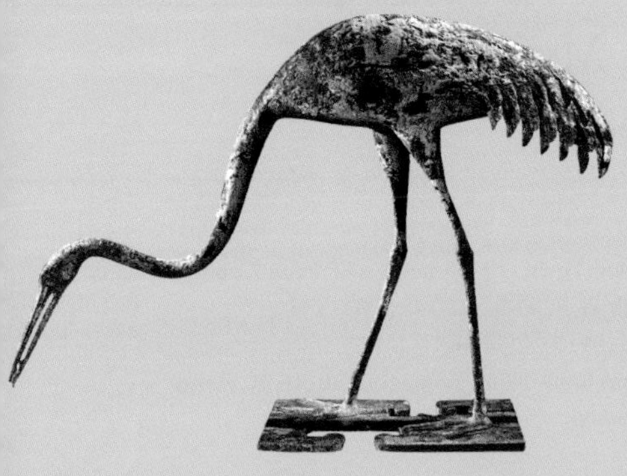

in boots with upturned toes. The sleeves of the generals'tunics are usually long enough to partly cover the hands, since generals directed their troops and rarely engaged in direct combat themselves.

Officers have simpler headgear and usually wear a little more armour, sometimes on the shoulders, but not on the chest. Boots are flat-toed and box-shaped. Sleeves leave the hands clear and free, for the officer both directs his troops and may need to lead them by example into combat.

Cavalrymen are seen dismounted in front of their terracotta horses. They can be recognized by their sleeveless jackets of armour, which appear thick and are composed of quite large, squarish plates that seem to be riveted together. Headgear is extremely simple and close fitting, and is secured with a chin strap to prevent it blowing off while riding. Shoes are the lightest and smallest of all the figures.

Archers usually wear simple battle robes with no armour, and their arms are in the process of drawing back their bows. Kneeling archers are more plentiful. They are crouched down on one knee in readiness for combat and wear quite heavy armour. Viewed from the rear, their boots can be seen to have a distinct tread.

The infantry wear either battle robes or bulkier armour. Their hair is usually tied into topknots and their hands are poised to carry spears. The charioteers are in more active poses, with both arms stretched out slightly so as to hold the reins to drive their vehicles.

Two magnificent bronze chariots are housed in a relatively new exhibition hall, which stands to the right as you first enter the museum complex. In December 1980, two chariots, each with two-spoked wheels and drawn by four horses, were unearthed-totally smashed, apart from the solid bronze steeds and charioteers. These chariots were about half the size of the actual chariots used by Emperor Qinshihuang on his inspection tours of the empire. They were certainly crafted specifically for Emperor Qinshihuang's afterlife. One was made of bronze, gold and silver components (about 3,462 separate metallic parts in all). The second chariot, the *gaoche*, which was found in front of the other, may have been a vanguard vehicle. It is also called a *liche* (a battle chariot), and like the second, is drawn by four horses. The chariot carries a pair of bronze shields, a crossbow and arrow, and a box containing sixty-six bronze arrowheads.

Both chariots highlight the excellent metallurgical and metal-shaping technology of the Qin period, as well as its high artistic standards. Most chariot fittings are of solid bronze, while the harness and reins are inlaid with gold and silver. A tassel hangs down from each horse's neck. The chariot drivers and horses are also of solid bronze, and yet appear very life-like.

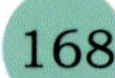

Famen Temple Museum

法门寺博物馆 *Famensi bowuguan*

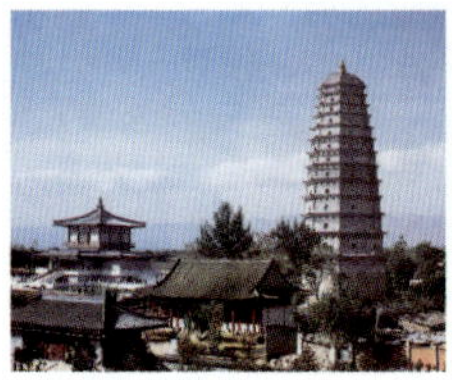

Famen Town, 10 km north of Fufeng County, Shaanxi
陕西省扶风县北10公里法门镇
Tel: (0917) 5254 465
Open: 8.00–18.00 summer; 9.30–16.30 winter
Gift shop

The Famen Temple, some 120 km (74.6 miles) west of Xi'an, dates back to the Eastern Han dynasty, between AD 147 and 189. However, the structure has undergone many renovations over succeeding dynasties. The temple houses one of Sakyamuni Buddha's finger bones, said to have been distributed by the Indian King Asoka (d. AD 232). During the Tang dynasty, the temple's pagoda was rebuilt and relics were tucked away in a crypt underneath it. In 1609, during the Ming dynasty, a 45-m octagonal brick pagoda was built above the crypt.

On 24 August 1981, the Ming dynasty pagoda partially collapsed, leaving exactly half the structure standing and the other half a pile of rubble. By 1987, the damaged pagoda had been completely cleared away, leaving the stairway to the underground vault exposed. Four finger-bone relics of Sakyamuni Buddha were discovered: one was found in the front chamber, in a reliquary known as 'the Asoka Pagoda'; one was discovered in a marble bier in the middle chamber; the back chamber held another in an eight-fold casket; and the last one was found in a secret shrine underneath the back chamber, in a five-fold casket. As only one of the bones is a genuine *sarira*, the other three are known as 'shadow bones'. They are meant to protect the genuine one in case of persecution of Buddhism. Visitors enter the renovated crypt via stairs leading inside and downwards.

The unearthed treasures are held in the museum, just next door to the temple. The museum is made up of three structures built in the architectural style of the Tang dynasty. The objects are nicely displayed and there are good explanations in Chinese and English.

A succession of emperors either visited the Famen Temple themselves or arranged for the famous finger-bone relic to be taken to Chang'an so they could view it. The temple underground vault included many artefacts for daily use offered by the royal families, such as tableware, tea items, censers, clothes, coins and jewellery.

The exhibition hall to the right of the Treasure Hall exhibits an excellent collection of Tang gold and silverware, demonstrating the advanced metalworking techniques and skills of the craftsmen of that period. Some one hundred of the gold and silver vessels, mainly imperial wares made in the royal workshop, were offered by Emperor Yizong (r. 859–873) and his son Emperor Xizong (r. 873–888). Examples include a gilded silver bowl with an overlapping lotus petal design; the four gilded silver ewers (ritual vessels for the consecration of the image of Buddha); an exquisite gilded silver basket decorated with geese in flight; eight small gilded silver plates with a peony design. In addition to the wares from the imperial workshops, there are also objects of tribute from southern China, and a special section dedicated to teaware.

These include a silver tea mortar decorated with a gold-gilt design of wild geese and a silver tea strainer with a design of an immortal on a flying crane, both dated 869.

Other rare objects include the *mise* or 'secret colour' celadon ceramics and more than 700 pieces of silk, including brocade, satin, embroidery, thin silk, gauze and many other types. Many of the textiles were donated by the imperial family or the aristocracy. Other textiles had been used to wrap objects. Some were imperially consecrated by Empress Wu Zetian (684–705). The best piece may be the miniature garment embroidered in gold-wrapped thread (even finer than strands of hair) and lined in red silk.

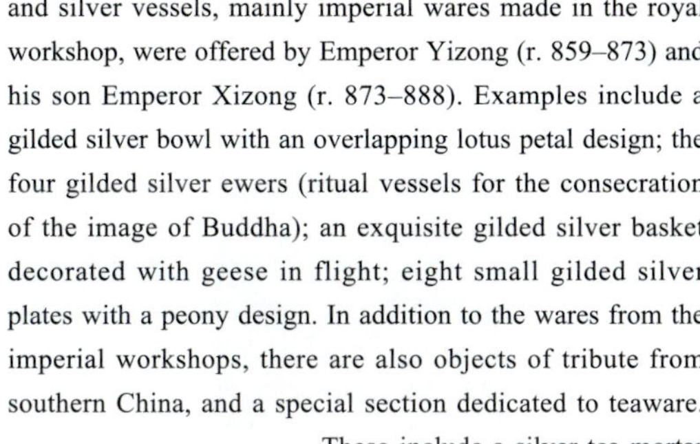

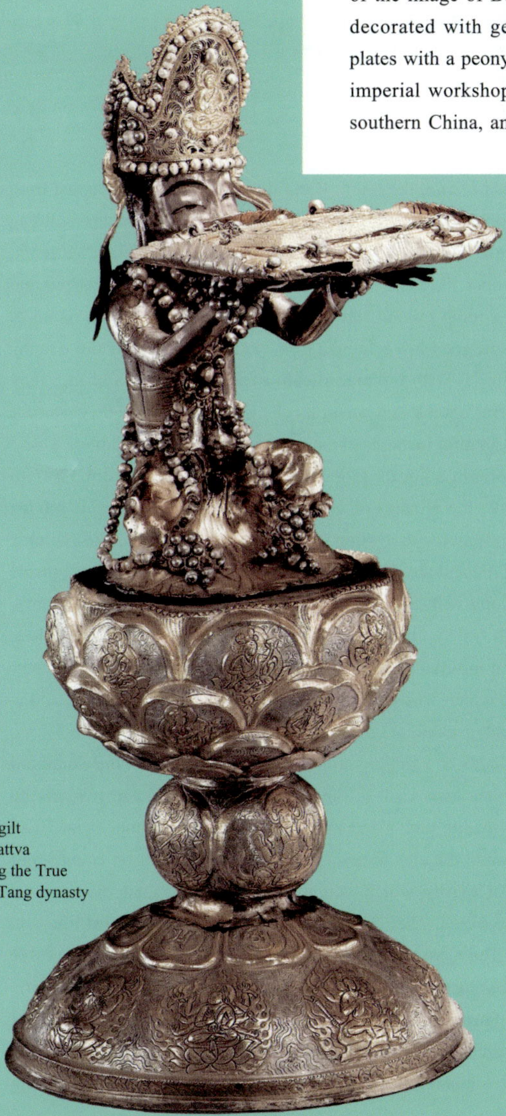

Ilver-gilt
dhisattva
fering the True
dy, Tang dynasty

Hanyangling Museum

169

汉阳陵博物馆 *Hanyangling bowuguan*

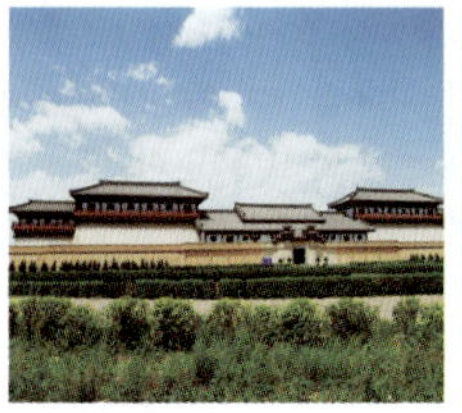

East side of the Xianyang International Airport Road, Xi'an, Shaanxi
陕西省西安市咸阳国际机场专线公路东段
Tel: (029) 8603 2883
Open: 8.30–18.00
www.hylae.com
Gift shop / restaurant

Yangling is the tomb of Liu Qi, the fourth Han Emperor Jingdi, who reigned from 157 to 141 BC. The tomb was discovered by accident in 1990, by workers building a road to the new airport. On the south side of the road is the Yangling Museum, which opened in September 1999 and is home to thousands of pottery figurines and animals. The Emperor's tomb mound sits on the north side of the road, opposite the museum. Archaeologists have focused on excavating pits in the nearby surrounding area and, as with the mausoleum of Emperor Qinshihuang, they have left the Emperor's tomb untouched for the time being while they wait for more advanced scientific methods of excavation to become available.

The mausoleum's south gate ruins were excavated from 1997 to 1998. Since 2001, the remains of the gate have been housed inside a large structure that resembles the original Han dynasty building. The rammed earth, pieces of tile and the post-holes of the original gate can be seen inside the structure, along with illustrations of gates throughout Chinese history. The Yangling South Gate is the first gate to be found; it is the most complete, and offers important information on traditional Chinese architecture. A pottery weiqi chessboard, which was found in the area around the south gate, and is the oldest of its kind, is exhibited in the main museum.

One of the highlights at Yangling are the pottery figures from the excavated tombs. A glass walkway has been built at the foot of the eighteen furrows, giving visitors a bird's eye view of the pits. Their number of figurines is impressive, with some 50,000 scattered around the site. When excavation work began on twenty-four pits containing the Emperor's army, which were to the south of the road, thousands of pottery warriors were discovered. Their bodies are approximately one-third life size, without arms and naked. Their arms and hands were made of wood, with moveable joints, but these, together with the leather armour and silk clothing they once wore, have long since decayed. There are, however, traces of red silk remaining on some of the figurines. There are patches of bright vermillion around the heads of some, with traces of woven silk fabric – apparently the remains of a kind of headband worn during

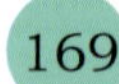
Clay-coated figurine in kneeling position, Han dynasty

this period. Some eunuch figures have also been found, providing the earliest known example of the existence of eunuchs in China.

All the figures were painted and many still retain at least their original basic ochre colouring, representing the skin. Features such as hair, eyebrows, moustaches and pupils were painted in black. Archaeologists have concluded that the nude figures, which were originally clothed, were intended as burial objects for the royal family alone, as they were found in pits accompanying the Emperor's tomb. It is thought that the practice of enrobing burial figures in textiles, which is characteristic in the Chu tombs, illustrates the influence of that culture, whereas the figures with sculpted clothes are similar to the figures in Emperor Qinshihuang's tomb.

The figures include soldiers, archers on horseback, servants, musicians and dancers. Some servant figurines have been unearthed in almost perfect condition, wearing moulded clothes with white painted robes and yellow belts. In some pits, the figures lay stacked on one another. In Pit No. 17 and No. 14, only the heads stick out of the earth, the bodies still buried from the neck down.

The excavated domesticated animals include horses, cows, pigs (some of which appear to be pregnant), sheep, goats, dogs and chickens. The horses have a slot along the back of their necks where a mane was once fixed, and a hole for a tail, but these have decayed, perhaps because they were originally made from real horse's hair. It appears that each pit represents a division or department of the Emperor's palace. In fact, some of the pits have revealed rooms complete with servants and everyday utensils. The inclusion of domestic animals is of particular interest to archaeologists as this is the first time such a quantity and variety has been discovered. Following the unification and standardization of the Qin dynasty, the Chinese under the Han Emperors experienced a relatively stable and prosperous period, in which the development of agriculture progressed rapidly.

At the end of your tour of the underground exhibit, visit the small theatre where a 20-minute 3D video is shown on the history of the tomb.

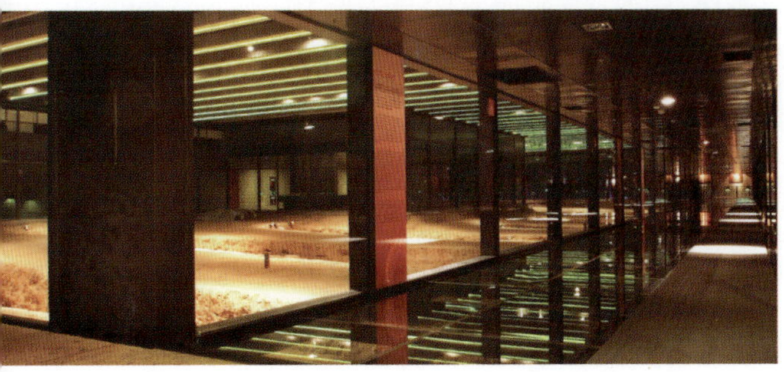

With its convenient location beside the airport road, Yangling is a convenient stop for tourists flying into or out of Xi'an.

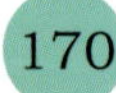

170

Shaanxi History Museum

陕西历史博物馆 *Shaanxi lishi bowuguan*

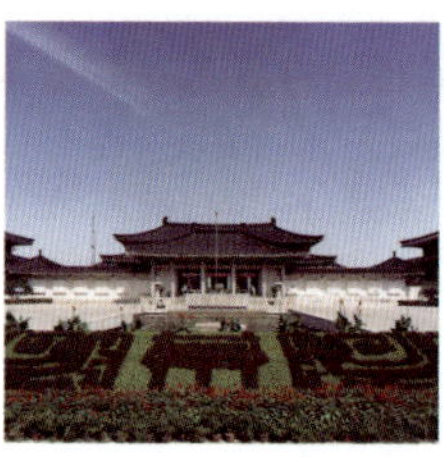

91 Xiaozai East Road, Xi'an, Shaanxi
陕西省西安市小寨东路91号
Tel: (029) 8521 9422
Open: 9.00–17.30, last entry 16.00, Nov 15–Mar 15;
        8.30–18.00, last entry 16.30, Mar 16–Nov 14
www.sxhm.com
Free pamphlet / wheelchairs available / English guide book

Maids in the imperial palace (detail), from the Tang wall paintings decorating Princess Yongtai's tomb

The creation of the Shaanxi History Museum, the final wish of Premier Zhou Enlai, began in 1983 and was opened to the public in 1991. It was the first major state museum built with modern facilities in China, designed in a mixture of traditional Tang and modern building styles. It is a massive structure with 8,000 sq m of exhibition space. Its remit is the explanation of the history and culture of Shaanxi Province, and the repository for its art.

Shaanxi, and its capital city Xi'an (originally Chang'an), was the heartland of ancient Chinese civilization. Details of its 150,000-year past continue to emerge from province-wide excavations in the loess – the dry sandy soil which has nearly perfectly preserved its past. Situated to the north and west, Xi'an had been the capital of the province, intermittently, since the time of the ancient Zhou. Thirteen dynasties had made their capitals here, as did the Qin Emperor, Qin Shihuangdi, who brought the period of the Warring States to a close by suppressing and unifying the other six states into a centralized China for the first time. It was outside Xi'an that he built his tomb with the famous Terracotta Warrior Army.

Xi'an reached the height of its wealth and power in the Tang dynasty, when it was laid out on a grid pattern, still extant today, with rectangular blocks of streets spreading out on the compass points from the Bell Tower at its centre. It was surrounded by walls, which were completed by the Ming and which still stand today. Situated at the eastern end of the Silk Road, which brought it great wealth, Xi'an alternated as the capital with Luoyang to the east for generations.

The permanent collection sets out to explain the rich legacy of Shaanxi's history and is divided historically into seven sections: prehistory, Zhou, Qin, Han, Wei–Jin, the Northern and Southern dynasties, and the Sui–Tang and Song–Yuan–Ming–Qing, giving a panoramic picture of Shaanxi's past, from the earliest times to the mid nineteenth century. The display of objects is enlivened by models of archaeological sites, explanatory drawings and photographs. Here, one can put into context painted Neolithic ceramics, bronzes that show the rise of the Zhou, the weapons, horses and

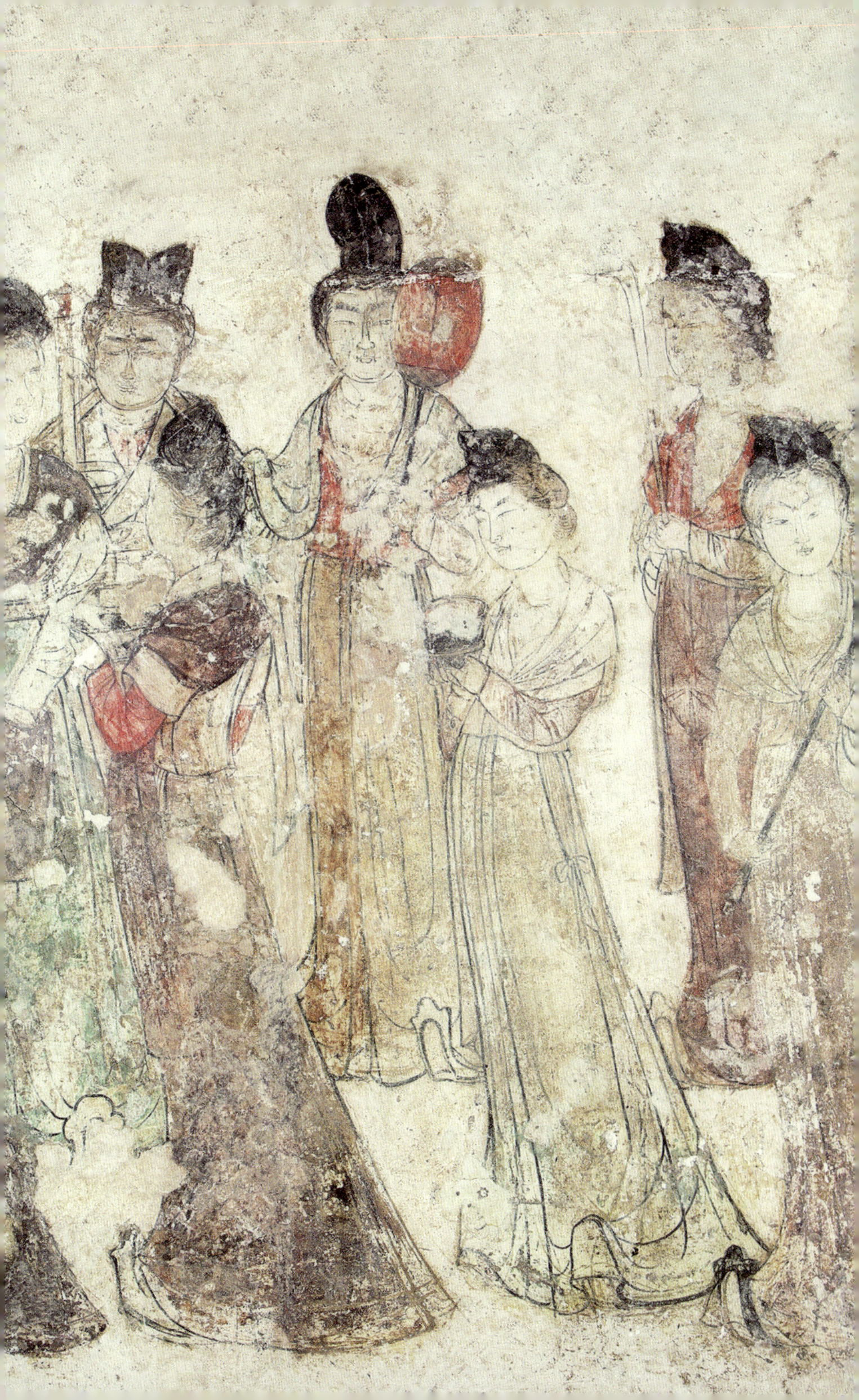

soldiers of the Qin, the daily life of the Han dynasty seen from the minute detail of its funerary objects, and the gold and silverware and sancai ceramics of the Tang.

It is no surprise therefore that over 370,000 relics have been unearthed in this province, including bronzes, pottery, stoneware, oracle bones, Han and Tang figurines,

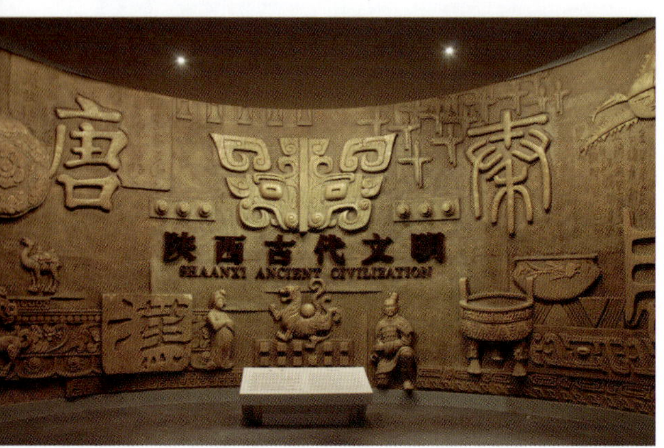

jade, copper, mirrors and brick tiles. There are pottery figurines from the Han and the Tang, as well as some of the finest gold and silverware, and a spectacular series of murals, from the Tang.

The collection contains 762 pieces of first class, 2,242 pieces of second class and 4,205 pieces of third class. The earliest exhibit is the prehistoric Lantian Apeman of 1,000,000 years ago; the latest relate to the Opium War of 1840.

The exhibition area of the museum is divided into three halls. The permanent collection is on display in the central Main Exhibition Hall, arranged historically and emphasizing some of the great achievements of art in Shaanxi, including the capital city Chang'an, the gold and silverware of the Tang dynasty, as well as its pottery figures, and the pottery figures and porcelain of the Song, Yuan and Ming dynasties. Throughout, the important role of the Shaanxi province in the development of Chinese history is traced.

One of the glories of the Shaanxi History Museum is a spectacular collection of Tang tomb frescoes, for which, at the time of writing, a new purpose-built exhibition hall is under construction. The murals come from more then twenty Tang tombs and cover more than 1000 sq m, delineating in vivid and elegant detail the court life, military, sports and pastimes of China's wealthiest dynasty. There are also pictures of foreigners who have arrived on the Silk Road. The tomb frescoes have been brilliantly preserved, having been peeled off the walls of the tombs to a depth of 5–10 mm, mounted on new backing and now conserved with the most advanced museum technology here – controlled temperature and humidity, and non-ultraviolet lighting system. The Tang murals alone are worth a visit to this museum.

Two other pieces are particularly treasured: one is a Tang dynasty animal-headed agate cup designed in the shape of a horn, with an antelope head and gold fittings. The other is the ingenious Dao Liu Hu pot; designed in one piece without any moveable lid, there is only one hole at the bottom of the pot through which it is filled, but which retains the contents when placed upright.

171

Xi'an Banpo Museum

半坡博物馆 *Xi'an Banpo bowuguan*

155 Banpo Road, Dongjiao, Xi'an, Shaanxi
陕西省西安市东郊半坡路155号
Tel: (029) 6281 5405
Open: 8.00–18.00, last entry 17.30, Mar 1–Nov 30;
     8.00–17.30, last entry 17.00, Dec 1–Feb 28/29
www.bpmuseum.com
Gift shop

Banpo is one of the earliest and finest Chinese archaeological site museums. The site itself is vast, with an excavated area of 50,000 sq m over various levels. The layout and topography is extremely interesting and there is so much to see, creating a vivid picture of the life of the original Neolithic inhabitants.

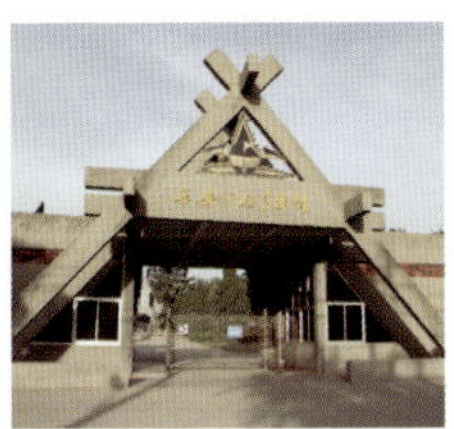
Red pot with nail pattern, Yangshao Culture

Banpo people lived 6,000 years ago, the biggest group yet known of the Yellow River Neolithic peoples. They were not only fishermen and hunters, but also early farmers. Some idea of their culture had been known about for some time, notably during the War of Liberation when Marshal Chen Yi had excavated some artefacts as his troops were digging trenches in the area, but the existence of Banpo as the major identifiable culture of the Yellow River Neolithic world was established only by the excavation of this site, which began in 1953.

Opened to the public in 1958, the site is elegantly covered in a steel and glass structure with walls in pale stucco reflecting the colour of the soil beneath. It was restored and re-opened in 2006. The grey-brown loess from which these remnants of Neolithic life emerge gives off a dusty impression of immense age, and, as always in Shaanxi Province, creates a sense of the layer upon layer of ancient civilizations lying underneath our own.

The visitor can choose whether to begin with the site itself at the end of the main courtyard facing the entrance, or to start with the two galleries of important excavated artefacts that are on the left of the main courtyard. There is much to be said for getting a feel for the site first. In any event, the two displays – the site and the artefacts – must be linked in the mind for the visitor to get the maximum from the experience.

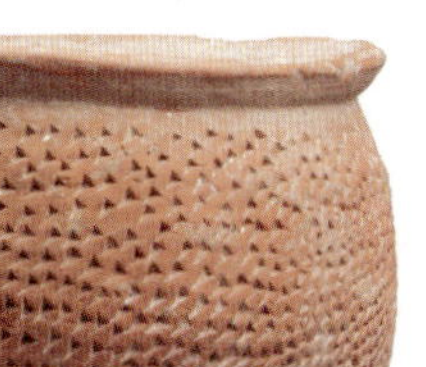
Red pot with V-bottom, Yangshao Culture

The site is surrounded by a huge trench, which covers an area of some 30,000 sq m containing residential areas within. These residential areas are clearly separated from others used for worship, pottery-making and burial. There are remains of more than forty houses, 200 cellars and storage pits, 200 adult tombs, some children's burial urns, two ditches, two pens, one worship site and six pottery kilns.

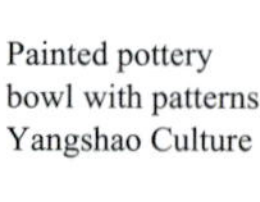

Painted pottery basin with fish and human face design, Yangshao Culture

The remains of the houses are semi-subterranean, some square, some circular; their outlines are clearly delineated by post-holes. Given the date and their physical nature, they give a fascinating insight into the evolutionary moment that mankind moved from cave dwellings into housing. In particular, it is easy to imagine the reality of the circular houses, which were supported by six beams, with sloping sides and a flat roof.

The square houses, with twelve posts arranged in three straight lines, are quite evidently the ancestors of the basic Chinese house and hall structure, which became the standard from the beginning of Chinese history to the twentieth century.

The storage pits were of many shapes and sizes and were scattered amongst the houses – some in the shape of a bag with a small mouth and big belly. Their inner walls were either plastered or burnt to help preserve their contents.

The kilns were either horizontal or vertical, mostly small, with space for not more than ten objects each. The most impressive remains of a kiln are housed separately in a building behind the main site.

There are two semi-circular pens near the ditches, which could have been fortifications or alternatively cattle pens. The function of the small ditch is unclear but the big ditch, sliced massively and deeply through the compacted soil, was clearly used for defence.

The graves were neatly dug, mostly individual but a few for group burial. Bodies were laid in deep soil facing west. Children were buried in small urns or jars.

There is also a standing stone pillar, 65 cm in height, which stands like a mystic sentinel with an apparently ovoid cross-section, and polished with striations on its surface. Its function is unknown.

Painted pottery bowl with patterns, Yangshao Culture

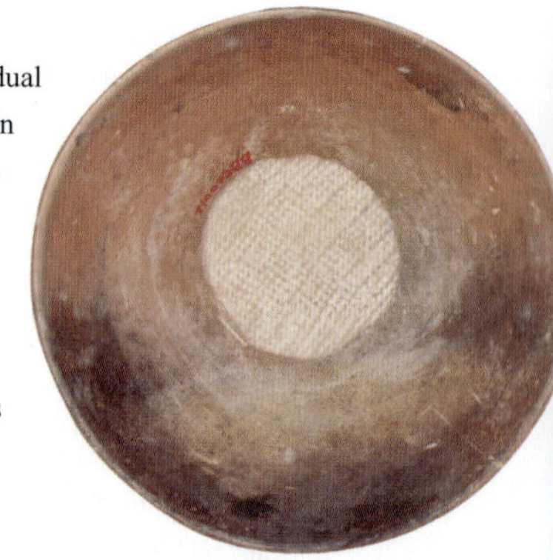

The Exhibition Galleries

More than 30,000 objects have been excavated on site; the finest, or most representative of these are displayed in two exhibition halls on the left-hand side of the main entrance. The first hall has objects such as stone tools, fishing implements, jade, and pottery rings. The second hall is dedicated to the very high quality red and black Neolithic pottery found at Banpo.

Almost without exception, the originality of the design and execution of these objects transcends their humble utilitarian function. Like the semi-subterranean houses of the site, they have a quality which exemplifies the emerging skill of 'man the designer'.

Amongst the artefacts illustrating the daily life of Banpo people are bone needles, bone shuttles and earthen spinning wheels, cooking ware, food vessels and pottery stoves for cooking, and fishhooks and other tools for fishing. There are also decorative pottery rings of elaborate design, and stone beads.

It is the pottery that is of the highest quality. Outstanding examples include a pottery basin painted with a human face and fish, showing a human face with a triangular headdress, with semi-abstract fish on each side of the mouth. The subject matter and the style of its execution is the source of intense speculation amongst archaeologists, both for the strength and originality of its imagery and also because of the light it shed on the possible role of the fish in the shamanistic religion of Banpo Culture.

Banpo pottery usually consists of black painted decoration – mostly of human heads, fishes and birds – on a reddish ground. The style is geometric. Also not to be missed are some quite extraordinarily realistic pottery sculptured human heads, and human and animal figures.

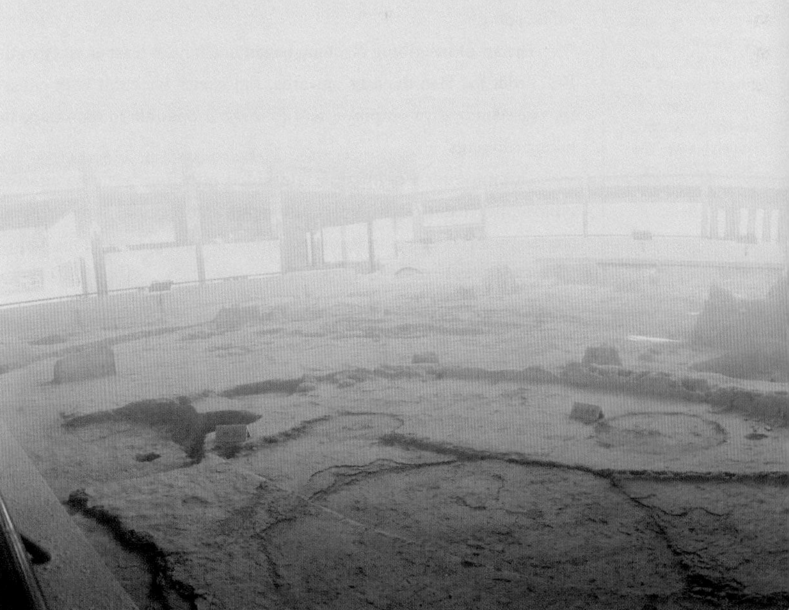

Xi'an Beilin Museum

172

西安碑林博物馆 *Xi'an beilin bowuguan*

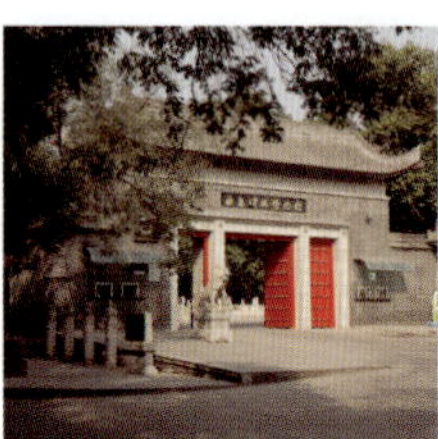

15 Sanxue Road, Xi'an, Shaanxi
陕西省西安市内三学街15号
Tel: (029) 87263686
Open: 8.00–18.15 summer; 8.00–17.45 winter
www.beilin-museum.com
English audio guide / Small book and gift shop

The Forest of Steles Museum, known in Chinese as the Beilin Museum, is one of the key depositories of Chinese culture – its core being an indispensable collection of classic texts and of masterpieces of calligraphy engraved on stones – or stele. It offers a graphic insight into the role of calligraphy – the most prominent art in Chinese culture.

Opened in 1952, in the former Temple of Confucius, it is located beside the southern section of the city wall. Its collection of more than 1,000 inscribed stones started in 1090, when a large collection of steles carved in AD 837 – of the oldest existing texts of the Confucian classics – was moved to the back of the temple for safekeeping.

The art of inscribing on stone began in China at least as early as the fourth century BC. From the Han dynasty onwards, flat stones were cut with either text or pictures for commemorative purposes, and to make it possible to reproduce them on paper by taking rubbings.

The museum's collection is divided into four basic categories: literature and philosophy, historical records, calligraphy and pictorial stones. Especially interesting are the pictorial stones in Room 4, almost all dating back to the Ming (1368–1644) or Qing (1644–1911).

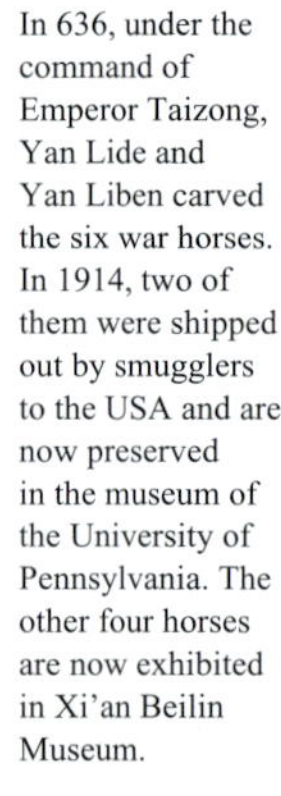

Six Steeds of Zhao Mausoleum: In 636, under the command of Emperor Taizong, Yan Lide and Yan Liben carved the six war horses. In 1914, two of them were shipped out by smugglers to the USA and are now preserved in the museum of the University of Pennsylvania. The other four horses are now exhibited in Xi'an Beilin Museum.

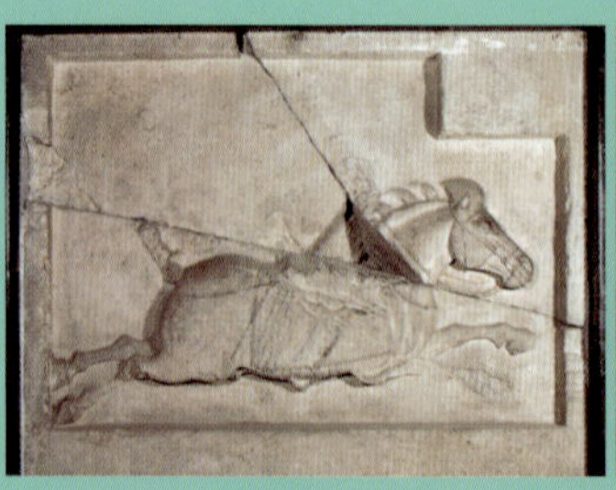

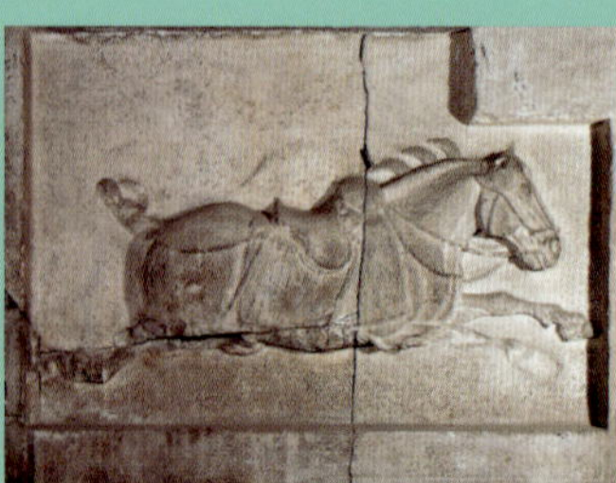

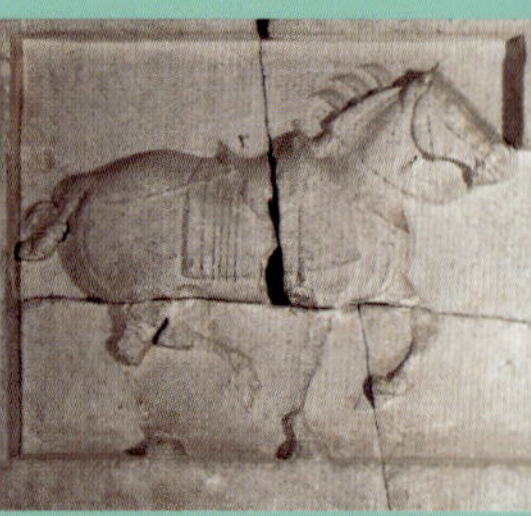

In Room 1 there is a set of 114 stones engraved in AD 837, which are known as the Kaicheng Classics. These include the Book of Changes, the Book of History, the Book of Songs and the Analects of Confucius. An impressive 650,252 characters are inscribed on the front and back of just one stele. Room 2 holds a valuable Nestorian stele, carved in 781. The stele bears the history of the Nestorian Christian community in

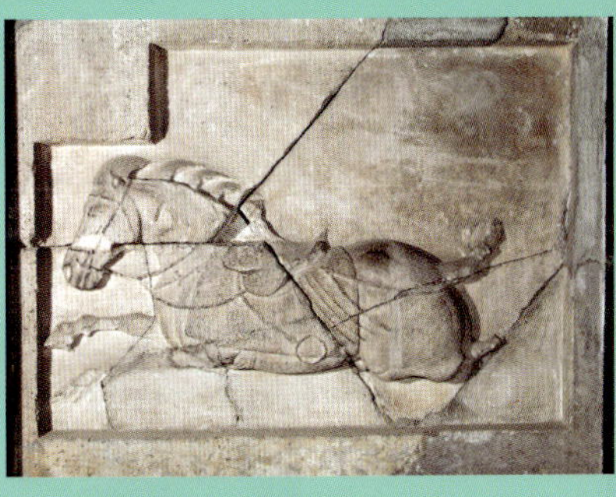

Chang'an, beginning with its founding by a Syrian missionary in the seventh century. Notice the small cross inscribed at the top, and the Arabic script at the bottom. There are also examples of calligraphy by many of the Tang dynasty's leading calligraphers. The stele have served as models for students practising calligraphy. Room 3 houses an important calligraphy collection. A stone carved by Shi Mengying in 999, during the Northern Song dynasty, bears characters in the ancient seal script, with the corresponding character in the later normal script inscribed immediately below each ancient character. Room 4 displays examples of poetry from the Song to the Qing dynasties, in the original handwriting of the authors. In Room 5 are stele of the Song, Yuan, Ming and Qing dynasties, primarily dealing with temple renovation and individual merit. Most of the inscriptions in Room 6 are poetry, written by the literati of the Yuan, Ming and Qing periods. Room 7 exhibits inscriptions by emperors, famous ministers and calligraphers throughout Chinese history.

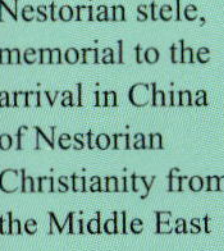

Nestorian stele, memorial to the arrival in China of Nestorian Christianity from the Middle East

The Stone Sculpture Gallery, just beside the museum, was built in 1963 and renovated in 1999. It houses some seventy excellent sculptures and relief carvings, the most famous among them being the six bas-reliefs from Zhao Ling, the Mausoleum of Emperor Tang Taizong. A number of large animals that once lined the approaches to imperial tombs of the Han and Tang are also on display, including lions, a tiger, a rhinoceros and an ostrich.

The exhibition also contains several Buddhist statues, including a very beautiful torso of a bodhisattva, showing the strong Indian influence typical of the Tang dynasty, and an Avalokitesvara on an elaborate lotus throne from the same period. Outside the sculpture gallery stands a collection of dozens of stone hitching posts, used during the Ming and Qing dynasties for tethering horses. The tops are decorated with carved animals and people.

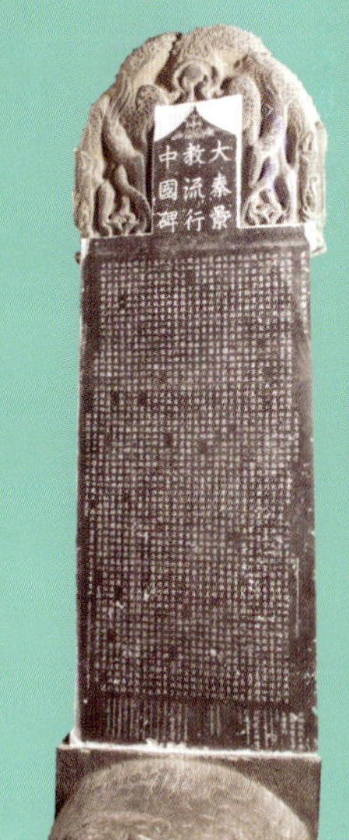

Xi'an Museum

173

西安博物院 *Xi'an bowuyuan*

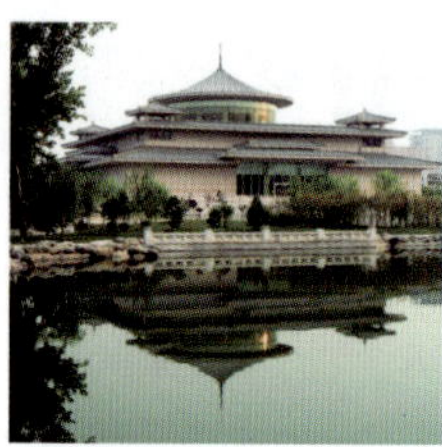

72 Youyi West Road, Xi'an, Shaanxi
陕西省西安市友谊西路72号
Tel: (029) 8788 8376
Open: 9.00–17.30 except Tues, last entry 16.30
www.xabwy.com
Gift shop / restaurant

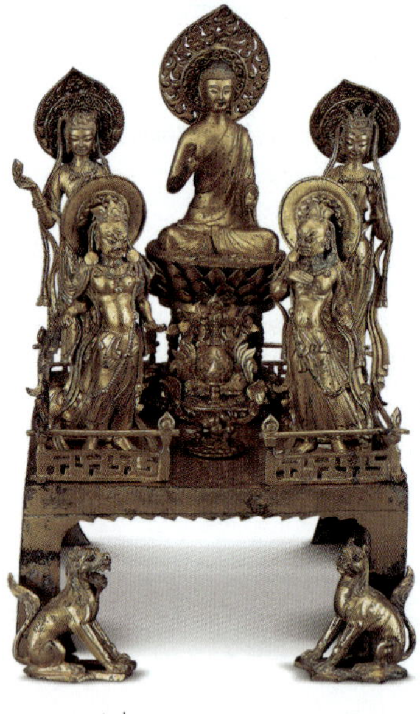

Gilt bronze
figure of
Buddha,
Sui dynasty

The very impressive new Xi'an Museum opened in 2007 in the park surrounding the Small Goose Pagoda. In the large lobby there is a marble map on the floor showing the layout of the city in different historical periods. Overhead, the ceiling is covered with a stylized lily.

The basement is a good place to begin a tour of the museum, presenting an excellent introduction to the history of the Xi'an city wall at different periods in Chinese history. Here, there are several wooden models of the ancient city. The first illustrates the walled city as it looked in the Han dynasty. The wall is not square, as it had to follow the contours of the Wei River. The Tang dynasty wall was quite large. The wonderful 1:1500 scale model shows a pagoda standing in each district of Chang'an, as Xi'an was then known. There were five gates in the wall and only the Emperor could enter through the south gate. Daming Palace, the home of the imperial court, can be seen in a separate enclosure to the northeast. Markets are visible outside the east and west gates of the wall. A third wooden model shows the city wall in the Ming and Qing periods, which represents the present-day shape of the wall.

The basement also has a section on ancient bronze ware from the Zhou to the Tang dynasties, including an elaborate bronze mirror. The collection includes a statue of a Qin charioteer, chariot parts, and tools, including axes, chisels and knives.

Of particular interest is a Hu pot in the shape of a silk worm, which was buried in the ground as a listening device to alert the military that the enemy was approaching. The museum also has what may be the world's first ever air conditioner – a metal box that contained pieces of ice.

An exhibition of pottery shows statues of the typically chubby women that were so admired in the Tang dynasty. The women wear long skirts and their shoes, which peak out from beneath their skirts, are curved. The elaborate hairstyles are particularly interesting. There are also tri-coloured galloping horses from the Tang dynasty. A number of foreigners can also be seen. One notable tri-colour features a foreign boy wearing a gown with a rounded collar while sitting on a horse. A model of a Ming dynasty funeral procession has seventy-seven figures, including one empty horse representing the deceased. Another Tang dynasty tri-colour shows a girl sleeping on the back of a camel. There is a coffin carved with intricate flowers and dragons and a coffin with a door.

The first floor has a wonderful collection of Buddhist statues. There is one stone statue from the Northern Wei dynasty and a beautiful statue of Guanyin, the Goddess of Mercy, from the Tang dynasty, which is gilded and painted, still showing traces of gold. The Buddha on display here is said to be the only one made of iron in China.

The second floor is devoted to Chinese calligraphy scrolls, including works by the legendary Zhang Daqian, as well as one Yuan dynasty scroll. There is also a collection of jade ware, including jade pigs from the Han dynasty, and all sorts of seals made from a wide variety of materials. Some of the characters on the seals are quite difficult to read, and so only recognizable to experts.

There are brief English descriptions with most exhibits.

There is also a 3D theatre here that shows a film introducing the history of the Small Goose Pagoda, a short walk from the museum in the park.

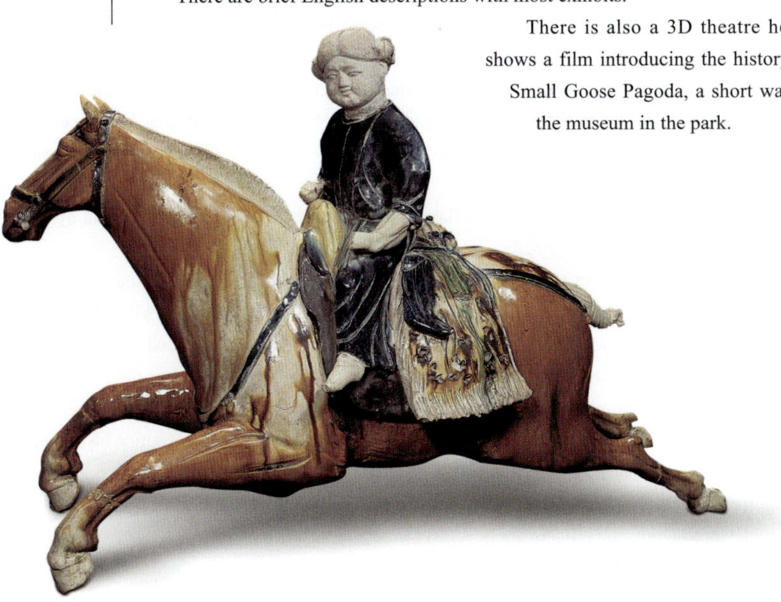

Tang tri-coloured glazed pottery figure of galloping horse and rider, excavated in the outskirts of Xi'an

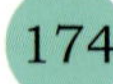

174

Yaozhou Kiln Museum

耀州窑博物馆 *Yaozhouyao bowuguan*

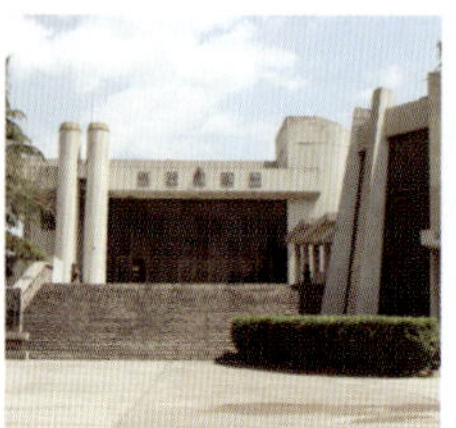

25 Xinyi South Road, Huangbao Town, Wangyi District,
Tongchuan, Shaanxi
陕西省铜川市王益区黄堡镇新宜南路25号
Tel: (0919) 7189 413
Open: 9.00–17.00 except Tues
www.yzybwg.com
Gift shop

If you have a special interest in ceramics and are visiting the sites of Xi'an, you can take in a trip to Huangbao in Tongchuan City, 80 kms south of Shaanxi's capital, to see the Yaozhou Kiln Museum.

Yaozhou pottery, sometimes called Northern Celadon, is mostly known for its olive green glaze, heavily covered in elaborate decoration consisting of flowers, clouds, dragons, phoenixes, fish, ducks and the like, although other glazes are also seen in Yaozhou ware.

The ware was first produced in the Tang Dynasty at which time the vessels appear rather coarse with an uneven glaze. Quality and varieties of shapes reached its peak in the Song Dynasty. The body of the vessels became thinner, the glaze even and the high fired pottery heavily decorated by carving and moulding. The richly coloured glaze often pools luxuriously around the carved design. In many objects the elaborate decoration covers the object both inside and out. Shapes included cups, bowls, censers, boxes, jars and more. The beauty of these objects made Yaozhou ware one of the most important celadon kilns in China.

The quality of the ware peaked in the Song, decreased through the Yuan dynasty and production was finally ceased in the mid-Ming Dynasty.

The museum's collection includes examples from all periods of production. Over 3 million pieces have been collected from the 200 workshops and kilns discovered over the archaeological site. In the galleries, the objects are displayed chronologically showing the development of the technology and artistry of Yaozhou pottery.

In addition to the exhibition of the wares and a visit to the excavations and kiln, the museum offers a hands-on area where visitors can see a demonstration of Yaozhou pottery production and even have a go at producing a piece in the pottery workshop.

Finally there is a reference and research section showing new methods of ceramic production and modern applications for ceramics.

For those who love to shop, modern Yaozhou ware made in the traditional fashion is widely available in town.

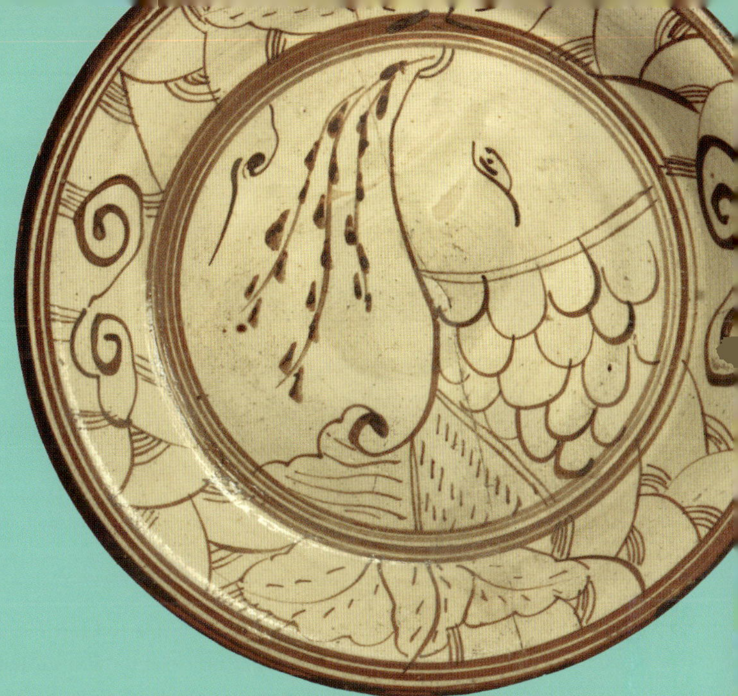

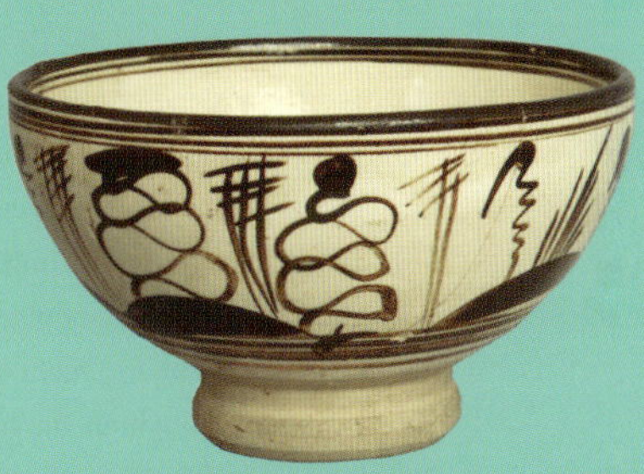

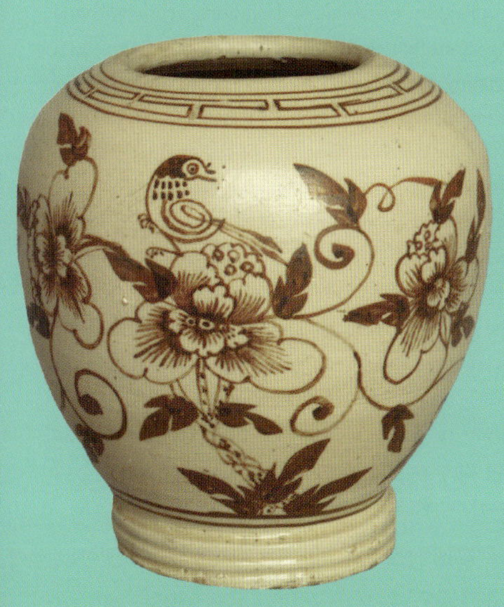

Ceramic ware, Ming dynasty

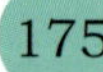

Inner Mongolia Museum

内蒙古博物院 *Neimenggu bowuyuan*

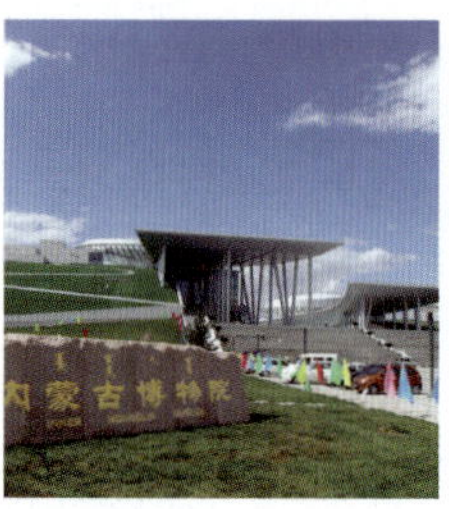

27 Xinhua East Street, Xincheng District, Hohhot,
Inner Mongolia
内蒙古呼和浩特市新城区新华东街27号
Tel: (0471) 4614 000 / 333
Open: 9.00–17.30 except Mon, summer;
      9.00–17.00 except Mon, winter
www.nmgbwy.com
Gift shop / café / restaurant

The Inner Mongolian Museum, formerly known as the Inner Mongolian Museum Institute, was founded in 1957, and is China's oldest museum to be found in ethnic minority areas. The museum combines distinctive ethnic characteristics and geographical features with modern museum techniques to highlight the history of the grassland-based ethnic groups, and vividly shows their development in contemporary politics, economy, culture and society. It constitutes in miniature an encyclopedia of the ecological vicissitudes of millions of years in the history of northern China, the history of grassland civilization of thousands of years, and the development of Inner Mongolia as a modern autonomous region.

The museum has an extensive collection of fossils and dinosaur remains found throughout Mongolia including the complete skeleton of a woolly mammoth. It possesses over 44,000 rare objects relating to the history of the northern tribes such as the Xiongnu, Xianbei, Qidan and Mongols, all of whom are of intrinsic interest and also resonate throughout the history of the northern frontiers of the ancient Chinese Empire. Of particular interest are the Mongol artifacts, including saddles, costume, archery and polo equipment; and also the collection of intricate Mongol bone carvings depicting and recording historical events.

Over three floors and fourteen displays, the museum tells the history of the Grasslands and their culture from the ancient fossils and into modern times with the exploitation of the region's mineral resources and its aerospace industry including the Shenzhou spacecraft.

The upper floor of the museum is dedicated to the great Genghis Khan (1162–1227), founder of the Mongol Empire and, at its height the ruler of much of Central Asia, creating one of the largest empires in history.

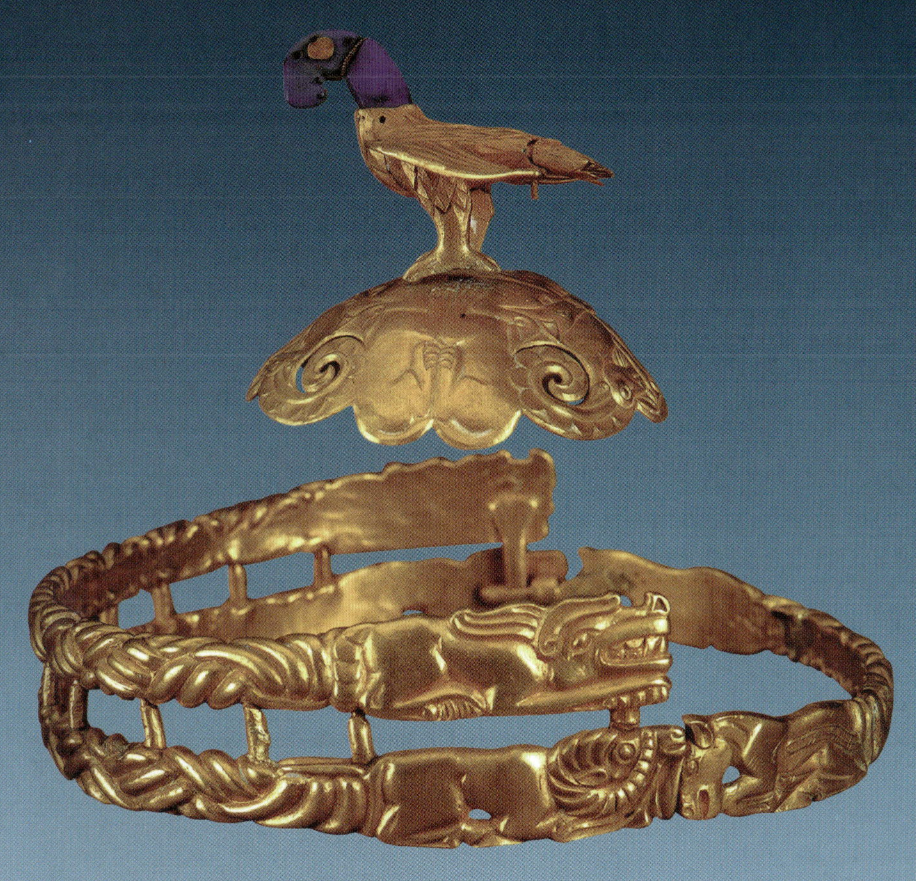

Golden crown of Xiongnu King, Warring States period

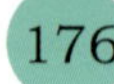

176

Ordos Bronze Museum

鄂尔多斯青铜器博物馆 *E'erduosi qingtongqi bowuguan*

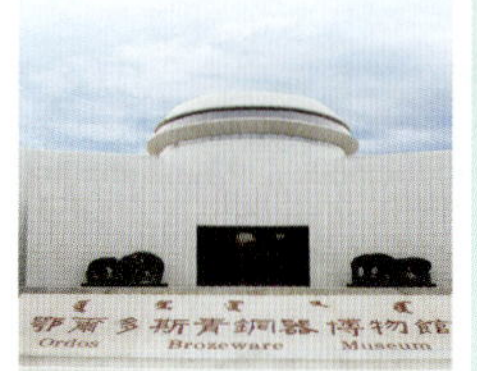

3 Zhungeer South Road, Dongsheng District, Ordos, Inner Mongolia
内蒙古鄂尔多斯市东胜区准格尔南路3号
Tel: (0477) 8323 026
Open all year round except Spring Festival
Gift shop

Ordos is located in the Inner Mongolia Autonomous Region of China.

From the first millennium BC, this region of grasslands and deserts was inhabited by nomadic tribes from the Central Asiatic Steppe. The fine metalwork of these groups bears a close resemblance to that of the Scythians and other west Asiatic nomads.

The Ordos Bronzes represent, for the most part, animal motifs and are usually decorative ornaments for horses, weapons, plaques or belt buckles and other small pieces to be attached to clothing. Very common are scenes of animals such as elk, oxen, horses, tigers – some shown in combat. This 'animal style' as it is called, reflects the nomadic life, and the importance of hunting in the culture.

The museum, built in 1989 and expanded in 2005, has a collection of over 10,000 pieces of which about 1000 are displayed.

Bronze ornament with the shape of ram

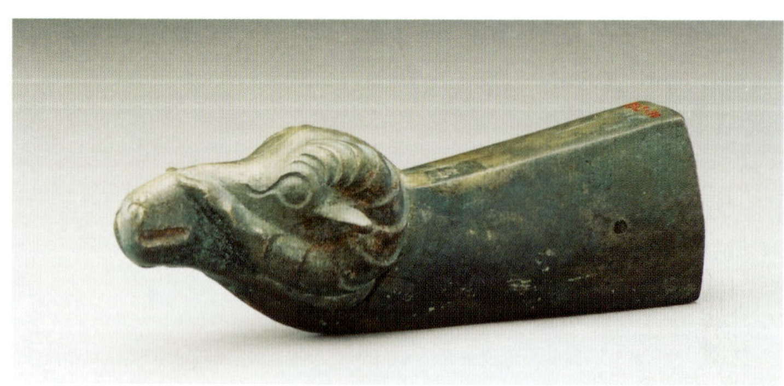

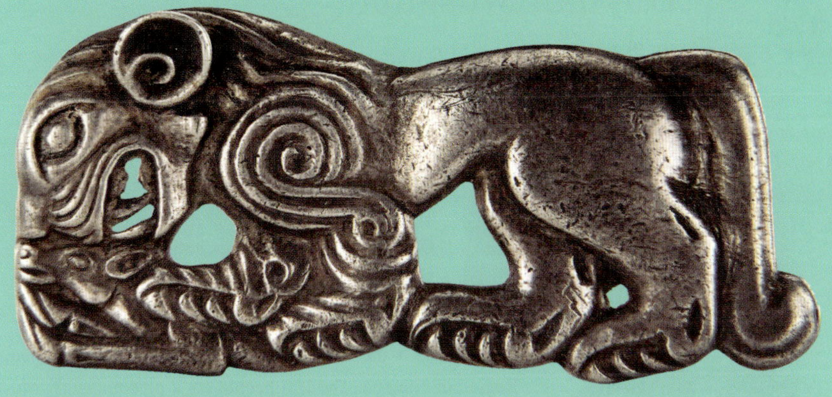

Silver plaque with tiger biting deer design,
Warring States period

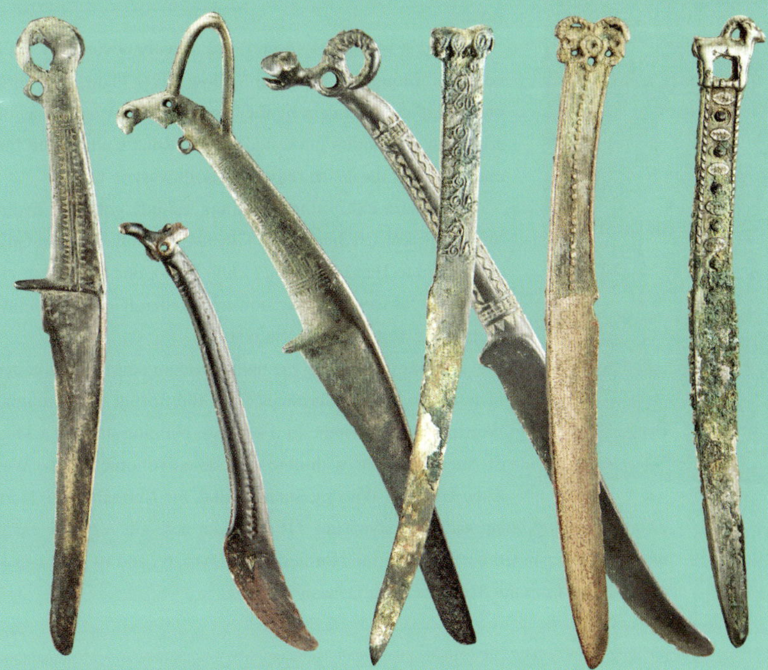

Ordos bronze weapons

Guyuan Museum

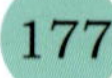

固原博物馆 *Guyuan bowuguan*

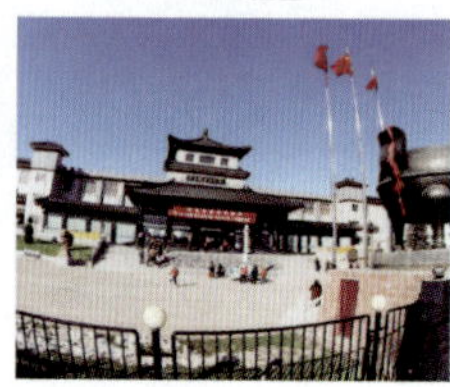

133 Xicheng Road, Guyuan, Ningxia
宁夏固原市西城路133号
Tel: (0954) 2698 189
Open all year round except holidays
Gift shop / bookshop

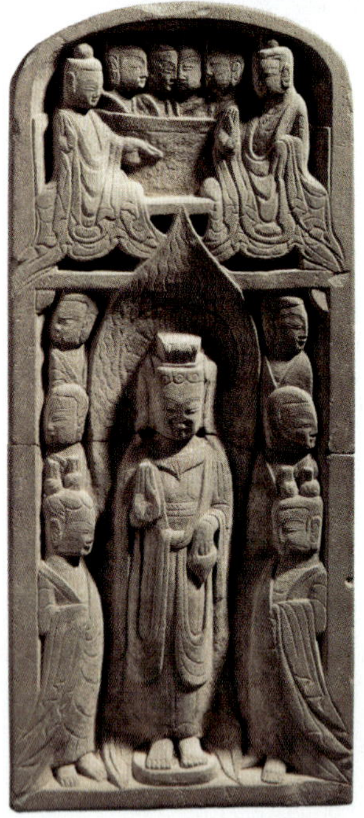

Northern Wei
dynasty stele

Guyuan is the southernmost region of the Hui Autonomous Region of Ningxia. The Hui people are a predominantly Muslim Chinese speaking ethnic group of some ten million found throughout China but predominantly in the North West and the Central Plains. Their culture shows the influence of Arabia, Persia and Turkic Central Asia as a result of their proximity to the Silk Road.

Ningxia is a largely desert area, mostly covered by the loess common throughout the great Yellow River Plain. It is bordered on its northern boundary by the Great Wall. Guyuan Museum will appeal to all visitors interested in Silk Road Culture and the life and culture of the desert regions of northwestern China.

The main exhibition buildings include galleries dedicated to the Ancient Civilization of Guyuan, the Silk Road in Guyuan, and a third to Han Liancheng (1909–1984), one of the four almost legendary 'hidden', hugely powerful generals of the Communist Party. He was a native of Ningxia.

The finest exhibit in the main museum building is a collection of northern Chinese bronzes from the Spring and Autumn and Warring States periods. In a separate building there is a Museum of Ancient Tombs with nine representative tombs of the Western Zhou Dynasty, Warring States Period, the Northern Wei, Northern Zhou, Sui, Tang, Song and Yuan dynasties. Of particular note are very fine examples of elaborated painted coffins from the Northern Wei Dynasty, and of gold and silver painted pots from the Northern Zhou Dynasty.

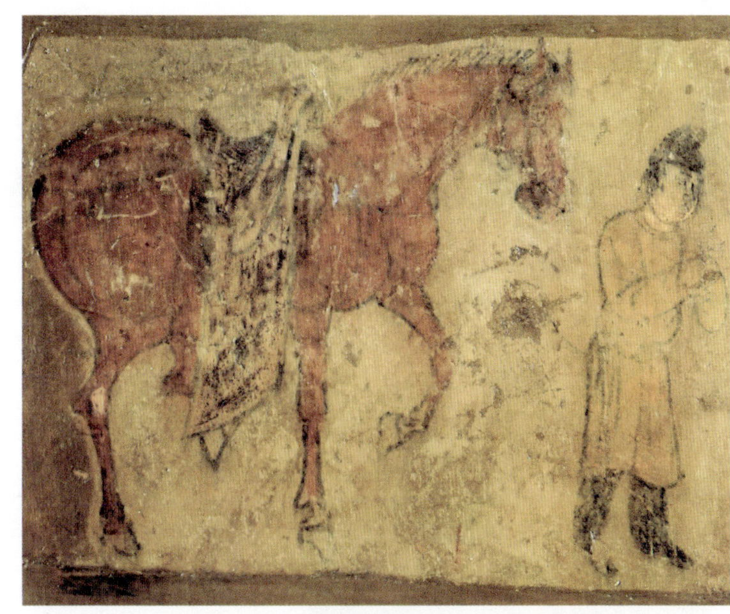

, Tang dynasty
all painting
detail)

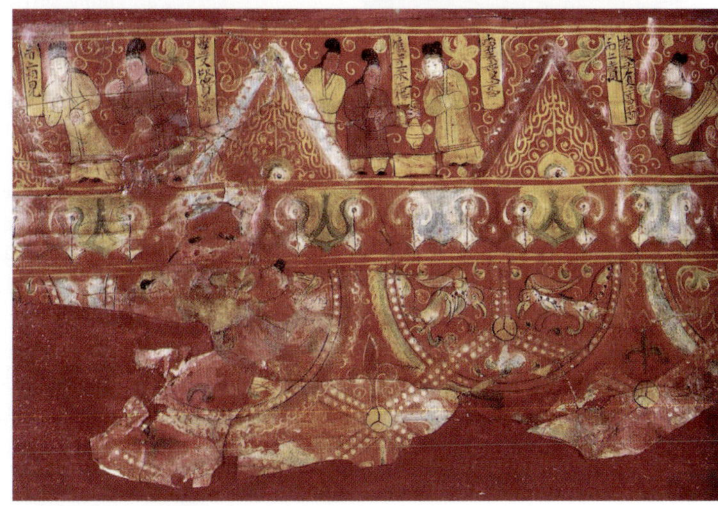

ainted coffins
om the Northern
Vei dynasty

Ningxia Hui Autonomous Region Museum

178

宁夏回族自治区博物馆 *Ningxia huizu zizhiqu bowuguan*

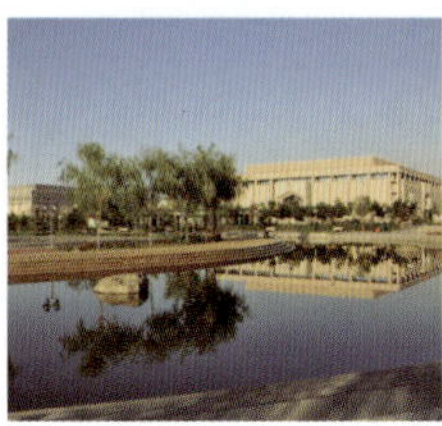

6 Dong Street, Renmin Square, Jinfeng District,
Yinchuan, Ningxia
宁夏银川市金凤区人民广场东街6号
Tel: (0951)5017 389
Open: 9.00–17.00 except Mon
www.nxbwg.com/en/index.asp
Gift shop / bookshop / café

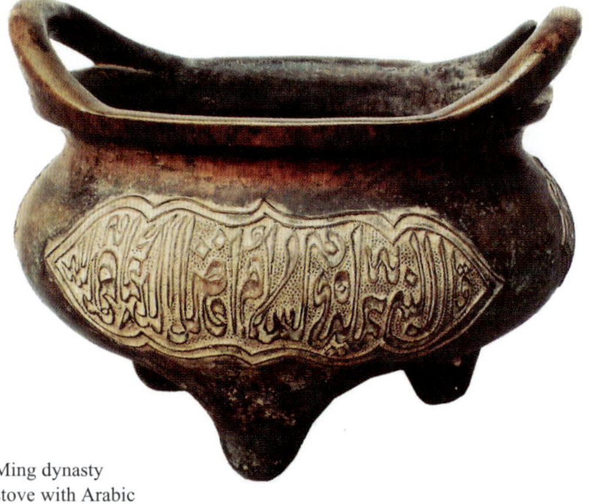

Ming dynasty
stove with Arabic
markings

Ningxia Museum is located on the grounds of the Chengtian Temple in the capital, Yinchuan City, of the Ningxia Hui Autonomous Region in the northwest part of China. This region is populated mostly by the ethnic Hui, Chinese Muslims who originally came to China from Persia and Central Asia.

Over four floors there are both permanent and temporary exhibition spaces providing sufficient room to devote complete halls to single key holdings, such as rock paintings, but also to cover the entire history of this region.

Among the stars in the collection are the displays featuring rock paintings from the Helan Mountains of Inner Mongolia. Carved into the rock are vivid images of mountain tigers, deer, wolves and some odd looking people decorated with horns or feathers. They date from the Spring and Autumn Period, as well as the Warring States Period and Western Xia Dynasty. They have been found in more than twenty places along a 200-kilometer stretch and are numbered in the thousands.

Additional displays include finds from the Western Xia Dynasty and folk art produced by the Hui. There is also a gallery filled with paraphernalia relating to the Red Army and the revolutionary base area of Shaanxi-Gansu-Ningxia set up to assist the Red Army with labour and resources in their fight against the Kuomintang from 1927–1945.

Dunhuang Museum

179

敦煌博物馆 *Dunhuang bowuguan*

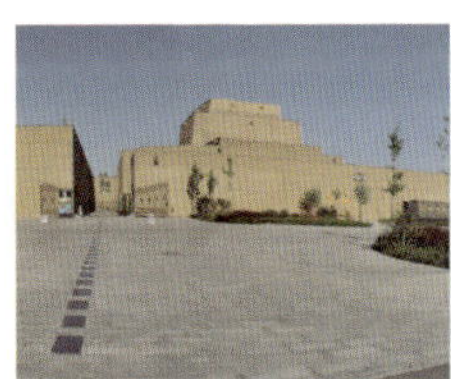

1390 Mingshan North Road, Dunhuang, Gansu
甘肃省敦煌市鸣山北路1390号
Tel: (0937) 8822 981
Open: 8.00–18.00 except Mon
Gift shop / bookshop

Opened in 2011, the new Dunhuang Museum is much more commodious than the previous one, which was rather cramped.

The collection encompasses the history of the city and county of Dunhuang and also the extraordinary wealth of objects found at the sites and excavations in the area.

The wealth of the local culture is illustrated in a display of local history spanning the Neolithic period to the nineteenth century; a miscellany including ceramics, old Chinese scrolls, coins, tools, tiles, bricks, bronzes, fabrics, jades and precious stones.

Of greater artistic and literary importance are some fine examples of classic Chinese and, in particular, Tibetan Buddhist manuscripts from the Library Cave (Cave 17) at Mogao, as well as hemp scrolls and other written and printed rarities.

There is a comprehensive and absorbing selection of locally excavated burial artefacts, including stone tablets, pagodas and pottery, and tomb guardians from the Han through to the Tang dynasties. Of particular interest are the decorative construction materials – lotus bricks and rare *qilin* bricks bearing a mythical deer-like animal sculpted in high relief.

The collection includes objects used for trade along the Silk Road, including fabrics, silks, Han bamboo strip documents, metal tools and weapons. There is also a reconstruction of the early Great Wall of the Han dynasty, together with objects and relics from its garrisons. Now in ruins, the wall once extended west even of Dunhuang to Yumenguan (the Jade Pass).

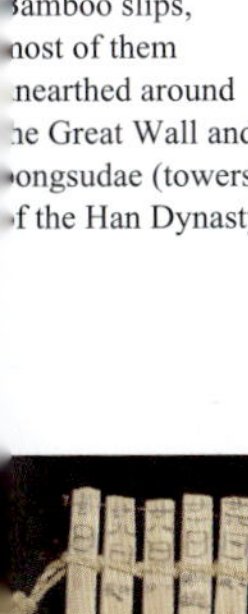

Bamboo slips, most of them unearthed around the Great Wall and fongsudae (towers) of the Han Dynasty

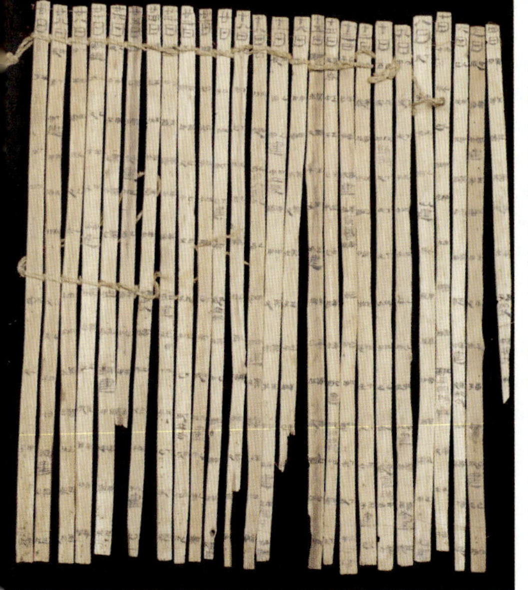

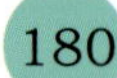

Mogao Grottoes / Dunhuang Academy

莫高窟/敦煌研究院 *Mogaoku / Dunhuang yanjiuyuan*

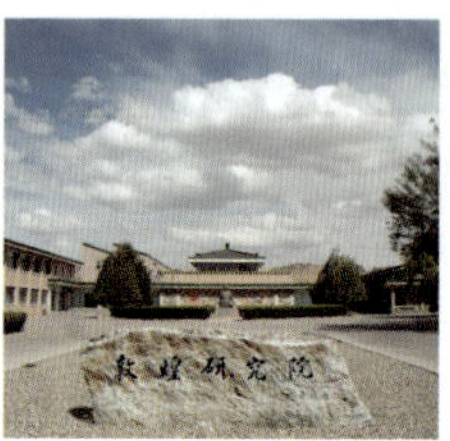

25 km from Dunhuang centre by bus or minibus, Gansu
甘肃省，距离敦煌市中心25公里
Open: 8.30–18.00, May 1–Oct 31; 9.00–17.30, Nov 1–Apr 30
www.mogaoku.net & www.dha.ac.cn & http://idp.bl.uk
English audio guide and written guide
Gift shop / book shop / restaurant / snack bar

The Dunhuang Caves consist of various Buddhist cave sites within the ancient county boundaries of the oasis trading city of Dunhuang, at the extreme western end of the Silk Road in China. Of these, the cave temples of Mogao, a World Heritage Site, provide one of the great experiences of China – indeed, one of the wonders of the world. The site itself, on the fringes of the Gobi Desert, is one of great beauty and resonance. The flat, reddish desert, pulsating with heat in summer, snow clad in winter, gives way suddenly to a wide valley carved out by the Daquan River.

On the west bank are cliffs varying in height from 15 to 30 metres. Into these, in four uneven layers, are carved a multitude of caves, of which 735 are extant, which contain no less than 45,000 sq m of wall paintings, more than 2,000 painted sculptures and some 50,000 manuscripts, works on silk and paper, and other precious artefacts.

Dunhuang is at the western end of modern Gansu Province – the western border of Chinese civilization. Beyond lay the barbarian world; and beyond that, the great civilizations of the Indian subcontinent to the southwest and the civilizations of western Asia and Europe in the distant west.

Dunhuang was not just a frontier town. It was a vital stage on the Silk Route – the great trading highway, arduous, perilous and time-consuming, but full of the promise of profit – that linked Rome, in the west, to Xi'an and Luoyang, the great capital cities of China, in the east.

Mogao was a meeting point for Indian Buddhist art and culture with Chinese civilization. The caves, founded by Buddhist monks in the fourth century, were inhabited as an isolated monastery for over 1,000 years. The murals with which they are decorated include some of the finest examples of Buddhist art in China, reflecting the changing style of Chinese art for more than a millennium, and ultimately, with a further move eastwards, providing the founding impetus for Japanese Zen Buddhism and for the creation of Japanese Buddhist art.

Five other major religions or systems are represented in the art of Mogao: Confucianism and Daoism from Central China, and Manichaeism, Zoroastrianism and

Nestorian Christianity from Persia and Central Asia.

Dunhuang was the place where the economy, culture, technology and social life of China met and mixed with that of Eurasia. This meeting had a dramatic effect on the appearance and development of Chinese Buddhist art.

The first cave was dug in 366 by a monk called Yue Zun from central China who had a vision of multiple golden Buddhas appearing in a cloud of golden light above the Sanwei Mountains. Shortly thereafter, a monk named Fa Liang joined him there from the east.

Mogao cave art flourished for more than 1,000 years, reaching its apogee during the early Tang period (618–755).

The essentials of Buddhist iconography had developed in India and Gandhara and changed little at Mogao, but the style and method of representation altered dramatically to create a uniquely Chinese version of Buddhist art.

The Mogao cliffs were composed of a friable conglomerate which defied carving – hence the decorative use of wall painting and clay painted statues as opposed to the earlier stone carved caves in India such as at Ajanta, or in Central China at Datong (the Yungang Caves of the fifth century).

The exteriors originally had wooden framed façades to simulate conventional buildings (although constant erosion has left only five caves with their external eaves intact). Inside, the decoration simulates a regular Chinese architectural structure with beams and rafters. There are five different types of cave, with uses ranging from group meditation, to cells for individual monks, to the great Buddha caves with massive figures, some over 35 m in height.

The cliffs on the west bank of the Daquan River into which are carved hundreds of caves

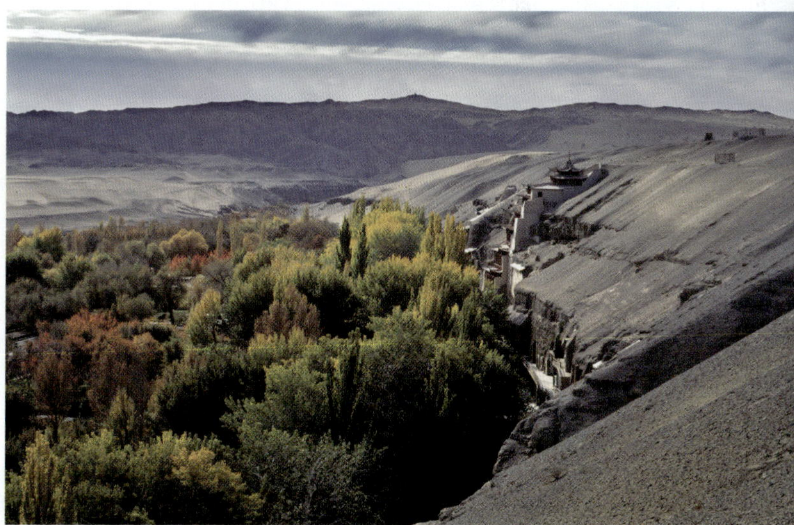

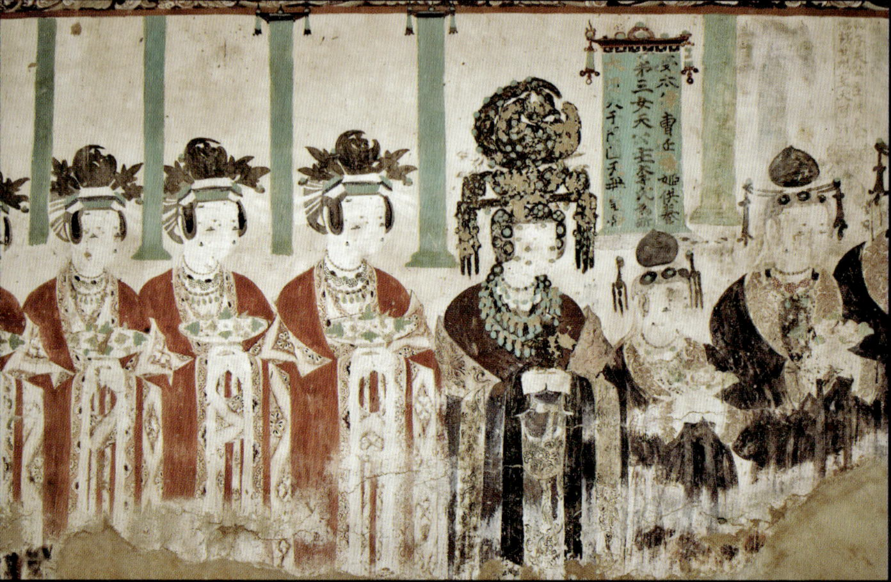

Cave 61 is on the ground floor of the middle section in the Southern District

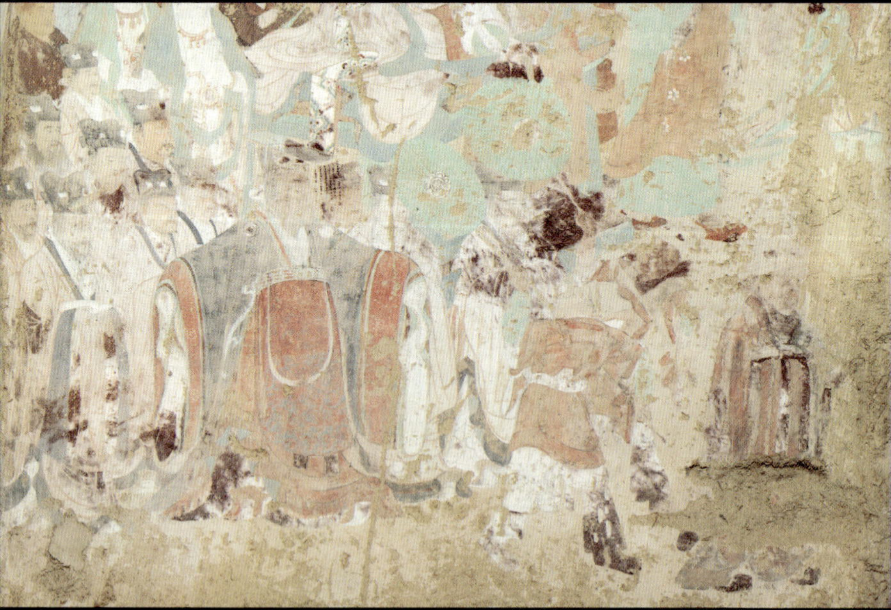

Cave 220 is located on the middle level in the Southern District. In 1943, the well-preserved Early Tang murals in this cave were revealed after the surface layer of the Song murals was removed

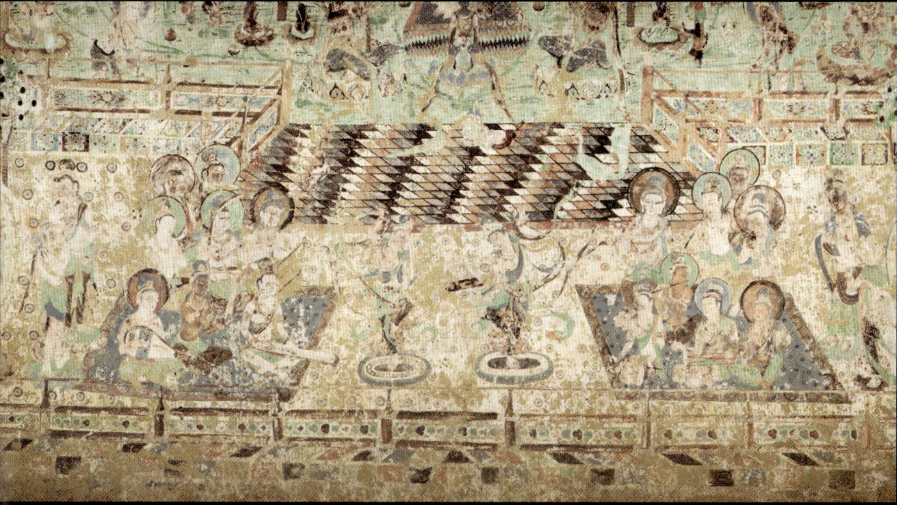

The south wall of Cave 220 is the earliest and largest Pure Land illustration at the Mogao caves

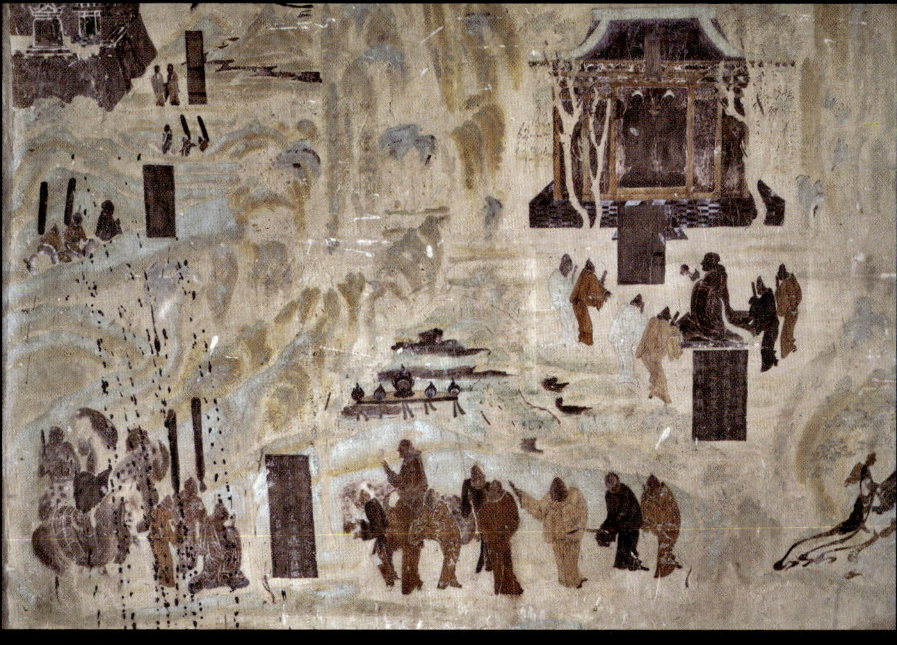

Cave 323: wall painting of *Zhang Qian's Travel to the West*

Apart from the giant Buddhas, which have stone cores, most of the statues have wooden skeletons, padded with reeds and covered with a mixture of clay and straw, which was then painted. Originally, the standing figures were broad-shouldered and Indian in style; over time they became more Chinese in appearance, with leaner, more square faces and flatter bodies. Under the Sui and Tang they come in groups of seven or nine. The mourners have exquisitely expressive features which contrast with the tranquil naturalness of Buddha's features as he enters *nirvana*.

The wall paintings were an integral – indeed the dominant – factor in the design. The cave walls were prepared with layers of mixed straw and clay which was then plastered. A great variety of both mineral and organic pigments were used to cover the whole area inside the cave. The total effect is truly extraordinary.

The paintings have seven different types of subject matter:

1. Paintings of Buddhas and other sacred figures such as boddhisatvas, disciples, *yaksas* (spirits) and *apsaras* (flying dancers and musicians who act as celestial servants to the gods).

2. Narrative paintings such as the *Jataka* stories of the life and acts of Buddha.

3. Paintings of gods and spirits, both Indian and traditional Chinese.

4. Sutra stories – the Buddhist scriptures visualized. At Mogao, these are transformed into large, complete series of narrative painting, illustrated here with a uniquely Chinese mastery of narrative and complex subject matter.

5. The story of Buddhism's journey east: the stories and myths of Buddhism's arrival in China, its power and efficacy, and the monks such as Xuanzang (602–664), who travelled to India in search of enlightenment and scripture.

6. Donor paintings: the portraits of the lay donors – both local and national – of Han, Tibetan, Tangut, Uighur and Mongol peoples, giving a fascinating record of the dress and appearance of men of power over a 1,000-year period.

7. Illusionistic architectural and decorative features of an extraordinary richness of detail and overall effect.

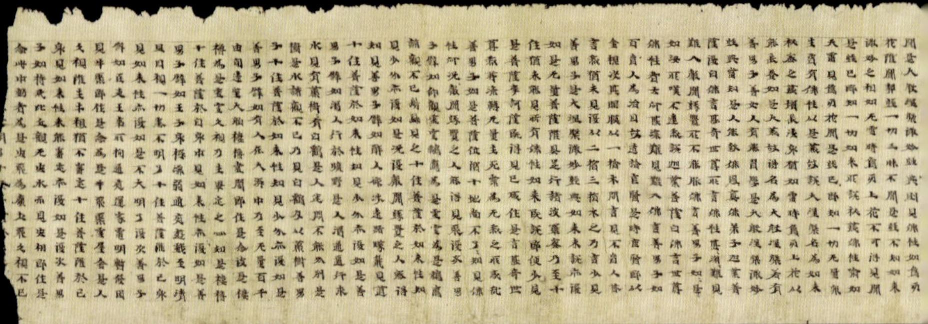

Mahaparinirvana Sutra, a Buddhist manuscript written on three-page white linen paper, Northern dynasties

Mogao has a major problem of conservation. Many of the paintings have over the years oxidized and become discoloured. Their preservation, and that of their ground, is a constant battle. Earthquakes and sand have taken a further toll. Wind erosion has weakened the ceilings of the caves and water has seeped down through cracks in the cliff, dissolving salts within the rocks near the wall paintings and causing further damage.

Furthermore, mass tourism would, if uncontrolled, cause the temperature, relative humidity and the carbon dioxide density within the caves to rise dramatically, further endangering the already seriously weakened wall paintings.

As a result, only twenty caves are open to the public, of which only ten can be visited, with a guide, at any given time. There is no choice offered as to which ones can be visited, although for a small additional fee a few more than ten caves can be seen.

The visitor should not be put off by this. Simply to visit some of these caves as part of a small group with an excellently informed guide in this remote site is experience enough.

In addition, there are eight reproduction caves, each beautifully executed and representing a significant period of art at Dunhuang, arranged by the Dunhuang Research Centre – together with an exhibition of objects from the caves. Both are highly recommended. Visit the museum that houses these after your tour of the actual caves.

The tour will definitely include a visit to Cave 17 – the Library Cave – the second reason for Mogao's international fame and importance.

In 1900, a small side cave was discovered off the corridor of Cave 16 during renovation work. It contained tens of thousands of ancient manuscripts, printed documents and paintings. The British and French explorers, Sir Aurel Stein and Paul Pelliot, with the help of a resident Daoist monk, Wang Yuanlu, acquired large numbers, mainly in Chinese and Tibetan, which were dispatched to the British Library

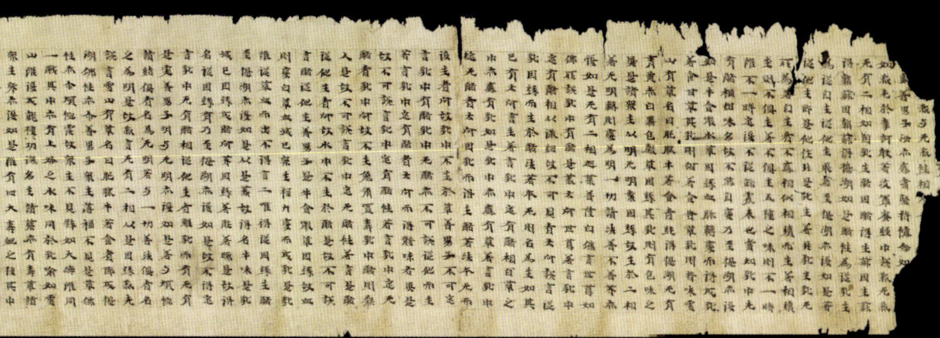

and the French Bibliothèque nationale in 1907 and 1908.

The cave must have been either a Buddhist library, or at least a source of ex-library copies from a local monastery.

Amongst its other treasures it contained the earliest complete printed book in the world, a copy of the *Diamond Sutra*, which was commissioned by a man called Wang Jie in memory of his parents in May 868. Outside, there is a permanent exhibition on the manuscripts related to the Library Cave.

There are a number of other cave sites in the Dunhuang region, although Mogao is justifiably the most famous and the most worthy of a visit. Of these, the visitor may want to take in the Yulin Caves (75 km west of Guazhou), with a site on the Yulin River almost as striking as Mogao itself; it is deeper and somewhat narrower. Yulin has forty-two extant caves, ranging from the seventh to the fourteenth century, containing 4,200 sq m of wall painting and 259 sculptures.

The true aficionado can also take in the Western Thousand Buddha Caves (33 km southwest of Dunhuang) and the Five Temple Site (40 km south of Mogao in present day Subei Mongolian Autonomous County).

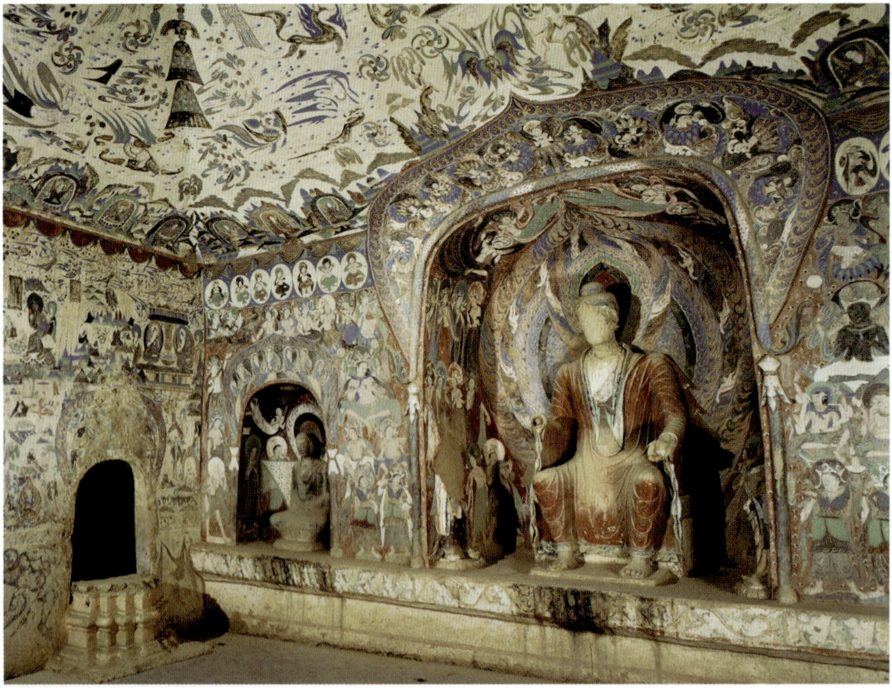

Cave 285 is located on the third level of the middle section in the Southern District. The ceiling centre features a parasol, while the four slopes represent images of the heaven, the secular world, and the universe

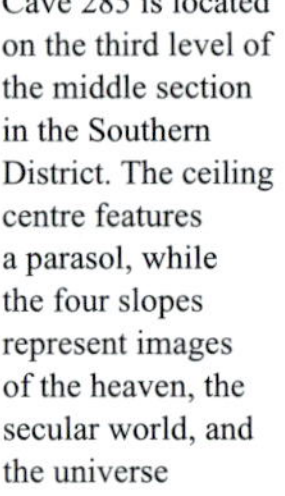

Jiayuguan Great Wall Museum

181

嘉峪关长城博物馆 *Jiayuguan changcheng bowuguan*

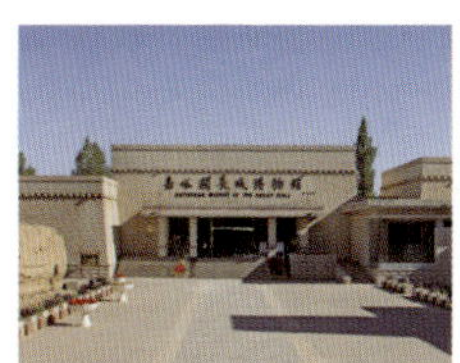

Yuquan Town, Jiayuguan, Gansu
甘肃省嘉峪关市峪泉镇
Open: 8.30–12.30 & 14.30–18.30 summer & autumn;
　　　8.30–12.00 & 14.30 & 18.00 winter & spring
www.jygcc.com.cn
Bookshop / gift shop

Jiayuguan was the Ming fort at the western end of the Hexi corridor in Gansu Province. With its 17-m towers with upturned eaves, it is one of the iconic images of Chinese history, situated at the western end of the Great Wall, the ultimate western frontier established in the Ming dynasty (1367–1644). Earlier, during the heyday of Dunhuang, the frontier extended westwards of that city to the Jade Gate Pass (Yumenguan).

Intermittently for 2,000 years, with a policy that operates once again in the twenty-first century, this frontier 'where Spring winds never blow' was re-populated by Han Chinese farmers relocated from central China, and defended by Han Chinese soldiers who lamented their lot of near exile and constant danger – their experience recorded in some of the most moving of Chinese poetry.

Bronze plate used to validate orders to border guards, Ming dynasty

The Ming fort at Jiayuguan has been heavily restored but it is still a potent symbol of the extremity of Chinese power, lying in an open valley with the snow-covered Qilian Shan mountains to the north and the black Mazong (horse's mane) mountains to the south.

The new Jiayuguan Great Wall Museum has a series of fascinating reconstructions of military life on the Great Wall, its defences, and the tools and artefacts that were used by its garrisons.

Border guard's identity plate

Jiayuguan may not be worth a special visit, but for the traveller by road coming westwards up the Hexi Corridor from Lanzhou to Dunhuang, it provides a breathtaking piece of historical evidence.

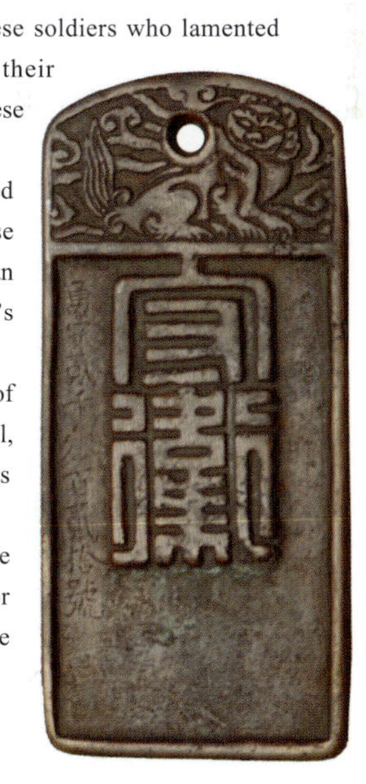

Gansu Provincial Museum

182

甘肃省博物馆 *Gansusheng bowuguan*

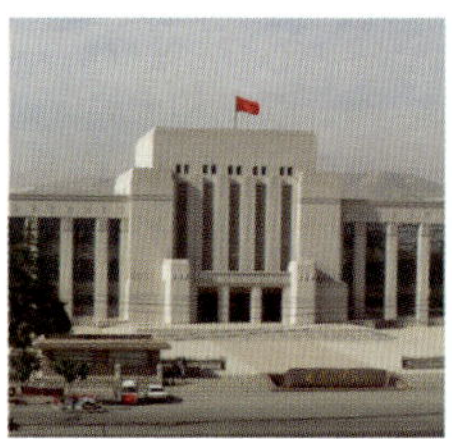

3 Xijin West Road, Qilihe District, Lanzhou, Gansu
甘肃省兰州市七里河区西津西路3号
Tel: (0931) 2339 131 / 133
Open: 9.00–17.00 except Mon, last entry 16.00
English- and Japanese-speaking guides are available
Shop / bookshop / coffee bar / restaurant

This massive, dour, Russian-style building covers 28,500 sq m of downtown Lanzhou. The new museum was opened in 2006. It houses a very important collection, reflecting both the historical and cultural importance of Gansu Province.

Gansu is old China's most northwestern province, a narrow strip of land that follows the course of the Yellow River from its emergence from the mountains eastwards for more than 800 miles along the Silk Road, taking in the Hexi Corridor – the 'throat of China'. It has proved a fertile source of pre-historic excavations, both of fossils and of very early cultural artefacts, in particular pottery. In historic times, Gansu came to prominence under the Han dynasty (206 BC – AD 220), with the growth of the importance of the Silk Road, and the Great Wall was extended westward through the province to Yumenguan (the Jade Gate Pass). Its importance declined during the Ming (1368–1644), in part due to the neglect of the Silk Road, but it became a separate province in 1666 under the Qing (1644–1911), with Lanzhou as its capital. In the 1920s and 1930s, Lanzhou was a centre of Russian influence and was very badly bombed by the Japanese during the war.

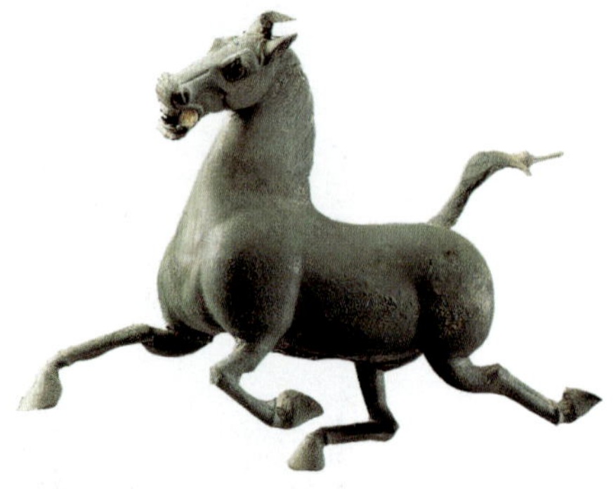

Bronze flying horse from Wuwei, Eastern Han dynasty

The museum directly reflects the cultural history of the province and the collection is divided into three main areas: the fossils of prehistoric animals; the ancient painted pottery of Gansu; and the culture and treasures of the Silk Road. All the objects have clear English signage.

The impressive fossil gallery houses some huge dinosaur skeletons along with what is reputed to be the largest complete fossilized skeleton in the world, of a mammoth (*Stegodon hunghoensis*), found in 1973.

Historically, the most important part of the collection is that of the primitive agricultural stone tools and early red-grey vessels from the Dadiwan site, which are 6,000–12,000 years old; and the Neolithic painted pottery, which is the chief local treasure of Gansu. The black and red painted pottery, some of it considerably sophisticated, includes magnificent examples from all the local cultures from 7000 to 476 BC – Yangshao, Majiayao, Miaodigou, Qija, Banshan, Siwa and Xindian.

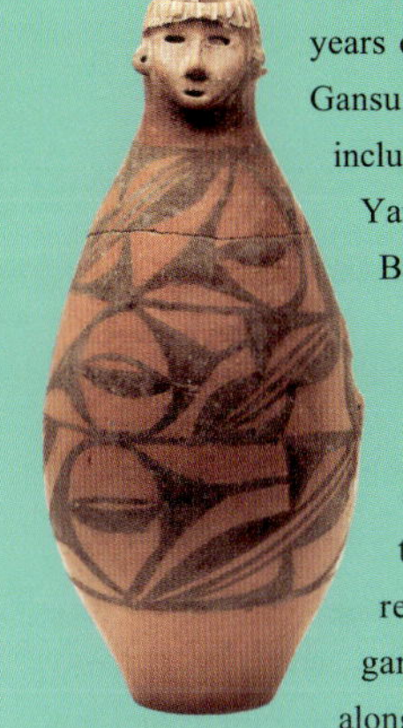

Painted pot, Yangshao Culture

The exhibition of the Silk Road treasures has its highlights in the Han dynasty. Of historical interest are more than 20,000 wooden tablets inscribed in ink recording the region's history, the fortunes of the garrisons, and events that took place along the Silk Road.

Of particular artistic interest are 220 Han bronzes excavated from the Leitai Tomb in Wuwei, including the world-famous Flying Horse of Wuwei (Eastern Han AD 25–220). This magnificent galloping beast, 34.5 cm in height, has one hoof on the ground, having trodden a small bird underfoot. This seems to have stopped the beast in full flight, as it were, and its neck and head have been thrown into an elegant sinuous contrapposto of almost Athenian fluency and subtlety.

There are many other national treasures, including many from the Mongol Yuan dynasty (1279–1368), the Mongols having conquered Gansu in 1235.

Stone statue of Avalokitesvara, Sui dynasty

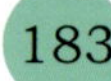

Liuwan Painted Pottery Museum

柳湾彩陶博物馆 *Liuwan caitao bowuguan*

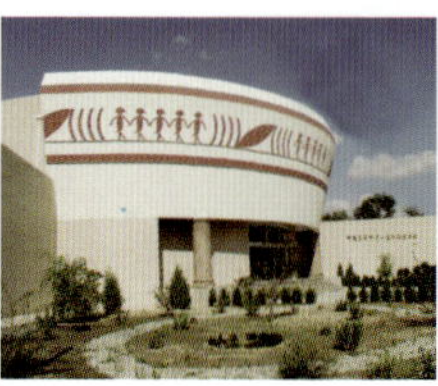

Liuwan Village, Gaomiao Town, Ledu County, Haidong District, Qinghai
青海省海东地区乐都县高庙镇柳湾村
Tel: (0972) 8658 151
Open all year round including holidays

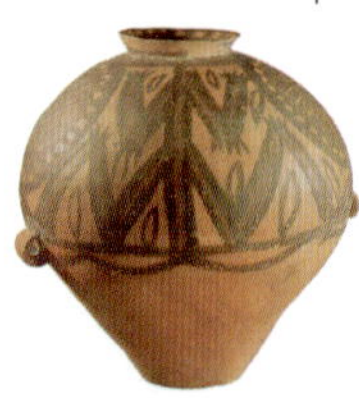

Located in Ledu County in the province of Qinghai, northwest China, this museum is the largest ceramics museum in the country with a collection of nearly 40,000 pieces, including over 20,000 examples of painted pottery dating from the Neolithic to the Bronze Age in Qinghai.

The museum is built near the large Neolithic burial site discovered near Liuwan village in the 1970s. Over 1,700 tombs from the Neolithic to the Bronze Age have been excavated yielding the majority of the finds in the museum. The painted pottery in the collection is from four distinct cultures: the Majiayao (ca. 3800–2000 BC), Oijia (ca. 2200–800 BC), Xindian (ca. 1500–1000 BC) and Kayue (ca. 900–600 BC).

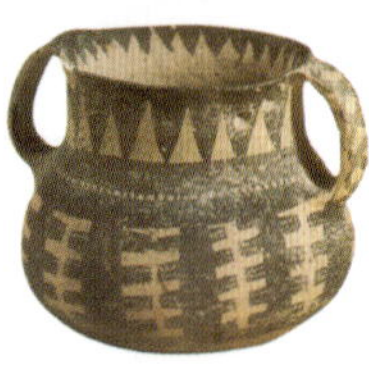

The Majiayao culture encompasses three phases each producing its distinct painted pottery. The Majiayao phase is characterized by spectacular, intricate spiraling designs produced in black ink on a red-buff earthenware body. The Banshan phase differs and is distinguished by its curvilinear painted abstract swirling patterns executed in dark red and black paint. Qijia culture, which followed the Majiayao at the juncture of Neolithic and Bronze Age development, produced pots that were sometimes unpainted and often imitations of metal vessels, indicating the introduction of metals at this time. Unique to this culture at the site are vessels adorned with an owl-like face with holes representing eyes and clay formed to produce the beak and ears. Characteristic of the Kayue culture were double-handled guan vases with large handles. Few pots from this culture were painted, but those that were decorated had simple lines and red triangular shapes.

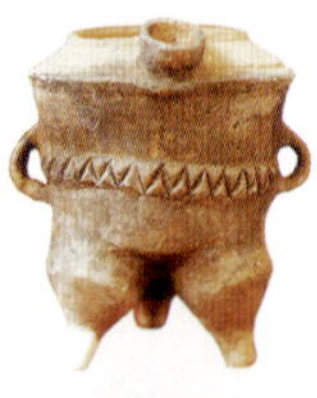

A majority of the artefacts on display are painted pottery. However, the museum also has examples of restored burial pits showing the placement of skeletons and surrounding vessels and other objects, such as stone spindle whorls, grinding slabs, axes, and bone awls and needles also unearthed from the tombs of the Liuwan cemetery. Two of the more distinctive finds are the trapezoidal stone axes with a single hole at one end and the bone shovels which were used to turn the soil and date from the Qijia culture. Their handsome display in well-lit cases permits the beauty of these finds and the painted decoration on the pots to be easily examined and appreciated.

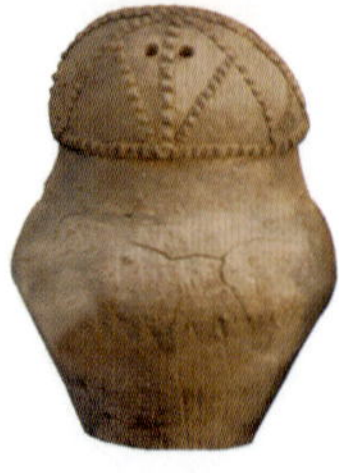

184

Hotan Museum

和田地区博物馆 *Hetian diqu bowuguan*

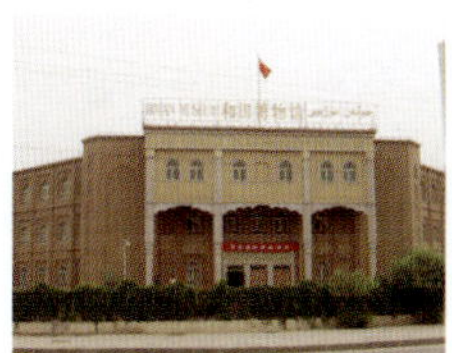

342 Beijing West Road, Hetian, Xinjiang
新疆和田市北京西路342号
Tel: (0903) 251 9286
Open: 9.30–13.30 & 16.00–20.00 except Wed, summer;
      10.00–14.00 & 15.30–19.30 except Wed, winter

The Southern Silk Road town of Hotan (Hetian) in the Uighur heartland has been renowned for its jade and silk products for more than 2,000 years. It is also home to the compact but rewarding Hotan Museum, comprising a ground-floor hall that highlights the development of human civilization along the southern edges of the Taklamakan Desert, and a first-floor display of all things related to Uighur Culture.

Downstairs, fossilized sea shells, Stone Age tools and Bronze Age pottery make way for Han period bracelets and carved pillars from the ancient ruins of Niya; wooden bowls, spoons and brocades showing intricate animal motifs and Chinese characters from the Sampul cemetery (created by the Udun people); and bone, jade, wood and clay artefacts from the ancient Silk Road cities of Karadong, Yotkan, Mazar Tagh and Rawak. Of special note are two Five Dynasties period (907–960) mummies from the Imam Musa Kazim cemetery and a fantastic ship-like wooden coffin still graced with colourful paintings of birds, dragons, snakes and tigers.

The upstairs Uighur gallery (photography permitted) has an excellent selection of carpets and jade carvings, as well as rows of *doppis* (Uighur caps), robes, a silk loom and examples of household goods and utensils, all of which help to create a picture of everyday life on the edge of the great Taklamakan Desert.

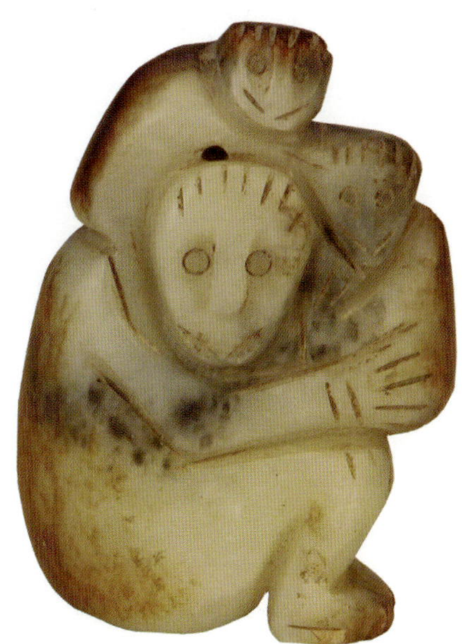

ng dynasty
de monkey

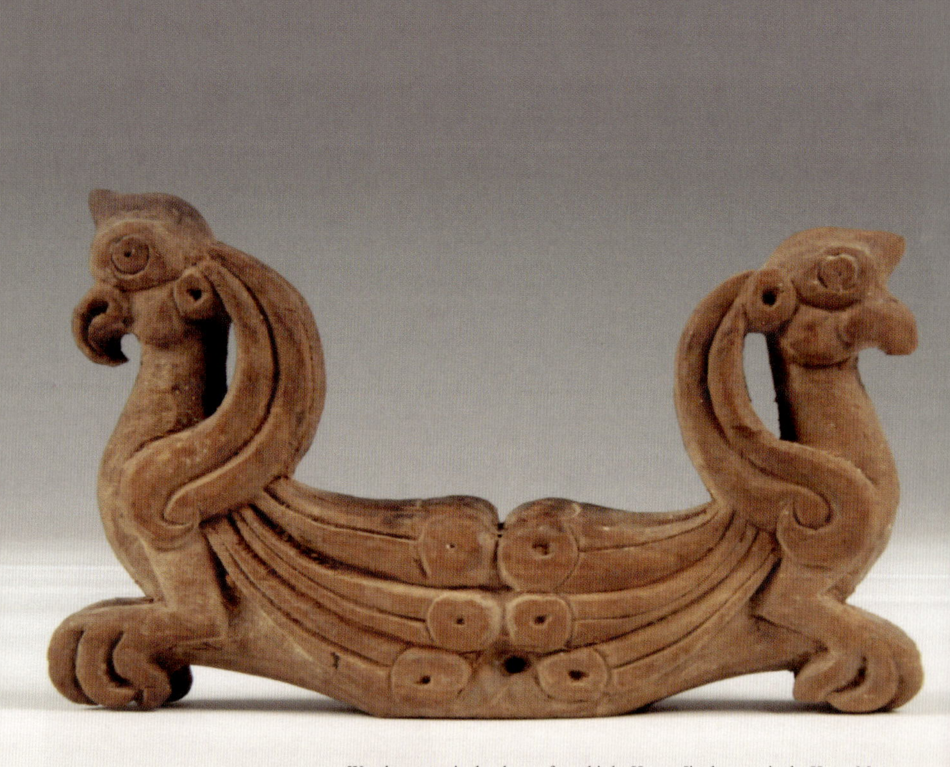

Wooden statue in the shape of two birds, Han or Jin dynasty, in the Hotan Museum

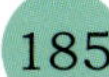

Turpan Prefecture Museum

吐鲁番地区博物馆 *Tulufan diqu bowuguan*

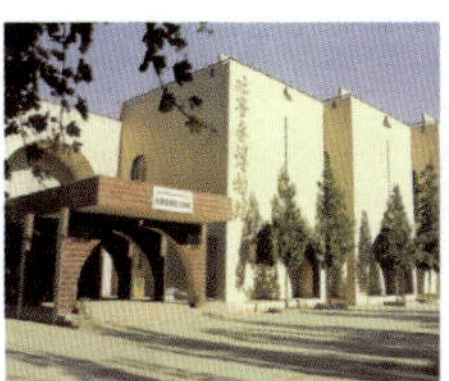

224 Gaochang Road, Turpan, Xinjiang (5-minute walk north of the main Public Square)
新疆吐鲁番市高昌路224号
Open: 10.00–19.00
www.turfanological.com

Turpan (Tulufan) is a popular Xinjiang tourist destination, but with so many nearby attractions its museum gets less traffic than it deserves (unfortunately, English is used only for exhibit headings and not for detailed explanations). Of the two halls on the ground floor, on the left is the Dinosaur Fossil Hall, containing a number of huge skeletons, the main one comprising actual bones discovered by railroad workers in 1993 of a 24-million-year-old creature named *Paraceratherium tienshanensis*. A first-floor open gallery around this shows the evolution of life and change in geography of the Turpan Basin, from lush swampy jungle 20 million years ago to dry desert today.

Also on the ground floor is the Culture and History Hall, with exhibits from archaeological digs at the major local sites of Jiaohe, Astana, Karakhoja and Gaochang. Upstairs is a room called The Ancient Corpses of Turpan, which were discovered only in the last few decades. There are twelve mummies in total (including two infants); a couple discovered in Astana cemetery in 1972 had documents buried with them showing dates (AD 502–640) and their family name – they are very well preserved, with the man's thin moustache still clearly visible. A nice touch is replicas of the couple in lavish Tang clothing standing next to the bodies, illustrating how they looked in life. Photography is allowed throughout the museum.

186

Xinjiang Ili Kazakh Autonomous Prefecture Museum

新疆伊犁哈萨克自治州博物馆 *Xinjiang yili Hasake zizhizhou bowugua*

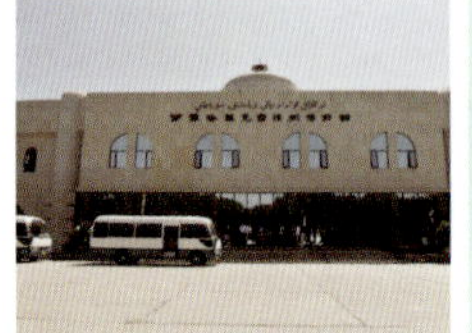

122 Feijichang Road (Airport Road), Yining, Xinjiang
新疆伊宁市飞机场路122号
Tel:(0999) 8222 907
Open: 9.30–19.30 except Mon, summer;
        10.30–19.00 except Mon, winter

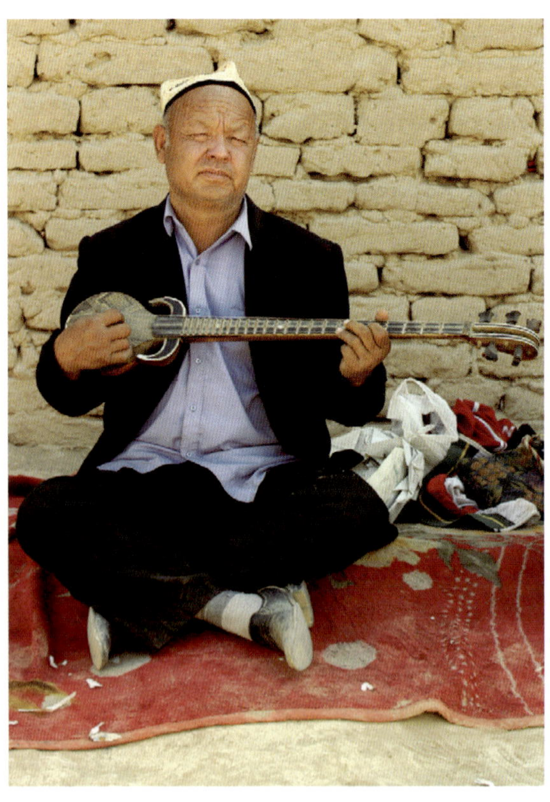

A street musician
in Xinjiang

A small but bright gem in a remote corner of China, this museum focuses on the history and culture of the Ili Kazakh Autonomous Prefecture, which includes all of northwest Xinjiang, from the fertile Ili Valley within the northern Tien Shan mountains to the Junggar Basin and Altai range in the far north. Of the three galleries, the first covers the prehistory period, displaying mammoth teeth from the Pleistocene era of a million years ago, petroglyphs from 8000 BC and early Bronze Age axes, sickles, arrowheads etc. The second details the rise of the great nomadic steppe cultures, showing skeletons, weapons, utensils and beautifully wrought gold work (look out for the superb fifth-century gold mask unearthed at the Boma Tomb in the Ili Valley), as well as a row of Altai anthropomorphic stone statues. The third gallery, the 'Gallery of Nations and Folkways', displays mannequins clothed in the various traditional dress of the thirteen indigenous ethnic groups (including the Han) of the region, with a centrepiece of a glorious Kazakh yurt surrounded by animal furs, horse harnesses, houseware and handicrafts. Photography is permitted only in the third gallery. A small but immensely interesting museum that is a must-see destination if you're in Yining.

Xinjiang Uygur Autonomous Region Museum

新疆维吾尔自治区博物馆 *Xinjiang weiwuer zizhiqu bowuguan*

187

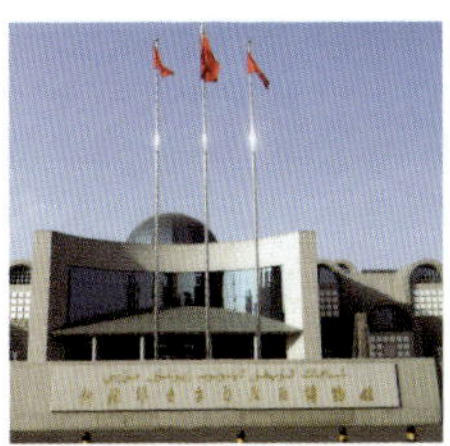

581 Xibei Road, Urumqi, Xinjiang
新疆乌鲁木齐市西北路581号
Tel: (0991) 4552 826
Open: 10.00–18.00 except Mon, last entry 16.30, summer;
10.30–18.00 except Mon, last entry 16.30, winter
www.xjmuseum.com.cn
Chinese / Uygur / English / Japanese guides are available

More than 2,000 years ago, as China began to develop into an empire of global significance under the Qin and Han dynasties, the empty land beyond its western borders was known simply as 'the Western Regions', a vast forbidding wilderness of mountain and desert, populated by 'savages' and all manner of demons. Today, the bulk of this region falls within the borders of the Xinjiang Uygur Autonomous Region.

The famous – and hugely important – Silk Road trade routes traversed Xinjiang's territory, skirting the infamous Taklamakan Desert and crossing high mountain passes on to farther lands. Along the way, caravans passed through oasis city-states that grew rich from the two-way traffic of merchant goods. These kingdoms also benefited from the ideas, technologies and religious beliefs that flowed between the major civilizations of East and West.

Over the centuries, the importance of the Silk Road waxed and waned, with the Xinjiang region's Buddhist kingdoms influencing Tang dynasty China (AD 618–907) heavily in religion, art and music, then playing host to the Mongol hordes of Genghis Khan, the conquering armies of Islam, and ultimately the military might of the Qing dynasty. But it wasn't until the late nineteenth and early twentieth centuries that foreign explorers began to unearth the immense cultural, historical and archaeological wealth that put Xinjiang at the forefront of Chinese anthropological exploration.

The best place to get a detailed overview of this fascinating legacy of many millennia of human civilization is in Urumqi at the Xinjiang Uygur Autonomous Region Museum. The museum's large new complex took five years to build, and was finished and opened in 2005. Its central domed entrance hall contains a 3D relief map of Xinjiang that immediately gives an insight into the importance of the region's topography in determining where and how humans could live and prosper.

The two-storey building is split neatly into four sections: on the ground floor, the subjects are the Silk Road and ethnic minorities, while upstairs a large room is devoted to Xinjiang's famous mummies and another contains memorabilia of the Chinese liberation of Xinjiang. It's best to visit the displays in chronological order, so first turn right and enter the 'Silk Road' down a tunnel-like corridor, walking on a Perspex layer over a sandy 'desert' floor.

This section actually covers a much greater time frame than its name implies – the first exhibit is an 8,000-year-old skull from Artux City, followed by pottery, wool and felt hats, and a dyed corduroy-style trouser leg from 1000 BC. A host of Bronze Age implements, colourful clothing and weapons are all in amazingly good condition and show excellent craftsmanship, but it is when you move on to the collection of items from the Western Han through to Tang dynasties that the incredible wealth of ancient artefacts becomes apparent. The dry desert conditions helped to preserve an amazing array of items that detail life in the oasis kingdoms, from silk brocades and copper seals to wooden tablets and official paper records; from Buddhist mural paintings to cakes and twisted dough sticks.

There are superb examples of Yuan dynasty horse halters, coins, gold figures and porcelain from the Middle kingdom, as well as rare Buddhist scriptures written in early Uygur Mongolian characters. The final section of the 'Silk Road' display shows Qing dynasty items such as jade and silver carvings, stone stelae and beautiful multicoloured silks from Hotan on the Southern Silk Road.

As comprehensive and compelling as the 'Silk Road' display is, above it on the first floor of the museum lies Xinjiang's highlight exhibit and its signature displays. A sign at the entrance to the temperature-regulated room says: 'Passed Away but Amaze the World Immortally [sic] '. This is your introduction to the famous Xinjiang mummies, and the first glass case contains the prize exhibit, the 'Loulan Beauty from Tiebanhe Riverside'. Excavated from Tieban River, north of Lop Nor, in 1980, with skin smooth and blackened by dessication, the corpse is a forty-five-year-old woman of Europoid origin, with red hair, a thin aquiline nose, and covered with a red-brown, rough wool blanket. Dated to 1800 BC, her features are delicate, her lips drawn back in a tiny, enigmatic smile, while fur-topped, leather-soled shoes cover her feet, and a feather, comb and woven basket are arranged around her exactly as they were when

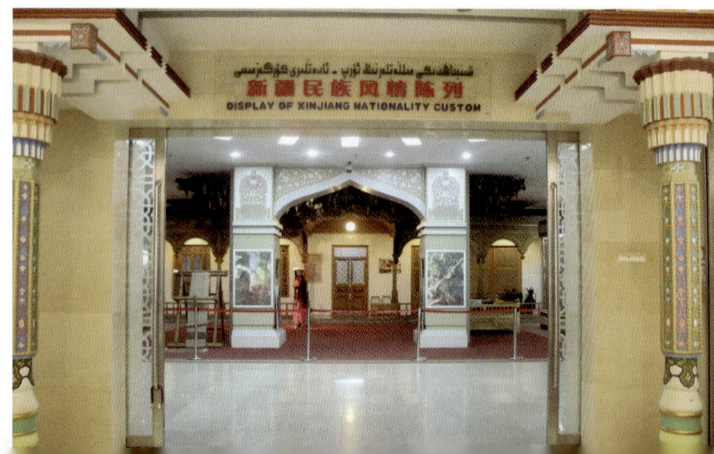

she was found.

Other mummies include a child, a boy of four to five years, swaddled in a wool blanket fastened with sixteen wooden pins; a long-haired adult female from 1800 BC discovered in the desert at the Xiaohe Graveyard and wearing a pointed felt hat with a weasel skin trim; and the dessicated corpse of one Zhang Xiong (583–633), whose feet retain incredible detail in the skin and toenails. Some of the mummies were excavated from the Astana tombs, Tang Chinese governors or military staff buried with bows and arrows alongside them, while a beautifully caparisoned male and female Europoid couple were exhumed from Qiemo in southern Xinjiang, buried alongside each other and dating to 800 BC.

After this emotive insight into Xinjiang's past, the 'Liberation' room on the same floor catapults you into the modern era. Unfortunately, where all the museum's other sections are clearly and informatively explained in English, this room has no English signage. So the military artefacts and memorabilia, including photographs and contract documents between the factions who fought for control of Xinjiang in the twentieth century, lose their potency.

Downstairs, however, the final section entitled 'Display of Xinjiang Nationality Custom', is well worth exploring in full, as it explores each of Xinjiang's twelve ethnic groups. You enter into a replica of a Uygur courtyard and house, with a wonderful display of Uygur musical instruments, and then pass through rooms highlighting each nationality's unique dress and customs, from Kazakh yurts to dummies of Mongolian wrestlers, Kyrgyz livestock and Xibe archers, and from Russian iron-and-brass beds to Daur hanging cradles.

A modern, well-planned museum, this is an essential stop on any Xinjiang tour, preferably visited before you move on to the region's main historical sites. The insight you gain here will augment your subsequent experiences.

Ethnic Minorities in China

The population of China is not a single homogeneous culture but is made up of many separate ethnic groups. The official count is fifty-six, the largest group of which is the dominant Han, making up about 92 per cent of the population.

A number of these groups, such as the Tibetans and the Uygurs, have their own territories, called Autonomous Regions, but in fact these regions are closely controlled by the central government.

The figure of fifty-six minority groups is a disputed number as there are countless subdivisions between some of these groups.

Some of these minorities have their own language (not a Chinese dialect). In addition, there are twenty-one unique systems of writing amongst China's ethnic minorities. Additionally, each group has its distinctive customs in terms of dress, religion, social mores, cuisine etc., giving them a strong sense of individual cultural identity.

CHINESE MUSEUMS ASSOCIATION GUIDE

BEIJING AND THE NORTH

THE NORTHEAST

SHANGHAI AND EAST CHINA

THE YANGTZE

THE SOUTH

THE SILK ROAD AND THE NORTHWEST

TIBET

HONG KONG, MACAO, TAIWAN

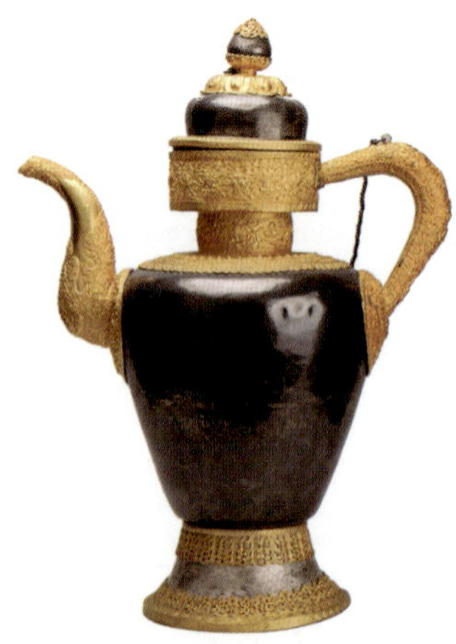

西藏

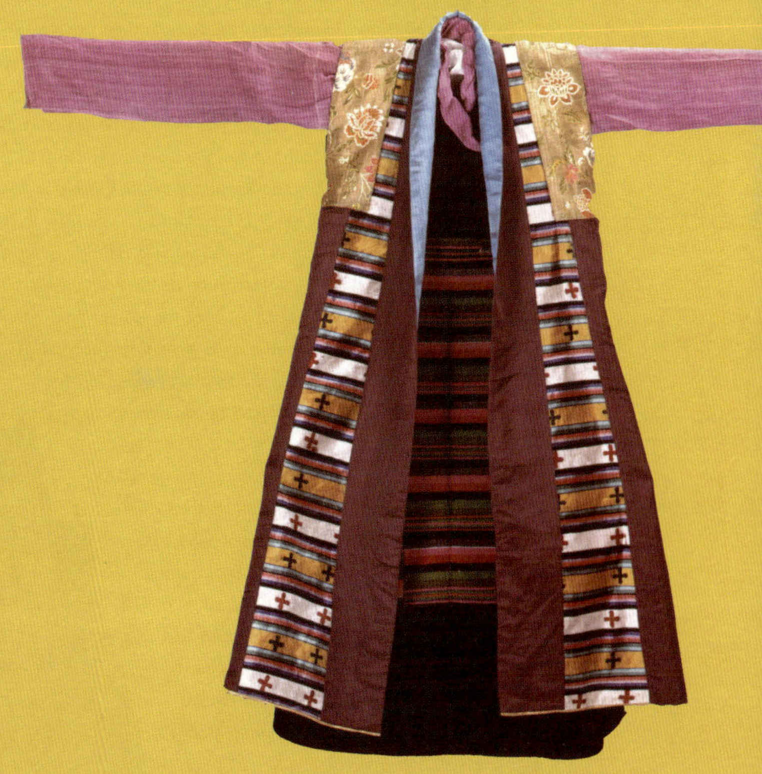

188

Potala Palace

布达拉宫 *Budala Gong*

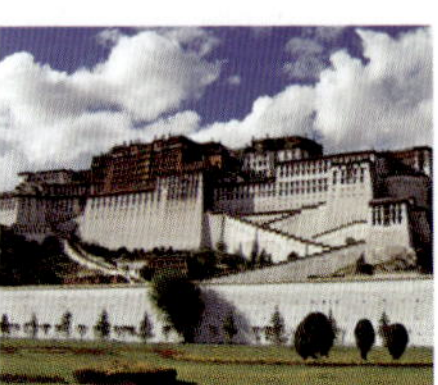

35 Beijingzhong Road, Chengguan District, Lhasa, Tibet
西藏拉萨市城关区北京中路35号
Tel: (0891) 682 2896 / 683 0427
Open: 9.00–12.00 & 15.30–16.30; tickets are limited, best to bu
a day ahead
Tibetan and Mandarin guides are available

With the increase in tourism, both Chinese and international, and the opening of the railway from Beijing, the number of visitors to the palace has increased to such levels that it has had to be rationed daily to about 2,300. Booking in advance is therefore recommended. A passport is required. The duration of visits is limited. Individuals have two hours and groups one hour. All bags (including cosmetics) must be checked. Remember that this is not just a museum but also a place of worship for many Tibetan pilgrims. Be respectful and honour their privacy.

The original palace that stood on this site was built by the seventh-century King, Songsten Gampo (r. AD 627–49), who also built the two holiest temples in Tibet – the Jokhang and Ramoche. A new palace was built in the same location 1,000 years later by the illustrious 5th Dalai Lama, Ngawang Losang Gyatso (1617–1682). Work began on the construction of the Potrang Karpo, or White Palace, in 1645. It was completed three years later, and in 1649 the 5th Dalai Lama moved from the Gelupa Order, Drepung Monastery, to his new residence. The building was then further enlarged with the construction of the Potrang Marpo, or Red Palace. The White Palace was used for secular purposes, both residential and bureaucratic, as it served as the seat of Tibetan government, while the Red Palace was used for religious affairs. It contains chapels, schools, libraries and even the tombs of several Dalai Lamas.

The 5th Dalai Lama was a charismatic and scholarly leader who united Tibet under the Gelug – or Yellow-Hat Sect – of Buddhism, made Lhasa the capital and was responsible for combining the secular and religious leadership roles of the Dalai Lama, which is maintained to this day. In an effort to avoid conflict or chaos, his death in 1682 was concealed for twelve years until the Red Palace was completed

The palace's sloping stone walls are 3 m thick and 5 m thick at the base

in 1694.

Since its construction, the Potala has been the home of all the Dalai Lamas, although since the building of the Norbulingka summer palace in the late eighteenth century, it has served solely as a winter residence. The 13th Dalai Lama undertook some renovation work in the early twentieth century, demolishing sections of the White Palace to expand some chapels and in 1959, the Potala sustained some damage during the Tibetan Revolt. The palace is now a UNESCO World Heritage Site.

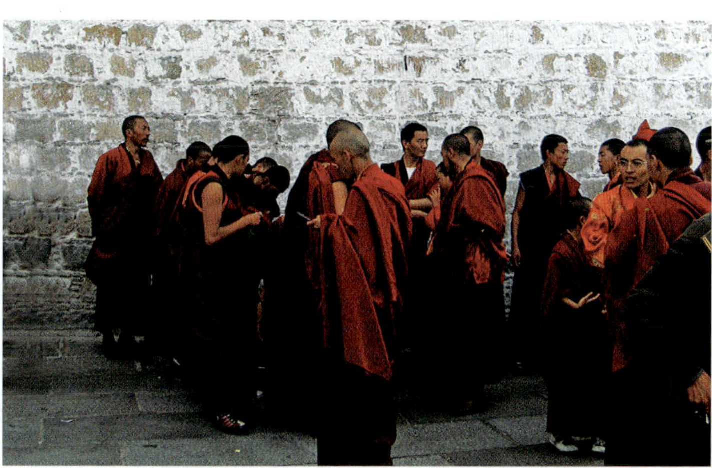

A visit to the Potala is overwhelming. The colourful palace is brimming with murals, paintings, pillars, statues, furniture, rugs, jewellery and more. The air is rich with the smell of yak butter which burns in the hundreds of lamps set before holy statues bedecked with the ubiquitous white ceremonial scarves; at their bases, cases stuffed with cash offered in the hopes of wishes being granted. The halls are crowded with an incongruous mix of Western and Chinese tourists and incessantly chanting Tibetan pilgrims, many of whom have travelled in arduous conditions to pray here. You will not see all 1,000 rooms in a visit of two hours – best to simply soak in the extraordinary atmosphere. For the voyeur, look at the private rooms of past Dalai Lamas, including that of the present 14th Dalai Lama as it was when he fled to India in 1959. And from the roof there is a magnificent view of Lhasa below.

The main attractions on the third floor are the Chapel of Maitreya, the Tomb of the 13th Dalai Lama, the Chapel of Three-Dimensional Mandalas, the Chapel of Victory over the World and the Chapel of Immortal Happiness.

The highlight on the second floor is the small, seventh-century chapel of Arya Lokeshvara – Potala's most sacred image. The chapel is one of the palace's oldest surviving rooms.

189

Tibet Museum

西藏博物馆 *Xizang bowuguan*

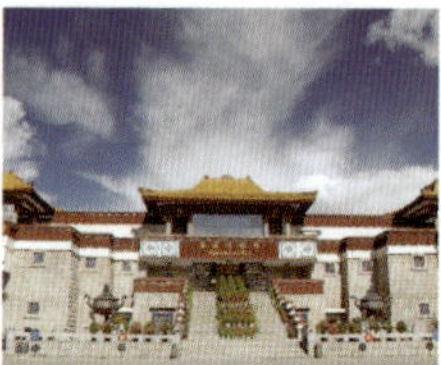

19 Luobukalin Road, Lhasa, Tibet
西藏拉萨市罗布卡林路19号
Tel: (0891) 681 2211 / 683 9222
Open: 9.00–12.00 & 14.30–17.30
Chinses / Tibetan / English / Japanese audio guide

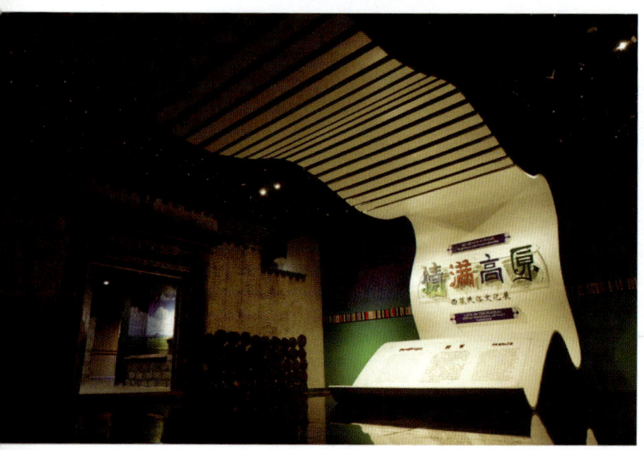

This museum building, in style a combination of Tibetan and Chinese, was designed by a Han Chinese architect from Sichuan Province and was opened in October 1999 with great fanfare. As the sign says at the entrance, the museum was 'built under the kind care of the Central Committee of the Communist Party of China'. The history of the Sino-Tibetan relationship, and reminders of China's righteous hegemony, is the message running throughout the museum's choices of exhibits as well as its signage. Notwithstanding the tremendously unsubtle political subtext, many of the objects here are of great interest.The Prehistoric Gallery exhibits material from the Paleolithic, Neolithic and Bronze Age, with the highlight being the Neolithic pottery excavated in the 1970s from the Eastern Tibetan site of Karo.

The Tibetan History and Culture Gallery has many highlights, among them the Golden Vase. There are two copies of this, one originally in the Jokhang Temple and one in the Lama Temple (Yonghe Gong) in Beijing. It was a gift from the Qianlong Emperor, and from it was drawn the lots determining the appointment of the Dalai Lama's reincarnation. This vase was also used in 1995 to determine the government-sanctioned selection of the 11th Panchen Lama.

Weapons from the Western Tibetan kingdom of Guge, which flourished from the ninth to the seventeenth centuries are exhibited. This kingdom was a centre of foreign trade and strong supporter of Buddhism, and was influential in the spread of Buddhism throughout Tibet.

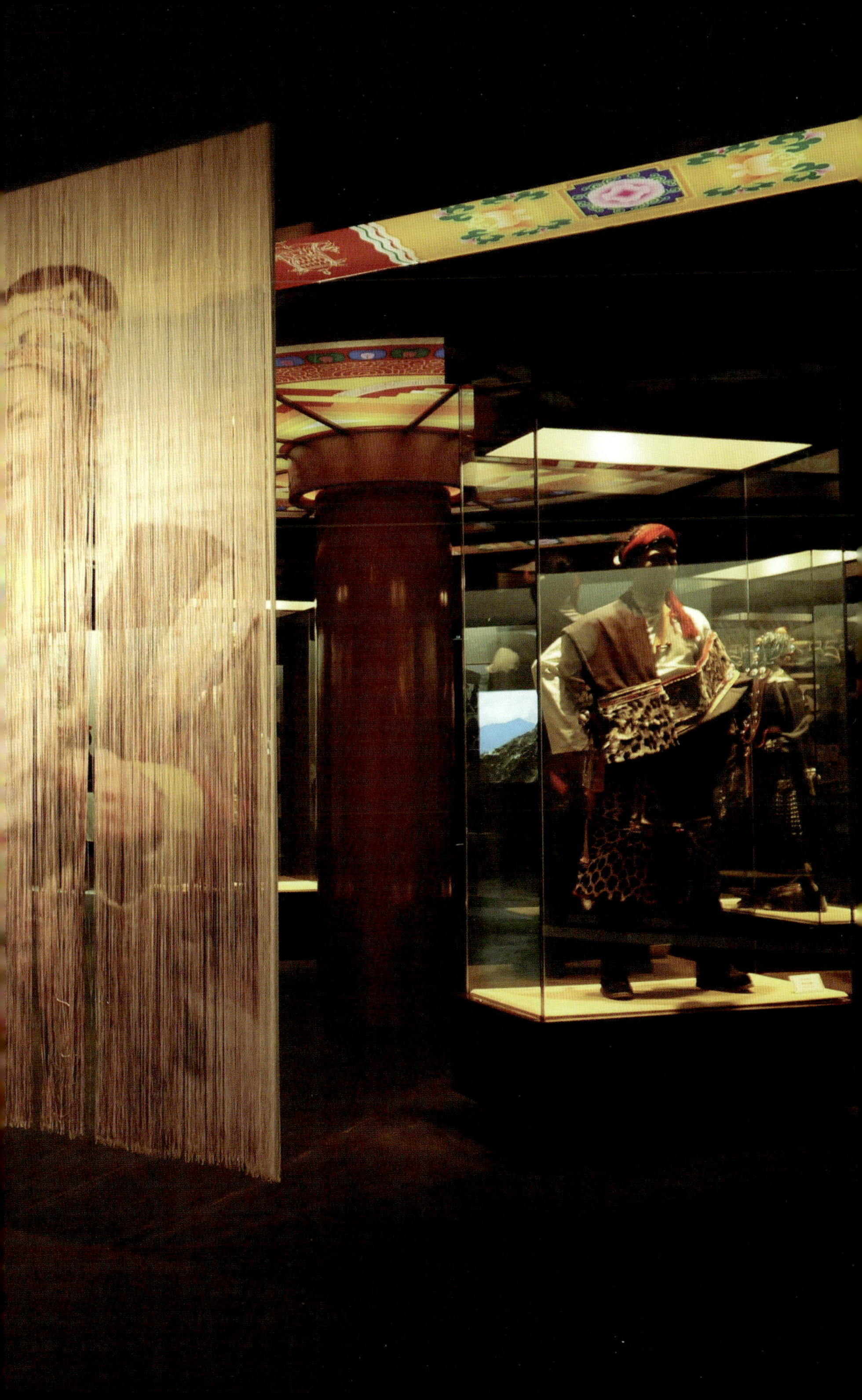

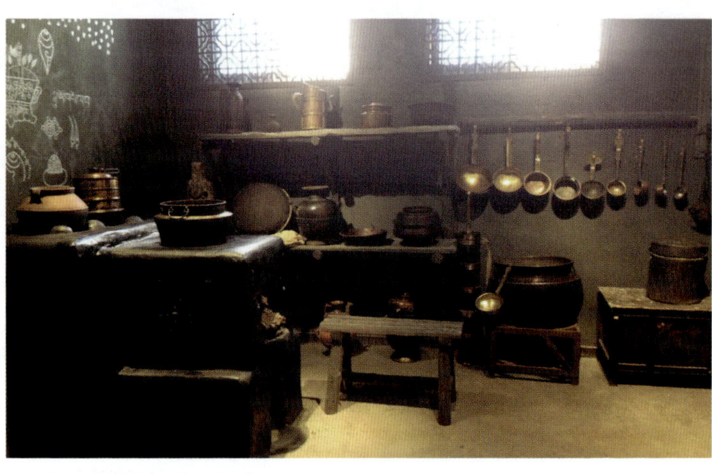

Rare pattra sutras – Buddhist scriptures written in Sanskrit on the leaves of the Indian palmyra palm – are also on display. Very few still survive. There is a birch bark Tang dynasty sutra which is labelled as the 'testament of Songtsen Gampo', who was the seventh-century King and founder of the Tibetan empire.

Tibetan golden bowl

The museum also holds a gold seal given to the 5th Dalai Lama, Ngawang Lozang Gyatso (1617–1682) in 1653 by the Shunzhi Emperor when he went to Beijing. He is one of the greatest and most revered of the Dalai Lamas and was responsible for unifying Tibet and combining the spiritual role of the position with political leadership. Among the accomplishments of this intellectual leader was declaring Lhasa the capital and being responsible for the rebuilding of the Potala Palace. Construction began in 1645 and wasn't completed until 1694. His death, which came before completion of the project, was kept secret for twelve years in order to prevent unrest.

Buddhist metal sculptures, musical instruments, astrological and cosmological paintings, mandalas and examples of Tibetan calligraphy are exhibited. One of the finest pieces in the museum is the Tsurphu Scroll, which was discovered in 1949 by the British scholar, Hugh Richardson, in the Tsurphu Monastery, west of Lhasa. This Ming dynasty silk-backed scroll is 15.2 m (50 ft) long and 76 cm (2.5 ft) high, with inscriptions in Chinese, Tibetan, Mongolian, Uighur and Arabic. The inscriptions alternate with elegantly painted panels depicting the miracles performed by the 5th Karmapa Dezhin Shekpa during his visit to the Yongle Emperor in Nanjing in 1407.

Painted, as well as *kesi* embroidered *thangkas* from as early as the thirteenth century are exhibited, some of which are very fine.

In the Folk Custom gallery, ethnographic handicrafts, jewellery, textiles and jade are represented. There is a reproduction of a typical Tibetan house, as well as a yak skin boat. On the third floor is a special display of imperial porcelain from the Ming and Qing periods, many of which were given as gifts to Tibet's nobles.

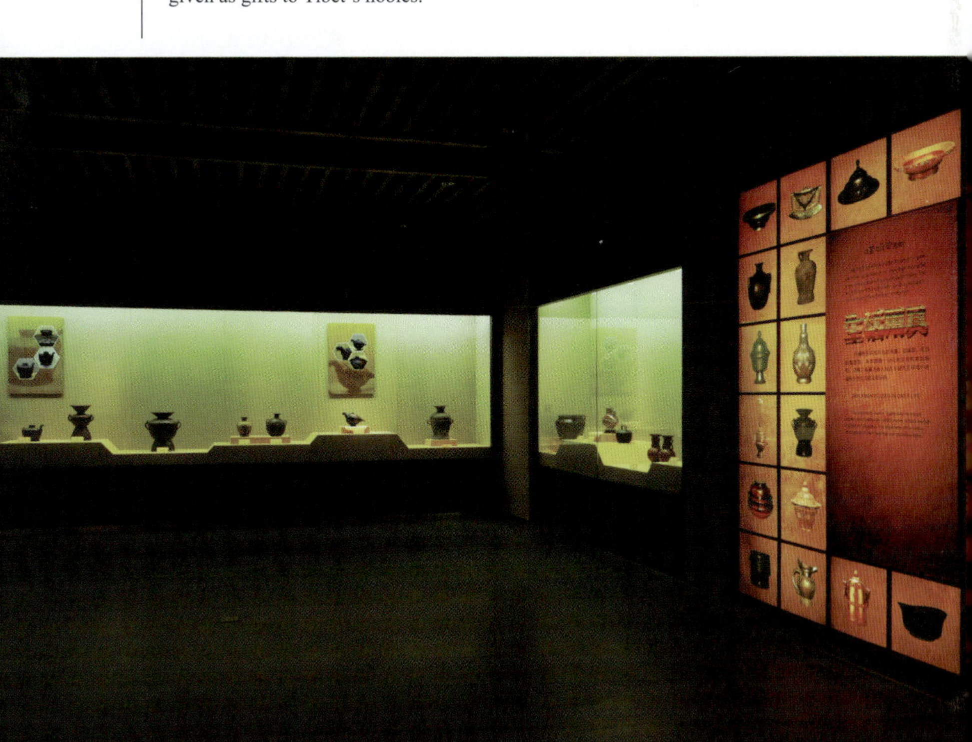

CHINESE MUSEUMS ASSOCIATION GUIDE

BEIJING AND THE NORTH

THE NORTHEAST

SHANGHAI AND EAST CHINA

THE YANGTZE

THE SOUTH

THE SILK ROAD AND THE NORTHWEST

TIBET

HONG KONG, MACAO, TAIWAN

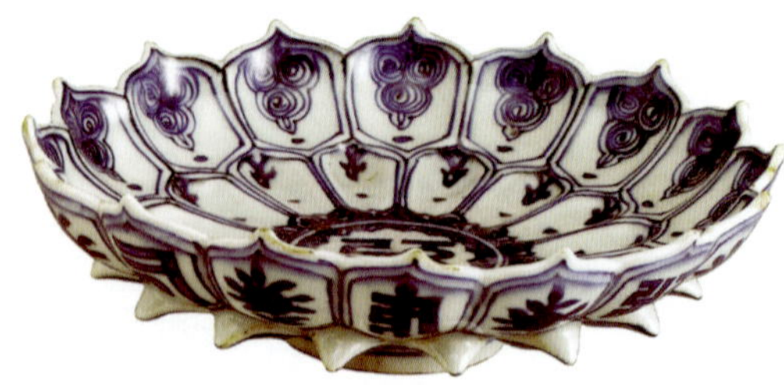

港澳台

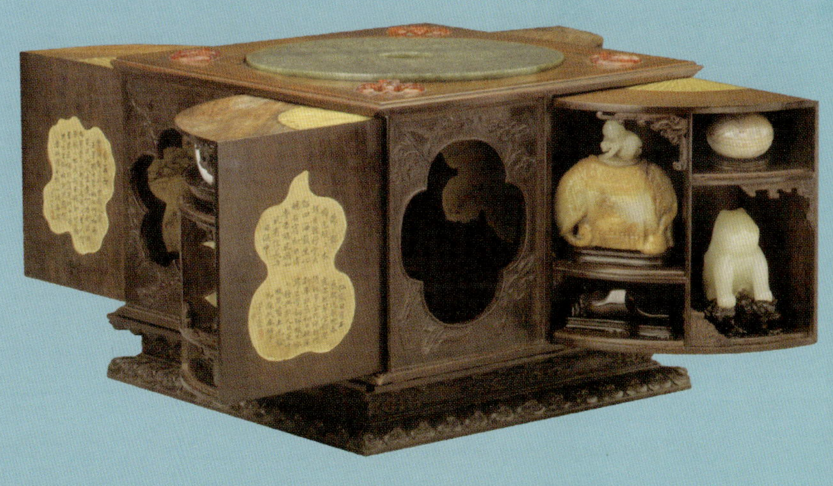

190

Hongkong Museum of History

香港历史博物馆 *Xianggang lishi bowuguan*

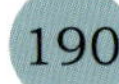

Chatham Road South, Tsim Sha Tsui, Kowloon, Hong Kong
香港九龙尖沙咀漆咸道南100号
Tel: (852) 2724 9042
Open: 10.00–18.00, Mon & Wed to Fri; 10.00–19.00, Sat, Sun and public holidays; closed at 17.00 on Christmas Eve and Chinese New Year's Eve
http://hk.history.museum
Gift shop / bookshop / café

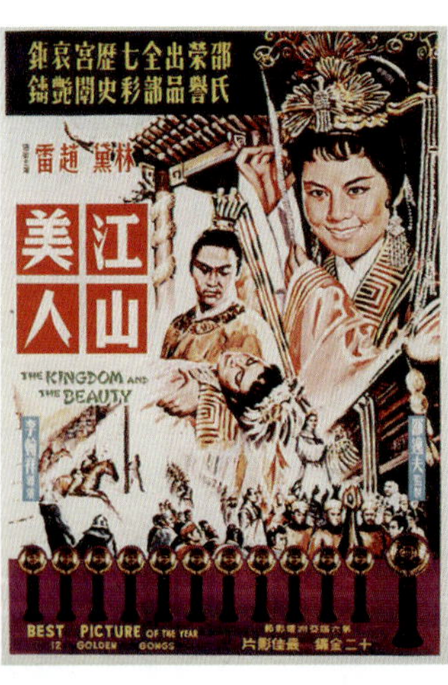

Old posters tell the city's history

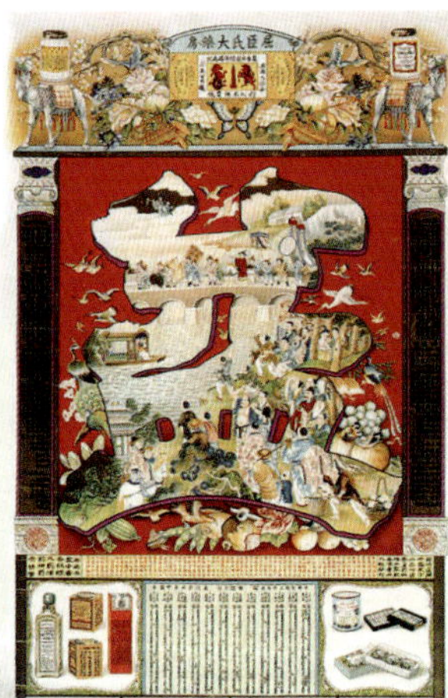

What do most people think of when they think of Hong Kong – shopping, great food, sophistication and extreme urbanism? But Hong Kong is so much more than that – as visitors always find out when they get here. The spectacular natural beauty of its many islands and beaches, its fascinating folk cultures, and its arts, music and history are at least as compelling as its commercial attractions.

The Hong Kong Museum of History is a wonderful introduction to this incredible city. After a visit, you will wander the streets of Hong Kong with a much enhanced understanding of what makes this remarkably vibrant city tick.

The story of Hong Kong is told in eight well-designed galleries on two floors comprising the permanent collection. The galleries are divided by subject – Hong Kong environment, Pre-history, Han through Qing Dynasties, Folk Culture, the Opium Wars and the British Colonisation, the Japanese Occupation, the Early City (pre-War to 60's) and the Modern City and handover to China. There are re-constructions of buildings, boats, shops and more, dioramas, objects in cases, videos (screened in English, Putonghua and Cantonese) and hands-on multi-media displays. Children will enjoy this museum tremendously, as will their parents. Whether you are new to Hong Kong or a long-time resident, a visit to this museum will certainly enrich your understanding of the city's cultural depth and dynamism.

Besides the permanent collection, the museum also hosts temporary exhibits which include local material concerning Hong Kong's culture and history as well as joint exhibitions with museums from mainland China and around the world.

For those with very specific interests, this museum runs five branch museums in Hong Kong: the Hong Kong Museum of Coastal Defence at Shau Kei Wan, the Lei Cheng Uk Han Tomb Museum at Sham Shui Po, Law Uk Folk Museum at Chai Wan, Fireboat Alexander Grantham Exhibition Gallery inside the Quarry Bay Park and Dr. Sun Yat-sen Museum at Mid-levels in Central.

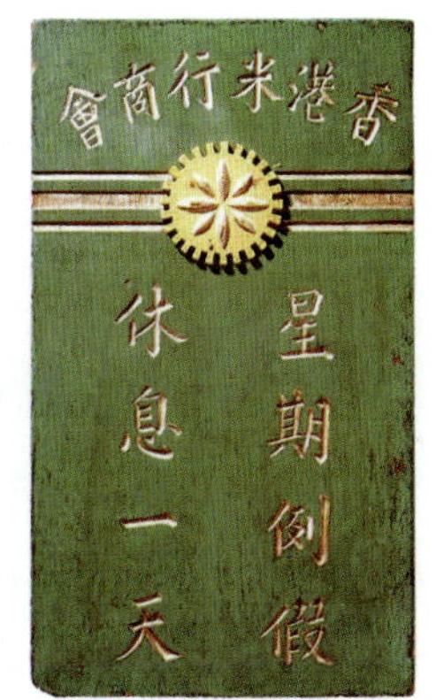

191

Macao Museum

澳门博物馆 *Ao'men bowuguan*

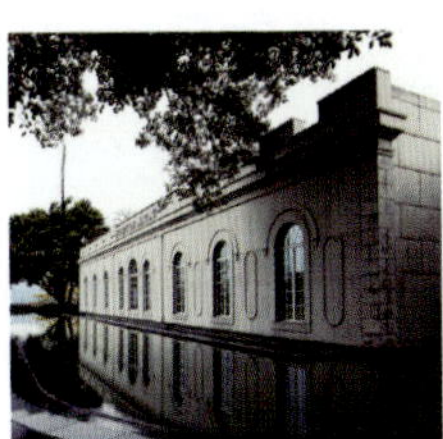

No. 112 Praceta do Museu de Macau
澳门博物馆前地112号
Tel: (853) 2835 7911
Open: 10.00–18.00 (ticket booth closes 17.30) except Mon;
free for public on the 15th of every month
www.macaumuseum.gov.mo
Mandarin / Cantonese / Portuguese / English guides

Strategically located on the western side of the Pearl River Delta across from Hong Kong and facing the South China Sea, Macao was the most important European trading port in China for three centuries until Hong Kong took over. It was under Portuguese sovereignty from the mid-16th century till 1999 when it became, like Hong Kong, a special administrative region of China. The Portuguese have left their mark. Trade was their main game, with slaves, silver and silk making their way to Japan and Europe via lucrative trade routes. Christian missionaries and Jesuit priests came too who lived and studied here before heading to mainland China. This East-West mix is reflected in Macao's historic streets and architectural ensemble of religious and public buildings such as hospitals, universities and a series of forts.

Today, one of the legacies of the missionaries, Mount Fortress built by the Jesuits in the 17th century adjacent to the 16th century ruins of St. Paul's, plays host to the

Macao Museum. It was first converted into a meteorological station dues to its hilltop location and decades later the museum. Recently the Fortress and the surrounding historic centre of Macao were inscribed on the UNESCO's World Heritage List. Views from the top offer visitors an outstanding panoramic vision of the territory consisting of the peninsula and two islands Taipa and Coloane along with Cotai, a reclaimed strip of land that joins the two and is known as the "Las Vegas of Asia" due to the numerous gambling casinos that have sprung up.

As a listed historic building, the museum had to configure its exhibition space to retain and preserve the architectural character of the Fortress. The result is three floors for permanent displays: two underground and the third at the top. Over these spaces the exhibitions unravel Macao's unique fusion of two disparate cultures, its diverse commercial activities, religions, as well as rituals and festivals, and provides a glimpse of present-day Macao. Displays focus on specific subjects, particularly the relationship between the Chinese and the Portuguese that coloured much of Macao's history and gave rise to its unique architecture, as well as many of its traditions.

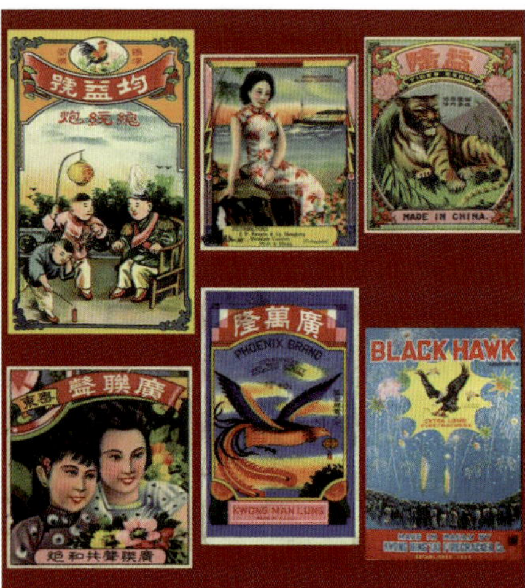

Boxes of firecrackers, once a major industry in Macao

Fascinating is the section on the sport of cricket-fighting which dates back to the 14th century and has its origins in China. Specially bred crickets are fed tofu and other supplements and then matched to size before they are pitted against one another. Brushing their antennae with a mouse whisker gets them in fighting mode. Betting is fierce and often with high stakes. And did you know that firecrackers were a major industry during the 20th century in Macao? Factories sprang up to serve the growing demands from China and abroad. The museum's displays of photographs and tools used to produce firecrackers, and other items give you a good insight into an industry that no longer exists, although today Macao is well known for its annual International Fireworks Display Contest, which should not be missed!

National Palace Museum in Taipei

192

台北故宫博物院 *Taibei gugong bowuyuan*

221 Zhishan Road, Sec. 2, Shilin District, Taipei, Taiwan
台湾台北市士林区至善路二段221号
Tel: (+886) 2 2881 2021
Open: 9.00–17.00, late opening Sat until 20.30
www.npm.gov.tw/en/
Restaurants / cafés / book & gift shop
English guide books / audio guide

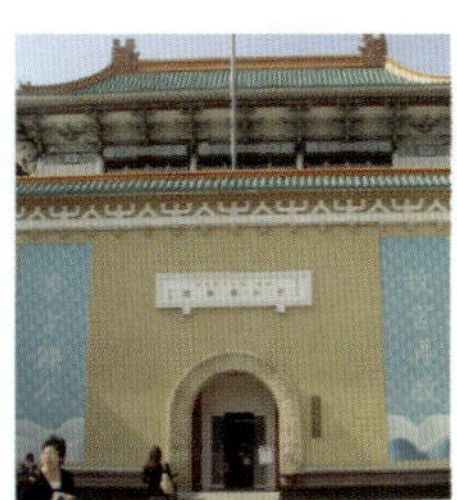

Han dynasty
bronze mirror

This museum houses some of the greatest examples of Chinese art from almost all periods. It contains many of the greatest treasures from the old imperial collection in Beijing. Even more than the imperial treasures that ended up in the Nanjing Museum after the end of the Civil War, these in Taipei represent *hua-xia*, a term that means 'China' both in a political sense and also in the broadest cultural sense – the representatives of Chinese art and culture.

The National Palace Museum in Beijing was founded in the Forbidden City in 1926 after the expulsion of the last Emperor, Puyi. When Beijing was threatened during the War against Japan, the Nationalist government of Chiang Kai-shek took with it as much as possible of the collection, first to Nanjing, then to Chongqing, then back to Nanjing. The possession of the collection was considered almost as a seal of power proclaiming the authenticity of the Nationalist government. In 1948, when the Civil War was drawing to a close and it was clear to Chiang Kai-shek that he would lose Nanjing, he ordered as much as possible of the cream of the collection to be shipped to the island of Taiwan. This included some sixty boxes of paintings and objects that had been exhibited at the Royal Academy in London in 1935–36 – a collection which had given to many in the West their first glimpse of the nature, quality and range of Chinese art. Between 1948 and 1949, no less than 3,248 crates were shipped to Taiwan, where on arrival they were stored in caves in the Taichung area of the island.

The building of the current museum was completed in 1965, and is situated in the northwest area of Taipei City, facing Shuangxi Park, in a luxuriously wooded and hilly area. The design of the building was based loosely on the Palace Museum in Beijing, with green tiles, yellow walls and white staircases. The museum has been constantly

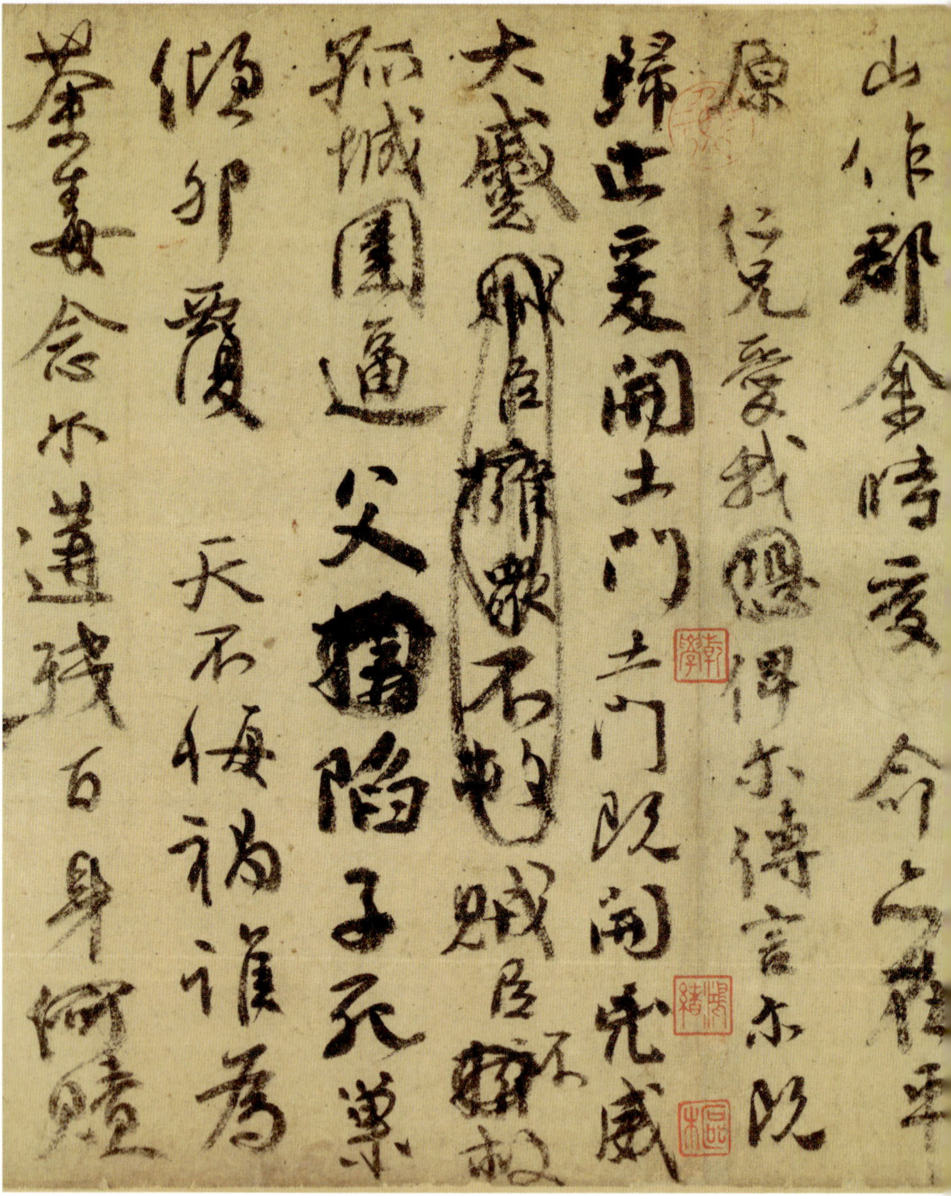

山作郡命上□王
原仁兄愛我俾爾傳言爾既
歸止爰開土門土門既開凶威
大蹙賊臣不救
孤城圍逼
父陷子死巢傾卵覆
天不悔禍誰為
荼毒念爾遘殘百身何贖

Yan Zhenqing's calligraphy

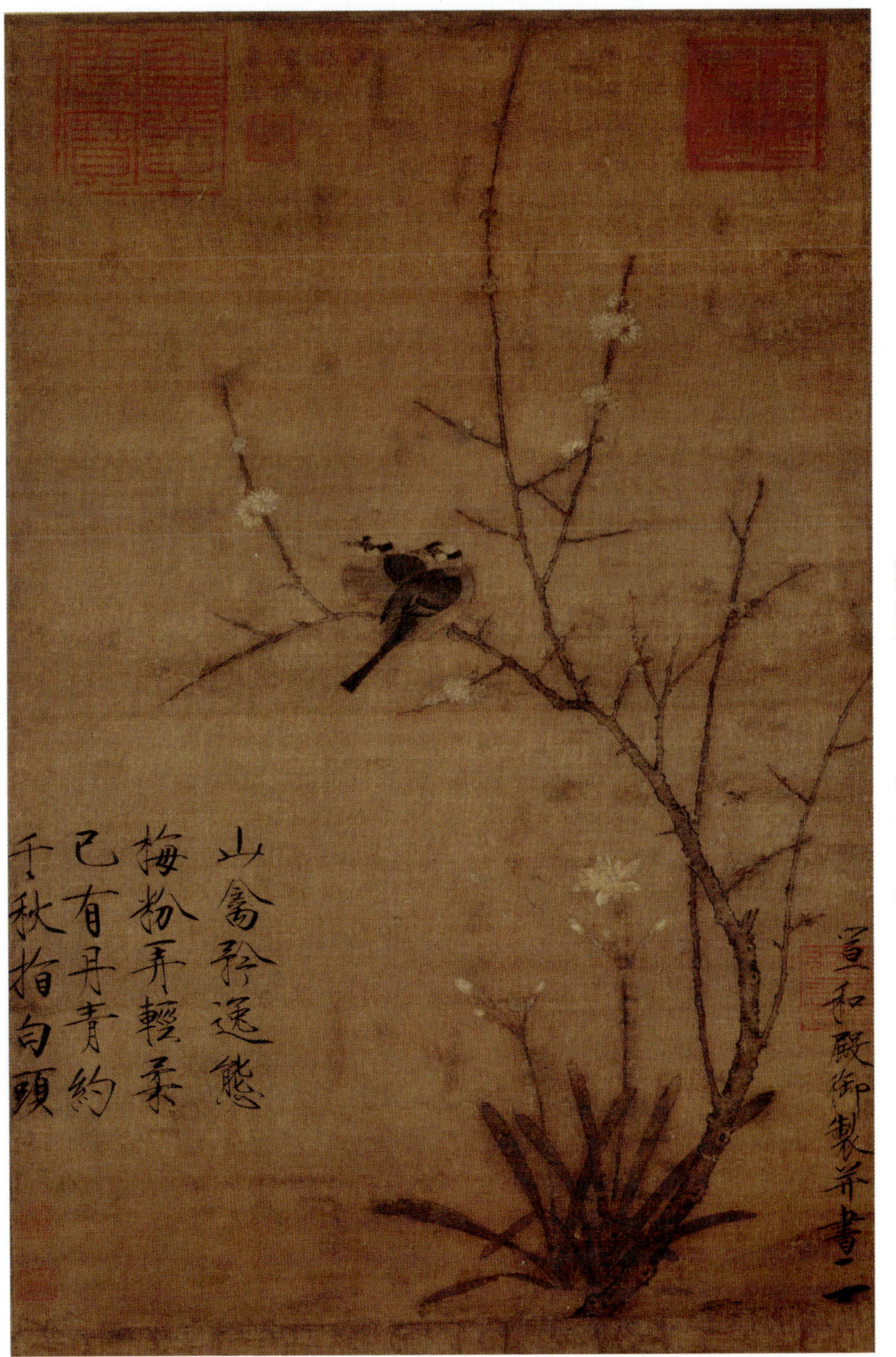

Hand scroll by Emperor Huizong (1082–1135)

expanded and improved, with the final restoration completed in 2006. Important pieces are shown for three months at a time over a ten-year cycle, to ensure that all the greatest of the treasures are seen by the public at least once in a decade.

The permanent collection is on show in the main four-storey exhibition hall (there is a high-quality restaurant on the fourth floor). There is another building for temporary exhibitions, and a library which is open to the public. The grounds contain three separate Chinese gardens and a memorial hall to the modern master from Sichuan, Zhang Daqian, built on the site of his former residence (booking is required for the memorial hall; it is closed Sundays and national holidays).

The main entrance to the museum is on the first floor, where the visitor is greeted by a bronze bust of Sun Yat-sen, the founder of the Republic in 1911. It is a replica of the bust at his tomb in Nanjing. Here, there is also a selection of some of the finest pieces of calligraphy and paintings in the collection, including the two most famous long scrolls in the history of Chinese art.

The national treasures in the collection include the Mao Gong *ding*, a Western Zhou bronze excavated in Shaanxi province in 1850. It is 53.8 cm in height, and while the interior and exterior decoration is relatively plain, on the inside is an inscription of 491 characters (the longest inscription known on any ancient bronze), making it a priceless record of ancient Chinese language and history, as well as a magnificent object in itself. The collection also contains a further 2,382 ancient bronzes.

Other galleries contain jades, calligraphy from the Jin and Tang dynasties onwards, paintings starting from the Tang and Song dynasties, ceramics from the Song and Yuan dynasties onwards, bamboo items, objects from the scholar's table, rare books and lacquer ware.

The outstanding national treasures include paintings and calligraphy by the master calligrapher Wang Xizhi (303–381); Fan Kuan (*c.* 950–1027, Song dynasty painter); Guo Xi (1023 to *c.* 1085, Song dynasty painter); Li Gonglin (1049–1106, Song dynasty painter); Qiu Ying (*c.*1509–1551, Ming dynasty painter); and Wang Hui (1632–1717, early Qing dynasty painter).

Among the scholar's objects is the inkstone of Su Dongpo (1037–1101), one of the most famous of the Song dynasty literati and a great calligrapher; and the inkstone of Zhao Mengfu (1254–1322), a famous Yuan dynasty calligrapher.

There is a magnificent collection of Northern Song imperial ceramics, and also representative collections of objects from all later dynasties. Among the most popular and well-known objects is the Qing dynasty imperial Jade Cabbage; 19-cm high and made of jadeite it is carved with exquisite virtuosity to show the green and white colours of a fresh cabbage, and two grasshoppers.

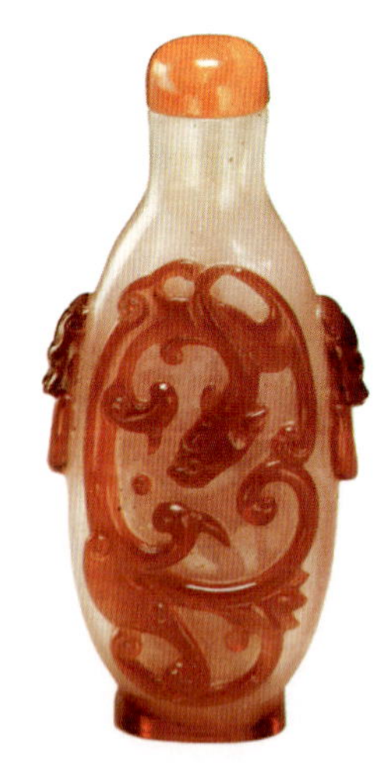

Exquisite snuff bottle with red dragon pattern, Qing dynasty

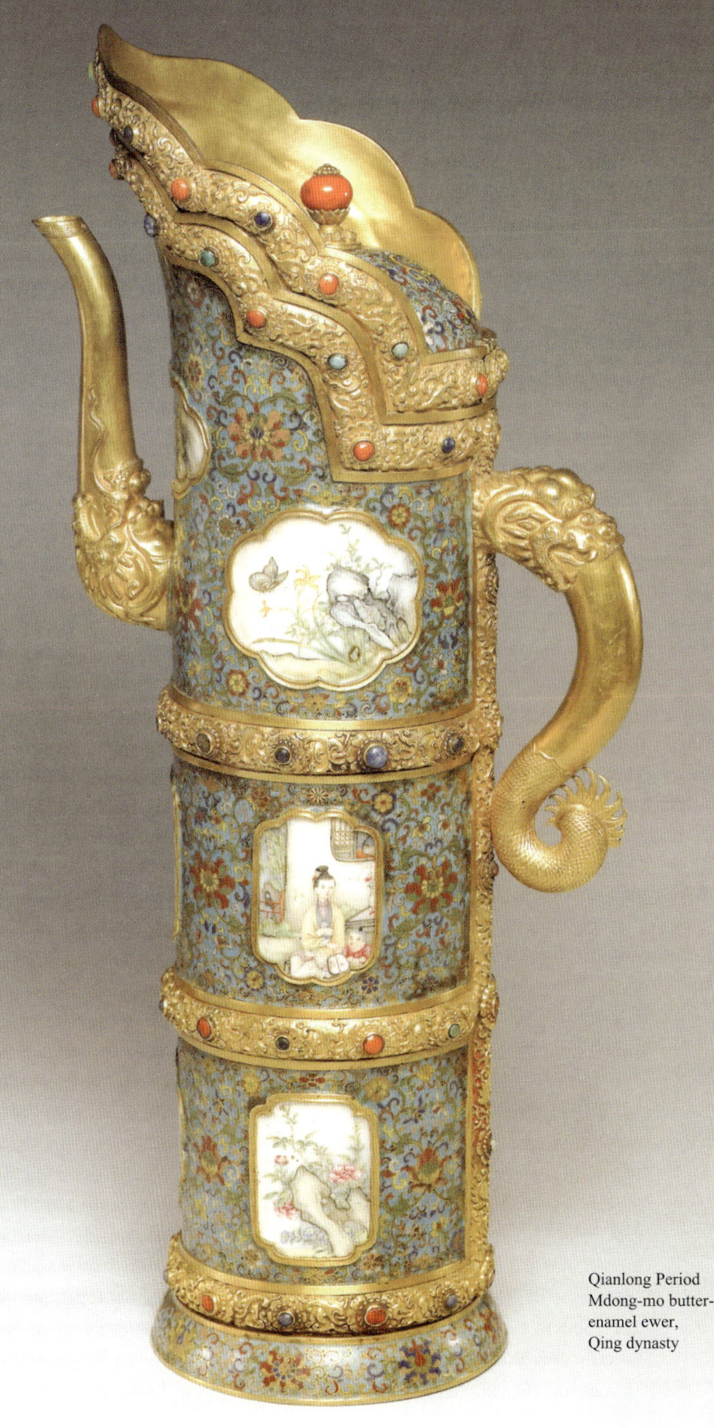

Qianlong Period
Mdong-mo butter-tea
enamel ewer,
Qing dynasty

Photographic Credits

The authors wish to thank all contributors for their kind permission to reproduce the images which appear in this book. Every effort has been made to credit and trace the copyright holders of all images and we apologize in advance for any unintentional omissions. The publishers will be happy to amend any errors or omissions in subsequent editions of this publication.

Except for those noted below all photographs are by © Miriam Clifford. All rights reserved. © Cathy Giangrande **7, 9, 21**. © Paul Mooney **14, 84 top, 270**. © Elissa Jaffe Cohen **72**. © Gavin A Fernandes **134 bottom**. © Edward Denison **166–67**. © Deke Erh **155–56**. © Jeremy Tredinnick **262, 292, 297**. © Kaizheng Yuan **358–59**.

Courtesy of the following individuals, museums, architectural firms, businesses, libraries and institutions: Beijing Ancient Coins Museum **10**. Beijing Art Museum **12–13**. Beijing Planetarium **18**. CAFA Art Museum **25**. Capital Museum **3, 26–27**. China Agricultural Museum **28–29**. China Millennium Monument World Art Museum **32**. China National Film Museum **33**. Shangai Postal Museum **34–35**. SOAS (School of Oriental and African Studies) Library, University of London **36–37, 56 top, 75 bottom, 79, 153 bottom, 228**. China Railway Museum **38–39**. Dabaotai Western Han Tomb Museum **40**. LEHK (London Editions (HK) Ltd) **41 top, 45 top, 46, 49**. Forbidden City and the Palace Museum **41 bottom, 42–43, 44 bottom, 48**. Guanfu Museum **52–53**. Lao She Museum **55**. Lu Xun Museum Beijing **56 bottom, 57**. Mei Lanfang Memorial Museum **58–59**. National Museum of China **2, 65–68**. National Museum of Modern Chinese Literature **69**. Soong Ching Ling's Former Residence **73**. Zhoukoudian Site Museum **76–77**. Tianjin Academy of Fine Arts Gallery **80**. Tianjin Museum **81–82**. Tianjin Science and Technology Museum **84**. Hebei Provincial Museum **85–87**. Chengde Imperial Summer Resort Museum **88–89**. Luoyang Museum **95–98**. Luoyang Museum of Ancient Arts **99–101**. Sino-Japanese War (1894–1895) Museum **108–109**. Qi State History Museum **111**. Shandong Provincial Museum **112–15**. Qingdao Municipal Museum **116**. Qingzhou Municipal Museum **118–19**. Coal Museum of China **120–21**. Pingyao Confucius Temple Museum **122, 123 top**. Shanxi Museum **124–27**. Aihui History Museum **130**. Harbin Architectural Museum **131**. Heilongjiang Provincial Museum **132–33**. Japanese Germ Warfare Museum Unit 731 **134 top**. Northeast China Revolutionary Martyrs Memorial Hall **135**. American POW Memorial Museum – Mukden Prison Camp **136**. Chinese Memorial Hall of the War to Resist US Aggression and Aid Korea **137**. Liaoning Provincial Museum **138–40**. September 18 History Museum **142**. Shenyang Palace Museum **143, 144 top**. Jilin Provincial Museum **144 bottom, 145**. Himalayas Art Museum **150**. Memorial Hall of First National Congress of Communist Party of China **152**. Shanghai Auto Museum **154**. Shanghai Kids' Museum **157**. Shanghai Lu Xun Memorial Hall (Final Residence / The Tomb of Lu Xun) **158–59**. Shanghai Museum **160–63**. Shanghai Museum of Public Security **165**. Soong Ching Ling Memorial Residence in Shanghai / Soong Ching Ling Mausoleum **168–69**. Sun Yat–sen's Former Residence and Museum in Shanghai **170–71**.

The Memorial Hall to the Victims in the Nanjing Massacre by Japanese Invaders **172.** Nanjing Cloud Brocade Museum and Research Institute **173.** Nanjing Museum **146, 174–78, 376–77.** Nantong Abacus Museum **180–81.** Nantong Kite Museum **182.** Nantong Museum **184–85.** Suzhou Museum **187–89.** Suzhou Opera Museum **190–91.** Xuzhou Museum **147, 193.** Yangzhou Museum / China Block-printing Museum **194–95.** China Grand Canal Museum **196.** China National Silk Museum **197–200.** China National Tea Museum **201–202.** Hu Qingyu Tang Traditional Chinese Medicine Museum **204.** Pan Tianshou Memorial Hall **205.** Southern Song Dynasty Guan Kiln Museum in Hangzhou **206–207.** Zhejiang Museum of Natural History **208–209.** Zhejiang Provincial Museum **210–13.** Ningbo Museum **214–15.** The Museum of Hemudu Site **216.** Liangzhu Museum **217–19.** Anhui Museum **222–23.** Hubei Provincial Museum **224–26.** Memorial Hall of Wuchang Uprising of 1911 Revolution **227.** China Lantern Museum **229.** Sutherland Hussey **230.** Chengdu Wuhou Shrine Museum **233–34.** Dayi Liu Family Estate Museum / Rent Collection Courtyard **235–36.** Jianchuan Museum Cluster **238.** Jinsha Archaeological Site Museum **239–41.** Liangshan Yi Ethnic Group's Slavery Museum **242.** Sanxingdui Museum **243–45.** Sichuan Museum **246–48.** Zigong Dinosaur Museum **251.** Zigong Salt History Museum **253.** Baiheliang Underwater Museum **255.** Chongqing Three Gorges Museum **220, 258–61.** Quanzhou Maritime Museum **265.** Guangdong Marine Silk Road Museum **267–68.** Guangzhou Museum of Art **269.** The Museum of the Mausoleum of the Nanyue King of the Western Han Dynasty **272–73.** The Museum of Dr. Sun Yat-Sen **274.** Opium War Museum **275.** Shenzhen Museum **276–77.** Hunan Provincial Museum **263, 278–79.** Jingdezhen Folk Kiln Museum (Hutian Kiln Site) **281–82.** Jingdezhen Imperial Porcelain Museum **283.** Jingdezhen Porcelain Museum **284–85.** Lushan Conference Site Memorial Museum **286.** Lushan Museum **287.** Bada Shanren Memorial Hall **288.** Nanchang Bayi (August 1st) Uprising Museum **289.** Jiangxi Provincial Museum **290–91.** Yunnan Provincial Museum **294–95.** Lijiang Municipal Museum **296, 297 top.** Guizhou Provincial Museum **298–99.** The Memorial of Zunyi Meeting **300.** The Museum of Guangxi Zhuang Autonomous Region **301–302.** Guangxi Museum of Natural History **303.** Hainan Museum **305.** Baoji Bronze Museum **308.** Emperor Qinshihuang's Terracotta Warriors and Horses and Mausoleum Site Museum **307, 309–13.** Famen Temple Museum **306, 315.** Hanyangling Museum **316–17.** Shaanxi History Museum **319–20.** Xi'an Banpo Museum **321–23.** Xi'an Beilin Museum **324–25.** Xi'an Museum **326–27.** Yaozhou Kiln Museum **328–29.** Inner Mongolia Museum **331.** Ordos Bronze Museum **332–33.** Guyuan Museum **334–35.** Ningxia Hui Autonomous Region Museum **336.** Dunhuang Museum **337.** Mogao Grottoes / Dunhuang Academy **339–44.** Jiayuguan Great Wall Museum **345.** Gansu Provincial Museum **346–47.** Liuwan Painted Pottery Museum **348.** Hotan Museum **349–50.** Xinjiang Uygur Autonomous Region Museum **354.** Tibet Museum **356–57, 360–63.** Hongkong Museum of History **366–67.** Macao Museum **368.** National Palace Museum in Taipei **364–65, 369–73.**

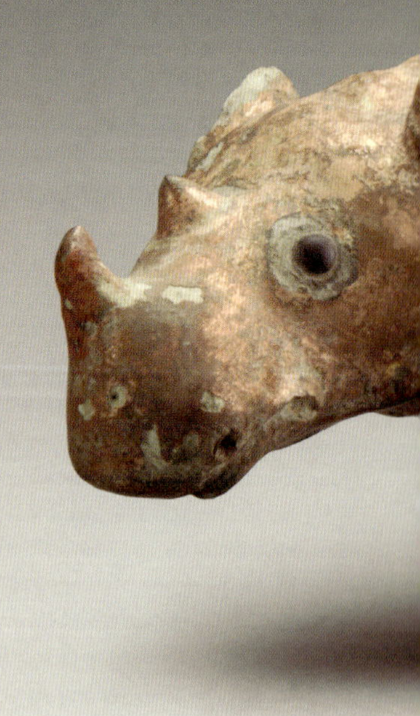
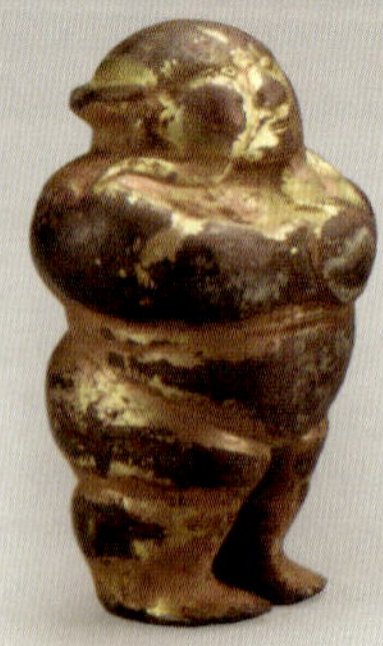

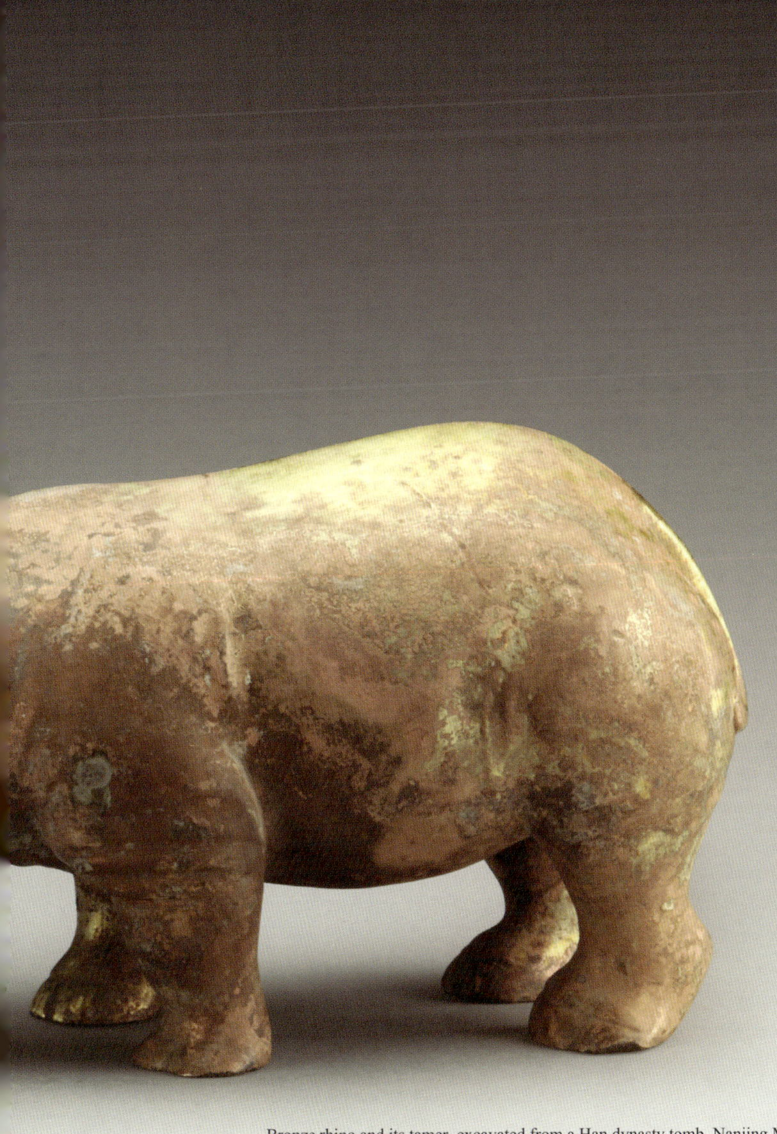

Bronze rhino and its tamer, excavated from a Han dynasty tomb, Nanjing Museum (no.95)

Glossary

bi	disc with a hole in the centre – often made of jade or stone
Bianzhong	musical instrument – a set of chime bells hung on a wooden frame
bixie	'averter of evil' winged mythological animal with two horns – often a tomb guardian
blanc de chine	white porcelain made in Dehua, Fujian Province and exported widely
celadon	a European term referring to a green glaze and ware, sometimes crackled, that became very popular as an export – green is most prevalent, but it also appears as yellow, grey, blue and white
cloisonné	decoration made using copper or bronze wire on a metal base and filled in with molten coloured enamel
cong	tall tube-shaped inner vessel with square outer walls, symbol of heaven and earth
ding	round or square ritual vessel or kettle – often three-legged, but also four-legged
dou	food container on a stem, usually bowl-shaped with bowl-shaped lid
doucai	designs on porcelain which are first painted in underglaze blue, glazed and then fired at a high temperature, with outlines then filled in with red, green, yellow and aubergine overglaze enamels and fired again at a lower temperature
famille jaune	predominance of yellow in decoration
famille rose	predominance of pink enamel in decoration
famille verte	predominance of green in decoration
fangding	is a square, four-legged *ding* vessel
fenghuang	Chinese mythological bird often translated as 'phoenix' although it is not the same as the Western version
fengshui	geomantic science of matching spaces to forces of nature
ge	a weapon, originally stone and later bronze blade attached to the top of a long staff
gu	wine container with tall, thin stem which flares into cup
guang	wine vessel – shape similar to a modern gravy boat
Guanyin	bodhisattva of compassion or goddess of mercy, one of the attendants of Amitabha Buddha – originally the male Indian god *Avalokitesvara*
gui	food container with handles; seen in a variety of shapes
he	box
hu	jar or pot
jia	wine vessel on legs for storing or warming wine
jian	double-edged sword

jin-silk	complex warp faced polychrome woven silks
jue	libation vessel
kaolin	a fine white clay, essential ingredient to create porcelain
kesi	highly prized and intricately styled woven silk
lei	tall wine jar with narrow neck – usually four-sided or round
leiwen	spiral pattern seen on bronze objects
li	round-bellied tripod vessel, more delicate than a *ding* in design
luohan (arhat)	disciple of Buddha
meiping	gracefully proportioned narrow-necked vase on a flat base designed to hold one flowering branch
nao	bell with curved lip
qi	battle axe
qilin	mythical creature with hooves and horns – a good omen
qingbai glaze	porcelain glaze that is a pale and delicate bluish-green colour
qipao	long, tight-fitting woman's garment often with high side slits, based on traditional Manchu dress – the modern version became very popular in 1930s Shanghai
Sakyamuni	'Sage of the Sakyas' – one of the names for Gautama Buddha, the historical figure
samite	heavy silk fabric often interwoven with gold or silver threads
sancai glaze	'tri-colour' glaze – although in fact not limited to three colours – particularly used in Tang dynasty
sarira	Buddhist relic
si	Buddhist temple – e.g. Famen Si
stela (e) also stele (s)	large upright inscribed stone or slab
sutra	the holy scriptures and teachings of the Buddha
yan	steamer – both utilitarian and ritual
you	wine container
yu	bowl-shaped food container with handles
yue	broad axe – often ritual
zhi	wine vessel or cup
zun	urn which can be in the shape of an animal

Chronology
(ancient China)

Neolithic period	*c.* 12000–2000 BC
Yangshao Culture	*c.* 5000–3000 BC
Hongshan Culture	*c.* 4500–2900 BC
Dawenkou Culture	*c.* 4300–2500 BC
Liangzhu Culture	*c.* 3300–2200 BC
Majiayao Culture	*c.* 3100–2700 BC
Shandong Longshan Culture	*c.* 2500–2000 BC
Central Plain Longshan Culture	*c.* 2500–1900 BC
Qijia Culture	*c.* 2400–1900 BC
Xia dynasty	*c.* 2070–1600 BC
Erlitou Culture	*c.* 1800–1600 BC
Ba	*c.* 2000–220 BC
Bronze Age	21st to 5th centuries BC
Shang dynasty	*c.* 1600–1046 BC
Zhou dynasty	*c.* 1046–221 BC
Western Zhou	*c.* 1046–771 BC
Eastern Zhou	770–221 BC
Spring and Autumn period	770–476 BC
Warring States period	475–221 BC
Qin dynasty	221–207 BC
Han dynasty	206 BC–AD 220
Western Han	206 BC–AD 8
Xin or Interregnum of Wang Mang	AD 9–23
Eastern Han	AD 25–220
Three Kingdoms period	AD 220–265
Western Jin	AD 265–316
Eastern Jin	AD 317–420
Southern and Northern dynasties	AD 420–589
Southern dynasties	
Song	AD 420–479

Qi	AD 479–502
Liang	AD 502–557
Chen	AD 557–589
Northern dynasties	
Northern Wei	AD 386–534
Eastern Wei	AD 534–549
Western Wei	AD 535–557
Northern Qi	AD 550–577
Northern Zhou	AD 557–581
Sui dynasty	AD 581–618
Tang dynasty	AD 618–907
Five Dynasties and Ten Kingdoms	AD 907–960
Liao dynasty	AD 916–1125
Song dynasty	AD 960–1279
Northern Song	AD 960–1127
Southern Song	AD 1127–1279
Western Xia dynasty	AD 1038–1227
Jin dynasty	AD 1115–1234
Yuan dynasty	AD 1206–1368
Ming dynasty	AD 1368–1644
Qing dynasty	AD 1644–1911

Acknowledgements

During the lengthy and demanding process of compiling the first edition of this book, ***CHINA: museums***, we collected along our journey a host of individuals to whom we owe a great deal of gratitude. Firstly, our sponsor, Gazeley – in particular Pat McGillycuddy, Chief Executive Officer – who believed in this project enough to finance it from its earliest days; a very big thank you!

Outstanding support in so many ways came from Dr. Paul Clifford; whose knowledge of China he generously shared from start to finish was so invaluable and much appreciated. MC and CG are profoundly grateful to Wang Yi our Project Assistant in China. His tireless and efficient help and guidance on museum matters, as well as his marvellous skill as an interpreter and facilitator on our travels are incalculable. Special thanks goes to Paul Mooney, an associate writer and researcher in China who, at the drop of the hat, travelled far and wide to reach museums we might otherwise have left out and did so with professionalism now rarely encountered: *quel homme!* Others who assisted with writing, photography and research include Edward Denison and Jeremy Tredinnick, thank you for your willingness and spirit of adventure. Space does not allow us to personally thank the numerous museum directors and owners, curators, assistants and archaeologists who, generously gave us their time to guide us through their collections, granted oral interviews, plied us with useful catalogues and DVDs and countless times many kindly invited us to share a meal; to all of them we offer a heart-felt collective thanks. Architectural firms and photographers kindly supplied us with images of artist's renderings of new museums, or out-of-the way ones without which this book would have been less visually pleasing. An endless stream of colleagues and friends helped us with their skills, encouragement, friendship and contacts; to them we offer our deepest appreciation. They include: Nancy Abella, Francine Auster, Clifford Coonan, Cindy Cui, Deke Erh, Ulrika Fornaeus, Amy Gendler, Wang Jie, Roger Keverne, Tang Liang, Robert Martin, Enrico Perlo, Jiang Ping (Charissa), Zhang He Ping, Guang Yu Ren, Yueying Shan, Dr. Wang Tao, Didi Kirsten Tatlow, Julie Upton Wang, Pat Wang, Ma Weidu, Suzhen Xie, Kaizheng Yuan and Dr. Xiaodong Zhu of the State Administration of Cultural Heritage. MC would personally like to thank Dr. Alfreda Murck for her encouragement and confidence from the very beginning of this project and sage advice throughout. To her family – Paul, Jasper, Hugo and Zoë who have been so supportive and patient throughout this very long process – she sends her love and thanks. CG would like to thank her husband, Paul and their sons, Chris and Alex, for their boundless support.

We are grateful to our agent Andrew Nurnberg for his skilful negotiations and for introducing us to Yilin, who presented ***CHINA: museums*** to the Chinese Museums Association. This new edition of our book has been recreated due to the constant support of Song Xinchao, President of the Chinese Museums Association and Chairman of ICOM-China. It is due to his enthusiasm that our book is now re-appearing as the ***Chinese Museums Association Guide***. Its new scope and purpose have dictated some deletions and many additions to our original text and the help and support in achieving this of Gong Liang, Director of the Nanjing Museum and Vice-President of the CMA have been invaluable. This book is based on the original design of Misha Anikst and his team whose talent is evident in the new edition. Finally our heartfelt thanks to Lu Chenxi and the whole editorial and design team at Yilin Press, without whose constant attention and hard work, this book would never have appeared and to Peter Brown our copy editor for his exacting editing skills and for stepping up to the plate at a moment's notice.

Index to Art Spaces, Museums and Sites

Abacus Museum, Nantong 180–1
Academy of Fine Arts Gallery,
    Tianjin 80
Aihui History Museum 130
American POW Memorial Museum
    – Mukden Prison Camp 136
Ancient Architecture Museum,
    Beijing 6–9
Ancient Arts, Luoyang Museum
    of 99–101
Ancient Chariots, Chinese, Linzi
    Museum of 107
Ancient Coins Museum, Beijing 10–11
Ancient Metallurgy Museum,
    Tonglushan 228
Anhui Museum 222–3
Archaeology, Arthur M. Sackler
    Museum of Art and
    Archaeology 4–5
Architecture Museum, Ancient,
    Beijing 6–9
Architectural Museum, Harbin 131
Art, Guangdong Museum of 271
Art, Guangzhou Museum of 269
Art Museum, Beijing 12–13
Art Museum, CAFA 25
Art Museum, China Millennium
    Monument World 32
Art Museum, Himalayas 150
Art Museum, National, of China
    (NAMOC) 64
Art Museum, Poly 71
Arthur M. Sackler Museum
    of Art and Archaeology 4–5
August 1st (Nanchang Bayi)
    Uprising Museum 289
Auto Museum, Shanghai 154

Aviation Museum, Beijing 14
Aviation Museum, China 30–1

Bada Shanren Memorial Hall 288
Baiheliang Underwater Museum 255
Bank Museum, Shanghai 155–6
Banpo, Xi'an Banpo Museum 321–3
Baoji Bronze Museum 308
Beijing Ancient Architecture Museum 6–9
Beijing Ancient Coins Museum 10–11
Beijing, Lu Xun Museum 56–7
Beijing Planetarium 18–19
Beijing Police Museum 19–20
Beijing Stone Carving Museum 21–2
Beijing Tap Water Museum 23–4
Beilin, Xi'an Beilin Museum 324–5
Brocade and Embroidery Museum,
    Chengdu Shu 231–2
Brocade, Cloud, Museum and Research
    Institute, Nanjing 173
Bronze Museum, Baoji 308

CAFA Art Museum 25
Capital Museum 26–7
Chariot, Royal Six-Horse, Museum of
    Zhou Capital and 102
Chengde Imperial Summer Resort
    Museum 88–9
Chengdu City Museum 230
Chengdu Shu Brocade and
    Embroidery Museum 231–2
Chengdu Wuhou Shrine Museum 233–4
China Agricultural Museum 28–9
China Art Museum 148
China Aviation Museum 30–1
China Grand Canal Museum 196
China Lantern Museum 229–30

China Millennium Monument World
  Art Museum 32
China National Film Museum 33
China, National Museum of 65–8
China National Post and Postage
  Stamp Museum 34–5
China National Silk Museum 197–200
China National Tea Museum 201–2
China Printing Museum 36–7
China Railway Museum 38–9
China Tobacco Museum 149
Chinese Medicine, Traditional, Hu
  Qingyu Tang, Museum of 203–4
Chinese Memorial Hall of the War to
  Resist US Aggression and
  Aid Korea 137
Chinese Opera, Museum of 79
Chinese People's Revolution,
  Military Museum of the 60–1
Chongqing Huguang Guildhall
  Complex 256–7
Chongqing Three Gorges Museum
  258–61
Cloud Brocade Museum and
  Research Institute, Nanjing 173
Coal Museum of China 120–1
Coins, Ancient, Beijing Museum of 10–11
Conference Site Memorial Museum
  Lushan 286
Costumes, Ethnic, Museum of
  BIFT 62–3

Dabaotai Western Han Tomb Museum 40
Dayi Liu Family Estate Museum
  / Rent Collection Courtyard 235–6
Dr.Sun Yat-Sen, The Museum of 274
Dinosaur Museum, Zigong 250–2
Dunhuang Museum 337

Ethnic Costumes, Museum of BIFT 62–3

Emperor Qinshihuang's
  Terracotta Warriors and Horses
  and Mausoleum Site Museum 309–13

Famen Temple Museum 314–15
Film Museum, China National 33
Fine Arts Gallery, Tianjin Academy of 80
Folk Kiln Museum (Hutian Kiln Site),
  Jingdezhen 281–2
Forbidden City and the Palace
  Museum 41–9
Former Residence *see* Residences
Funerary Horse Pit Museum of the Eastern
  Zhou, Linzi 106

Gansu Provincial Museum 346–7
Geological Museum of China 50–1
Germ Warfare, Japanese, Museum
  Unit 731 134
Grand Canal Museum, China 196
Great Wall Museum, Jiayuguan 345
Grottoes, Longmen 94
Grottoes, Mogao, Dunhuang
  Academy 338–44
Guan Kiln Museum, Southern
  Song Dynasty in Hangzhou 206–7
Guanfu Museum 52–3
Guangdong Marine Silk Road
  Museum 267–8
Guangdong Museum of Art 271
Guangdong Provincial Museum 270
Guangxi Zhuang Autonomous Region,
  the Museum of 301–2
Guangzhou City Museum 271
Guangzhou Museum of Art 269
Guizhou Provincial Museum 298–9
Guyuan Museum 334–5

Hainan Museum 304–5
Hanyangling Museum 316–17

Harbin Architectural Museum 131
Heavenly Kingdom Historical Museum,
    Taiping 179
Hebei Provincial Museum 85–7
Heilongjiang Provincial Museum 132–3
Hemudu Site, Museum of 216
Henan Museum 90–2
Himalayas Art Museum 150
Hong Kong Museum of History 366–7
Horse Pit Museum of the Eastern Zhou
    Linzi Funerary 106
Horses of Emperor Qinshihuang's,
    Terracotta Warriors, and Mausoleum
    Site Museum 309–13
Hotan Museum 349–50
Hu Qingyu Tang Traditional
    Chinese Medicine Museum 203–4
Hubei Provincial Museum 224–6
Huguang Guildhall Complex 256–7
Hunan Provincial Museum 278–9
Hutian Kiln Site, Jingdezhen Folk
    Kiln Museum 281–2

Ili Kazakh Autonomous Prefecture
    Museum, Xinjiang 352
Imperial Porcelain Museum,
    Jingdezhen 283
Inner Mongolia Museum 330–1

Japanese Germ Warfare Museum
    Unit 731 134
Japanese Invaders, The Memorial Hall
    to the Victims in the
    Nanjing Massacre 172
Jianchuan Museum Cluster 237–8
Jiangxi Provincial Museum 290–1
Jiaozhuanghu Underground
    Tunnel War Remains Museum 54
Jiayuguan Great Wall Museum 345
Jilin Provincial Museum 144–5

Jingdezhen Folk Kiln Museum
    (Hutian Kiln Site) 281–2
Jingdezhen Imperial Porcelain
    Museum 283
Jingdezhen Porcelain Museum 284–5
Jinsha Archaeological Site
    Museum 239–41

Kaifeng Museum 93
Kids' Museum, Shanghai 157
Kiln Museum, Folk, Jingdezhen
    (Hutian Kiln Site) 281–2
Kiln Museum, Guan, Southern
    Song Dynasty 206–7
Kite Museum, Nantong 182–3
Kunming City Museum 292

Lantern Museum, China 229–30
Lao She Museum 55
Liangshan Yi Ethnic Group's
    Slavery Museum 242
Liangzhu Museum 217–19
Liaoning Provincial Museum 138–40
Lijiang Municipal Museum 296–7
Linzi Funerary Horse Pit Museum of
    the Eastern Zhou 106
Linzi Museum of Chinese Ancient
    Chariots 107
Literature, National Museum of
    Modern Chinese 69
Liuwan Painted Pottery Museum 348
Longmen Grottoes 94
Lu Xun Memorial Hall (Final Residence
    / The Tomb of Lu Xun), Shanghai 158
Lu Xun Museum, Beijing 56–7
Luoyang Museum 95–8
Luoyang Museum of Ancient Arts 99–101
Lushan Conference Site Memorial
    Museum 286
Lushan Museum 287

Lüshun Museum 141

Macao Museum 367–8
Marco Polo Bridge / Sino-Japanese War
    Memorial Museum 72
Marine Silk Road Museum,
    Guangdong 267–8
Mausoleum of the Nanyue King of
    the Western Han Dynasty,
    The Museum of the 272–3
Mausoleum, Soong Ching Ling /
    Memorial Residence in
    Shanghai 168–9
Medicine *see* Chinese Medicine
Mei Lanfang Memorial Museum 58–9
Memorial Hall, Bada Shanren 288
Memorial Hall, Lu Xun / Final Residence
    / The Tomb of Lu Xun, Shanghai 158
Memorial Hall of First National
    Congress of Communist Party
    of China 152
Memorial Hall of Wuchang Uprising
    of 1911 Revolution 227
Memorial Hall, Pan Tianshou 205
Memorial Hall to the Victims in the
    Nanjing Massacre by Japanese
    Invaders 172
Memorial Museum, Mei Lanfang 58–9
Memorial Museum – Mukden
    Prison Camp, American POW 136
Memorial Museum, New Culture
    Movement 70
Memorial Museum, Sino-Japanese War
    / Marco Polo Bridge 72
Metallurgy, Ancient, Tonglushan
    Museum 228
Military Museum of the Chinese
    People's Revolution 60–1
Millennium Monument World
    Art Museum, China 32

MoCA Shanghai 151
Modern Chinese Literature,
    National Museum of 69
Mogao Grottoes / Dunhuang
    Academy 338–44
Mukden Prison Camp, American POW
    Memorial Museum 136
Museum of Art, Guangdong 271
Museum of Art, Guangzhou 269
Museum of Chinese Opera 79
Museum of Ethnic Costumes 62–3
Museum of Hemudu Site 216
Museum of Natural History, Beijing 15–17
Museum of Oriental Musical
    Instruments 153
Museum of Public Security,
    Shanghai 164–5
Museum of Zhou Capital and Royal
    Six-Horse Chariot 102

NAMOC (National Art Museum of
    China) 64
Nanchang Bayi (August 1st)
    Uprising Museum 289
Nanjing Cloud Brocade Museum
    and Research Institute 173
Nanjing Massacre by Japanese
    Invaders, The Memorial Hall to
    the Victims in 172
Nanjing Museum 174–8
Nantong Abacus Museum 180–1
Nantong Kite Museum 182–3
Nantong Museum 184–5
Nantong Textile Museum 186
National Art Museum of China
    (NAMOC) 64
National Film Museum, China 33
National Museum of China 65–8
National Museum of Modern Chinese
    Literature 69

National Palace Museum, Taipei 369–73
National Post and Postage
  Stamp Museum, China 34–5
National Silk Museum, China 197–200
National Tea Museum, China 201–2
Nationalities Museum, Yunnan 293
Natural History, Beijing Museum of 15–17
Natural History, Guangxi Museum of 303
Natural History, Tianjin Museum 83
Natural History, Zhejiang
  Museum of 208–9
Naval Museum, Qingdao 117
New Culture Movement
  Memorial Museum 70
Ningbo Museum 214–15
Ningxia Hui Autonomous Region
  Museum 336
Northeast China Revolutionary
  Martyrs Memorial Hall 135

Open House Museum, Shikumen 166–7
Opera, Chinese, Museum of 79
Opium War Museum 275
Ordos Bronze Museum 332–3
Overseas Chinese Museum 264

Palace Museum, and Forbidden City
  41–9
Palace Museum, Shenyang Imperial 143-4
Pan Tianshou Memorial Hall 205
Pingyao Confucius Temple
  Museum 122–3
Pingyao Museum (Qingxu Temple) 123
Poly Art Museum 71
Potala Palace 358–9
POW, American, Memorial
  Museum, Mukden Prison Camp 136

Qi State History Museum 110–11
Qingdao Municipal Museum 116

Qingdao Naval Museum 117
Qingzhou Municipal Museum 118–19
Quanzhou Maritime Museum 265–6

Sanxingdui Museum 243–5
September 18 History Museum 142
Shaanxi History Museum 318–20
Shandong Museum 112–15
Shanghai Auto Museum 154
Shanghai Bank Museum 155–6
Shanghai Kids' Museum 157
Shanghai Museum 160–3
Shanxi Museum 124–7
Shaoshan Mao Zedong Memorial
  Museum 280
Shenyang Imperial Palace Museum 143-4
Shenzhen Museum 276–7
Shikumen Open House Museum 166–7
Sino-Japanese War (1894-1895)
  Museum 108–9
Sichuan Museum 246–8
Sichuan University Museum 249–50
Sino-Japanese War Memorial Museum
  / Marco Polo Bridge 72
Soong Ching Ling's Former Residence 73
Soong Ching Ling Memorial Residence
  in Shanghai / Soong Ching Ling
  Mausoleum 168–9
Southern Song Dynasty Guan Kiln
  Museum in Hangzhou 206–7
Sun Yat-Sen's Former Residence
  and Museum in Shanghai 170–1
Suzhou Museum 187–9
Suzhou Opera Museum 190–1

Taiping Heavenly Kingdom
  Historical Museum 179
Tank Museum 74
Tianjin Academy of Fine Arts Gallery 80
Tianjin Museum 81–2

Tianjin Natural History Museum 83
Tianjin Science and Technology
    Museum 84
Tibet Museum 360–3
Tobacco Museum, China 149
Tonglushan Ancient Metallurgy
    Museum 228
Turpan Prefecture Museum 351

Xi'an Banpo Museum 321–3
Xi'an Beilin Museum 324–5
Xi'an Museum 326–7
Xinjiang Ili Kazakh
    Autonomous Prefecture Museum 352
Xinjiang Uygur Autonomous Region
    Museum 353–5
Xu Beihong Museum 75
Xuzhou Museum 192–3

Yangzhou Museum / China Block-printing
    Museum 194–5
Yaozhou Kiln Museum 328–9
Yinxu Museum 103–5
Yunnan Nationalities Museum 293
Yunnan Provincial Museum 294–5

Zhejiang Provincial Museum 210–13
Zhoukoudian Site Museum 76–8
Zigong Dinosaur Museum 250–2
Zigong Salt History Museum 253–4
Zunyi Meeting, the Memorial of 300